PENGUIN BOOKS

SERIOUS PLEASURES

Philip Hoare was born in Southampton, England, and educated at no less than three Catholic establishments. Since then
he has been a cable fitter's mate, a record-shop assistant, and
a pop-group manager. He has written for the *Sunday Times*,
the *Independent*, and the *Daily Telegraph* newspapers in London, as well as contributing to *Harpers & Queen* magazine.
Serious Pleasures is his first book, and he is currently writing a
biography of Sir Noël Coward. Philip Hoare is thirty-three
and lives in Shoreditch, London.

Serious Pleasures

THE LIFE OF *Stephen Tennant*

BY PHILIP HOARE

PENGUIN BOOKS

PENGUIN BOOKS
Published by the Penguin Group
Viking Penguin, a division of Penguin Books USA Inc.,
375 Hudson Street, New York, New York 10014, U.S.A.
Penguin Books Ltd, 27 Wrights Lane,
London W8 5TZ, England
Penguin Books Australia Ltd, Ringwood,
Victoria, Australia
Penguin Books Canada Ltd, 10 Alcorn Avenue, Suite 300,
Toronto, Ontario, Canada M4V 3B2
Penguin Books (N.Z.) Ltd, 182–190 Wairau Road,
Auckland 10, New Zealand

Penguin Books Ltd, Registered Offices:
Harmondsworth, Middlesex, England

First published in Great Britain by Hamish Hamilton Ltd. 1990
First published in the United States of America by
Viking Penguin, a division of Penguin Books USA Inc. 1991
Published in Penguin Books 1992

1   3   5   7   9   10   8   6   4   2

The acknowledgments on pp. 421–4 constitute an
extension of this copyright page.

LIBRARY OF CONGRESS CATALOGING IN PUBLICATION DATA
Hoare, Philip.
Serious pleasures: the life of Stephen Tennant/by Philip Hoare.
p.   cm.
Includes bibliographical references and index.
ISBN 0 14 01.6532 0
1. Tennant, Stephen.   2. Eccentrics and eccentricities—Great
Britain—Biography.   3. Great Britain—Social life and customs—20th
century.   I. Title.
CT788.T424H36   1992
941.082'092—dc20   91–743

Printed in the United States of America
Set in Linotron Sabon

To my mother and father

Contents

Contents

. . . the exact limitations of one's taste should be an intense pleasure . . . Most people are never sure what they like. Pleasure should be a deep, as well as a light thing. You should name the book of your life 'Serious Pleasures'.

Stephen Tennant.

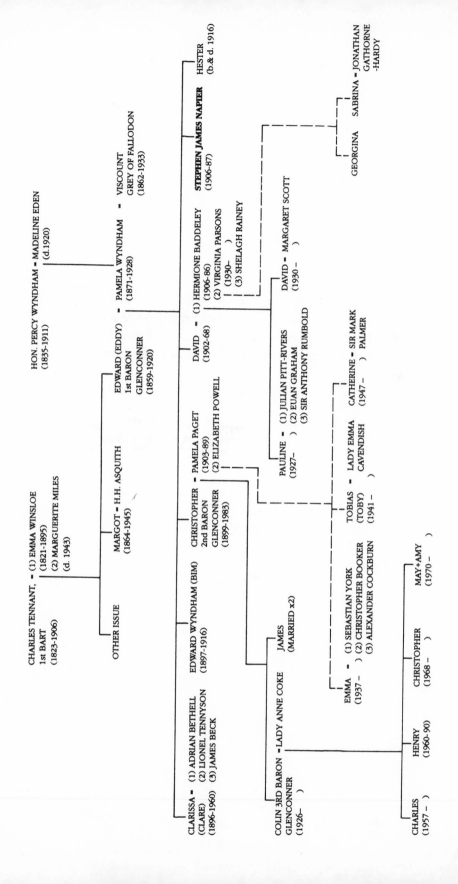

The Tennant Family Tree

Introduction

DRIVING DEEP INTO the heart of the Wiltshire countryside, on a minor 'B' road north of Salisbury, you travel along the winding lush valley of the upper Avon, past stone and thatch cottages, wide water-meadows with their stunted, pollarded willows, and through tunnel-like beech lanes. The air itself seems to become green, and the omnipresent lowering grey clouds above press one further down into soft landscape. Wilsford-cum-Lake is announced by a metal county council sign, around a steep bend. A straggle of farm-workers' cottages suddenly gives way to a much more imposing edifice – the gables of Lake House, sunning itself in the dip of the road. A little later, a war memorial to the right indicates the parish church of St Michael's. To its left is a little driveway with two or three respectable-looking brick houses – to its right is an altogether more mysterious pathway. Parking by the church gate one late autumn afternoon, I walked along this yew-shaded driveway, unevenly covered in old gravel, pot-holed and obviously little used; at its end was the chequer stone and flint frontage of Wilsford Manor.

It was my third visit to the house. Previous expeditions had found it empty – the local cleric told me no one was at home, but that I should have a look at the garden anyhow: 'I'm sure Mr Tennant wouldn't mind.' Then I had found a completely overgrown expanse of mature trees and long grass, peppered with ancient statuary and tumble-down disused fountains. To the right stood a building rather like a large greenhouse, its glazed roof and sides smashed intermittently, and a murky concrete pond inside, overshadowed by clumps of bamboo run wild. Those grasses were also dotted around the grounds, but even more exotic were the tall Chinese palms nearer the house, surrounding a conservatory in a similar state of disrepair. In it stood a wire garden chair, ornate and rusting, long since abandoned by its occupant. Where the conservatory abutted the house, the soft grey stone had been painted a bright pink which, despite its peeling surface, still looked brash and distinctly unEnglish. The whole garden looked like a decayed Mediterranean film-set.

Taking care not to put my foot through a rusty white-painted metal drum, or to tread on a fallen bust of a Roman emperor, I peered in through one of the windows. Very little was distinct, but there were intimations of precious things: a Chinese lacquer cabinet, and one or two old photographs, framed in gilt and pastel pink and blue. An empty bed stood in the middle of the room. I later learnt that the legendary incumbent of Wilsford was ill, and recuperating in a Wiltshire nursing-home. I toyed with the idea of trying to visit him there, but decided that it would be too much of an intrusion. Better to wait, and see.

I had begun to write long letters to Mr Tennant, rather too enthusiastic ones perhaps, full of praise for him and his work. I knew that they might appear insincere, but they were in fact completely truthful, for I had become fascinated by the man's mystique, his servitude to a life of truly applied art; that is, an exclusion of all else but beauty from his existence. I saw the Beaton photograph of him in his black mackintosh, his smouldering eyes looking out from 1927 across sixty years, and it seemed that this one image, this one person, encapsulated all that I thought glamorous about that time. And when I had discovered, in Hugo Vickers' biography of Cecil Beaton, that Stephen Tennant was very much still alive, and living in the time-warp of Wilsford Manor, I became determined to meet him.

Vickers had struck up a friendship with Stephen during his research on Beaton's life, and had persuaded Hamish Hamilton to reprint Stephen's comic book, *Leaves from a Missionary's Notebook*, that autumn. I had written two articles publicizing the book for my new hero, one in *Blitz* magazine – illustrated by the mackintosh photo – and a full page piece in *The Observer*, which appeared to have brought him to fame once more.

All this had only served to heighten my interest in Stephen Tennant and his life, rather than exorcize it, and one morning I woke from an extremely vivid dream, wherein I had been travelling to Wilsford to meet its occupant, but had learnt, *en route*, that he had died. Only a few minutes after waking, the telephone rang. It was Hugo Vickers, telling me he had dreamt Stephen had died. We agreed it must be an omen of sorts and, in Stephen's own words, decided to 'galvanize circumstances'. A plan was agreed with Hamish Hamilton, whereby I should personally deliver to Mr Tennant his six 'author copies' of *Leaves*, and Hugo undertook to write me a letter of introduction to the artist/author.

It was a very nervous would-be biographer who knocked on the side-door of Wilsford Manor that dark October afternoon, clutching a brown paper parcel of books in one hand, and a bunch of tiger-lilies and a letter in the other. After what seemed an age the door opened and Sylvia Blandford, Stephen's nurse-cum-housekeeper, answered. A Scottish woman in her late thirties, she seemed an oddly 'everyday' sort of person to be looking after such an extraordinary man. I explained my mission, and Sylvia looked askance. 'Um, I don't know – I'll have to go and see.' Having given her my letter of introduction, I stood waiting, apprehensively. She returned from some inner sanctum and said I would be seen, but just for ten minutes.

Sylvia led the way, past her homely part of the house, along a white-painted corridor, then, quite quickly, into the misty darkness of a curtained hall. I followed her up a wooden stairway, past open doors faced with pink and gold-starred wallpaper, with glimpses of golden things in dimly-lit rooms. Then we were out on a wide landing, incredibly stuffed with ornate furniture. There was no time for closer inspection, as Sylvia gave a tap on a side door, and showed me into a bedroom. The room was heavily curtained, and very dark. The first thing I saw was a dull, unshaded electric light bulb dangling from the centre of the room. Then, as my eyes grew accustomed to the dimness, I realized that to my right, propped up on a divan bed, covered by fur rugs and with a cup of tea and a Bakewell tart on a tray on his lap, was the Honourable Stephen Tennant.

He was much thinner than I had expected – probably because I was relying for recent visual imagery on reports from Hugo, who had seen Stephen before his latest illness. Now he was gaunt, quite bald with only a straggle of long steel-grey hair, and obviously weak. Yet as he sat up in bed, and extended a long, elegant, turquoise-beringed hand in greeting, I suddenly became aware that this was really him – that that face, with its noble cheekbones once more in evidence, belonged to the same person who had charmed a generation years before, and obsessed me now.

His toy monkey sat up beside Stephen as I handed him his books, whilst Sylvia put the flowers I had brought him in water. I told him how much he was appreciated in London. 'Am I famous?' he enquired modestly. 'Oh, terribly famous!' I replied. 'Really!' he said, almost in mock-astonishment. I gave him news of Hugo, and asked if he might sign our copies of *Leaves* for us. 'Yes, yes . . . of course,' he replied. 'Now what date is it?' he asked, answering himself before we could correct him, 'the very last day of October, I think . . .'

As he proceeded diligently to sign the books with his blue felt-tip pen, I looked around the room. It held a veritable clutter of things – all the totems that I had heard of: the rainbow-coloured fishnet, now draped over a screen, and shells, seemingly everywhere. Piles of letters, books, stuffed toys, jewellery boxes and fur rugs lay nonchalantly about the bed.

'Tell me what I've written now,' said Stephen as he finished, squinting in the semi-darkness to read his writing. Then I showed him the article I had written. 'You wrote about me? Oh, that's a lovely picture of me!' 'Isn't it lovely?' I agreed. 'Beautiful! That's lovely!' he exclaimed, bidding Sylvia to take it to the window so that she should scrutinize it all the better.

We said goodbye. 'Oh, what a cold hand!' said Stephen. 'Give him a nice hot cup of tea,' he instructed Mrs Blandford. But tea was the last thing I wanted as I stood in that incredible place, trying to convince myself I – or it – was really there. I asked Sylvia if I might have a look round. 'Of course,' she said – and vanished down another staircase. I was alone, in that great empty house, apparently undisturbed for years. Gingerly I groped my way round, amazed at each new sight. The gathered silk curtains, the swags of the borders high up on the walls. The rococo sugar-candy glass mirrors, the bearskins and brocade cushions and marble plant tubs and framed photographs. And piles of paintings, scattered like gigantic confetti across the rooms, on the floor, along consoles and up windowsills.

I climbed to the top of the house, up the limed staircase and its heavy balustrades, on which yellowing straw hats were piled (last worn by Stephen's Bloomsbury guests in 1929), to the attic rooms, dusty and unswept, apparently still waiting to be decorated. A grotto bench, gilt wood with fantastic undersea carvings, was stored in one corner, and an empty four-poster bed in the farthest corner reminded me that it was in one of the upper rooms that Cecil Beaton had stayed on his first visit to Wilsford in 1927. Back downstairs, I dutifully admired the photographs of Stephen by Beaton and Paul Tanqueray that stood alongside the portraits of his mother, Daphne du Maurier and Willa Cather on the grand piano. More metallic tinsel cushions, more chintz-covered sofas, more mirrors, chairs and tables cluttered every room. The ceiling was silver-foil, the walls wreathed in gold. And everything so still, so untouched.

Suddenly, I felt a little scared. Here I was, left alone in this house, with its strange occupant, and the housekeeper in some distant room. I had no idea of how to descend to ground level – which staircase had I been led up? Then I realized I was back by Stephen's bedroom, and I could hear him talking and laughing to himself. Downstairs, the front door shook with the wind and threatened to blow open, scattering the straw hats and shells like the autumn leaves it whipped up outside. Around the house, through rooms full of silver satin chairs and stacks of paintings, his voice echoed, laughing down the century . . .

The last letter that Stephen Tennant received, on the morning of his death, was one in which I announced, with a mixture of wary joyfulness, that Hamish Hamilton had agreed to publish the book I wished to write about him. Stephen was read the letter by his nurse, and an hour or so later, when Sylvia Blandford's daughter Louise came up with his morning tea, he told her the news. 'Isn't it exciting?' he said, and lay back on his pillows. Yes, he was famous; of that he could be sure.

Chapter 1

The Web of Childhood

Who mothered me? Who fathered me? No earthly parentage surely blessed me thus?
— Stephen Tennant's journal

IN the late nineteen-fifties, Diana Menuhin came to visit Stephen Tennant at Wilsford. He asked her to come up to his bedroom. 'There was no impropriety in that,' she recalls. 'He took me upstairs, and in one corner of the room was a sort of shrine to his mother. Stephen pointed to a photograph of him as a boy, in a dress, in Pamela's arms, looking adoringly into her face. "Look, Diana – there never really was any hope for me, was there?"'[1]

It is perhaps too easy to take a Freudian viewpoint of Stephen Tennant's childhood. A commanding, over-protective mother, a father who receded so far into the background that Stephen could remember very little of him. Therein a recipe for disaster? Perhaps. But also the grounds for the creation of a very extraordinary personality, one who would influence and inspire, as well as irritate and exasperate.

The world into which Stephen was born was one of luxury and privilege. The Tennants had reached their zenith simultaneously with the success of the British Empire. The Industrial Revolution was concomitant with their rise to aristocratic power, and they stood firmly amongst the great families in turn-of-the-century Britain. London society exhibited all the particular signs of this glory – a glittering round of elegant balls and artistic salons, within which Stephen's mother, Pamela, was an equally glittering figure. She was a Wyndham, a product of older and nobler breeding than the rich Scots family into which she had married, with the romanticism of French blue blood running in her veins. Stephen was fond of relating how his mother's antecedence could be traced to Philippe Égalité, an influential cousin of Louis XVI.

1

To Stephen, his father's family seemed positively drab and dour compared to Pamela's ancestors, an inheritance still evidenced by his maternal grandparents. Percy and Madeleine Wyndham counted amongst their friends artists like Edward Burne-Jones, Philip Webb and others of the Arts and Crafts Movement. Their home, Clouds, in Wiltshire, was the product of William Morris' precepts – aesthetic truth to form and materials – and the family's attitudes followed similar lines, with relaxed discipline extended towards Pamela and her siblings. There, contrary to accepted Victorian views, children were seen and heard. Her parents loved their children; 'those wild Wyndhams' spent as much time as possible with their offspring, cultivating their talents, an example that Pamela followed with her own children.

Born in 1871, Pamela grew up to be a strong-willed woman of great beauty (immortalized by John Singer Sargent in his famous painting of Pamela and her two sisters, dubbed 'The Three Graces' by an admiring Prince of Wales). Possessed of sharply-defined good looks and imperious bearing, Pamela was an excellent candidate for admission to an aristocratic 'club' of rebels that prevailed amongst the more liberated circles of her youth. These were 'The Souls', a group of about fifty young aristocrats which included members of both Pamela's and Eddy Tennant's families, as well as the Charteris and Lyttelton families. Their gods were the Pre-Raphaelites and William Morris; they eschewed facile London smartness, instigating their own liberated brand of wit and wisdom. When they assembled, most notably at Glen, there were intimate discussions of art, literature and life that shocked their tight-corseted parents. Amongst this incestuous company, Pamela's beauty, and her fiery nature, marked her out for particular attention – especially that of the opposite sex.

Pamela's first serious romance was probably her only true love affair. Harry Cust was a handsome Edwardian rake and literary editor who fell for Pamela as deeply as she fell for him. When the affair came to an abrupt end – Cust had to admit responsibility for another woman, who was pregnant by him[*] – there were recriminations on each side. H. G. Wells is said to have discovered Cust weeping in his office, whilst Pamela wrote to her lost lover letters full of grief, yet still implicitly faithful. She was sent to India to recover and met Eddy Tennant shortly after, in 1894. They

---

[*]Cust is said to have strewn Leicestershire with his bastards – Diana Cooper, whose family lived at Belvoir Castle in Rutland, acknowledged him as her father – and there have even been allegations that a certain grocer living in Grantham, by the name of Roberts, married the daughter of a Cust child.

married quite quickly; Pamela was eager to start a family and establish another life. She was in her mid-twenties, he thirty-five. It was not a match made in heaven, rather one of convenience. Her new husband was well-established, respectable, handsome, but little else. He could not, and would not, replace Cust.

Edward Priaulx Tennant was the first son of the great industrialist Sir Charles Tennant ('the Bart') to survive childhood, and he bore all the responsibility for carrying on the Tennant line. This new dynasty had had humble origins – as hill farmers in Ayrshire – but through the ingenuity and acumen of Eddy's ancestors had risen to become one of the wealthiest families of the nineteenth century. The prosaic basis for this rise was a successful formulation of a bleaching process, an invention which, when tied to the linen manufacture that was Scotland's major contribution to that explosion of capitalism, the Industrial Revolution, allowed Sir Charles the wherewithal to build his mock-baronial pile, Glen, in Peebleshire, an outward expression of their financial grandeur.

Glen must have seemed like a fairytale castle to the young Tennants. The main building, of grey stone, was erected in 1858, with twenty-nine bedrooms and six reception rooms; a large tower was added later. The garden was landscaped into wide terraces, and created the effect of a huge house nestling in the hills of Peebleshire, miles from road or rail. It was also far enough away from 'Tennant's Stalk', the huge factory chimney that dominated Glasgow's skyline, to distance the Tennants from their industrial roots. Glen was a remote kingdom, presided over by the bewhiskered Bart, who would outlive his first wife and eventually father a further three children, the youngest being born only two years before his death in 1906 – the year in which Pamela and Eddy's youngest son, Stephen James Napier Tennant, was born.

Eddy's childhood under the Bart's rule had not been entirely happy. His strong-willed and eccentric sister Margot (with whom he got on best, and who later married the Liberal Prime Minister, H. H. Asquith) recalled that the boys' tutor used to beat them viciously, inflicting mental and physical scars for life. Sir Charles seemed to relish only his eldest son's prowess with a gun, and was known to get Eddy out of bed late at night to show off his skill. Raymond Asquith observed in 1902 that the Bart was 'one of the most extraordinary men' he had ever seen, '78 years old . . . and a very decent shot, though he shot poor Eddy the other day in the bone of the eye, and another man in the balls . . .'[2]

Glen was the one constant in Eddy's life. Here he indulged his great passion, forestry, an escape from business duties in London, and the land around Glen gave him ample opportunity to experiment and plant, especially after Sir Charles' death, when the property became his. Eddy was an introspective, shy man, who could have had little in common with either his wife or his youngest son. A portrait painted at the time of Stephen's birth shows him tight-lipped against the world, his eyes fixed on a far horizon. Perhaps he was never happy – his career, such as it was, failed to take off. In 1900 he had campaigned for a parliamentary seat for the Liberals in Glasgow, but without success. Margot remarked, 'Eddy lacks drive, and as Pamela is born without it . . . they are not the people to conquer votes with.'[3] Yet six years later, Eddy won the seat for Salisbury, helped once more by his wife. A man who met Stephen in later life recalled the campaign. 'Mr Baillon then said how much like my mother I looked – said apropos of her beauty – "There was many a Tory turned Liberal when they saw her – she was the most beautiful woman I ever saw."'[4] Eddy finally accepted the title of Lord Glenconner in 1911, after three other such offers had been made to the family by the Crown. In the same year, he became Lord High Commissioner to the General Assembly of the Church of Scotland. But these were all duties; he would have been quite content to have left it all to manage Glen's forests.

With the more prominent profile of the family engendered by their new title came a move south. The Glenconners already had a London address, 34 Queen Anne's Gate, overlooking St James's Park, a grand town house with a large annexe housing the famous Tennant Collection of paintings (the first private collection to be opened to the public). But a country home was needed, and for Pamela there was no location more desirable than her home county, Wiltshire. She wanted to be near Clouds, but also to be far from the Bart's domination of Glen, and the Tennants' coarse Scottish antecedence. Pamela found the tiny village of Wilsford-cum-Lake, up the winding Avon valley north of Salisbury. Lake House was the only substantial building nearby, renovated in 1898 by her mother's architect friend, Detmar Blow. Thus Lake, with its gables and mullioned windows, became the model for Wilsford Manor.

Blow and his builders demolished an old farmhouse which stood on the site – a gently sloping expanse of ground, surrounded even then by a protective bank of mature trees that shielded it from the Amesbury road. 'Truth to material' demanded that all the stones of the old building be reused in the new building, as if to give it a 'race memory', a patina of age which would not trumpet its newness. The creepers which had covered its walls were preserved, as were the box-yews, holm oaks and ancient lawns, and the new house was erected around these natural obstacles, a corner of it carefully angled to accommodate a venerable old yew. The house was to sink into its setting, a metaphor for Pamela's ancestry over the 'new money' of the Tennants.

Nikolaus Pevsner gives the building's provenance as 'built with local labour and without a sub-contractor. The style is that of the local 17c. Chequer flint and stone, gables, mullioned windows. Late 17c. staircase with strong banisters.' (Writing in the nineteen-fifties, he adds acidly, that 'the woodwork, made by Ernest Gimson, has all disappeared'.)[5] The staircase had been ripped out of a house in Blandford Forum, bought by the Tennants for that purpose alone; the shaped timbers of the top floor and Gimson's panelling had the effect of giving the interior a warm 'homely' atmosphere. The interior of Wilsford Manor reveals an asymmetrical structure that added to this feeling of cosiness. Each room leads into another, and walking through large reception rooms, up the graceful staircase and along expansive landings to the well-appointed bedrooms, a newcomer to the house had the impression of constant discovery, as though on an expedition through a maze of pleasing spaces, each turn designed to bring a leafy leaded window into view. On and up went the house until, reaching the upper rooms on its third floor, the disorientated visitor was not at all sure how to regain ground level.

Each of the rooms was individually decorated and assigned a name under Pamela's direction – 'Blue Tulip', 'Jessamine', 'Little Rose Leaf Room'. Some rooms were left unfinished, so that Pamela could decide their characteristics later. But Wilsford Manor was designed as a family home, with Pamela's four (soon to be five) children in mind. There was a cottage-like nursery wing, thatched and low-built, with solid oak timbers and sloping roof, abutting the main house. Adjoining it was a tiny round two-storey children's playhouse, complete with a staircase up to a first-floor hideaway and a conical thatched roof. Even inside the 'grown-ups'' house, there was a 'Pirate's Stronghold' and a 'Cave Room'; and the 'Stone Parlour' below, one side of which opened out on to the garden, was furnished like a country kitchen. Here Pamela could live a simple life with her brood, as though Wilsford Manor were still the old farmhouse that this large mansion had replaced.

The land around Wilsford was the Tennants', almost as far as the eye could see. As well as the manor's grounds themselves, extensive enough to require the services of sixteen gardeners, there was the neighbouring farm, Normanton, and its land, acquired by Eddy, with fields stretching west and north as far as Stonehenge. To the east was the Avon, with its fishing rights. And southwards was Lake House, which Eddy also bought, and let out to the Bailey family.

The Tennant children were brought up in the Thatched Wing, its compact little rooms connected to their parents' bedrooms by a long corridor. Along this narrow passage Pamela came, to talk and play with her children. Clarissa, known as Clare, was the eldest, born in 1896, a beautiful, wayward girl who would grow up to rival even her mother's looks. A year later came Edward Wyndham, nicknamed 'Bim', very much his mother's child. Christopher was born in 1899, then David in 1902. Pamela's last surviving child was Stephen, who came into the world on 21 April 1906,* shortly after the family had taken possession of their new home. It was significant that Stephen should be born at Wilsford, for the home and its mistress would determine his life completely.

Even Pamela could not take on all the duties involved in rearing four sons and a daughter, and Rebecca Trusler was a nanny whose services came highly recommended – her previous employers had been the families of both Philip Burne-Jones and Rudyard Kipling (cousins and family friends of the Wyndhams). A rotund, affable London widow in early middle-age – she was forty-nine when she joined the household, in the year of Stephen's birth – Nannie Trusler was beloved of all her charges, the younger children in particular. With her broad Cockney accent and kindly, large-featured face, she was the ideal no-nonsense *in loco parentis*. Even Pamela, whose standards were set so high, approved.

Rebecca Trusler would come to be one of the most important people in Stephen's life, ever-present, always consoling, sometimes stern, but never less than 'belovèd' – Stephen liked to accent the second 'e' to stress her preciousness. If parted, they would communicate almost daily by letter, and Stephen would ask friends such as Elizabeth Lowndes, whom he knew from early childhood, to look after her for him. To Susan Lowndes, Elizabeth's younger sister,† Rebecca Trusler was 'the sort of nanny every child would love to have. She was stoutish, homely, old-fashioned – comfortable. Grey-haired and cosy, she never got cross with you.'[7]

*There is a story that Stephen was the product of a Dr Aaron, who had a method of artificially inseminating society women who could not conceive with their husbands. In one version, the doctor had a stud of eligible footmen waiting outside the door. In another, a teaspoon was used to carry the husband's semen to impregnate his wife. Lady Diana Cooper alleged that Stephen was an 'Aaron's baby',[6] although there exists no evidence for this other than the fact that Eddy's relationship with Pamela was always a fragile one, and had grown yet more distant by 1905.
†Their mother was the famous crime writer, Marie Belloc Lowndes (1868–1947), sister of Hilaire Belloc, and a great friend of Pamela's.

Nannie might admonish her charges for some small misdemeanour, but seldom was a harsh word heard.

Nannie Trusler supervised the day-to-day upbringing of all the Tennant children, but Stephen – 'Steenie' as he became known to the family – she loved most of all, with his bubbly halo of golden curls, his bright blue eyes and angelic, chubby face. He had a sweet nature which would appeal to any would-be mother, and to Nannie Trusler he seemed almost her own. Trusler's special fondness for Steenie would cause his mother not a little concern, as she saw her employee gradually become a rival for Stephen's affections, and even took steps to limit Nannie's influence over her youngest by adopting a village orphan boy, Barnaby Keel, to be 'Nannie's boy'. But Pamela could never break the bond that had been made between the two, and her own relationship with Stephen suffered as a result. As Susan Lowndes observed years afterwards, 'Pamela was the star, but Nannie was the rock – I think, truly, Stephen loved his nanny more than his mother.'[8]

Osbert Sitwell, who was to befriend Bim Tennant during the Great War, wrote that Pamela loved her children 'in a French and not an English way; she wished to be with [them] throughout the day – the last thing, as a rule, that an English parent of her kind would desire – and to regulate absolutely their lives.'[9] Her children were an extension of her own charm, an adjunct, almost a fashion accessory. Peter Quennell noted that visitors to Glen would be received in the hall, 'so that by the time you arrived upstairs, Lady Glenconner had assembled her family around her in a sort of photographic pose – Clare looking pretty, Stephen on her knee, and so on'.[10] Stephen himself later noted down a caustic comment from his Aunt Margot's lips: 'I never care for a woman draped in her children – let them go.'[11] The fact that Pamela never did let go would be the root of their problems, as she herself acknowledged in her book, *The Sayings of the Children*: 'For the child is still then an exquisite plaything for its Mother, presenting no problems as yet. Nevertheless these are the years when a Mother may learn a great deal, for problems are all there, latent; and if she listens, she will have a guide to later years . . .'[12]

Pamela was a paradox – a dreamy beauty, yet with a steely will. She lived simply and poetically, yet entertained the Prime Minister at dinner. Susan Lowndes observes that Pamela's temper 'would not be tolerated nowadays. Sometimes it became so extreme that she would literally be on the floor biting the carpet in rage',[13] and Osbert Sitwell was shown 'the marks on her wrist she had made where she had dug the nails of the other hand into it, in order to prevent herself from being rude to a visitor she had disliked . . .'[14]

To Edith Olivier, Pamela 'seemed to pour ideas into one's mind like wine into an empty glass',[15] whilst to others, like Cecil Beaton, she was a fairy godmother, remote and beneficial, overlooking the younger people with a guiding eye. Edith's niece, Rosemary, remembers her as 'a very grand figure, draped in furs – I was rather frightened of her, actually.'[16] Pamela was formidable, yet tender. She oversaw her children's education, a subject in which their father had little say. Like some avid gardener caring for early blooms, Pamela would allow nothing to stand in the way of the pursuit of their cultivation.

Soon after recovering from Stephen's birth, Pamela made Wilsford host to all her friends. Regular visitors included Arthur Balfour, Henry Newbolt, Arthur Conan Doyle and Philip Burne-Jones. Pamela disliked the London season, which she referred to as 'murdered summers'.[17] Wilsford Manor, her own creation, became something of a retreat, a refuge from the hubbub of the London salons.

In this atmosphere Stephen spent his formative years. With 'Mummie' and 'Nannie', he lived an early life of comforting daily routine, playing in the garden with his older brothers, and helping his mother in the Stone Parlour. He also had friends like Tossie Ford, one of Pamela's adopted village children, but Stephen's real company was the nature around him. In the grounds of Wilsford, and in the quiet country life of the village, he came to know natural things. Trees and flowers fascinated him, as did the fauna. Mary Hartley, one in a long line of governesses, used to take young Stephen butterfly-hunting in Teagle Lane in the village: 'Her agility far surpassed mine,' recalled Stephen.[18] With his mother's encouragement, a close examination of the natural world held limitless fantasies for him; frogs and toads became the populations of fairytales.

Pamela's fostering of his burgeoning imagination was manifested in her recording all the babyish phrases, naive utterings that she interpreted as having other meanings more mature than their speaker's age. She had already made her offspring famous in *The Children and the Pictures*, tales she told to explain the events portrayed in the great works of art in the Tennant Collection. In *The Sayings of the Children*, her offspring are given numbers instead of names – One to Five, in order of their ages. Pamela unashamedly states that 'Five was almost certainly the best Baby of all. To Five and Three, the Mother gives the highest praise. Invariably happy, sweet-tempered, contented, gentle, and amused. When Five was two years old he cried because he had stepped on the dog's foot, and he thought he must have hurt it. "What a soft-hearted Baby," exclaimed the Irish Cook, who had witnessed the happening; and she added she had not known "a Baby could be pitiful".' Here is the formative Stephen: 'Five very early in life saw design in what was around him. At about four years old he perceived the countenance in the blossom of a pansy. It actually arrested him as he ran down the garden path. "Oh!" he cried: "Something's looking"; and he pointed at the flower's face. Then he crouched down on the path with his cheek almost at the level of the box edging: and the Mother watched both creatures gazing into each other's face closely.'[19]

Examples of Stephen's wisdom crowd the book with knowing insights into his childish view of the world: 'Five was astonished when he found Cain and Abel were both boys . . . Five would always allude to a pair as "husband and Mother", when putting his Noah's Ark out two by two. And when looking at a pair of doves, he asked: "Are they mister and a she?"' Many of the sayings attributed to Five recurred in Stephen's later life. (He describes a flower as having 'such a forgiving blue', a phrase which he used as an adult, presenting a bouquet to Elizabeth Bowen.) The effect of Pamela having published her children's sayings was to inculcate a feeling of import to their early lives. When she relayed Stephen's exclamation: 'While I was running fast over the flowers on the Downs, I heard all the flowers saying: "Stephen, Stephen"', Pamela acknowledged that 'what may be self-centred in later life is prettily cloaked in childhood'.

The book describes the children's caravan expeditions, which Pamela saw as escapes from the 'daily routine [that] clamps us. Few people are strong enough, or even willing, to go away for long from the cares that concern them. It is the small duties of life that pin and hamper.' As early as this, Stephen began to realize that there were duties the world would demand of him, and perhaps, like Peter Pan, the Boy Who Never Grew Up, he determined even now to avoid them. When she wrote that 'Five has a pleasant fancy that beguiles much of his time', Pamela foresaw a life of poetic aspiration for her youngest son, away from the smoky business of his father's father, and away from the responsibilities of the world.

Chapter 2

The Never-Land

'I don't want ever to be a man,' he said with passion. 'I want always to be a little boy and to have fun. So I ran away to Kensington Gardens and lived a long long time among the fairies.'

— J. M. Barrie: *Peter Pan and Wendy*

THOSE years before the Great War were 'sweet and carefree', according to Osbert Sitwell, then a young man in his early twenties. 'Never had Europe been so prosperous and gay.' He saw in the flowers that decorated the grand houses a symbol of lustrous epoch, 'a profusion of full-blooded blossoms . . . that lent to some houses an air of exoticism'.[1] Wilsford was one such place. All England seemed like a hot-house, and Stephen was growing up in this perfervid environment, bottle-fed by Pamela on a rarefied diet of culture and beauty.

In London, Diaghilev and Bakst had 'splashed the city' with their colours. New young talent came from people like Osbert and Edith Sitwell, already champions of the avant-garde, establishing their own poetry magazine, *Wheels*, which published Bim Tennant's verse (and was partly edited by Nancy Cunard, with whom Pamela's eldest was romantically linked). Ronald Firbank was beginning to weave his own exotic mystique and baroque prose, and the 'Corrupt Coterie' of Diana Manners and her friends – the children of the Souls – danced a new social tango. Entertainments in the London houses of the rich 'grew in number and magnificence . . . Champagne bottles stood stacked on the side-boards.'[2] In such fecundity Society glittered, basking in the affluence and security of imperial Britain.

It was a heady legacy for Stephen to inherit, but one which was all too soon to be violently curtailed by the events of 1914–18. Within a year of Diaghilev's *L'Après-Midi d'un Faune* opening in London, Stephen's father Eddy would be standing with Sir Edward Grey, the Foreign

Secretary, in his office in Whitehall. 'The lamps are going out all over Europe,' Sir Edward told Lord Glenconner. 'We shall not see them lit again in our lifetime.'

[handwritten annotation: GREY & CHURCHILL WERE FOR WAR OTHERS RESIGNED AT DECLARATION MORLEY & ... SHAW DAMNED GREY]

Stephen grew long-limbed and tall, despite the apparent sickliness which had been present from birth. Early photographs show the change from podgy baby into a straw-hatted toddler, playing in the sunny garden whilst his mother writes inside. The features began to appear that would make him into a handsome young man: strong chin and cheekbones, a well-shaped, longish nose, an elegant almond-shaped head – a refinement, in fact, of Eddy's looks, even to the curly blond hair ('that poisonous wave',[3] as he later referred to it). Most striking of all, though, were his mother's eyes: solemn, sultry, piercing blue-green, looking knowingly out at the world, even at that tender age. They were the eyes of a boy ready to see the world's beauty, and to exclude all else. Eyes of intelligence, of selectivity, exhibiting a certain disdain behind the charming, disarming smile.

A tale is told of Eddy, Lord Glenconner, lining up his younger sons to ask of them what they would become. Each reported the usual boyish aspirations: Christopher to be a businessman, David an engineer. Eddy nodded approvingly. Then came Stephen's turn. What did he want to be when he grew up? 'I want to be a Great Beauty, Sir,' he apparently replied.[4] How could Eddy ever have influence over such a child? Even Pamela was aware of the difficulties: 'Don't tell Eddy Steenie plays with dolls,' she asked of her niece, Kathleen.*[5] Was she culpable? There is a telling piece of childish talk, intended for publication in *Sayings*, but excluded for reasons known only to Pamela: 'Stephen and Malcolm,† talking together, Glen 1913. Malcolm: "Don't tell Nannie or anyone, but you know I'm a little girl really, all the time!" Stephen: "How do you know?" Malcolm: "Don't you know I wear a ribbing in my hair at night?"'[6]

Anyone could be forgiven for mistaking Steenie for a little girl. With his pretty face and long blond hair, and the fussy dresses in which his mother clothed him up to the age of eight, he looked like the daughter her friends said she wished Stephen had been. Sir Steven Runciman remembers seeing Stephen walking in St James's Park in skirts: 'Stephen was a substitute Clare, I think.'[7] When William Chappell's journalist mother

---

*Kathleen Tennant, later the Duchess of Rutland. Stephen was pageboy at her wedding in 1916.
†Son of Lord Glenconner's best friend, General Arthur Wolfe Murray, to whom he left a sizeable bequest in his will.

interviewed Pamela at home in 1914, she came back with a story of 'the most beautiful child she had ever seen', almost impossibly a boy.[8] With gifts of jewellery from his mother and her friends, such things shaped a young mind.

Once, when Eddy was away, Pamela turned the large racquets court at Wilsford into a theatre, where a production of *The Sleeping Beauty* was staged, directed from its wooden gallery, with Stephen in the leading role. With no young females to rival his claim on the part, Stephen launched himself into his role. It was his *métier*, he decided – to be on display – and Pamela did nothing to dissuade him of these inclinations. How could she protest, then, when he came down one day with a beauty spot carefully positioned on his cheek? Her reprimand to his posing brought the reply, 'But Mummie, I always pose.'[9]

Pamela lovingly recorded the growing progress of all her children as would a gardener, in a book of their weights, naked and clothed, summer and winter: '13 July 1915. Stephen Tennant (in clothes): 4st 6lb . . . 1916. Stephen in summer clothes: 5 stones . . . 24 April 1917. Stephen – in sleeping suit: 5 stones – in clothes: 5st 6lb.' And so on, even up to 16 April 1924, when Stephen was nearly eighteen: 'Nude – 9st 6lb to 7lb'[10] – as though her children were orchids grown under glass.

Stephen was eight years old when the Great War began – and as it ground to an uneasy halt, he was already approaching puberty. They were turbulent years in which to grow up, but apart from certain economies, it seemed the war would hardly affect him – though both his elder brothers enlisted.

Whilst young Steenie drew clever scenes of Zeppelin raids over London, Europe soaked in blood. In 1916, twenty thousand young British men died in the first day of the Battle of the Somme in France, and Stephen's poet brother was there. 'Death and decomposition strew the ground,'[11] wrote Bim to his worried mother on 18 September. A few days later, he became another of those dead men in a muddied field, felled by a sniper's bullet. He died with four photographs of his mother in his pocket.

It was a shock from which Pamela never recovered, and one which had reverberations for young Stephen. With this object of his mother's affections gone, much of that love was invested thereafter in David and Stephen. Bim's death had compounded a sorrow already grieving Pamela: in May she had given birth to a sixth child, Hester, her longed-for second daughter, but she died within hours. Pamela buried the child at

Queen Anne's Gate, then went to the Salisbury Infirmary. 'I've lost my baby,' she told the Matron. 'Have you any orphans?'[12] That night a tinker woman called Hope had died giving birth to a son. He was named Oliver, and taken back to Wilsford to be brought up with the Tennant children, but he was not a successful import into the family. ('His breeding worked out' they said, and he grew rebellious. Eventually Christopher put him into the Merchant Navy.*)

Stephen had one legacy from Bim – his new school, West Downs, which he entered that autumn. Bim had written only a month or so before his death to his old housemaster to warn him that he would 'not find S. an easy chap in some ways. He's a non-combatant, by nature, and a conscientious objector to things essentially manly, such as jumping on other little boys' faces and having his own jumped on.' Bim could not 'overcome a wish to go to you rather than elsewhere',[13] fearing what his little brother's peer group might make of Steenie.

The fact that Stephen had apparently had to be taken away from another preparatory school, Sherborne, because he had cried too much did not bode well for West Downs or its new pupil. Living, eating, sleeping amongst other boys, with the added privations of war, made prep school an uncomfortable experience. A contemporary at West Downs, the Reverend A. E. Ford, recalls 'a very shadowed time'. Heating during that winter was strictly limited – 'I never had so many chilblains in my life.'

The Reverend Ford remembers Stephen as 'a very slender, fair-haired boy, quite delicate . . . He was clever, I think – but not keen on games.'[14] Nor would Stephen have been keen on the activities of the school Scouts, who were detailed to dig practice trenches on the playing fields. One time he pricked his hot water bottle with a pin, to make staff believe it – or he – was leaking. Just two months of school life were enough for both parties, and Stephen was taken away by Pamela before Christmas.

Stephen was much happier at home, doted upon by Mummie, cared for by Nannie. Thereafter lessons were given at Wilsford, by a stream of private tutors (twenty in one year alone), or in London, where Elizabeth and Susan Lowndes sometimes joined his dancing class at Queen Anne's Gate. Here Stephen would perform in a long smock-like shirt, learning his dainty steps along with his young friends. The Lowndes children often

---

*It appears that Stephen kept in contact with Oliver Hope in later life, still sending presents of a pipe and tobacco to him in Alexandria, Egypt, as late as 1935.

stayed with the Tennants during the war, partly because Wilsford was safer than their parents' London house, but also because Stephen and David were their ages, and good playmates. Susan Lowndes recalls 'great games of "kickapeg"',[15] a sort of hide-and-seek, and in the grounds at Wilsford they would slide along the thick hedges on tea-trays, much to the annoyance of the gardeners.

The dancing lessons stood Stephen in good stead for one of his first public appearances on stage a year later. He had already been in one of the 'Tableaux Vivants' at the Royal Albert Hall in 1914, dressed in a satin gown and cradled lovingly in his mother's arms, but this new role was more demanding. He was a main character in a ballet devised by the family friend and author of *Peter Pan*, J. M. Barrie. Entitled *The Origin of Harlequin*, it was staged as a charity performance at Wyndham's Theatre in August 1917. Stephen remembered the rehearsals vividly, not only because he enjoyed any kind of theatricality (later he would declare: 'I'm very like a stage person, really – I think I have a talent for acting'),[16] but because visitors included the society beauty Lady Diana Manners, and the sophisticated actress Gladys Cooper. The latter's beauty staggered him, with her 'doe-eyes and heart-shaped face', and yet this goddess sat on a chair 'like an ordinary woman and spoke in a chattery voice'.[17] Many of his early childish drawings featured these heroines of the theatre, icons of beauty and glamour.

Daphne du Maurier also took part in the performance. 'I remember you well!' wrote the author of *Rebecca*, sixty years later: 'You danced so well in that ballet, and I can see you now at the few rehearsals we had, wearing dark grey trousers and of course in those days hair quite short, and I remember thinking how terribly clever it was of a boy of 13 or so, which you seemed to be, to be able to dance so admirably!'[18]

Bim's death had turned Pamela's interest toward spiritualism, the drawing-room hobby made fashionable in the late nineteenth century, and which the losses of the Great War served to popularize. Sir Oliver Lodge, famous for developing wireless technology, was one of its scientific exponents, and was also a family friend of the Glenconners. Eddy had leased a house across the lane from Wilsford Manor to the scientist, allowing him to build a large room on top of it in which he could carry out his experiments. Distraught as Pamela was after Bim's loss, she turned to Lodge to help her try and contact her son 'on the other side'.*

* Pamela seems to have had a good grounding in the subject as her father, Percy Wyndham, was, according to Lodge, 'one of the earliest investigators into psychical phenomena'.[19]

Together, she and Lodge carried out a psychic contact method in which a medium goes into a trance and contacts a spirit guide, who indicates messages from the deceased loved one by naming pages and numbered lines in books in the house library. Pamela was convinced that through these 'book tests' she had contacted Bim. A medium, Mrs Leonard, was supposed to have used an Indian spirit guide, 'Feda', to bring Bim back from the dead. So convinced was Pamela that in 1921 she published the results of her seances in a book, *The Earthen Vessel*, which set out to prove 'our conviction that we have spoken with our son'. Such misplaced hope was readily grasped at by grieving parents, and Pamela's book was a success.

The atmosphere at Wilsford Manor must have been very strange then, with Pamela entertaining odd people and conducting mysterious experiments in darkened rooms. Although young visitors like the Lowndes girls recall that they were kept out of such goings-on, David Tennant was drawn into his mother's spiritualist sessions – with Stephen sometimes as their subject, as a transcript of a later session indicates: 'Good morning! Good morning! Very glad, very glad to see you,' went one message from 'Feda' (via Mrs Leonard). '. . . The Lord is here, and Bim is here . . . He wants to help now . . . and he seems as though he rather wanted to help David and Stephen and Christopher . . . He says he has an idea he is going away with Stephen. Oh! What a nuisance; Bim seems to have an idea he is going away with Stephen somewhere. Well, Feda thought it would be nice for him to stay here . . .'[20]

These sessions did not impress Aunt Margot. 'I always knew the living talked rot,' she said to Henry Channon after listening to Sir Oliver lecturing on such experiments, 'but it's nothing to the nonsense the dead talk.'[21] Nevertheless, at large spiritualist meetings, Pamela – and even Eddy – testified to their belief publicly. Pamela would pursue spiritualism throughout the rest of her life.

As the war ended, a family expedition to America was planned for winter 1919. The family friend, Sir Edward Grey, now Special Ambassador to Washington, promised an informed tour – and introduction to the best society and entertainments New York could offer. So Stephen and his siblings packed their bags for the New World.

They sailed from Southampton and arrived in New York in December. Below the windows of their luxurious Waldorf Astoria hotel suite were the bustling streets of a city untouched by war. New, vibrant, exciting, for Stephen it was the first physical contact with an almost unbelievable new world. Pamela was also impressed by America, and wrote – a little sardonically – in her journal: 'How pleasant it is! I never knew I was so delightful! or could be so clever! – how overlooked I have been until now! What have the people in London been thinking about? – didn't they know then that I was with them? – here, people seem hardly to have existed till we came among them! – my room is a bower of roses, the table groans under cards . . .'[22]

One glamorous treat for Stephen was his visit to the Metropolitan Opera House to see the famed Enrico Caruso, 'the man with the orchid-lined voice', perform. Stephen sat entranced. 'All too glorious for words,' he wrote later, and recalled it in a snippet of verse:

When I heard Caruso sing
So long ago – in New York City
He woke the Goddess of Spring . . .
An English boy was happy then . . .[23]

The Tennants' social success in New York was compounded when they began to travel round the country, on a Pullman chartered by Lord Glenconner from New York to Chicago. The thrill of sitting in the observation car on that long ride out West must have been memorable for a thirteen-year-old; across Pennsylvania and Ohio, past the Great Lakes and wilderness of North America, sights later stirred by the prose of his favourite author, Willa Cather. There were stops in snow-covered Denver and Boston, where Pamela consulted local mediums. Stephen was 'very impressed; Truth, with a touch of charlatanism'. One medium told them 'things unknown to us both, which we checked in England. She couldn't have read our minds,'[24] he observed.

From Chicago they went to Santa Barbara, California, where the announcement of their arrival in the local newspaper highlighted the distance between father and son. 'Scottish Magnate is now staying at the Ambassador's Hotel', read the report. 'I remember saying to my father, "If you're a magnet, may I ask what you're a magnet for?" It wasn't well received at all,'[25] recalled Stephen. The newspaper also announced that the Tennants' youngest son was giving dance recitals at their hotel; young Steenie was showing off the steps he had learnt at Queen Anne's Gate.

Stephen loved California, discovering there the beauty of sea-shells which would become a near-obsession for him, finding on the beach 'the kind with bluegreen iridescence' (abalones) that fascinated him. He went shopping with Pamela, buying crêpes de Chine and wonderful silks.

On their return to England, Stephen confessed to feeling down-hearted.

'I feel that American gaiety is somehow more convincing and infectious than the London species... I remember thinking New York and California parties stupendous compared to English ones... in London one feels everyone is very tepid afterwards compared with the cordiality and zest of American friends.'[26] He longed to go back to a land where he felt 'so appreciated'.

'I suppose at times I've been very conceited,' admitted Stephen towards the end of his life, 'because I have dazzled many people with my talk. When I first grew up I had a very rich vocabulary, a very wide, wide outlook altogether.'[27] Pamela thought her son inspired by William Blake, while Stephen came to think of himself as talented, someone special, even before he had begun his adult life. A precocious artistic talent was already emerging (a watercolour of the Wilsford garden done in 1917 seems very proficient for an eleven-year-old), and it was this facility that was first to establish him as a 'phenomenon'.

But in 1920, tragedy struck the Tennant family once more. Eddy, Lord Glenconner, died quite unexpectedly after a relatively routine operation, aged just sixty-one. If their mother had been any less of a person than she was, the family might have fallen apart, but Pamela found it surprisingly easy to cope, especially with her faith in spiritualism, which had taught her that no one was lost for ever. The effect on Stephen is difficult to judge. Certainly he hardly missed Eddy: 'My father was such a dull man, I can't even remember what he looked like,'[28] he later remarked. He felt no guilt at this. For Stephen, Eddy had just been a shadowy figure who provided, and little else.

In his will, Lord Glenconner left his Wilsford and Queen Anne's Gate properties, and the bulk of his sizeable assets, in trust to Pamela.* Glen went to Christopher, who inherited the title (after Bim's death) of second Baron Glenconner. Clare, already into her second marriage, was left a large lump sum, the residue to be eventually divided between David and Stephen. Disproportionately for the two youngest sons, Stephen was also specifically bequeathed Lake House and a newly acquired Tennant property, Dryburgh Abbey, in Berwickshire. Monies were left, too, to Sir Edward Grey, now Lord Grey, and to Nannie Trusler 'as some recognition of her services faithfully performed to my children' an

*Lord Glenconner's unsettled property was valued at £819,479 gross, with £640,899 net personalty. The will, written in 1916, also indicated that Lord Glenconner's body was to be cremated, 'and my ashes placed in an Oak box of such a size that it can be readily carried by one man'.

annuity for life. A codicil refers to Dryburgh Abbey, a tenth-century monastic ruin, with Sir Walter Scott's tomb in the church of St Mary's Aisle, to be left for 'national purposes', but the rest of the property was to be held 'as real estate in trust for my son Stephen James Napier Tennant'.[29] Despite his dullness, Stephen's father had left him an embarrassment of riches.

The Tennants left 34 Queen Anne's Gate to live in Pamela's house at 4 Buckingham Street. With David at Cambridge, Clare married and Christopher busy at Tennant & Co., Stephen could enjoy his mother's company alone. On one trip to Stratford-upon-Avon they met the best-selling novelist Marie Corelli. Author of innumerable romantic novels, Corelli was a friend of the Burne-Joneses and the Wyndhams, and lived nearby in Maison Croft, an elegant Georgian house. Now 'frankly grotesque'[30] in appearance, she was nonetheless a town celebrity, and her eccentric ways emphasized her reclusiveness. She dressed like a young girl despite being over sixty, and often talked in a kind of baby language – when Philip Burne-Jones had a fit of exhaustion on a visit to her, she laid him out on the sofa and administered brandy and warm water in spoon-fuls, saying: 'Now ickle droppie more . . . and then a snooze till dinner-time, and bright as a button again.'[31] Not for nothing did E. F. Benson draw upon Corelli's idiosyncrasies for the character of Lucia in his *Mapp and Lucia* novels. Such qualities did not go unobserved by the young Stephen. He later described her as 'the most extraordinary sort of fixation . . . She liked being with a very dark woman'[32] (her 'companion', Bertha Vyner). One afternoon, as they sat having tea, Pamela wandered off into the garden. Corelli turned to the young Stephen and said, 'Would you like to see a hollow tree at the back of the house? It's a hollow tree that I've made a little spiral staircase in, and I go up it when I'm alone and have tea with my dolls, all around me.' 'Lovable! Lovable!' exclaimed Stephen, but when he told it all to his brother Christopher on returning home, 'he thought I was inventing it! He said, "She sounds dotty to me!"'

Stephen also recalled a stay with the Earl of Strathmore, at Glamis Castle, whilst the family were at Glen. There he met their young daughter, Lady Elizabeth Bowes-Lyon, later to become a close friend of his brother Christopher. The enormous castle was the legendary home of the Monster, said to be a hugely deformed figure which lived in a secret room. Stephen noted 'rotting tapestries' and 'hideous Danish furniture' at Glamis, and found his room decorated with 'spinachy green and sour yellow tapestries'.[33] Lady Strathmore told him that one wing of the building was never used, yet, coming down to dinner that evening, he and Pamela evidently saw a footman cross the hall, go under the rope that separated it, and up a staircase. In his hands was an enormous tray of steaming hot food. Speculating on the nature of the Monster, Stephen was told that it took the shape of 'a huge sheep-dog' or was 'half-man, half-baboon'.

Although Stephen often seemed a shy and introspective boy – he described himself as having 'eyes like a panic-stricken fawn or gazelle'[34] – he was already an entertainer, overcoming innate shyness to perform in public or private. His love of stars like Anna Pavlova and Sarah Bernhardt was matched only by his worship of the fabulous Russian Ballet, interests which developed into active preoccupations, and he often acted out – or danced – scenes for the benefit of family and friends.

Stephen's own friends were select and few. First and foremost came the Lowndes girls: Elizabeth, six years older than Stephen, dark-haired and attractive, and her younger sister Susan, just as pretty; Stephen loved them both. Other occasional playmates included the Herbert boys, sons of the Earl of Pembroke who lived at nearby Wilton House, and Rosemary Olivier, niece of Wiltshire author and Pamela's friend, Edith Olivier. But Stephen's idea of fun sometimes included some very naughty behaviour. Already exhibiting a certain attraction to his own sex, and evidently quite precocious in physical matters, he began experiments which for other boys would have been restricted to school dormitories, but which for him had a more public display. At fourteen, he would approach soldiers from the nearby training camps at Bulford and Larkhill with cigarettes in return for a kiss. Even worse, the young teenager would sometimes wait until a charabanc full of tough soldiers was passing, then lower his trousers to bare his bottom at them. News of this behaviour soon reached Pamela, and was ignored, even when Stephen was later caught by a policeman, doing something he shouldn't with one of His Majesty's military personnel. Stephen was frogmarched back to the Manor; discretion meant no further action was taken by the local constabulary, who believed the parents would deal with the matter – yet not a word of comment was passed at the dinner table.

Stephen's tutors tried to teach him the orthodoxies of the world, but as the youthful doodles on his textbooks show, he was more interested in his pet toads, or contemporary fashion. In *Victor and Victorine*, his French reader, he sketched elegant ladies' hats and shoes; in his French primer, profiles of lovely women. And in an earlier *Scripture Verses*, the margins are covered with crocodiles, snakes, dragonflies and butterflies, along with religious figures – 'Jesu is tempted by Saten [*sic*]'. The habit of marginalia, which ran riot over Stephen's library in subsequent years, started early with him.

By the beginning of the 1920s, however, Stephen's artistic talents had blossomed into quite acceptable paintings and drawings – good enough,

The Toad wore a toque.

thought Pamela, to exhibit publicly.* So at fourteen the artist Stephen Tennant was given his first London show. It was held at the Dorien Leigh Gallery at Cromwell Place, in South Kensington, and attracted more than its share of publicity, because of both the youth of the artist, and his family name. The private view, held on 5 April 1921, attracted all of Pamela's friends, erstwhile Souls, relations and a number of national pressmen.

The *Daily Mail* commented on the exhibits: 'They are well above the average of the clever child's dabblings,' adding that 'the really interesting point of it all is the indication of the modern child's sophistication. The modern child is an habitué of the Russian Ballet, and forms first ideas of draughtsmanship from collections of Aubrey Beardsley prints. The Yellow Book is clearly popular nowadays in the nursery.'[35]

Margot, as ever, was on hand to deliver her verdict: surprisingly good. 'She was surprised to see that he could do such good work,' noted the *Daily Mirror*, 'and expressed the opinion that he ought to go in for a

---

*Pamela also had Stephen's line drawings of animals privately published that year in a children's book of some charm, *The Bird's Fancy Dress Ball.*

course of training.'[36] The *Mirror* noted that the artist 'commenced drawing hard when he was nine, and has never had a lesson. He is now going to set up a studio and study art seriously.' Margot actually bought one of the pictures, 'Design for a Magazine Cover', whilst another was bought by Princess Victoria, King George V's spinster sister. And on 31 May, no less a person than Queen Alexandra gave her royal approval to Stephen's work, when she visited the exhibition and purchased 'The Boy Who Saw the Fairies'.

Fame so young! There were reproductions of Stephen's work in the *Daily Sketch* and the *Graphic* – one rather strangely entitled 'Fish and Chips' (so-called after the Winchester School magazine of the same name, to which both Pamela and Philip Burne-Jones contributed), accompanied by a photograph of the artist in a thick cable-knit sweater, slicked-back hair and, surely, a trace of maquillage? Perhaps it was around this time that Stephen was at tea with Aunt Margot, and was ordered from the table. 'Stephen dear, just go and wash your face.'[37] Margot was, if anything, even more formidable that Pamela. She certainly daunted young Stephen, and even in later life treated him as a child. 'I can't understand your dislike of politics,' she barked at him once. 'Politics are life.' 'Hell to me,' said Stephen, *sotto voce*.[38]

On 22 September Pamela enrolled her son in the Ashburnham House of Westminster School. Stephen's education had fallen behind in the wake of his artistic endeavours and frequent illnesses, and Pamela thought it would be worth trying him once more at a public school. The college was only a few hundred yards from their house in Westminster, and Stephen went as a day boy. But in April, after only two terms, he was taken away by Pamela; once again he had not found school to his liking.

Meanwhile Pamela had been sharing much of her life with Lord Grey, now nearly blind and quite ill from the strain he had undergone as Foreign Secretary during the war. A close friend for many years, Grey's relationship with Pamela had deepened since the death of her husband. He had been a constant visitor to both Queen Anne's Gate (his own London home was on the same street) and Wilsford. They shared an inordinate love of birds, and, on 4 June 1922, they married in St Michael's at Wilsford.

Stephen was nothing less than pleased. He too was very fond of 'Sir Edd'ard', as he called Lord Grey, and shared his interests in nature. The new family began to stay at Fallodon, Grey's house in Northumberland, where, as at Wilsford, there were extensive aviaries full of exotic birds. Pamela would sit at table with one perched upon her hand, and was often seen shopping with a parrot on her shoulder. Fallodon House was an undistinguished and unostentatious building, but it had a happy atmosphere, less dispiriting than Glen's. Situated far up the north-east coast of England, between the great conurbation of Newcastle to the south, and the Holy Island of Lindisfarne to the north, Lord Grey's country home provided fresh sea air – always thought good for sickly children like Stephen – and the nearby beach to play on.

Close by, at Doxford, lived family friends, the Runcimans. Their young son Steven was deemed a suitable companion for Stephen, despite being three years older. Both were tall boys, and the elder Steven was quite as good-looking as the younger. Together they would go down to the beach to play games, or be entertained by Stephen's theatrical impersonations. 'He was great fun in those days,' recalled Sir Steven Runciman, a distinguished scholar of the Byzantine. 'My sisters and I loved him. He was full of fantasies. He was – it's a terrible cliché now, I know – but he was life-enhancing.' Stephen was 'an obvious mother's boy . . . One wondered what would happen to him, if he would ever get free of Pamela. He was this hot-house flower, and one couldn't tell what might happen if the glass in the conservatory got broken.'[39]

While Stephen amused the younger Runcimans, Pamela expounded her theories on spiritualism to the parents, and 'bored them terribly with it', noted Sir Steven. 'Pamela was very good with birds, though – they would fly to her finger when she called, which she thought was marvellous. She was very vain . . . she would pose with her index finger just resting pensively on her cheek, so as not to make a dent!' He liked Lord Grey better: 'I think because I shared his passion for ducks. Being nearly blind, he would ask me to identify his favourites for him.'

Lord Grey was 'a marvellous man, quiet and unassuming, but with his own wit and much charm', wrote David Tennant's first wife, Hermione Baddeley. 'He was sometimes a long-suffering husband – Lady Grey was not renowned for her punctuality. She would flutter back and forth while he waited, looking at his watch, ready to leave. "I'm just going to be two minutes," she would cry; then ten minutes later: "Just another minute!" "Darling," Lord Grey would wearily say, "I do wish you'd stop 'justing' and get into the car." And then on one occasion, once they had finally climbed into the car, the chauffeur closed the door just a little too quickly and caught it right on Lord Grey's ankle. It must have been extremely painful, but instead of letting out a yell of displeasure . . . Lord Grey said quietly, "Please don't do that again." '[40]

*

In the summer of 1922 Pamela decided to send her youngest son to Paris, to learn French and, it was hoped, to engender some sort of ambition – one proposal, for him to enter the diplomatic service, having being encouraged by her new husband. That trip to Paris was a crucial step in Stephen's development, but not in the way that Pamela wished. It instilled in him a love of France and travel in general, and, as if to prove it, years later Stephen fictionalized the experience in a thinly-veiled piece of autobiography entitled 'Parc Morceau'.[41] In it, he portrays himself as Edward, the young boy taken to Paris by his mother, Lady Brandon:

'"You will try, Edward, to – to justify us, our belief in you, won't you?"' says Lady Brandon/Grey. '"You know, taking you away from Chancellbury – " she looked away helplessly. His open loving face drew only tenderness from her. He was so much younger than his years – and yet, in some ways, disconcertingly aloof and adult . . . She sometimes felt almost unnerving wisdom behind that searching pellucid gaze . . . "I will learn French," he said, "and anything else you like." "Not only that," she went on. "We want you to try and develop a sense of responsibility. You know, some boys of your age are already much more – well, interested in . . ." She faltered, the gravity of his face made her words sound oddly inappropriate. "You aren't a child any longer, darling."'

It is an acute record of Stephen's adolescence, and the problems he was already facing. Lady Brandon is seen as a remote figure, whom Edward loves – but not passionately. That is reserved for his Nannie Hallett. The portrayal of his mother shows how far estranged he felt from Pamela – and apparently always had done. (Rosamond Lehmann observes that in the early twenties, Stephen told her that 'the only person he ever loved as a child was his old nanny: he spoke of his mother with great bitterness. Perhaps he felt she had ruined his life.')[42]

Lady Brandon is exasperated at her son's lack of practical aspirations. His face only lights up when observing nature, 'the veinings of a fresh leaf – watching clouds . . . dipping his fingers in clear water'. At such times he seemed alive, 'but his powers for contacting practical issues – everyday life – were nil'. She, on the other hand, 'liked to think herself literary – but her true sphere was the more cultivated conventional *beau monde* . . . Hermione Brandon, whose charm and beauty had greeted her in the glass every morning now for more years than she cared to number, was greedily exacting as to the admiring allegiance of her family and immediate circle.' This was true enough. Pamela insisted on being the last to be kissed before bedtime, and David Tennant recalled looking at his mother's arched foot one day, and thinking it ugly. She asked him what he was looking at, but he dared not tell her. The idea that any part of Mummie might be imperfect was unallowable. 'She had never faced the fact that Edward's feeling for her was more in the nature of the admiration evoked by a work of art – in the esteem of a connoisseur [rather] than the affection generally existing between mother and son. His devotion to his nurse, Nannie Hallett, had, she felt, outstayed its welcome and should have faded to a suitable temperature with schooldays and adolescence. She was very jealous of Nannie Hallett.'

The adolescent Stephen revelled in the Paris of 1922. With Pamela he visited the parks and the shops, and bought a pair of tortoises for the little hotel garden. They shopped at Poiret's and Chanel's 'discreet sumptuous salons', ate ice creams in the Champs Elysées and dined at Foyots. Before Pamela left, she took Stephen to see the ageing Sarah Bernhardt, at her own Théâtre Sarah Bernhardt. By now the divine Sarah was sixty-nine, and appearing in a wheelchair, having had her leg amputated years previously. Stephen remembered the experience well. In their hotel suite, he found a notice in the newspaper. '"Mummie, do you see who's acting in Paris now? Sarah Bernhardt! She must be 102!" And Mummie said, "We'll go tonight." And we went, and oh, she was so wonderful . . . an eternal beauty.'⁴³ Pamela was evidently unimpressed. Stephen recalled that his mother 'for some reason never took us to the ballet – she always liked a good straight play – Mummie didn't like musicals, musical comedy tunes or songs – she just thought they were sort of, too commonplace . . . too ordinary. My mother had a very serious side to her – a serious-minded side.'

This was the difference between Pamela's sensibility and her son's: she saw Bernhardt as 'an old woman, with a cracked voice . . . obscene, struggling in a bath chair, screeching at a world that had forgotten her', whilst Stephen's vision was of 'a star-dusted festival, a legend of incomparable romance', which made him sigh in rapture – he was a true child of the theatre. 'I never could see anything in her,' said Lady Brandon/Grey. 'Don't keep kicking me, darling.'

Then came Nannie, and 'when Lady Brandon, with her maid and her many trunks had, at last, really gone, they couldn't believe their luck – so neither attempted speech . . . they were both too happy to talk, really – outside, all Paris was theirs, like a vast impossible present . . .' Stephen's first stay in Paris elongated into one long dream. He spent his time being taught French, whilst Nannie sat sewing at the window. Or else the French mistress would be dismissed, and he sat reading his books at Nannie's feet, or playing with his tortoises in the garden. On the hot summer nights they would talk there, of the travels they would undertake in the future, together exploring the world.

Then there was a flurry of excitement when Stephen and Nannie saw Anna Pavlova* arrive at their hotel, and Nannie told him the famous dancer had stared at him. She was surrounded by 'five or six Russians in rather flashy clothes and straw boaters – enigmatic dissipated faces . . . subtle Mongolian cheekbones and slit eyes – bored sensual hard faces but all with the fascination that the stage brings.' Pavlova herself had a 'little blue-white mask of a face, like an enamelled pip . . . so artificial that it looked as if a greenish spot light played on it'.

Perhaps this brief time spent alone with Nannie, in that romantic city, was one of the truly happy times of Stephen's life. 'Edward would glance lovingly and proudly at Nannie Hallett's fine head, bent over her sewing. She sat very upright and her forehead was nobly sculpted, the grey hair drawn neatly back in a small knot on her neck, in the fashion of thirty years before . . . Edward thought Nannie Hallett was the most beautiful person he had ever seen . . . he knew that he would never meet again another human being with so fine a character, so brave and selfless and humorous, so strong with the salty strength of the earth . . . His own composure was a delicate perilous thing – an iridescent fabric shot with fears. And Nannie Hallett's equable bluff outlook was a kind of vicarious fortress: of course he knew it couldn't save him, nothing could. But the knowledge was there – made his own fate more bearable . . . Years of prolonged delicacy of health had impressed on him the fact that there is not much time to be happy in, so perhaps it is more practical to be gay – also, it costs less when you lose it. To be happy sets a premium on your ability to sustain it.'

*Anna Pavlova (1882–1931), probably the most famous ballet dancer of the century, had just returned from a hugely successful American tour that spring, and would take off for a tour of Japan in September.

Chapter 3

The Kingdom by the Sea

It was many and many a year ago,
In a Kingdom by the sea,
That a maiden there lived whom you may know
By the name of Annabel Lee;
And this maiden she lived with no other thought
Than to love & be loved by me.

— Edgar Allan Poe: *Annabel Lee*

*I*N the summer of 1922, arrangements were completed for Stephen's entry into the Slade School of Art, part of University College, London. The move was possibly initiated by Stephen himself – he would complain in later years that his family never realized 'one's full significance'. Now perhaps he could show them all just what he could do. Stephen announced that he now wished to be known by his third name, Napier ('Steenie' being unsuitable for an art student). He wrote to Elizabeth Lowndes, who had herself announced that she wished to be addressed by her full name, that 'I comply with this dramatic and inspiring change on one condition and on one condition only – that you call me Napier (my third name) for evermore, till Hell freezes and charcoal sprouts.' In a special concession to this special friend, he allowed that 'you may have the choice of James, my second name. Let me know your views on this solemn and intricate subject. Love from – No name as yet. P.S. I tend towards Napier. P.S. I LOVE "Elizabeth".'*[1]

In the long echoing corridors and high-ceilinged rooms of the Slade, Stephen spent months vital to his creative youth. Art school epitomized freedom for a young boy – to paint, to draw, to create. For someone like

---

*'Napier' had a certain kudos in the twenties. Michael Arlen used it for the hero of his bestselling novel, *The Green Hat*, whilst Napier, Lord Alington, the bisexual object of pursuit of Tallulah Bankhead, gave it real-life romantic overtones.

Stephen, who had spent most of his time closeted at home, here was a chance to experience a greater life. The Slade also introduced him to another young student who would become one of his best friends – Rex Whistler.

Professor Tonks was the absolute ruler of the school. A gaunt figure who gave 'short shrift to the swarms of aspiring students',[2] his criteria for admission was always high draughtsmanship. Stephen, although one suspects a little family string-pulling (Tonks was a close friend of the Asquiths), satisfied this with his clever sketches and nimble lines. Just to come into a class at the Slade must have required all of Stephen's courage. He was still an essentially shy person, despite the posturing, and Rex Whistler spoke for both of them when he recalled the dreaded first day in the Antique studio, where Tonks expected his students to gain proficiency drawing classical statues and busts before they could be allowed the privilege of sketching from 'Life'.

'The Antique presents a most terrifying spectacle to anyone with the courage to open the door,' wrote Rex in a letter to Stephen. 'One packed vista of orderly and artistic ladies in serried rank upon rank – peppered sparsely with the more sombre hues of diligent and intimidated males. A veritable phalanx of industrious scholars! As of old (you remember) when anyone enters, a thousand pairs of cold, unemotional eyes are raised piteously from their drawing boards, and survey the foolhardy intruder with silent reproach.'[3]

Rex Whistler was a year Stephen's senior, and already destined to be an exceptional artist. The Royal Academy had accepted him in 1922, but he was 'sacked for incompetence',[4] as he put it. Happily Tonks took another view – he pronounced Rex's extraordinary facility for draughtsmanship close to genius, and in the words of another contemporary Slade student, Oliver Messel,[*] Rex became 'the apple of his eye'.[5] Rex was born in Chingford, Essex, in 1905, and his father was a modest builder. He had a stable, quiet childhood, and had gone to Haileybury school, where his proficiency at covering his French Grammar with 'thumbnail horrors and grotesques' had outstripped his intellectual pursuits. Rex preferred practical jokes and rugby-playing to the classroom. Now he was at the Slade, and determined to make the most of the advantages laid before him.

'Term had been running a fortnight or more, when a new student appeared in the Life room,' wrote Rex's brother, Laurence. 'In the silence

---

[*]Theatre designer and later rival of Beaton's, Messel (1904–78) later lived in Barbados, designing villas on Mustique for Stephen's nephew, Colin, the third Lord Glenconner.

of the sombre room he looked around, wondering who would be congenial. There sat Rex, seeming different from the others and more interesting . . ."[6] But Stephen hesitated, and it was some time before they began to talk together during one lunch break, 'sitting in winter sunshine under the columns'. Stephen recalled that first meeting to Laurence. 'What you call the "Enchanted Slade" period is here in my memory. Please say those same wonderful words about Rex stepping into a world of "unbelievable beauty" when we became friends first.'[7]

To Stephen, Whistler appeared 'plump, thickset, very boyish . . . with a manner both impulsive and diffident'.[8] Rex's own initial impression of Stephen was that of a 'slender figure and extraordinary beauty, like a more delicate Shelley';[9] and it was poetry that established the bond between them. Over sandwiches in the Quad, Stephen read aloud from Walter de la Mare, while Rex 'made pictures of "Peacock Pie" and of "Henry Brocken", and the book we loved best of all was *The Secret Garden*' [Rex depicted Stephen as the sickly hero of the book]. Edgar Allan Poe's verses were read aloud, '"Ulalume" and "Annabel Lee" – we often recited "The Raven",' recalled Stephen.

The boys shared a love of legends and mythology, and found a 'strong reciprocal bond in the passionate vividness of our imaginations'. Not all was so high-flown, however. Stephen and Rex would devise Chinese tortures, with 'the thoughtless luridness of young people'. Rex would cover sheet after sheet of drawing paper with endless inventions – 'cars, cowboys, mad gadgets, heavenly Rackhamesque old tramps in lichen coats and mossy rags . . . We adored Dulac and Rideau.'[10]

They also loved American cars and Hollywood movies, westerns being particularly favoured. They hummed American pop songs of the day, and mooned over white-faced heroines of the silver screen. When signing-in for the morning, Stephen would write alongside Rex's name comments such as 'Disgracefully late', 'Report on arrival' or 'Unnecessarily early'.[11] Or he would rush up the steps and bar the way of a 'swarm of lady students' who seemed always to appear at the door when he was there. The boys also pretended to be in love with 'a plump mulatto lady' in the girls' Life Room, off-limits to male students (there being twice as many girls as boys at the college): 'They swept in one day with a bouquet of white roses, to the delight of the class, and presented it to the lady with such winning grace that she too was enchanted.'[12]

As to work, that was a different matter. A fellow Slade student, Mary Adshead, who later did mural work with Rex, recalls that Stephen did not appear to be a regular attender of Life classes. 'I never saw him actually drawing at the Slade – he didn't seem to be a serious artist. He only ever came in with Rex . . .'[13] One reason was recurrent illness; another, Stephen's shyness. He preferred a one-to-one friendship, or a limited gathering where he was sure of his own ground. A third explanation was that, on his own admission, the Slade daunted Stephen; Tonks' stress on draughtsmanship and application can be seen as pivotal to what happened to Stephen's own art. He found in it a need for good drawing – but also found it difficult to 'follow through', to apply himself with any degree of self-discipline.

Stephen and Rex undertook expeditions together, to the Department of Egyptology at the British Museum, or on boat trips down the Thames, to the Pool of London, in 'romantic moonlight . . . dressed as bargees'. There were wild parties with friends in Hampstead, afterwards walking on the Heath 'for miles in the dawn, singing – all arm in arm – in the summer dawn'.[14]

For the two young boys, it was their 'Kingdom by the Sea' – a line from Poe's 'Annabel Lee'* that they used on the backs of envelopes in letters to each other:

> *I was a child and she was a child*
> *In this Kingdom by the sea:*
> *But we loved with a love that was more than love –*
> *I and my Annabel Lee . . .*

Rex wrote out the poem and decorated it in his *Anthology of Mine*. The illustrations in this little compilation of favourite poems, with their decadent ladies and ghostly figures, showed how closely entwined were the friends' creative imaginations (Stephen's own face can be discerned as another dead lover, in Tennyson's 'Tears, Idle Tears', lying white and seraphic at the foot of one of the pages). Later Lady Aberconway would say to Osbert Sitwell, 'Stephen owes a great deal to Rex.' 'The other way round, you mean,' replied Osbert.[15] It was thought that Rex copied his handwriting from Stephen's florid, elegant script. He told Stephen later, as his friend struggled with one of his pictures, 'Always put your handwriting with your painting.' 'He believed in my talent,' said Stephen, 'and said, "You know, you draw as well as Aubrey Beardsley, and he was world-famous." Professor Tonks thought I was very talented – he said "You have no idea how gifted you are."'[16]

*The doomed heroine of Poe's poem is his first wife, Virginia Clemm, who died of tuberculosis at the age of twenty-four.

Soon Rex was writing excitedly to an old school friend: 'I'm going down this weekend to stay at Lord Grey of Fallodon's house in Wiltshire!!!... the Hon. Napier Tennant is at the Slade and we've got rather a "case" (to use the college expression).'[17] That weekend was the first of many; Pamela saw Rex, not only as a charming and talented young boy, but as a stabilizing influence on her son. Not everyone thought the new and ever closer relationship a good idea. With Rex's visits to Wilsford and introduction to high society, his brother thought he had been 'pulled a little off-course by that alluring friendship'.[18]

Rex wrote 'Napier' an elegant letter on vellum, inscribed in 'Court Hand', thanking him for the loan of a white shirt during his stay at Wilsford, which he had forgotten to return when leaving. Over the next few years, Stephen and Rex would almost live in each other's clothes – swapping them, or discussing new acquisitions – as their intimacy grew. Were they then lovers? Laurence Whistler writes: 'By this age [Rex was 19, Stephen 18] any homosexual leanings he had were not towards a male more feminine than himself.'[19] For either, the idea of putting their friendship on anything more than a 'spiritual love' level would have been difficult to imagine. Rex was undecided and nervous about his sexual orientation, Stephen still apparently too ethereal to consider anything physical. Years later, when their 'case' had faded, Rex wrote an epitaph to their relationship: 'Thank God it grew and lasted all this time owing nothing to unhappy and destructive SEX . . . physical love.'[20]

The beginning of 1923 saw Stephen on the theatrical boards once more. He played 'Thinima', wife to the wicked pirate Blue Beard, in a pantomime, *Blue Beaver*, which had two charity performances – at Wilton House on 23 January, then again the following day at the New Theatre in Salisbury. Stephen himself designed the costumes for the play, which had been written by Edith Olivier.

Miss Olivier was an early female graduate of St Hugh's College, Cambridge, and lived with her sister, Mildred, in the Daye (dairy) House, in the grounds of the Pembrokes' magnificent seventeenth-century house at Wilton. They were the daughters of the Rector of Wilton, and Edith was described by Pamela as coming from an old Huguenot family and 'a figure in the archeological and ecclesiastical life of Wiltshire.'[21] She was also to become a talented writer, with her vaguely Gothic novels set in Wiltshire. Cecil Beaton saw her as 'a rather swarthy and formidable middle-aged woman', whilst Stephen thought her 'utterly adorable' and possessed of 'rare gifts'.[22] She gathered artistic and literary figures to her house at Wilton, many of whom came to regard the Daye House as their 'spiritual home'. Edith was percipient about Stephen and his family. She once told Rex, to whom she became devoted after meeting him the following year, that Pamela's Wilsford had never had a truly easy atmosphere – 'in spite of her graciousness and love of God, there was always the sense of steel in the caress'.[23]

Edith, although in her late forties, had a child-like sense of fun, and could engage in all the dressing-up that *Blue Beaver* entailed. It was the time of the charity performance, when aristocratic altruism resulted in endless *tableaux vivants*. *Blue Beaver*'s cast list included various members of the Pembroke family – young David Herbert (blacked up as 'a realistic representative of an Eastern bodyguard');[24] Sir Michael Duff, handsome young son of Lady Juliet Duff; and Miss Olivier herself. Stephen's performance was, by all accounts, a great success. Clad in a silk gown, with strings of pearls around his neck, and heavily made-up as the heroine Thinima, he prompted members of the audience to ask whether he was a boy or a girl, so convincing was the disguise.[*] 'And he was very beautiful,' admitted Rosemary Olivier, Edith's young niece.[25]

Beautiful enough to merit a large photograph in the *Daily Graphic* on 5 February ('The Hon. Stephen Tennant being assisted in his make-up as Thinima by Lord Herbert . . .'),[26] Stephen stands, arms outstretched, as David Herbert adjusts his exotic costume. The local newspaper reported that 'the fantastic scenery and dresses were designed by the Hon. Stephen Tennant, who as "Thinima", the wife of "Blue Beaver" . . . was a principal character, the one, in fact, upon whom fell the most work . . . It was a very happy thought of Lady Pembroke to gather her young friends together for such a good purpose, and one and all of them appeared to thoroughly enjoy their appearance in public.'[27]

Rex's visits to Wilsford continued until the following spring. On the first weekend of April, 1924, he was there to meet Meraud Guinness, and Anne Douglas Sedgwick;[†] the former one of a pack of beautiful Guinness

---

[*]Although he looked the part, according to the *Salisbury & Wiltshire Journal* Stephen did not quite sound it: 'The Hon. Stephen Tennant was responsible for a meritorious performance,' it noted on 26 January, 'and his movements were adequately ladylike, although he was not able to simulate the feminine voice with equal success.' Stephen's voice, once broken, had become something of a baritone.

[†]Anne Douglas Sedgwick (1873–1935), New Jersey-born writer who spent much of her life in England, was a friend of, and much influenced by, Henry James. Her husband, Basil de Selincourt, edited her *Portrait in Letters* (published in 1936), which included a number of her letters to Stephen.

girls; the latter, a writer, close friend of Pamela's, and greatly admired by Stephen. Described by Edith Olivier as 'an enchanting talker' with 'white hair and bright-blue eyes',[28] both she and her sister, Alice Sedgwick, were frequent visitors to Wilsford. It was through Anne's literary connections in New York that Stephen would later make contact with Willa Cather.

Wilsford seemed a very grand country house to Rex – not that the family's wealth was flaunted. Susan Lowndes recalls a distinctly unpretentious atmosphere: 'Life at Wilsford was not luxurious at all – it was comfortable, yes – but no luxury.'[29] In the aesthetically white-panelled drawing room, hung with Sargent's charcoal drawings of the Tennant children, and a few good oils left over from the Tennant Collection, the young friends would sit discussing art and poetry, or take part in less serious pursuits; word games and charades were particularly popular.

Some people (notably Stephen's cousin, Ursula Wyndham)[*] have observed the similarity between Stephen and Rex's relationship and the fictional friendship of Sebastian Flyte and Charles Ryder in Evelyn Waugh's *Brideshead Revisited*. Ryder, the middle-class boy, is taken up by the ethereal and aristocratic Flyte, who habitually carries his teddy bear about with him. He takes Ryder to his parents' stately home, and introduces his friend to his old nanny, whom Flyte still dotes upon. Ryder is masculine, quiet and an exceptional draughtsman, who paints a mural at Brideshead. Their youthful and innocent love-affair blossoms in the languid days spent at Sebastian's splendid home – but the friendship falters when Charles comes to feel increasingly distanced from Sebastian's lack of realistic values. There is no evidence that Waugh drew directly from Stephen and Rex for his book (although he certainly satirized Stephen and his friends in other books), but, given that he knew both of them, quite possibly theirs was the kind of relationship he was using in Brideshead to epitomize his theme of *temps perdu*.

Like Sebastian, Stephen exuded an air of frailty but, unlike Flyte, there was a physical reason for this. Tuberculosis, the King's Evil, had manifested itself in his lungs. The disease was still prevalent in the 1920s, although by no means as endemic as it had been the century before. It was, however, still the most feared of afflictions, in the days before antibiotics, and a major killer. (There was an idea that a genetic disposition to TB had been introduced into the Tennant family by Robina Atholl, the mixed-blood, common-law wife of Stephen's great-

[*]In her memoirs, *Astride the World* (Lennard, 1988), pp.137–8.

great-grandfather, John Tennant; four of Charles Tennant's children had succumbed to the disease in childhood.)

Treatment of TB still consisted largely of a prescription of dry, clean air, and other respiratory therapies which seem quite eccentric nowadays. Katherine Mansfield was advised by Professor Gurdjieff, in October 1922, to take deep breaths over a cow manger at Fontainebleau – only to die there a year later. The medical advice Pamela sought for her son was not so strange – the severity of Stephen's condition did not yet merit such extremes – but nonetheless there was concern enough to send Stephen off with his brother Christopher and Nannie Trusler for a short holiday in Spain in late May and early June. They stayed at the Ritz in Madrid, and visited, amongst other places, Seville, 'tawny Spain, by moonlight, with a June breeze bringing orange blossom and the satisfying click of castanets', wrote Stephen.[30]

On their return Stephen's health did not appear to have improved, and the local family physician, Doctor Kempe, advised a lengthy stay in a sanatorium. Stephen was to spend most of July, August and the first two weeks of September at the Sanatorium at Mundesley, on the far eastern coast of Norfolk, undergoing a strict regime of diet and lung-clearing treatment. On 12 July he wrote to Elizabeth Lowndes: 'I do honestly feel this place is doing me good.' He passed his time making human observations. 'One patient here, a young man with a beard, kisses roses in the garden! And our Head Doctor, who for many years having been single, [has] married in peculiar circumstances . . . One day the scullery maid broke a lot of china and was sent for by Doctor P. to be reprimanded. She burst into tears and the next day he married her!' Stephen felt 'quite resigned to these months', and was 'fairly happy because my beloved nanny is visiting me this weekend'. The warm weather was helping, and he was already discovering how much better he felt in the summer: 'I am coming to life at last, I feel . . . I should like always to be in the sun.'[31]

Stephen and Rex started up a fervent series of 'Kingdom by the Sea' letters whilst he was convalescing, each beautifully illustrated by the young artists. Rex was busy working on his first mural in a boys' club at Shadwell in London. When Rex sent out photographs of the work-in-progress, few of their friends could have failed to notice the resemblance between Napier and the willowy youth in one corner of Rex's wall-painting, positioned in a proscenium arch. With a hooded skeleton figure leaning towards him (inspired by their mutual love of Poe) once more making the mortal connection, Rex's portrait indicated that he took

Stephen's illness as lightly as did the patient himself. Little did either realize how serious the condition was to become in the years that followed.

The stresses of Stephen's protracted incarceration were beginning to show by the end of August. Rex told Stephen that he had been 'looking & praying for some word, some token of your repentence . . . And your admonition about "tantrums" – can I not even more aptly apply that to you ?' (The cause of this contretemps appears to have been a disagreement over the merits of Hollywood child-star Jackie Coogan.) Rex was the first to bury the hatchet. 'But I will reprove you no longer; already I can picture your flaming cheeks down which are coursing the tears of remorse, and I too begin to regret my harshness – I had a long letter from Nanny this morning and was delighted to hear you were so much better.'[32]

Stephen's exile was drawing to a close. Pamela came to spend a weekend at the Sanatorium at the beginning of September, and was able to tell Stephen that he could come home at the end of the month, but for a few days only. Further recuperation was needed in a foreign clime; Stephen was to be at Wilsford long enough only to pack his bags. He was off to take the mountain air of Switzerland – and Pamela had agreed that Rex might go too, as travelling companion.

The rising excitement for both boys as they prepared for this great adventure could not be disguised in the flurry of letters that flew between Rex's Farnham Common home and Mundesley. Stephen had written to Mrs Whistler to ask her approval for the plan. Rex replied to Stephen that if he could have his way, 'I'd pack my toothbrush (and Euthymol) right away and follow you to the moon !'[33]

Their respective travelling wardrobe details filled Stephen and Rex's correspondence in the days before their departure. '. . . As a matter of fact, I've got jade green jerseys & scarves,' admitted Rex, '(I hope you don't mind) and bright magenta – at least I've sent one away to be dyed bright magenta . . . I haven't got any white . . . I always thought white looked rather dirty . . . when seen against the virgin whiteness of the snow.' Rex had acquired soft brown trilby hats for Stephen and himself at Charles Barker's in Tottenham Court Road, and 'How about these snow caps ? They really are meant for ski-ing, I believe, but they look rather lovely and rakeish – with huge peaks . . .'[34] Rex imagined them on the train, which would provide 'unlimited thrills – I think it would be wiser & more discreet if we three travelled well masked as though we were decamping croupiers or abdicating royalty.' The usual witty sketch – of Stephen, Rex, and Nannie Trusler in masks and armed with pistols, to the horror of other passengers – accompanied the letter.

Stephen had beautiful suede dressing-cases made for each of them, sporting their gilded initials, outer covers of canvas, and with a selection of gold-topped glass bottles, each monogrammed; 'cases quite heavy in themselves before anything was packed in them, and presupposing a world of manservants and porters'. His brother noted that Rex's 'recent friends of the West Herts Rugby XV, now discarded and forgotten',[35] would have been uneasy at all this ostentatious peacockery.

On 20 October the *Daily Mirror* announced in its social column: 'Mr Tennant's Reading Interlude . . . Mr Stephen Tennant . . . is going with a reading party of two or three other young men and a tutor to Switzerland. There they will study and indulge in the winter sports. Mr Tennant has interrupted an art course at the "Slade" to do this . . .'[36] The Channel crossing was scheduled for 23 October, and Stephen, as the 'seasoned traveller' (a transatlantic trip and one or two to Paris being adequate qualifications), felt he could advise Rex on the rigours of the journey. However, Stephen had a great propensity for *mal de mer*, and confessed to his diary that for once he hadn't actually been sick. Rex, on the other hand, looked 'rather silent and lemon-coloured'.[37]

On arrival in France, all arrangements were smoothly undertaken by the valet, leaving Stephen, Rex, and Nannie ample leisure to settle into the train for the journey to Paris. Stephen pointed out a ruined château 'I always look out for'. They drew into Paris in early evening, and were painlessly checked into the famous Hotel Meurice on the rue de Rivoli. The next day they explored the city with wonderment, going to Stephen's favourite sweet shop, 'Au Palais des Gourmandises', then driving past the Arc de Triomphe, along the Bois du Bologne, and out to Longchamps. In the Louvre, Stephen watched Rex standing before Watteau's painting of the Pierrot, 'with a wonderful faint, ironic smile playing on his lips'.[38] Stephen might have been playing the indulgent, gracious host, and serious Francophile, but he wasn't above 'wowing' the staid Parisian pedestrians. According to Rex, they spent a good deal of their time 'strolling, curiously attired, in the rue de Rivoli, the cynosure (or so we hoped!) of all eyes! – with strange little felt hats over one eye AND PLUS-FOURS!'[39] Rex might have felt a little self-conscious, but Stephen strode ahead, quite oblivious to any sarcastic Gallic remarks.

35

Soon the two friends and Nannie were off on their travels again, heading south-east on the night express to Montreux. Then they were on the narrow-gauge mountain railway, 'crawling up into picture-postcard land, green, blue, purple, white – fir-trees, sky, shaggy slopes, white caps', and surprisingly hot, so that (Stephen wrote in his journal) the floor of their compartment was soon 'ankle-deep in discarded scarves and coats'.[40] He had resumed his diary, a habit begun at the age of fifteen and maintained sporadically during his early years. Now Stephen was recording his ecstasy at his first sight of Mont Blanc. The train climbed higher, taking them up the Berner Alpen, above Lake Geneva and the Rhône Valley to Villars, a tiny village nearest to the villa that was their destination. At the station, they were met by Doctor Macfie, the Scottish 'doctor-cum-tutor' in whose charge the two boys were to be placed. He was plump and affable, a middle-aged Scotsman who besides his teaching and doctoring wrote verse of his own.

The Villa Marie Louise was to be their home for the next few weeks. A large Swiss chalet, it had just three other paying guests, and was run by an English couple. It was all very homely, and Stephen and Rex were soon settled into a routine of work (very little), rest (a great deal for Stephen) and play (as much as either boy could persuade Dr Macfie to allow them).

Macfie soon realized that neither of his charges was very interested in learning what knowledge he had to impart to them, especially during what they had come to regard as a holiday of the most enjoyable kind – that is, without parents. Literature, history and geography lessons were soon allowed to lapse by mutual agreement, although French lessons were adhered to. A 'demure and rather charming young Swiss',[41] Mlle Cremieux, had been engaged for this purpose, and although Rex couldn't speak French, he enjoyed reading it. Stephen, who possessed some proficiency in the language, proceeded to interject some fun into the proceedings. Poor, innocent Mlle Cremieux was asked, with all the sincerity Stephen could muster, the exact meaning of the less salubrious passages in Verlaine and Baudelaire, whereupon she would shake her bowed head and say she couldn't tell them: 'It is bad.' Such ragging was never ill-mannered, however, and Mademoiselle took all in good heart. She even took part in Stephen's and Rex's amateur dramatics out on the slopes, acting out scenes from their favourite Hollywood movies, with Mlle Cremieux as the endangered heroine. Photographs show her slumped on stone steps, having murdered her lover, or carried over Rex's shoulder as he shoots his way out of a fight.

Stephen made friends with one of the English guests at the villa, a Mrs Knowles, and found her an excellent person to discuss the literature he had grown up with, 'the kind of prosey, domestic books that I love so much', sharing 'a little private moan of reminiscent pleasure' over Marie Corelli, 'that queen of tosh'.[42] Stephen's reading was getting more adventurous – taking in the Symbolists – although a copy of Baudelaire's

Les Fleurs du Mal was decorated in a moment of idleness with two Eton-cropped females, one smoking a cigarette through a long holder, the other kissing a cherub. This habit of desecrating books, even in such a pretty manner, was vexatious to Mlle Cremieux. Teaching the boys from Verlaine's *Cent Meilleurs Poèmes*, she discovered that Stephen had scribbled on her copy 'during an abstracted moment' in the lesson. 'This infuriated her and she would not take it back, so I bought her another.'[43]

With the Alpine winter coming fast upon them, Stephen and Rex eagerly awaited the ice so that they might *début* their skating outfits. But lack of expertise and a thawing rink meant that they were forced to subdue their 'toilettes' until they were more proficient in the sport. Stephen's health was improving, the fresh air clearing his lungs and bringing colour to his wan cheeks. Soon they were able to set off on day-long expeditions with Dr Macfie, by train or car, to 'some sun-dazzled height',[44] there to look down on glorious, breath-taking valley scenes.

Pamela arrived on 21 December to spend Christmas at Villars, and soon celebrations were under way. She eschewed the modest rooms of the villa for the grander accommodation of Villars' Palace Hotel, and there threw a number of parties over the holidays, bringing London elegance to the little Swiss village. Rex was glad he had packed his evening suit; Stephen, as always, was well equipped, and had his valet to look after such things. The dress for the party given on Boxing Night demanded something different from white tie and tails, however; this was to be a lavish costume ball, and Stephen, as usual, whipped up a little something – a chequered costume of a swirling cloak and Eastern-style turban in green, blue and silver.

Pamela now proposed that they take a house on the Italian Riviera, and thus Dr Macfie was dispatched to find a suitable place near Rapallo. He succeeded in locating a villa near San Remo, and whilst he engaged local staff, Pamela and Stephen set to compiling a list of suitable house-guests to join the boys there. Number one on any such list for Stephen was Elizabeth Lowndes, and it was to her that the first invitation went.

'Will you come out & stay with us . . . ?' implored Stephen. 'You must say yes! Please! please do; it will be such fun; Rex, you & me, & lilac & roses & mimosa & sunshine . . . Mummie is writing particulars . . .'[45] Once more parents had to be consulted – Mrs Belloc Lowndes was perfectly amenable – and the day was set. '. . . Three cheers for the 13th!!! The day of your arrival at the Villa Natalia! I shall meet you at the station waving palm branches and mimosa!' wrote Stephen, as he watched the snow falling outside his window, drawing a white curtain across the Alps. A postscript, 'Do you still love mah-jongg????',[46] referred to the current board-game fad which had almost fanatical popularity in the early 1920s, and of which Stephen and his friends were avid players.

Pamela returned to London in mid-January, to attend the opening of David Tennant's new club, the Gargoyle. Stephen and Rex stayed on at Villars, until, in the third week of February, they broke camp and set off for the south.

San Remo, a pretty little coastal village twenty miles or so along the coast from Nice, was part of the newly discovered and highly fashionable Riviera. It was hot, even in February – Mediterranean and sun-drenched – and, most of all, chic. Stephen and Rex, arriving in advance of Lady Grey, found the Villa Natalia rather noisier than she had been led to believe by Dr Macfie, situated as it was close to the routeway of the international express which thundered past day and night. Despite this, the house seemed like heaven, with its steep garden running down to the bluest of blue Mediterranean seas, a fabled sea which would capture Stephen's imagination for the rest of his life.

Stephen gave the villa good advance publicity in a letter extolling its charms to Elizabeth: 'A creamy villa in a grove of palms and delicious trees; our garden goes down to the sea and there is a heavenly terrace of stone actually in the sea where we sit and play mah-jongg or draw. Such a beautiful town, San Remo – white & red & glittering in the hot sunlight ... the sea is roaring in my ears as I write and through the windows palms are tossing.'[47] Rex wrote to thank his beneficent, as yet absent, hostess for this paradise: 'Rooms deliciously cool and lofty,' he reported; 'Stephen looking much better ... It [the Villa] is a beautiful sunny pale yellow, with lovely long shuttered windows';[48] and he marvelled at the incompetent Macfie's ability to have found such a place.

Their guests arrived in turn. First to come was Pamela, followed by Elizabeth. Then there was Edith Olivier, due at the end of March, and, soon after, Alice Douglas Sedgwick. What had started as a short 'reading trip' to Switzerland ended in a gathering of all Stephen's favourite people on this marvellous Mediterranean coastline. Few eighteen-year-olds could count themselves so lucky.

Elizabeth Lowndes was met at the station by Stephen bearing flowers. She had come to be one of his greatest friends in recent years as they together grew up, and this charming, vivacious girl was as intimate a confidante as Rex had become. Elizabeth's maturity – she was, after all, six years older than Stephen – only increased her attractiveness in Stephen's eyes; she was no silly flapper, but a highly intelligent and witty young woman. 'Eloise', as 'Napier' now addressed Miss Lowndes, had become an important part of his life.

With Elizabeth at the Natalia, the fun resumed. There were outings along the jewelled coast, and into the Italian countryside, where the simple rural beauty seemed so romantic. Then it was on to Nice, to sample its cosmopolitan charms. Showing his passport at the French border, Stephen solicited the usual reaction – his startling looks would make anyone glance twice. The guard could not believe that the tiny head and shoulders of Stephen in his British passport was the same figure who sat in the car before him. 'I shall never forget his face,' wrote Nannie Trusler. 'He looked at the photo then at Stephen, not quite sure if it was Stephen and whether to let him pass or not.'[49]

Elizabeth's stay was a comparatively short one, and all too soon she was on the train back to Paris once more. But the hiatus created by her departure was temporary. At the end of March, Edith Olivier arrived at San Remo station, to be greeted by Stephen bearing a large bunch of freshly-picked violets. For Edith, the dazzling beauty of the south was 'almost too theatrical', but the sun and light helped dispel sombre thoughts, for her beloved sister Mildred had only recently, and suddenly, died at Wilton.[*]

Eager to forget her grief, Miss Olivier launched herself into the holiday life of the two young boys. It was her first meeting with Rex, with whom she felt an immediate sympathy. He struck her as 'a delightful keen boy, who loves talking',[50] and Rex, on his part, was immediately attracted to this 'short-sighted, vivacious' woman.

The following morning Stephen took Edith on a walk into the town. Together they drank hot chocolate in a little shop, and to Edith 'everything seemed so gay and coloured . . . marvellously tropical'. They returned to the villa for lunch, and spent a leisurely afternoon sitting out on the terrace, reading or writing in the sun. Stephen filled his diary with pictures of everyone. After tea, Edith produced the new poem by Edith Sitwell, *The Sleeping Beauty*, which she had brought from London, and read aloud to Rex and Stephen.

Then it was off on a train journey to Cap d'Ail, in the continuing blazing sunshine. Stephen bought two red butterfly nets 'and stepped along with his enchanting speeding leaping movement', his nets over his shoulder, whilst Rex took care of the 'business part of the journey'. Nannie kept her eye on them all: 'very careful but also delightfully unconventional and unfussy', thought Edith. Cap d'Ail was a riot of flowers, and they called at the Eden Hotel, high above the sea, its garden full of bougainvillaea, pansies and marigolds.

The boys had 'the most governessy governess', but she appeared to have little opportunity to exert any beneficial influence. They were too busy on trips into town with Edith, who was proving great fun, and not at all the blue-stocking she first appeared. One evening Stephen led them on an expedition to find tree frogs 'who sang in chorus rather like shrill ducks quacking'. These peculiar amphibians were traced to a water-butt in someone's garden, and as Stephen led his hunters towards the butt, the owner ran out with a large and rather fearsome dog. 'But the man was too delightful, an amused laughing fat Italian who, when he grasped what we wanted, helped Stephen to catch the frogs. Stephen wildly excited over this,' wrote Edith.

One afternoon, the three ended up at a *thé dansant* where they found Italians, French and Germans sitting around watching 'some terrible German danseuses – very naked', with ballet skirts 'and bare dirty legs with garter marks at the knee. Busts wobbling horribly in little sateen

[*]Edith Olivier's first published book was dedicated to Mildred's memory – *The Mildred Book*, privately printed at Shaftesbury, and illustrated by Stephen and Rex.

bodices. No grace or gift for dancing' here, they surmised. After the performance, there was ordinary dancing, and Stephen and Rex took it in turns to dance with Edith. They were glad to get back to their terrace, where she read from Walter Pater, a new discovery to both of them – 'both revel in every sentence'.*[51]

They had decided that Edith must be modernized, as she had so suddenly lost twenty years and become a contemporary. She was persuaded to have her hair cut short – a bingle, a variation on the highly fashionable shingle. Stephen took this spinster in her fifties, prescribed short skirts and lipstick, and with the renovation of that schoolmistressy 'bun' – hey presto! A new Edith emerged, butterfly-like, to accompany her young beaux to a motor race. Her family's reaction, on Edith's return to England, was reported to be the source of some misgiving, not to say shock.

Stephen's health continued to improve. Strenuous travel was still proscribed, and although Dr Macfie's pronouncements were usually greeted dismally by Stephen, his favourable report to Pamela (now back in England) pleased Stephen. Nannie wrote about her charge to Elizabeth, just two days before Stephen's nineteenth birthday, telling her he was in San Remo buying socks. 'He loves shopping as you know – if Stephen wants to save any money, he must not go where there are any shops as he cannot keep himself from buying or spending.'[52] She bought him a birthday cake in town, and told Elizabeth that they had been frog-hunting and had fallen off some stepping stones 'which caused me and Stephen fun and me a wetting . . . There has only been one more outing to Monte Carlo since you left which was rather a late one. Her Ladyship wrote or wired to Doctor Macfie to say there was not to be any more until after Easter. He got very angry, said he would not be dictated to from an outsider, would give up the case, he knew quite well what to do having had care of sanatoriums for many years.'[53]

Stephen stayed on until the end of April, relishing his last few days in San Remo. He felt more alive now in the reviving, exciting beauty of that Mediterranean climate, and it compounded the opinion formed earlier that summer in Mundesley. He was, he decided, truly a child of the sun.

---

*Walter Pater (1839–94). Critic, aesthete and homosexual, he idealized male friendships in *Marius the Epicurean* (1885). He died writing a candid homoerotic poem, 'Gaston de Latour'. Oscar Wilde was one of his most fervent aesthetic disciples.

Chapter 4

Napier and Eloise

> *He sought*
> *For his heart was tender, things to love,*
> *But found them not, alas! nor was there ought*
> *The world contains, the which he could approve.*
>
> — P. B. Shelley

STEPHEN and Nannie returned home to England in early May, breaking their journey in Marseilles, where they stayed one night, providing Stephen with a tantalizing glimpse of a city that would become an obsession for him. Then it was on to Paris, visiting an old family friend, the writer and poet Mary Duclaux, who interested Stephen because of her connections with two of his favourite writers: she and her sister, the novelist F. Mabel Robinson, had known Thomas Hardy and his first wife, Emma, and they had also lived in the Brontës' Yorkshire village of Haworth.

Back at Wilsford Stephen released a Mediterranean cache of water-snakes and geckoes into the Reptillery first started by his brother, now maintained entirely by him. A large glazed building a few yards from the west side of the Manor grounds, replete with bamboo plants and a terrapin pool, here he could play with his new animals – glad now to be rid of the attentions of the tiresome Dr Macfie.

However, sadness greeted the travellers. Nannie's daughter, Nellie, who lived at Wokingham with her husband and nine children, had contracted tetanus which had gone beyond the point of treatment. Nannie rushed to help, but was too late 'for me to know her . . . It was septic poison which caused lockjaw – & went to her brain – it was terrible to hear her raving.'[1] Poor Nellie was taken to hospital because her behaviour was frightening the children, and died there a few days later. Stephen exhorted friends to console Nannie in her distress, and letters of

42

sympathy came from Elizabeth and Rex. Practical help was provided by Pamela and Christopher, who arranged for the family to be taken care of financially. Stephen took it as hard as Mrs Trusler. He had a new tutor, yet another, by the name of Babb, 'very nice but I am too heavy hearted over Nannie's sorrow to like anything or anybody at this moment', he wrote to Elizabeth on 14 May.

Soon Stephen's unhappiness was dispelled by a new project of his own, sparked off by his stay in San Remo, and his observations of Riviera high society. 'I am writing a novel & adoring it,' he told Elizabeth. 'I hope first to bring it out (if it will be taken) in the *Daily Mirror* as a serial. It is high life with a capital H & full of crude impossibilities – however one has to begin like that. I hope one day to be a great novelist. It is I think going to be called "The Monkey House". I am undecided between this & "Gutters of Gold" (the last is most suitable to the daily M. don't you think ?).'[2]

Stephen finally alighted on the title *The Second Chance* for his first attempt at prose, a novella written in pencil at what looks like feverish pace. It is the tale of Marcella Maine, a vamp in her thirties whose husband is a good-for-nothing racehorse owner. Her lawyer, Roderick Hankey, a childhood friend, falls in love with Marcella and leaves his dull wife and equally dull daughters in the country to travel Europe and America with this glamorous *femme fatale*.

The book compares with the early works of Evelyn Waugh or Nancy Mitford in subject matter and treatment; beneath the social frivolity is an attempt to satirize the hedonistic nineteen-twenties. Stephen's naive characterization of Marcella still rings true, with her selfish vanity and careless treatment of those who love her, yet with a certain sense of self-doubt and guilt. She appears to be drawn from life – it is obvious that both Pamela and Stephen's sister Clare (who liked to bathe daily in milk to 'feed' her skin) were role models for his heroine's behaviour.

'Marcella was a high-priestess of that fashionable cult, chronic unpunctuality,' wrote the author. 'Roderick hurried her and worried her till she turned on him and said, "Really! If you say another word I shall have ten fits! I can't and won't be hurried. I want gloves! a handkerchief. Louise, do be quick – lipstick, powder, all that! Now my pearls! Quick! Oh, don't hurry me, Roddy. It hasn't got any arms" – this to poor Roderick, who was delving feverishly in her fur cape for non-existent sleeves.'[3] The scene recalls Hermione Baddeley's tale of Lord Grey's subjection to Pamela's tardiness. One can also see a similarity to Eddy, Stephen's father, in Mr Maine, 'a cardboard figure, who was absent-minded at breakfast and ruled by her'.

Strewn throughout the twenty-two chapters of this tragi-comic romance are various sub-plots. Roderick's daughter, Ada, besotted by
Marcella's sophistication and her continual appearance in the society
columns, leaves home to live with her father and his mistress. Ada's crush
on her heroine has the young Miss Hankey devouring every published
mention of Marcella available. One is 'a peculiarly trite article in an old
monthly magazine which stated that the lovely Mrs Maine never wore a
pair of stockings twice, always wore garters of alligator-skin, and never
travelled without an Ethiopian courier who guarded her priceless
entourage wherever she journeyed. For all she understood the garter
might have been Ethiopian and the Courier an alligator . . . If one day a
telegram should arrive saying, "Come at once to Switzerland and join your
father and myself in our gay life", the Ethiopian alligator will conduct you
here. I shall receive you in my Italian palace, etc. etc!'

The book could not have been written in any other period, so 'twenties'
is Stephen's vocabulary. He uses the adjective 'ultra' a great deal, as in
'Paris was ultra-dusty', and chapter-titles such as 'Jazzomania'. The
account of Marcella's procession across the Atlantic on the SS *Amputania*
entails a constant presence of hairdressers and manicurists to attend to Mrs
Maine's toilette, whilst almost all the first-class passengers suffer
appalling sea-sickness. Written from personal experience, it was a joke
Stephen very much enjoyed: 'Over our hero's racked form the writer
must draw a merciful curtain.' A new character, Prince Tuad Mossuk
Muraldenez Rey, another Marcella camp-follower, is seen immured in his
cabin, suffering too – his 'yellow hand . . . lay like a bunch of wizened
bananas on the quilt'.

On their arrival in New York, Marcella and company are besieged by
reporters and drooled over by her American friends – again, Stephen's
own observation of hospitality in America, where, he later noted, one is
'pelted' with bouquets. Stephen's description of Marcella's levee in her
New York apartment is worth recording in full, not only for its humour,
but for its prescience of Stephen's own later habits *au lit* that he would
develop into a lifestyle and an art in itself:

'Ada, on entering the bedroom, perceived at once that the bed was
performing all its pet tricks which . . . are invariably called forth to rile
and exacerbate the hapless rest-seeker. The present occupant of the bed in
question was in the last stages of exasperation. The pillows had strangely
minimized themselves to give the least support to Marcella's aching back;
all her books had crept out of arm's length, with the paper-cutter and the
scissors (always the cunningest evaders of weary arms). Crumbs were

playing their gritty tremolo in each most un-get-atable portion of her body. The cloak of invisibility which the fountain-pen can assume on the least and minutest provocation was in this instance of the most impregnable character; not even Ada, flat on her stomach beneath the bed, could plumb its fastness. "Never mind, I shall get up now. This dreadful bed has thwarted my every wish! Ada darling, come out! It's not there. If you kick the bed again I shall just give one screech and explode!" She leapt from the bed, upsetting a box of marrons glacés, a white enamel telephone, a plate of biscuits, a basket of peaches and an avalanche of books. With purple cheeks and much puffing, Ada emerged from the brocade valance and immediately, as if by magic, each desired object revealed itself, lying in feigned innocence on all sides.'

There is not a little of Stephen in Marcella. She receives reporters from *The Modern Home* magazine and tells them that 'perfume is as necessary to my existence as warmth to the orchid. I fade and grow listless if the air I breathe is not constantly sprayed with some rare fragrance. Attar of lilies or amber . . .' In later years, Stephen Spender would recall Stephen's manservant being sent to his master's London rooms in advance, to spray them with Stephen's favoured scent in readiness for his arrival.

Marcella's audience is a ruse, designed to impress the two female reporters with her 'decadence'. She is in a darkened room, dressed in black velvet, with white maquillage and gold dust in her hair. Absinthe and iced caviar are served, and the whole scene is reminiscent of the Marchesa Casati, the epitome of the twenties vamp. Tall, gaunt, and with eyes heavily made-up, she would lead her two pet panthers by their diamond leashes through the Piazza in Venice, where the crowds would nervously part to let them by. Schiaparelli recalled sending a girl over from her boutique to the Marchesa's apartment in Paris. 'She found the Marchesa in bed, fully made-up in the old vamp style, covered with a rug of black ostrich feathers, eating a breakfast of fried fish and drinking straight Pernod while trying on a newspaper scarf.'[4]

It was Stephen's penchant for such figures which later led him to create the same kind of legend around himself, as he became more like these 'fixations' he so admired. Marcella's departure from Grand Central station, 'with seven trollies of vast trunks', was echoed years later by Stephen's amusement on hearing that his friend Barbara Hutton (whose qualifications for this category of woman were impeccable) travelled to Morocco from Paris with 'six crates of scent'.

Stephen finished his book in September 1925, with what he called 'a shattering roar of chaotic tragedy and grief-stricken drama',[5] but which actually read rather more tamely. It ends abruptly, as if he had become tired and wished to send it off as soon as possible. Marcella muses on her cold-hearted ways, wondering what she should do about Roddy, Ada, the future. As her train pulls out of the station, she looks up at the decoration on the tiny ceiling of her Pullman compartment, and becomes transfixed by the 'fruit, roses, a harp, a mask, a peacock, then flapping ribbons delicately binding a repetition of the last garland . . . fruit . . . roses . . . a harp'.

During its writing, Stephen had already been approached by one publisher, John Murray (told of the book by Doctor Macfie, 'the first good thing [he] has ever done for me !').[6] Stephen announced he could not think of publishing yet, and proceeded to seek Marie Belloc Lowndes' advice on publishers and possible newspaper rights. But there was no serialization of Stephen's would-be blockbuster in the *Daily Mirror*, or anywhere else, for that matter. Whether he lost heart, or lost faith in the book, it is difficult to say. Whatever happened, it merely gathered dust in a trunk, as would his later, more mature efforts to write fiction, victims of their creator's vicissitudes. At the last minute – despite the obvious hard work that had gone into its creation, and its flashes of true humour and acute contemporary observation – Stephen lost the impetus, or perhaps the courage, to follow it to a satisfactory conclusion.

Stephen's close friendship with Elizabeth Lowndes grew yet closer in the summer of 1925 – so close, in fact, that Miss Lowndes was petitioned for her hand in marriage by Stephen James Napier. Elizabeth's visits to Wilsford became more frequent in those early weeks of summer, after Stephen's return from San Remo. A love of animals bound them – Elizabeth was always eager to rush into Stephen's Reptillery on arrival, to see his newest acquisition, often with a new addition to the menagerie of painted toads, lizards and African frogs, brought down from London by Elizabeth herself, who never hesitated to fetch a grass snake from pet stores for Stephen and carry it down in a box on the train.

Elizabeth stayed in her favourite Rose room, and after tea Pamela would send them off in the Victoria for an evening drive, unchaperoned, in the Wiltshire country lanes, across the wilderness of Salisbury Plain, then 'wild and unfenced with dewponds filled with great crested newts, and Stonehenge standing stark and deserted'.[7] Discussing Stephen's novel, or Elizabeth's attempt to write short stories – 'the coachman must have listened with astonishment', observed Elizabeth's sister – they would bowl along, Stephen waving to children as they passed, or covering Elizabeth's legs with a rug lest she catch cold in the cooling evening.

Pamela was well aware of Stephen's increasing affection for Elizabeth, and actively encouraged the relationship. When arrangements for Elizabeth's visit to San Remo were being made, Pamela had written to the girl's mother: 'I have been very touched to realize Stephen's deep affection for your Elizabeth. It has come over me with a sudden impact that this is a very real and growing feeling. You know all I feel about your child! So I need not dwell on that – but let me first add that it might be a very blessed time for them all . . .'[8] Then, on the evening of 23 June, Stephen summoned up the courage to ask Elizabeth if she would marry him. Elizabeth, not particularly surprised by this new turn of events, could give her suitor no definite answer; she asked for time to consider. Stephen, on his part, announced that he would wait and, in the meantime, try to prove his 'great and enduring love'[9] for her.

Stephen wrote to Marie Belloc Lowndes to assure her of his devotion to her daughter. 'I do feel that never yet have I met or known a girl who combined such charm, such humour, such wit and such wisdom as your precious daughter. Quite apart from my own knowledge of the perfection of her character, the universal liking and admiration of all who meet her is a unique indication of something more unusual. Never, until I saw her coming down the stone path on arrival here last time, did I feel so certain that if I could earn her love I should be the happiest man in the world.'[10]

Stephen announced, to both mother and daughter, that his 'first wooing present' would be a pair of single-pearl earrings. 'Do use your supreme influence,' he asked Mrs Belloc Lowndes, 'and get her ears pierced . . .' Not only this, but Stephen thought Elizabeth should, like Edith Olivier, undergo another transformation. '. . . Your mother consents to you having your hair shingled and you can guess what exstasy [*sic*] I am in!!!' he wrote excitedly to Miss Lowndes on 8 July. 'I have written to enquire of the finest shingler in Europe . . . About your ears being pierced your mother agrees. I shall have the pearl studs for you as we pass through London en route for Fallodon. Will you lunch or dine with us at the Gargoyle?' Stephen boasted that 'your Beloved mother and I are having delicious talks and laughs. She is invaluable in all matters appertaining to the Novel and our happy friendship.' Marie Belloc Lowndes' attitude to the whole affair was, according to her younger daughter, typically French. 'She did not believe in the "falling in love" syndrome at all – being a Catholic, she knew marriage was for life, and everything had to be taken into account. She stayed very much on the sidelines, and left it up to Elizabeth to make up her own mind.'[11]

Added to that, there were dark hints from Nannie Trusler, who told Mrs Belloc Lowndes that her 'Steenie' was 'not right, physically'.

And Miss Lowndes herself? She was, she recalled, 'very fond' of Stephen – but never in love with him. Besides that emotional hurdle, she also realized, being six years Stephen's senior, that the match was not realistic. 'It just wasn't feasible,'[12] she decided. Elizabeth wanted a normal marriage, with children and a stable future, none of which Stephen could offer. But Elizabeth respected the fervency of her friend-turned-suitor's desires, and there was, somewhere within, a doubt. His touching display of devotion convinced her of his sincerity. On 14 July, an envelope containing two pressed handkerchiefs, embroidered with roses, arrived at 9 Barton Street: 'The charm and lovely freshness of them reminds me of you; when you wear them, think of your – Devoted Stephen.'

The letters, addressed with their respective love names, Napier and Eloise, passed between their respective homes with often daily frequency (with Elizabeth living literally around the corner from Smith Square, this was a real boy/girl-next-door romance). The shingle and shingler were of great import. A Mr Leonard in Coventry, who had given Clare Tennant

'the best shingle in London',[13] was recommended, but Elizabeth's decision was eventually swayed by her mother, who took her along to get both shingle and ear-piercing operations done on 21 July. Stephen was delighted, and longed to see 'the darling head in its shingled beauty', only then adding: 'You don't say whether you like [it]? (the most important person!) . . . The pearls shall be pinkish and creamish as you wish. I agree they are prettyer (what odd spelling!!!). N.'[14]

By the end of July, Stephen had gone up to Fallodon with Pamela and Lord Grey for the rest of the summer. He was determined, though, not to be parted from his Eloise for long; she seemed to be looking favourably on his proposal. 'I was moved (and joyously moved) by your letter, my dearest,' he wrote from Northumberland on 28 July. 'If we are, as I hope and pray, destined for each other, what golden realms we'll wander in! what treasure troves of material and spiritual glories will unfold for us!' Stephen envisaged an idyllic life together: 'I shall write the greatest books! the most beautiful poetry! paint the finest pictures! and you will help me and advise me and do the lady bountiful (like Amy) [the heroine of *Little Women*] and spread the wonderful good that is in your heart and we will visit and travel in all the most wonderful countries! It will be heaven! You, me and Nannie. She loves travelling more than anything! We three will sail around the seas together tasting the myriad wonders and sights of this beautiful world!' Wonderful plans indeed – and who but Stephen would propose taking his nanny on honeymoon?

Waiting for Elizabeth's planned visit to Fallodon, Stephen occupied himself with local life. Steven Runciman, who had earned the nickname 'the fringed rose leaf-eater' from Stephen,[*] was there with his family, and together they faced the 'Northumberland frumps' who were in 'frightened array already'[16] (the same frumpish debutantes who occasioned Stephen's ire by breaking into his room one day and jealously scattering his collection of make-up). Stephen was also concerned with sending enraged letters to the editor of the *Tatler*, who had printed one of his sketches without permission – or payment: 'this I mind the most!'

Elizabeth arrived at Fallodon in time for the grand pageant which was to take place at Alnwick Castle, the seat of the Duke of Northumberland. A huge sprawling castle, Alnwick was an impressive stage for the recreation of the siege of Bamburgh Castle which was to open the fête. Organized by Steven Runciman's mother, this dramatic set-piece was to feature various members of the Runciman family, and their daughter-in-law, Rosamund, who had married Leslie Runciman in 1922. Half-American, and described by Stephen Spender as 'one of the most beautiful women of her generation',[17] Rosamond Lehmann was at that time putting the finishing touches to her first novel, *Dusty Answer*, and would become a great lifelong friend of Stephen's. She played 'first herald', while Wogan

---

[*]'In my undergraduate days I shocked the respectable world by wearing my hair in a sort of fringe,' recalled Sir Steven, 'a coiffure that nowadays would be perfectly acceptable but that then was somewhat *outré*. I also, when friends came to tea with me, provided them with rose-leaf jam, which I obtained from a little Greek shop in the East End . . .'[15]

Philips (later her second husband) was the Earl of Northumberland. Rosamond's brother John Lehmann took the part of the Captain, and lastly there was a motley crew of 'Men-at-Arms, Retainers, etc.' which included the name of 'the Hon. S. Tennant', 'a very fetching young soldier', Sir Steven recalled.

It was a grand affair, with long reports in the local paper, the *Alnwick & County Gazette & Guardian*: 'No more appropriate setting could be imagined . . . than the spacious lawns at Alnwick Castle, with their enclosing walls of ancient masonry and historic towers.'[18] Episode One of the pageant began thus: 'Men-at-Arms are seen on the battlements of Bamburgh Castle now besieged by the forces of King William II. A herald arrives demanding surrender. Matilda, Countess of Northumberland . . . refuses to yield. A captain of the King's Army then brings before the walls her husband, Earl Robert, who has been captured unknown to her, and threatens to put out his eyes. Matilda in horror flings down the keys and the King's men enter in triumph.'

A photograph accompanied this description of the drama, and on one side of the imploring Matilda, perched up on the battlements, is the unmistakable figure of Stephen, attired in rough tunic and holding a pikestaff, with an unconvincing military bearing. He gasps in mock-horror as he and the Herald, Rosamond, recoil from the threat to their master below. Miss Lehmann later recalled that afternoon, observing that she had 'the demeaning role of a (male) herald, with little to do except to run along the battlements at one point, looking out for the enemy. Stephen was to play a similar part. As we sat in our rough male sackcloth and cross garters awaiting our brief moment of glory, we fell to discussing our favourite colours. Blue, I said, then red. Then pink. 'Oh, pink! I almost faint when I think of pink,' said Stephen. 'Such was our laughter,' recalled Rosamond, 'that we totally missed our cue. I don't think we were forgiven.'[19] Certainly Stephen's behaviour was an eye-opener to locals, as the Duke of Northumberland was later to note, complaining that Stephen caused 'considerable comment' in those parts, recalling Edward VII's (?) dictum, 'I don't care what you do, so long as you don't frighten the horses.' HIS MISTRESS 'JERSEY LILY' SAID IT

Elizabeth's visit came and went, and Stephen stayed on at Fallodon. He had begun to realize that his dream of wedded bliss with Eloise was not to be, yet there was no diminishing the closeness of their friendship. In between garden parties at the Runcimans', and a visit from his sister Clare, Stephen wrote to Elizabeth: 'I miss you so frightfully! I can't tell you what your visit meant to me. This morning I go down to the sea alone.'[20] However, beach outings with his brother David, Leslie, Rosamond and Steven Runciman were fun, Stephen gossiping with the latter two as Leslie and David dug in the sand.

The family had to return to London in mid-September, for Stephen's eldest brother Christopher, Lord Glenconner, was about to be married to Pamela Paget.* *Vogue* dubbed their wedding, at Wells Cathedral on 30 September, 'one of the most important social events of 1925'.[21] It was important for Stephen too – he had designed the bride's and bridesmaids' dresses. The *Sketch* reported the great occasion with a photo-spread: 'The bride wore a gown of gold-and-silver patterned lamé adorned with a narrow edging of gold tissue, and had curious and fan-shaped draperies of gold tissue, as well as a white veil. The elder bridesmaids wore velvet dresses of the same period as that of the bride – those of Miss Sylvia and Miss Angela Paget carried out in golden yellow; of Miss Alison and Miss Nancy Tennant, in sapphire blue; and of Lady Mary Thynne, in jade green.'[22]

Stephen had drawn on medieval costumes for inspiration, using bright colours to reflect medieval stained glass. The designer himself arrived at the cathedral with a toad and a snake, habitual accoutrements at this time. There was another budding young artist in the crowd, a Mr Cecil Beaton – he knew Pamela from Cambridge – who wrote in his diary of his disapproval of the bridal costumes, but thought their creator rather interesting. Elizabeth and family were there too, having come down on the specially-chartered train. Stephen hoped that it had not tired his beloved, 'but it was rather fun! wasn't it?'[23]

For the Armistice Celebrations that year, Stephen planned an intimate dinner party at his brother's Gargoyle Club, which had opened earlier that year. At a loose end after leaving Cambridge, David had hit upon the idea of opening a night-club specifically aimed at the literary and artistic crowd. Situated in Soho, the Gargoyle, with its rickety lift up to mirrored dining and dancing rooms, quickly became extremely fashionable. For Daphne Fielding, it transformed 'conventional people into Bohemians . . . It was easy to imagine David Tennant's first wife, Hermione Baddeley, kicking her well-turned legs in a can-can *à la* Goulue, for in its infancy the Gargoyle had a Toulouse-Lautrec atmosphere',[24] while Edward Burra liked its 'dainty Tudor atmosphere . . . a

---

*Pamela Paget (1903–89) was one of the first women to attend Cambridge University, and was famous for having thrown herself backwards off a moving bus in Park Lane to prove her father's theory that she would stay upright.

little bit more expensive than our dear old Maison (Lyons)', he told Barbara Ker-Seymer, 'but still when you are surrounded by lovely Matisses whose price runs into 4 figgers and get a squint at *Vogue* without paying it's not so expensive . . .'[25]

Stephen had made one or two visits to his brother's club since its opening earlier that year, and was particularly taken by its interior, decorated by Hugh Gee (husband of Hermione Baddeley's sister, Muriel). There were dark blue floors and a ceiling studded with silver stars – a theatrical effect which was matched by his own 'Silver Room' in the new London home the Greys had taken that year. Stephen organized a celebration of 'grand success' at the Gargoyle for the evening of 29 November; with 'very precious chosen people',[26] the two most precious being Elizabeth and Nannie.

Most of Autumn 1925 was spent at Wilsford, with occasional trips to London to visit the theatre – and Elizabeth. Stephen was yet hopeful, writing on 26 November that he had loved seeing her: 'Thank you for the glove and the word it rhymes with ———— . . . Our understanding is a heavenly thing, but my dear, never let it cramp you or make you feel anything but free as the wind, it is only that I am here – a mite of unworthiness.'

Winter came, and snow fell at Wilsford. Stephen caught a cold, and wrote to Elizabeth from his sick-bed to ask if she would perform a favour for him. He was buying a white rat from Gamages – could she send it down by train? Or better still, someone from the family tailors, Lesley and Roberts, was coming to measure him for a suit, and 'if you would buy the rat I would tell them to call for it at No. 9 and bring it down with them . . . ask when they are coming . . . & to call for "the package". Better not mention contents – some people do not take to Rats!!!'[27] Elizabeth did as she was bid, and the following Monday received a card from Stephen: '. . . The tailor begged to see what he had conveyed thither, and was much interested!?! Are you sending the house by post?'[28] Evidently the house for Stephen's new pet was not needed. To Nannie's surprise, the rat spent most of its time in his pyjama pocket – 'Oh, Master Stephen, you don't want to keep that dirty thing in there!'[29]

A week or so later, Stephen and his mother saw the fruition of a project which they had collaborated upon together – their illustrated book, *The Vein in the Marble*. Published by Philip Allen as a quarto-sized edition, the contents of *The Vein* are pure period whimsy. Using Pamela's poems, epigrams and morality tales, the book is half text, half illustration;

Stephen's harlequins and Regency ladies vie with fairy-tale characters, drawn with a certain exuberance, if not with consistent talent. The drawings show what he could do, but do not quite break out of untutored naivety; there is no maturity to these languid faces and florid figures.

The Vein in the Marble has a dedication: 'To the most perfect of collaborators in great as in little things – My Mother'. Following it come thirty or so parables of modern life, often couched in historic settings. 'France, 1795 ... the very atmosphere must weep', is one caption to a lurid Revolutionary scene of beheaded aristocrats (a reference to Pamela's French ancestry), while 'After the Circus' has a 'common trollop, rather elderly, in a daring crinoline'. 'Sod and Soil' – 'principals, not individuals' – recalls Pamela's erstwhile association with Arts and Crafts, and in 'Drive On!', an eighteenth-century carriage scene has a lady descending to kiss a beggar. (An old Wilford retainer remembers that Pamela used to encourage beggars and tramps to call at the front door, where they would be given money – thus ensuring that in the local fraternity Wilsford became known as a 'good house', and not one to rob.)

Some scenes are almost surreal; '"I don't like your story" said the Moon to the Nightingale' – a woman weeps while her young son lies dead on a table by the window, the moon in the sky, a bird in a cage – inevitably seen as a reference to Bim's death. Overall, there is a cloying feel of sentimentality to the book which only just escapes being embarrassing.

However, when Pamela and her youngest took delivery of their first proof copies that winter's day, they sat from lunch till teatime 'hardly speaking . . . deaf to the world, now & then murmuring madly, in a sort of trance!' To see one's work published in a book for the first time was a magical moment. 'We almost wept with excitement as we each finished our book! The child of our endeavours at last launched upon literature's perilous seas!'[30]

The reviews of *The Vein in the Marble* were surprisingly good; its sales were not. When Philip Allen passed on the disappointing figures, Stephen admitted, with a certain business acumen, that the market for such books was very small, but he could rejoice in reviews, 'all to a degree laudatory'.[31] Steven Runciman felt at the time that Stephen was rather embarrassed after the book came out – and made it known that it was his mother who had been responsible for it.

That winter, Pamela and Sir Edd'ard proposed to spend Christmas abroad. The *Daily Mirror* reported on 3 November: 'I hear that Viscountess Grey is shortly taking her son, the Hon. Stephen Tennant, to Madeira . . . Unlike his brothers, who are both very robust, the Hon. Stephen Tennant is rather delicate, although the delicacy is due, I believe, to long hours spent in art schools at a time when he was growing very fast. He is a young man of insatiable energy.'

Thus Stephen was encouraged to consider himself of fragile health, a young artist suffering for his art. He would not have forgotten Aubrey Beardsley's untimely demise. Like his later friend, E. M. Forster, who was convinced of his own youthful delicacy until he realized in middle age that his health was actually quite robust, Stephen assumed throughout his life the state of ailing, of a lack of vigour which would never have occurred to him as being at all hypochondriac. Yet this six foot two inch tall young man who had such curtailed expectations would, in the event, outlive most of his contemporaries.

Pamela, however, continued to be concerned for Stephen's health. He had been examined that autumn by London specialists, and the Salisbury physician, Dr Kempe, and the conclusion was that a spell in winter sunshine would do him good. Thus the family set off on 18 December,

boarding the Union Castle ship *The Saxon* at Southampton, *en route* for
Madeira.

The Saxon was a small ship 'decorated with the vigorous hideosity that
is the prerogative of "passenger boats" and has painted heliotrope,
mauve and orange funnels. A very nice mixture too,' observed Stephen
critically.[32] They lunched on board, greeted by the Captain as a 'nasal and
swift-playing band' played 'God Save the King'. At four o'clock, they
pulled out of Southampton Docks, which 'slithered away into the
distance and we turned our half-happy, half-melancholy attention to
cabins, bunks etc . . . This touching sentence suggests emigration for life,
but we are simply going to Madeira for Christmas!'

Stephen sought suitable company among the passengers, but found few
to please, though many to amuse. 'An enormous widow with a scarlet
face, ginger wisps of hair protruding from a musty black crêpe toque, and
a mouth like a coal scuttle' caught his eye amongst the 'brisk platitudin-
ous mothers' and young men 'with assumed deep voices and ill-fitting
clothes'.

The Greys and their son stayed at the renowned Reid's Palace Hotel in
the capital, Funchal, and found Madeira lush and exotic. Soon they were
launched into Madeiran society. 'Very claimative,' noted Stephen;
'lunches & mah-jongg teas & casino parties envelop one on every side'.[33]
One hostess learning of Stephen's dancing skills invited him to perform at
a party. Stephen lunched with her to discuss arrangements 'and choose
where I shall dance! My dear!' he told Elizabeth, 'the most lovely place, a
sort of terrace bowered in exotic plants with great jars & a flight of stone
stairs and she is going to have it all illuminated.'[34]

A principal joy of the island for Pamela and Lord Grey was the
abundant bird life. In a market they bought several varieties, including
parakeets and finches. Stephen had a personal parrot, a green Amazon
named Jonathan Jewel whom he declared very tame, despite the fact that
Jonathan had bitten his master three times. Pamela's particular pet was a
grey African dubbed Poll Squallor: '"Poll Squoll" for short because she is
so dirty & untidy & unkillingly greedy'.[35] Stephen was later to transfer
his affections to Poll when Jonathan died.

They intended to leave Madeira, birds and all, in early February, but
more bad weather delayed them. In the meantime Stephen had met a
doctor, a Portuguese specialist who had performed a small operation on
his nose to help his breathing. Stephen rather liked him, and boasted that
he had dined 'with him and 18 others! mostly Portuguese . . .'[36] Thus it
was a sad Stephen who boarded ship for the return to England, but

arriving home at the end of February, he was glad to supervise the Reptillery and settle a new consignment of birds into the aviary.

'We are oh so hilarious at being home again,' he told Elizabeth.[37] 'All the Parrots are safe and well. "Poll Squoll" has had tea with us – she has such personality. "John" has been out on the balcony all day – he talks in Portuguese and makes lovely noises.' The spotted plant he had brought from Madeira looked just right: 'It is very reptillian [*sic*],' concluded the correspondent. 'I've just had a delicious "sit" & play in the Reptillery,' where he spent hours watching Java sparrows in the bamboo. 'They look so decorative! One hopped onto a common terrapin's back & jumped off very quickly when the head shot out angrily!'[38]

Chapter 5

Overture . . .

And certainly, to him life itself was the first, the greatest, of the arts, and for it all the other arts seemed to be but a preparation. Fashion, by which what is really fantastic becomes for a moment universal, and dandyism, which in its own way is an attempt to assert the absolute modernity of beauty, had, of course, their fascination for him.

— Oscar Wilde: *The Portrait of Dorian Gray*

IN the spring of 1926 Stephen, not yet twenty, wrote an extended letter of critical praise to an unknown American author whose books he had discovered[*] and had been avidly reading since the latter part of the previous year. The author was Willa Cather. 'I think *A Lost Lady* a deeply beautiful book,' Stephen had written to Elizabeth Lowndes on 18 November 1925, 'so well written that it is like a life experience frozen into a day's reading. It is gripping & supremely moving in the fine, hard, remote way that all emotion should be conveyed.'

Fine, hard and remote could equally well describe Cather herself. A child of Virginia, she had spent most of her youth in the wild country of Nebraska, where her family moved when she was just nine years old. This sudden uprooting from the genteel South to the remote Western landscape was pivotal to her work, which used that countryside, then an endless sea of red grass, as a basis for her elegiac, lyrical books. 'There was nothing but land – ' writes the hero of *My Ántonia*, one of her greatest works ' – not a country at all, but the material of which countries are made.'[2]

Willa Cather shocked her home town of Red Cloud, Nebraska, with her boyish ways (she dressed like a young man, and had her hair crew

[*]Sir Steven Runciman is of the opinion that Baba Brougham (p. 67) first brought Cather to Stephen's attention. 'She certainly gave me copies of Cather's books,' he recalled.[1]

cut), by her experiments into vivisection, and her general disregard of the social expectations of a young girl. But as soon as she entered Lincoln State University, she began to make her mark in another way – by writing. Starting out on student publications, she rose quickly to editing jobs on local periodicals. Cather's stage critiques for the *Nebraskan State Journal* pulled no punches – Sarah Bernhardt was one of the few actresses to meet with her approval – and soon drew the attention of *McClure's Magazine* in New York. By 1906 Cather, clad in 'tailored shirtwaists and mannish ties',[3] was living in the very heart of East Coast Bohemia, New York's Greenwich Village, and had already become a force to be reckoned with in the literary life of the city where she would spend most of the rest of her days.

But Cather's fictional territory was the pioneering West and other virgin lands. Her books dwell on the past as a lost country. The inscription on the title page of *My Ántonia*, Virgil's *Optima dies . . . prima fugit*, sums up the narrator's feeling: 'the melancholy reflection that, in the lives of mortals, the best days are the first to flee'.[4] *A Lost Lady* draws on these emotions too, with its tale of the fey and beautiful Marion Forrester, doomed to love and be loved, one of Cather's most haunting creations. The fictional heroine appealed greatly to Stephen's sensibility. 'I feel such a power to live in me, Niel,' she tells the young boy/narrator (Cather customarily uses a male voice to tell her stories). 'Her slender fingers gripped his waist. "It's grown by being held back."'[5] Marion's mere presence is magnetic. 'The voice he heard behind him . . . burned through commonplace words like the colour in an opal.'[6]

Stephen was fascinated by Willa Cather, and the books which described her world. He felt he had to know more. In March, inspired by an article written by Hugh Walpole drawing attention to Cather's work, Stephen sat down and wrote his first fan letter to Willa Cather. 'It was eight pages of very brilliant criticism,'[7] Stephen modestly recalled, 'me at my very best, and I sent it to a great friend of my mother's, another famous writer, Anne Douglas Sedgwick. I wrote this long letter and Anne wrote to me and said, "I thought your letter so remarkable that through a mutual friend I've sent it to Willa Cather."'

Within a few days an envelope arrived from America, addressed to Stephen in an unknown blue hand. 'It was my first letter I ever had from Willa Cather!' exclaimed Stephen. 'My mother had a houseparty – every guest room was filled – and I was so excited about this I rushed before breakfast – people were hardly awake, hadn't been given their tea or coffee – and I jumped onto them, leapt onto them, jumping up and down shouting "I've got a letter from Willa Cather!" And none of them had heard of her or knew anything about her.'

This was an ignorance which Stephen would spend the rest of his life attempting to correct. And the letter itself? Well, Miss Cather was 'surprisingly open and confidential', according to Cather scholar Patricia Lee Yongue.[8] 'She expressed a great deal of pleasure at his astute and sensitive observations about her work, but also pointed out some of the flaws in the novella [*My Mortal Enemy*, which Stephen had just read]. She told him, too, that he was sure to like her newest work, *Death Comes for the Archbishop*.' Stephen replied at once, saying how much he looked forward to reading this new book. Her reply, written from Jaffrey, New Hampshire, where she spent her summers writing in a tent in a meadow, 'reveals some of the deference to Stephen that was to increase over the years: maybe he would not like *Archbishop* at all: the work was curiously limited by its theme and hence might not appeal to a mind as probing as his.'

It was another eighteen months before Stephen's critical eye could make its judgement of *Death Comes for the Archbishop*, an evocative tale of Catholic missions in New Mexico. He first saw it announced in a bundle of American papers he had delivered to Fallodon when he was there in September 1927. 'I could shout for joy!' he exclaimed. 'She is my favourite living writer,'[9] he added without equivocation. That would remain his opinion for the next sixty years.

The weekend parties at Wilsford continued throughout Spring 1926. In April he and Pamela were at rather a loss: '. . . Such an awful thing! David is unable to come this weekend for long enough to make it worthwhile, so Mummie and I have had to seek wildly for another man,'[*][10] he told Elizabeth, who was herself invited that coming weekend. It was to include two girls who she hadn't met before. 'Isn't it funny?' said Stephen, regarding his brother's absence. 'And all those Mitfords asked for him!!!'

'Those Mitfords' had to make do with David's brother, who proved to be just as entertaining. Stephen warned Elizabeth in advance that he wanted to play a lot of mah-jongg that weekend: 'Will you be an angel and bring your incense-burner with you . . . Also your Chinese coat. Of course if the Mitfords don't play we'll make them.'[11] Elizabeth arrived by the three o'clock train that Friday – along with the mice Stephen had

* Other guests included the diarist and parliamentarian Henry 'Chips' Channon, Frances Stonor, and Sophie Parker.

ordered 'in their château' (she had also been dispatched to Derry & Toms' department store at the last minute, to seek out European terrapins, 'six, if they have them').

The two Mitfords selected to come for the weekend (their mother having decided two of her daughters quite enough) were the eldest, Nancy, and her younger sister, Pamela. Nancy was twenty-two, and, like Stephen, had studied at the Slade briefly, but was back living with her parents having tried to escape 'Farve' in London. She had begun that year to write her first novels, *Highland Fling* and *Christmas Pudding*, and Stephen himself would become the basis for one of her most endearing characters, Cedric, in *Love in a Cold Climate*.

But in April 1926 Stephen was a rather gauche-looking boy, Nancy only slightly more worldly-wise. They posed for photographs in front of Wilsford, she with her arms folded, in long sweater and skirt, he resplendent in his new pepper-and-salt plus-fours suit, and very white, pointed shoes, smiling nervously before the tyranny of the lens.

In May Britain was plunged into industrial uncertainty, quickly followed by chaos, when the miners' strike led to an all-out General Strike. Stephen thought it a 'frightful thing',[12] after listening to his stepfather speaking on the wireless on 9 May. Fearing for Elizabeth's and Susan's safety in town, Stephen offered them shelter at Wilsford for the duration, although he acknowledged that he felt 'so gloomy at being in the country. I long to be ladling soup in a canteen or striding about with a truncheon.' Stephen was more realistic when he added, 'What a ruin and a desolation it will end in !'

Once the strike was settled, and London back to normal, there was excitement at the new Diaghilev production, *Les Noces*, which premiered on 14 June at His Majesty's Theatre. Stephen was at the opening night, in company with other society notables such as Lady Diana Cooper and her great friend, Viola Tree, the painter Augustus John, and the fashionable playwright Noël Coward. It was a gala occasion, and a new friend of Stephen's, William Walton, the young composer 'discovered' by the Sitwells, had his *Portsmouth Point* performed as the musical entr'acte. Stephen already knew of the young man and his work – back in 1921, Osbert Sitwell had arranged for Walton to be invited to perform one of his songs at a concert at 34 Queen Anne's Gate – but it was only now that he became properly acquainted with the youthful genius.

Initially Stephen found it hard to talk to Walton, whose shyness was not helped by his sponsors' high public profile. 'I think the Sitwells a little bit swamped his personality,' Stephen was to recall, 'they were all so conceited and exhibitionistic! But we must honour Osbert for discovering and nurturing his genius.'[13] Stephen thought that the awesome trio teased Willie, reproving him 'for his Oldham background, as being too "low" & vulgar (half in fun, of course)'.

Stephen had always been a huge fan of the Ballets Russes, and could later boast that he had known a number of Diaghilev's dancers very well, and of having been taught to dance by one of their greatest choreographers, Léonide Massine. His favourite was the ballerina Tchernicheva, whom, after one performance, he fêted with a huge shield made of flowers which he had designed for her. 'I remember how lovely she was,' rhapsodized Stephen years afterwards, at the same time recalling that she had to give up dancing later 'because she walked like a duck as she grew older! Her behind drooped down, you know . . . she was like a duck drawn by a comic person.'

Lady Grey did not accompany Stephen on such outings. She did not quite approve of the ballet, nor did she approve of her son's increasingly acerbic tongue. 'She used to say to me "You know, you're too critical, Stephen. It does wither life so to be as critical as you are." I'd be describing someone's appearance, and I suppose making fun of them. My mother had a very serious side to her . . . and she didn't want me to become drier and drier as a talker,' he admitted. 'I was tending to become rather superior and pleased with myself when I hadn't any reason to be so.'[14]

Glorious summer broke out towards the end of June, and Stephen was off to Wimbledon with Elizabeth on the 30th. Then there was Lady Colefax's party for Mary Pickford, the immensely successful Hollywood star, visiting London with her equally famous husband, Douglas Fairbanks. 'Heavenly' was Stephen's judgement of both party and guests.[15]

The following weekend at Wilsford was so full that Nannie's room had to be commandeered as a dressing-room for guests. There was a new name for the visitors' book, that of the American novelist Elinor Wylie, enjoying the reflected glory of her successful novel, *The Venetian Glass Nephew*, published the previous autumn. An attractive but highly-strung woman, Wylie made her appearance at Wilsford that weekend in a new Poiret gown. Edith Olivier recalled her regal progress down the staircase, 'wearing a dress made of stiff shiny silk, and it looked like frozen water'.[16] Elinor herself was a little disdainful of the dream-like properties of the house: 'This is a lovely place,' she wrote to her husband from the Manor on 18 July, 'beautiful, peaceful – not too grand – but just too calm and easy. It would kill the soul.'[17]

Stephen was impressed by the American, as much by her slightly hysterical nature as by her literary talent; but all this frenetic socializing was taking its toll on his health, and Nannie Trusler expressed her worries to Elizabeth: 'He has been looking tired & white for the last week or so, so is not coming to London for a time – he does so much when there.'[18] Poor Stephen: commanded to stay at home, when he had already ordered his costume for the Duchess of Sutherland's ball. Still, it could not be helped; Mummie's – and the doctor's – word was law. Soon it was time for the annual visit to Fallodon, where once again Stephen hoped to gather his friends about him. 'Three weeks if you can,' he told Elizabeth. 'I'm putting aside "duty" & "pleasure" books, Tolstoi & Dostoevsky in the first . . . *Vogue* is SUCH a good paper now we are taking it in.'[19]

Elizabeth came up to Fallodon for another protracted visit, staying on into September. She and Stephen had decided to take a Pelman course, the memory training method which used cards to improve the recall of facts, figures and faces. They worked together at the exercises, sitting together at a table in the drawing room, happily testing each other's memory. Stephen seemed keener on Pelmanism than his companion, and two months later he declared it was the only thing that was preventing him from vanishing 'away into a mist with sheer ennui'.[20]

Elizabeth returned to London, leaving Stephen to make his first visit to Glen for six years. He found it changed 'in some ways for the better, & in some ways not'.[21] Christopher now lived there, and had a house party consisting of Anne (Nan) Tennant, Stephen's aunt on his father's side; the Marquess of Queensberry, Francis, and his new wife Kathleen; 'Also Captain Barton and his fat daughter. Such a funny party!' said Stephen. 'Oh how I hate Scotland!' He felt 'cold and heartless, like a stranger' now that Glen meant nothing to him, and longed to return to 'London & heavenly Wilsford'. Like his mother, Stephen winced at Scottish barbarity, a sensibility exacerbated by the fact that here were the family's coarse industrial origins.

Just driving back to Fallodon after that dismal weekend cheered him. 'I am so thankful to be in England again – even if it is the north. It's paradise after Scotland, which repelled me more than ever.'[22] There followed a dance given by the Runcimans at Doxford, 'a very gay scene, loud band & every floor gleaming & bare'.[23]

Stephen was with the Runcimans again a week or two later, when the younger members of the party 'were very naughty about the Doxford-ites, really naughty!!!'[24] Stephen was tiring of the country social scene

— and the locals were feeling the brunt. But by 6 October he was southbound once more. 'Hallelujah! Hosanna! & everything else!'

However, 'bleak and blank' was the mood Stephen found himself in on his return to London, despite the joys of the new town house acquired by Pamela and Sir Edd'ard. Mulberry House stood on peaceful Smith Square, in Westminster, just south of the Cathedral close, an area which still retained something of Victorian London, with its narrow gas-lit streets and ancient buildings.

Stephen approved of Mulberry House, partly because of its size — although it was a large home for a dwindling family (with Clare and Christopher married, and David in a flat of his own in Sloane Street). Designed by Sir Edwin Lutyens, it had spacious Edwardian rooms, a panelled library and marble dining-room. Stephen had the luxury of a big bedroom on the first floor, along with an annexe designated as his studio, in which he could work at his paintings. He was having some small success selling these — and as Nannie Trusler noted, this gave him great pleasure 'as he loves making money on his own. When he gets a cheque for a picture he is ever so pleased.'[25]

The current mood of dullness and the impatience he felt with his 'dreamy self'[26] probably stemmed from the fact that his creative life had reached stasis. Whilst Rex had gone on to great things, recognition of Stephen's abilities had stalled a little. In one of these moods, Stephen had launched himself into the embellishment of his room — and a lifelong preoccupation with the outer limits of interior décor began. He began to order exotic fabrics, paints and furniture. The result was the 'Silver Room', an extraordinary flight of fantasy. To begin with, all the walls were covered in gleaming metallic silver-foil paper, and the ceiling was painted a dreamy sapphire blue. Then a plush, velvety black carpet was laid. Next, Stephen demanded silver-topped tables, and a silver brocade cover for his bed. Silver satin curtains were hung, and one or two non-silver finishing touches added — a polar bear skin rug or two. The whole luminous effect — Pamela likened it to an iceberg — was set off by massed bunches of Arum and Madonna lilies.

Stephen was proud enough to allow a *Vogue* write-up a few months later, which also revealed the unique method of illumination. 'And shall we decorate for the gloom and fog that is past or for the sunshine that is to come?', it reported in its March issue. 'Stephen Tennant's silver and crystal room, devoid of colour, in which he turns off all light and lets it be lit only by the queer upturned light of the street lamp in the square outside, how romantic and enviable that seems when we visit it only by clear starlight, how shuddery cold when a clammy fog touches us. Even the alligator tank behind seems cheerful in comparison, the parrots on the stoop a revelation of happy colour.'

The alligators and parrots with whom Stephen shared his rooms proved impractical, to say the least. Jonathan and Poll Squoll had little respect for his carpet, and the reptiles, which had been named after Hollywood stars, grew rather too large. Soon the sad day came when 'Gloria Swanson' and friends had to be taken to the zoo; they were getting 'rather snappy',[27] observed Nannie, who was afraid Mr Stephen might get bitten.

London life was exciting for Stephen – he was being sculpted for a bust by Mrs Hilton Young, and told Edith Olivier of her 'vicious mania for men . . . Stephen says she dances before him as she sculpts, waving her hands invitingly till he realizes that she is inviting him to join her!'[28] – but he enjoyed the weekends at Wilsford best. One, on 18 December, brought Elizabeth and Susan Lowndes down, together with that other chic pair of sisters, Meraud and Tanis Guinness. The Guinnesses were family friends, their mother, Mrs Benjamin Guinness, being one of London's most notable society hostesses. Tanis had her own particular charm, later ascribed by Beaton to her 'simply gigantic eyes' and 'nice slow voice . . . rather like a stolid Greuze',[29] whilst Meraud was the more rebellious, but just as handsome, sister. Tanis, later Mrs Phillips, recalled seeing Stephen quite often around that time, being particularly pleased that weekend when her host wrote in her autograph book: 'Her bows are only rainbows.'[30] Elizabeth was at her best that weekend, noted Stephen. 'I've never loved you so much as I did this time – you help so . . . Wasn't the weekend fun?'[31]

That weekend Tanis had spoken of a photo-session she had just had with the new young photographer Cecil Beaton. Now Stephen longed to meet him, and to be 'snapped', as it seemed everyone was receiving the Beaton treatment nowadays.

Cecil Beaton came from an undistinguished family, and since leaving Cambridge had been struggling with a tedious job in a City office. Two years Stephen's senior, he had been, like Stephen, obsessed with fashion and the stage since childhood, and found photography a good medium in which to express himself. By dint of hard work and self-publicity, he managed to work himself into the world he longed to be a part of; 'anything for the "uprise"',[32] he declared. Soon he had a queue of society figures waiting to be photographed. His unusual techniques – he would put his sitters under a glass dome, or photograph them from above, perched precariously on stepladders – caught the *zeitgeist* exactly; an experimental, head-over-heels modernism – and people loved the results. It was Allanah Harper, one of the young social leaders of the time, who introduced Cecil to so many parties and people that year. Through her he met and photographed the Jungman sisters, Zita and Teresa (Baby), society beauties who epitomized the twenties' bobbed hair and flapper look. On 21 December, Cecil had arranged to deliver prints of the session with Baby to her personally, at Oliver Messel's studio, where Messel was himself painting a portrait of Miss Jungman.

Cecil found the Oxford aesthete Brian Howard there, 'the Queen of the troupe – with his floppy eyes and fish face', a 'superficial smartness' that made Cecil long for 'open spaces and ploughed fields!' Baby raved over his photographs, but Cecil felt out of place. He telephoned Allanah Harper 'as I was expected there to tea. It was difficult to get away from here but I would go if I could. Troupes of smart people came to the telephone to say a word of love to Allanah. It was disgraceful, insincere, disgustingly smart and was so dreadfully like the party in a Noël Coward play! Then someone said Stephen Tennant was in London – screams and then more telephonic rot.'

Beaton made his departure, noting later in his diary, 'I'd like to have met Stephen Tennant but in those circumstances it would have been difficult.' That wish was to come true that same evening, as Cecil went to the ball. It was the coldest night of the year, and he arrived at a dance given by Mrs Benjamin Guinness. Cecil wrote proudly: 'I enjoyed the party as here I met Stephen Tennant for the first time & liked him enormously & I felt puffed with pride that he so gushed at me.' Beaton was 'already a name' with Stephen, he said. 'He'd noticed masses of things I'd done – & seen things in the papers & for years had wanted to know me just as I'd wanted to know him.'

They spent the whole of the party getting to know each other. 'We sat in a corner with Tanis & Meraud and talked wildly & made elaborate plans for photographs of us all to be taken doing ballets – matelots or something like that.' The youthful vanity of these boys was not to be underestimated; it reflected the spirit of their age. After such a thrilling evening, Cecil was 'very happy & tomorrow would very likely be lovely too, as I am invited to go with Stephen Tennant, Tanis & Meraud to the Circus'.[33] For Beaton it was a 'crucial step in his uprise', wrote his biographer, Hugo Vickers. 'Everything he had aspired to for so long was suddenly his.'[34]

Cecil arrived at the Gargoyle the following afternoon, after a rushed lunch, with the added anxiety of being financially embarrassed. He found 'a hearty crowd', with Stephen looking 'so well cared for, in beautiful clothes & him fun & glossy'. Cecil felt his position dreadfully. All the 'names' seemed to be there, including Brian Howard once again, 'with that most . . . affected young man, Acton. The brother Harold is nice, but this elder one' (William, the painter) Cecil found 'too bloody for words. Tanis & Meraud were eating scrambled eggs & bacon.' Cecil wondered what the party would be like, hoping that 'these smart young boys' wouldn't tag along and ruin it all for him. Then, 'luckily Stephen offended Brian Howard by saying he didn't like the Dunn Twins,* who'd been asked for the Circus Party, and there was a scene which resulted happily by just the 4 of us going.'[35]

In the Christmassy atmosphere of late December 1926 the Circus at Olympia was an exciting place to go. The cavernous building held fairground rides, and circus acts like the famous acrobat Babette, apparently an elegant woman performing daring feats, who shocked the audience at the finale by removing his wig to expose his true identity. There were side-shows and freak-shows and roundabouts and coconut shies. Here Stephen 'rode the papiermaché horses . . . surrounded, as usual, by an adoring group of Guinness girls',† wrote Cecil in his published diaries. 'He wore a black leather coat with a large Elizabethan collar of chinchilla.‡ As he blew kisses to left and right, he created an unforgettable sight.'[38] (On that subject, Stephen would later recall some advice from Osbert Sitwell: Osbert said, 'When you are about to enter a room, turn and blow kisses at imaginary people. This convinces the new party that you are so popular.'[39])

Stephen's appearance at Olympia almost rivalled the circus itself, with its 'terrific glut of gilt – & bright pinks & blues & silver'. Rex had recommended the Great Switchback, and the boys went wild with delight. They also ventured into the freak show, which was so 'strangely Elizabethan' and horrific it made them feel ill. Stephen bought Tanis a balloon, but it burst on a nail, 'evidently too lovely to last', said Tanis.

The entertainment they liked best was the rocking-horse ride, where

---

*Offspring of Sir James and Lady Dunn, who also lived in Smith Square.

†Stephen, reminiscing about Cecil after his death in 1980, wrote that 'all the Guinnesses, dead or alive, milled around him! Sachie (Sitwell) said, in a loud voice, "There are too many Guinnesses." (6 or 7 near him were not amused!)'[36]

‡This was Stephen's romantic leather mantle, derived from his brother's flying jacket, with a fur addition to its collar – exotic for the time, but not without precedent. The minor Bloomsbury figure and 'dress-fetishist' Gerald Heard was reported to have worn one with a leopardskin collar, along with purple suede shoes.[37]

they hung on to brass bars and hogged their brightly-painted wooden steeds for twenty 'goes'. Cecil was the only one to notice that 'people stared & glowered & even laughed at us'. Stephen and the Guinness girls couldn't have cared less. It was the difference in class; they, the aristocracy, would give no quarter to such public astonishment, whereas Beaton, acutely aware of his background, did.

The party returned to town, to plan other outings over tea and bread and jam at the Guinnesses'. Upstairs in the girls' bedroom, they looked at old photographs and inspected their wardrobes for clothes suitable for a session with Cecil. In the old nursery they sang 'sentimental songs' and 'gave imitations of awful people' and played games, 'saying who was like what flower – Stephen said my material was "expensive taffeta" . . . We chatted for such an age & were so happy that it came as a bitter blow for us to find that it was nearly 8 o'clock & we must part."[40]

Two or three days after Christmas Stephen wrote his first letter to Cecil Beaton, agreeing that 'the Circus afternoon was divine & had a quality of strangeness that was haunting & indescribable.' He added as a PS: 'I want to be photographed drowned in picturesque rags like this', accompanied by a sketch of himself lying like Ophelia in a pool, hollow-cheeked and eye-shadow'd ' – or would it be too funny? A sham moon would be such fun! & your lighting always looks like moonlight anyway & is the loveliest lighting I've ever seen in any photographs.'[41]

Meanwhile, Cecil was having tea with their mutual friend Eleanor 'Baba' Brougham,* whose assembled company considered Stephen a

---

*The Hon. Eleanor Brougham (1883–1966) was formerly lady-in-waiting to the Queen of Spain, author of *Varia* and various anthologies of English and Scottish poetry. On 13 September 1925 Stephen had written to ask Elizabeth down for the weekend to meet Baba: 'Her father thinks she's pretty & her mother thinks her clever and as she is neither it's rather a joke! isn't it? Not for her, of course, but for us!'

subject of intense interest; they all agreed how much they adored him. Cecil described Baba as 'about 45 years old but is essentially young in ideas – and it is rather extraordinary her making remarks to young men such as "I can see you're the sort of stuff the British Empire is made of . . ."' She talked 'in sharp jerks – she spurts out amusing remarks at a great rate & is intensely fidgety & moves in jabs'.[42] Stephen, who conducted a sort of love/hate relationship with Baba, later recalled her saying, 'Nobody is rude to me twice.'[43]

Cecil was soon to have a chance to consolidate his new friendship, thanks to the gossipy Baba. 'I was mooching around the house dully after lunch when the telephone rang & Stephen Tennant rang me up to know if I would stay the weekend with him on the 15th . . . My heart leapt with delight . . . Evidently he likes me as much as I like him & he & Baba Brougham were lunching together today & had worked one another [up] about me by saying lovely things about me and now oh joy of heaven I was asked to stay at Wilsford.'[44] Stephen Tennant's world seemed so glamorous and privileged – another level of existence altogether, and one to which Beaton desperately aspired. Cecil lost no time in preparing for the great event.

On Saturday 15 January, Cecil began his day by getting a haircut and face-massage at Selfridges. On the way to Waterloo, he called for Baba, who 'rather unnecessarily took her old maid with her . . . We talked fast & amusingly & at the station met Steven Runciman looking extremely foreign & intellectual.'[45] (Cecil had known Runciman at Cambridge, where he had been one of Cecil's first male photographic subjects. Steven had been teaching in Peking, where he had met the last Chinese Emperor, and had returned exuding charm of 'jade and porcelain', said Stephen.)[46] Dorothy Wilde, niece of Oscar and a writer herself, was the fourth member of their party, and seemed, to Beaton's ever-critical eye, 'rather vulgar' with 'bad style smartness'.*

At Salisbury station they were met by a car, and whisked along the Wiltshire lanes to Wilsford. Cecil saw the Manor for the first time, mistaking it for 'a lovely Elizabethan house', but rightly judging it as 'obviously the home of artistic, clever people'. He noted the profusion of Pamela's bird-cages hung on the walls, and 'the most exquisite & delicate flowers'. Inside lived up to expectations, too. 'The scene was a large long oak room, very comfortable & informal with enormous soft chairs,

---

*Dorothy (Dolly) Wilde (d.1941), daughter of William Wilde, was also a drug-addicted lesbian – parodied by Djuna Barnes in her novel *The Ladies' Almanack* (1928) – whose affair with Natalie Barney drove her to two attempted suicides.

bowls of fat hyacinths, freesia, & a lovely untidy litter of books.' And there was Lady Grey herself, beaming a smile of welcome for her son's guests. Cecil found 'eyes bright & small', a face a little like a parrot's, hair 'grey-tinged wisps'. And beside her, Stephen, 'incredibly lovely . . . in plus-fours & a jumper with a lizard-skin belt'.

The Jungman sisters were already there, 'both looking very countrified in wool & tweeds. There was a terrific screaming & yelling & frantic screams of delight from Stephen . . . wild screams and a very loud voice – a rather affected empty deep voice shouting – girlish screams from Zita & Baby & more vulgar screams from Dorothy Wilde.'[47] Zita Jungman noted that the diaries she kept in those days were filled with references to everyone 'screaming with joy' : 'We were all so over-excited. We were all talking about ourselves always.' To have been within earshot of such a crowd must have been true purgatory for anyone of a nervous disposition.[48]

'My whole visit from beginning to end was like being at the most perfect play,' wrote Cecil. 'Here Stephen was saying glorious things the entire time – funny, trite, vital, importantly exact things.' Together guests sat in front of a blazing winter fire, burning incense in a long spoon. They played writing games, and 'lovely precious brilliant things were said every second'. Stephen, 'very social mannered & kind & polite', then showed Cecil to his room, the Celadine Room at the top of the house, with its four-poster bed and oak-beamed ceiling, '& masses of fresh flowers'. Stephen's solicitousness seemed 'almost embarrassingly social' to Cecil. 'It was a part of him that was so unlike most young men. I am more polite or normally social than most, but Stephen is incredible – one cannot get within him at all.'[49] Beaton's judgement was well-observed and confirmed by other friends. Stephen's almost excessive good manners seemed to conceal an underlying edginess.

When Cecil published his edited diaries, he wrote that it was impossible to put into the printed word the brilliance of Stephen's 'verbal fireworks display . . . His ability to make people laugh was brought out, not in repartee, but in declamations on a definite subject.'[50] Edith Olivier also wrote that Stephen was 'the most sparkling talker' who ever came to her house, 'and perhaps the most amusing. He dances like a will-o'-the-wisp where other people stick in the mud . . . He can be by turns poetic, malicious, and nonsensical. His talk is very pictorial and he handles words as if they were paint on a brush.' But, she added with characteristic insight, 'when Stephen is alone with one friend he is often drawn to speak of very grave and profound subjects, and then he becomes unhappy, for he is never sure about what he loves and believes in, and he would like to love and believe in so much'.[51]

Cecil's first evening at Wilsford drew to a close when Stephen, on account of his delicacy, had to retire early. Beaton went to his room, savouring the Morris wallpaper, 'vases of delicate jasmine, columbine, roses & violets [and] the lovely piles of all the books I wanted to read. I undressed & wore a flimsy pair of speckled pyjamas which completely went with the room . . . I wanted to eat all the books & all the flowers & Stephen as well: I am sure I went to bed with a beam of happiness on my face.'[52]

Sunday morning was spring-like, and Stephen, Cecil and Steven had breakfast together. Stephen was full of energy, 'so alive & alert', evidently a morning person, unlike Cecil who habitually felt 'quiet & dull' early in the day. Stephen took his guests into the garden to show them the parrots and his exotic collection in the Reptillery. Then the ladies appeared: 'Zita & Baby very fleet & agile – Dorothy Wilde in vitriolic purple & her face plastered with powder.' There followed a short and rather muddy walk along country lanes, singing 'amusingly silly songs', returning early so that Stephen could rest before lunch. By this time Baba Brougham had finally surfaced, 'wrapped up & swaddled in rugs' against her worsening cold.

Another guest had arrived, Bordie Harriman, 'that good-looking rich young American boy', whom Cecil feared might spoil the perfection of the party, but was 'quietly charming' and quite amenable.* At lunch Cecil sat next to Pamela, cowering in the presence of a 'superior being', and observed that the amusing table talk produced an extraordinary reaction from Lady Grey, whose face 'screwed up into uncontrollable laughter which was without a sound'. Cecil was accordingly nervous for the photo-session scheduled for that afternoon.

After Pamela had been photographed, the rest of Stephen's guests clamoured for the Beaton treatment. When he announced that he had only three exposures left, 'the scream was so terrific that it was almost ear-splitting'. They set off, running round the house to find suitable costumes, producing some 'extraordinary garments'. Stephen began striking poses which 'in anyone else would have been disgusting but which in him was innocent & amusingly childlike'. After tremendous

*Harriman was of an ambassadorial family who were friends of Lord Grey's. He was an actor, appearing in *Corinne* in London, and a casual friend of Stephen's during the mid-twenties.

preparations and delays, the photographs were taken. 'Crowds lay upside-down on the floor. Screams of laughter in the middle of most exposures.' The resulting few shots show a bundle of beautiful people lying every which way, each over-made-up face looking limpidly out to the lens. Continuing the spirit of the game, Stephen proceeded to give his imitation of high-kicking chorus girls, and Cecil joined in. 'We tried desperately to do a scene of *The Last of Mrs Cheney*, with Stephen as Gerald du Maurier & myself as Gladys Cooper but this was a hopeless failure.'[53]

All too soon it was Monday morning. Snow lay outside when they woke, and a happy communal breakfast saw everyone as talkative as they had been the night before. Stephen, having avoided all such nocturnal gossipings, was 'particularly vivacious & looking particularly lovely' again. 'It was awful to go away. We sat in the flower-filled sitting-room & listened to "Bye Bye Blackbird" being played on the gramophone. Zita & Baby were full of effusive regrets.' A cold wait on Salisbury station ensued, and a packed train meant they had to spend the journey to Waterloo in the luggage van, all looking 'hideous – cold & tired'.[54] And so to the cold reality of London.

Chapter 6

. . . *And Beginners*

The first night I was in Paris I went to the Opera, and I don't mind
telling you, my darling, that all eyes were upon me, in my box; the
poor artistes might just as well not have been on stage at all.

— Cedric in Nancy Mitford's *Love in a Cold Climate*

IN January 1927 Stephen's name was once more in the national press.
The *Sunday Express* commented on the unusual décor at Mulberry
House, 'where his originality has expressed itself in a Silver Room.
Smith Square is known as "Baby Belgravia".'[1] The same column also
noted that Mr Cecil Beaton was 'leaving London for Cap Ferrat, where he
is to stay with another clever young man – Stephen Tennant'.

By the beginning of February, Stephen and Pamela were packed up and
ready to leave for the Riviera. The fashionability of the resort had grown
throughout the twenties, so much so that sometimes it seemed there were
more English and American visitors than the native French. Late winter
and spring was the high season there, and during those few months the
whole of the south coast became a playground for the *beau monde*.

Soon Pamela and Stephen were installed at the Villa La Primavera, an
optimistic name which they hoped Cap Ferrat would live up to, although
the weather was distinctly un-springlike for the first weeks of their stay. It
was larger than the Villa Natalia and also had a garden that ran down to
the sea. Elizabeth and Nannie were sent reports soon after arrival.
Stephen told Nannie (in consolation for her absence, perhaps) that he
didn't like it as well as San Remo, and wrote of 'icy weather, leaden skies,
roaring sea', to Elizabeth.[2] 'We wear our thickest clothes, tweeds &
woolens & do not venture out. Mummie has made some of the rooms
very nice, but the "taste" of the owners is a nightmare of dullness &
vulgarity.'

The continuing cold gave Stephen 'the blues', despite a visit to Nice on

11 February, and the fact that beloved Nannie wasn't there added to his vague unhappiness. His friends seemed to be enjoying themselves without him in London; Elizabeth and Rex, now getting on famously, had been to an exhibition together, which made 'a great wave of misery' roll over Stephen. But he was already spotting the stars of Nice and Monte Carlo, and at the latter he met Lily Langtry. 'A "big moment" as you can imagine – I hope to get to know her soon.'*[3]

The arrival of Mrs Belloc Lowndes and Elizabeth was followed by that of Edith Olivier, who was given a separate flat in a wing of the house. She felt out of place at first, inhibited by the younger people. 'Stephen's liberated friends think they have a monopoly of modern ideas.' One girl talked 'of prostitution lightly as a possible way of getting money'.[4] She found that Stephen was working on another idea for a novel, about the memories of a seventy-year-old woman reminiscing on her past. Edith thought it highly original, 'but feared it might be too subtle for publication'.[5]

Towards the end of February the weather improved, and Stephen implored Cecil to hurry on down. 'I can't tell you what it's like now! A sea like gentian glass, a sky of crystal clear madonna blue, and flowers that make one shriek! – and look again! . . . I must stop now & float out into the garden . . . Come to this Hesperides as soon as you can!'[6]

Cecil arrived a week or so later. To him, the company was as wonderful as the place. Pamela, 'always so intensely busy communing with birds and stars, was vague about mundane matters; only fitfully did she think of introducing her friends to one another'. So Cecil made his own introductions: to Marie Belloc Lowndes, 'a french pastry cook's version of Queen Victoria'; to the 'dozens of Guinness and other exquisite girls' who appeared for Stephen to be 'cherished' by; and Rex, who arrived at La Primavera shortly after Cecil, impressing the young photographer with his air of 'exaggerated retirement'.[7]

Here Pamela ruled rather dreamily over her guests, spending her time putting sprigs of peach blossom in the bird cages and talking about Emily Dickinson, creating theatricality in an already theatrical setting; the garden with its profusion of bougainvillaeas, primulas, roses and tulips burst forth with Mediterranean spring abundance. The days were spent laughing and talking in the sun, the evenings in guessing- and writing-games and reading aloud; 'existence seemed to consist of day to day delights.'[8]

*Lily Langtry (1852–1929). Actress and mistress of Edward VII, a great beauty of her day, she lived her later years in Monte Carlo.

The rocks beyond the villa's garden were chosen by Stephen and Cecil as a setting for some remarkable photographs. Wrapped in thin imitation leopardskin (from which Cecil had had a dressing-gown made for his Wilsford visit, much admired by Stephen), Stephen and Rex posed as classical figures sprawled out on the rocky shore. Rex, his costume tied heroically about him, resembled Hercules – or Johnny Weissmuller – washed up after a shipwreck. Stephen, who lacked the physique of a former rugby player, sat with his leopardskin twisted into a sort of halterneck toga, looking romantically out to sea, revealing his exquisite thinness.

They looked quite similar, these three handsome young men, as they paraded their summer suits on the promenade; a photograph taken by Loelia Ponsonby (later Duchess of Westminster) has them interposed between Stephen's female guests, showing off their Riviera chic: 'The young men certainly look smarter than the girls!' she noted. Loelia had wanted to meet this 'much-discussed young man' for a long time; she found Stephen 'too entrancing to look at, like a delicate Byron – also very intense and amusing'. She soon discovered Stephen's ability to improvise dramatic vignettes at the drop of a panama hat. They acted scenes from a film, 'most improper . . . one scene of rape and seduction following the other. I reckoned it would never be passed by the censor!' Loelia added later: 'Stephen was very funny and very good-looking. He used to do a marvellous Nijinsky stunt, taking hours dressing up as LE DIEU BLEU. He would come in to take his applause, then pretend to say goodbye for ever, then in a flash return for more applause.'[9]

Stephen's 'crowd' were all there: Zita Jungman and Dorothy Wilde were staying at the villa, while Loelia, and Tanis and Meraud Guinness came over from their own place at Cannes. Cecil employed his photographic skills to pose them 'generally upside-down', records Edith,[10] 'on the floor – in a flower bed and what not', all encouraged by Stephen to do more reckless and outrageous things for Beaton's lens.

The stream of grand visitors to La Primavera was endless. The Stanleys of Alderley came to stay, the Douros to lunch, and the Scarbroughs and the Islingtons all called. Such was the profusion of titled folk that when Princess Louise, Duchess of Argyll and artistic daughter of Queen Victoria, arrived for lunch, Edith was the only person to recognize her and rushed forward to curtsy, their hosts, Stephen and Pamela, being otherwise occupied. 'Very bad of them,' judged Edith.

All too soon it was time for Pamela to take Stephen home. On their return, Stephen found Cecil's snaps from Cap Ferrat published in various gossip columns – he, Cecil, Rex and Elizabeth strolling on the prom – and he determined to have a session with Cecil all to himself. Over the next few months Stephen would pose for photographs that made of his striking looks an icon, and that helped establish him as a star of society in his own right.

At Wilsford, Stephen was frustrated by appointments with doctors and dentists from meeting Cecil for lunch on the one day he was able to spend in London, and the photography 'for which I yearn will have to be postponed'.[11] Not for long, however. Soon Stephen was in front of one of the silver-foil backgrounds which had become one of Beaton's trademarks, gazing lovingly at the lens, as though in a mirror. Stephen was encouraged to bare his upper torso, to show off his pale marble body, given just the slightest of tans by his Mediterranean holiday. 'Oh! I can't tell you how lovely I think the big silver ones are!!!' wrote the model. 'I sit & gaze & gaze at the full face one. I have not shown them to Mummie as I shall produce one for her as a radiant Easter present. What do I owe you for them? You cannot continue to give me exquisite enormous photographs.'[12]

A further glut of photography was in order for the next big event – a lavish charity pageant, to be staged on 6 May, with major roles for both Stephen and Cecil. Such events typified the 1920s obsession for dressing-up, as *Vogue* noted in its spring edition: 'Nothing is more fun than dressing-up and overpainting one's face, for, as Tallulah Bankhead says, "One can never use enough lip-rouge."' In the same magazine, Cecil wrote of the phenomenon, the Charity Matinée: 'The prime reason for this function is dressing-up – the official excuse a maternity hospital . . . There is no actual rehearsal, because, as the whole of the British aristocracy believes itself to be histrionically gifted, this deficiency in no way interferes with the riotous pleasure of the performance.' This particular show, which was to open the London Season, ran under the theme, 'Great Lovers through the Ages', and was scheduled for perform-ance, in front of royal guests Princess Mary and Princess Arthur of Connaught, at the New Theatre.

Stephen and Cecil set to work, feverishly designing their costumes. Stephen was to be Prince Charming (to Joan Barry's Cinderella), and Cecil, Lucien Bonaparte (his sister Nancy playing Heloise). *The Lady* magazine anticipated great things, with not a little flattery: 'Stephen Tennant should look marvellous as Prince Charming: he has the clear-cut features and the rather wavy hair of his handsome mother as well as her charm.'[13] Certainly Stephen's costume would draw notice, an eighteenth-century concoction entirely fashioned in his favourite colour. 'The Hon. Stephen Tennant gambolled away in a pink wig and pink satin coat,' reported one paper, 'but had some difficulty with the slipper of his Cinderella.'[14]

The pageant was a wild success. 'Queen Victoria' was played by Megan Lloyd George, daughter of the former Prime Minister, whilst Stephen's sister Clare took the part of 'Madame Recamier'. Zita Jungman and Lady Pamela Smith were 'Romeo and Juliet' respectively. Cecil took photographs of Stephen and the others before they took the stage; Oliver Messel and his sister, Anne Armstrong-Jones, were Bacchus and Ariadne, vying with Stephen and Cecil for rococo splendour.

'Naturally there were one or two amusing contretemps,' observed the *Westminster Gazette*, 'but the amateurs were as self-possessed as the professionals, and the medieval ladies managed their dresses admirably. The fringe of Tallulah Bankhead's dress caught on to the gold wig of one of her slave girls and all but removed it. And those who did final hitchings-up and powderings before coming down the steps to the stage had their movements reflected on the green backcloth to the amusement of the audience.'[15]

After such tiring excitement, both mother and doctor put a strict limit on Stephen's London visits for the rest of May. At such periods, Stephen had to rely on visits from friends. Edith would bring Cecil over, and noted how he was excited by 'the eccentricity of life at Wilsford'. One afternoon they arrived 'to be told that Stephen was gardening. They found him nailing sham bark to a sapling to make it bigger.'[16]

Edith was privately becoming 'exasperated by the way [Pamela] seemed to be turning Stephen into a chronic invalid. As soon as he developed the slightest cough or sore throat he was stopped from going to balls, and he was rarely allowed to visit London. Instead she brought London society to Stephen's bedside where he lay, most decoratively, surrounded by his poetry, paints and boxes of medicines.' She refused to believe that such 'fussing' would do any good, 'and thought that if he was really ill he should be sent away for a year or two for a consumptive cure'.[17]

For the next few weeks, Stephen had to rely on the reports of town gossip from Cecil, Rex, and Elizabeth. The latter wrote of Mrs Hilton Young's exhibition of sculpture, though not of the work; Elizabeth was more interested in talking about animals with the artist's son, who, she informed Stephen, was fascinating. The latter said they must get him down for a weekend, as the young man – Peter Scott, later Sir Peter, the naturalist – was obviously very interesting.

No mention was made of the bust Hilton Young had done of Stephen at the exhibition, but his profile was already being studied anew, for Jacob Epstein had agreed to sculpt Stephen early that summer. Stephen came to London for his first sitting on 10 June. Probably commissioned and paid for by Pamela to mark Stephen's coming of age (he had turned twenty-one that April), Stephen relished the idea of sitting for an artist of such standing. Epstein, a modernist of sometimes shocking talent, had only recently caused an uproar with his *Rima* in Hyde Park, commissioned for a bird sanctuary (and after which Elizabeth mischievously named her cat). His commissioned bronze busts, however, were more traditional, larger-than-lifesize, yet still dynamically modelled.

Throughout the summer Stephen sat on a number of occasions for Epstein, watching his bust take gradual shape under the master's hands. The clay model was finished by the end of July, when Stephen heard that Elizabeth had met his 'beloved Epstein . . . I mourn the end of such richly enjoyable sittings to the greatest living sculptor.' But the consolation was great, for 'now I am immortalized, put forever beyond decay & this world's "slow stain", to gaze with sightless [eyes] at myriads of future generations – lovely thought . . .'[18] The *Daily Express* printed a photograph of Epstein and his work-in-progress on 19 July – as the sculptor works, his daughter Peggy Jean looks on – and the inanimate Stephen sits surreally on a pedestal.

The Epstein bust captures the essential poise and grace of the young Stephen Tennant better than any photograph. Looking out to a far horizon, one long, elegant hand clasped lightly to his breast, Stephen's pose unequivocally bespeaks a poetic sensibility. It was cast in bronze, and two months later Epstein wrote to thank Stephen for a cheque, £100 on account. 'The silver room sounds beautiful & I would love to see the golden bust placed in it. Let me know when you come to London & I will bring it to you.'[19]

Stephen was nervous: 'It will be my first sight of it since it was in Clay – I feel torn with apprehension [that] in Bronze it may be less beautiful! It is in bright gold bronze now & should look divine in my silver room.' He was not disappointed, and, indeed, grew positively ecstatic contemplating his image. 'I shall never forget the magical sensation of being sculpted by this great sculptor as I sat, to feel this lovely wraith growing beside me & when during rests I turned and met this exquisite grey creature looking like a drugged, drowned Parsifal – it is flattering, but this is as it should be. When I am dead & forgotten its loveliness will live, gazing back into the past at me – when Ghost meets Ghost.'²⁰

It was the ultimate 'kick' for Stephen, to have this dull gold icon of himself, for eternity; even Epstein was pleased with the result. He thought Stephen one of the best-looking subjects who had ever sat for him, and when his nephew, the painter Michael Wishart, asked him years later who was the most beautiful person, 'male or female, he had ever seen', he said, 'Oh Stephen Tennant, Stephen Tennant, absolutely without a doubt.'²¹ He showed the bronze at the 27th Exhibition of the London Group at the New Burlington Galleries in autumn 1927, whence it passed into Stephen's possession.[*]

In June Stephen was once more playing host at Wilsford, this time to quite a literary party. Sacheverell Sitwell (with his wife Georgia), and Eddy Sackville-West were esteemed poets of the time; Rosamond Lehmann's newly-published *Dusty Answer* had received critical acclaim, and the guest of honour was Elinor Wylie, back in England to visit old friends. Rex, Cecil, Zita and Bordie Harriman made up the numbers.

It was early summer and Wilsford could not look more beautiful. Stephen was showing off his new hair style, 'finger waves', which made him look very *à la mode*. But idle minds fell to naughty thoughts, and someone suggested – while she was upstairs dressing elaborately for dinner – that Elinor's excessive vanity might be the subject of some entertainment that evening. In truth, Wylie had been getting on people's nerves, with her incessant preening. Rosamond Lehmann remembers her as 'pathologically neurotic and self-centred – really a pathetic "case". She arrived with a trunkful of costly and elaborate toilettes and the game (in which I took no part) was to see how many times a day she could be persuaded to change. Every hour, so far as I can remember! And the jokes centred upon how much flattery she could swallow.'²²

After dinner, when there were supplementary guests – the eccentric composer and artist Lord Berners, and the Colefaxes – a midnight trip to the mysterious stones of Stonehenge was suggested. The guests packed themselves into a car, and drove off in a 'wild dash' to Salisbury Plain. It was Midsummer's Eve, and a magical time to be at this ancient site, Elinor was told. Clambering over the barbed wire, Rosamond watched as 'some of them hoisted her up to a stone and pretended to worship her as the

---

[*]He was later to lend it to the Tate for some fifteen years, it being returned to him in 1967. The bust was sent for sale by auction in the late 1960s, but failed to reach a reserve of £2,000 at Sotheby's. It was sold for £24,200 at the Wilsford Manor auction by Sotheby's, to the Fine Art Society, who subsequently resold it for £40,000 – the highest price yet paid for an Epstein bust.

Moon Goddess in an evening gown of silver lamé.' Elinor began to recite some of her poetry 'in a strong New Jersey accent', inviting 'anyone to strike her dead', so inspired was she by 'this monstrous "Temple of the Winds"'.[23]

'The joke was beginning to wear a bit thin by the time we got back,' remembered Miss Lehmann.[24] 'She suddenly burst into tears and said they were all making fun of her and demanded to be taken straight back to London. There was a good deal of awkwardness after that, and I have a strong memory of having to spend a great deal of the night trying to comfort her.' Rosamond was treated to 'long recitals of Elinor's history, tales of dead babies and of the ceaseless hardships she had endured'.[25] Even Miss Lehmann's patience was tried. 'No one had warned [her] there would be such a performance and her generous pity quickly turned into disgust,' observes Wylie's biographer. The incident became so infamous that by the time it reached Wylie's friends in the States, it was changed 'to include Elinor dancing nude in the moonlight'. She did not forget the slight easily. Writing to Stephen after her return to New York, she ended her letter: 'Give my love to any of my friends who want it . . .'[26]

That weekend saw Cecil out with his camera once more, snapping one of his strangest 'groups', the whole house party lined up on the floor, covered with the ubiquitous imitation leopardskin. It can hardly have been the most comfortable of poses, but each face looks remarkably composed as hair fell back and facial muscles relaxed flatteringly. And Stephen, of course, is on top. With his immaculately waved hair glowing gold, a well-cut window-pane check suit and lavish gold tie, he presides over this glamorous human sandwich of friends with consummate ease.

Chapter 7

Stage Centre

'It seems to have been very splendid: Cedric changed his dress five times; he started with tights made of rose petals and a pink wig and ended as Doris Keane in *Romance* in a black wig; he had real diamonds on his mask. Your mother was a Venetian youth, to show off her new legs, and they stood in a gondola giving away wonderful prizes to everybody – Norma got a silver snuff-box – and it went on till seven. Oh, how badly people describe balls.'
    'Never mind, there'll be the *Tatler*.'
    'Yes, they said it was flash all night. Cedric is sure to have the photographs to show us.'

— Nancy Mitford: *Love in a Cold Climate*

SUMMER, 1927, marked the height of activity for a group dubbed 'the Bright Young People' by some prescient journalist. It was a club which no one would ever admit to membership of, least of all its real initiators, but one to which Stephen was laterally aligned, if not an active member. Definite activists were the Oxford contingent: Harold Acton, said to be the first to sport lavender-coloured 'Oxford bags' and to initiate the fashion for early Victoriana; and his close associate Brian Howard, equally flamboyant, and a frequent guest of Edith Olivier's[*] – both aesthetes of the highest order. Then there was Cecil, who knew a good publicity vehicle when he saw it. Stephen's brother David played host to the party at the Gargoyle, and was a Bright Young Person by association and deed; he and his wife Hermione were given the credit for inventing the Pyjama Party, whilst Loelia Ponsonby initiated the (Bring a) Bottle Party.

    Parties were the key entertainment, and the wilder, the sillier, the more

---

[*]Stephen's relationship with Howard was equivocal, and he told Edith in 1926 that Brian was 'notorious and *not liked*'.[1]

The Tennants, c. 1910. Left to right: *David, Clare, Pamela with
Stephen, Bim and Christopher*

Eddy in uniform of the
Scottish Archers, 1903

Glen, Innerleithen

Wilsford Manor, 1906

Stephen and Nannie, 1908

*Stephen on a fishing expedition,
early teens*

Stephen by the Stone Parlour. The nursery balcony above

Pamela at Wilsford, early 1920s

Fallodon Hall, Northumberland. Home of Lord Grey

Lord Grey by Harold Speed

Stephen the youthful suitor,
mid-1920s

Elizabeth Lowndes and 'Rima'

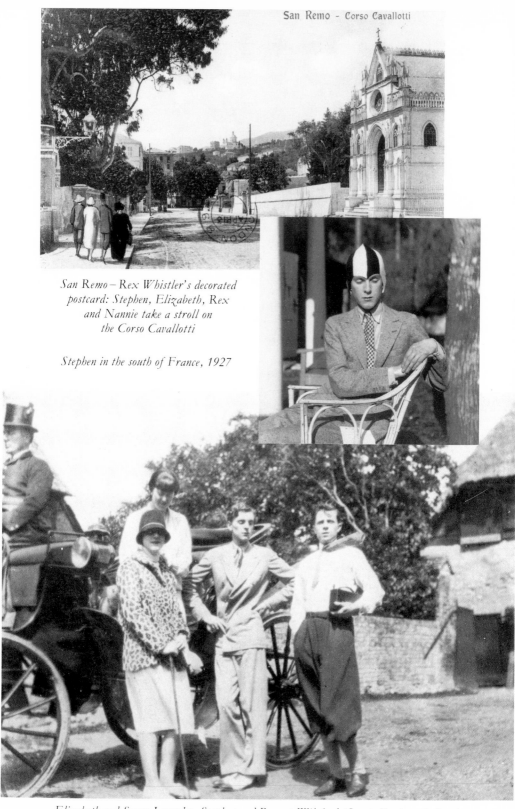

San Remo – Corso Cavallotti

*San Remo – Rex Whistler's decorated
postcard: Stephen, Elizabeth, Rex
and Nannie take a stroll on
the Corso Cavallotti*

Stephen in the south of France, 1927

Elizabeth and Susan Lowndes, Stephen and Rex at Wilsford (Louis Ford on the box)

Cecil Beaton and Stephen, 1927

Laurence and Rex Whistler: 'Uniform as penguins'

Cap Ferrat: Cecil, Stephen, Zita Jungman, Edith Olivier and Rex

Stephen on the rocks

elaborate the better. Swimming-bath Parties, Mozart Parties, Treasure Hunt Parties, parties of every sort and form. And it cannot be denied that Stephen, with his high-profile good looks, impeccable breeding and background, was pre-eminent on Fleet Street's list of Bright Young People.

In the late nineteen-twenties Stephen represented the very extreme of fashion – for a man, at least. His feminine manner and appearance were not played down by the tasteful, well-cut double-breasted and pin-striped suits, which should have made him look like any other young blade about town. Stephen's physical presence alone counteracted any such supposition. He was tall and imperious, yet walked with a pronounced, affected gait that has been described as a 'prance', or as being apparently 'tied at the knees'.[2] His every movement, from his facial muscles to his long limbs, seemed calculated to an effect: not for nothing, did he boast, had the great Léonide Massine trained him in his dance studio in Bloomsbury. (Massine was reputed to be something of a sharp practitioner, and it is likely that in Stephen he saw the chance of easy money, rather than a serious performer.)

Stephen's hair, naturally fair, looked unnaturally gold now; he would gild it with a sprinkling of gold dust, and used certain preparations to keep dark roots at bay. It was finger-waved, almost a marcel, and probably the elaborate product of a chic Bond Street salon, busy that year administering every kind of crop to the fashionable female head. Indeed, given the bustless, languid silhouette of the time, Stephen might well have been mistaken for a *Vogue* illustration – perhaps by Lepappe – come to life.

It was almost excusable for a Bright Young Thing to look the way Stephen did, just as homosexuality was tolerated (if not actively condoned) within his social group. Even though his co-respondent black-and-white shoes might mark him down in an army man's book as a bounder, his breeding and impeccable manners provided a shield. One could not be rude to him, even to his face – there would simply be incomprehension – who would dare to criticize? Had they no beauty in their lives that they had recourse to nervous laughter in the face of others? William Henderson, the artist, told of seeing Stephen enter Boulestin's chic and expensive restaurant in Covent Garden. Henderson had been to the theatre with his uncle, a rather peppery naval man, Admiral Sir Lewis Clinton-Baker. They looked up as Stephen and his guest went to their table. The Admiral turned to his nephew and said, 'I don't know if that's a man or a woman, but it's the most beautiful creature I've ever seen.'[3]

But there were already complaints. Edith Olivier heard of parents who did not think Stephen a suitable companion for their children, and noted in her diary for 14 June 1927: 'Helena Folkestone spoke distressingly of the way he is misunderstood and people hate him and say such beastly things about him. As I say it's *vieux jeu* on their part, as now-a-days so many boys are *girlish*, without being effeminate. It's the sort of boy which has grown up since the war.'

In mid-July Mrs Benjamin Guinness threw a fancy-dress ball at which Stephen 'tried to impersonate a beggar but was "elegant as a fairy", making a dramatic entrance in a billowing silver cloak which hid the rags below'.[4] The 'beggar' disguise was to become one of Stephen's favourites, which he recommended to Cecil and Rex. The latter, however, was less comfortable than the others in such costume, more especially so when someone complained that too much flesh could be seen through the strategically-torn rags; Rex didn't mind the fact that Stephen used make-up, but was worried that his friend was over-doing it, noting that he 'puts on as much as a girl'.[5] Others less tolerant than he frowned when Stephen took to the floor at these dances, holding a book in his hand: 'This was outrageous on a formal occasion when the men must be as uniform as penguins while the girls could be as polychrome as butterflies,' wrote Rex's brother. 'The men must not draw attention to themselves. That was the real charge against Stephen, an irrefutable one.'[6]

But Stephen would not be fazed by the hearties or the censorious. He was in nautical gear for a party on 18 July; then, on the 21st, the *Evening Standard* reported on the previous evening's fancy-dress ball given by Mrs Edward Grenfell at Cavendish Square. All Stephen's crowd were there – the Sitwell brothers as 'Heavenly Twins', Cecil as 'Aries', and 'Mr Stephen Tennant, who favours impersonation of beggars, was on this occasion dressed in what looked like green rags.' The more socially conscious of newspaper readers might balk at this 'poor little rich boy' imitating poverty which was an insufferable reality to miners' families, and call it all flagrant and arrogant decadence. No matter to the Bright Young People, however. Their class had won the General Strike, and the casting-off of Victorian mores was the order of the day. The decade for fashionable political conscience was yet to come.

'London's Bright Young People have broken out again,' the *Daily Express* reported on 20 July. 'The treasure hunt being passé and the uninvited guest already *démodé*, there has been much hard thinking to find the next sensation. It was achieved last night at a dance given by Captain Neil McEachran[*] at his Brook Street house. All the guests had to represent some well-known personality. The Hon. Lois Sturt arrived as

---

[*]Later to marry William Walton's lover, Imma Doernberg. McEachran's homosexuality and alcoholism made the match an unhappy and short-lived affair.

Tom Douglas in "Fata Morgana". Miss Tallulah Bankhead also essayed the masculine mode, assuming the character of Jean Borotra, wearing flannels and a shirt. Sir Matthew Wilson's son Martin showed courage by choosing Lady Diana Duff-Cooper as his original. The Hon. Stephen Tennant was only less daring in his portrayal of the Queen of Roumania.'

Stephen, as usual, had taken a great deal of trouble over getting his costume just right. *The Tatler's* report on the 'Living Celebrity' party published a group photograph of the revellers taken in the street outside McEachran's house, and Stephen's efforts raise him leagues above his fellow impersonators, who look positively amateur next to his 'Queen Marie of Roumania', with high-necked Edwardian dress of white silk, replete with pearls, gloves, and elaborate coiffure. Elizabeth Ponsonby's[*] red wig (she came as Iris Tree) and the host's 'Lloyd George' look prosaic, slightly silly; Stephen is undoubtedly the professional.[†]

There was one young aspiring writer at the Brook Street party, Evelyn Waugh, who would make use of this material in his first novel, which he began to write two months later. *Decline and Fall*, and its sequel, *Vile Bodies*, satirized the whole phenomenon of the Bright Young People – and Stephen was an easily recognizable target. It was at such parties that Waugh made his mental notes. He wrote of this particular spree: 'I don't know who the host was. Everyone dressed up and [for] the most part looked rather ridiculous. Olivia [Plunket Greene] had had her hair dyed and curled and was dressed to look like Brenda Dean Paul.'[7]

Waugh at one point worked on the gossip column of the *Daily Express*, which gave him further fuel for his modern satire. The same paper was always full of the goings-on of the rich and notable. On 29 July, it had occasion to report that 'Viscount and Viscountess Grey of Fallodon are staying longer in the south this year than usual owing to the celebration of the coming of age of Lady Grey's eldest [*sic*] son, the Hon. Stephen Tennant, fixed for August 8. After that date they will be leaving for their Northumberland seat.'

To celebrate Stephen's birthday, a new photo-session was commissioned from Cecil. Stephen booked in for a Saturday session at the end of July. The results were some of the most stunning images yet produced of young Mr Tennant. Once more against the silver foil, Stephen wore his

---

[*]Hon. Elizabeth Ponsonby (1900–1940), cousin of Loelia Ponsonby and Olivia Plunket Greene, and a prominent Bright Young Person. Evelyn Waugh modelled Agatha Runcible in *Vile Bodies* (1930) on her. Her father, the first Baron Ponsonby, was an upper-class socialist who was a member of Ramsay Macdonald's 1924 government.

[†]*The Tatler's* photograph was placed next to a picture of the real Queen Marie of Romania, an indiscretion which earned its editor the sack.

dark pinstripe suit, a long-collared striped shirt gathered by a silk tie, and a jewelled stick-pin. Then, in a moment of inspiration, he threw on his black leather mackintosh with a fur collar. The effect was electric. Stephen sits half on a stool, hand on hip, staring straight into the camera.* There is make-up – a touch of lip gloss, some vaseline on the eye-lids, perhaps – but the effect was not of some painted, effeminate creature. Rather, it is an unworldly alien, unused to twentieth-century dress codes, who has appeared in front of the lens, an approximation of what a young man should look like. 'Too beautiful,' cried Stephen, as they proceeded to shoot rolls of film, he disavailing himself of his clothes to bare his torso for some more revealing exposures.

'I'm nearly crazy at their beauty,' he said when his prints came. 'I just go on looking at them in a dream of bliss, the mackintosh looks so romantic & the positions are nearly all good, I think ... About 7 or 8 are quite perfect, luscious & dazzling & melting & the bare shoulder ones are like sculpture, too beautiful for words! The one that looks down yet sideways takes my breath!' Stephen sketched the shot, half-naked and posed like a Hollywood temptress, to illustrate his point.[9]

The following weekend held much in store for both Stephen and Cecil. On Friday 5 August the Earl of Pembroke held a grand ball at Wilton House, to celebrate his son Sidney's coming-of-age. Guests who could not be accommodated in the house itself were put up by friends in the vicinity. Beaton was lodged with Edith Olivier at the Daye House, whilst Loelia Ponsonby was staying at Wilsford. Preparations for the evening were taken seriously at the latter; Loelia recalls Stephen leaving his guests to

---

*Stephen's later Wiltshire neighbour, the artist Henry Lamb, told him: 'You've got what the French call "*Regard de Venus*" – one eye looks in one direction, the other in another – that is thought beautiful by the French.'[8]

get ready as early as four o'clock. He eventually came down 'looking like a gilded butterfly, long lashes and gold dust in his hair'.[10] Thus they drove the few miles to Wilton, to be received by the Pembrokes in their lofty marble hall.

'It was a grand occasion, and I was over-awed,' wrote Cecil. Guests included Rudyard Kipling, Lord and Lady Anglesey, the Cecils and the Guinnesses. All was going well, until 'out of the darkness a group of tail-coated young men surrounded me . . . With a tremendous splash and plopping of stones, I found myself standing hip deep in the Nadder.' A considerable exaggeration, perhaps – David Herbert remembers the river being very low that summer. But one of the hearties who had been incensed by Cecil's flamboyant appearance shouted out in the darkness, 'Do you think the bugger's drowned?'[11]

The bugger hadn't drowned, but re-entered the ballroom, soaking wet. Neither Stephen nor Brian Howard, who could both have expected similar treatment, were aware of what had happened until later. Indeed Howard, had he been faced with the situation, might have dealt with it in the same way his fictional alter-ego, Anthony Blanche, does when faced with a mob of college hearties in Waugh's *Brideshead Revisited*, inviting them to throw him into the college fountain. '. . . Nothing would give me greater pleasure than to be manhandled by you meaty boys. It would be ecstasy of the naughtiest kind.' Blanche calls their bluff by stepping into the water himself: 'And you know it was really quite refreshing, so I sported there a little and struck some attitudes, until they turned about and walked sulkily home.'[12]

Lord Head was one of those responsible for Beaton's ducking: 'not something I review with pride . . . Cecil was primarily a homosexual, and much encouraged by people like Stephen Tennant.'[13] In the ball-room, meanwhile, Loelia had been 'obliged to dance with [Stephen], and he swooned about on the floor. She noticed the heavies moving in – Laycock, Feversham, Head – and feared they would be propelled into the river too, but as the storm rose so it dissolved.'[14] Edith Olivier noted that it was thought Stephen had escaped by saying 'it would kill him'. Girls as well as boys were involved in the teasing, thinking that Lady Pembroke shared their dislike of the 'pansies', only later to receive a demand from their hostess for letters of apology.* Edith added: 'What an amazing thing is this hatred of the unusual – from Shelley onwards.'[16]

---

*Lady Pembroke later told Edith 'she would thrust her hand into the fire to prove her faith in Stephen in spite of his appearance.'[15]

Stephen later observed that Cecil's face 'was very "made-up"' that night. 'Mascara, rouge, face-powder. The Bullies who ducked him were no doubt annoyed with his painted face. They were "put off" by his maquillage.'[17] Stephen's love of powder and paint was no less than Beaton's, and would grow more prodigious over the years as Cecil and other friends forsook its aid to beauty. From the moment he had placed that first beauty spot on his cheek as an adolescent, Stephen had begun a love-affair with cosmetics that never abated, even into old age. Aristocratic privilege allowed him to 'get away with it', while lesser mortals like Beaton were given a hard time. 'I love the feel of it on my face', said Cecil to Stephen, who agreed, 'I adore cosmetics', adding later, 'I want to have bee-stung lips like Mae Murray.'[18]

Soon after Stephen's coming-of-age party, a low-key affair with a select few friends, it was north again, to Fallodon, this time with a new holiday project for Stephen. Pamela had decided to revise and reprint her collection of chosen verse and sayings, *The White Wallet* (named after the white file in which she used to collect her pieces), and after Stephen's successful dust jacket for Lord Grey's *The Charm of Birds* published that year (which featured an intricate design of birds' wings), had suggested that Stephen illustrate the new edition.

The White Wallet came out the following year, and proved a better seller than *The Vein in the Marble*. Stephen's drawings were better too. Instead of heavy-handed parables, there are delicate, lightly-drawn heads of clowns and Bacchus, Adam and Eve by the Tree of Knowledge on the

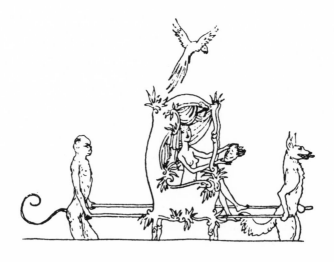

title-page, and a pretty flight of parrots on an end-paper. All very fanciful still, but the attention to detail and stylistic devices made these admittedly slight offerings attractive.

Despite that slightness, it seemed the complexities of working with publishers would never end. Stephen wrote a telling *cri de coeur* to Elizabeth on 12 September: 'I am swamped with business – I don't know where to turn from bills & work – oh the Hell of being grown-up!'

At Fallodon, Cecil remained Stephen's contact with the 'civilized' world. The northern country, the rain, the 'nightmarish people' conspired to aggravate Stephen. He sought diversion in a 'glorious bundle of American papers', and the latest from D. H. Lawrence, Katherine Mansfield and Virginia Woolf. Other diversions were more energetic. On a visit to a circus, Stephen had actually performed: 'starting up on a horse & going round the arena really!!!'[19] The acquisition of a new toy, a cine-camera, proved highly diverting, as he told Cecil: 'I've got the most lovely films of myself taken here – I'll show them to you directly I get South – William takes them so well.'[20] William was the young man observed the following summer at Wilsford when Lytton Strachey came on a visit: 'We were filmed almost the whole time by a footman (a dark young man in spectacles)',[21] and was pressed into service down on the beach. David Tennant had a new and even faster car – an Isotta Fraschini, an Italian racing model – which he drove down to the sea-shore, and together they were filmed, David as 'a black Demon', and Stephen 'buried in leather and fur'.[22]

Cecil had duties to perform for Stephen: 'My dear! please hurry to Selfridges for the elixir as I am becoming a mournful sight, daily navy blue hair sprouts from my head – do be an angel & send it quick!'[23] wrote Stephen, referring to the preparation he used to 'help along' that golden wave of hair, unobtainable in philistine Northumberland. When it finally came, it was very welcome indeed: 'A million thanks for the marmalade. I was about to go mad with suspense when it arrived.' Stephen was already looking forward to a new season of fun in town. Suggestions for the upcoming 'Porcelain Tableaux' were swapped with Cecil. 'Can't we have Leda & the Swan & Europa on the Bull?' asked Stephen, '& Cupid & Psyche & Aphrodite – rising from the foam? Cardboard foam & a sham pinbody & crimped hair to the waist. I've really no ideas. I may have some when I get South. This icy seabitten place is impossible to think in but I am chubby with health, bent on conserving & perfecting my person for the Silly Season.'[24]

That season began for Stephen with a visit to the Albert Hall with Christabel McLaren, later Lady Aberconway. Wife of Lloyd George's private secretary, Henry McLaren, Christabel was a family friend whose company Stephen enjoyed and whose wider acquaintance made her attractive to him. Together they saw the great Russian singer Chaliapin perform. A day or so after their musical evening Stephen invited Christabel to Wilsford for the weekend of 14 October, along with another new friend whose acquaintance Stephen had recently made and who interested him a great deal. He was forty-one – almost old enough to be Stephen's father – rugged, masculine, an ex-army man. He was also a renowned pacifist and even more famous poet. He was Siegfried Sassoon.

Siegfried Sassoon, born in Kent in 1886, had been educated at Marlborough College and Cambridge. His father, the first of the great Jewish Sassoons from Central Europe to settle in England and marry a non-Jewish woman, had left Sassoon's mother when he was three; like Stephen, Siegfried considered himself a 'mother's boy'. Theresa Sassoon was part of the great Thornycroft family – farmers, shipbuilders and sculptors – whilst the Sassoons were known as 'the Rothschilds of the East'. Siegfried wrote that 'my artistic talent derives from the Thornycroft side. But . . . the daemon in me is Jewish.'[25] His early passions were equally divided between literature and fox-hunting, both of which he pursued avidly until the Great War. He enlisted at the outbreak, and distinguished himself as a second lieutenant, being awarded the Military Cross for bravery; he had rescued one of his wounded men by carrying him back from the battlefield to safety, despite being wounded himself. So reckless was Sassoon that he was known to his Division as 'Mad Jack'.

But soon the senseless carnage in the mud of France prompted him to protest against the Allied strategies, which seemed to him to be wasting unnecessarily the lives of countless young men – mere boys, like Stephen's brother Bim, dying before they had a chance to live. He renounced his commission, refused to fight, and sent a letter of protest to his commanding officers which was later read out in Parliament. Judged to be suffering from a nervous breakdown, Sassoon was sent to a nerve hospital, Craiglockhart, near Edinburgh. There he came under the care of a progressive, understanding doctor, W. H. Rivers, who diagnosed 'anti-war complex'.

The poetry which was the result of Sassoon's strongly felt convictions, and which expressed his anger and frustration at the 'Jingos' and the 'complacent moderates' and the war profiteers, was a strident, literate and effective voice of protest which brought praise as well as condemnation for its author. Sassoon's most bitter collection, *Counter-Attack*, was written whilst he was at Craiglockhart. By the time the war had ended, and the cost was counted, the reputation of Sassoon – a protester, yet a brave fighter too (having returned to the front line, despite his protest) – enhanced the public standing which his work had secured for him.

By the mid-twenties, Sassoon was reaping the financial and social rewards of his acclaim. When Stephen first met him – at one of Osbert Sitwell's dinners at Carlyle Square – Sassoon had just published *Satirical Poems*, the latest in a sequence of hard-hitting pieces that had an underlying tone of social criticism (Sassoon had joined the Labour Party, and was literary editor for the left-wing *Daily Herald* after the war). Yet he was much in demand socially. A later biographer wrote of the paradoxes of Sassoon's life now: 'Sassoon the Socialist in sandy-coloured tweeds, yellow waistcoat, and a pink shirt was . . . coming on quite terrifically, as he more and more frequented the company of "titled blokes and blokesses" rather than that of the workers on the march waving the red flag.'[26]

Sassoon had known Osbert Sitwell since his army days, and had been instrumental in introducing William Walton to his new sponsors when he had got to know the composer at Oxford in 1919. Sassoon's relationship with the Sitwells in general, and Osbert in particular, was ever one of equivocation. He wrote in 1922: 'I suddenly realized my attitude towards O. Sitwell is strongly sadistic. I saw, quite coolly, that my (supposed) stab at his feelings this afternoon aroused in me acute sexual feelings toward him (I'd never before been conscious of any sexual feelings toward him, except a slight repugnance). Does it help one to "realize" these things? And are the Sitwells worth worrying about? And is there anything in life which can be disconnected from this curse of sex?'[27]

Sassoon's convoluted attitude to his own sexuality had always created interior struggles for him, more especially so for a man whose homosexual feelings towards the men under his command during the war were put under additional strain by the fact that these comrades could be sent to their deaths by him, an officer. Since the war Sassoon had had serious love affairs with two men, one a German prince, Philip of Hesse,* the other, Gabriel Atkin, an artist whose reprehensible behaviour had caused the

---

*Prince Philip of Hesse, b.1896, grandson of Frederick III of Prussia. He married Princess Mafalda in 1925, and later became a Nazi stormtrooper, having a distinct predilection for violence. He was a go-between for both Mussolini and Hitler, and was involved in negotiations between them and the Duke of Windsor during the war, but fell from favour and was interned. His wife died in Buchenwald concentration camp in 1944. He was released from the camp in 1945 and died a year later.

poet a great deal of pain. Sassoon's own mother had 'always disliked and distrusted G.', observed Siegfried in his diary. 'His half-frivolous & wholly pleasure-loving temperament repelled her (as it often repels me).'[28] Sassoon hated the side of this wayward lover who represented 'green chartreuse and Epstein sculpture' to him; Siegfried later told Stephen that Atkins 'enjoyed torturing me'.[29] Meeting the ethereal, beautiful, pure Stephen seemed a breath of fresh air to him, although friends who had witnessed the unfortunate course of Sassoon's affair with Atkins might have advised caution in embarking on a new romance; it was Osbert who told Siegfried once that the latter was the worst judge of character he knew. After the unhappy Atkins affair, Sassoon had begun a new relationship with the theatrical director Glen Byam Shaw, whom he had met in October 1925. 'Our happiness together seems so spontaneous and natural,' wrote Sassoon in his diary, 'that there is nothing to be said about it.'[30] Yet Sassoon's satisfaction with his new love was to last barely a year. Soon he would be launched into a love that would alter his life.

Siegfried Sassoon was a highly desirable name on the guest lists of the literary and artistic salons of the twenties. Lady Ottoline Morrell, the eccentrically attired Bloomsbury hostess, prided herself on her relationship with the poet, and Siegfried could often be found at the dinner table of such women as Emerald Cunard, mother of the rebellious Nancy, and one of the top names in that rarefied strata of gracious ladies.* Which is not to say that Sassoon altogether approved. He took their hospitality, and was entertaining – sometimes – but would go back to his flat in Campden Hill and write a poem such as 'A Breach of Decorum', after a vexing evening at Lady Cunard's, satirizing the double standards he found in such women:

> *Such dreadful taste! 'A positive blasphemer!'*
> *'He actually referred to our Redeemer*
> *As the world's greatest Socialist teacher!'*[31]

Sassoon appeared dour, with his somewhat craggy yet undeniably handsome features seldom seeming relaxed or at peace. Ottoline Morrell, on her first encounter with the poet, described 'the lean face with green

---

*He also knew Margot Asquith quite well, staying at the Asquiths' country house, The Wharf, Sutton Courtenay, on a number of occasions; another opportunity for him to have met Stephen, who was at The Wharf during the first weekend of June, 1927. It would have been impossible for either to have missed the other in London in those days, and their social circle so nearly coincided. One of the earliest identifiable occasions for a sighting of Stephen and Siegfried in the same room would have been Sibyl Colefax's party for Douglas Fairbanks and Mary Pickford the previous July, which both attended.

hazel eyes, his eyes large and rather protruding, and the nose with wide nostrils, that made me think of a stag's head or faun. He was not exactly farouche but he seemed very shy and reserved; he was more sauvage; and, as I looked at his full face I said to myself, "He could be cruel." '[32] Robbie Ross, Oscar Wilde's loyal friend who took Sassoon to Garsington to meet Morrell, told him after the visit: 'But you really must try not to look so like a shy and offended deerhound next time you are talking to her.'[33] Sassoon generally lived a quiet life, going out from his flat only occasionally to be entertained, preferring to order his life around his writing. Even on those first few meetings, he appeared exceptional to Stephen, who also had recourse to anthropomorphic terms in describing his new friend: 'He had very little social sense,' he wrote later. 'He was like some charming wild animal – one never felt he was really tame (or tameable).'[34]

It was significant that Osbert Sitwell should be instrumental in bringing the two together, in the light of the consequent trouble caused by Siegfried's relationship with Stephen within the Sitwell camp. Osbert had known the Tennants since the Great War – he had met and befriended Bim in the army, and was a regular visitor to Wilsford. It was logical and obvious that, as he came out in London society, Stephen should be on the periphery of the intense cultural circle dominated by Osbert and his siblings.

The ritual of courtship began. Stephen flaunted his charms; his beauty, youth, and quick-witted ebullience. Sassoon was entranced, and offered in return his fame, his talent, his position; the people he knew, the standing he had in contemporary English letters – his success. He was of a slightly older generation, but had rebelled against it (perhaps seeing in Stephen's effeminacy a reaction against the masculine values of war), and could be at once avuncular and aesthetic. All very tempting to the impressionable young Stephen. Each had flattered the other and, in the multi-coloured splendour of Osbert's Italianate dining-room, it was difficult to tell whose web had ensnared whom.

This was no ordinary physical attraction. Sexual desire, the one for the other, was obvious, although no record of its consummation exists, and it is therefore difficult to make judgements. Most people who knew Stephen well could hardly believe the physical act possible for him, so much above such earthy matters did he appear.* Rather, it was a passion of minds and

---

*Despite this the structure of their physical relationship appears obvious: Stephen, with his near-hermaphroditic presence, was the beautiful woman; Captain Sassoon the rough-hewn man. As Sassoon scholar Patrick Quinn observes, Siegfried's intimate relationships required him always to be the dominant partner: 'As long as it was him who was in control, he could feel that his masculinity wasn't threatened.'[35]

ideals; for Stephen, the idea that a world-famous poet should be in love with him was enough to make him return the compliment. Full-fledged love was yet to come, however, and when Stephen invited Sassoon to Wilsford that weekend, it was as a new friend (Stephen would always, almost naively, plunge into new friendships without a second thought), who had enormous charm in every way.

That country weekend was to be a milestone for both Stephen and Siegfried. Osbert Sitwell and his younger brother, Sacheverell, with his wife, Georgia, were there, bringing Willie Walton with them. There were Zita and Baby Jungman, of course, and Rex and Cecil made the gathering complete. The latter's presence was crucial, as his camera was to record the *fête galante* Stephen had devised to amuse his guests. This was to be an eighteenth-century tableau, after the style of the painters Watteau and Lancret, fashionable favourites of Stephen, Cecil, and Rex. The whole weekend was to be devoted to dressing-up. On the first evening the three principal boys and the twins appeared dressed as nuns, which was followed by a swift costume change in darkness, for them to reappear in pyjamas, and dancing to the gramophone. Siegfried was not overly impressed: 'It was very amusing, and they were painted up to the eyes, but I didn't quite like it,' he wrote in his diary.[36]

This antipathy meant that on no account could Sieg[*] be persuaded to don the elaborate period costumes Stephen had assembled for his guests. Each had long brocade waistcoats, satin blouses, breeches and stockings. Immaculate silk cravats and heavily applied maquillage completed the ensemble. Not so much authentic eighteenth century as an interpretation, via Stephen's fancy, and Rex's rococo confections, done for the benefit of Cecil's lens. The 'Lancret Affair' held up a mirror to the prevailing Bright Young Person mentality; the penchant for fantasy and masquerade had become an expression of the disregard they felt for the immediate past or the immediate future. They lived – or tried to live – outside their time.

Stephen judged that Sunday morning parade 'moderately successful'.[38] He marshalled his players into various scenes – Cecil, Rex, Zita and Baby by a haystack; the same group, *en fête champêtre*, on the lawn. Then William the footman was employed to photograph the entire group on the rickety wooden bridge that spanned the Avon at the edge of the grounds. The result was 'the creation of what have become probably the

---

[*]As his friends addressed him. Stephen had a special nickname, 'Kangar', for Sassoon, although he later considered: 'I think S.S. looks more like a moose than a Kangaroo.'[37]

most evocative images of wealthy young England in the 1920s',[39] as John Culme wrote. Only Walton seems ill at ease in his disguise, perched on the rustic rails with his friends; Beaton is a natural poseur, whilst Whistler is solemnly aesthetic in his portrayal. The Jungman sisters look amusing and amused, quite used by now to these pantomimes, and Georgia Sitwell, the Canadian newcomer, has taken to it all in the whimsical spirit of its instigator. And then there is Stephen, unmistakably at the centre of proceedings, eyelids heavy with shadow, exquisite, at the height of his beauty and power – the unchallenged Prince of the pageant. Sachie Sitwell wrote to him a few days later: 'Those two days at Wilsford were too heavenly and idyllic for words! The Lancret affair was unforgettable and I shall remember it all my life. What a marvellous gift you have for making other people happy; in some ways the most wonderful quality that anyone can be possessed of. The whole time was one unending joy and now it is over I feel nearer tears than laughter . . .'[40]

The morning's play-acting over, Siegfried suggested to Stephen that they drive over to visit Lytton Strachey, who lived at Ham Spray House in the north-western part of the county, between Newbury and Hungerford. Osbert and Christabel were eager to come too, and the four of them set off late from Wilsford, driving in darkening afternoon across country in Siegfried's two-seater 'dickey'. It was the first time Siegfried had Stephen as a passenger in his car. Soon the cold winter's dusk was upon them, and somehow they got lost on the downs, and ended up driving into a haystack.[*] Thus shaken and quite late, they arrived at Ham Spray to be greeted by that High Priest of Bloomsbury, Lytton Strachey. He had immured himself in this eighteenth-century house to work, and told his lover, Roger Senhouse, that he was 'impervious to all temptations, among them a most strange eruption of unexpected visitors from the expensive classes, including Osbert Sitwell, Christabel Aberconway, Siegfried Sassoon and Stephen Tennant, all of them entirely occupied with "dressing-up". The night before they had all dressed up as nuns, that morning they had all dressed up as shepherds and shepherdesses, and in

---

[*]Siegfried was, by all accounts, a precarious man at the wheel. He once collided with an island in the middle of an empty Bayswater Road, out of distracted irritation with a boring dinner guest he'd just left. When driving Stephen across Europe the following Autumn, he 'swept round corner after corner' along precipitous mountain roads, and wrote blithely to a friend, 'Why people say I am a bad driver I can't imagine!'[41] Salisbury's courts could: on 20 March 1932 Siegfried was charged with reckless driving at Barford St Martin, his second offence in a week. The policemen at the scene gave evidence that 'Captain Sassoon' was driving at speed on the wrong side of the road, and that 'the defendant seemed hardly responsible to be in charge of a car'. He was fined £3 with £1 3s 6d costs, had his licence endorsed, and was told 'if he was before the Court again something rather drastic would happen'.[42]

the evening they were all going to dress up as – God knows what – but they begged and implored me to return with them and share their raptures.'[43]

Stephen recalled wearing his dark brown plus-fours to Ham Spray – surely quite sensible country wear? They stayed an hour or so; Christabel entertained them by quoting from the poetry of Stephen Phillips. Unable to entice Strachey to join the fun, the party set off back to Wilsford. 'I shudder to think of the horrors of their return journey,' wrote their host, who was left with an impression of 'strange creatures – with just a few feathers where brains should be. Though no doubt Siegfried is rather different . . .'[44]

When Strachey's letters were later published, Stephen remarked on his comments with some humour. 'All invented really, I think – "I enjoyed meeting Stephen Tennant but I did not care for his magenta lips." ? I'm sure my lips have never been magenta! There's always been colour in them . . . He was rather a mixture of things really,' he said of Strachey. 'I never felt comfortable with him. He liked me much more than I liked him . . . He wanted to be like me. Somebody said, "He can't forgive Destiny for not making him look like you."' However, Stephen conceded certain things in common. 'We had a great love of clothes, love of a certain amount of publicity but not too much – just a little bit. I think in some ways he rather looked like me. I think his profile and his face was rather like mine.'[45]

Siegfried, to their relief, got his passengers home safely. Stephen had decided that it was to be a fancy-dress dinner, but as Edith Olivier noted in her diary: 'Hours passed and the guests grew hungrier and hungrier while Stephen dressed.' At 9.30 Osbert and Sachie, Siegfried and Willie led them 'and plied us with champagne before we actually died and then came a message from Stephen telling us to begin dinner . . . At last he came in a white Russian suit with a silver train and bandeau round his head. He moves like Mercurius, with winged feet.'

Dinner was 'very amusing', with films shown afterwards by William the footman, 'who, at his own request, had dressed up as an Indian and pretended he didn't know English.'[46] Afterwards a game of hide-and-seek was proposed. The labyrinths of the attic rooms and the nursery wing were perfect for the game, although it resulted in the second accident of the day, when, down in a dark cellar, Christabel hit her 'pretty little nose' on a door.[47]

Stephen's admitted predilection for 'a certain amount of publicity' was fulfilled over the next few weeks when, once more back in the swing of things after the enforced peace of Fallodon, he threw himself upon the mercy of London society. On 2 November, *Vogue* published Beaton's

Wilsford 'upside-down photo', and that week the papers noted Stephen's presence at an exhibition of Honoré Daumier's work at the Lefevre Galleries. '[It] attracts almost every high-brow in London,' commented the man from the *Daily Sketch*. 'The other day I met Osbert Sitwell, Cecil Beaton and Stephen Tennant there.'[48] By the end of the month, Cecil's own exhibition at the Cooling Galleries would be filling the gossip columns with his and his friends' names.

There was tremendous interest for Beaton's first one-man show; at a private Private View, 'the chosen few were privileged to wander round the rooms, waving a cocktail glass in one hand and one of those Tunbridge Wells wafers, than which there is no more fashionable food stuff today, in the other', noted the *Sunday Times* on 20 November. 'Miss Edith Sitwell, mysterious and enigmatic as ever, Mr Stephen Tennant, and one of the two lovely Lady Curzons were other sitters who were discussing their portraits.' Cecil's show included, apart from his wondrous photographs of Stephen, the Epstein bust, which Stephen had lent to give a three-dimensional elegance to the exhibition. It also had the added effect of making Stephen one of the faces of the whole event; that demanded more than just one visit to the Cooling Galleries. *The Lady* saw him there in company with Oliver Messel and Oswald Mosley, noting that 'the first two, with Mr William Walton, the composer, and Mrs Sitwell, were at the first night of *Sirocco*.'*[49]

It was impossible for even the most casual peruser of the gossip columns, were there such a person, not to notice Stephen's name cropping up at every fashionable event. He had become one of those stars of society whose immediate significance was not quite evident – one assumed they must do something. In this respect, he resembled the currently high-profile Sitwell trio, with whom he was increasingly seen. Edith, Osbert and Sacheverell Sitwell excited the sort of comment in the twenties that would in later years be accorded to multi-media 'superstars' like Andy Warhol. The appearance of either or all of the Sitwells at a private view such as Cecil's endorsed that artist as indubitably fashionable, and their comments were sought by reporters as the ultimate litmus-test of art *à la mode*. They also aroused a great deal of animosity from people who considered their modernist stance no more than a pose. Lord Beaverbrook declared 'this family is less than a band of medio-

---

*Stephen had been in the stalls for Noel Coward's new play. It had an uproarious first night, with Ivor Novello booed and audience laughter at the line: 'One of my greatest friends died of consumption.' The leading lady, Frances Doble (Georgia Sitwell's sister), broke down in tears at the final curtain.

crities'⁵⁰ and demanded no publicity be given to them in his papers. But for Stephen and his friends, they represented the shock of the new, and were very welcome for that.

The *Daily Herald* reported that at Beaton's show 'the crowd grew denser with the arrival of the Sitwells. "Do you approve of cocktails at an art show?" I asked Mr Osbert Sitwell. "Of course" he replied, "but more I musn't say at the moment, for I am giving my views on cocktails in my play 'First Class Passengers Only' which is being produced next week."'⁵¹ Stephen naturally attended the opening night, which was not well received. He was offended when he discovered that Osbert hadn't wanted Stephen to attend the dinner afterwards, given by Mrs Ronnie Greville. This, and the lameness of the production, did not stop him making further visits, and he wrote to Elizabeth: 'How bad the Sitwell play was!!!–wasn't it? I long to discuss it with you, although I am sick to death of everything to do with it having seen it three times (spiritual not intellectual loyalty).'⁵²

Stephen's relationship with the trio was as bumpy as that first night. Osbert could be extraordinarily vicious, even about his closest friends, and Stephen's relations with Siegfried caused a deal of enmity. Rex Whistler reported to Edith Olivier: 'Yes I too like Osbert very much, though of course my liking is lessened by knowing him to have been so double-sided to Stephen and Cecil.'⁵³ Stephen knew perfectly well the sort of things Osbert said behind his back. He had witnessed the latter's nastier side when at dinner at Carlyle Square; Stephen was sitting next to Edith Sitwell (whom he described as 'a huge old baby vulture' with 'pale lemon hair and scrawny thin hands').⁵⁴ Whilst waiting for the last guest to arrive, Osbert launched into a monologue. 'You will find she smells of camphor balls – she will be wearing an old lace curtain from some Notting Hill lodging house. Would you like to know the form her madness takes?'⁵⁵ Stephen spoke up: 'Osbert, how can you say such obscene and vile things about Virginia Woolf's madness – about a guest – who will arrive any minute – you Beast!'⁵⁶ When Virginia arrived, she proved that she too was well aware of Osbert's bitchiness, and declared aloud: 'I keep hearing from my friends the horrible things Osbert says about me!'⁵⁷ (Morgan Forster told Stephen that Virginia could be just as vituperative – 'She's like the Pope – she excommunicates you!')⁵⁸

This internecine squabbling always bubbled below the surface of Stephen's relationship with Osbert, Edith and Sachie. The Sitwells were to weave in and out of Stephen's life in these years like characters in an

E. F. Benson novella, as relationships took uphill and downhill turns. Stephen got on best with Edith (who had been to stay at Wilsford that spring, and appeared to have a penchant for artistic homosexuals, despite her avowed dislike of sexual inversion), and attended one of her famous afternoon tea parties at her flat in Bayswater that December, where he revelled in the intellectual talk, the strong tea and penny Bath buns. He was also able to report to the guests that Siegfried had taken him to meet 'the uncrowned King of Wessex' – Thomas Hardy.

Sassoon had known Hardy for many years, and was a regular visitor to the writer and his second wife, Florence, at their large house, Max Gate, outside Dorchester (this visit, on 6 December, would be Sassoon's last; Hardy died just a month after, aged eighty-eight). Virginia Woolf, who had visited him a year or so before, described him as 'a little puffy cheeked cheerful old man, with an atmosphere cheerful & businesslike in addressing us, rather like an old doctor's' and her: 'She has the large lacklustre eyes of a childless woman; great docility & readiness, as if she had learnt her part . . .' They had asked Virginia about their dear friend Siegfried – had she often been to his flat? 'I said no. Then she asked about him & Morgan, said he was elusive, as if they enjoyed visits from him.'[59]

Which they did, and looked forward to Siegfried and his new young friend's arrival that Tuesday. Sassoon drove Stephen there from Wilsford, arriving in time for lunch. Stephen was surprised at how short the author of *Tess of the D'Urbervilles* was: he had to stand on a stool to carve the roast goose. But both he and his younger wife were 'angels', and Stephen had a long talk with him about his work. He was pleased when the old man presented him with a printed copy of Henry Glassford Bell's *Mary Queen of Scots*, which he signed to Stephen.

Hardy had his own impression of Stephen, which Florence recorded in her diary after the two visitors left that afternoon: that Stephen was the only other man he had ever met who walked like Swinburne. When they arrived back at Wilsford, Stephen ran in to report on his encounter with the greatest living novelist to his mother. But Pamela seemed uninterested and, according to Stephen, hardly bothered to look up from her spiritualist tract. It was already evident that she did not approve of Stephen's new intimacy with Sassoon – or, possibly, feared for its consequences.

After Hardy's death, Stephen remained in contact with his widow Florence, visiting her with Siegfried, and corresponding frequently. She 'never realized the truth of Sassoon's relationship with Tennant',[60]

observes Hardy's biographer Robert Gittings, even though she saw both
up until her death in 1937. It appears that Stephen was involved in the
furore that broke out after Hardy's death, when Somerset Maugham
published *Cakes and Ale*, which commented satirically on a young wife of a
famous author capitalizing on her husband's fame. It seemed to draw on
detailed observations of Max Gate and its inhabitants, although
Maugham had never been there. 'It seems likely that the channel, without
himself being conscious of the process, was Siegfried Sassoon, through a
friend he had brought to Max Gate before Hardy's death, and who is
mentioned more than once in Florence's letters to him.'[61]

Robert Gittings is still of the opinion that Stephen was the most likely
culprit, and certainly Stephen would have met Somerset Maugham at any
number of parties during the twenties – quite possibly at his wife Syrie's
fashionable gatherings at their house in the King's Road. To be fair to
Stephen, it may only have been gentle bragging – his meeting with the
famous writer and his charming wife – but Stephen's good memory and eye
for detail would have been stored carefully away by Maugham, who
became infamous for taking up such information and caricaturing people
in his writing.

Back in London at the weekend, in his Silver Room at Mulberry House
'surrounded by white azaleas . . . mauve orchids and scarlet carnations',[62]
Stephen looked forward to his next stage appearance. The 'Porcelain
Tableaux' organized by Olga Lynn took place at the Savoy Theatre on 11
December, properly entitled 'China Groups Through the Ages', and it was
noted that only three men were among the cast of fifty: Stephen, Cecil, and
Oliver Messel. Nonetheless, Stephen managed to keep the side up amongst
beauties such as Viola Tree and his sister-in-law, Pamela, Lady Glenconn-
ner, who arrived only just in time 'to take her place as a Muse'.[63] Stephen
was also pleased that month by the new *Vogue*, in which Cecil described a
photo-session he had recently conducted with Siegfried. He noted that the
poet was in 'a state of nerves and misery' as he faced the lens. 'He groaned;
tears welled up into his eyes and flowed down his rugged cheeks! And when
it was all over he sighed with relief and shook himself like a dog after a
bath.' Stephen loved this description, and was amused by Cecil's comment
on his other most eventful sitting, with Stephen himself, when 'somehow
every light I had, save one, was broken'.[64]

1927 had certainly been an important year for Stephen, and as it drew to
a close there was yet one flattering tribute to be paid. When Rex Whistler's
Tate Gallery restaurant mural had been opened on 30 November,

Stephen's friends discovered that Rex had portrayed him as the epicurean hero of the tale he had told so masterfully in oils around the walls. *The Pursuit of Rare Meats* even had a 'guide', written by Edith Olivier: 'The Crown Prince Etienne' – for it is he, Stephen, with a Gallicized name – 'was the first to appear on the steps. He was a youth of rare beauty and promise, an aristocrat from the top of his high brow, to the tips of his long and pointed finger-nails. Narcissus-like, he was often seen bending over the fountains and pools of water in the Park, but this was not in order to admire his own beauty – admirable as it was. He was only seeking for newts, tadpoles, and other such rare creatures, to add to the collection in the Royal Reptillery and Aquarium which he had presented to the Duchy in commemoration of his twenty-first birthday . . .'[65]

Chapter 8

Intermezzo

Who, then, it is natural to ask, are the Bright Young People?... It would be unfair to terminate this list without including in it the name of the Hon. Stephen Tennant. His appearance alone is enough to make you catch your breath – golden hair spreading in flowing waves across a delicate forehead; an ethereally transparent face; clothes which mould themselves about his slim figure. And should he favour you with speech, with an epigram, perhaps, that reveals an intuition as searching as a woman's, you will feel that condescension, indeed, can go no further.

— *Daily Express*, 14 September 1928

THE winter of 1927–8 was once more spent abroad, for the sake of Stephen's health; Pamela was convinced that he needed winter sunshine, and the fact that London had been particularly fog-bound in late 1927 confirmed her view. She had heard, from her cousin, Nan Tennant, of a suitable German pension in the Bavarian Highlands. Quiet, well appointed, with nursing facilities and fresh mountain air, it was ideal for her youngest. Haus Hirth was named after its owners, Walter and Johanna Hirth, a well-to-do German couple impoverished by the country's economic collapse, who had now taken to letting out rooms to paying guests. Over the next two years Stephen was to become very attached to the place and people. Johanna Hirth would nurse him with dedication, even to the point of contracting tuberculosis herself.

Stephen's Aunt Nan proposed to accompany him to Bavaria, and they set off for the Continent in late January, reaching Paris on the 23rd. The two stayed at the Hotel Crillon on the Place de la Concorde, and shopped 'mechanically', Stephen much regretting not bringing a valet with him: 'It is not the clothes so much as the myriad small fatigues that they save one,' he told Elizabeth.[1] His relationship with his 53-year-old aunt had never been close, and without Nannie Trusler things were very dull. Even a visit to the Casino de Paris didn't cheer him up, nor was Stephen looking forward to his imminent departure for Southern Germany, even though there they would be joined by William Walton. With both Rex and Cecil busy with their burgeoning artistic careers, and Siegfried likewise occupied, the latter had suggested that he pay for Walton — ever in need of financial help, as well as peace and quiet in which to compose — to stay at Haus Hirth with Stephen. Besides being company for Stephen, Walton would act as a locum for Siegfried's affections; in effect, Sassoon had sent the composer over as a 'minder'.

Stephen's first impression was of a 'queer place, everything so German! German! German!' he told Elizabeth. The Hirths had the qualities of kindliness, simplicity, and exceptional hospitality, but 'the scenery is hideous', which Stephen endeavoured to ignore by burying himself in his writing, painting and drawing. The basic requirements were there; hot water, electric light, and the one real attraction, solitude, meant that, for a few weeks at least, 'it shouldn't be too unbearable'.[2]

After a few days Stephen's zest for new places and people returned. With the windless sunshine, and Willie to keep him company, he began to enjoy Bavaria. Together they sun-bathed all day on the chalet balcony, in 'Lido' dressing-gowns, gossiping idly. Meals were 'a hubbub of Germans, on every side . . . Hamburgers & Wurtemburgers & Dusseldorfers . . . all so divine, hideous & unceasingly genial. They take photographs of me all day, which delights me & encourages my halting German sallies.' Stephen reported to Cecil that he was 'conserving what remnants of youth I possess. I have a chic sunburn (so has Willie)'; tanned skins were newly fashionable, Riviera-style. Stephen boasted that he lived on fruit and salads, with daily doses of cod-liver oil, 'never touching cakes, sweets or pastries, or chocolates . . . I go to bed early & emerge upon my sun-soaked balcony about 11.30. I take a ration of exercise and I hope that all these "health & beauty" precautions will by the end of March produce the desired results.'[3]

Herr Hirth, in his suede lederhosen and white shirt, made Stephen laugh with his funny English, while 'Tante Johanna' was more caring and devoted than any mere landlady. Clad in pink crêpe de chine shirt and flannel trousers, his feet bare, Stephen wrote his diary and letters while contemplating 'green fields, dark woods and white snow peaks against a sizzling sapphire sky'.

He still longed for London news, but instead he had to make do with Willie's stories, which actually turned out to be very good, particularly concerning 'private scandals . . . his details are hair-raising.' These included wild speculation about Michael Duff and Teresa Jungman (com-pletely unfounded), as Stephen noted Willie's 'indiscreet secrets about our London friends – I knew Michael Duff at one time, he was practically "wanting", I thought, but it's ideal for Baby. I've always thought the half-witted millionaire the perfect husband, such *laissez-faire*, such *carte blanche*, but, joking apart, I believe he's terribly nice, & I think, good-looking . . . When do they marry?'* he enquired of Cecil, sure he would know all the latest. 'If by chance you hear of any Borzois for sale, tell me, won't you????... Do tell me about your tea with Ottoline, isn't she a marvellous creature?? I put her very high, don't you? She has I know (although I don't know her) the kind of mind I love and her beauty is frightening isn't it???'4†

Meanwhile, Stephen and Willie decided to explore Munich, a two-hour drive away, although they decided to stay for three days. Operas, plays and shopping were all packed in, together with a dose of 'ptomaine poisoning' (a type of food poisoning then thought to be caused by putrefying animal tissue). Having recovered from that, and leaving Willie to take care of hotel and taxi business, Stephen 'swept about hoping to be sighted by film producers, hungry for talent',6 but Munich seemed bereft of movie moguls that spring.

Hollywood was very much on Stephen's mind as, via Beaton, he had been commissioned to write a piece for *Vogue* on the cinema. The resulting article was published in the late spring edition, but since writing it Stephen had become dissatisfied with the piece. He told Cecil it was 'so bad!!! (I haven't been to the movies for months!!)',7 but yet he hoped they would use one of the 'mackintosh' photographs for the 'author shot'. This did not transpire, but Stephen's article did, and ran to a hefty four pages.

Entitled 'Concerning the Cinema',8 its bold premise was that 'The condition of the cinematograph to-day is restless and volcanic. The screen-child, the "Pollyanna" of the rolling blue eyes and barley-sugar curls, is growing up . . . Until a few years ago the screen merely aimed at entertainment of the rudest description; to-day it endeavours (however

---

*Sir Michael Duff married Lady Caroline Paget, the beautiful daughter of the Marquess of Anglesey (with whom Rex Whistler fell in love) in 1949.
†Stephen met Lady Ottoline Morrell, the great literary hostess, soon after, probably through Sassoon. Her daughter, Mrs Igor Vinogradoff, recalled that 'Stephen was a great friend of my mother's . . . He used to send her beautiful drawings, and they exchanged letters about which were the best face creams to use – he often came to her Thursday afternoons at 10, Gower Street.' She remembers Stephen as 'a very tall and elegant homosexual – I can barely remember meeting a normally-sexed man at my mother's in those days.'5

unsuccessfully) to combine intelligence with entertainment.' Stephen's cinematic survey is a humorous, light gallop through the 'state of the art', penned with the same panache and exuberance that made his spoken word so entertaining. Perhaps in journalism he had found his true voice? Pamela did not think so. 'My mother hating *Vogue* said, "That's not the pulpit or forum I wish for you",' recalled Stephen years later.[9]

Stephen put off asking friends over to Bavaria to stay, as he had done at San Remo and Cap Ferrat in the years before, as he didn't expect to remain long. He was longing to acquire new pets when he returned to England, and asked both Cecil and Elizabeth to look out for a pair of Borzois. 'I want two, a pure white one and a beige one . . . why haven't I had them before?' he mused. 'Think of them on the downs, & in my Silver Room! Don't you want to swoon when you think of them?'[10] Stephen imagined these elegant Russian hounds running full pelt about the lawn at Wilsford, finally subsiding around him like a pair of chorus girls in ostrich plume costumes; borzois were the chicest animal accessory of the twenties, and Stephen was 'starving' for them.

Stephen's appreciation of the Germans remained equivocal. While he was excited at being written about in a Berlin newspaper, the *Berliner Tageblatt*, after being spotted at a carnival ball in the nearby town of Garmisch, he still found them, as a race, impossibly greedy. When Frau Hirth told him of a famous musician who had 'thanked her with tears in his eyes' when she had presented him with a tray of German sausages, Stephen just couldn't believe it, especially as he himself was on a new diet which had made him realize that 'we all eat too much! I now eat apples spread with honey for tea, nothing else! no tea to drink, & I feel a different person!'[11]

Stephen stayed on at Haus Hirth until late March, visiting southern baroque churches, becoming interested in the 'Mad King' Ludwig II, whom he thought a delightful character. He made an attempt to learn German, and became captivated with a German girl staying at Haus Hirth 'with Tahiti blood! She looks like a Gauguin . . . Also, there are two pleasant Americans . . . a bullying wife who says "B–O–Y–D, now you must be quiet" if her husband aged 65 talks too much at meals. I heard him say in a melancholy voice the other day "America is a woman's country."'[12]

Travelling back via Paris a week or so later, Stephen made the acquaintance of the Russian emigré painter, Pavel Tchelitchew. Alerted to this new artist's work by Edith Sitwell, his champion in England,

Stephen found both man and pictures fascinating. Tchelitchew, one of Gertrude Stein's three 'geniuses' (in company with Ernest Hemingway and the painter Francis Rose), was a colourful character whose sporadic mastery of English and quixotic nature endeared him to Stephen, and thereafter he counted the painter one of his true friends. Tchelitchew found in Stephen a charming Englishman – and one who could afford to buy his paintings. They became great buddies, visiting the Medrano circus in Paris together; Tchelitchew's imagination was stimulated by it, and circus imagery figured heavily in his work around that time. Stephen implored Pavlik, as his friends called him, to paint his portrait when he came to England that summer, and Pavlik agreed.

Stephen wrote to Edith Sitwell with the news, and she was pleased, and hoped she wouldn't be away when Tchelitchew came for she was already developing a strong attachment to the painter. On Stephen's return from Europe, she told him how much she was looking forward to Tchelitchew's visit, and lectured him on how great an artist he was, instructing Stephen to visit Pavlik's show at the Redfern Gallery in Bond Street, where he was to inform the owner of the artist's genius likewise. Edith also sent Stephen copies of her poems 'The Strawberry' and 'The Greengage Tree'; she had written the former whilst staying at Wilsford the previous spring. Stephen was proud that the poem, later acknowledged as one of the best works of Sitwell's 'romantic' period, had been inspired by his home.

Back in London for the start of the new season, Stephen found his brother David was about to marry the young actress Hermione Baddeley. They had met at one of Syrie Maugham's parties in 1925, and had since conducted an affair, much to Pamela's disapproval. But when David brought Hermione to Wilsford, Stephen had liked her very much. Unlike his mother, Stephen positively approved of stage people, and got on well with Baddeley. Hermione noted that 'all the family were witty, amusing and like David, very good-looking. I remember his younger brother, Stephen, leaning towards me once and saying: "Of course we have the fatal gift of beauty, darling."'[13]

David married Hermione at the King's Road Registry Office on 16 April 1928, and Stephen enjoyed the party afterwards, at the Gargoyle. Four days later, Stephen was the co-host (it being close to Stephen's twenty-second birthday) of a party with Brenda Dean Paul (a friend of David's, later a 'society drug addict') and his cousin Olivia Wyndham, at the latter's house in Sloane Square. It was the return of the Bright Young

People. Tom Driberg, who, in his guise as the *Daily Express*'s 'William Hickey', did as much to publicize his friends' activities as any other gossip columnist of the time, wrote: 'Intelligence – determined and natural – and Beauty turned up in crowds.' Stephen and his friends had drawn up a guest-list of impeccable taste. Cecil, Rex, and Willie were at the top, together with Constant Lambert, Walton's composer 'rival'. Then there were Harold Acton and Brian Howard, along with Oliver Messel, wearing one of his fantastic papier-maché masks. The then highly-popular artist Cedric Morris was another star, as was Ernest Thesiger, the effete actor well known for his exquisite *petit point*.

But the real star was Stephen, whose arrival and appearance were calculated, as ever, to impress. 'Mr Stephen Tennant, who wore earrings and a football jersey, told me about his new book, *The White Wallet*,' reported Driberg. 'Mr Tennant, when in London, drives about in an electric brougham of the Edwardian period. He says it is like riding in a bow-window.' The columnist related how 'a friend of mine saw him off at Waterloo on Saturday, and their drive to the station in the brougham was a piece of high-class entertainment which the Cup Final crowds seemed to appreciate enormously'.[14]

Peter Quennell was the friend who arrived with Stephen at the party in that extraordinary motor vehicle. An aspiring writer and poet down from Oxford, he had been 'discovered' by Stephen, who offered to give him a lift to the party. Quennell had certainly not imagined a ride in such a vehicle. He lived in a 'very modest flat' at the time, and was surprised when Stephen sent round his car and chauffeur. 'It was like a semi-circular shop window on wheels, lit from within, and I was perched up on the back seat, as high as one is in a hansom cab. The chauffeur was very old and very venerable with proper livery.' Arriving at Mulberry House, Quennell was shown up to Stephen's bedroom, there to await his tardy host, delayed with costume preparations. He recalls the Silver Room, 'very luxurious, with a great cornucopia of fruit beside the bed'. Stephen was a long time coming and, when he did arrive, Quennell heard his sister Clare downstairs telling him: 'Stephen, your little friend has been waiting for you for a very long time!' 'I think she rather mistook my errand!' jokes Quennell.[15] Once more in procession, they set off for Sloane Square and the party. There Stephen found all his friends, looking almost as good as he. 'William Hickey' noted his cousin Olivia Wyndham, in 'a conventional frock of silver tissue', but 'one girl impressed me deeply with her bravery. She had gilded her hair.'[16]

London that year was full of amusing entertainment. At last Stephen was able to go and see *This Year of Grace*, and the record of the hit song from the show, 'Dance Little Lady', was never off the Wilsford gramophone. 'I'm Mad About You' and 'Try to Learn' were favourites too – even Sir Edd'ard loved them; 'we hum them or play them all day long . . .'[17] From Wilsford, there was a visit in late April to the health farm Preston Deanery Hall, near Northampton, for dietary therapy: 'sugar forbidden – no tea allowed, noiseless nurses pacing the corridors, bored patients dragging through a game of croquet'.[18] It was an advanced sanatorium which relied on special diets to give its upper-class 'patients' a new lease of life, and Stephen appears to have spent most of his time there abed, waited upon by nurses hand and foot, being fed orange juice and fruit.

Three weeks of diet '*à la* Preston Deanery' convinced Stephen of its beneficial qualities, and he felt enough of an expert on the health-giving virtues of brown bread ('so tonicky', as he later told his niece Pauline), fresh fruit and vegetables that he told Elizabeth and Susan that he would put them on the same diet when they came to stay at Wilsford. Another excitement whilst at the health farm was a request from Richard de la Mare of Faber & Faber for Stephen, on Sassoon's recommendation, to illustrate one of the Ariel poems in their series of small poetry pamphlets.[*]

The relationship with Siegfried was fast intensifying. Sassoon (together with Zita Jungman) visited Stephen at Preston Deanery that month, and drove his young friends to nearby Weston Hall, to visit the Sacheverell Sitwells at home. Stephen's diary for the time appears to have vanished, but it is obvious from other evidence that he saw more and more of the poet as the year progressed. A newspaper reported a sighting at His Majesty's Theatre in July, where the Diaghilev ballet was performing, and Stephen had taken a box for the season. Here observers wondered why Sassoon was in a lounge suit, rather than evening dress.[†] Nannie went to the ballet later too, 'and sitting beside Stephen in his box opposite that of King Alfonso of Spain, she made an interesting contrast to the other women in their satins and scintillating metal brocades'.[20] The young poet Stephen Spender heard reports too of the gold dust which Stephen used to

---

[*]Eventually Stephen would work on three such commissions, each one a Sassoon poem: 'To My Mother' (Ariel Poem No. 14, pub. 1929), 'In Sicily' (No. 27, pub. 1930), and 'To the Red Rose' (No. 34, pub. 1931).
[†]Siegfried's token gesture against Society. In 1925 he had recorded in his diary an invitation from his friend Frank Schuster to the opera, when out of annoyance he refused to wear evening dress: 'The thought of that smart crowd of "society people" – all there because it's a social event – irritates me, and makes me want to be different from them!'[19]

brighten his hair on these almost royal public appearances. There was no concealing this friendship for Sassoon as he was seen about town with the brightest of the Bright Young Things.

The London season of 1928 was Stephen's last foray into the world of the Bright Young People, as indeed it was their swansong; the coming Depression would seal the fate of such cavortings. For Stephen, the year was to end sadly, and begin a cycle of anxiety, illness and upheaval that would thereafter blight his life. The abandoned enjoyment of this final party sequence had within it its own obsolescence.

Stephen swam through these events with his usual grace. At Elizabeth Ponsonby's party in Royal Hospital Road, he appeared 'a fantastic figure in silver grey', along with Cecil as 'an Edwardian dude, with golden wig and topper'.[21] The beautiful dancer and actress Tilly Losch, later to marry the surrealist patron and millionaire Edward James, was there, dressed boyishly in a carmine sweater; her presence made Stephen swoon, for she was the star of *This Year of Grace*.

The parties came in quick succession, as if the hosts and hostesses knew it was their last chance to outdo each other in innovation and extravagance. David and Hermione Tennant threw a pyjama party, a post-honeymoon celebration, at Adelphi Terrace. Hermione claimed that David initially proposed dress should be *au naturel*, but they decided that would be taking things too far, and settled upon nightwear instead. The *Evening Standard* observed that 'the host's brother began the evening in white satin, but changed halfway through into green'.[22] J. M. Barrie, who lived below, was sufficiently roused by the noise to call at their door – not to complain, but to ask if he might join the party. He ended deep in conversation with Stephen's cousin, Greta Wyndham (Dick Wyndham's Scandinavian wife), whose androgynous blonde crop appealed to the author of *Peter Pan*.

Towards the end of May, Stephen and Cecil were weekend guests at Savehay Farm, the country home of Oswald Mosley and his first wife, Cynthia.* There they dressed up in Cynthia's mother's old Edwardian

---

*Sir Oswald (known as Tom) and Lady Cynthia (known as Cimmie) Mosley also lived at Smith Square, and were thus neighbours of Stephen's. Savehay Farm was frequently host to the Sitwells, William Walton, Oliver Messel and others of Stephen's set, his cousin, Dick Wyndham, being one of Mosley's best friends. Mosley was serving in Ramsay MacDonald's Labour government at the time, later to leave and form his own New Party, which attempted to bring together such disparate figures as Aneurin Bevan and the Sitwells. The Party's eventual failure led to the development of Mosley's British Union of Fascists. Cynthia Mosley died of appendicitis in 1933, and three years later Mosley married Diana Guinness (née Mitford), with whom he had been conducting an affair for some years.

clothes and 'did the most fantastic dances as passed description for effeteness, tho' brilliance was in every line'.[23] Both boys had stayed with the Mosleys before, and on one such summer visit Oswald Mosley had his cine-camera on hand to film their escapades. The result was the only such film of Stephen to survive from the period.

An outdoor performance was decided upon, and a story-line devised. Beaton was the powdered Madam of a brothel, engaged in tempting the men of the party, John Strachey and Dick Wyndham. Cimmie was one of the girls in Cecil's charge; and Stephen, in one of his favourite costumes of the time, was a mysterious blind beggar boy whose significance to the plot remains unclear. Cecil had assembled a disguise of false nose and bouffant wig to caricature Margot Asquith, and towards the end of the drama runs off to drown him/herself in the river, a sequence made hilarious by the fact that his wig began to float off in the fast-running stream, completely ruining the dramatic effect. Stephen too wore make-up, but his was a pale white mask, with pencilled eyebrows and those bee-stung lips with which he sought to emulate Hollywood starlets. Staggering daintily about, clad in silken rags, he holds his arms out, feeling his way as he imagined a blind boy would. He sits and makes daisy-chains by the river; and later plunges in too, only this time looking more like Ophelia than Cecil's amusing performance – with echoes of Narcissus, Shelley, and presaging Jean Cocteau's art films – he tips his head back into the water, over the river bank, poetically drowning. Only from this filmed evidence can the unreality of Stephen's presence be judged. With long, fine limbs and a graceful gait, he resembles a whitened stick insect, stalking his way through the crackly black and white silent film.

On 22 May there was another pageant, the last of such *tableaux* in which Stephen would appear. It was held at Daly's Theatre, and Stephen's guise was to be that of his favourite poet. He appealed to Rex for costume ideas. Rex wrote back from Rome, where he was studying at the British School, with sketches of two alternative views of Shelley: 'Very loose sleeves to the shirt, or perhaps this would look too much like a sailor?', the accompanying sketch showing a romanticized, meditative poet; 'Or the rather healthier socialistic Shelley?', a second drawing of Percy Bysshe, waving his hat with bravura in one hand, the other clutching a bag of pamphlets slung over his shoulder.[24]

Stephen's love affair with Shelley, evidenced by Rex's gift of the *Collected Poems* in 1926, had continued apace. Rex painted a miniature watercolour of Stephen as the poet, standing with his hand in his blue tailcoat, gazing wistfully to one side. Stephen liked to see himself in the 'beautiful, sensitive imaginative boy' of whom he read, 'unsuited to the rough-and-tumble of public school life . . . known to his classmates as "mad Shelley"', and he loved the description of the poet as 'gold-dusty with tumbling amidst the stars'.[25] Stephen's assumption of his favourite persona was also recorded in an impossibly fey and poesy-laden photograph of the costume he had made up for the 'Hyde Park Pageant', with his hair tumbling down in curls over a face thick with built-up eyelashes and powder, his thin neck framed in a loose ruffled shirt, looking like one of Rex's drawings come to life. Nancy Mitford, who went to the performance with Patrick Balfour, had to admit that Stephen was 'very beautiful as Shelley'[26] and rivalled only by Oliver Messel, who had come as Lord Byron.

Once more Stephen's likeness was preserved for posterity in three dimensions that summer as Maurice Lambert, the bearded and Bohemian brother of the composer, Constant, sculpted Stephen. 'It is very startling . . . the fur collar of the coat looks like a huge dead snake, the face has a null, poisonous beauty that I like,' wrote Stephen after seeing a photograph of the finished bronze printed in the *Daily Express* that autumn.[27] A more staid representation than the extravagant Epstein work, the bust still had its charm in the etiolated features of the young Stephen rising from the exaggerated chinchilla collar of his leather jacket.

The party season continued. On 8 June there was the Chelsea Arts Ball, at which – unusually – Siegfried was spotted with the others, 'a large group in fantastic rags of chiffon and velvet, showing the Picasso scheme of colourings'.*[28] 'Who are the young men of to-day?' asked the *Sphere* a week later, in one of those idly-written articles that seemed to fill the papers, then as now. 'Or rather, who are the models on whom they are bidden to mould their personalities? Let us take the Hon. Stephen Tennant, who cut so dashing a figure at his brother's bottle and pyjama party: and his friend, Mr Cecil Beaton. Both these young men are in their very early twenties, are slender, with a knowledge of clothes that embraces the female wardrobe, with a most definite artistic sense which their predecessors in the rough old days might envy.'[29] The readership of the popular papers took such approbation seriously; there must have been many a young provincial man who aspired to Stephen's standards, who looked longingly at the photographs in the tabloids and the

---

*A later photograph of Sassoon, dressed in Elizabethan doublet and hose at a Wilton pageant, indicates just how painfully uncomfortable the poet was in the unaccustomed role of dandy-aesthete.

magazines, and attempted to buy a tie like that, or persuaded their tailor to cut a suit so wasp-waisted.

As a leading man of fashion, Stephen had published his views on 'Chic' earlier in the year, in a follow-up to his previous journalistic venture for *Vogue*. His 'Word of Counsel for "Today's Lady"' piece in the *Evening News*,[30] which gave its writer authority by virtue of his having 'designed many lovely dresses for women', took as its starting point that 'woman's dress to-day is a uniform without a uniform's reticence. But as we are alive to-day let us dress like to-day!' Stephen exhorted his readers. 'I love fashion: the fashion of every age is a summing-up of everything most *réussi* in that age.'

Stephen had no thoughts of liberation when he declared with the unequivocality of a Poiret: 'Only one woman in a hundred can be trusted . . . Far better to look like the dullest Chanel mannequin than the intense beauty-loving Englishwoman whose wardrobe consists of bernouses, saris, mandarin coats, antique velvets, painted wooden beads, huge dull silver plaques, and so forth.' Stephen's fashion diktat demands 'lines severe and colourings cool! Have a sleek neat head, and austere street coats! In the evening let your dress be luxuriously simple and your wrap luxuriously complicated! With diamond bracelets from wrist to elbow, an expression of vacuous boredom on your face, and the steel of your heart tempered for conquest – life ought to be fun, oughtn't it?'

Yes, indeed, as a caveat stressed: 'A note as regards the "bored" expression. Do not overdo this.' Stephen advised *News* readers not to be 'insolent and frosty; the High-hat and "Ritzy" air is always ridiculous; but do not beam fatuously or leave a smile on your face or look breathlessly enthusiastic like a dog with its tongue out – it's a question of poise, not pose.' Stephen would always have such fanciful ideas of how a lady ought to look and behave; later, in America, he noted how few women left their faces in repose, like he did: composure was so much better for the wrinkles. Or, yet later, how flat shoes really didn't suit one of his female relations; they looked so dowdy. For him, even close women friends had to consider their decorative values first and foremost. Then, as in old age, Stephen could sound like the mistress of a Swiss finishing school.

The season continued in frantic pace, and Stephen's contribution to the parties of that year was a gathering held in his own Silver Room, where, under the midnight blue ceiling, a list of celebrities came to pay homage to Elinor Wylie, the guest of honour who had warned her host that she could not stand for any length of time, having suffered a fall. Rebecca West was there, and watched Wylie hobble in and lie 'down on the wide bed . . . with her head on a silver pillow'. Stephen's assembled guests included the American singer Paul Robeson (appearing in *Showboat* in Drury Lane that year, and, coincidentally, another subject of an Epstein bust), and the usual crew of Cecil and friends. Stephen requested them to brush their signatures on his silver-lacquered walls in black ink,* and Wylie struggled to her feet to examine each name, 'looking up wistfully and crying, "Oh, that is beautiful! I shan't be able to do it half so well."'[31]

Wylie's bathetic character, a mixture of ludicrous egotism and helpless beauty, was well illustrated by the scene. Sadly, it was the last Stephen saw of her. In November she left her house at Henley, to sail back to New York on the SS *Berengaria*, and on 16 December her mercurial mind was defeated by her weakened body. She suffered a stroke, and died within minutes. But this unhappy news would be overshadowed for Stephen by another and altogether more drastic bereavement that autumn.

As the Bright Young People danced across the ballrooms of Mayfair (and, in one case, the shop counters of Selfridges) that summer, Stephen's social whirl was to suffer a rather less pleasant public exposure in the nation's papers. Current tabloid press attention on the Youth of England was running high, and new stories of their excesses were demanded daily – and Stephen happened to be in the wrong place, at the wrong time. What became known as the 'Ellesmere Ball Row' splashed his name across a thousand breakfast tables, as an offending, or offended, party in a social contretemps in which he was subjected to the most intense degree of press interest – albeit unwelcome – yet. It seemed the knives were out for Stephen.

The occasion for all the fuss was a ball held in honour of the Countess of Ellesmere's daughters at Bridgewater House, one of the huge town houses on Park Lane. Guests included Princess Andrew and Princess Aspasia of Greece, Prince George of Russia, Lady Maud Carnegie and her husband, among others (Osbert Sitwell was another guest, and was to meet the great love of his life, David Horner, at the ball). The hostess, 'resplendent in gold and green lace',[32] graciously received arrivals in the hall, but had left her station by the time Stephen and his friends arrived.

He had taken Elizabeth, Nancy Beaton, and David Plunket Greene to

---

*A method of decoration hitherto employed by Oscar Wilde in his rooms off the Strand, where he had visitors such as Sarah Bernhardt and Lily Langtry sign their names on the white-panelled walls. Cecil Beaton was to go one better a few years later at his country retreat, Ashcombe, where his guests were invited to trace the outlines of their hands on his bathroom wall.

the Russian Ballet at His Majesty's Theatre, and, having himself been invited to the Ellesmere Ball later that evening (as was Plunket Greene), Stephen proposed that he and David should take Elizabeth and Nancy as their companions. He could not have foreseen the trouble this would cause: it was quite natural for the two young men to bring the ladies, and the girls themselves did not think of themselves as other than welcome.

This, however, was not the case. Lady Ellesmere had the subject of 'gatecrashers to the forefront of her mind, because the previous year an American debutante, Charlotte Brown . . . had been brought uninvited by Lady Muriel Paget, who, as everybody agreed, should have known better'.[33] Lady Muriel Paget also happened to be the mother of Lord Glenconner's wife, Stephen's sister-in-law, Pamela. Thus, as Stephen and his party made their (probably flamboyant) entrance, Prince George of Russia saw the girls and remarked to Lady Ellesmere: 'I didn't know you knew Miss Beaton?' 'Upon which the irate Lady Ellesmere swept up to the girls and asked them: "Why have you come?" "Oh! We came with Mr Tennant." "Would you kindly leave the house."'[34]

As Hugo Vickers observes: 'The affair might have rested there but Miss Horner, a journalist, happened to witness the scene and the story broke in the newspapers.' The week-long stream of press reports began with an inflated account of what had happened. Lady Ellesmere declared to the *Daily Express*: 'I wish the fullest publicity to be given to the names of my uninvited guests as I consider this to be the only way of dealing with a nuisance which I understand many hostesses have suffered from this season.' The same report concluded that 'as a result of what was said, Mr Tennant withdrew his party'.[35]

Years later, Stephen intimated that in his youth he had been 'fond of shocking his genteel, aristocratic society by crashing its elegant balls . . .'[36] But he cannot have been aware of what the Press would make of it, and neither he nor Pamela was very pleased by the resultant publicity. The *Star* asked him for his comment: 'Here is a simple statement of facts. Mr David Greene and myself, who had received invitations to Lady Ellesmere's Ball, took two women as our partners. Lady Ellesmere has made a mistake as to the identity of the three women to whom she spoke.'[37] The next day, the *Morning Post* printed an open letter from him to the hostess: 'Dear Lady Ellesmere – Last night I took my party of four on to your ball. David Greene and myself had received invitations. Miss Lowndes and Miss Beaton had not. Any blame must fall entirely on me. I asked them to come with me and when they said they had not been asked, I said I did not think it mattered if they were with two men who were asked. I apologise for this quite inadvertent mistake, and it was entirely my fault. Yours, Stephen Tennant.'[38] That the reports contradict themselves was indicative of the fact that, as Vickers notes, 'this was the first time a society hostess had spoken publicly, with the result that the squabble was vaunted in the press with the open collaboration of all concerned. As a result of this incident, more than any other, have the Nigel Dempsters of today gained their freedom.'[39]

The *Daily Express* of 12 July printed, via Tom Driberg, Stephen's 'retorts courteous' (it should also be noted that Lord Beaverbrook, the proprietor of the paper, was a friend of Pamela's). 'What I object to,' said Stephen, 'is that Lady Ellesmere should have implicated my partner, Miss Beaton, and Miss Lowndes.' He considered that she had 'taken an unwarrantable line'. These remarks were accompanied by a large photograph of Stephen, as were many of the other articles on the affair. The *Daily Mail*, the *Express*'s rival, weighed in with an alleged quote from Stephen too: 'I admit I was to blame . . . It is true that I first said when the trouble began that I was asked to bring a partner. I confess now that this was untrue. I think all the trouble was caused by Lady Ellesmere hearing with her own ears Miss Lowndes saying "Isn't it a joke? I have not been invited." She may also have heard one or two slighting remarks that I made myself about the dance.'[40]

Stephen denied saying any of this. The *Evening Standard* (an Express newspaper) gave him the chance to speak in that evening's edition, his comment having been sought by reporters ringing round for follow-up stories that morning: 'The alleged "interview" with me published in a morning newspaper to-day is an invention. I did not see any reporter from that newspaper, and I cannot imagine how this invention came to be published . . . Neither Mr Greene nor I nor either of the two young ladies we brought was turned out, nor did I make any "slighting remarks" about the dance. As for the remark attributed to Miss Lowndes, she never said anything of the kind.'[41]

Elizabeth's mother, Marie Belloc Lowndes, told the same reporter that her daughter was unwilling to speak about the subject, 'for it has occasioned a good deal of personal distress. I can assure you she was the innocent victim of an unfortunate incident.' Susan Lowndes recalls that the whole affair was very traumatic for her sister. 'It was perfectly natural for a young man of the time to take any young lady with him at dinner on to a ball, to "drop in" for a dance. Lady Ellesmere was obviously put up to making such a fuss by other hostesses, who had become angry at the practice. It was all rather silly, really.'[42]

Back at Wilsford, Pamela was 'in a panic, quite broken', according to
Edith Olivier. 'She and Lord Grey have been warned that it's the
beginning of a "Round-up" of Stephen and his foppish friends.' She told
Edith that she feared Stephen 'would be suspected of real immorality if
he continues to be written of in the papers in this company'.[43] Edith
agreed that the best thing to do would be to write to Stephen and his
friends, including Sassoon, to ask him not to go to any more parties that
Season.

While Fleet Street continued to thirst for new information, letters came
in from every quarter, with support for either side. Lady Ellesmere
received one such from the Duke of Northumberland, who, alluding to
Stephen's sojourns at Fallodon (and probably to his appearance at the
Alnwick pageant), noted that: 'The principal culprit is a youth whose
strange behaviour has caused considerable comment in Northumberland.' Lord Lambourne called them 'howling cads', whilst another peer,
raising the notion of the Tennants' social standing, declared that
Stephen's letters make 'his conduct more disgusting. When I think of his
breeding, I don't wonder however, and after all, blood does count for
something! Money only will not always carry everything.'*[44]

The episode even ended up as a music-hall joke: 'Where are you going
to, my pretty maid?... Nobody asked me, Sir, she said', and witty
party-givers greeted their guests with 'Good evening, everyone, I did not
send you an invitation as I knew you would come.'[45] Stephen's new
sister-in-law Hermione recalled that she hadn't been on Lady Ellesmere's
list. 'David was furious that his marriage had been overlooked and we
didn't attend ... "Lady Ellesmere's List" became the laughing-stock of
London society. David insisted that on the invitations to our next party
we put "Gate-Crashers Welcome".'[46]

The last party of the season proved the most extraordinary of them all.
The 'Bath and Bottle Party', arranged for the Friday evening following the
Ellesmere Ball, was 'justified, if by nothing else, at least by the weather'.[47]
In the heat of that midsummer, St George's Swimming Baths on
Buckingham Palace Road was a cool place to be – in both senses of the
word. The invitations read: 'Mrs Plunket Greene, Miss Ponsonby, Mr
Edward Gathorne Hardy and Mr Brian Howard request the pleasure of
your company at St George's Swimming Baths, Buckingham Palace

---

*This particular jibe may well allude to Stephen's Aunt Margot, whose *Autobiography*
scandalized her peers with its frank reminiscences.

Road, at 11 o'clock, p.m. on Friday 13th July, 1928. Please wear a Bathing Suit and bring a Bath Towel and a Bottle. Each guest is required to show his invitation on arrival.'[48]

The latter stipulation, in the light of the previous week's events, was apposite in the extreme, and reporters noted that 'invitation cards were very carefully inspected at the door'. The invited guests arrived wearing bathing suits 'of the most dazzling kinds', and danced 'to the strains of a negro orchestra . . . The Hon. Stephen Tennant was on this occasion an honoured (and invited) guest. He wore a pink vest and long blue trousers.' As the party hotted up, the more adventurous, or drunken, guests leapt into the pool itself, the water having been slightly warmed for the evening. They splashed about among the huge inflatable rubber horses and flowers that decorated the water, illuminated by coloured spotlights trained on the pool. Some people – guests included Cecil, Peter Quennell and the Bloomsbury artist Clive Bell – had brought 'two or three bathing costumes, which they changed in the course of the night's festivities'.[49]

The gallery of the baths was converted into a cocktail bar, and a special drink, 'the Bathwater Cocktail', had been concocted for the occasion, although 'the cocktail mixers evidently found the heat intolerable, for they also donned bathing costumes at the earliest possible opportunity'. To the outside viewer, it must have all seemed like the last days of Rome, as these 'beautiful people' cavorted on that sweltering summer night. The party was still going strong in the early hours of the following morning, and 'bedraggled guests were playing up to the astonished gaze of the world's workers passing by', when the police were called 'to encourage the last guests to depart'. The constables' efforts were thwarted when 'the more rapacious' of the late revellers dragged the officers into the changing-rooms, 'in the hope of a general disrobing'.[50]

It was obvious this kind of event had reached its saturnalian peak with the Swimming Bath Party, and Stephen, worn down by the Ellesmere row (and warned off by his mother), was beginning to tire of the antics of the Bright Young People. Allanah Harper recalled that one of the last parties of that time, given by David Tennant, ended 'in a free fight. I found myself in the middle of a jealous fracas, scuffle and scrimmage, which although it had nothing to do with me, resulted in my dress being practically torn off and tufts of my hair held up as trophies. After that experience I never went to parties of this kind again.'[51]

Chapter 9

Southern Baroque

The Charity Matinée was over, I felt; the impresario had buttoned his astrakhan coat and taken his fee and the disconsolate ladies of the company were without a leader ... For a few happy hours of the rehearsal, for a few ecstatic minutes of performance, they had played splendid parts, their own great ancestors, the famous paintings they were thought to resemble; now it was over ...

— Evelyn Waugh: *Brideshead Revisited*

WITH summer into its second half, Stephen was bound once more for Fallodon. Sadness befell him with the demise of the borzoi, named Norma, he had acquired, for which he felt a certain desolation – although 'the heavenly photo' which Cecil had taken of Stephen with his elegant hound was a testament to her short-lived beauty. His holiday reading – the novels of Ronald Firbank, on the recommendation of friends – was to be a new discovery. 'I must read Firbank,' noted Stephen in a letter to Cecil written the week before he left for the north. 'I'll read *Caprice* first.'[1]

Although there is no record of Stephen Tennant ever having met Ronald Firbank, the similarities between the two were far too evident to ignore for many of Stephen's own friends – especially Sassoon, who had been introduced to the eccentric novelist by Osbert Sitwell in Oxford in 1919. It was 'My oddest experience there', averred Siegfried,[2] who found Firbank's appearance 'as orchidaceous as his fictional fantasies'. Both Siegfried and Cecil urged Stephen to read Firbank in the mid-twenties, by which time he had already become a cult figure to people such as the Sitwells. Firbank, like Stephen, was fascinated by Anna Pavlova and Anna de Noailles, the French poet, and also had a penchant for Negro themes, once announcing to the Sitwells: 'Tomorrow I go to Hayti. They say the President is a Perfect Dear'[3] – one of many travel plans which, like

Stephen's in later years, Firbank did not fulfil. Novels like *Prancing Nigger* must be seen as direct precursors of Stephen's *Leaves from a Missionary's Notebook* and *Lascar*; certainly their influence, and that of their author, is undeniable. And there was one last quality he shared with Stephen: tuberculosis; for Firbank died of consumption in 1926. To Harold Acton, Stephen was a Firbankian character himself, and he recalls that when he met 'the juvenile Tennant with his buddy Cecil Beaton . . . my impression was that he had wriggled out of one of Ronald Firbank's novels I was reading at the time, either *Valmouth* or *Caprice*, I forget'.[4]

When Sassoon met Firbank, the novelist informed the poet, in one of his rare communicative moments, that 'I am Pavlova, chasing butterflies . . . You are Tolstoy, digging for worms.'[5] Perhaps Stephen reminded Siegfried of Firbank; whether conscious of the similarities or not, Sassoon was quite smitten by Stephen's own particular charms. He was to spend the next six years of his life chasing this particular butterfly. His mistake was to try and pin it down.

Once at Fallodon, Stephen looked forward to a visit from Sieg, whiling away the time writing and drawing, in 'Arctic' weather.[6] Elizabeth was due too, but for a short visit only, for Sassoon had new and adventurous plans for Stephen and himself that autumn, and had come to Fallodon to seek Lord and Lady Grey's approval. The idea was for a mini Grand Tour, staying first at Haus Hirth for the mountain air, then going south to stay with the Sitwells at their father's Italian palace at Montegufoni, to coincide with the music festival to be held in Siena. All this under Siegfried's supervision – and in his Packard car; he would drive out to join Stephen and Nannie in Germany in early September.

Elizabeth and Siegfried joined Stephen at Fallodon and were soon off on picnics and visits to the beach. The disparity in ages between Sassoon and his younger friends did not seem to bother them, although Elizabeth found him a little difficult to get on with, veering from playful skittishness to sullen childishness. She was surprised when, out on a picnic, he accidentally upset a cup of tea over one of Lord Grey's valuable books. She couldn't understand why, instead of admitting to it and apologizing, as any 'adult' might do, he tried to deny he had been responsible. 'Very strange behaviour,' thought Elizabeth.[7] Stephen was still getting to know Siegfried, and did not see such behaviour as a portent. He rather enjoyed the fact that Sieg appeared happy with his friends and family; Lord Grey and Sassoon struck up a friendship, which Siegfried later commemorated in a poem, 'Fallodon Memory'.

*

Stephen, Nannie and William, as valet, crossed the Channel on 29 August. They took the Orient Express from Paris, arriving in Munich the next day. They rendezvous'd with Siegfried, and spent a few days in Munich, going to a performance of *Figaro*, 'through which Nannie and her charge sat spellbound by the voice of Elisabeth Schumann'.[8]

On 4 September they arrived at Haus Hirth, to be greeted as old friends by Tante Johanna and Onkel Walter, and just in time for Siegfried's forty-second birthday, which was celebrated at breakfast with a cake stuck over with little red candles. Sassoon liked the Hirths, who seemed to him to prove how nice people became when they lost their money. Upstairs in his bedroom, Stephen spread his belongings about – dressing-gowns in pink hues, books, magazines, letters, perfumes by Worth and Molyneux, a bunch of violets, and his toy bull terrier, Franz.

Down below, William was learning German from the kitchen maids, amidst hoots of laughter, whilst Cook announced to all and sundry that Captain Sassoon was 'England's greatest poet'. Nannie Trusler sat quietly in a corner, sewing or pasting postcards in her scrapbook. The guests were amenable, and included the Mounseys – he a director of Barclays Bank, who had been at Cambridge with E. M. Forster, and a devotee of Wagner, playing *Parsifal* before dinner each night. The Mounseys' four-teen-year-old son Patrick was there too. He remembers that for most of the time Sassoon was upstairs, tending to Stephen, and seemed to appear but seldom for dinner with the others. The invalid was spending much of the day on his sunny balcony, trying to get his body 'sandal-wood colour'.

There were outings in a carriage drawn by two ambling grey horses, through countryside alive with the sounds of bees and cow-bells. One expedition was to find King Ludwig's schloss, Lundendorf, which Stephen thought 'quite mad, but beautiful in a crazy way', with its grotto and blue underground caves, and the lake 'with a swan-boat on it in which the mad King played at being Lohengrin'. The castle itself was 'incredible, a toy palace, so exotic & gilt, tiny salons packed with ermine curtains & ostrich plumes & Sèvres china & french paintings'[9] – an exuberance with which Stephen was to feel a certain affinity in later years. In the evenings Stephen played Strauss on his gramophone, and read, whilst Siegfried arranged his travelling library, and smoked his pipe in peace. Already the two were falling into a shared life together.

Siegfried mapped out their imminent Italian trip with great care, working out a route which would display the scenic beauty of Northern Italy in all its glory. On the morning of 9 September, Stephen and Siegfried sped off in the red Packard, waving goodbye to the Hirths.

At last, thought Stephen, the adventure had begun . . .

They drove from Garmisch to Borzen in blinding sunshine, and on along wildly zig-zagging mountain roads through the Mendolo Pass, Male, the Madonna di Campiglio and Fiona. As Siegfried negotiated precipitous corners, Stephen scanned the majestic scenery through binoculars. Once in Italy, the landscape levelled out into cultivated hillsides, and by 11 September they were at Lake Garda, sitting in a café by the beautiful blue water. Stephen sat spellbound as Siegfried told him stories of the American lecture tour he had undertaken in 1920. 'It was absolutely absorbing, & what Mrs Belloc Lowndes calls a "human document".'[10]

On 13 September, having stayed overnight in Cremona, they drove to Bologna, stopping in the little town of Busseto for lunch. In one of the shops, Stephen discovered a veritable treasure-trove of old photo-post-cards of adored film and theatre stars, and soon he was snatching up handfuls of Mae Murray, Gloria Swanson and Rudolf Valentino. While Siegfried picked out cards of Verdi, he wondered at his friend's curious ability to veer from good taste to the tawdry.

How extraordinary that progress through Northern Italy of the two friends in the bright red Packard car must have seemed. When they stopped, huge crowds would gather around like flies to a jam pot. Luckily their fascination for the car distracted their attention from the occupants, which was just as well as Stephen's costume was not conventional, consisting mainly of a sailor's jersey, a pair of gym shoes, and a green eye shade, although Siegfried persuaded him not to wear the coral necklace which he had bought in Riva.

Arriving at Bologna that evening, they checked into the Grand Hotel Brun. Here, Siegfried complained with good humour, he had begun to discover that he was a first-class valet, unpacking Stephen's varied and fantastic wardrobe, and unwrapping numerous bottles and jars from a sea of tissue-paper. Meanwhile Stephen would read Shelley's letters, gargle, eat a peach, or hold an enormous mother-of-pearl shell up to his ear. They were in Bologna for just one night, and as Siegfried looked forward to two more blissful weeks, he wrote: 'Sometimes I wonder whether it can be true that I am so happy,' adding ominously ' – and I wonder what the future has in store for me to balance it.'[11]

The smooth progress *en route* to Siena, where Stephen and Siegfried were due to meet up with the Sitwells, William Walton, Constant Lambert,[*] and others, was halted somewhere along the line. As they raced towards the town on 14 September, Siegfried realized they would not be in

[*]Constant Lambert (1905–51), brother of Maurice, and the first British composer to write for Diaghilev.

time for *Façade*, scheduled for performance at the International Festival of Contemporary Music in Siena that morning. As the Packard drew into town it was already late afternoon, and Stephen felt an acute sense of bitterness at having missed Willie's brilliant setting of eleven of Edith's poems, declaimed at tongue-twisting speed to a surreal jazz and waltz-influenced canter. 'I thought I should die of temper. I felt eaten up with rage & hate. RAGE & HATE',[12] wrote the vexed Stephen in his diary, indicating that it was not only his mother's beauty he had inherited, but her temper as well.

After dinner with the two composers, Walton and Lambert, Stephen's anger subsided. Here they were in romantic Italy, guests of Sir George and Lady Ida Sitwell in their huge eleventh-century castle, and here too were friends, invited by the Sitwells to enjoy the three-week-long house party: Christabel Aberconway, Zita Jungman, Arthur Waley, the poet and translator of Chinese literature who had recently become a good friend, along with his friend, Beryl de Zoete. And, of course, the Sitwells *en masse*: Edith, Osbert, Sachie and Georgia.

Christabel Aberconway recalled that Montegufoni seemed host to 'a continual coming and going of guests for luncheon and dinner, and one evening there was a great invasion of about eight busloads of people who came for supper – the food and wine was always delicious. Who organized it, I can't imagine.'[13] Stephen was not convinced of the luxuries of which Christabel had spoken. Warned by Edith of the possibility of encountering scorpions in the passage, he quipped: 'You do offer such kind hospitality!'[14] Added to that, there was no electric light in the castle, and 'the mosquitos are frightful'.[15] Christabel came into Stephen's room – her hair in two plaited 'tails', he recalled – to tell him what he had missed at the performance of *Façade*, and to tell him that Edith had been very angry that they had been too late for it. An inveterate gossip, she later gave details of the scenes at Siena to Virginia Woolf, who in turn passed it all on to Vita Sackville-West, 'a vast panorama of the Sitwells in Italy, Zita saying "And I'll have a tray in my room", the bath not locking, Lady Ida, Stephen Tennant with his old nurse' (for Nannie had come too, at the express invitation of Osbert) ' – what I call, perhaps foolishly, "real life".'[16]

Evenings amongst such company were bound to be entertaining. They ate out on the terrace, Edith in best Plantagenet chic (Elizabeth Bowen later described her as a 'high altar on the move'),[17] in one of her silk turbans and a Florentine brocade dress; or, on one occasion, the company found themselves dining in the kitchen, entertained by Willie playing jazz and popular songs on the piano. To Stephen, Siena was dramatic, illuminated at night with 'burning stuff so that the flames flickered behind the castellations',[18] as they wandered about in the hot night air. Then, on the morning of 22 September, three carloads of the Sitwells and their guests set off for Viareggio, on the west coast of Northern Italy, near to where Shelley had drowned in 1822. The proximity of his hero's resting-place cast Stephen into gloom. He thought of the poet all day, and felt 'a sort of dull agony' sweep over him, yet at the same time feeling grateful 'for his help, & for his beauty'. The following morning he was sitting up in bed, in his 'shrill green check pyjamas & pink ice dressing gown', reading and thinking of Shelley again.[19]

Guests began to leave on the 23rd, and by the 24th, Stephen, Siegfried and Nannie, in company with Willie and Constant, had journeyed on to Florence, where they stayed at the Hotel Helvetia. Together they spent the days exploring the beauty of the medieval city, having tea at Doney's, eating wondrous white grapes. Here Siegfried found a copy of Firbank's *Sorrow in Sunlight* for Stephen.

Thence to Venice, Stephen's first encounter with the Dream City. From the Hotel d'Italie, Bauer-Grunwald, he had time to write to friends. 'It is too good to be true,' he told Cecil. 'We have sight-seen voraciously clutching our Baedeker . . . I can't begin to describe it here.'[20] He told Elizabeth on 29 September that he and Nannie had spent that afternoon in a gondola. 'The Doges' Palace rising from the sea – the cries of the gondoliers – the lap-lap of the water against the walls . . . Yesterday we visited St Anthony's church at Padua.' As he wrote, Venice was 'bathed in blue dusk, sapphire twilight'. Sieg added a PS: 'Haven't lost any maps while abroad' (a reference to a Fallodon outing) – and Stephen enclosed the tiniest photograph possible, less than a centimetre round, looking healthy and radiant, his hair in a huge golden wave.

Sitting in St Mark's Square, drinking hot chocolate and watching the pigeons circle in the blue sky above them, the travellers couldn't be happier. Siegfried found an enthusiastic review of his newly-published *Memoirs of a Fox-Hunting Man* in the *Observer*, the first of many press-cuttings sent by his publishers. There were thrills in the publishing world for Stephen, too, when the Ariel booklet 'To My Mother' appeared: verse by Sassoon, decorations by Tennant. The frontispiece was a line drawing of a rosy-cheeked and blond-haired child (rather like Stephen himself as a baby) in his mother's arms, surrounded by lilies, daisies, and roses.

Soon after, Stephen and Nannie returned to Haus Hirth by train, leaving Siegfried to undertake the tiring road trip back on his own. When he arrived, he was found to be suffering from bronchitis, and so now it was his turn to be the pampered invalid.[*] His illness meant that their stay at Haus Hirth was extended, until he was well enough to drive on to Paris. This was no bad thing, as Stephen found the Bavarian country 'molten in the Autumn blur', with 'dazzlng days, mountains glittering like bride-cakes, gentians & the last late goldenrod'. He lay out in the sun all day, and once again heard Strauss waltzes played 'faultlessly . . . *Wiene Wald*, do you know it?' he asked Cecil; ' – it saps the melting marrow from one's bones!!'[22]

Yet Stephen was considering the future, too. 'When I get back to London I hope to renounce society & become a recluse. How well I am able to fulfil this resolution remains to be seen. I am going to draw & work very seriously,' he declared, indicating that the endless round of parties (and the unpleasantness at the Ellesmere Ball) had taken their toll, and, possibly, that his mother was making warning noises. In the wake of Cecil's and Rex's current successes, he had now to think of 'a career' for himself. Stephen asked Cecil to Haus Hirth the following February, when he was due for a return visit. 'Everybody knows you & there are always cries of admiration at your photographs in my scrap books – 'Ach! Ceecil Beaton! ach! ach!' – they cry when I mention you. Apparently your photographs have been seen in German papers – is it true you & I appear in a novel by Waugh?'[23]

Stephen referred to *Decline and Fall*, which was published that autumn, and parodied the very hedonism he was now attempting to renounce. The bizarre adventures of its hero, Paul Pennyfeather, among the Bright Young People drew on Waugh's personal experience of that world. Cecil was unmistakably David Lennox, the society photographer who snaps Mrs Beste-Chetwynd from behind (Cecil's real-life portrait of Margot Asquith was likewise a rear view), and Stephen could be excused for thinking himself portrayed as Lennox's friend: 'The first to come were the Hon. Miles Malpractice and David Lennox, the photographer. They emerged with little shrieks from an Edwardian electric brougham and made straight for the nearest looking-glass. In a minute, the panotrope was playing, David and Miles were dancing, and Peter was making cocktails. The party had begun.'[24][†]

[*]Edith Sitwell complained to Edith Olivier in November that she 'had been very angry with Stephen . . . says that Siegfried has two patches on his lung and blames S[tephen] for this as he made him do rash things abroad'.[21]
[†]A later scene has Miles Malpractice enjoying a 'wicked' game of cards with a military guest of Margot's: 'Such *naughty* faces,' he observes, much in the 'Cedric' manner. Waugh's illustration for the scene in which Pennyfeather gets lost in the Vieux Port of Marseilles also bears a distinct similarity to Stephen's later observations of *louche* life there.

Evelyn Waugh's son Auberon observes that 'there are various other candidates for the Miles Malpractice slot, and I don't think there is too much mileage in it, if you will excuse the joke.'[25] But one can understand Stephen's suspicions. The fact that *Decline and Fall* quickly became a best-seller didn't help. With Waugh's attack on the frivolity of his set, Stephen thought it time his life took a more serious turn.

By the second week of October Sassoon's health had improved, and on the 15th they left Haus Hirth, Stephen and Nannie taking the train to Paris, where Sassoon would join them later. They stayed at the Hotel Foyot at first, and Stephen met up in town with Meraud Guinness and Brian Howard. Together with Madame Picabia, wife of the painter Francis Picabia, they spent 'an amusing evening at the *Boeuf sur le Toit*', the extremely fashionable café patronized by Jean Cocteau and his friends. It was the very centre of the Parisian *haute bohème*, 'and we saw such exhibits, among them Lady Mendl, Zena Taylor, Mrs Geossens, the Willie Kings etc . . . I adored it,' Stephen told Cecil. 'Meraud has the most perfect "crop" & looks heavenly & is more perfect than ever.'[26]

One evening Stephen went to see the legendary Mistinguett perform. She was the dancer and actress whose viperish tongue and hot temper had made her a major personality of the Folies Bergère in the 1910s. Now aged fifty-four (although she kept her age a closely-guarded secret), she was a little over the hill. She also was extremely jealous of other artists; she once spat at Josephine Baker (whose dressing-room Stephen also

visited whilst in Paris) in the street. Stephen thought her 'the most outrageously pathetic thing'. She appeared twice in the show, 'once as a little girl like this – ' Stephen drew a caricature of a wizened actress for Cecil's benefit ' – the curtain goes up and finds her sitting on the floor & looking exactly like an old Baboon, dressed like Jessie Matthews in a Mae Murray wig – her other appearance is a scream!! – she staggers down some stairs in a ten foot high headdress weighing a ton, it topples & tips over her wisps & yellow fringe & creased mauve forehead. She lifts her leg stiffly once or twice & croaks out "Pariselle" (which is supposed to be her "big hit" song of the show). She's really worth seeing' concluded Stephen, ' – so tragic so absolutely "gone" . . . She looks like the female impersonator at the Chiswick Empire.'[27]

From Paris, Stephen and Nannie moved out to Versailles, to stay at the Trianon Palace Hotel. Autumn made every tree flame red-gold, and he and beloved Nannie wandered around the palace and the Petit Trianons. Siegfried then joined them, and they visited Stephen's old friend Mary Duclaux and her sister, Mabel Robinson, to hear their recollections of Hardy, Sassoon having been asked to write his life for Macmillan's *Men of Letters* series. On a day trip to Chartres, they found themselves in the midst of a village wedding party, which moved Siegfried. 'I looked at his face,' wrote Stephen, 'while the peasants danced & the fiddle scratched, his eyes bright & his whole aspect was one of absorbed delight.'[28] Back in Paris, Stephen took Nannie to the *haute couture* salon of Paul Poiret, where they agreed how lovely the pale blue walls painted with white doves and sprays of roses were – a visual memory perpetuated many years later in Stephen's painted mirror bathroom. Stephen told Anne Douglas Sedgwick of his happiness. She replied: 'Your little letter almost brings tears to my eyes; the loveliness of its evocation so makes me long for Versailles and Fontainebleau, and you give them to me at a season when I've never seen them: black coral trees: – perfect; and the under-the-sea feeling. I've often had that, a sort of 1st act of "Rheingold".'[29]

The happy, lazy days continued. Stephen read Virginia Woolf's *Orlando*, deeming it 'very lovely & charming' on 9 November, but within a week had changed his opinion. 'I am reading "Orlando" with rather puzzled distaste now.'[30] Perhaps he sensed something in the air, for among all the jokes and laughter with Nannie, while he and Siegfried were visiting Mme Duclaux, 'talking gaily & well'[31] until seven o'clock in the evening, Stephen had unknowingly suffered a terrible loss. Pamela had become unconscious after undergoing a severe stroke in the garden at

Wilsford. Within four hours, without regaining consciousness, she was dead.

The telegram was waiting for Stephen when he returned to the hotel. It was painfully ironic that he and Nannie had planned to return to England the next day; just hours before, he had been looking forward to coming home, after his long European sojourn. Now it was a sorrowful pair who left Versailles for a harrowing two-day trip back to England. 'It was a golden winter morning, but my heart was lead & ice, lead & ice,' Stephen wrote on the morning of his first day home, in a house in which his mother's dead body was laid out in her bedroom. 'Now as I wake this [morning] my great grief shadows backwards over it all & I seem to have been in a trance, a trance of mingled despair & hope.' As he had arrived 'at Wilsford's front door that is like a Bible', so tired that he felt madness was upon him, his brother Christopher was there to meet him, and hold him in his arms ' – nothing after that but dazedness & unreality . . .'[32]

News of Pamela's death had been received by Stephen's friends as a great shock. Cecil, who was at a dinner party in New York, heard a fellow guest relaying the news in a matter-of-fact manner, not realizing Beaton's connection. 'My life stopped still – I ceased to go on living for several moments,' wrote Beaton. 'I couldn't believe it was true – she must be mixing up names . . . Why, Lady Grey had been so particularly well of late. I know that she had suffered from her heart but she had since her visit to her pet cure hospital felt so well, looked so well . . .' Cecil painfully summed up the implications of Pamela's passing: 'There would be no one to look after the ill-birds, there would be no one to look after the parrots – no one to look after Stephen – poor Stephen – & how false & frivolous my letters written to him last week would seem at this moment – poor, poor Stephen.'[33]

The funeral at Wilsford, on 22 November, was a muted affair. The family filed out in procession from the Manor, behind Lady Grey's plain oak coffin, to the church, where the Bishop of Salisbury presided over the service. Mourners included Viscount Gladstone, Marie Belloc Lowndes, Lady Violet Bonham-Carter and Dr & Mrs Kempe. Lord Grey and his stepsons stood holding wreaths of flowers as Pamela was laid in a moss-lined grave. Stephen wrote to Cecil a day or so later: 'When you get this you will have heard of my great loss. Grief turns one into a queer being, but through the unhappy days that pass so strangely the thought of one's friends is very lovely & makes the loneliness a little better & it is because of our friendship that I wrote to you because I know you will grieve with me . . .'[34]

Already Beaton was thinking that Stephen's health would suffer, without Pamela's steadying influence 'to keep him from doing silly things'.[35] There was a memorial service in London, at St Margaret's Church. Pouring rain made the occasion even sadder, and Baba Brougham had to dash through 'a band of merciless reporters and cameramen' with her coat collar turned up. She saw Stephen, 'absolutely quiet but very white . . . I believe he is going away with Lord Grey to look after him, which is the best thing he can do – Clare is terribly upset – I don't think they can take it in at all – She [Pamela] was perfectly cheerful a few days before – everybody is profoundly shocked.'[36]

Siegfried returned from France, and was 'shouldering the burden nobly, oh! so nobly',[37] said Georgia Sitwell, who told Cecil that she too was worried about what might happen to Stephen. Sassoon saw him on the night of 30 November at Mulberry House, whence Stephen had returned after spending three days with Anne Douglas Sedgwick* in Oxfordshire. Edith Olivier came to stay at Mulberry House while Stephen and Lord Grey were in London, where she helped with arrangements. She thanked Cecil for his letters of condolence. 'It really meant a lot to him. When one is unhappy, it does really help to know that one's friends care.' She observed that 'no one could be more bereaved. His whole life broke up with her going. Everything changed. He is so lonely, having to arrange everything for himself – all the little household details which he didn't know existed! And yet in spite of this – & in spite that he feels it all at every moment – he is being quite marvellously brave – & is full of entire faith & joy & confidence in the knowledge that she is happy. She never saw death, but was quite well & happy – playing with her birds – writing letters – & then lay down & died. No suffering. No sorrow at leaving them all. No anxiety over their future. All this makes Stephen happy alongside of his personal grief.'

Edith stressed that Stephen was not ill, as expected, 'though I can't help fearing that this courage must be costing him more physically than one can see as yet'.[38] The tragedy appeared to have brought out new reserves in Stephen, which many would not have believed possible of a person hitherto so flighty. In later life, Stephen wrote to a friend that he believed 'sorrow can be an ennobling thing – that we can be better people because we have suffered so acutely. We all need courage.'[39]

The immediate matters of business had to be attended to. Christopher, Lord Glenconner, was to take over Mulberry House '& he & Pamela will have Stephen's bedroom!! – they will paint its walls a quiet cream colour,

---

*To whom Pamela had left her outstanding papers and manuscripts to edit and publish after her death.

& that silver dream will burst like a kettle' – as Stephen's life seemed to have done. 'We have made up our minds that this is rather a wonderful end for it,' wrote Edith Olivier. Meanwhile, Stephen would need a London residence. Edith had been helping him search, but so far they had found only 'the most vile & foul rows of dens or dog-kennels, offered at enormous rents, in disgusting "mansions"'. They had pinned their hopes on Olga Lynn's 'dream of a house': 'Stephen would make it perfect. It is the house for him.'[40] But Lady Erroll (wife of Jocelyn Erroll, of *White Mischief* fame) had her bid in first, and hers was the offer accepted.

The contents of Pamela's will were read out, and it was discovered that David was to have Wilsford.[*] Edith observed that the latter was 'utterly hard & heartless & has only one idea, to sell it to the highest bidder. He is quite without sentiment for the house his mother built & loved so much.'[41] David's daughter, Pauline, observes that her father had a compulsion to make money – but only because he saw it always about to disappear. His impulse to get rid of Wilsford was also born of a need to free himself of his mother's influence, which he had increasingly found suffocating. His Cambridge philosophy lecturer advised him he must 'cut his mother's apron strings'[42] if he were ever to live a full life. By selling his childhood home, David hoped to do just that.

Thus a plan was decided upon. Stephen would sell Lake, the original model for Wilsford, to the Baileys, '& if he can get rid of the rather large amount of land & farms, shooting & fishing which goes with Wilsford – he will buy just the house & grounds. This will be perfect,' said Edith '& I think it is practically arranged.'[43] But David had a turn of conscience about selling his mother's beloved home, and instead agreed with Stephen's trustees an arrangement to lease the house to his brother. Wilsford became Stephen's – in all but title – for ever.

On 10 December Stephen and Lord Grey – 'the two who really care',[44] noted Edith – left for Fallodon, there to recover from the awful business arrangements and duties that had followed Pamela's death. They spent Christmas at Glen, with Christopher and his wife, and Clare and her third husband, James Beck. Clare's three sons by her second marriage lightened Stephen's first Christmas without his mother, as he listened to the resounding shouts and 'puffings of toy engines' as his nephews played with their presents. 'Spaniel puppies and bicycles trip one up & bustling

---

[*]Stephen having been well provided for in his father's will (he now inherited Lake), there was little left that Pamela need bequeath him.

competent Governesses & nurses hurry forward & abduct or produce their charges with a lot of brisk by-play – Miss Russell is hot stuff after a football – but equally she is admirably motherly in the drawing room after tea.'⁴⁵

To all appearances Stephen was back to normal, putting a brave face on his grief. Perhaps the only person who underestimated the long-term effect of Pamela's death on his life was Stephen himself. He may have felt that a great weight had been lifted from his shoulders, but the release was not yet absolute.

Stephen was convinced that his mother had not left him, but remained, in spirit, beside him. The spiritualism which had dominated her life had affected both his and David's attitude to their loss. Hermione Baddeley recalls the first night they spent at Wilsford after Pamela's death, when she and David were in their bedroom, Pamela's body in hers. 'She looked asleep and completely at peace. There was not a line to be seen on her face and her profile was noble.' Having gone to bed, Baddeley says she was woken by someone coming into their room. '"Is that you, Stephen?" I whispered. No one answered. There was complete quietness in the room. I sat up terrified.' She woke her husband, who is supposed to have replied, quite matter-of-factly, 'It must have been Mummie coming in to wish us goodnight.'⁴⁶

'A long time later I went with Stephen to a spiritualist meeting,' she adds. 'Through the medium came a message for me. It was: "Hermione, why were you upset when I came into the room? I just wanted to be close to David."'⁴⁷ The fact that the tale of Pamela's 'return' had got into the papers as 'Actress Sees Ghost' could well explain this 'uncanny' statement from beyond the grave. Yet Stephen believed implicitly in these things. It is plain that such a powerful influence as Pamela's was difficult to exorcize after so sudden a death. So strong that, according to Edith Olivier, it was the idea of Pamela's spirit being displeased with David's intention to sell Wilsford that convinced him, 'though sceptical . . . to leave well alone'.⁴⁸

At Glen that Christmas, only a month after her death, Stephen told Elizabeth that Mummie had been with him: 'I have received many wonderful messages – also I have some book tests for Fallodon! but the loneliness without her physical presence is by and all things awful & fills me with longing to die and she knows this & is always making wonderful signs – they are all singing downstairs in the drawing-room – and I could not bear it so I flew up to my room & thought how brave I am – but no one has ever helped as she has helped me!! She has rained messages on me. I'm going to "sit" once a month . . . Soon I go to Fallodon & there have the joy of the book tests!!! – a great sublime joy!! – such as Mummie had with Bim's book tests – now I know why her face used to look so wonderful, so uplifted, & happy.'[49]

Chapter 10

The Siegfried Idyll

Because to-day belongs to you by birth
For me no other day can ever bring
The wildflower wonderment of wakening earth.
And so, till now, I have not seen the spring.

— Siegfried Sassoon, poem written for Stephen Tennant on his twenty-second birthday.

TWO days after Christmas Stephen sent Cecil, still in the USA, news from Glen: of Edith Sitwell's new poem, 'Gold Coast Customs' – 'the most significant thing she's done. I'm crazy about it'; of Rex's latest pictures, and his imminent departure for India with Sir Edwin Lutyens (which did not actually transpire); and of Siegfried's new book, a sequel to *Memoirs of a Fox-Hunting Man*. Stephen's sister Clare, in 'very funny tea-gowns of pink satin trousers & coat & bunny fur' was nagging her husband Jimmy 'from dawn till dusk – poor man',[1] while Stephen maintained his sanity by reading French history. At the end of January, Stephen was back briefly at Mulberry House, and feeling ill. He had a stream of visitors, however: Lady Ottoline Morrell, Angela Baddeley (Hermione's actress sister), Meraud and her new husband, Alvaro Guevara, Sachie Sitwell, Zita – and Sassoon.

Siegfried had spent an unhappy winter without Stephen. He had last seen him in December, when he had told Edith Olivier of his 'great love and *comprehension* of Stephen'.[2] Now, in the latter's absence, he had turned to Rex for consolation, and the two had become close through their mutual affection for the boy. Rex started on a pencil portrait of Siegfried, and throughout the sitting, Sassoon spoke of Stephen. The drawing was finished at Rex's studio off Tottenham Court Road, where the poet, faced with one of Cecil's photographs of Stephen, 'kept glancing at it wishing he were with me'.[3] Later, after a weekend with Rex and Edith at the Daye House, Sassoon confessed to his diary: 'Am feeling rather worried about R., who is showing signs of falling under my spell . . . It would be easy enough to succumb, but would be no joke, once it began . . . R. is desirable, but I can't divide my heart into partitions, and if I were to try the experiment, I should find myself betraying [Stephen], who has given me his whole heart. I don't want to be unkind to R. So far he has said nothing, but his behaviour has given the whole show away.' Driving to and from Salisbury in his Packard, 'every milestone seemed to belong to S. I can see an emotional crisis looming ahead of me.'[4]

Siegfried spent New Year with Stephen at Wilsford, and, sensing his loneliness, decided to stay on for the first weeks of the year – crucial weeks in which Stephen came first to depend on Sassoon's support.

The latter was eager to introduce him to all his friends, one of the greatest of whom was Max Beerbohm, famed caricaturist and Edwardian dandy, and author of *Zuleika Dobson*. Both he and his American-born actress wife, Florence Kahn, took to Stephen at once. They met at Siegfried's flat at 23 Campden Hill Road, on 9 January, and all four were soon engrossed in conversation; Siegfried noted that Max 'never sat down the whole time . . .'[5]

Quite quickly, most of Sassoon's friends became Stephen's too. During the summer, they had visited Sir Henry Head and his wife, Ruth, at their Dorset home, Forston House. Head was an old friend of Sassoon's (they had met through W. H. Rivers, Siegfried's doctor at Craiglockhart), and he remained one of the most highly regarded scientists working in his field, famous for having volunteered to undergo a unique brain operation in 1908 to test its efficacy.[*] Sir Henry was a radical neurologist, well known to the Bloomsbury set. Roger Fry recommended the Woolfs consult him when Virginia became suicidal in 1913, which they did, with some success. (Virginia Woolf noted in her diary for 1 September 1928, talking 'of sodomy and sapphism' with Morgan Forster: 'This was started by Radcliffe Hall and her meritous dull book . . . Morgan said Dr Head can convert the sodomites. "Would you like to be converted?" Leonard asked. "No" said Morgan, quite definitely.')[6]

Stephen got on well with this cultivated couple, in spite of the disparity in their ages, and they in turn looked on him with parental affection. Sir

---

[*]Henry Head was born in 1861, and was brought up as a Quaker. He married Ruth Lawson in 1904 ; they had no children. He was knighted in 1927. Head was interested in literature and 'mysticism', and in addition to his medical works published two volumes of his own verse, and a translation of Heine's poems, *Destroyers and Other Verses* (1919). Ruth died in 1939, Sir Henry a year later.

Henry was a bluff and friendly figure; Sassoon described seeing him by chance in Hyde Park one day, 'tripping along in his baggy blue suit and looking more like an ex-sea captain than a famous scientist',[7] and his wife was as amiable, and understanding. She had written to Stephen shortly before Christmas: 'And though this must be a sad anniversary for you you have discovered the secret of forgetting sorrow by giving joy . . .'[8] Receiving a copy of the Ariel poem 'To My Mother', with Stephen's illustration, she wrote on Boxing Day: 'I do hope you will go on with your work. You see I write like a tiresome old friend, but I do want you to have that sort of root in the world that work gives, else you know like a too charming thistledown seed you may [blow] away into summery nothingness . . .'[9]

T. E. Lawrence, Lawrence of Arabia, was another impressive figure to whom Stephen was introduced by Siegfried, at the adventurer's odd little cottage, Clouds Hill, in Dorset; another, the painter William Nicholson, whom they visited at Sutton Veney. Gradually, Sassoon came to be indispensable to Stephen, placing himself emotionally and physically at his service.

Peter Quennell notes that to him and his friends it all seemed very sudden, this blossoming affair. 'Sassoon had never seen anything like Stephen before. He thought of himself as a simple, straightforward man. He wanted to pretend he was a simple man observing the rich. Then suddenly he came into contact with [Stephen] . . . It was a tremendous *coup de foudre* – Sassoon was like the worthy vicar of a parish coming to town and meeting this great society beauty . . . But it was rather ridiculous, really – these stories of Sassoon being sent back to the hotel to fetch Stephen's pearls, things like that,'[10] whilst Lady Ottoline Morrell's daughter avers that 'no one was in the least surprised when he and Siegfried Sassoon took off on holiday together'.[11] Anthony Powell recalled that Edith Sitwell had a title for the new relationship: 'The Old Earl and Little Lord Fauntleroy';[12] meanwhile Cecil discussed the suddenness of the relationship with Rex over dinner at Boulestin's. Quite what Stephen and Siegfried knew of all this is not clear, but they must have known such friends as Osbert Sitwell would be spreading news of their intimacy all around town. One thing is quite evident, however: neither the Earl nor Lord Fauntleroy much cared for what anyone else thought.

Stephen left for Germany at the end of January, after a last-minute 'orgy of photography at Lenare's',[13] where, with Cecil still in America, he,

Siegfried and Rex had to make do with a lesser artist, although the results were 'divine'. Stephen, Nannie, William – and Poll the Parrot – arrived at Haus Hirth in early February, to enjoy 'day after day' of 'hot sunshine & dry snow & the bluest of turquoise skies!'[14] Nannie, who had been unwell (and was becoming confused in her old age) was on the mend already, he heard* – and Poll sat out in the sun, in her golden bell-shaped cage, 'like a Phoenix on her nest with water instead of flames about her'.[15] Stephen overate and overslept, and crowed to Elizabeth of having a double-chin, and of being able to sunbathe nude on his own balcony.

The house had new guests; two Hessen Princes, who rather caught Stephen's eye, and an American girl, 'Alice from Moatz? (I don't know how to say her name) – a crashing bore & exactly like a million billion American girls, her conversation passes beyond belief!'[16]† Stephen was looking forward to the arrival of friends; Siegfried, Rex, Willie and Edith Olivier were all due to join him later in the month. Meantime, he had a new project with which to occupy himself. 'I've just finished a book on missionaries, all drawings, very improper,' he told Cecil on 15 February; 'I think [it] divine – but it's a little too much for my teutonic audience.'

What became Stephen Tennant's only commercially published work was *Leaves from a Missionary's Notebook*, the pictorial adventures of the Reverend Felix Littlejohn, a well-meaning man of the cloth who goes to convert the heathens of the South Seas, meeting two spinster assistants there to help him in his mission. He discovers, however, that his audience is most definitely unreceptive to the Christian Gospel, but rather fond of the two old ladies, one of whom is quickly seduced by a drunken seaman in a 'censor'd' scene of lust. It is a hilariously-drawn adult comic book, full of the beefy sailor types who would gradually become part of Stephen's visual stock-in-trade. The influence of Firbank is clear, particularly of *Caprice*, which Stephen had been reading some months before. In that book, Mrs Sinquier shudders when she hears her daughter's ballad about 'those scandalous topsies that entrap our missionaries! . . . The horrors that go on in certain places, I'm sure no one would believe.'[18] Due to various problems, Stephen's book was not published until 1937, by Secker & Warburg. *Leaves* was reprinted by Hamish Hamilton in 1986, to celebrate the author's eightieth

*It appears, however, that as early as February it was clear to Stephen's closest friends that Nannie was much more seriously ill than he was given to believe, and that her real condition was being kept from him for fear that it might make his own condition worse.
†In fact she was Alice Leone Moat, a *risqué* young American girl, later to become William Walton's lover, described by Edith Olivier as '*not* immoral, but the indecency of the public schoolboy'.[17]

birthday, when it incurred the wrath of Lambeth Council, who decided not to stock it in their libraries as it seemed to them to be racially stereotypical in its portrayal of large-bosomed native women.

But Stephen's attitude to other races was hardly racist; he was far too interested in them for that. 'I ache to have your news,' he wrote to Cecil four days later. 'The very thought of Harlem music & New York sets my nerves in an erotic jangle – I have always thought you impossibly virtuous but New York will mend that I dare say – if it has not already done so!' Stephen's estimation of such joys was simple. 'What in life could be more extatic [*sic*] an occupation than putting orchids in an ice-box & then taking them out again?' What indeed – other than a love affair? '. . . You must become less "cold" & try to fall in love,' was Stephen's advice, speaking as he did from new experience, 'it makes the whole difference to life! – I could not live without it – you must "take" a lover, as they say. I cannot think of you "spinstering" in that amorous bower!' Stephen had discovered love – and sex. 'I have always heard that "love life" in N.Y. is very hot & I long to savour it (I hope perhaps in the Autumn). I am sure there is no aphrodisiac like a negro's voice . . . here the two Hessen princes are so divine, & dreams of beauty – Donatus & Ludwig – they are too delightful & will be here in April if you pass through then.'[19] Too delightful to resist, apparently, for later Stephen hinted to Cecil of having had an affair with one of the German charmers.

The effects of tuberculosis on a person's character and emotional responses have often been observed to be a definite vivacity, and a propensity for emotional excess. TB victims are known to be likely to have sudden love affairs, and to accept their illness (which, after all, exhibits no initial physical symptoms other than tiredness or shortness of breath) as something on a spiritual plane, being a 'disease of the breath' rather than of the body. Pulmonary tuberculosis, from which Stephen suffered, was only frightening when the victim coughed up blood, which was usually in the more serious stages. For Stephen, it was yet a disability for which the prescriptions of fresh air and plenty of rest coincided with (or encouraged) a life-style which he could easily adopt, and come positively to enjoy. It was the legacy of TB that would make him a recluse in his latter years, and explain his self-imposed lassitude. Could his TB have been responsible, too, for the increasingly passionate – and erratic – nature of his affair with Siegfried?

The sudden recurrence of the disease, brought on by the emotional stress of Pamela's death, was the most severe yet; in fact, according to Siegfried, it was life-threatening. He wrote dramatically to Robert Graves that the doctor's diagnosis in London that January was that Stephen would 'probably be dead of consumption within a year'.[20] Yet Stephen remained unnaturally calm about the prospect. At Haus Hirth that winter, he appears to have wallowed in the pampering accorded his invalid status more than ever before. The deliciousness of being waited upon hand and foot never failed to enthral him, as he lay back on a deckchair in the blazing sun, 'plump & pink . . . & very golden about the head'.[21] Added to which a new doctor, Dr Kaltenbach, 'a Heidelberg professor, blond, young & fascinating', had taken over Stephen's medical care. Telephoning 'passionately' from Heidelberg when he couldn't come in person, he had written to Frau Hirth that Stephen was 'a mixture of a Fra Angelico angel & a Botticelli something or other; of course I am on the crest of a wave!!'[22]

The swinging between moods continued. Whilst at one moment Stephen could feel full of exuberant joy in his Bavarian retreat, another would bring back black memories, of Pamela, and the gaping hole her loss had left in his life. One Sunday night, towards the end of February, Stephen wrote in maudlin mood to Elizabeth: 'Nannie & I have been through some dark days, & my heart has been now & then more deeply shadowed than ever before in my life . . . The older one gets the more arbitrary time seems, doesn't it?'

Stephen was growing philosophical. 'Tonight I have been eating apricots, such lovely Bavarian ones! & I worshipped the source of their creation anew . . . the marvel of inhabiting even for so short a time a world so rapturously filled!' As he looked at the fruit, with their 'gold juice, their veining, their velvet coats', Stephen felt that in such earthly pleasures there was 'a promise of the scent of white jasmine – that is a divine promise – in all flowers & fruits & trees – they are symbols to me . . . I have had two wonderful dreams – now! just as I wrote those words! came a rap!! at my side – dear Lady Lodge!' (who had just died and was buried near Lady Grey at Wilsford). 'What a welcome waiting for her – now I must stop, I get tired easily, which is part of my illness & I try to write as little as possible – rest is the greatest cure for it you know . . .'[23]

But there were other more drastic remedies necessitated by the serious progress of the disease. In March, Stephen had to have a pneumothorax performed on his lung, a surgical technique whereby one lung was collapsed by introducing air between the chest-wall and lung, thus allowing it to rest. A painful operation, but it appeared to be successful in restoring his breathing difficulties – and, as Siegfried told Robert Graves, it saved Stephen's life.

William Walton and Edith Olivier were the first of Stephen's friends to arrive at Haus Hirth. Walton had been staying in Amalfi with Osbert and Sachie Sitwell when Stephen had written to invite him in February. Having obtained from the ever-beneficent Siegfried 'the brass for the ticket',[24] he made his way over to Bavaria. Edith arrived soon after, and soon saw the good that Haus Hirth and Tante Johanna and Onkel Walter were doing for Stephen. 'I feel anyone who is guided to this place . . . must be a chosen person,' she wrote. 'Stephen has been led here for a great purpose – that the loveliness in him may grow and the other side vanish.'[25] Nannie confided in Edith that she had 'deplored Pamela's lack of discipline with her children . . . As a matter of fact, I think Stephen is amazingly unspoilt by it. Its lack has given his genius – spiritual and artistic – full play.'[26]

Edith was surprised when Sassoon came to Haus Hirth on 4 April: he seemed an entirely different man from the 'rather grim alarming aloof poet of London'. The Hirths doted on him, as did all their staff, and Siegfried himself was in an almost childish state of excitement at being back – at Haus Hirth, and with Stephen, who was noticeably improving. Edith saw Sieg running in and out of the room 'saying again and again how happy he is'. And Stephen, equally relishing the attention of his loved ones, sighed: 'What a happy day!' as he lay back after an evening's talk with Siegfried.[27] Rex was the last perfect piece to the picture, and he came in time for Stephen's twenty-third birthday. Although the patient was still sickly, and continuing to receive the pneumothorax weekly, the Heidelberg doctor was performing miracles, and his prognoses had a guarded optimism about them now. Looking at this frail Fra Angelico angel, he wondered poetically 'how anyone so heavenly – so *unerdlich* – so spiritual' could 'face this rude world?'[28]

Arrangements to celebrate the angel's anniversary were complete, bowls of gentians in profusion, a circle of chairs and presents around the birthday cake. 'The candles were lit and then word came that his highness wouldn't be down for ten minutes,' wrote Rex to his mother, 'so they were blown out again hastily.' Onkel Walter and Willie were posted outside the door and halfway up the stairs. 'Twice false alarms . . . Tante Johanna's taper leapt.' Then, at last, Stephen appeared at the top of the staircase, in long velvet dressing gown, 'of orchid mauve with silver braid', and mauve silk pyjamas. A regal descent, then 'moans of delight and kissings for everyone. The goggling faces of rosy country maids could be seen stuffed round the crack of the door while Stephen knelt on the floor.'

Stephen set to opening his presents, 'saying lovely things to each giver'.[29] The best was a pearl-encircled locket from Tante Johanna; it had been given to one of her ancestors by the mad King Ludwig himself. Siegfried's gift was a precious copy of Gerard's *The Herball or Generall Historie of Plantes*, a seventeenth-century work with wonderful hand-coloured woodcuts.

The weeks in bed had resulted in a new Stephen; like a butterfly emerging from its chrysalis, he boasted of new skin 'too lovely – feet & hands like carrarar marble – & face rested & charming'.[30] Stephen's Heidelberg doctor continued his good work: 'He's a peach,' Stephen told Cecil, saying he was inviting him to Wilsford in the autumn. Now Stephen was well enough to go for carriage rides in the countryside, 'well-stocked with "Albert Hall Ball" peasants' and 'rapturous' spring flowers. An artist named Willi Pretorious was about to start work on a portrait of Stephen – 'one isn't painted nearly enough, is one?' – and Rex was to paint a big group of them all. 'Competition for prominence will be a very touchy business I foresee,' noted Stephen; 'my tongue is already flickering like an adder, lest one iota of foreground be denied me – in fact I have suggested such a nice idea – i.e. – that I should recline in the foreground & behind me, knee deep in a Buttercup field, a group in the distance of you all . . .' The Bavarian shops also demanded Stephen's attention, and on a trip with Alice Leone Moat, who must have exhibited some redeeming qualities since Stephen's last assessment of her, they found the Kaufhaus Hartstein, where they spent the afternoon 'turning over silks . . . so many stamped satins – & shot silks that reduce one to pulp – there's nothing like turning a stuff-shop upside-down is there?'[31]

Stephen's letters to Cecil exhibited the influence of the American novels he was reading. He declared he was now 'a simple homespun – & my eyes get large & round when I hear of the great big wicked cities & the gay life . . . the English governess with her water-colours pales before me – sketching gentians here – the spring flowers here are so darn stunning – now you big stiff so long – aw shucks! I'm reading Dodsmith & it's a wow!'[32]

Thus passed the days, the house-guests out on day-beds, soaking up the sun, or going on expeditions. Siegfried, newly rich from the sales of *Memoirs of a Fox-Hunting Man*, discovered that the roof of Haus Hirth had been damaged by the weight of winter snows, and that Walter Hirth wanted to build a further two guest rooms, but hadn't the financial wherewithal. So Siegfried wrote off to his banker for £500, and Stephen 'hearing that – matched it'. So, on his birthday, Herr Hirth was presented by Stephen with one roof tile. 'This means your new roof, given to you by Siegfried and me!'[33]

Rex, in turn, contributed a beautifully drawn advertisement for the guest house to be placed in English magazines: 'Bavarian Highlands: Haus Hirth, Untergrainau bei Garmisch. A Holiday or Rest Home – under ideal conditions. Two hours from Munich; Winter Sports till April; A Paradise of Flowers throughout the Spring. Excellent Doctors locally, and special Comforts for Convalescents. Rooms from 11 marks. Recommended by: Lady Balniel, Prince Ludwig von Hessen, Miss Edith Olivier, Capt. Siegfried Sassoon, Sir Squire Sprigge, Hon. Stephen Tennant, Mr William Walton, Mr Rex Whistler.'

As spring gave way to early summer, the circle of friends separated. Rex, Edith, and Willie had to return to England, and so Stephen and Siegfried were left together, with Nannie, in Bavarian bliss.

Although Sassoon had duties in England, the present attractions were too great. He was working well on his new book, *Memoirs of An Infantry Officer*, when he heard that his *Memoirs of a Fox-Hunting Man* had won the prestigious Hawthornden Prize. 'He is not returning for it, but angelically staying with me,' Stephen told Cecil proudly, asking his friend if he would go to the ceremony. 'It's in July, I think, & should be very funny, with Lord Lonsdale & Eddie Marsh etc. on the platform – do go . . .'[34]

Stephen and Siegfried stayed on at Haus Hirth until the end of May, when Siegfried proposed they move on; he had discovered a house available for rent at Breitenau, not far from Garmisch, and it seemed ideal for a prolonged stay. It would be cheaper than living at Haus Hirth – he, Stephen and Nannie could live self-sufficiently there – and had the bonus of isolation; good for both Stephen's and Nannie's health, and for Siegfried's work. The house at Breitenau was not much more than a cottage, situated on a river-island, the only access a swinging wooden bridge. All around cool, clear water lapped on shallow gravel shores, the streams full of trout. On the island itself were lawns 'ankle-deep' in gentians and wild lily-of-the-valley, amongst glades of silver birch. Behind was 'virgin pine forest, hot and scented in the sunshine, full of giant butterflies, snakes and lizards . . . it's paradise!!' exclaimed Stephen.[35]

Nannie had her own room, and a large verandah below Stephen's own. She was being looked after by a nurse, and her eyes, which had been causing her problems, seemed to have improved. Siegfried had the 'bibliothèque', a library converted into a bedroom, where he was able to work on his book in complete quiet. Stephen's room was alongside, and opened out onto a glorious view of snow peaks 'fading from rose to violet against the evening's dying blue'. It too had a large balcony, on which he soon assembled 'a medley of reptiles, butterflies, orchids, wildflowers, shells and aquariums', as well as Poll's cage, its occupant now fluent in German. The days were now so hot that all he and Siegfried wore were old clothes, Stephen in a torn pair of sailor's trousers and a vest; only Nannie looked respectable, 'like a fairy-tale nurse',[36] in her Bavarian costume. While Siegfried worked, Stephen read; Emily Dickinson seemed particularly suited to this life: 'The soul selects her own society / Then shuts the door.' Or he worked on 'a cynical tiny scrap of a short story',[37] two thousand words long, rather in the vein of *The Second Chance*, which he thought *Vogue* might be interested in.

Sometimes Siegfried would take a break, and come down to cut logs for the fire for cold evenings. He posed for photographs, bare-chested, looking like a real woodsman. Stephen posed too, by the river, in vest and trousers, thin as a birch sapling. Copies were sent home to friends in England. 'You can hardly guess with what pleasure we gazed at those lovely pictures of the S.S.S.,' wrote Ruth Head. 'H.H. begs humbly at intervals for a sight . . . and positively gloats over the Siegfried head with raised arm. He nearly weeps at the thinness of your shoulders which is a real Physician's point of view.'[38] Stephen went hunting for wild-life, finding ten different kinds of orchid. He came back from these forays – 'underfoot one cannot walk for wild scarlet strawberries' – loaded with acquisitions for his two verandah aquaria: fire-bellied toads in one, alpine newts in the other.

All was idyllic, save Nannie Trusler. Her health had deteriorated (Siegfried told Robert Graves that during their time at Garmisch she was 'always on the edge of a stroke'),[39] and by mid-June she had to return to England. She looked quite well when Stephen bade her goodbye; he could not know that the next time he saw her, she would be dying. But with Sieg beside him, Stephen did not even feel Nannie's departure so badly. Ruth Head wrote to him: 'It is not surprising that S.S. should give you his dear society all this time, because I feel sure he is quite as happy to be with you as you to have him . . . Also I somehow feel that in spite of hosts of friends, S.S. is rather a lonely sort of a man, so I refuse to think he is giving up everything he really values by being with you at Breitenau.'[40]

The Hawthornden prize-giving took place on 12 July, and Sassoon's friend Eddie Marsh* reported that 'Edmund Blunden† received the prize for Siegfried and made a pleasant little speech, nervously. His arse is as sharp as a fin, & he doesn't look well – but says he will be alright when he gets his life of Leigh Hunt off his chest . . . Thank you very much for the two photographs – both so beautiful. Yours is so radiant, it is difficult to realize you had even had a day's illness,' he told Stephen. 'It is grand that your spirit is untouched by all you have gone through.'[41]

Rex too received photographs, whilst in Rome, finding them amusing: 'Yes, amusing, particularly Siegfried at the window with flowers at his waist! But of course the seabird on the beach' (i.e. Stephen's striking riverside pose) 'is a dream of loveliness isn't it? (I'm not going to be rude enough to say how did you manage it?)'[42] Privately, Rex felt he'd lost Stephen to Siegfried, remarking wryly to another friend, of Stephen's absence throughout that summer: 'I suppose he's lost in Europe with that fox-hunting man.'[43] And later he commented to Stephen himself, of Sassoon: 'He doesn't want to share you, does he?'[44]

Stephen's condition still necessitated the lung treatment which he had been having every week since March, 'a jading, irksome ordeal for one whose physical courage is not great,' he admitted. He was being given the pneumothorax at a nearby hospital for poor people, run by nuns who looked on Stephen as 'a strange beatific phenomenon. I am called the "Jungle Lord" – they are so sweet & they finger my orchid coloured shirts so reverentially.' When one of the hero-worshipping sisters (who appeared to regard Stephen as a Bavarian Lord Greystoke) found Stephen's monogram on a scarf, 'tremendous excitement ensued, like savages with an alarm clock'.[45]

For both Stephen and Siegfried, Breitenau was heaven on earth. Long summer days of indolence slipped into one another, and all obligations and worries back home receded. Siegfried spoke to Stephen of the bliss of poetry: 'Just one line! – is pure heaven!' and the latter wrote himself: 'That summer night which must always be in the future: The magnetic zone where memory stands with hope, two brothers arms entwined.'[46]

It was cruel of Fate to heap upon Stephen another soul-destroying loss that summer, within a year of the last. They received word in late July that Nannie Trusler's condition had suddenly worsened; it had become

*Edward Marsh (1872–1953). Patron of the arts, early friend of Sassoon's.
†Edmund Blunden (1896–1974). Poet, and one of Sassoon's closest and lifelong friends.

critical and she was in hospital in Chelsea. Siegfried decided to take Stephen back. Once again it was an unhappy journey home by train and boat to England. Rebecca Trusler was old and infirm; Stephen could not have expected her to go on for ever. But why now? Once more his life was upturned, and this death would affect him as deeply, if not more so, than Pamela's death just nine months before.

Back in London it seemed as though there might yet be hope for Nannie's recovery. Stephen saw her on 2 August, then left for Wilsford, happier under the illusion that she might recover. Siegfried had had difficulty getting him through the past few days, so upset was he, although his brother Christopher had been 'very kind and helpful'[47] too. Rex and Edith Olivier came to visit Stephen at Wilsford; when they left, to Edith Stephen looked 'very tragic',[48] standing at the front door as they drove off.

Within a few days Stephen had dashed back to town, knowing now that his beloved Nannie was dying. He went to the hospital, to visit her for the last time. It was almost too heartbreaking for him to see the one stable thing left in his life slip away from him. She died peacefully on 14 August, aged seventy-one, and Rex came to draw her on her death-bed the following day; Nannie in repose, a farewell to the old lady who had looked after him as well as she had Stephen, since his first visit to Wilsford. From his lonely hotel room Stephen sent a note to Elizabeth, on the evening after Nannie's death. 'I'm here till Saturday. I'd love to see you – I'm crazy with unhappiness. I don't know what to do.'[49] Elizabeth, the long-loyal friend, consoled him, sharing his grief; Rebecca Trusler had been part of her life for almost as long as she could remember. Together they cried over Nannie's death.

The following day, Stephen felt well enough to dine with Siegfried at the Union Club, where they accidentally met up with Lytton Strachey. The latter noted Stephen's appearance: 'Extremely beautiful – but frail beyond imagination', and he noted that Sassoon appeared to have become Stephen's 'garde malade'.[50] Edith Olivier, even in her admiration for Rex, compared him unfavourably with Stephen that week, 'exquisitely beautiful and bronzed ... His face beside Rex's looked marvellous.'[51] Stephen left London and returned to Wilsford the next day. Faced with that huge empty house alone, he was glad of the knowledge that Siegfried would be joining him the following week. Slowly Stephen would come round to normal life once more – and to the daunting prospect of running his new home.

Sassoon was a near-constant fixture at Wilsford that autumn, sleeping in a room on the second floor of the thatched wing, close to Stephen who spent his days and nights on the loggia, in the open air. Siegfried brought friends like Edmund Blunden to visit Stephen, who took to Blunden – he visited again in early September – and Stephen maintained contact with the poet even after his friendship with Sassoon had cooled, as he did with so many of the people he met through Siegfried.

Sassoon was at Wilsford for his forty-third birthday, pleased to find Stephen looking well after the recent sunny weather, and four days of 'complete quiet'.[52] Stephen was already seeking the help of his friends in the mammoth task of renovating Wilsford. He asked Rex to look out for statues and rococo dressing-tables. Rex apologized for having neglected him, although he himself had been put off from coming to Wilsford for the weekend, and could not make the next, as he was going to stay at Weston with Sachie and Georgia. In reality, Rex was no longer willing to be at Stephen's beck and call; he had 'that fox-hunting man' to look after him now.

Others felt put out, too. Edith Sitwell suspected Sassoon, with whom she had hitherto been very close, of cancelling arrangements at the last minute in favour of Stephen. The late arrival at Siena the previous year still grated, and fermented into positive unpleasantness. She accused Sassoon of disloyalty and had given him 'blazes': 'I have told him Osbert, Sachie and I perfectly realise his attitude towards us, that we have understood it since last summer,' she told her sister-in-law, Georgia.[53] Siegfried in turn spoke of the spat to Edith Olivier. 'He is angry with them for their spiteful tongues. I see his friendship with Stephen has driven a wedge between the Sitwells . . . I suppose [they] are jealous, also they do like to use their friends as subjects for *bon mots*.'[54]

Stephen tried to stay out of such wranglings, preferring instead to discuss furniture ideas for Wilsford with Cecil. They met in early September, when Cecil told his friend that he was about to be sculpted by the artist, Frank Dobson, whose shiny modernistic head of Osbert Sitwell had received such acclaim in 1922. Stephen thought this a grand scheme, and told Cecil to go ahead and commission one of him, too. 'It would be such fun! – & give us satisfactory feeling to leave England with two dreaming blind echoes of us in stone – left behind – something definitely accomplished.'[55]

However, all did not go smoothly. A week later Stephen was still excited: Cecil was already sitting for the sculptor, whilst Stephen wanted to be 'a voluptuous skeleton' for his bust, 'just cheekbones & a navel really', conceding that Dobson was 'very expensive – but I suppose his name is very famous'. [56] Even so, Cecil had managed to haggle down Dobson's price, but Stephen's subsequent sittings began to go disastrously wrong. Evidently there was a clash of personalities. Stephen complained of the artist's complete lack of interest: 'He doesn't shew he even likes doing me at all. I might be the dreariest client for all he shows! . . . all he says is "you are like Puffin"[*] – Just when I'm feeling like Lina Cavalieri in her prime.'[57] As a consequence of Mr Dobson's lack of interest in his client – when Epstein, Stephen pointed out, had been ecstatic – the commission was abandoned, and the project never completed.

Beaton made a more successful introduction when he recommended Stephen go to Syrie Maugham's shop with a view to buying for Wilsford. 'Syrie's', on Duke Street, already a Mecca for the fashionable, was full of her plaster-cast palm tree decor, limed and whitened Louise Quinze pieces (mostly nineteenth-century reproductions, which didn't stop the outcry that Mrs Maugham was ruining antique furniture), and made-to-order rugs by Marion Dorn. Stephen's first order was tall lamps for Wilsford (he later bought a large pink palm tree standard lamp from the shop), and he was thinking of having a rug woven with his face on it – and perhaps Siegfried's too. Another shop, Denham McLaren's, supplied seating for his new Pink Room, which Stephen bought whilst in town for another photo-session, at the Becks' studio, with Cecil. The two friends posed together, in black and white hooped rugby jerseys, looking quite sporty, although Stephen rather regretted the 'poisonous wave' in his golden hair.[†] Siegfried too had been persuaded to undergo the torturous process of photography before Cecil's lens; 'large heads', requested Stephen, as though he were a mother sending her son to the barbers. 'I want one marvellous full face & one marvellous profile looking his very best – not the tortured, scarred hermit . . . and could the faces be pale against dark instead of the reverse? – but I leave it all to you.'[59]

Stephen was very pleased with the results, a 'continual joy . . . the one that manages to be deer-eyed & quizzical-mouthed is really ravishing,' he noted.[60] More Syrie pieces arrived; delivery was slow, but Cecil, the wonder-worker, hurried them up. Stephen was now on the lookout for a

---

[*]Margot's son Anthony 'Puffin' Asquith (1902–68), who was making his name as a film director.
[†]Stephen's appearance continued to draw attention. 'We spoke much of dear Stephen and of the spiteful things said about him,' wrote Edith Olivier after seeing him with Sassoon on 23 October. '[Stephen] evidently does mind very much the way people talk and he *won't* do anything which looks as if he minds. Rex and Cecil tonight were saying that his hair is more becoming if flat to the head and not waved but they daren't tell him so because it *also* is "wiser".'[58]

tall cheval glass, preferably with a coronet on top, and Mr McLaren was invited down to Wilsford to give his personal advice on further requirements.

Siegfried continued to lavish presents on Stephen, who appeared to be buying enough for himself. One of Sieg's tokens was Swainson's *Exotic Conchology*, in which he wrote:

> *Stephen*
> *War has its idiot Shells:*
> *How different are these,*
> *designed by diligent Nature*
> *For her Devotees . . .*
>
> from SS, Oct.3, 1929.[61]

Throughout October Stephen's health improved. The Heidelberg doctor had arrived earlier, and pronounced his lungs clear of infection, although the patient would still need nine months of rest and recuperation. 'All we can do is surround him with our love,'[62] said Siegfried, which he did.

Stephen busied himself being parochial, with 'the Vicar and his wife to tea, "waifs & strays" bazaars – & designing the garden which is going to be divine!!' he told Elizabeth.[63] On the first weekend of November, the weather still unaccountably hot as an Indian summer prevailed, Rex was at last able to come down for a visit. Siegfried was away, but William Walton and Arthur Waley were there on the Saturday, when Lytton Strachey drove over from Ham Spray, where E. M. Forster was staying with him and Dorothy Carrington.[*] After a 'lovely drive', Strachey and friends arrived to find 'no Siegfried', but the others out in the garden:

'We had lunch on the lawn, in such blazing sun that our host was given an excuse for sending for a yellow parasol for himself and a series of gigantic plaited straw hats for his guests. We were filmed almost the whole time by a footman (a dark young man in spectacles). We inspected the aviary – very charming, with the most wonderful parrots floating from perch to perch and eventually from shoulder to shoulder. Finally, we went indoors, and in a darkened chamber were shown various films of the past, worked by the footman, who also turned on a gramophone with suitable records. Stephen was extremely amiable, though his lips were

---

[*]Lytton Strachey was to live only two more years before dying of stomach cancer at Ham Spray, where Carrington, obsessively but unrequitedly in love with him, attempted suicide twice in the days after his death – the second time successfully, although in botched manner, taking a shotgun to her body.

rather too magenta for my taste; Arthur Waley was positively gay; Morgan shone as required; W.W. said absolutely nothing; and I, sitting next to Rex Whistler, couldn't make up my mind whether I was attracted or repelled by his ugly but lust-provoking face . . .'[64]

It was a measure of Stephen's magical properties that he inspired such serious figures as Arthur Waley to be 'positively gay' in his company. The visit also marked one of Morgan Forster's first encounters with Stephen, the beginning of yet another close friendship between author and aesthete.

But in these autumn months waves of depression hit Stephen in between such pleasant garden parties. At his low points, he felt ill and wretched and, with nobody left to fuss over him, he tried to impose some sort of self-discipline; he desperately wanted to avoid falling so ill again. He told Cecil: 'You can't imagine how lonely it is without my mother & Nannie . . . I am in some ways so completely desolate.' He felt the whole definition of his life had changed. ' . . . In a way, luckily, I don't feel able to have fun like I used to – or to tire myself out – & think it more than worth it – which I used to do.' Stephen acknowledged that 'all this is silly & gloomy but to anyone as feverishly social in their temperament as I am ill-health is a crushing tragedy'. Bidding goodbye to Cecil, who was off to America again, he looked forward to meeting up in the spring, to knock Wilsford 'to bits . . . & flood it with Borzois – & start a stable & ride on the downs – & live in white glass rooms confected by Syrie & be oh so beautiful & gay!!!'[65] But even as Cecil got ready to sail from Southampton on the *Aquitania*, Stephen was hurriedly packing his own bags at Wilsford: he and Sieg were off on their travels again – to Paris, and then Sicily.

Chapter 11

In Sicily

Let us be true to what we have shared and seen,
And as our amulet this idyll save.

— Siegfried Sassoon: 'In Sicily'

THE last truly happy period of Stephen's relationship with Siegfried Sassoon began with their journey to Paris that November. There they took a suite at the Plaza Athenée, on the Avenue Montaigne. One of the purposes of coming to the city was to meet André Gide, the great French writer, who paid them the honour of visiting the two at their hotel.

The city itself had revitalized Stephen. He felt 'gay & fresh', he told Cecil. 'My new suits (all copied from yours!) are dreams – the whole of Paris "gawps" at me.' A better reaction than that which he and Siegfried had been experiencing in their home capital: 'Osbert was unbelievably catty in London,' Stephen told Cecil. 'His book is dull . . .'[1] (Sitwell's novel *The Man Who Lost Himself* is about a young writer who meets himself as an old man. Osbert's 'cattiness' was part of the general Sitwell disapproval of Siegfried's friendship with Stephen. One explanation put forward was that Stephen had had a brief affair with Osbert's new love, David Horner – not impossible, given Horner's golden good looks and family connections with the Tennants. However, Osbert's love/hate relationship with Sassoon explains much; when Stephen had left Osbert and company in London, the latter 'was in a very suspicious queasy state bordering on the mania housemaids have for key holes'.)[2]

Stephen also felt the loss of Nannie when in the city both of them loved. But he told Elizabeth that he was 'profoundly conscious of her nearness . . . that of course makes the lack of her physical presence the more unbearable – but I often feel her presence so strongly that I am compelled to speak aloud to her and then I get waves of happiness most strange and wonderfully – such is the power of love!'³ Stephen would never travel without a framed photograph of Rebecca Trusler to put beside his bed.

On Friday 22 November, Stephen and Siegfried left Paris and sped comfortably south to the Italian coast, where Sassoon had arranged to see Max and Florence Beerbohm in Rapallo. They booked into the Excelsior Hotel on arrival, and the following day went to the Beerbohms' Villino Chiaro for lunch, 'an enchanting experience' for Siegfried, 'of which one can only say that it is as enjoyable as reading his books and looking at his drawings'.⁴

The Villino Chiaro's terrace was on the roof, 'with the blue expanse of the sea beyond the parapet wall creating an illusion of our being suspended in the sky, high above the world',⁵ wrote Siegfried. They spent all afternoon exchanging news and gossip and literary chat; only as twilight began to fall did the two travellers take leave of their solicitous hosts, and return to the hotel. Stephen and Siegfried spent most of their stay with the Beerbohms. 'Their liking for me and Stephen so blissfully comforting,'⁶ wrote Sassoon after their visit of 26 November. The weather had continued to be bad: 'The sun never shone,'⁷ recalled Siegfried years later. That afternoon it rained and the wind blew. At lunchtime, the curtains of the villa were drawn, 'and we sat around the table by soft electric light, in a homely little universe of our own'.⁸

Stephen and 'Mrs Max' got on very well: he had 'won her heart entirely',⁹ noted Siegfried. Stephen would sit with Florence Beerbohm in rapt talk, often of Florence's stage career. Siegfried was proud of his beautiful friend; Stephen's good manners and his ability to get on with people, especially those more advanced in years than he, made him the perfect guest. Despite the continuing rain, Siegfried managed to take Stephen along to visit W. B. Yeats, who lived nearby. Sassoon confided in Max Beerbohm that he personally thought the poet 'a bit of a poseur',¹⁰ but Stephen got on well with the great Irishman, who told him: 'I love the French language – because I understand it so little; the charm would go if I spoke it well.' 'I love mystery,' added Yeats.¹¹

The weather was one factor in Siegfried's decision to seek the sunnier south. On 7 December they had arrived at Naples, 'unbelievably lovely'¹² in hot sunshine. They stayed high above the town, in hotel rooms looking out over the sea to Capri, Vesuvius, and down to the roofs of Naples itself. Poll the parrot sat in her gilded cage on the balcony rail, and listened 'to the multi-coloured hum of the town',¹³ cocking an eye at the azure seas. Here Siegfried bought Stephen a copy of *English Eccentrics and*

Eccentricities by John Timbs, a Victorian study of 'Strange Sights and Sporting Scenes', 'Delusions, Impostures and Fanatic Missions', which together they customized by sticking into the back pages various Sitwell newspaper clippings – 'Never heard of the Sitwells', etc. – with cut-out heads of Edith stuck on to other pictures, and the addition of a pair of glasses here, a bright pink nose there.* This greatly amused both of them, though Osbert, who kept his own press cuttings on public display in a bowl in the drawing room of Carlyle Square, would have been outraged by their impudence.

From Naples the two adventurers set off by boat for Sicily, and came to the capital city, Palermo, in mid-December. They stayed in the Grand Hotel des Palmes, on the Via Roma, where Wagner had completed *Parsifal* in 1882. Stephen's imagination was fired by the old city and its distant views of Stromboli and Etna, volcanoes which smoked under a brilliant blue and cloudless sky. This potent seascape burnt itself into his creative memory, a montage of mountain peaks and vivid blue seas which would become the obsessional centre of Stephen's paintings, from the snow-capped volcanoes and still bays of the cover he drew for his 1935 diary, to the luminous ink paintings of his old age – 'the blue of redemption'.

So 'southern and divine' did Stephen find Palermo that all time appeared different. The palmy town, with their 'great white hotel', was 'all cactus & hibiscus & nostalgic-eyed loungers – the verb "to lounge" is symbol of everything'. Every sense was stimulated; the brightly-painted carts were 'smothered with bells – everywhere you are deafened by tinkles & barrel-organs'. Even here, in this 'R. Firbank city' where Europe ended, high fashion, courtesy of the couturier Charles James, came. He had made Stephen 'the stunningest fancy-dress – black trousers that seem glued to every fissure & ripple of thigh & bottom & an ineffably limp shirt of creamy satin like ultra, ultra Devonshire cream mixed with mother-of-pearl'.[14] Stephen's near-fetishistic description of a uniform, for which there must have been very little practical use in a mainly rural Italian island, is characteristically intense, typical of his lavish appreciation of beautiful things.

From Palermo, Stephen and Siegfried set off to explore the island. A valley on the way to Noto, where Stephen recalled an almond tree in blossom 'all humming with bees & yellow swallowtail butterflies',[15] was to be Siegfried's inspiration for a poem drafted in those hazy, happy days,

---

*Their skit was prescient, for three years later Edith Sitwell published her own survey of *English Eccentrics*.

written to encapsulate his love for the time, place and person of that winter 'honeymoon' – 'In Sicily':

Because we two can never again come back
On time's one forward track,
Never again first happily explore
This valley of rocks and vines and orange-trees,
Half Biblical and half Hesperides,
With dark blue seas calling from a shell-strewn shore:

By the strange proven power of Spring's resistless green
Let us be true to what we have shared and seen,
And as our amulet this idyll save.
And since the unreturning day must die,
Let it forever be lit by an evening sky
And the wild myrtle grow upon its grave.[16]

Siegfried wrote out the verse in his careful, precise hand, and proudly presented his lover with the token. This 'amulet idyll', another island paradise, provided both travellers with ceaseless joy in those weeks of winter and early spring in Sicily. At Siracuse, staying at the Hotel Villa Politi high on a rocky outcrop north of the city, by the Cappuccini church, Stephen recorded the 'musical comedy "maid of the mountains" – all caves – & tropical creepers & swarthy peasants and sunsets made for Jose Collins'. They spent a quiet time in the hotel, Siegfried continuing work on *Memoirs of an Infantry Officer* and Stephen sitting on the balcony, 'wrapped in dirty white velvet',[17] sunbathing, or sketching the Cappucci convent. From here came a photograph of the two, idling on their sunny Sicilian terrace; Sassoon sits up on one wall, a Venus ear sea shell clasped to his own ear, whilst Stephen leans back in his silk Charles James beach pyjamas, his delicate face turned upwards to the Mediterranean sun.

On the shore, Stephen would watch as Siegfried waded into 'that delicious sea' to find him those shells, 'Venus Ears and Corals and Coral fans – like in Boucher's pictures'.[18] These were the jewels Sicily had to offer, the amulets the lovers shared, which stayed by Stephen's side throughout his life. Sassoon was completely, irrevocably, obsessively in love with Stephen: 'You are the person I've most loved in my whole life,'[19] he told him. And then Stephen loved him too. 'The plates we filled with Venus-ear shells . . . the Bee orchids we painted,' recalled Stephen eight years later. 'I shall never forget that lapis sea beyond orange groves, or S.S.'s head silhouetted against the lamplight in his bedroom as he pared & cleaned the sea-shells . . . & on top of the wardrobe Polly snoozing in her cage.'[20]

But that was in the hindsight of time, at once the most corrosive and healing of forces. The years had already advanced upon Stephen; he was shocked to find he was, at the age of twenty-three, going grey – or white-haired, at least. 'One side is nearly grey & silver glimmers everywhere!!' he told Cecil. 'In spite of all this I'm enjoying myself hilariously – but feeling ill every few days.'[21] In Siracuse, Stephen acquired a copy of E. M. Forster's *A Passage to India*, and on the fly-leaf he wrote out the quotation: ' . . . But really, that was all, so light did he travel.' This was how Stephen thought of this holiday; careless and carefree, out of time and worry, and the responsibilities for his own life and future that his recent bereavements had forced on his shoulders – shoulders too weak to bear such a burden.

Friends were just across the water: Osbert Sitwell, David Horner and William Walton were all staying in Amalfi. Walton was in financial difficulty once more. 'The question is how am I going to exist between April 17th, when I leave here for Berlin,' he wrote to Siegfried, '& April 24th when I get paid (Mks 500) for my concert, & incidentally how to get there even . . . Stephen may well blame me for my insipid letters, but I have no equivalent of the exciting Siracusan life to describe so he can hardly expect anything else. It is good news to hear that he is so well – so pink & chubby & I hope you are the same.'[22] Uncle Sieg came to the rescue, and Willie wrote back from Amalfi to thank him; and Stephen too, for the latter had bestowed on the composer an important present – he had provided the wherewithal for a new piano – his one stipulation being that its legs should resemble those of Mrs Belloc Lowndes.

Meanwhile, William the footman was at Agrigento, filming his employer against ruined Greek temples. 'Sieg's in grand form,' Stephen reported to Cecil. 'He gives you a horse-bite on your behind in return for the large tweak I gave him from you. Georgia & Sachie are on the Duke of W[estminster]'s yacht at Barcelona,'[23] he noted, adding a note of personal doubt as to the suitability of the match between his old friend Loelia and the immensely wealthy Duke.[*]

Seeing out the rest of that stay in Sicily left Stephen with strong impressions which would recur to him over the years. 'Sicily, Siracuse. The Latominas,' he wrote in the margin of a book years later. 'The low hedges of Rosemary, the freesias – Iris – Anemones – Almonds in flower. The fountain at Palermo – with mauve nephar.'[25] Such inscriptions appear on Stephen's books and papers over the rest of his life, the marginalia of memory, stored away to relive again and again in future years.

With the beginning of April, Stephen and Siegfried left their paradise island to return to Rapallo and the Beerbohms. Florence had booked them into a different hotel, the Bristol, and hoped they would find them more comfortable rooms, offering softer pillows and mosquito nets. The two joked about half the contents of the Villino Chiaro ending up at their hotel. Back chatting with his friends, Siegfried noted that he was 'quite rusty as a talker, after conversing with no one but Stephen since December 2nd!'[26]

Spring came to Rapallo, and filled their room with 'a bower of clotted-cream carnations'. Cecil sent Stephen a caricature of Edith Sitwell – 'I laughed so much at Edith S's smudged eyelids! – Siegfried's laugh echoed through the hotel . . .'[27] Back in London, the Sitwell feud simmered on. Edith wrote sourly of Siegfried that he had 'found it hard to condone any luxury until the last two years, in which he seems to have suffered a sex-change'. Asked by the Sexual Reform Society to help campaign for greater freedoms and support for the legalization of homosexuality, she replied: 'I shouldn't have thought anybody needed encouraging,' adding, 'and really we have quite enough of it without training fresh ones.'[28] It should

---

[*]Loelia Ponsonby married Bendor, 2nd Duke of Westminster, 'in a blaze of publicity'[24] on 20 February of that year. The Duke of Westminster made an unpleasant name for himself, hounding Earl Beauchamp from the country by informing the King he had created a known homosexual a Knight of the Garter. Beauchamp lived in exile thereafter, and his misfortune prompted Evelyn Waugh to characterize the Earl (father of Hugh Lygon, the real model for Sebastian Flyte) as Lord Marchmain in *Brideshead Revisited*.

be remembered the sort of relationship Stephen and Siegfried were conducting was still very frowned upon by the majority, and carried stiff prison sentences in England – which was why foreign travel was so attractive to homosexual men of their class.

Virginia Woolf had her own observations on homosexuality to make that month when she had spent an evening talking at Raymond Mortimer's,* 'chiefly upon the atmosphere of buggery'. Lytton Strachey, Morgan Forster and Eddy Sackville-West comprised the company. 'Anyway, he said, Ensor (I forget) looked very pretty in a white suit – the rest oh so hideous. At this the other buggers pricked up their ears & became somehow silly. I mean rather giggly & coy. An atmosphere entirely secluded, intimate, & set on one subject . . . A photograph of Stephen Tennant (Siegfried Sassoon goes to the same dressmaker) in a tunic, in an attitude was shown about; also little boys at a private school. Morgan became unfamiliar, discussing the beauties of Hilton Young's stepson [Peter Scott]. "His skating is magnificent" (then in an undertone deploring some woman's behaviour). This all made a tinkling, private, giggling, impression. As if I had gone in to a men's urinal.'[29]

But Stephen and Siegfried cared little for the opinions of friends and acquaintances at home. The former had discovered 'stunning sailor clothes . . . Italian fisherman's – gaudy scarves & sashes – coarse, striped utterly divine stuffs – smelling like stage fishermen & endowing one with sizzling sex-appeal the moment one puts one on,' he told Cecil.[30]

Another recipient of Stephen's missives from Rapallo was the society hostess and interior decorator Sibyl Colefax (at whose salon Stephen was amused to be asked, by a rich American woman, 'Are you one of the Sitwells?'[31]). As a friend of Pamela's, she had a 'soft spot' for young Stephen, and would carefully glue into her scrapbooks the photographs and cards he sent her. Stephen was also to become a customer at Sibyl Colefax's shop when furnishing Wilsford in the mid-thirties. Lady Colefax's social engineering was prodigious (for which reason she was widely regarded as a model for Benson's Lucia); Margot Asquith remarked that one could not even refer to the birth of Christ without Sibyl claiming to have been in the manger. Of Colefax's character, Stephen was percipient. A year or so later, when Siegfried was musing on the

*Bloomsbury art critic (1895–1980). The *Oxford and Cambridge News* of 13 June 1928 noted: 'Raymond Mortimer had a successful party in Gordon Place, at his house which has a room with walls painted by Duncan Grant and a dining-room papered with foreign newspapers varnished. Here Stephen Tennant made a good "late" entrance in white . . .'

inadvisability of naming roses after people, and wondered aloud if there was one called 'Lady Colefax', Stephen replied: 'There ought to be a BLACKCURRANT named after her.'[32]

Stephen told Sibyl of 'heavenly days' at Rapallo, 'eating peerless food to an accompaniment of peerless quips & cracks – leaving one's nose in freesias & wallflowers for as long as one wants – sitting in the summer's warmth on the terrace . . . Mrs Max is almost more kind than any human being ought to be – my hotel bedroom doesn't know itself – as it is practically refurnished from Villino Chiaro.'[33]

At the end of April, Stephen, Siegfried, William, and Poll set off for a leisurely trip to Paris, stopping at Aix-les-Bains, then Biarritz (where once Stephen overheard someone say, 'No, I don't like him, but if I were a Mum he'd be the only boy in the world for me.' 'I was very made-up,' noted the boy, '& beautiful as a vision').[34] In Paris, Stephen saw Tchelitchew again, who completed one of many portraits of Stephen, 'full of the esprit Anglais'.[35] The result of one of Stephen's sittings was 'such a wicked ivy-leaf shaped face – so lovely'.[36] A later Beaton photograph has Stephen lying face up, with an upturned table behind him pinned with Tchelitchew's ink sketches of his head, done from every conceivable angle. Stephen bought at least two Tchelitchews in Paris that spring – 'The One Who Fell', a strange, typically Tchelitchevian view of a corpse-like male body from the feet looking up to the head; and 'The Dream', described by James Thrall Soby* as one of the artist's 'wine red paintings . . . showing a group of figures peering from beneath the horizon at an outstretched nude male figure'.[37]

Stephen and Siegfried stayed at the Pavillon Henri IV, at St Germain-en-Laye, just outside Paris, until the second week of May. While they were there, Stephen sent a message of congratulations to his old friend Elizabeth, who was about to become the Countess of Iddesleigh. 'Please give a special smile to me and Nannie at your wedding – we shall be there smiling through tears of pure happiness for your happiness',[38] and he sent a bracelet of sapphires, diamonds and seed-pearls as a wedding-present – along with a flower brooch which he had made – for the woman who might have been his wife.†

*In the catalogue (in which Stephen's Tchelitchews were illustrated) to the 1942 Tchelitchew exhibition at the Museum of Modern Art.
†Elizabeth married Henry Stafford Northcote, third Earl of Iddesleigh (1900–1970), who served as a major in the Welsh Guards in the Second World War. After the trials and traumas of bringing up her family in wartime London, she and her husband eventually settled down to quiet rural life at the Iddesleigh country seat, Pynes, outside Exeter, where she still lived in 1990.

There was an altercation between Stephen and Siegfried at Saint Germain, their first recorded argument, when, after a long drive in the rain, they squabbled over some small point, and ended up not speaking to each other. Stephen's irritability may have been ascribed by his friend to his tiredness after months of travelling away from home, and the recurrence of illness, of which there were already disturbing indications. But Sassoon was also witnessing signs of Stephen's capriciousness, and his inherent instability, that would prove disastrous for their relationship in the next few years.

Chapter 12

There's Something Wrong in Paradise

She would say: 'Other people rule my life,' and it was true. But she allowed them to do it only because her superstitious fancy had invested them with magical importance regarding her own destiny, and never because their personalities awoke any profound sympathy or understanding in her.

— Paul Bowles: *Let It Come Down*

ON 14 May Stephen and Siegfried returned to England. Back at Wilsford, its newly-planted gardens full of 'creamy, gold-dusted lilies'[1] (the owner having grown yet fonder of the funereal flowers, a decadent symbol of his own mortality), Stephen found much work to be done to achieve the high standards of renovation he had set himself. But there was an impediment to the ongoing dynamism of Wilsford's redecoration; its young owner's health was once more at risk. Siegfried was seriously worried. Without Nannie or Pamela, who would arrest Stephen's impulsive behaviour enough to impose the strict regime of rest and quiet that was absolutely necessary to keep the tubercle germ in abeyance, there was now only one candidate for that onerous duty: Sassoon himself.

In Rapallo in April Siegfried had expressed an anxiety for a London doctor to X-ray Stephen's lungs; but Stephen was already over-exciting himself. At Wilsford, he ran excitedly round his house, with armfuls of cut flowers, arranging his sea treasures from Sicily. Siegfried made his move, to install himself there as *garde malade*. But where, in the light and air of the Mediterranean, Siegfried's companionship was vital and required, here, in Stephen's shadowy country retreat, with its memories of childhood and Nannie, depression took hold again, and the part of

Stephen that Edith Olivier had hoped would disappear under the influence of Haus Hirth re-emerged. His selfishness, and wish to be his own master, introduced an insidious thought; perhaps Siegfried's attentions were not as necessary or desirable as he thought them to be.

Stephen was even beginning to doubt his own taste. 'I'm making Wilsford hideous,' he told Cecil. 'I've no taste suddenly & a pit of doubt in my stomach about every colour & now I am so ill & apathetic . . .'² Beaton had just acquired his own country house, and it pleased Stephen that his friend would be near to him. '"Ashcombe" is such a lovely name!' wrote Stephen on hearing of the rural paradise Cecil had discovered in the Wiltshire downs. 'What fun it'll be exchanging & alternating visits – I shall be very catty if your salon is prettier than mine – and I shall stolidly imitate all your ideas.'³

There was a constant interchange of such ideas; white-painted side-drums were to be found in both establishments, as were baroque and rococo pieces chosen more for their exuberance than for their utility. In many cases, the similarity between the decoration of Ashcombe and Wilsford was the result of the meeting between the Vogue Regency styles of Syrie Maugham and Sibyl Colefax with the theatrical originality of Stephen and Cecil's tastes, present since youth. Arbiters of taste often return to the prevailing aesthetic of their childhood for inspiration (Beaton was to draw on Edwardian memories for *My Fair Lady*). Stephen too remained inspired by that time; indeed, the mixture of his mother's Edwardian house and his own fancies resulted in something quite close to the boudoir of the actresses Gaby Deslys or Sarah Bernhardt, of whom both he and Cecil remained devoted admirers.

The redecoration of Wilsford became all-important to Stephen. When Pamela had died, leaving him with an income of around £15,000 per annum, what was a boy to do with a huge house (and staff) all to himself? What to do, but decorate; to impose his own taste upon his childhood domicile, an attempt to exorcise its ghosts. Unable to take part in London society, Stephen threw himself into the task of directing the refurbishment of his house from his bed, and that autumn was immersed in ideas for 'chic, amusing lighting' for the drawing room: 'I want shafts of light & coloured light & all sorts.'⁴ He sought more Syrie pieces, wondering how to cope with white carpets ('don't they all get black in a week?'), and told Cecil he would be in town in a week or so to seek out 'silver & white baroque or Louis XVI furniture – I want fat carved console tables for the drawing room . . . Also I want any silver mirrors or lustre or silver wood in any form – I say this just in case you see any or hear of any for sale – for Wilsford is all upside down at the moment & empty as I am struggling with convalescence to start setting it right . . . This is what I look like now only thinner.' Stephen included a self-portrait with his letter, an awful skull-like head with stretched and drawn skin over gaping eye-sockets.[5]

'I'm very dull to meet,' Stephen added, 'but the skin on my hands is like fine snow over brittle sticks & I've much to show you – a sapphire ring!! – shells – coral – the new lily garden – the new loggia & fountain . . . my room as I write is all tuberoses & three varieties of vast lilies.' Wilsford's burgeoning charms were somewhat tarnished by staff problems, however. 'I've an Ass of a nurse,' he reported, who was 'ghoulishly bright – I snub her from morning to night'. He had also heard from his sister Clare – a rare occurrence – that she had enjoyed a photo-session with Cecil, and was 'much impressed by your cleverness',[6] said Stephen with a degree of surprise. (Years later, he observed that Beaton's good manners were so impressive that 'even her acid tongue spared his "mystique"'.[7]) Clare disapproved of her brother's effeminate ways, preferring fox-hunting men – an irony which would not have occurred to her. She told friends stories of how her eccentric brother nursed his tortoise, and grieved over its death, and laughed aloud over the newest tale of his silliness in her drawing room. There was no love lost between Pamela's eldest and youngest.

Stephen continued to sleep outside, as he had done when he was a child. The summer night air was good for his lungs: 'Great fun! – and so refreshing – my hair is always in thick bright curls,' he told Cecil, '& I hope to get very plump & very fetching.'[8] It was in the new loggia that Cecil photographed Stephen on a rare visit that summer (Siegfried having imposed strict limitations on his charge's social life) – Stephen lying abed, looking immaculately ill, the pallor of the consumptive sitting well on his fine features, enhanced by a little lip colour and powder. Nannie's framed photograph is on one side table, whilst on the wall behind him a *Daily Telegraph* fly-poster advertises Siegfried's new book.

Beaton's letters that summer were full of the new love of his life, Peter Watson. They had met in Vienna, and Cecil was 'hypnotized' by this tall, dark, and handsome playboy of the arts. 'I long to know P.W.,' said Stephen. 'He sounds perfect – I adore little behinds too – and am always drawing sailors with tiny tight behinds like terriers.'[9] When Stephen did meet Watson, he established a friendly relationship with the wealthy patron of the arts, a diffident, cultured man who was to found the Institute of Contemporary Arts and finance *Horizon* magazine. 'I liked Peter very much,' recalled Stephen of Watson, 'an aesthete of great distinction.'[10]

But for the present, such socializing was strictly forbidden. 'I'm not sure if I shall be allowed to see you & Rex,' Stephen wrote when Cecil proposed another visit, to talk about his plans for Ashcombe and its gardens. Stephen could not even apply himself to his own household tasks now. 'I shall not go on with Wilsford till the Spring – as I shall be unwell till then,' he announced, 'unable to cope with anything – & I hate "half-doing" things – I'm not going to see anyone either . . .'[11] No one except Sassoon, that is.

'I would gladly die for him,' announced Siegfried,[12] and as Stephen weakened and slipped into a decline, so his lover took control. Further visits from friends were summarily curtailed. A planned weekend with Rex was diverted to the Daye House, with an invitation to come over for an afternoon if Stephen's health was up to it. But Rex declined, resenting Sassoon's influence over his old friend. He confided a dislike of 'pipey men'[13] – a veiled reference to Siegfried. Cecil was likewise put off by an apologetic letter from 'S.S.': 'But you will understand how essential it is that Stephen should avoid all excitement & fatigue. He has started his systematic treatment, & until his temperature is down & he has put on a little weight he must be quiet.' Siegfried was in no doubt that 'his life depends on the disease being checked'.[14] Even in the early thirties, tuberculosis remained the most dreaded infectious disease, killing between 30,000 and 40,000 people a year, many of them Stephen's age.

Susan Sontag's essay, *Illness as Metaphor*,[15] cites 'febrile activity' and 'passionate resignation' as features of this disease of extreme contrasts. 'Having TB was imagined to be an aphrodisiac, and to confer extraordinary powers of seduction,' she observes. It was 'a disease of time; it speeds up life, highlights it, spiritualizes it'; indeed, TB was thought of 'as a decorative, often lyrical death' to undergo. The romantic notion, of a literally consuming passion, was very much encouraged by the poetic nineteenth-century victim; it became almost glamorous to look sickly. The idea that only 'sensitive' people suffered TB must have occurred to Stephen, whose favourite writers – Shelley, Keats, Katherine Mansfield, Emily Brontë – were thus smitten. Sontag quotes Shelley's letter to Keats: 'This consumption is a disease particularly fond of people who write such good verses as you have done.'

Sontag's ideas on the psychological effects of TB explain much, especially in the light of later developments. She observes that sex could be prescribed as a therapy to sufferers. 'Like all really successful metaphors, the metaphor of TB was rich enough to provide for two contradictory applications. It described the death of someone (like a child) thought too "good" to be sexual: the assertion of an angelic psychology.' Thus, Stephen as the faerie-child, either too frail for these physicalities himself, or seeing them childishly, as a game. Even the foreign travel necessary for its treatment made the sufferer 'a wanderer in endless search of a healthy place'. As Sontag observes, 'It was a way of retiring from the world without having to take responsibility for the decision.'

Stephen had Siegfried to take responsibility for him. In the eight weeks since their return, Sassoon had had a progressively more harrowing time, attempting to control both Stephen, and his doctors, whose behaviour was 'enough to send one crazy'.[16] He had spent all summer at Wilsford, with only short visits to his London flat. On 12 July he was in town to see the Beerbohms, who were in England, and proposed that they come down with Sibyl Colefax, who was driving to Wilsford the next day. 'You could combine Stephen with Stonehenge, which is only two miles away.'[17]

It was this apparent selectiveness that annoyed Stephen's old friends. Rex was eventually allowed a weekend visit, when Stephen happily showed his friend the shells he had collected from Sicily, which he had been sketching. On the Sunday evening, however, Stephen became tired and despondent, which communicated itself to Rex. Rex tore up a shell drawing Stephen had done, 'because he thought it would discourage S. from drawing shells', wrote Siegfried in his journal. 'So I was up late with the two of them, in succession, straightening out their sorrows!'[18]

A subsequent visit from Whistler was recorded as though Sassoon himself were the doctor. 'He talked to S., 2.30 – 3.'[19] Rex found out days later that while he could have only half-hour bedside talks with Stephen, Siegfried had invited his friend, Glen Byam Shaw, to stay the weekend. Rex liked Byam Shaw, but admitted he was resentful. He had come to feel a stranger, 'uncertain and shy, in a house full of memories'.[20]

The progression of Stephen's illness that summer – indeed, for some summers to come – consumed all of Sassoon's energies. Doctors came from Salisbury, London, and even from Germany, in an attempt to check the TB germ. Influenza was an additional hazard, and in late May, with Stephen's temperature rises being plotted in detail, Siegfried became worried that his friend was not receiving the proper treatment.

Christopher Glenconner had called in Dr Kempe, the family surgeon from Salisbury (seen as a 'mismanager' of illnesses by Sassoon, and who, according to Edith Olivier, had allowed Stephen to go on for six months in consumption five years previously, without diagnosing anything serious), who had permitted Stephen to take his own temperature and to eat ordinary food, which had resulted in acute constipation. Siegfried also noted that a tubercular cow had been discovered at Wilsford, and yet had not been destroyed, thus exposing Stephen to yet another source of the tubercle germ. It was only when Lord Grey visited Sir Oliver Lodge, and the latter's daughter expressed surprise that there was no nurse in attendance, that one was called. This on the seventh day of Stephen's fever (the worrying symptoms of the secondary stage of TB being swinging temperature changes in the sufferer). Dr Chandler, a London lung specialist, was sent for, and he diagnosed paratyphoid.

Chandler also took three sputum tests, the last of which indicated TB; yet he told Sassoon there was no trouble in Stephen's lungs. Siegfried appealed to Henry Head and his wife, Ruth, for help. Sassoon complained that Stephen's family were ineffectual, saying that Christopher was decent enough in his own way, but was casual in his attitude to his youngest brother, and when he had visited Stephen on 24 May, had spent two hours smoking cigarettes in the invalid's bedroom. Christopher trusted Dr Chandler, observed Siegfried, and was prejudiced against all Germans (Sassoon wanted to send to Heidelberg again – it was no coincidence that his hero, W. H. Rivers, had trained there). Frustrated by the bungling, Sassoon came to regard himself as the only competent person in a situation he saw as increasingly serious. He was outraged when Dr Kempe told Stephen that the last TB test had been positive, 'to make him understand that he must keep quiet',[21] and the doctor was distinctly off-hand with Siegfried when he asked the doctor questions about the patient.

Stephen himself appeared to be above these medical shenanigans; 'that is Stephen's glory,' said Sieg, 'that he can somehow cause us to remember the joy of life & to share in his amazing ecstasies! I am beginning to realize how much that means in this weary world.'[22] Stephen ate the first strawberries of the season on 15 June, and declared them to be 'all summer in a sniff'.[23] A new Scottish nurse, found by the Lodges' daughter, had a nice face, and was doing sterling work.

But the doctor problem continued to exacerbate Siegfried's worries. Dr Kempe announced that Stephen must go to London to be X-rayed by Dr Chandler. Siegfried protested that his friend was in no condition to make such a journey; why couldn't the X-rays be taken in Salisbury, where there were perfectly good facilities? The friction between Sassoon and the doctors was not helped by the fact that he considered the new German methods for treating TB far in advance of their parochial English treatments; he noted that at Haus Hirth Dr Kaltenbach had forbidden salt in Stephen's food, a dietary procedure dismissed as worse than useless by Kempe and Co. Stephen was sleeping out in the new loggia now, surrounded by tall lilies in white tubs. Here Siegfried would take tea with him in the afternoon, and read to him for half an hour each evening. Stephen was accordingly grateful for his friend's ministrations, and when he told Siegfried, 'I don't mind being ill, because I'm hoarding up my enjoyment for when I'm well again',[24] it brought pricking tears to Sassoon's eyes.

Dr Hausen, that 'nice German doctor', was now summoned (Sassoon noted that Dr Chandler was now being directly rude to him). The German specialist knew Stephen's case history better than anyone, and had recommended protective injections two years ago, which Pamela had forbidden – partly, Siegfried suspected, on the advice of Dr Chandler, who didn't want to lose one of his lucrative high-class patients to a foreigner's care. Into this tragi-comic opera scenario of doctors various came yet another, a Doctor Snowden, from the sanatorium at Linford, near Cadnam, who at least gave Sassoon some of his time. The new doctor was surprised that Dr Chandler hadn't been to see Stephen since 27 May, although he had written to Snowden, giving a brief outline of

Stephen's medical history. Siegfried told him that he had arranged for another X-ray, and hoped to get 'the proper treatment' started as soon as possible. Suggestions to send Stephen to Linford were inadvisable, said Sassoon, and could result in a deleterious psychological effect; better to make Wilsford itself into a sanatorium. As he left the doctor at Wilsford, Siegfried apologized for bad-mouthing other members of his profession, adding that it was all getting too much for him. Dr Snowden advised: 'Don't let your anxiety react on the patient.'[25]

On 9 July Lord Grey wrote to Siegfried from Fallodon: ' . . . The news of Stephen is serious . . . it seems to me that the right thing for Stephen to do is to make an end of half-measures and go to a Sanatorium . . . It is a very disagreeable conclusion & Stephen may feel that life on such terms is not worth having. That you can be with him must be a boon greater than words can express. For it is only someone to whom he is greatly attached & whose presence is a pleasure & no effort to him, who could help . . .'

The patient himself was having lunch out on the loggia, under its striped awning. There was a heavy shower, and he remarked to Sieg: 'It looks as if I'm going to be blown on and rained on – and snowed on!'[26] The unintended pun seemed a good omen for the new doctor's role in the case.

So Stephen watched summer drift into autumn from his bed and, as cooler weather came, he retreated back into his bedroom. The regular routine continued, with Sassoon staying in the house most of the time, only leaving when Stephen's condition appeared to have improved in late September. Worn down by the worry of the past few months, Siegfried returned to London to recharge himself in London society.

The change in Stephen's and Siegfried's relationship began to be obvious in the autumn of 1930. Stephen's natural eagerness and vivacity – which Siegfried saw as 'typical consumptive vitality' – declined from then on, partly a result of the colder weather, thought the poet. But then there was Stephen's 'intense pride', which Sassoon ascribed to the Tennants in general: 'Like all his family, Stephen cannot be driven. He can only be led.'[27] Now Siegfried had real glimpses of Stephen's duality. He saw, on one side, the charm and intelligence that had inspired his devotion – and, on the other, the vanity, the worldly sophistication and temperamental traits that seemed to be exacerbated by his illness. The amenable 'other side' was quickly being taken over by the negative half of Stephen's character, and Siegfried, in the defensive front line, was the first to suffer. Stephen stopped keeping his diary in 1930, and his last entry, dated 25 October, read : 'Emerson says "Today is a King in disguise." When I'm with Sieg there is no disguise. I do miss him – but I'm better alone.'[28] It was a statement of intent.

Great pain was in store for Captain Sassoon, as perhaps he knew. Realistically, he could not have expected his relationship with Stephen to evolve into a happy future life together; all portents were against that. Sassoon, almost with a romantic notion of doomed love (and self-pity, perhaps, for which he undoubtedly had a predilection), saw an ill-starred future. Yet he acted out his part, as if it were a fate-determined plot in one of Hardy's novels. Sassoon should have known that nothing so intense as his few months of joy with Stephen could last, that such affairs have an inbuilt obsolescence, by reason of the temperature they raise. And like Steenie's temperature rising and falling, so Siegfried's favour rose and fell.

When Siegfried arrived back at Wilsford on 16 December, he found Stephen well, but concerned that he had been left on his own for six weeks. The bad winter weather had coincided with a change in temperament, noted Sassoon; Stephen wasn't sleeping well, his tempera-ture was up, and he was again showing the symptoms of 'flu. Stephen begged Sieg to stay until after Christmas, which he resolved to do.

It was a quiet Christmas, that of 1930, the last Stephen and Siegfried would spend happily together. Stephen was overcome when Sieg gave him his Christmas present – eighteen volumes of *Conchologia Iconica*, the most comprehensive study of shells available. Siegfried handed him the first volume, and when Stephen learnt that seventeen more awaited him downstairs, he was quite overcome, and began to cry. At a loss as to what to say, he paused for a moment, and then announced that a special bookcase must be built for them in the newly decorated drawing room. All that afternoon, Stephen pored over the beautiful hand-coloured Victorian illustrations.

Sieg's Christmas card was as delightful, and even more touching. He had written out his poem 'December Stillness' on a card decorated with a cross made from blue coloured paper, and illustrated his lines with a naive watercolour of a solitary figure looking out to a distant winter landscape :

December stillness, crossed by twilight roads,
Teach me to travel far and bear my loads.[29]

Such happiness seemed to make Stephen physically better, as his temperature dropped down to normal. Settling back on his pillows, he exclaimed : 'Oh Sieg, am I really getting well ?'[30]

*

'Siegfried's fall was not immediate,' observes Laurence Whistler. 'It was tragic, being brought about by himself and not the situation : a noble mind made abject.'[31] The deterioration was accelerated by Siegfried's over-solicitous behaviour that Christmas, when Stephen realized that his friend's attentions were exceeding his duties.

Stephen began to dwell on the less attractive aspects of his famous friend. Often in later years he recalled the poet's 'boastfulness'; Stephen alleged that Sassoon would remind him that he was 'one of the great poets of his time', admonishing him, 'Don't you realize I'm a Faber author ? . . . I'm one of their big names.' At his most bitter, Stephen would recall S.S. telling him : 'When you are famous, everyone wants to meet you' – the implication being that Stephen should feel accordingly honoured. 'He was only happy talking about himself,' said Stephen, 'so vain and conceited.'[32] Which is precisely what Sassoon thought of Stephen, at times. Yet he persisted. In 1961, after his conversion to Roman Catholicism, Sassoon wrote to a friend : 'In the past I had no rule of life to live up to . . . I have come to the conclusion that in human relationships it is sometimes virtuous to be tough. And I never could be, to my cost. As Shelley said, "Our whole life is an education of errors."'[33]

Siegfried was also very aware of the (perceived) difference in status between him and Stephen, the grandness of Stephen's family, of which he stood half in respect, half in disapproval. He referred to 'the money-loving Tennants',[34] yet was paradoxically in love with the youngest and most ineffectual member of them. Stephen represented to many social-istically-minded men (as Sassoon had been) all that was decadent about British aristocracy after the first war. Sassoon found it difficult to square his devotion to Stephen with the latter's preoccupation with the free-spending and fashionable lifestyle of his contemporaries, that same glittering society which the poet had lambasted in his satirical verse.

Edith Olivier wrote at the time that Stephen was 'like a half-fairy creature – captivating and cruel'.[35] Reproachfulness had superseded caring love that winter, and Siegfried had to withdraw. He had reason to quarrel with Nurse May, who was becoming over-protective of her charge, and was frightening Stephen with stories of the dire consequences of seeing Siegfried. Edith Olivier was convinced that the real reason for the nurse's anger was that she had fallen in love with Sassoon herself, and hated to see him being affectionate towards Stephen. Sassoon told Edith that he knew people thought that Stephen was a bad influence on his creative life, but 'he would far rather have this affection . . . than write books'.[36]

Yet Stephen insisted on keeping Nurse May, who could not be persuaded to have Siegfried back at the Manor. There was additional trauma when Faber sent back Stephen's illustrations for Sassoon's Ariel poem, 'In Sicily', saying it would be too expensive to reproduce in colour. Stephen, who hadn't read the covering letter, burst into tears, thinking they had not considered his work good enough. Siegfried remedied the situation by paying the extra cost himself.

Edith Olivier was a great source of support to Sassoon in those trying months. She dined with him at Wilsford on 1 September (Siegfried having been reinstated, much to Nurse's fury), and heard that Stephen had been coughing blood-tainted phlegm. Nurse May said she oughtn't to see Stephen, but she insisted. 'I thought him nervous, more fidgetty [*sic*] than I have ever seen him at first, then he became his delicious creative self . . .' She and Siegfried talked till midnight. 'He says he can't fancy S. as ever *old*, and yet he can't face the thought of his death . . . Talked so touchingly of their love and said he always wanted to *do things* for people he cared for and now he has someone he can do *everything* for.'[37]

But after Christmas Nurse May succeeded in getting Siegfried banished once more, after causing a tearful scene with Stephen which resulted in Sassoon having to spend the night at the Pembroke Arms in the village. Siegfried made up his mind to go abroad, to try and forget about it all. William Walton was staying with Imma Doernberg, his lover, at Casa Angelo in Switzerland, and wrote to Sieg telling him he should come and stay : ' . . . Imma has heard from Edith about Stephen's I hope temporary set-back and of the catastrophe with Nurse May. What a bitch. I am sure she's made him ill on purpose. I think Imma had better see her handwriting'[38] – Imma being an amateur graphologist. (She later analysed Sassoon's, and found a 'racked, sensitive, shattered spirit . . . by nature homosexual'.[39]) Thus, at the end of March, Siegfried packed up and left for Ascona, near Locarno, where he spent the whole of April and May. Walton had suggested it might be a good place for Stephen to convalesce, but he soon realized that the relationship was under great strain, and that the blame he put on Nurse May lay in fact with Stephen's own instability. Even his reassuring and sensible companionship could do little to alleviate Sassoon's preoccupied mind; seldom in those weeks away did he stop thinking of Stephen, ailing at Wilsford, without him.

The pull was too great. Back in England in June, Siegfried attempted a reconciliation, only to find Stephen quite altered. They went out for a drive in the Wiltshire countryside, as in happier times, but Sassoon was pessimistic. He found Stephen's mind as sick as his body; everything was changing. The vacillation continued. He was about to set off for Wilsford on 7 July, when a telegram came from Stephen, putting him off. Sassoon wrote optimistically to Max Beerbohm that Stephen's feverishness was slight – 'he is much better lately' – although conceding that he had seen little of Stephen recently, giving the 'five weeks season of Opera and Sitwells and asking old friends to lunch at the Hyde Park Hotel' as his reason.[40]

Stephen's illness and attendant incarceration dragged on through the summer. He did not move from his bed, and wrote few letters. On 29 August he managed to scribble a note to Elizabeth, now Countess of Iddesleigh : ' . . . oh dear, I often wonder how to face the crushing unhappiness (it's partly sleeping drugs – & not very good sleep). I pray & talk a lot to St Therese which is comforting – & Nannie is with me every night & often in the day . . .' He was seemingly slipping into delirium.

Siegfried kept his distance, told now by Edith Olivier that Stephen had expressed a wish that he would stay away, that he had to stick with Nurse May if he were to get better. Sassoon wrote reproachfully to Stephen, and caused tears. Siegfried in turn was upset when he heard that Stephen was entertaining visitors. He had invited Morgan Forster, his new friend, to stay at Wilsford, and Siegfried felt as Rex had done when Byam Shaw had stayed. The cat-and-mouse game that Stephen seemed to play with people was wearing him down.

In October, Sassoon rented Fitz House, in Teffont Magna. This little Wiltshire village was but a few miles from Wilsford, and just along the road from Teffont, where David Tennant rented a manor for himself and his family. This rural location was chosen ostensibly for work purposes, but actually for its proximity to the loved one.

Along these quiet country lanes Siegfried wandered in the evenings, contemplating the turbulence of his life. Here the drama of the next few months was played out, as letters of hope and hopelessness travelled across the county. 'I have rented this rafted and reconstructed residence for the winter and am more or less morose and singularly solitary in it,' Siegfried told Max in October. 'Wilsford is exactly fourteen miles away.'[41] A photograph sent to Rosamund Lehmann (one of the few friends to understand what was going on) of the poet sitting on his courtyard wall shows his mood exactly : grim-faced and as morose as his report to Beerbohm indicated.

By the end of that winter, things remained painfully unresolved, as he reported once more to Max, and at length : 'You will wish to hear some news of Stephen, so I will condense it for you (it is a tale which I am apt to enlarge on, with my "long grey beard and glittering eye"). He has made very little progress this winter, and has been in bed since October. His illness has become an obsession with him, and he will see no one. I suppose that such a monotonous existence has made him feel that the easiest way is to shut his eyes; and he has become so low in mental aliveness, through lack of nutrition from other minds, that anything in the nature of an idea tires him. Even orchids over-excite him, he announced recently, and he is sick and tired of arum lilies. No one can persuade him to make an effort to be less lethargic, because he refuses to take any suggestion of any kind, and rules his nurses and doctors inflexibly. Five weeks ago he had a haemorrhage, but it doesn't seem to have been a serious symptom, though it caused him to exist in a sort of vacuum of carefulness ever since. I fear that he will soon have become, in the minds of his friends, a pressed flower between the pages of a book of memory. But he could never be moderate in anything he did; and as at least half of me is always loitering about in his locality waiting for him to get well, I am not an impartial judge of his methods of enduring this dreadful illness. But if only we could do something to help him! Obstinate little creature that he is! "O that we two were Maying (at Villino Chiaro)". But nil desperandum, as the classical scholars say. I must be gay; though "By Gum, I usually feel about as jolly as a prairie-oyster", as some Yankee humorist might say.'[42]

Throughout spring and summer Stephen lay in bed, seeing no one, writing nothing, doing nothing. Sassoon grew impatient, and weary. Walton wrote advising him to take 'a couple of days' "festive gaiety" each week' to avoid depression. 'It does seem that there is still some life yet left in Steenie,' he said encouragingly. 'I imagine that Lord G[rey] is the one who might use most influence with both Snowden & Christopher . . .'[43] That lack of any influence was proving disastrous for them both.

In October, Stephen had visited Linford Sanatorium, near Ringwood in Hampshire, as the accounts for Wilsford Manor reveal. They also indicate the day-to-day expenses that he incurred during this long period of illness – the bottles of 'Lait du Jour' and 'Special Cream' delivered from Merritt's of Berkeley Square, the Roger et Gallet violet shaving cream from Douglas's of Bond Street, the bottled French plums from Fortnum's. The bills for these extravagances sit uneasily alongside receipts for the disinfection of bed linen from the Salisbury and District Isolation Hospital, and Harley Street consultants' fees. A bill for a dozen red roses sent to Cecil at Ashcombe in November and the tailor's expenses for enlarging Stephen's velvet court dress trousers indicate some sort of awareness of an outside world – as do taxi fares for visits by Nan Tennant on 9 and 13 October. But life had ground to a virtual halt at the Manor now, and the birds and reptiles fluttered and crawled in their outhouses, unattended by their master.

Chapter 13

The Fatal Gift of Beauty

He had always the look of one who kept himself unspotted from the world. Men who talked grossly became silent when Dorian Gray entered the room. There was something in the purity of his face that rebuked them. His mere presence seemed to recall to them the memory of the innocence that they had tarnished. They wondered how one so charming and graceful as he could have escaped the stain of an age that was at once sordid and sensual.

— Oscar Wilde: *The Portrait of Dorian Gray*

GIVEN the vexatious course of events, it is surprising that Siegfried remained phlegmatic about his relationship with Stephen, and the steep decline it now assumed. But what he came to realize, over the next few months, was that it wasn't just the physical illness that had changed Stephen; his friend was now becoming mentally ill, too.

There was a new nurse at Wilsford now, to replace the tyrant Nurse May, and she had 'lovely blue eyes',[1] but for some reason Stephen's household servants – possibly infected with the 'hyper' atmosphere of the house – were so rude to her that she was reduced to tears within two weeks of her coming. At last, Siegfried was allowed back for a brief visit, bearing lavish gifts – to no effect. Stephen would not be swayed. Rex came down for two nights, 'wearily trying to bring peace'. He stretched out on Stephen's bed, 'among the necklaces and bibelots', languidly chattering nonsense with his friend. Nurse did not approve of such 'lying about, talking in this absurd way – very modern, I suppose'. Then Siegfried arrived, to find Stephen without his make-up. This caused further scenes, at which Rex attempted to impose a truce, to no avail, and took refuge in the outbuildings, where he distractedly paced about the garage. Siegfried sought Edith's advice – 'Where did I go wrong?' –

but even she was growing tired of the never-ending scenes and agonized sighs.

From Fitz House, Siegfried once more tried to control the progress of Stephen's medical treatment. Henry Head had recommended a new specialist, Dr George Riddoch (with whom he and W. H. Rivers had collaborated on neurology work in 1920). Both Sir Henry and Siegfried hoped that Riddoch's expertise in matters neurological and psychological would help Stephen to face his growing problems. But Sassoon knew Stephen would resent his or anyone else's interference (noting privately that Stephen had become very suspicious in character over the past two years – especially of Siegfried himself), so he asked Head to make sure the new doctor disguised his provenance, saying it should appear that he had come to Stephen via Dr Snowden.

A proposition to move Stephen to Hampstead for treatment was made, but Siegfried reasoned that he would not want to be so near his brother, Christopher, who lived there. Instead, Sassoon suggested a house be rented for him near Maidenhead, for the end of July, when Wilsford became too hot and unsettling. Rosamond Lehmann lived only fifteen miles away (at Ipsden, in Oxfordshire), and remained one of the few people who could see Stephen without tiring him, said Siegfried; he had already asked her to look for a suitable house.

On Sunday, 25 June, Dr Snowden examined Stephen, and rebuked him for 'playing up' his illness. Stephen had taken to insisting that Nurse lift him up in bed, complaining that to do it himself gave him chest and back pains. Nan Tennant also visited that afternoon, and found him acting up too, but also 'nervy'. He appeared with 'unbrushed hair and a wan martyred smile' when she arrived, although she was told afterwards by Nurse that he was perfectly normal when with the doctor, and spent most of the day putting a lot of 'preparations' on his face.[2]

Stephen's aunt told him he should see this new doctor (Riddoch), but Stephen flatly refused, saying that if it had been his idea, then he might have done it. But he would think about it. He told Nan that she seemed to be doing a lot of things behind his back, which he didn't like. She replied that she would continue to do them anyway; it was for his own good, and he should stop play-acting and obey good medical advice. Stephen then became self-pitying, said he was lonely, and tried 'artfully' to discover where Nan was staying (actually with Siegfried at Fitz House). As she left, the butler told her that 'Mr Stephen' was eating very well. It appeared to Nan that Stephen's spoilt behaviour was pure childish mischief. It was also obvious that Stephen's illness was mental as well as physical. The pent-up emotional stresses of the last few years – Pamela's and Nannie's deaths – had been held back to some extent by his affair with Siegfried; as that began to break down, so the trauma of past loss manifested itself.

That summer, a very hot one, Sassoon continued to follow Stephen's progress daily. In August, the TB germ was diagnosed as completely eradicated from Stephen's lung. Willie Walton wrote hopefully to Sieg, saying he would try his luck with a visit to Stephen that August: 'I am sure he will begin to get more normal once he can assure himself that no more haemorrhages will occur.'[3] Meanwhile, Stephen's cousin, Violet Bonham-Carter, managed to gain admittance to the Manor in early August, and discussed Siegfried with him.* The result was that Stephen allowed two visits from Sassoon, on 16 and 19 August. On the first meeting, Stephen appeared constrained and defensive, but on the Saturday he relaxed into his old self, and chatted with Sieg quite happily for over an hour.

But Stephen's worsening mental state was giving rise to great concern (as was his physical behaviour, which had become unstable and led to trouble with the law), and by the late summer of 1932 steps were taken to deal with it. Dr Riddoch diagnosed Stephen's illness as 'nervous', and in consultation with Henry Head recommended that he be sent to the 'nerve hospital', on whose management committee Sir Henry served. The Cassel Hospital for Functional Nervous Disorders, in Penshurst, Kent – known as 'Swaylands' – was founded in 1919 by the German-Jewish philanthropist Sir Ernest Cassel, financial adviser to Edward VII and one of the richest men in Europe,† and drew on the lessons learned from shell-shock cases of the Great War to treat psychiatric problems in civilian life. The Cassel Hospital was run along the same lines as the hospital at Craiglockhart, to which Siegfried had been sent during the war (and which he was writing about at the time, in *Sherston's Progress*, published in 1936), and was using inno-vative therapies, as well as Freudian psychoanalysis, to treat its patients. Swaylands also happened to be just ten miles to the east of Siegfried's family home, Weirleigh, in the Weald of his youth.

Its situation was one of quiet, country house comfort, set in textbook rural prettiness. The straggling pile of Georgian and neo-Elizabethan red brick buildings, with its panelled dining and music rooms and grand

---

*This relationship was further complicated by the fact that Violet Bonham-Carter was herself in love with Sassoon.

†Cassel died in 1921, leaving a fortune of almost £2 million to his grand-daughter, Edwina Ashley, who married Lord Louis Mountbatten the following year. According to former domestics at the hospital, Lady Mountbatten kept up the association with Swaylands, sending Christmas presents to patients and staff, and there is evidence to suggest she may have met Stephen there.

staircases, had originally been the Drummond family home, and Edward VII had often been entertained there. There was a huge Palm Court, in which patients could spend recuperative afternoons, and expansive landscaped gardens. (An ornamental lake had been drained so as to prevent possible suicides, although this did not prevent one aristocratic inmate hanging himself from a pole in the hop gardens that bordered the grounds.) Patients occupied elegant first-floor rooms with beautiful views across the Medway valley, attended by a staff of five doctors and twenty or so nurses. Swaylands was non-profit-making; ward patients paid three guineas a week, whilst wealthy patients were charged seven guineas and upwards. Sir Ernest Cassel's intention had been for it to 'assist chiefly educated persons of slender means',[4] but in fact, because of its situation and reputation, many of its inmates came from well-to-do families. To the ill-informed, Swaylands was known as a place for 'family skeletons', such as Lady Streatfeild, known locally as 'Mad Flo', and was also a temporary home to one of the Bowes-Lyon family, similarly afflicted with a genetic disposition to mental problems.[5]

Yet the methods used at Swaylands were absolutely up-to-date, and the medical director, Dr Thomas Arthur Ross, who was to be Stephen's personal doctor (much as Rivers, who was a friend of Ross's, had been Siegfried's at Craiglockhart), was held in high regard; he wrote two seminal works on neuroses,[*] and was a founding father of the hospital. He had helped develop new techniques for dealing with the causes and effects of mental problems, which were only now being seen as illnesses which could be treated rather than ignored (and having been a physician at the Royal National Hospital for Consumption, at Ventnor, he was eminently well qualified to deal with Stephen's problems).

Despite such liberated ideas, mental illness still carried an undeniable social stigma in the early thirties. Stephen himself was concerned that his illness should not be generally advertised, although he hadn't the irrational fear of it that others might have shown. But the social implications of his spending a year of his life in a hospital for nervous disorders could not be ignored. The most important part of him, his acutely active mind, was at risk, and with that threat came attendant damage to the way he would react thereafter to the greater world. Stephen's social ability would be drastically curtailed by his illness, just as his future expectations were. He would spend the rest of his life in fear of

---

[*]*The Common Neuroses* (1923), and *An Enquiry into Prognosis in the Neuroses* (1936). Dr Ross (1874–1941), Edinburgh-born, coincidentally lived at Smith Square, only doors away from Mulberry House.

slipping in and out of a neurosis which, hard to define as it was, had effects quite evident to both him and his friends.

So Stephen was settled in at Swaylands, where Dr Ross's methods of treatment prescribed an initial period of rest in bed, with as few visitors as possible. 'Here the doctor must use his common sense,' he wrote. 'While he is in bed the patient may, of course, have books and sober newspapers. The yellow press is better forbidden at first, and so also are sensational books.'[6]

But as he had admitted to Max Beerbohm, Sassoon was unable to stay away from the 'locality' of his loved one, and he resumed his visits to Stephen on 2 November, finding that further lung problems had been diagnosed and that Stephen was being kept quiet.

On 18 November, however, Siegfried found Stephen sitting up in bed, having enjoyable talks with the doctor. 'Dr Ross says I am much shyer than most people,' he told Siegfried proudly, 'and not nearly so boastful about myself!'[7] Ross diagnosed 'shyness' as a symptom of 'anxiety reaction' in neurotic patients. His daily conversations with the patient (the hospital regime prescribed one-and-a-half-hour sessions each day) were in fact a gently applied form of psychoanalysis, by which he sought to discover the true, subconscious reasons for Stephen's behaviour and current problems. The new treatment was doing Stephen good, Sassoon concluded, and the Salisbury nurse had been replaced by a Swaylands one, which had made both patient and poet happier.

Further communication in what was left of 1932 was by postcard and letter. Cards came from Sassoon, initialled 'K' (for 'Kangar'), telling Stephen he had passed Wilsford 'swathed in white mist – a robin sitting on the old water-butt in the Kitchen garden',[8] and that Sassoon had seen Morgan Forster and Edmund Blunden in London, both of whom enquired after Stephen's health.

During the winter, Swaylands continued its good work. Dr Chandler visited before Christmas, and seemed pleased with the patient. A quiet festive season for Stephen was spent yet again in bed. Would the coming year see him restored to a normal life? Friends and physicians knew the answer: only if he wanted it.

In January, Siegfried broke his collar bone whilst out riding on the downs above Wilsford, and was gratified to receive a parcel of invalid jellies from Fortnum and Mason's, sent by Stephen. He was upset Sieg hadn't been to see him recently, he said; but besides his accident, Sassoon explained that he was staying away for Stephen's own good, as his visits seemed to upset him. He promised to come the following Thursday, when he found Stephen drawing once more – an encouraging sign that his mental state was stabilizing – but Dr Ross reported that the tubercle was active again. However, the patient had gained four pounds in the past week or so, despite a depressed period; Stephen had complained that his friends were neglecting him, after an invitation to 'one or two'[9] had met with no takers. Ever since childhood he had been used to being given attention whenever he demanded it; Stephen now found it hard to understand why summonses to his bedside might not be obeyed. And when he found out that Glen Byam Shaw had been staying at Fitz House, he was distinctly jealous.

During that three-hour visit, Stephen let slip that Dr Ross had, during one session of analysis, 'tackled the tragic disability' which Siegfried noted had been the source of Stephen's difficulties, '& the cause of most of his irrational restlessness'.[10] Quite what he referred to is unclear, but the probability is that the 'disability' was sexual in nature, very possibly impotence. (Whether this was real, or feigned – in self-defence when with Sassoon – again cannot be determined.) Ross was of the opinion it had been caused by a shock in early childhood, and proposed that a course of hypnotherapy could cure it. (He notes in *The Common Neuroses* that 'the causes of fear of impotence may [be] deeply seated. They may be dependent on childhood fixations which have become unconscious. The procedure then will have to be analytic . . .'[11] Ross's threefold psycho-therapies at Swaylands consisted of 'hypnotism, persuasion and analy-sis'.)[12] Both Stephen and Siegfried appear to have been very grateful to the doctor for this suggestion, although the nurse attending Stephen disapproved, saying that Dr Chandler had told her 'the boy is in no fit state to undergo auto-suggestion',[13] an opinion most probably coloured by a traditional resistance to progressive medicine. Hypnosis as a treatment for psychosexual problems, as pioneered by Freud and Jung, was still in its infancy, and hardly accepted by the Harley Street establishment. Chandler had instead prescribed gold injections, of which Stephen had had three.

It was perceptive of Dr Ross to attempt to treat Stephen with a therapy that relied so much on an exploration of his own past, for it was in Stephen's childhood and upbringing that the real problems lay. Although there may have been no one great shock as Ross diagnosed, the whole of Stephen's formative years had subjected him to a dominating force – his mother – and an unrealistic environment – Wilsford – which really were the root causes of his neurosis (Ross's telling Stephen that he was 'much shyer than other people' indicates the doctor's genuine understanding of his patient's precarious condition). Stephen's mental model of the world outside, constructed during his early development, did not tally with reality. It could not deal with the real world, as Dr Ross soon discovered (despite his comments about his patient's 'boastfulness', he privately diagnosed Stephen as a 'romantic liar', and an exhibitionist).

Stephen told Sieg that the nurse frightened him, but Dr Ross was so different: 'It is so nice to have a doctor who thinks you are good for me,' he told Sassoon.[14] Ross's investigation into Stephen's 'tragic disability' had already lightened the load. With the prospect of a cure, they could be happy together again; it seemed to Siegfried now that at last things between him and Stephen were on a more level footing, that their relationship could yet survive. All of his dreams about Stephen were happy ones now, he told Henry Head, and he looked forward to a return to the old days. He visited Swaylands on 1, 8, and 15 February, propping up Stephen in his bed so that he could see the afternoon sunshine over the Wealdonian hills, and wrapping his 'little woollen coat' around his friend's shoulders. When Stephen said, 'Isn't it fun spreading coats out for picnics!', Siegfried thought, 'How can one help loving a person who says things like that after 3 years of illness?'[15]

But Sassoon was deceiving himself. He did not hear from Stephen for a month, and received word that his TB had flared up again, making him additionally miserable. On Stephen's twenty-seventh birthday, he asked Violet Bonham-Carter to visit him, not Siegfried. Yet Sassoon's devotion remained, almost unembittered. When he saw Margot Asquith in town that month, and heard her abuse Stephen and his capriciousness – 'The Wyndhams have no heart'[16] – he leapt to his friend's defence. Deep down in his own heart, though, Siegfried discerned a bitter kernel of truth.

In May Siegfried, teased beyond endurance, was driven to write an open and frank letter to Swaylands, putting things 'on the line'. He declared he would no longer be bullied by Stephen: 'Can't you hear the best thing in your life being strangled, while you lie locked in with your obsession?'[17]

There was no reply. Siegfried made daily visits to Wilsford, riding a horse from the stables there, and visiting the garden, where he had befriended the two spinster sisters, the Misses Hunter, Beryl and Eileen, who, dressed in smart green uniforms, looked after the Wilsford gardens. He liked them enormously, not least for their sense where their employer's seemed to be lacking. 'Really and Truly', as he nicknamed the middle-aged ladies, were down-to-earth (literally) and full of sound advice. Fans of his poetry (they had actually bought and read his books, noted Siegfried, unlike people of a 'higher station' who only *appeared* to appreciate his work), they gave him plants for Fitz House in exchange for signed editions – a fair barter, thought Sassoon.

Twelve years in employment in the Wilsford garden, they were 'the best thing England can produce', said his manservant. They told Captain Sassoon that it was only because of his stabilizing influence that they had remained under 'Mister Stephen's' employ, and that if he went – as now looked inevitable – then they would go too. Siegfried counted such loyalty high, and determined to employ them himself, in that event, or set them up in a flower-growing business. Then at least something constructive might have been gained from this unhappy period.*

Violet Bonham-Carter persevered with her cousin meanwhile, pleading Siegfried's case with 'the young lord',[18] reminding him of what a great poet Sassoon was, and how unreasonable he was being. Such arguments cut no ice with Stephen, however, who, in his weakened physical and mental state, had in his head the idea that he must resist Sassoon's threatening encroachment on his present and future existence. At Fitz House, Siegfried tried to work, but couldn't; despite the fact that he wrote to Swaylands several times a week, it was five weeks since he had had a message from Stephen. Then he discovered from 'Really and Truly' that their master was due to return home soon, a fact concealed from him. Sassoon wanted to remain aloof, but could not, admitting his obsession was too far gone. The fourteenth of May, he noted wryly, would be the third anniversary of their return together from abroad

Later in May, Stephen's discharge having been put back another four months, Siegfried received a letter from Dr Ross, telling him he could not visit. Greatly annoyed, Sassoon yet pledged:

> Oh Steenie I have promised
> To serve you till the end.[19]

His pride was affronted. Why did the doctor give him no news of Stephen's physical state, or when he might return to Wilsford? Sassoon replied with an outspoken letter to Stephen, warning him that he could stand to lose all his friends if he continued in this way; and that he should remember this one's years of devotion and care.

Siegfried was also worried that without him, Stephen would be taken advantage of. He had already discovered that David Tennant had brought Dick Wyndham down to Wilsford for a long weekend, in Stephen's absence. They had appeared with 'hot-house strawberries',[20]

*The Misses Hunter did leave Stephen's employ soon after. Devoted and inseparable, Eileen Hunter died on 23 April 1944, and her sister Beryl ten days later, on 3 May.

Wilsford house party, 1927. Left to right: *Rex, Baby Jungman, Sacheverell Sitwell, Edith in Stephen's arms, Osbert Sitwell, Elinor Wylie, Zita and Rosamond Lehmann*

On the rug at Wilsford, 1927. Left to right: *Sacheverell, Stephen, Rosamond, Osbert, Baby, Elinor, Cecil, Rex, Bordie and Zita*

Stephen as Prince Charming, 1927

Edith Sitwell

Edith Olivier by Cecil Beaton

On the bridge, Wilsford, October 1927. Left to right: *Rex, Cecil, Georgia Sitwell, William Walton, Stephen, Baby and Zita*

Haus Hirth

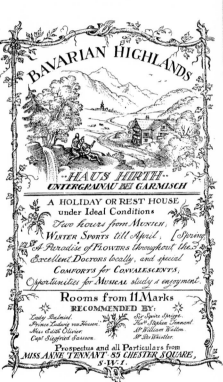

Rex's advertisement for Haus Hirth

Siegfried and Stephen, Garmisch 1929

Rebecca Trusler (Nannie)

Cover for Leaves from a Missionary's Notebook, *1929*

Garmisch, July 1929.
'This lurching nautical pose is
misleading (I scarcely paddle!)'

Sicily, April 1930

With 'that fox-hunting man', Sicily, 1930

Stephen in Charles James, Polly in cage

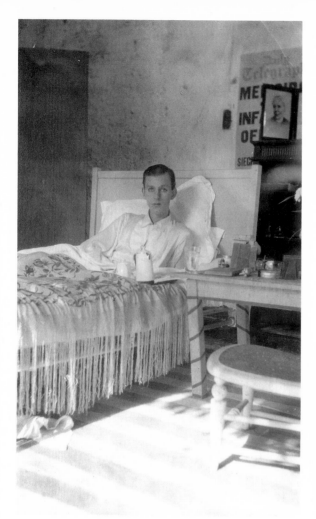

Stephen ill in bed, 1930

Swaylands, the Cassel Hospital, Penshurst

Stephen in Victoria with Sir Oliver Lodge, Louis driving, 1935

Stephen's Christmas card, 1934

1935 journal cover

had drunk champagne which David maintained was his father's, and had been rude to Stephen's trusted housekeepers, Mr and Mrs Gale. David had left instructing Mrs Gale to put the expenses down to Stephen. Siegfried's concern seemed justified. (The house expenses at Wilsford were certainly made free with by other members of the household during these years, although Stephen declined to prosecute when he later learnt of their petty thievery.)

Unconscious of all this, laid up in his bed at Swaylands, the invalid dictated a reply to Siegfried's ultimatum. Sassoon received the letter on 22 May:

'Dear Captain Sassoon,

Thank you for your letter. Mr Tennant told me that he received a letter from you, but he has not read it and I do not think he intends to. What I am going to say is something I have nothing whatever to do with, except that I have been asked to pass it on to you as a message from him. I do not know why, but since your last visit his feelings towards you have not been what they were. He says you upset him and make him feel ill, and that he cannot see you again. I know that he has done this before, and that you will probably feel he is a very impossible person. He is of course not well, and that is about all there is to be said for it. I know also that I encouraged you to come in the Autumn, because I thought that your visits did him good: but as he says he does not wish to see you now, I can obviously do nothing further in the matter.

Yours sincerely, T. A. Ross'.[21]

Siegfried was devastated. Had he spent four years of devoted service to this person, who could now turn round and dismiss him in such an insulting manner? No one else would have done the same for him, or tolerated such whims and selfishness – not even his family, thought Sassoon. He could not believe it, and, on the basis of that slim disbelief, wrote back to Dr Ross, asking him to ask Stephen to reconsider; his whole future was at risk, because of these temperamental outbursts. Stephen had sent the same sort of message to Clare, Siegfried noted.[*] Could this really be the way Stephen wanted to run his life?

[*] Clare had visited Stephen, and burst into tears as soon as she entered his room, which frightened him as he had immediately assumed Dr Ross had told her he was dying. Afterwards, he had a Swaylands nurse ring her and ask Clare not to visit again as it had upset him so much. 'Clare has a pebble for a heart, and has always spoken of Stephen in a most unfeeling way,' Violet Bonham-Carter told Sassoon.[22] Stephen apparently also told his sister that people had been throwing stones through his window, and that his doctor had consoled him by telling him he was like Saint Stephen, which left Edith Olivier wondering who was 'the patient, who the physician?'[23]

It was a rhetorical question, but Siegfried could not take 'no' for an answer. Violet Bonham-Carter advised him to 'invest less feeling' in Stephen, but to Sassoon that was like telling the sun not to set in the evening. She agreed that Stephen was 'the most inconsiderate person in the world',[24] but what could he do about it? That evening, Siegfried sought consolation in the company of friends, and went to the local circus with the Misses Hunter and Edith Olivier; but he admitted that his heart was breaking.

In the meantime, Dr Ross had decided not to try any psychological treatment on Stephen, as he thought he might be unnecessarily 'bullying'. In fact, he confessed that he was only allowing Stephen to remain at the hospital because he did not know what to do with him. The patient seemed content merely to drift apathetically from day to day. Stephen spoke to Violet Bonham-Carter of Wilsford as the place he would like to be more than anywhere else, yet appeared to have no strong desire to go back. Eventually, however, that was the only alternative, and Stephen was duly returned to his home.

From there, he made it known that he would not see Siegfried for a year, but when told that the poet might go to America, Stephen at once wanted him back. Sassoon had made that well-worn journey from Teffont Magna to Wilsford-cum-Lake too many times, only to be turned away at the door. Wandering round the house, he had peered in through the window, 'observing unobserved a supine Stephen'.[25] Months of pent-up emotion made a fist of his hand, as Siegfried smashed the leaded glass. It was all over.

The immediate aftermath of the affair was anticlimactic; judgements were made on either side, recriminations that would last into both Stephen's and Siegfried's old age. Lady Juliet Duff sympathized with Stephen, telling him Sassoon had 'no social sense' and illustrating her opinion by example: 'When he dines with me – if he's bored he leaves at 9 – if he's enjoying the gramophone he stays till 2 o'clock – he'd never ask you if you were tired – or think that he might be boring you.'[26] William Walton went further, and told Stephen some years later, when the latter confided in the composer a certain desire to make peace with Sassoon, to apologize: 'But why?' said Walton. 'It was he who behaved badly, not you, he was so stupid & dense: he behaved abominably.'[27] Morgan Forster wrote to Stephen soon after, asking, 'Have you had an emotional and physical overturn? Your news, though I accept it as good news, startles me.' And Aunt Margot put her pennyworth in, telling her nephew: 'There's nothing so dead as a dead love-affair.'[28]

Siegfried suffered, in Stephen's eyes, one of the greatest character defects: not knowing when he wasn't wanted. Even Sassoon's later sympathetic and cautious would-be biographers, like the nun Dame Felicitas Corrigan, had to admit that 'no one who knew S.S. well could cherish any illusions: at no time could he have been an easy man to live with, and there were moments when unconsciously he made heavy demands upon his friends.'[29]

But Siegfried had on his side a huge body of friends, mutual friends of both parties, who could neither understand nor forgive Stephen's actions. Sassoon's friend and executor Sir Rupert Hart-Davis remains convinced of Stephen's monstrous behaviour, a paradigm of all that was vain, selfish and cruel; heartfelt criticism from one who knew what Sassoon suffered. Yet Stephen was quite well aware of what Siegfried's friends thought. On the occasion of Maynard Keynes' death in 1946, he told Laurence Whistler: 'You knew he had, for years, a bad heart? After my break with S.S. I had a card from Maynard – saying "I am having to lay up, & rest a lot now, my heart, unlike yours, not being whole." He could never resist a dig at one – malicious creature.'[30]

It is quite paradoxical that having so summarily dismissed Siegfried, Stephen should seemingly spend the rest of his life regretting the action – or, at least, continually recalling the years he spent with Sassoon as an idyllic lost past. 'I miss motoring with S.S.,'[31] he wrote in his journal, and would entitle poems: 'I like to be in love – Sicily, 1928',[32] choosing to forget that it was he who had terminated the affair. He liked to remember Siegfried as his champion and protector, as on the occasion when someone complained about Stephen's use of make-up. 'I think it's rather courageous of him,' retorted Sassoon. But he was at the same time bitter. 'He wasn't deferential enough to me,' noted Stephen in one of his many notebooks, and in another, a more specific observation: 'S.S. hated lady writers – "They write their works sitting on their suitcases in railway stations" – this was so like him – his hates were virulent – Titanic.'[33]

Stephen seldom wrote as revealingly in his 'public' letters as he did in his impetuous scrawled comments, to be found crowding the margins of his books. 'I could never care for anyone deeply unless they asked too much of me,' he wrote in one. 'Love must make outrageous demands – or it is not Love. Love is not mild, considerate or precise. And it wrecks every preconception of what it is!'[34]

Perhaps they were just too different, these men. The masculine poet, who had lived through a bloody war, knew too much of reality: Siegfried had wrought a career for himself; he had achieved his reputation by talent and determination. Stephen's position was almost entirely due to his family's wealth. He lived an unrealistic life of fancy-dress, and had no past, present, or future career. Sassoon's ascetic life-style could in no way dovetail with Stephen's flitting, flirting existence. When Firbank had compared Siegfried to Tolstoy digging for worms, and himself to Pavlova, chasing butterflies, he was addressing the same dichotomy.

The emptiness in Stephen's life left first by Pamela's death, then Nannie's, and now Siegfried's ejection, gaped like an empty chasm. It sent him to his closest friends for support. To their credit, people like Rex Whistler forgave past injustices, and pledged themselves anew. He wrote to Stephen that summer, apologizing for not writing before: 'Anyway, whether you know it or not, I have loved you all the time & I think I always shall. You see I may perhaps be different for some people: with them possibly not writing means forgetting, but it really doesn't with me. I have thought of you continually during these months & sometimes felt very near to you . . .'[35]

Siegfried, on his part, broke away as sharply as could be thought possible. At the Wilton Pageant on 5 June he first encountered a friend of Edith Olivier's, Hester Gatty, whom Edith described as 'exquisite . . . and very like Stephen'.[36] They met again in September, and within weeks Sassoon was expressing his love for her; within months, they were married. Siegfried told Edith he had seen a swan flying slowly away above them at Wilton; it was a symbol of Stephen passing out of his life, he said.

In September 1933 Sassoon published a limited edition of his collected poems from the past few years. *Vigils* contained 'In Sicily' and 'December Stillness', poems written very much under Stephen's spell. The illustrations were by Stephen Gordon, and Siegfried wondered aloud if 'his' Stephen would be jealous. He had heard his health was improving, but predicted the coming winter would slow him down again, as it always had done – this, however, without malice. The bitterness was reserved for the fact that Stephen seemed completely unaffected by the death of his stepfather, Lord Grey, who had died that month. Sassoon noted sourly that Stephen now avoided 'all strong feeling'.[37]

In October, when Siegfried announced his engagement to Hester, he still found himself thinking of the effect of his actions on Stephen, almost as though the match were a slap in the face for his 'ex'. Indeed, it seemed as though Siegfried was marrying on the rebound: barely three months separated his introduction proper to Miss Gatty, his protestation of love, and their marriage, on 18 December, at Christchurch. (By 1941 it seemed to Rex that the marriage was already on rocky ground, not least because it was obvious to the artist that Mrs Sassoon had fallen in love with *him*.) But Siegfried was, for the first few years at least, happier with Hester than he had ever been, often telling friends that he could not imagine how he had gone through such pain, worry, and emotional blackmail.

Meanwhile, Stephen's recovery gained apace in the Sassoon-free months of late summer and early autumn. He left Swaylands in late August, to resume recuperation at home.* On 17 September, Edith Olivier called on him. 'He looked well in a way, certainly fatter,' she wrote in her journal, 'but he's lost his air of dazzling other-worldliness when he seemed a transparent lamp holding a brilliant *shaking* flame. He looked down a good deal so that his face had less expression . . . He begged me to back him up in staying on at Wilsford.' (Lord Grey's recent death had apparently put Stephen's tenure at the house in some doubt.)

But by October, Stephen was enjoying 'quite a revival of health', and was ready to see friends again. He invited Cecil to Wilsford, the first time for more than a year. The visit was highly successful. 'This was, as always, one of my great joys,' Beaton told his diary, 'for Stephen is one of the few people I have ever met who have genius, who seems apart from the ordinary rut, & in comparison he makes the rest of the world seem squalid.' Yet another nurse, in that long line of suffering medicos, greeted Cecil and gave a good report of the patient. Shown into the library, Cecil found the interior of Wilsford much changed. There were walls of books, 'covered, as is the floor, with ice-cream pink – the chairs & furniture white, flowers abounding'.

Then Stephen appeared, excited to see Cecil, 'giggling and laughing with a handkerchief up to his mouth'. There was a great deal to discuss, Siegfried being an obvious subject. Here Cecil had to tread carefully, for he knew that Sassoon had just announced his engagement to Hester. Beaton merely referred to the fact that Siegfried had a girlfriend, 'to which Stephen said he hoped she was not attractive'. (Cecil himself was

---

*Stephen seldom subsequently referred to his time in hospital. His one acknowledgement of his eleven-month stay at Swaylands was an often-recalled conversation with one of the nurses he had befriended, who had wondered aloud, 'You know those birds called Bats?' The significance of this odd remark, apparently important to Stephen, remains obscure.

dabbling in heterosexual love in a brief affair with Doris Castlerosse, and was advocating it as a good cure for homosexual affairs.)

They spent the afternoon looking through Stephen's scrapbooks and the old photographs Cecil had taken, and together 'moaned at our beauty'. Stephen had started drawing again, and Cecil thought it not up to his previous standard, although 'this could not be expected after so many years of rest' and he still found it 'full of genius'. Stephen's beauty, charm and 'exquisite sense of humour' put new life into Cecil's veins: 'His appreciation makes one realize how dumb & numb one has been until the moment of discovery.' Cecil, still smarting after Peter Watson's rejection of his affections, found being with Stephen a great pleasure. 'He makes one enjoy ordinary things so that they become wildly exciting. We looked at some pages of my albums & swooned at the beauty of Garbo whom Stephen in character & personality resembles a great deal.' This would have greatly flattered Stephen, had he known it, especially as Beaton spoke from personal experience, having been lucky enough to have a close encounter with the legendary actress on his visit to the States.

They gossiped about Joe Ackerley, the writer, critic, poet (later editor of the *Listener*), and a friend of Morgan Forster, who had introduced him to Stephen. Ackerley had – probably at Stephen's request – sent his photograph. This caused Stephen and Cecil a certain amount of amusement, for, as Stephen pointed out, Ackerley looked very much the 'same type' as Siegfried; handsome in a stern, rather military way. They laughed so much at their jokes that Stephen nearly choked, '& we gossiped about our love affairs & it sounded like a Peter Arno drawing . . . when Stephen interrupted me & said "Afterwards don't forget to remind me to tell you about my conference with the German Prince!" How we laughed.' Cecil found Stephen 'every bit as precious & valuable as ever he was', and valued Stephen's criticism of his own work, when he declared Beaton's photographs better, and 'deeper . . . He told me he had seen my Peter once or twice but had not found him an interesting character.' (This was not strictly true, as later Stephen would relish Watson's company.) Stephen complimented Cecil's figure – and gave 'graphic descriptions of the scenes with Siegfried'.

Beaton overstayed his allotted time, listening to Stephen's 'rapt whispers'. When he finally got up to leave (Nurse hovering in the background), Stephen presented him with a camellia, picked from a tree he had growing in a huge white wooden tub in his room, '& we laughed at the idea of a tree growing indoors & wondered why it should appear so normal.'[38]

Cecil followed up the visit with gifts of photographs, and a silk tie, 'so chic with my guinea-fowl tweeds – how clever of you!' said Stephen. 'The photographs of Toklas & Stein are incredible.' With Christmas approaching, Stephen had plans for his card, and enlisted Cecil's help. 'I want to super-impose a profile with the garden behind – is this possible?'[39] But thoughts of Christmas were tarnished by the year's surprising culmination of the Sassoon saga. When Stephen heard of the marriage, with Edith, Rex, and T. E. Lawrence the only guests invited, he wept. Other 'friends' were typically cynical; Edith Sitwell commented to her sister-in-law Georgia, 'And I suppose the bridal pair will want to adopt S.T.'[40]

Chapter 14

New Horizons

It was not till the third day that he ventured to go out. There was something in the clear, pine-scented air of that winter morning that seemed to bring him back his joyousness and his ardour for life. But it was not merely the physical conditions of environment that had caused the change. His own nature had revolted against the excess of anguish that had sought to maim and mar the perfection of its calm. With subtle and fine wrought temperaments it is always so. Their strong passions must either bruise or bend. They either slay the man, or themselves die. Shallow sermons and shallow loves live on. The loves and sorrows that are great are destroyed by their own plenitude.

— Oscar Wilde: *The Portrait of Dorian Gray*

CHRISTMAS at Wilsford Manor was celebrated with a fireworks display on the West Lawn, mostly for the benefit of local 'waifs and strays'. The house accounts list the wonderful pyrotechnical developments of the thirties: 'Animated Fountain, Pyramids of Lace, Asteroids, Snow Flakes, Transformation Fountains, Whistling Rockets, Vertical Wheels', and, of course, the 'Octopus Star'. Fred. Sutton, 'Bakers of Salisbury', supplied fancy cakes and buns, along with the hire of china to cater for the village children. Stephen continued a tradition started by his mother, and would love to throw such parties, held inside the Racquets Court.

The running of Wilsford, as with any large country house, was an expensive business, and becoming more so with the financial constraints of the thirties. It became less viable for Stephen to manage the estate by himself – especially given his precarious health – and so his brother Christopher negotiated the sale of 2,000 acres, land which then had little commercial value and went very cheaply by today's standards. Stephen still retained a full retinue of staff – cook, valet, housemaid, chauffeur and two gardeners – but hired a car from Amesbury (the garage's bill indicates much use in January 1934, Stephen visiting Cecil at Ashcombe, and Edith at Wilton). There also appear to have been a number of 'staff movements' at the Manor in 1933–4. Both Mrs Wise and Mrs Selby had reason to leave Stephen's employ, Mrs Selby's removal expenses being charged to the house. The staff turnover at Wilsford was certainly high: Stephen and his whims made him a difficult master to serve. In the 1940s, Elizabeth Bowen recommended the services of a Normandy chef, Yves, 'an elderly obstinate Breton used to petit bourgeois and smaller establishments',[1] who was completely bewildered by Wilsford and its master, and left in high dudgeon, after much throwing of kitchen implements.

The mid-thirties saw the beginning of Stephen's wandering years, a restless time when he travelled both Europe and America, looking for new experiences, indulging his curiosity about the world and its people. It was also the gestation period for his creative work, when his projected novel, *Lascar*, would emerge as an *idée fixe* to obsess him for the rest of his life. A book that was never to be, yet it would co-exist with Stephen's daily life, as much as a human partner might have done. Stephen would channel his unspent emotional energy into *Lascar*, but it was energy that seemed to dissipate even as it formed the shape and substance of his dreams.

That winter, Stephen decided that the best way to forget about Siegfried's 'unreasonable behaviour' would be to get away from England entirely. The parochial attractions of Wilsford, after years of lying there abed, had palled, and its redecoration no longer seemed vital.

But there were still relapses in the next few months. In April 1934, Morgan Forster visited Stephen for the weekend, and found his host too ill to spend more than twenty minutes twice a day with him, unable to be sociable for longer periods. They did manage to drive into town together, although even then Stephen had to cover his eyes with a bandage, lest the passing scenery made him giddy. Then, one cold night later in the month, Edith Olivier was surprised to receive an unexpected midnight caller. It was Stephen, who had been driven over to the Daye House wearing a suit coat and trousers over his pyjamas, 'looking bloated'. Edith was shocked, but still found as they talked that Stephen remained 'so utterly his wayward self in spite of the disguise of the fat'.[2]

Only by early summer 1934 did Stephen emerge fully from the years of illness and emotional upheaval, seemingly unscarred, and with a new social thirst. Lady Juliet Duff was one friend whose company he particularly sought. Her mother, Lady Ripon, had been instrumental in publicizing Diaghilev's ballet in England, and as Lady de Grey was one of the great society hostesses of the Edwardian era. Juliet had inherited her social skills, and at her house, Bulbridge, in Wilton, one might meet any of England's great names, from Winston Churchill to Somerset Maugham. Stephen relished her company, and that of her good-looking and engaging son, Sir Michael Duff. By virtue of her wide acquaintance, Lady Juliet was also a superb source of gossip and news (which, said friends, was her primary function in life). Meeting up that June, Juliet told Stephen she had recently seen Siegfried, who had told her that Stephen had 'irresistible, compelling charm', to which Stephen replied 'Attaboy Stephen !'[3] in his recently-resumed journal, where he also noted that he had been compared to Wilde's Dorian Gray.

On 8 July Stephen went with Edith to a bathing party in Bulbridge. Edith found him in an odd mood, not wanting to bathe, but instead sitting and watching with her, and gossiping about Rex. '*Someone* abuses Rex to him. Who is it?' she wondered, noting that on three separate occasions recently Stephen had 'told things against him.(1) He speaks cruelly about people.(2) He sees *only* Tallulah Bankhead.(3) Now, he has taken to drink and is *carried to bed*.' Thus Rex could well understand Edith's judgement of Stephen when she wrote (having heard that he had written to Siegfried wanting to 'come back into his life') that Stephen had a 'prankish wickedness . . . that human hardness of a jewel or elf'.[4]

At last Stephen was ready to take off from dreary England; and in the first week of August, he made his first proper flight in an aeroplane. He and Cecil flew from Croydon Aerodrome, on Imperial Airways' fashionable '12.30 to Paris'. Anyone who was anyone – from the Prince of Wales to Mary Pickford, from Feodor Chaliapin to Barbara Hutton – flew this route. Passengers were treated to the utmost in-flight luxury then available during the two-and-a-half-hour journey to Le Bourget. Lunch was served, and uniformed stewards calmed nervous passengers who sat white-faced in their bucket seats. On arriving smoothly and swiftly in Paris, Stephen and Cecil checked into the famed Hôtel Prince des Galles, to spend a few days hard shopping in the capital. Schiaparelli's boutique on the place Vendôme was a first, essential stop. Then they bought huge armfuls of yellow nasturtiums, cornflowers, and zinnias, which Stephen floated in his bath, as though he were Millais painting Ophelia.

Although Beaton had to leave his friend to meet up with Tchelitchew in

Spain, that summer bloomed golden; from the days of sickness had come days of delight. Stephen journeyed south to Avignon. Here he found the white-walled courtyards of Provence, and the romantic Roman ruins, Les Antiques, at Saint Rémy. He stayed at the best hotel, Le Prieuré, on the place du Champêtre, in the shadow of the ancient priory, and from there explored the town of Avignon and its environs. Cecil rejoined him, glad to escape the bickering of Tchelitchew and his boyfriend, Charles Henri Ford, in Seville. Together they revelled in the hot weather, and Beaton took snapshots of Stephen perched on one of the Roman walls, the very epitome of South-of-France chic in his black vest and pants. He was also flattered by Cecil telling him, 'I can't imagine anybody not liking you.'[5]

But Beaton had all too soon to return to London to begin work on a Cochran show, leaving Stephen to move on to the Hôtel Riviera at Aix-en-Provence, visiting Mont Saint-Victoire with its pine woods and 'rose-red soil',[6] much painted by Cézanne. Here he felt the pull of the south, and had soon made up his mind to go yet further, to Marseilles – a momentous decision, as this first real contact with the city would spark off *Lascar*.

The descriptions of Marseilles that were to pepper the manuscripts of his 'Story of the Maritime Boulevard' stem from that initial experience, of a 'glittering jungle of sound and colour'.[7] A brief glimpse confirmed what he had heard from other visitors like Brian Howard or Constant Lambert,[*] who had been there a year or two previously. Here was a potent mixture, seething with exotic life and the promise of every kind of experience. Stephen wrote of 'the first impression Marseille made on me, when my book, *Lascar*, first stirred – awakened in my mind. The dock . . . the smoke; the decorative braves; the warehouses and ship-yards; the pleasant clamour – all this made my heart sing – as if the pulse of this sad world . . . had quickened, become more healthy.'[9] These first impressions were to swirl about in the recesses of his memory, the images sticking in his mind's eye, to percolate and ferment over the next few years until he gave them a chance to surface as literal descriptions.

Stephen set off for Palma after a few days; he flew from Marseilles on a seaplane, which, as it rose and banked, gave him a new perspective on

---

[*]Lambert wrote in 1928 that ' . . . the only difference between Marseilles night life and a Great Ormond Street party is one of expense. One feels that at any moment the homely figure of Dick Wyndham may emerge from a bordel or that Wadsworth [Edward Wadsworth, the painter] will be seen trying to retrieve his hat from some old hag or other. All the female whores look like Greta [Wyndham's wife!] and all the male ones like Brian Howard.'[8]

the city that already obsessed him. In Majorca the sun reigned, and Stephen did little more than make tentative forays from his hotel. It was a peaceful isle still, yet to become a manic tourist trap, and he could wander empty coves and along great stretches of sandy beaches quite alone.

He returned to Paris on 18 September, staying at the Hôtel Raphael to sample the further delights of his favourite capital. Once more he lost himself in shopping expeditions, buying a turquoise tortoise which sat on his table as he sketched it. Stephen felt the pangs of remorse at his lack of thrift. 'And now Stephen darling that you have bought the turquoise tortoise you must cease to bask in the illusion that you are economical.'[10]

Old friends in Paris beckoned. The following day Stephen saw Mistinguett again. Six years had mellowed his former harsh judgement of the singer, and he found her performance at the Folies Bergère 'charming & lovely – I loved her completely . . . her smile completely survived the years.' Sixty years later, Stephen recalled the scene for his friend, the Earl of Pembroke. 'A most extraordinary woman!' he declared. 'I met her through Lino Carenzio – who was then her boyfriend. He was playing with her at the Folies Bergère – and I met him shopping near the Etoile, and he said, "You must come and see Mistinguett, because she loves you and calls you her *amour! c'est mon amour*!" . . . I couldn't quite rise to that altitude of splendour!' noted Stephen. 'She was frightfully rich. I went to lunch with her and the house was so cold that we had to have lunch in a sort of telephone box, sitting on each other's knees! Freezing! We couldn't stand up! And she had dyed hair, rather a lovely brown, over one shoulder . . . she had a husky voice and a famous song – "My Man" – I knew it in English – it was sung in New York quite a lot . . . and she winked and tried to be frightfully vulgar but she never managed to be vulgar at all.'[11]

By October 1934 Stephen was back at Wilsford, albeit briefly. Wanderlust still prevailed, even if his next trip was only to rural Dorset. Here he visited T. E. Lawrence for the second time, at his tiny and primitive cottage, Clouds Hill, near Bovington Camp where he was stationed. Lawrence led an ascetic life, glad of visitors such as Morgan Forster and Siegfried Sassoon. Stephen was much taken with the adventurer's 'mystique', and the two got on well together, talking of Noël Coward, amongst others: 'His music's no good,' said the Arabian hero, 'vitality is all that he's got really.' Lawrence told Stephen that only simple pleasures inspired him now – like cutting fresh gorse and heather, then stacking it to dry by the fireside. He said that quite soon he would be leaving the Air

Force, where he served as Corporal T. E. Shaw. 'Do come and see me,' he said. 'I shall need to be diverted, and amused.' Stephen noted that the soldier talked in short bursts, like Morse code. They spoke of mutual friends – of Forster especially, with Lawrence making the cryptic remark: 'He's the one – but people don't know.'[12] They talked of Morgan's latest work; one story, of a love affair with a ghost ['Doctor Woolacott'], Lawrence particularly loved, and he told Stephen he wished Forster would publish it. This was to have a sad importance for Stephen, for only a few months later Lawrence had a fatal accident riding his motorbike from Clouds Hill, and died in May 1935.

Stephen stayed during October in the Cove Hotel, Lulworth, close to the picturesque Dorset coastline. 'You should love this place!' he told Cecil. 'This morning I walked to unbelievable white cliffs & beaches – seagulls – ruby weed and a sea-wind that made me want to cheer for joy. I came back so hungry: 2 helpings of boiled mutton & onion sauce, "tasty" like ambrosia.' Stephen described his fellow guests. 'All "ladies" – in the genteelest sense – some are damp-nosed & knit all the time, one is very old and like a peppery old colonel – she hates me & glares when I come into the room.'[13] Stephen illustrated the scenario with a sketch portraying three elderly ladies with pinched features, assiduously knitting in the hotel lounge. Above was a self-portrait, Stephen in his new sou'wester, with which to brave the autumn sea gales. No fisherman ever looked this chic.

That evening he took Florence Hardy to a nearby circus, and was full of his news; he had decided to spend the winter in America. Cecil had written out introductions to Madame Karinska, the Russian dress designer whom he knew there, and to the manager of the Waldorf Astoria, recommending the best accommodation for his friend.

So New York called, and Stephen came. Passage booked, he set sail on the Cunard liner, SS *Berengaria*, from Southampton. Nothing could be more glamorous or exciting than setting off on a transatlantic voyage in those days. At Southampton, one received the hospitality of the shipping line as soon as one alighted at the terminus station, coming into the art deco splendour of the South Western Hotel, where Press photographers lay in wait for the newest movie star arrivals or departures. Time for a drink as one's luggage was whisked on board (in Stephen's case, a plethora of trunks, dressing-cases, books and make-up boxes), then an ascent to the huge floating hotel that was to carry one effortlessly across the Atlantic.

The *Berengaria* was the flagship of the Cunard fleet, boasting a large ballroom and a Palm Court, the latter 'skilfully schemed to give the Berengaria passenger the illusion of being in a patio at Monte Carlo' — or so said the brochure blurb. First-class accommodation was unashamedly sybaritic: marble-panelled bathrooms, reception rooms that would not have been out of place in the Paris Ritz, and the largest public room of any ship afloat.

Coincidentally, the *Berengaria* had been the ship on which Sassoon had made his return voyage home from his American lecture tour in 1920. 'I suppose that most people, while travelling on a large well-behaved boat, are luxuriously detached from ordinary existence,' he observed. 'To this obvious sensation I surrendered unconditionally.'[14] This was certainly Stephen's experience too. With any necessary duties taken care of either by his new valet, a twenty-five-year-old Italian named Vittorio Bracco, or by the white-uniformed and noiseless stewards, he could lie back on the promenade deck, enjoying the late autumn sun and invigorating mid-Atlantic breeze.

Then, almost miraculously, the towers of Manhattan and the Statue of Liberty loomed on the horizon. As the white superstucture of the ship nudged towards the quay, it seemed as though they were entering into the very heart of New York. A broad plank with handrails, and a flash of bright sunlight, was all that stood between Stephen and the New World.

The story of Stephen's arrival in New York that autumn of 1934 has been described by David Herbert in his memoirs, *Second Son*. Herbert had gone to New York against his parents' advice, and had fallen in with the New York café society, along with his compatriot, Michael Duff. Tallulah Bankhead, Mrs Patrick Campbell and the Vanderbilts were all part of his social circle, which prided itself on its more Bohemian members; Olivia Wyndham, Stephen's cousin, lived in Harlem with a black actress, Edna Thomas. This was the New York which Cecil had experienced on his previous trips to America. He had in turn relayed all such gossip to Stephen, who came looking forward to experiencing it all himself. However, according to Herbert, New York was not prepared for Stephen Tennant. It seemed that Rex's fear, expressed before his friend's departure – that Stephen would 'seem very odd to the Americans'[15] – was justified.

According to Herbert, he was sitting in his Waldorf Towers apartment when a telephone call came through from mid-Atlantic. 'I couldn't think who it could be. Then I heard a familiar and tremulous voice, something between a contralto and bass, faint and far away, saying: 'David, David, I'm coming to the New World for the first time! Meet me at the boat. Cherish me and introduce me to the glories of New York!'[16]

Herbert met the boat. 'The passengers left in streams, but there was no sign of Stephen. Did I dream up the telephone call? . . . I waited until the stream became a trickle . . . and then, at last, he appeared, "Marcelled" and painted, wearing a large black felt hat trimmed with flowers, a gold tinsel tie and a black shiny mackintosh trimmed with a fur collar. This may not sound odd now, but in the thirties it was electrifying. He walked down the gangway delicately holding a spray of cattelya orchids. "Pin 'em on!" shouted a tough customs officer "Oh, have you got a pin?" exclaimed Stephen. "What a wonderful welcome! I've searched the whole ship for one." Quite out of his stride the burly customs man fumbled behind the lapel of his coat and handed Stephen what he wanted. "You're a darling!" cried Stephen. "What a lovely start to my visit! You kind, kind creature!"' Herbert reports that he felt 'covered with embarrassment, but Stephen's total naturalness and complete disregard for the reactions of others carried him through any situation, no matter how hostile. His charm was irresistible.'

Stephen certainly seems to have fallen very quickly into the swing of things Stateside (and America to his charms: one new acquaintance by the name of Dick Wilson told him, 'You are more like Royalty than any Royalty.'). He checked into the Waldorf, where Cecil's recommendation had secured him one of the best suites, and from there he explored the city and the sights he remembered from his youth. The Fifth Avenue shops (especially La Vieille Russie), Central Park and its zoo, the cabs and the street sellers all fascinated him. The sheer excitement of the fast-moving metropolis transfixed him. There were friends too: Charlie James, the couturier; Michael Duff and David Herbert; and Pavel Tchelitchew, there to organize his first one-man show at the Julian Levy gallery. David Herbert threw a cocktail party in Stephen's honour, 'being careful only to invite friends who I thought would understand'.[17]

'Stephen was at his best, brilliant and witty, and the party was going extremely well when the doorbell rang. In walked a manicure girl with her trolley. "I'm afraid you've made a mistake," I started to say. "No. No!" cried Stephen. "It's for me." He sat down, talking all the time while the girl manicured his nails. Quite suddenly he exclaimed, "My dear! your nails are in a terrible state! I suppose you never have them done yourself." And, whisking round the trolley, he got to work. We thought the poor girl would be cut to ribbons. Stephen, however, just continued gossiping. The girl was turned to stone with apprehension and astonishment. After a while a seraphic smile appeared on Stephen's face and he said, "There! That's better! Now you can go anywhere!" The result was perfect.'

Herbert maintains that this was all 'more than I had bargained for . . . A week or two later we were all nervous wrecks. Luckily the New York air did not suit Stephen's delicate health and he departed for Hot Springs.'

The portrait his childhood friend gave did not please Stephen on its publication in 1972. According to friends at the time, he was positively vexed by Herbert's somewhat snide comments on his effeminacy. But there was a certain degree of rivalry between Stephen and David Herbert, probably stemming from their younger days; Stephen gave as good as he got. When, back in England, David had painted the interior of the Park House, his eighteenth-century 'Pavilion of Pleasure' at Wilton, a deep shade of black throughout, he recalled David asked him not to tell his mother, the Countess of Pembroke. 'It was rather silly, really,' said Stephen. 'All she had to do was to walk round the corner and look in the windows.'[18]

'The Homestead' hotel, situated by one of the warm springs of the Appalachian mountains, was aimed at wealthy city dwellers who came south to take the waters. Stephen did not partake of the 'medical baths and pool' in Hot Springs, however, preferring a leisurely five days of inactivity – in fact, becoming just a little depressed. America had not fulfilled his expectations second time around, and on the basis of 'reasons of health' – it was all so exhausting, he announced – Stephen cut short his stay. Soon he was on the return passage to England, there to spend a quiet Christmas.

In January Stephen resurfaced in Wiltshire society. He talked to Edith Olivier 'of his loneliness and of Siegfried, seeming so glad to know S really wishes him well and does not hate him'. Stephen said he'd like to see Siegfried 'some day but not yet as he would feel *left out* because Sieg has "a rock to return to". He honestly thinks he *only* chucked Sieg because he felt it good for his health and this is true – tho' not *all* the truth,' observed Edith, noting that he 'often told Rex that Sieg had begun to bore him to death! and this because he *would* possess him entirely and keep everyone else away'.[19]

Used by now to spending the late winter abroad, however, Stephen took off to Switzerland, then Italy, settling on the Casa Angelo at Ascona, a small *pensione* with a marvellous view of the Italian Alps, recommended to him by William Walton. The Italian spring suited Stephen, for he travelled on south, staying in Turin during March.

Nonetheless, Stephen was beginning to feel world-weary, and a little lonely. He still valued his friends, yet never seemed convinced of their affection. He was always seeking reassurance of devotion from Cecil or Rex. He wrote to the latter that spring, somewhat frantically, accusing him of forgetting their old friendship. The truth was that he and Rex had drifted apart: gone was that romantic correspondence of their youth, the ink sketches and intricately-doodled envelopes which gave their letters to each other the flavour of a Victorian love affair. It had not happened in any purposeful way, but merely because Rex was busy pursuing an active career, and could not drop his brushes the moment Stephen called, even if he wanted to. Whether or not Rex knew of Stephen's gossip about his private life, as relayed to Edith, is not clear; certainly Rex remained loyal himself.

It was with some frustration, then, that he replied to Stephen's letter on 12 April. Begging forgiveness for not writing, he told Stephen how the burden of work depressed him. 'How I hate illustrating,' he confessed. Then: 'Darling Stephen, I do love getting letters from you – you are so wrong if you think I am indifferent about whether you write or not. I love being with you and always shall, and therefore letters are the next best thing. I too value our friendship more than I can express & feel sure that it will always always remain. & why should it not? As thank God, it grew and has lasted all this time owing nothing to unhappy destructive SEX. I say thank God because I am sure that if the affection we have for one another had been based on physical love – or sex – it would . . .'

Annoyingly, the second page of the letter is missing. But the message, despite all protestations, was clear. Their Kingdom by the Sea had sunk, and would never now be salvaged.

With Beaton, it was another matter. Stephen still held him in his thrall, and Cecil would readily give up his time. He felt inspired by Stephen, emotionally and artistically; whenever they met, Cecil took something away with him, an idea for a surreal photo-set, an acutely-observed fashion detail, or a piece of witty badinage, that could later be recycled. Thus, when one evening that May Stephen rang up 'at the eleventh hour' to suggest a trip to the theatre, Cecil jumped. *Stop Press* was the chosen production, and Cecil looked forward to an evening of 'Stephen's fancy & wit', as he knew his friend would be stimulated by the 'archlights, footlights, the grease paint', which 'goes to his head – & he becomes more fantastic than [ever] before.'[20] What Beaton had forgotten, however, was that Stephen's appearance was likely to elicit a 'barrage of rude remarks from total strangers', an indignity which Cecil himself had left behind in his younger days.

That hurdle over, Cecil and Stephen settled down to enjoy the musical. It was not a brilliant one, but the 'blaring tunes' and chorus-kicking fired Stephen. 'He produced some very funny remarks. Before Dorothy Dickson, the leading lady, had appeared he looked impatiently at the programme to see in which item her first entrance was made & seeing that it was next said, "I suppose she is putting on the last lot of skin lotion now?"'

In the interval they went backstage and witnessed the reality of theatrical glamour – dressing-rooms like rabbit warrens, a cast 'rather like hooligans'. In the second half Stephen, gossiping to Cecil in the stalls, described Katharine Hepburn – one of his current 'flames' – as 'that wild yell that is synonymous with the bell ringing for break in the preparatory school – the scream as all the pencils are downed & the children rush to the playground'. Less abstractly, he enthused over the 'intense, boyish look' of Garbo, 'surprised, looking over one shoulder with the hearth rug lock of hair hanging over one eye'. Cecil concluded in his diary: 'Stephen still retains the poetry of the theatre that used to bless my childish days & which has now turned to different interest in the theatre.' In other words he, like Rex, had grown up. Stephen, like Peter Pan, had not.

Chapter 15

Bloomsbury-by-the-Sea

We're just off to see what Stephen Tennant has done to Monk's House. Bath salts – scents – everywhere I expect, if not Stephen himself.

> — Virginia Woolf to Lady Tweedsmuir, 5 July 1935

THERE were new friends for Stephen in 1935. His relationships with the Bloomsberries and their greatest literary exponents – E. M. Forster and Virginia Woolf – in particular became more important, as his maturity and the increasing desire seriously to enter the literary arena became uppermost in his conscious mind.

Given Stephen's literary upbringing and milieu, it was logical that he should affiliate himself to the Bloomsbury group, who remained the most important artistic influence in his world. Bloomsbury was an artistic community, with ideals of Beauty and Culture above all else; sympathetic ideals to Stephen, who was a new recruit, somewhat warily welcomed. (He was regarded by Virginia Woolf as very much part of the 'Mayfair' set – in which she included her own lover, Vita Sackville-West, Lord David Cecil, and the Sitwells – and therefore to be suspected on grounds of money and power.)

In the mid-thirties Stephen strengthened his connections with the Woolfs, the Bells and others. He began to inhabit their territory (living in Sussex, and Bloomsbury itself), to assume their habits (his journal-keeping and copious correspondence followed their set patterns of communication and creative work); he even spoke like them. Lytton Strachey made the 'high-pitched whinney' fashionable amongst his set; Stephen talked in similar fashion, albeit in a lower register. Even in the late nineteen-eighties it was possible to detect the same echoes of 'artistic' inflection in his speech, from a culture already flourishing eighty years before, at his birth. V. S. Naipaul, whose landlord Stephen became in later years, was told by a Wilsford gardener: 'He doesn't say peony like you and me ... "He says peony." The word in his pronunciation rhymed with "pony". Somewhere ... I had heard or read of this Edwardian affectation, an affectation known to be an affectation.'[1]

In the spring and summer of 1935, Virginia Woolf was hard at work on her new novel, *The Years*. Woolf struggled with its creation, moving between her London home at Tavistock Square (where Stephen had first been taken to visit the writer by their mutual friend, Arthur Waley, in 1929), and the Woolfs' country home, Monk's House, at Rodmell, a little village on the Sussex South Downs. Quentin Bell dubbed this landscape 'Bloomsbury-by-the-Sea' with good reason. Harold Nicolson and Vita Sackville-West lived at Sissinghurst, the Woolfs at Rodmell, Clive and Vanessa Bell, and Duncan Grant, at Charleston. During his time at Swaylands, Stephen had come to know that countryside too, and in the years before the war he was to become a virtual fixture at hotels in Piddinghoe (close to Rodmell), Seaford, and Wych Cross.

Virginia Woolf notes Stephen's name in her diary entry for 5 June 1935. The writing of *The Years* was weighing heavily: 'It's beginning this cursed dry hard empty chapter again. Every time I say it will be the devil! but I never believe it. And then the usual depressions come. And I wish for death ... after the queer interlude, at once life — that is the telephone beginning — starts. So that one is forcibly chafed ... Vita; Stephen Tennant; Julian; dressmaker; going to Rodmell for Whitsun.'[2]

In her diary entries, Virginia's encounters with Stephen often appear as telephonic ones, and usually the tone suggests slight exasperation at having to leave her work once more. But as with most writers, what Virginia Woolf complained of as interruptions she also welcomed as diversions — and to observe life and people was part of her stock-in-trade. When asked about Virginia's opinion of Stephen, Stephen Spender replied that 'she only really *liked* Bloomsbury people; everything outside her world was, to her, a spectacle. People were fish in a tank — and Stephen would certainly have been a fish in a tank to Virginia.'[3] Woolf was herself told by her friend and lover, Vita Sackville-West: 'Oh yes, you like people better through the brain than through the heart.'[4]

Whatever Virginia's true opinion of Stephen, she thought affectionately enough of him to lend him their country house for the last weekend in June, 'in an access of generosity', as she put it, adding, 'Thank God we are alone this weekend.'[5] (Which recalls Stephen's favourite Woolf comment: 'Do you enjoy visits from friends?' asked young Stephen.

'Dubious – very dubious. "Yes –" then her face lighted up – "it's so wonderful when they go." ')[6] Stephen went to Monk's House ostensibly to get some writing done, Virginia having recommended it as a peaceful place. But Virginia knew Stephen better than to expect him to have 'buckled down' to any work. She and Leonard were due to return on 5 July, and Virginia hoped she wouldn't find their guest still *in situ.** Her fears were unfounded. Stephen had moved on to Kiln Cottage, a guesthouse not far away in Piddinghoe, run by a Scottish family, the Burnsides.

Throughout the summer Stephen was stationed in Sussex, gathering together his literary thoughts. He saw the Woolfs on a number of occasions. His visits appear to have been a point of contention between Virginia and her husband. 'L. in a stew about Stephen,' she wrote in August, 'that is he wants to come; why have S. 3 times & not Kingsley Martin. A very old, sorry, but not serious story'[8] (Stephen being Virginia's taste in friends, the more prosaic Martin, editor of the *New Statesman*, being Leonard's). Stephen later recalled telling Virginia how much he enjoyed arriving at Kiln Cottage in Piddinghoe. Virginia turned to Leonard and said, 'What can they think, when this bird-of-paradise arrives?' Stephen was very pleased: 'After that, I decided I must cultivate her acquaintance!'[9]

Stephen's attitude towards Virginia Woolf was, whilst being an honest bit of lion-hunting on his part, not completely full of unequivocal admiration for a writer whose work was already being seen as amongst the most important modernist literature produced so far. Writing about her in 1978, Stephen proved he was as used to aquarium-gazing as she was: 'Virginia Woolf was like a Magic Priestess – with a maze & labyrinth – she neither knew the way in – or out of it,' he noted. 'But the excellence isn't sustained really – She is a "Cult" – that must remain a little ambiguous, I think.' Stephen had the benefit of hindsight, his personal recollections cutting through time, a result of his razor-sharp memory: 'She had an angry laugh! (I told E. M. Forster and he was amused) & was at times formidable – too upset by petty trivial things – unworthy of her splendid aesthetic insights. She could talk dazzlingly – & also very spitefully. Her essays, I prefer, on the whole.' Later he added, 'Virginia Woolf is a genius *manqué.'*[10]

---

*Woolf's nephew, Quentin Bell, recalls that Stephen sent his hostess a present after borrowing Monk's House. 'This took the form of a very expensive looking oblong parcel which in its glossy splendour made one suppose that it must contain something of the highest value. When my aunt opened it she found two pieces of bark from a tree which were, according to Tennant, of the most exquisite and subtle beauty. Virginia didn't agree and was rather cross.'[7]

'How infernally sad all loneliness is,' said Virginia to Stephen. Yet she complained to her sister Vanessa on 29 July that Stephen had already been round that morning: 'What can be done about people?'[11] The distance between Stephen and Monk's House, which allowed such casual and (apparently) annoying calls, widened in August, to Virginia's relief. By the end of the month he had moved on to the quiet seaside town of Seaford. From here he boasted to Sibyl Colefax of having 'seen Virginia and lots of heavenly people. Vanessa Bell I like enormously.'[12] He had also drunk to Sibyl's health when visiting Maynard Keynes and his wife, Lydia, for lunch at their home in Tilton.*

On 15 September, Stephen was comfortably settled into the Bay Hotel, Seaford, and bought a large scrapbook intended for use as his new journal. On its cover he carefully painted a neo-romantic landscape, to one side a classical bust, framed in a draped window at which stands a dressing-table. It is typical of the kind of composition Stephen had invented for his pictures: a distant exotic view, surrounded by some of his favourite things. All around are stuck perfume bottle labels – Worth, Roger et Gallet – and in the mid-distance a matelot waves a salute. The colours are muted greys and blues, with white gouache details, such as the pair of evening gloves laid neatly on the dressing-table, as if the occupant of this hotel room were off out for the evening, or had just returned.

That night, Stephen was woken by a tremendous crash. A sea gale had blown his window in. Seizing his toy plush monkey, he ran out into the corridor, wondering what to do. From the landing window, he anxiously watched giant waves crash against the esplanade. Eventually the hotel owner came to his rescue, and found him a new room on a quieter side of the hotel. Yet the storm did not abate, and through his dreams Stephen heard windows banging and the rain spattering the ground.

At breakfast the next morning, Stephen was cheered by letters from Morgan Forster, and from his new secretary-companion, a reassuring 50-year-old woman from Cheshire by the name of Josephine Wilkinson (known as Wilkie). The letter from Morgan planned a visit to Seaford for later that month. Stephen's friendship with the author had grown over the past few years, and now it was at its closest.

Forster was forty-six, and a well-established and highly respected writer in 1935. His background was very much more humble than

---

*Keynes, the radical economist (1883–1946), had married Lydia Lopokova, star of the Russian Ballet, in 1925, and lived on the neighbouring farm to Charleston (home of the Bells, and Duncan Grant, his ex-lover).

Stephen's, but they did share certain similarities. Forster's father had died from TB a year after his son's birth, and Morgan was thereafter brought up exclusively by women – 'the classic Freudian recipe for subsequent confusion about his sexual role', observed his friend, Francis King.[13] Forster's mother, Lily, was accordingly protective, especially over his health – she feared he too might contract TB – and for years Forster assumed his health was, like Stephen's, precariously balanced.

At Cambridge, Forster became one of the Apostles, the free-thinking brethren which included Lytton Strachey, Maynard Keynes, Roger Fry and Leonard Woolf; predominantly homosexual – although neither Fry nor Woolf were of the persuasion – the group defined the beginnings of Bloomsbury. In 1901, Forster and his mother went on a European tour that was to inspire *A Room with a View*, published seven years later, followed by *Howard's End* in 1910. There was a long hiatus before his next major novel, time which Forster spent in India and Egypt, discovering those countries, and his own sexuality. His early lack of such fulfilment has been seen as the motivating factor behind his writing, loneliness and isolation breeding the intense, constrained emotional atmospheres of his early works. It is a marked contrast with Stephen's early life and indicates, perhaps, the reasons why a writer like Forster, struggling with his background and personality, achieved creatively what he did, while Stephen's energies (such as they were, given his periods of illness) were dissipated. While Lily Forster said of her son, 'I never saw anybody so incapable',[14] Pamela had expected of hers the highest artistic achievements.* As her grand-daughter Pauline observes, Pamela was an artist, and expected her children to live like artists. Stephen had all that Morgan had not – extreme good looks, a privileged upbringing, money – but it was Morgan who had the drive (in much the same way as had Cecil). As his friends achieved their ambitions, so, conversely, Stephen's great expectations slowly lost impetus, and gained inertia.

Stephen Tennant's appeal to the homosexual literary 'Gang' (as Arthur Waley called them) of Forster, J. R. Ackerley and William Plomer, and their appeal to him, was defined by the difference in class and life-style. By being so opposite to the hard-working lives these men led, Stephen – the leisured aristocratic host – was an attractive notion in himself. To men who worked in dusty London offices all week, Wilsford was a welcome escape (it was Cyril Connolly who said that a writer ought to have a rich friend). But most of all, there was a liberated feeling about being with

---

*When Stephen first started up a friendship with the author, Pamela was not impressed, and in one of her scathing asides observed to her youngest son that Forster was 'ugly'.[15]

someone like Stephen, with whom they could open up and talk unhindered, sometimes in extravagant ways (P. N. Furbank, Forster's friend and biographer, notes that Stephen was percipient in seeing Forster's 'suppressed love of the exotic').

Although Furbank observes that Forster sometimes suspected Stephen of 'upper class caprice',[16] Morgan's relationship with Stephen was evidently an affectionate one. In his letter that autumn, Morgan told Stephen he had been out walking on Folkestone beach with Joe Ackerley, and the latter had found a pebble which he had named, 'the shape of things to come'. Morgan promised to bring it with him to Wilsford, 'And perhaps I shall not be able to stop myself from dropping it down your neck,'[17] he wrote playfully.

Waiting for Morgan's visit, Stephen lost himself in the quiet charms of the local shops. He was captivated by a miniature chest of drawers, which he thought perfect for storing his portable treasures, the talismans which he carried about with him – shells, rings, love-letters, pressed wild flowers. From the same antique shop, he emerged clutching a china portrait of Shakespeare. Elsewhere he found an embroidered cushion, which he bought as a present for Alice Douglas Sedgwick's new cottage at Enstone, Oxford. The last acquisition of the day was perhaps the most important: Stephen's first bow-tie, which he wore that evening, 'with sexy results'.[18]

We are not privileged to know with whom this accessory was so successful, but Stephen's diary opens the next day with a quote: ' "Yes, we were very much in love," she said – "We used to look at each other with the terrible wonder that is love; and when we kissed & embraced, the whole world faded and thundered in our ears." '[19] It hardly matters to whom this refers (more likely to Sassoon than any other); all of Stephen's emotions have a nostalgic, lost tone, as though he cannot expect love affairs to last. Certainly, by the beginning of the following year, he announced to his diary that he had forsaken love and sex altogether.

On Sunday a Dr Parsons came to check on Stephen's health, and pronounced him 'very well'. Parsons advised art as therapy: 'If you sketch from morning till night it will be the saving of you. Create! Create!'[20] That evening, this pleasing advice still with him, there was an exciting expedition to the fair at Newhaven, with Stephen's recently engaged valet and chauffeur, Burnside (from Kiln Cottage), driving him in his new Rolls.

Even Seaford itself, which seemed ugly at first sight, redeemed itself with fuchsia hedges and magenta veronicas in the little gardens. Outside the town limits, in rural Sussex proper, Stephen liked to walk, discarding his Norfolk jacket in the heat of the midday sun, dallying with field-workers and carters, watching women set out for the shops. Their ordinary tasks and the bustle of everyday life pleased him as much as any of his more sophisticated interests. His joy in commonplace things – from lichen on the walls to the horses' fine brasses – was a basic appreciation of existence. He told Alice Douglas Sedgwick that he was now 'principally solitary, which I prefer; the rare imprint of a passing day settles more deeply & variously when I am alone.'[21] For the rest of his life, Stephen would be essentially alone. He liked his own company, to sit and watch the world without the world bothering him. 'I've never found the companion as companionable as solitude,' he declared. Alone with his thoughts, he could feel that he had no responsibility to anyone or anything, but it would mean sacrificing many things, the most important of which was real friendship. All relationships after Siegfried were conducted at a distance, even when Morgan or Cecil or Rex were with him. Stephen shut out the world to enjoy it further.

Stephen still could not decide to which exotic land he would next sail – California? South Africa? He planned his packing: new white linen shorts, his tiny cabinet for shells, his two lapis lazuli rings, all in readiness for 'hippos and humming-birds'. Yet by 27 September he still hadn't made up his mind. Then, just before setting out for a driving lesson (under Burnside's direction, Stephen had become eager to pilot his shiny new Rolls himself), Stephen received a letter which suddenly determined his autumn destination for him. Willa Cather wrote from Paris, where she was visiting her friend Isabelle McClung, who was dying from a liver disease. Out of this misfortune came luck for Stephen – for Willa suggested he come to New York to visit her, and then spend some time in her favourite countryside of New England.

Thus fortified, off Stephen went, dressed in grey polo jersey and flannel trousers, his hair wavy and newly washed, for a happy lesson in the Rolls, excited by the possibility of meeting his literary heroine at last. That evening he dined in Lewes, and was delighted by the appearance of a scampering baby mouse on the window sill. Where other diners might have expressed outrage and called for its removal, Stephen merely counselled it to be careful, or 'some trap-minded person' might see it.[22]

Such child-like delight filled his journals with trivial and amusing incidents, written in his elegant hand and multi-coloured inks, alongside sketches of flowers, friends, street scenes. Souvenir tickets were stuck down beside envelopes of letters from Vanessa Bell or Virginia Woolf; all mementoes to take their place in his iconographia, arranged at leisure in a leisurely life. Greater events do intrude – Stephen notes the first Italian battle in Abyssinia – but the political implications of far-off wars meant little to him.

Morgan Forster came to Seaford that weekend on his promised visit. He was not surprised to see Stephen's Rolls waiting for him at Groomsbridge station on Saturday morning ; he might even have expected to find bouquets of roses, carnations and gladioli arranged inside the car. But he had to blink when he looked again, for there, poised quiveringly on the flowers, were two huge tropical butterflies his host had acquired in East Grinstead. Forster arrived at the hotel to be greeted by Stephen, who thought the writer looked tired and rather sallow. Having recovered from the journey after a cup of tea, they sat down to chat. Stephen showed Morgan his latest journals and was particularly proud of the entries on T. E. Lawrence, which described his last evening with their friend, when they had spoken of Morgan's unpublished stories. Forster complimented Stephen on his descriptions, praise the latter rated very highly as he knew well that the writer never said such things just to please.

They dined together that evening, both in high spirits. Morgan gleefully described a recent party of Sibyl Colefax's, at which Noël Coward had been guest of honour, and had talked drivel all evening. Stephen laughed out loud, in his staccato fashion, and as the wine bottle emptied they became quite uproarious. Morgan also talked of a visit to Amsterdam with Bob Buckingham, his policeman friend, Christopher Isherwood, Klaus Mann (son of Thomas), Brian Howard and Gerald Hamilton, the 'Mr Norris' of Isherwood's Berlin novel, *Mr Norris Changes Trains*.

As he sat opposite his friend, Stephen assessed Forster. He thought him ageless rather than youthful, a man of genius ; slightly mysterious, certainly secretive. Stephen sympathized with Morgan's attitudes to humanity – the empathetic yet admonishing tone which he took with modern values, the writer's gentle liberality. 'In his writing there is something more terrible than sadness, a kind of vast, neutral wisdom ; rich, pellucid, yet desultory . . . E. M. F.'s greatness lies in his odd tenderness and abstract cynicism.'[23] The two discussed literature – William Plomer had recently suggested Forster should publish a collection of essays and criticism, and Stephen thought this a good idea, although he liked Morgan's fiction best. Retiring to the music room, Forster read aloud a new story he had just written, 'You Never Really Know', which Stephen considered improper but very witty. Morgan got a little annoyed when, on telling Stephen he could only stay till Sunday, his host asked him why he seemed to spend his life leaving people, quoting Virginia Woolf on the subject: 'Morgan's always in such a hurry to leave me.'[24] Stephen saw that Forster was not pleased, and so desisted. They spent the rest of the evening eating bull's-eye sweets and chatting, and later Morgan played the piano – pieces from Beethoven, Mozart and, on Stephen's request, César Franck. He lay back, with eyes shut, and revelled in Forster's playing. When the evening drew to a close, and they went up to their respective bedrooms, Stephen leant out of his window to pick two passion flowers from the creeping vine that grew there – one for Morgan, and one for himself.

The next morning Forster was in unexpectedly high spirits, waking Stephen at a quarter to nine. 'I hope you don't mind me being so gay?' he said, and added deprecatingly, 'It's not that I feel well.'[25] No reason was forthcoming. They lingered over coffee in the hotel restaurant. Discussing films, Forster extolled the beauty and talent of Garbo, saying that this was one of the few occasions when public opinion was actually right. After breakfast, talk turned to Stephen's *Missionary* book, which was still in abeyance. (It would not be published for another two years, and was dedicated to Forster, who wrote to Stephen in early March 1937, accepting the dedication: 'I hope you are not making it too improper or I shall lose my place with the Earnest Left.')[26]

They drove back to Groombridge in time for Forster to catch the midday train. Stephen sketched them both, waiting on the platform, he looking tall and svelte, very elegant; Morgan short and stumpy, yet genial. Stephen stood waving from the platform, until the train, and Morgan waving from it, disappeared round a bend.

The following day was a red-letter one, literally, for in red ink capitals Stephen triumphantly recorded the fact that he had driven the Rolls for the first time on the main road. He wrote excitedly to Cecil on 9 October: 'Yesterday we went on the main road for the 1st time!!! lorries roaring by: Stephen the tough little guy at the wheel; and to my chauffeur's thrill & joy I turned in to the hotel drive & "swept" up to the entrance! & cashiers were seen clinging & shrieking to each other as the car approached & then, when I got out fainting with triumph, my pants came down!!! with all the cashiers watching – oh dear!'

The next night, Stephen and Burnside were out for a moonlight lesson, a two-hour drive to Groombridge and back, Stephen being complimented on his new-found skill by his chauffeur. He came in dog-tired, yet still

took notice of the evening headlines: sanctions against Italy, in an effort to halt the Abyssinian war. In his journal, Stephen stuck a picture of Sir Samuel Hoare and Anthony Eden.*

The next two weeks were spent at Forest Row, near East Grinstead, where he was consulting Dr Parsons, who now wearied Stephen. A visit to the circus near there introduced Stephen to a mandrill, which he loved, especially when it kissed its keeper on the lips; but by 20 October he was back in Seaford, and feeling depressed by the uneventfulness of his life.

So it was in search of a happier mood that a week later Stephen arrived in London to lodge in his favourite suite at the Hyde Park Hotel (complete with its pet pigeon, Matthew, which he liked to feed with corn). He had gone straight to the theatrical costumiers Nathan's (later Berman and Nathan's), where he had commissioned an extravagant fancy-dress outfit, a powder-blue Hussar's uniform, to take to the States.

A gathering was scheduled for Saturday evening at Peter Watson's chic town flat in Shepherd's Close: Peter, Stephen, Charlie James, Geoffrey Gorer – and, last but not least, Pavel Tchelitchew. Stephen counted the

---

*Within a month, the crisis had escalated into full-blown war. Hoare resigned his position as Foreign Secretary, replaced by the handsome thirty-eight-year-old Eden, one of the 'Glamour Boys', on 23 December.

latter one of the few people who really mattered to him, so it was a gay evening he spent there. He sat on a sofa, Gorer to one side, Pavlik the other. Whilst Stephen drank his milk, Tchelitchew playfully tried to pop pieces of chocolate cake in his mouth. Peter Watson, his dark hair turned light brown by a recent holiday in the sun, was looking smart in an Austrian shirt (Austrian clothing being in vogue at the time – both Stephen and Cecil sported short coats with rounded lapels, embroidered shirts – even to the point of wearing lederhosen-style shorts).

Stephen presented Tchelitchew with a maroon and white check scarf, in a gardenia-decorated box. He had visited Pavlik's show that morning, at the Arthur Tooth galleries, and enthused over the latest collection. And to his delight, Stephen discovered that both Pavlik and Peter would be in New York that winter.

Back at the flat, Peter had to get ready to leave for Ashcombe, where he had been invited by Beaton to spend the weekend, along with Syrie Maugham and Charles Henri Ford. Stephen offered Charlie James a lift back to his flat at Bruton Street, and James invited Stephen in, to see his studio. There, by candlelight, beneath a photograph of Jean Cocteau, they tried on some of the couturier's latest creations. James, the designer of Stephen's Sicilian wardrobe (though he did not generally design for men and often modelled dresses for intimate clients), was a notoriously effeminate young man of Oriental appearance, the same age as Stephen but considerably more *outré*. The idea of these two in *haute couture* trailing round his all-white studio, with its dyed pampas grass in huge vases, must rate high in images of between-the-wars camp.

The next morning Pavlik was on the telephone for an age, analysing the effect Stephen had on people: 'To them you are a strange inexplicable flower,' he told Stephen in his broken French/English. (Another time, the artist told Stephen he was at his most beautiful when angry!)

There was one last afternoon of London appointments: afternoon tea with his new sister-in-law Elizabeth (Lord Glenconner's second wife), a fitting at Nathan's, and shopping at Schiaparelli's, where he bought a blue jersey with red zips.* Then it was back to Seaford; London was too hectic for Stephen's nerves. Two painful visits to the dentist later, he fetched up at the Burley Grey Hotel at Seven Sisters, feeling very ill and sorry for himself, after two anaesthetics two days running. It was only the thought of the nearness of his departure for America that raised Stephen's spirits at all.

---

*Cedric in *Love in a Cold Climate* accurately recognizes a short red jacket Fanny wears nonchalantly as a cardigan as a Schiaparelli design. 'Schiap' had shown zipped jumpers in her Spring collection that year, in which Salvador Dali had collaborated.

Chapter 16

O Pioneer

The sky was burning with the soft-pink and silver of a cloudless summer dawn . . . he came upon thickets of wild roses, with flaming buds, just beginning to open. Where they had opened, their petals were stained with that burning rose-colour which is always gone by noon – a dye made of sunlight and morning and moisture, so intense that it cannot possibly last . . . must fade, like ecstasy . . . He would make a bouquet for a lovely lady; a bouquet gathered off the cheeks of morning . . . these roses, only half-awake, in the defenselessness of utter beauty.

— Willa Cather: *A Lost Lady*

'CUNARD White Star. Aquitania Library. Sunday 24th November 1935. Wilkie & I embarked at Southampton, 20th – & I write this in mid-Atlantic somewhere near the Gulf Stream – for a warm, stuffy wind is blowing. Rex is on B deck – we are on A. We three have the greatest fun. He is going on contract to design sets & dresses for Helen Hayes – Victoria Regina (NOTE. Remember cable Willa Cather today.) We like this boat.'[1] Given Stephen's susceptibility to sea-sickness, it was quite obvious that the latter opinion would change during the voyage, although his suffering on this trip was exceeded by his amused observations. 'Stephen writes of a rough crossing,' noted Cecil in his diary, 'with old ladies having to be "aided" to their compartments – Rex says "How he does enjoy the subtleties of such a joke!"'[2]

Stephen's entourage comprised Wilkie and a new valet, George Wade (at forty-eight, an older man than usual as his manservant), who apparently doubled as a masseur and male nurse. They were joined, by happy coincidence 'and good arrangement', by Rex, who was to design Gilbert Miller's production of *Victoria Regina*. He had booked the same passage on the *Aquitania*, but was not looking forward to his first visit to the States.

Stephen, on the other hand, positively relished America for its glamour and high-paced living. The only slow aspect of this adventure was getting there.

Stephen spent much of the voyage drawing with Rex, and they would have dinner together, with Wilkie. One evening Stephen sat at table, reciting a poem to Rex, and his voice 'grew sibilant with drama' as he spoke the lines which seemed to refer to 'old faces' and 'old voices'. It was only when he looked round that Stephen suddenly realized that the American matrons at the next table thought he was referring to them.

As the ship got out into the Atlantic swell, Stephen fell victim to his old travelling nemesis, nausea, and he felt very weak. He was only just able to read – Cather's latest, *Lucy Gayheart* – as he lay in his cabin, listening to the strains of the ship's band playing one of his favourite tunes, 'Red Sails in the Sunset', until, on the evening of 26 November, they sighted the lights of New York.

The *Aquitania* came into dock the following morning. That evening, Stephen was ensconced in his nineteenth-floor suite in the Hotel St Regis, high above the 'vast subdued roar of the city'. Sitting up in bed, surrounded by his framed photographs of Mummie, Nannie, and Sir Ed'dard (in parliamentary robes), with the plush monkey at his side, Stephen contemplated the stupendous view from his window. At 6.45, whilst Stephen was deep in a life of William Beckford, the telephone rang. It was Rex, who had been all day at the theatre, exhausted after directing scene painters. Should they dine together? No: Stephen was too tired to do anything but dine abed, and he told Rex he should do likewise. Rex agreed, and they both decided to put off seeing Tallulah Bankhead for another day. Rex expressed surprise at the squalidness of New York: 'Every street reminds me of Tottenham Court Road.'[3]

Laurence Whistler considers this telephone call between floors, 'bedroom to bedroom, Rex halfway down in some canyon' (actually the fifth floor), a sharp reminder of the difference between the two friends. While Rex had come to work, Stephen was 'pillowed up high in the St Regis, cushioned, as everywhere else, in hired cars and lovely homes and shops, from any contact with the harsh, uncaring city'. When Rex took breakfast in bed the following morning (on Stephen's advice), his polite English solicitation to the newspaper boy was taken for a pass, and he got a terse 'Wadpaybrjawant' in reply from the sullen boy. 'To Stephen, had this happened, it would not have happened,' observes Whistler. 'It would have been wiped from the record instantly.'[4] Or perhaps Stephen would have been lost for words, as he had been on the drive from the docks to the hotel the previous evening, when Wilkie had innocently asked what the word 'phallic' meant. Stephen replied with unanswering silence.

America stretched before Stephen like a lion ready to be tamed by his unyielding charm. It was autumn, and he found the very air of New York glorious. At the St Regis, he dined in the softly-lit dining room, with its pickled oak 'waffle' panelling, all very becoming. Stephen sat at table, in his smart new blue suit, crisp white linen shirt and bow tie, alone, tired, and ready for bed. Then Rex and Wilkie joined him – eating before going on to a play. The former was looking 'very distinguished and aloof, with an ambiguous pucker at the corner of his mouth',[5] while Wilkie sported a white frill, designed for her by Stephen. Suddenly, Peter Watson was discovered dining in another corner of the room, and after an enthusiastic reunion, tried to persuade Stephen to join his party. He was greatly tempted, as Peter's guests were Madame Karinska and the Russian composer Nicholas Nabokov, both of the Ballets Russes, but he resisted the invitation, preferring his bed to burning the midnight oil.

New York
Tough.

Central Park the next morning was cold and fresh, and Stephen's walk took in children pony-riding, with a 'street-tough' leading them along. He bought chocolate dragees and sat up on a high stool at a vending stall, to drink hot chocolate and watch the world go by. He bought three toy monkeys, of pink fur and tinsel, on strings, and took them back to the hotel. There he was excited to find a message from Willa Cather, inviting him to call at her apartment at 570 Park Avenue soon. Stephen could hardly wait to meet his favourite writer, and felt sure he would not be disappointed. There was also a note from Tchelitchew (who had arrived in New York on the same day as Stephen), on the back of which Rex had pencilled a warning: he had seen a reporter knocking on Stephen's door that morning. It transpired that they wanted to photograph Stephen as a 'new society arrival', which he could hardly understand, modestly claiming that he was no celebrity.

Stephen spent happy hours at the hotel, sitting with Rex in his bedroom, writing letters and his journal whilst Rex worked on his designs. Stephen also noted with satisfaction that Rex still used one of the dressing-cases they had had made to take to Villars in 1924; he had his with him, too. He decided to go and rest – 'When I want solace I think of racoon's faces,' he declared. He also confessed a fear that he might, in this relaxed hotel life, one day descend in the lift and emerge 'into that golden lacquered laquey'd hush of marble & velvet & Mammon'[6] . . . with his fly-buttons undone.

Stephen was enticed from this hall of Mammon to dine with Tallulah Bankhead at her suite in the Gotham Hotel. 'I felt awfully uncomfortable,' he recalled. 'She was having one of her eclipses – rather forgotten about.' Bankhead's wild career had taken her to London in the twenties, where Stephen had met her socially. Rex too had become an intimate friend: David Herbert once called at Tallulah's London hotel room, to be told by her maid Edie, 'Miss Bankhead is in the bath with Mr Rex Whistler.' 'I'm just trying to show Rex I'm definitely a blonde!' said the actress. Bankhead had a predilection for well-bred young Englishmen; she had pursued Napier Alington obsessively around London, and later said that Rex had come to New York just to see her. But at forty-three, an habitual abuser of alcohol, cocaine and amphetamine, the actress was past the sultry temptress stage, and fast becoming a parody of herself. Yet she retained an undeniable allure, especially for Stephen, who was intoxicated by any creature of stage and screen.

Tallulah got off on the wrong footing with Stephen that evening, however, by criticizing his appearance. 'She looked at my hair and said "You needn't wave and dye it like that, because you don't need to at all . . . You know, a man doesn't want to look pretty." And I said, "Well,

some men, I think, do want to look pretty. And nicer still, beautiful!"'
Stephen's discomfort stemmed from his assessment of Tallulah as 'one of
those people who always expects people to make love to her – I had a sort
of feeling that she did, rather.' Nothing could have been less likely with
Stephen, whose susceptibility to this ageing actress's sexual charms was
barely above zero.

Stephen had made a valiant attempt to please his hostess, by bringing
'bowers of flowers' to her room, though he felt outclassed by the gardenia
tree which Peter Watson's new friend, Robin Thomas,* had brought her.
'But that evening Tallulah – I wish I'd been sweeter to her now, I can be
very cold and distant – she said "Now, Stephen – I've ordered for you –
spread all around us – all the most American dishes I can think of, to
please you, and you've eaten hardly anything at all!"' Stephen could not
admit that his lack of appetite was because he felt the last course on the
menu might be him. 'I was deeply ill at ease with her – I felt she was a
man-eating vampire, really.'[7]

On Tuesday, 3 December, Stephen had made his long-anticipated
pilgrimage to Willa Cather's flat at 570 Park Avenue, where the novelist
lived with her companion Edith Lewis. The apartment was at the rear of
the building, and its heavily curtained windows all faced the blank walls
of the Colony Club, one of New York's most exclusive gathering-places,
next door. But Cather's abode could not have been further in spirit from
the high society of the club, or the *haute couture* of Fifth Avenue. As her
flat physically turned its back to that life, so did Cather. (In her last
apartment, she had even rented the rooms above hers so as to ensure
peace and quiet.) To the public, as to her readership, Cather was 'an
ingrown genius', as George Seibel had called her.[8]

Stephen could thus feel justifiably honoured to gain an invitation to this
inner sanctum. When Cather opened her front door herself: 'In a flash as I
saw her eyes I knew this was the writer of *My Ántonia* & *A Lost
Lady*.[9] They spent an enchanted hour together and Stephen's impressions far exceeded his expectation of what she would be like. Two days
later, the telephone in his hotel room rang before breakfast, and her
'strong, truthful, splendid voice'[10] asked him to tea again that afternoon.
Stephen danced for joy around his bedroom.

He went out and ordered a bouquet of pink roses to be sent to 570 Park
Avenue, and a few hours later presented himself promptly at the door.

---

*Robin Thomas was the son of 'Michael Strange', a beautiful lesbian who dabbled in the arts.

Known for her love of bright and exotic clothing, Willa received him wearing black satin pyjamas, a brilliant flamingo-pink tunic, and a cream shirt. An imposing, broad figure, with a strong face, she was not an easily forgettable person. Stephen's description of her stayed with him even into his old age; he recalled her 'gentian blue eyes' and 'famous Irish red hair', with 'dark eyelashes, so that she looked made-up though she never had'.[11]

Every now and again, Cather would lay her hand on Stephen's arm, to stress a point – and the affection she felt for him. They discussed everything. Willa produced old photographs of herself, and of her travels in New Mexico, where she had set her 1927 novel, *Death Comes for the Archbishop*. Stephen in turn had brought his photographs of Pamela, and Cather asked a lot of questions about her. They spoke of the West, and how, for Cather, the film industry had spoilt California. Stephen evinced his high opinion of Greta Garbo, but the stern authoress denied Garbo's intelligence. 'She can't be . . . or she wouldn't be a film actress. To waste the best years of one's life on trash like that.'[12]

Many people have commented that Willa Cather couldn't have been a very 'nice' person to know. Her strength of will and opinion set her up as a rather hard-faced and unbending woman who knew what she liked and what she wanted from life; and, importantly, what she expected from other people. Strange, then, that she – the strenuous literary perfectionist, prolific in her output – should 'click' with someone like Stephen. The explanation, as both Hermione Lee and Patricia Lee Yongue comment, was Cather's inherent snobbishness. Quite simply, Stephen's aristocratic pedigree made him an attractive symbol of Old World charm and sophistication. Cather, the hard-bitten pioneer of the West, was softened by what has become a clichéd appeal to Americans: the real English gentleman.

How then did Cather react to Stephen's obvious homosexuality? She had always disliked effeminacy in men, having spoken out against Oscar Wilde's 'artificiality, his flippant epigrams and mannered witticisms', and admired only 'the healthy commonplace'[13] in art. Yet she herself was a lesbian, although her relationships with Edith Lewis and Isabelle McClung did not appear to be physically based. 'She just wasn't interested in sex,' notes Lee. 'Cather seems to have been one of those truly "asexual" people.'[14] That neither her own orientation, nor Stephen's, intruded on their friendship indicates its sincerity. Cather could have explained Stephen's feminine manner and appearance by his Englishness; more important to her was his mind. She plainly respected his opinion of her work, and had realized, even from those youthful early fan-letters, that here was an acute critic whose considered correspondence actually meant something, was not just flattery.

Thus when the two discussed literature on these initial meetings, Cather listened as hard to Stephen as he did to her. Willa's observations of New York literary life were graphic; she hated the commercial publicizing atmosphere of the town. Even more feared was the prospect of what Hollywood would do to her books. She told Stephen she relied on her publisher to protect her fictional children.

She was vexed too, that November afternoon, by the *New York Herald Tribune*'s request for a 'Christmas prayer' from her. 'If you believe in prayer – how degrading,' she told Stephen. 'If you don't, what a travesty.'[15] As they talked, he noted the 'stormy, rebellious shape of her mouth, and the strength of her chin, so stubborn'. He added that, when talking of the little zoo in Central Park, Cather announced she liked the llama best: 'I like the disdain on its face.'[16]

Happier talk was of vacations. Willa suggested Stephen go to New England now, to catch the last of the Fall in the countryside which had inspired *My Ántonia*. She hoped, perhaps, to join him there, and became animated when proposing that they both buy fur coats in preparation for the winter. Willa showed Stephen four rough turquoise nuggets she had found in New Mexico, and Indian bracelets and necklaces of Spanish coral. As the time came for him to leave, Cather saw him to the lift. 'Put that in your vest pocket,' she said, pressing into his hand one of the rough lumps of blue stone; 'one of Tom Outland's* turquoises.'[17]

On the morning of 6 December, Stephen had breakfast with Rex in his room. Rex, still in his pyjamas, ran about, answering telephone calls across a floor strewn with costume designs for Helen Hayes and telegrams from Gilbert Miller. He hardly had time to hear where Stephen was off to. 'Send me a cable, when you arrive,' was Rex's exhortation, ' – and paint!'[18]

Stephen left New York, with Wilkie and Wade, and travelled north to Massachusetts. They arrived in the little town of Jefferson, to stay at Mount Pleasant House. Stephen was in the heart of rural America, and loved it; yet memories of his past drifted into his dreams. On 9 December, Stephen records that he and Wilkie had a long conversation about Siegfried, and he had cried a lot. 'They are such real things, tears,' wrote

---

*Fictional hero of Cather's novel, *The Professor's House* (1925).

Stephen. 'I who shun emotion – so dread it.' He added, on the evening of the 14th: 'Who was it who said that until all sexual desire was past, no peace could be found – boy, you've said it!' A few days later, out shopping with Wade, Stephen bought a bottle of Emeraude eau-de-Cologne. As he opened the bottle, the New England winter's day suddenly became Palermo five years ago: 'beloved Sicily'.

Stephen spent a bad night, and in the morning Wade came in to massage his chest and back. At lunch, he and Wilkie laughed about the hotel's primitive lavatories, which resembled sheep pens. Added to that, the place was tremendously over-heated, and the bathrooms mere cupboards, without electric light. But Stephen could bear any privations when he heard comments such as the waitress's to Wilkie: 'What a beautiful boy! – what a lovely personality!'[19]

Stephen revelled in the American experience. The newspapers were 'a blizzard of hold-ups, stick-ups, murders, fights', with only 'faint whispers of the European crisis – Laval, Eden, Ethiopia – behind the din of Chinese "magos" killing their wives in vast letters'.[20] It was already snowing in Jefferson, and Stephen awaited word from Wilkie, who had gone on to Jaffrey to make arrangements for their stay there.

Snow continued to fall, and Stephen set off for Worcester, the nearby town, on the local bus. Here he indulged in his favourite pastime: shopping. He bought country-style belts studded with fake gems, a blue jacket – 'Very snappy,' said the man in the shop – and two rodeo shirts. Stephen admired the hanks of bootlaces and farmers' breeches piled up in the shop: all America's mystique seemed invested in these Western working clothes – the pioneer spirit in outfits for heroes.

Back at the hotel, he busied himself with Christmas drawings for his friends, and reading Cather's *Obscure Destinies*, which made him think of his own. On the evening of 20 December, he looked up at a starry sky and wondered if it were the same over Wiltshire.

The next few days Stephen spent buying and doing up parcels of Christmas presents for Cecil, Rex, Pavlik, Charlie, Wilkie, Wade and Burnside, for which task he had found some silver ribbons and blue wrapping paper covered in silver stars – one of his favourite colour combinations. The celebration of the season seemed to Stephen more enthusiastic in this country, where streets were lined with large Christmas trees, with the snow making it all look very festive.

On Christmas Eve, Stephen arrived at Shattuck Inn – where Cather had written *My Ántonia* – run by a friendly couple, the Austermanns. Any friend of Willa's was a friend of theirs, and the Austermanns made Christmas a charming New English one for him, with presents of candy and baskets of fruit. On Christmas Day George took him for a drive through town, which looked positively fairy-like, with coloured candles and lights in every porch and window.

Stephen explored Jaffrey's limited but charming amenities: the library and the local café. He made friends with a Norwegian ski-master, John Knudson, who called on New Year's morning with oranges in his hands, and, being tall and dark (and handsome), the residual Scotsman in Stephen hoped he would bring good luck. John doubled up as a woodcutter too, and took Stephen off for a day's foresting. Together they set out with an axe and clippers to clear the trail Knudson was working on. Stephen was set to clipping off overhanging branches, and even chopped down a birch tree. 'Boy, take care you don't cut your foot,' said John. 'Keep your feet apart.' (Stephen began to feel remorseful three hours later. He disliked people cutting down trees, as did Cather, who wrote to him shortly afterwards: 'I wish I had poisoned John 2 years ago. I knew he would go on & on chopping down trees.') After his exertion, Stephen felt tired, and sat down on a pile of logs to watch his friend chop wood. They walked back together in the twilight, Stephen to a relaxing hot bath. He oiled himself – just one of his many ritual 'beauty' treatments – and dined in bed, 'aching deliciously'.[21]

During that week he went on many expeditions with John, enjoying his masculine company. George Austermann pleased him too, with his 'wisecracks' and 'gay, friendly voice'. He would take Stephen into Jaffrey in the Packard, and drink 'cawfee' with him at 'Whipples Cosy Lunch'.

But by the end of the week, Stephen felt he had to get out of this rural backwater. He and Wade left Wilkie at Shattuck Inn, and went to Boston, where he checked in to the Copley Plaza on 16 January. His spirits soared at once. Boston was cosmopolitan, enchanting, very English in its civilized tone. It also boasted sophisticated shops; Stephen was delighted when he found a favourite, the Japanese shop Yamanaka, which Pamela and he used to visit. Fuelled by a newly arrived letter of credit from home, Stephen had his cab stop and he dashed in to buy two rings – one cornelian, the other a great lump of amber – along with perfumed incense sticks.

That afternoon he strolled over to the square, where there was a merry-go-round, and he listened to its tinkling tunes from a red satin tent, where he sat drinking *crème de menthe*. As a blizzard blew in Copley Square, the hotel barman persuaded him to try a 'Pousse Café', an elaborate, rainbow-hued cocktail. Its strength was belied by its pretty appearance; soon Stephen felt very drunk and rather peculiar, and had to take to bed for the rest of the afternoon.

Early nights and clean living kept Stephen a smart boy. Entering his thirtieth year, he could flatter himself that he was weathering time's onward march very well indeed. Stephen attributed his continuing good looks to the recuperative qualities of his long periods of rest. Observing that his newly-washed hair was looking 'silky soft – with honey brown lights where the large wave curls round to the temples', he adjudged himself 'rather beautiful still. In a soft light I look as youthful & lovely as ever I did, but not in the hard daylight. I like to say "Today I am beautiful". I do not like to think that a day will come when I can no longer say it – and so endeavour with every means I can contrive to propitiate & divert time – as Scheherazade did her Caliph – Time is my Caliph.'[22]

Stephen thought the casual peruser of his journal might like to avail himself of his beauty secrets. 'You would like to know some of my precautions, my schemes & methods for delaying the passing of youth?' These procedures included: washing his hair with fresh eggs followed by a lemon rinse; applying nourishing creams made especially oily for his winter trip; an absolute ban on facial grimacing or harsh, wrinkle-forming laughter – aided by a series of facial massage exercises. Stephen shaved with Roger et Gallet 'Savon à la Violette', which smelt like 'all the purple violets in the world pressed to one's cheek'. The inner man was as well cared for, with a diet of as much milk and butter as possible. Plenty of water and no highly flavoured sauces were an additional and rather more modern precaution. He would rub olive oil over his body after bathing, then perform small exercises designed to relax nervous tension. Then it was early to bed and early to rise. Quite impatient with the demands of his reader, Stephen's final beauty tip was the memorizing of lovely poetry to help put one in a lovely frame of mind. 'And still you are insatiable! still you want more – more! And you are quite right – because Beauty is divine.'[23]

By the end of March, Stephen's reading had switched from *Howard's End* to the travel pages of *Vogue*, which made him long for Paris, society, Europe – civilization. The thrill of American rural life had palled, to be replaced by loneliness; a tiny snapshot taken of him walking along a New England lane shows Stephen tall but less willowy now, a little more substantial in build. His neck is muffled, his head bent in thought, and his hands dug deep in his pockets against the cold.

The underlying mood of despondency he felt, principally caused by unhappy memories, and exacerbated by homesickness, caused Stephen a deal of pain that late winter. More than thirty years later, he recalled that time in a letter to Mildred Bennett, the keeper of Cather's 'Pioneer Memorial' and a great friend: 'The winter I spent at Shattuck Inn I had a very severe depression,' he told her. 'Almost alarming in its intensity. Rosamond Lehmann gave me a doctor's address at Stockbridge, Mass. – but as spring came, the Depression went completely.' It may have been, as Stephen explained, that 'Cold doesn't suit me – or Northern Scenery. I need Mexican Beauty, or Palm Beach – or my Home.'[24] But it was also a foreshadowing of things to come, that would precipitate deeper depressions in the future.

By April, he had returned to New York. His American tour having drained his resources, this time he booked into a small hotel, the Lowell, which had the advantage of being quite close to Willa Cather's apartment. He dined with her at 570 Park Avenue, where there was 'gay, vivid conversation'. He had brought her from Yamanaka presents of jade and cornelian fruits and animals. He and Willa chatted in her library for two hours, about Cather's books. Stephen rhapsodized over *A Lost Lady*, and Willa commented that her heroine had 'fooled herself', adding, 'Can't you hear that woman laugh?'[25] She was also pleased when Stephen told her that Thomas Hardy had spoken so highly of the book on Stephen's visit to Max Gate, as she admired him as one of the greatest novelists of their time.

Practically everything Willa said lodged in Stephen's memory, to be recalled for years to come. 'She was very easily offended,' he remembered; when Cather gave him a copy of *One of Ours*, she said: '"It's full of typographical errors." The look of disgust and scorn on her face made me realize how disillusioned she was about such things . . . The critic in her was never quite dormant.' Infinitely precious about her own work, she was encouraging about others'. Stephen complained that only rarely did he feel 'the writing ability' was with him. 'She laughed and said, "Give the mood a chance."'[26]

In his letters, in which Stephen's literary impulse flowed best, he exhibits an awareness that not all readers would appreciate Cather's chosen terrain – as he himself had found, with his stay in the American countryside. 'I see why some people think her dull,' he told Mildred Bennett. 'She plays down her material, rather; making it all quieter than it need be.'[27] And later: 'there is a curious "purity" in her stories, a self-discipline on a gargantuan scale. A part of her longed to luxuriate, but the hedonist was always curbed by the austere, exquisite Guardian Angel who never relaxed his vigilance – "The Artist is never free", she says herself.'[28]

Unfortunately, little remains of Willa Cather's and Stephen's correspondence, with which they carried on their friendship after Stephen left for England that spring. His letters to her were summarily burnt by Edith Lewis, in accordance with her friend's wishes, after Cather's death in 1947. Those of her letters to Stephen that survived his constant re-reading and attendant wear and tear give little glimpses of their transatlantic discussions. Often *Lascar* would be the subject: ' . . . to write a great book ? A Masterpiece ?' said Willa of Stephen's ideas. 'If so you were very foolish. Nobody ever wrote a masterpiece by resolving to do so . . .'[29] Perhaps Cather saw in her friend something of her own fictional creation, the intellectual tutor Gaston Cleric in *My Ántonia*, whom Jim Burden thinks had 'narrowly missed being a great poet, and I have sometimes thought that his bursts of imaginative talk were fatal to his poetic gift. He squandered too much in the heat of personal communication.'[30]

Cather's judgements did not cease to be scathing. Allowing only her favoured authors, Flaubert and Turgenev, unalloyed praise, she later told Stephen that she thought the work of his friend, Elizabeth Bowen, 'cold, calculating trick writing'.[31] Elsie Mendl, one of his society hostess friends, and an American, she called 'the most commonplace sort of social climber', and Willa deplored the 'very mediocre set poor Mrs Simpson had round her'.[32] But Stephen himself could do no wrong. Writing from her Maine retreat, Whale Cove Cottage at Grand Manan, she thanked Stephen for his Christmas card: 'Weren't you a smart boy to make your Christmas letter to me arrive on Christmas eve ?' Receipt of *Leaves from a Missionary's Notebook* solicited the cabled acknowledgement: 'Book outrageous but delightful. Splendid drawing' in November 1937,[33] and when she received a copy of *The White Wallet* from her aristocratic, aesthetic friend, Willa wrote back in encouragement: 'Go right along, my boy, as we say in the South.'[34]

Such words meant much to Stephen, who held her opinions as the ultimate approbation. For the rest of his life, he would tirelessly exhort friends to read her work and ask publishers to republish it. By such persistence, Stephen sought to repay something of Cather's undoubted faith and belief in him as an artist and a friend.

Chapter 17

Palazzo Wilsford

There, isles of summer seemed to drift away – the pale blue spaces – the part of the sky that opened in the clouds was a soft greenish blue . . . it seemed to tell of ineffable things, to remind you of dreams undreamt – of time having ceased to function.

— Stephen Tennant: notes for *Lascar*

SO Stephen returned to Europe, stopping in Paris in late spring, then travelling on to Rhodes. The Greek isle was new and fresh to him, and he watched sailors mend their nets 'on Aegean evenings, by May's tender moon'. He found the beauty of the island almost overwhelming. 'Even when I was there, it seemed unbelievable,' he wrote years later. 'I felt that I had stolen a march on probability – it had a quality that usually only distance & longing can give; now that it is in the past – it is sheer romance – like Siracuse.'[1]

The Balearic Isles ended a brief sunny interlude before the final homecoming to Wilsford in mid-July, 1936. Here a thousand and one jobs awaited Stephen, after his absence of nearly six months. Old friends came to visit; one weekend he had Arthur Waley to stay, along with Penelope Betjeman, wife of the future poet laureate. Stephen delighted in taking his guests out on a boat on the Avon, and besported himself in the garden, being photographed by Penelope as he lay back on a pillow on the grass, his head surrounded by magnolia flowers.

But there was trouble brewing in Bloomsbury that autumn, and Stephen was the cause. On a visit to Lady Ottoline Morrell at Gower Street, Stephen had been shown a series of letters from Lytton Strachey to Virginia Woolf, written years before, in which he repeated indiscreet stories about Virginia's engagement to Leonard Woolf.* Stephen wrote

---

*Strachey himself asked Virginia to marry him after his affair with Duncan Grant had ended, and was much taken aback when she accepted. He withdrew the offer.

about it later in his journal, recalling Virginia's 'beautiful voice on the telephone, perhaps the loveliest voice I ever knew, so low and soft, such a fine articulation, so much more than charm . . . the letter [mentioned] her engagement to Leonard Woolf . . . it was a huge book of letters – first rate reading.'[2]

When he sent back the Strachey letters in September, Ottoline wrote: 'Don't mention that you send Lytton's letters to me, as Dorothy [Carrington] is Touchy & Jealous about him. Virginia was very angry with me that I had shown you those letters.'[3] Evidently Stephen had mentioned the fact to Woolf, commenting on Strachey's remarks about the engagement, and Virginia's 'extraordinary appeal'. She was indignant, and wrote in her diary on 27 November, awaiting Lady Ottoline after tea: ' – & am I to tell her about Stephen Tennant & Lytton's letters? She will erect herself & puff out her cobra hood if I do.' Ottoline arrived, and was 'attenuated, & abashed. She put up no fight; was all shyness & anguish, & agreed with me about S.T. & the letters.' Lady Ottoline maintained that she had forgotten there had been anything 'intimate' in the letters; that Stephen had arrived at Gower Street by chance with 'a little rucksack. So she took pity on him.'[4] Stephen himself was interested to learn later from Stephen Spender that 'Ottoline Morrell had been represented to him as a mischief maker by Morgan Forster'.[5]

It was something of a storm in a teacup, perhaps, with Lady Ottoline as much to blame as he; but once more Stephen's love of literary gossip had got him into hot water. He would have to be careful in future, if he were to keep the friendship of such eminent (and egotistical) personalities. Not all of them had Siegfried's patience.

Earlier that summer, before he had incurred her transitory displeasure, Stephen had rung up Virginia, to hear her beautiful voice, and to ask her to come on a country ride in his Victoria, 'talking intimately',[6] as she complained to her diary. This was one of Stephen's favourite occupations, to bowl along Wiltshire lanes in his mother's carriage; perched up high on the leather upholstered seat, with Lewis Ford to drive the horse in front, Stephen could chat away to his guest as they processed around the countryside in Ascot fashion. Sir Alfred Beit remembers visiting Stephen around this time. He had been staying with friends not far from Wilsford, and went over on 'a beautiful July evening' to have dinner with Stephen. 'After dinner he asked me would I like to come for a drive and on my saying "yes", he called for a Victoria with an old coachman and old horse and we ambled around the charming countryside on a perfect warm night.'[7] The renowned soldier, Field Marshal Sir Gerald Templer, and his wife were living at the time in a cottage in Lake, and were secondary witnesses to Stephen's processions: 'We used to see him, wearing a green suede coat, driving down and back through the village of Lake in a Victoria, but never spoke to him,' Lady Templer remembered. 'He wore, always, I think, the green suede coat.'[8]

Queen Elizabeth the Queen Mother also recalled Stephen's carriage rides. 'Oh! Stephen. I'd love to see him again. It brings back so many memories of when I was young . . . Stephen used to ride over the downs in a carriage, thinking lovely thoughts or whatever one did in those days.'[9] She recalled fond memories of Wilsford in early times (having often come to visit Stephen's brother Christopher there).

The day after Edward VIII's abdication Stephen wrote to Cecil that work on Wilsford had resumed, and it was now 'filled with men hammering – wiring – altering'. The upheaval made a peaceful life impossible, so Stephen had taken himself off to Dorset. He stayed in Dorchester, where he discerned a 'surrealistic' charm: 'men on bicycles with very long ladders fore & aft – and such like'.[10] He spent his time drawing and writing, with occasional visits to Florence Hardy.

Stephen also wrote of plans to travel back to the States, and perhaps even further, to Bali, Java and Sumatra. But he realized how much he had missed England and friends like Cecil (and blamed his Wilsford staff for not passing on telephone calls: 'They ought to be lynched – they never give me messages.'). He felt rather out of the swing of things now, promising a newly-designed Christmas card only if it were 'tolerable . . . really I am now such a back number, I hardly dare to raise even the mildest dust with a feeble drawing – how I despise amateurs.'

Stephen did not travel in those next few months, for Wilsford needed him. The house had been neglected of late by its spiritual son, and now it required all his attentions to make it come alive once more. It would be the immediate natural surroundings of the house that would determine its interior, he decided. 'If at first Stephen had a plan for Wilsford Manor,' wrote John Culme, 'rather than allowing each new fancy to predict its development, then it was to create in its interior fresh, airy spaces where sunlight, diffused in its passage through climbing clematis and rose, might flicker on some ephemeral arrangement of rock crystal and pearly nautilus, some exquisite plaited basket of snowdrops and aconites, or perhaps the shoulder of an ice-blue satin-covered sofa.'[11]

Already Syrie Maugham's renowned love of white pervaded the place.

That spring, Stephen commissioned a bed from her shop, and the schemes he had worked out for Wilsford with Maugham were being carried out to an extravagant degree. The shells which Stephen had lovingly collected since Sicily were to provide another natural motif for the house. He noted the arrival of 'a huge shell for flowers & a shell above for concealed lighting';[12] soon plaster scallops were to stud the dining-room ceiling, the maritime theme being echoed in swags of white plaster ropes. Shells were a predominant feature of Syrie Maugham's decorative work of the period. She made great use of Regency furniture, often decorated with shell motifs; and Venetian grotto furniture, with its bizarre gilded oyster- and barnacle-encrusted rococo forms, suited both Stephen's and Syrie's aims. In 1935 Maugham had declared: 'I am specializing in everything to do with shells – shell printed fabrics, shells for table decorations, shells as flower vases.'[13] One such item from 'Syrie's', a huge plaster and wooden Nautilus shell, supported by stylized dolphins, stood as the centrepiece of Stephen's new library, reflected from behind by a tall mirrored panel.

Stephen claimed to have been the first person to get Syrie Maugham to use colour; whilst not strictly true, Maugham's work for Wilsford certainly indicated a great deal of Stephen's taste in the pinks and blues she used for the furnishings and materials.

Nothing escaped Stephen's or Syrie's renovating eye. He wanted to sweep away what he saw as the 'gloominess' of the Arts and Crafts influence of Pamela. Thus, where Syrie might have left rooms white and modernistically bare, Stephen proceeded to overlay fancy and plumage, as if to assert his own unique stamp. He loved the flattering effect of concealed lighting and had it installed everywhere. The bathrooms were fitted with pink chiffon curtains, metal swags made to decorate radiators. Everything was embellished. It became a never-ending task.

In April, Stephen went south to enjoy the late spring in Torquay – that very Victorian resort which he had first visited with his mother years before. Here he found the Imperial Hotel almost unspoiled, a great nineteenth-century edifice secured on the red rock cliffs of Torbay. There were long terraces – 'great quarter-decks of molten light overlooking the sea' – and outside his bedroom window, '3 double flowering pink cherry trees, freighted – pregnant, miraculous with blossom'.

Amid sunshine and 'shimmering seas', Stephen reported to Sibyl Colefax that the American ambassador was staying. He paced the terrace, calling his dog 'in a charming lazy voice – I want to know him (ambassador, not the dog). Do you know him?' he asked Sibyl. 'He looks very nice – & except for the cherry blossom I don't know anyone here . . . Have you read René Guyon "Sex Life & Sex Ethics" – Bodley Head? – a vitally brilliant study: (this letter will make you laugh – I know – a *mélange* of cherry blossom, ambassadors & sex!')[*][14]

Stephen also made a visit to Bath, where he bought a pair of huge medieval Gothic windows. After returning from London, where he lunched with Cecil and Doris Castlerosse, Stephen found his windows had been installed in the wall of the bedroom that had been his mother's, with lights concealed behind so they appeared to be real. He told Cecil, 'They are so beautiful – I nearly fainted, they open into the room and mauve magnolias, white lilac & pinks are massed in them & floodlit – no words can describe the loveliness of the juxtaposition of fresh foliage & petals with the 14th-century stone & the light through the old glass.'[15]

The gardens at Wilsford were also being restocked with exotic inhabitants for the Reptillery, much neglected of late. The *Daily Express* noted on 7 May the following comments on 'prices for reptiles and batrachians' to be found in the May–June issue of *The Aquarist and Pond-Keeper*. It listed 'current prices for Natterjack Toads (1/3), Robust Plate Lizards (30/-). Three Toed Skinks (1/3), and Baby Spanish Terrapins (1/-) . . . Among subscribers who've over-subscribed sums from 6d up,' noted the paper, 'is the Hon. Stephen Tennant (3/6). Tall, dark, 31 years old, Tennant paints, writes, and rated as one of the bright young people back in 1926 . . .'

'Sky-blue velvet. Syrie,' was Stephen's note to himself on 14 May.[16] Over the next few years he continued to acquire an enormous catalogue of furniture, fittings and ornaments, and shops like Syrie's and Cook's of St Christopher's Place readily encouraged his collecting. It would not have been in Mrs Maugham's interest to advise her client that a pair of Venetian rococo looking-glasses might suffice, or that he had enough gilded console tables. Stephen, as a fashion victim, was at the mercy of the society decorators of his day – Elsie Mendl, Sibyl Colefax, Syrie Maugham – all of whom he counted as friends.

[*]The ambassador was Robert W. Bingham, replaced (due to ill health) by Joseph Kennedy the following year. The book was *Sex Life and Sex Ethics* by René Guyon (1933), a radical study leaning heavily on Freudian psychoanalyses of sexual repression, infantile sexuality, and neuroses. Guyon advocates the release of homosexuality 'from the absurd charges of immorality', and rationalizes that every kind of sexual habit is permissible. The sale of the book was 'restricted to members of the Medical, Legal and Educational professions and students of Social Science', according to a warning note on the dust-jacket.

Syrie Maugham was already at work in early summer on a new acquisition of Stephen's; he had at last found a suitable London *pied-à-terre*, and the flat at 19 Mecklenburgh Square was right in the heart of Bloomsbury. A quiet corner to the east of the Foundling Hospital, bordered on the other side by Grays Inn Road, the square had all the advantages of being in central London, with the added consideration of the proximity of the Woolfs at Tavistock Square, the Bells and the Waleys at Gordon Square, Lady Ottoline Morrell at Gower Street, and Morgan Forster at Brunswick Square. Number 19 was part of a Regency terrace; elegant with iron-railed balconies, it overlooked the private gardens of the square, full of leafy trees.

During preparations for the decoration of his new apartment, Stephen planned a trip to Paris, to reconnoitre fashionable interiors there. On 16 May he wrote to Cecil: 'I want very much to see one or two very smart modern flats with Bérard furniture etc . . . In March Vogue there was a shell bathroom in a Paris flat of Capt. Louis Weiller? . . . I do hope to do a shell one here.'[*] In the event, Stephen had to forgo Cecil's company, for the latter was summoned to the Château de Candé on 2 June, to take wedding photographs for the Duke and Duchess of Windsor.

Back in London, Stephen attended a concert conducted by Toscanini. But the London season's social events were to be put very much in the shade of an extravagant party held that summer in a remote part of Wiltshire.

Cecil's *Fête Champêtre* at Ashcombe was a magnificent exposition of thirties fantasy. It was a high society rural pageant in the tradition of Marie Antoinette, and a logical progression from Stephen's own 'Lancret Affair'. The arrangements for its celebration were detailed and extensive. A full Restoration scenario was composed by John Sutro, to be performed on the sloping lawns of Beaton's romantic wilderness. Salvador Dali inspired the animal face masks for the waiters, and Madame Karinska furnished costumes and dresses. Cecil ordered boxes of artificial flowers and ribbons from Paris to decorate his eighteenth-century house and outbuildings.

The party was set for 10 July, and buses were hired to transport guests up the steep hills of Tollard Royal, and down the equally precipitous rough chalk track to the house itself. Alighting from his chauffeur-driven Rolls, Stephen was outstanding in a vivid blue satin sailor outfit, of shirt

---

[*]Paul-Louis Weiller (b.1893). The shell bathroom still exists at 85 rue de la Faisanderie, a house he loaned to the Duke and Duchess of Windsor.

and shorts. A dozen sheep had been penned in front of the house, and 'urchins' shepherded goats with magnesium flares. The party went on all night, with fireworks to herald the dawn. Stephen loved it all. 'I shall never forget the beauty of the mise-en-scène for the play,' he told Cecil. 'The lime-blossom vivid . . . the roses & candles . . . It was a feast of fun & beauty – delicious food . . . the play was so funny – I hope you enjoyed the party too?'[17]

Stephen left in the early hours of the morning, having met a young photographer who had come over from Germany to make his name in England. Francis Goodman (then Franz Gutmann) recalled Stephen looking 'a little plumper than he had been, I suppose – I seem to remember that he filled the shorts rather well – but he still looked stunning . . .' Stephen took a shine to the handsome young German, and offered him a bed for the night at Wilsford. Next morning, Stephen left Goodman to breakfast alone. 'I remember the butler looked at my shorts as if I were some sort of harlot,' recalled Goodman. Stephen returned later, and gave Franz a red and white slipover as a present – 'very pansy for those days!'[18]

Later that month Stephen returned Cecil's grand hospitality with a rather quieter lunch party. Beaton noted in his diary that Stephen had 'come back into circulation again. He has been so ill for so long that when he recovered physically he was mentally many years younger – He was so much less brilliant than he used to be – It was sad – & one had to make so many allowances. Now it is wonderful to know that he has almost completely recovered & his mind is as alert & astonishing as ever.'[19]

Cecil found more changes at Wilsford than he could have imagined, wrought by Stephen and Syrie, 'and the effect is very gay. Lots of pale colours against white walls, flights of fancy that are very typical & often entirely successful – Huge tubs of rare flowers – the whole atmosphere very *fleuri, parfumé* – very Stephenish.' Among the other guests – who included the Henry Lambs and Edith Olivier – were Laura and Violet Bonham-Carter, the latter with a 'face like an Etruscan horse, voice affected like all protruding Bloomsbury intellectuals, eyes shut, shoulders swaying to & fro, she is the ideal sort of person to bring Stephen out as I like him best . . . With her he assumes that hard, dry, annihilatingly cold voice which means he is choosing his words with special care.' Violet and Stephen discussed various bird cries, one 'a startled somnambulist's cry', said Stephen, 'like someone murmuring in their sleep'. Another pre-prandial topic of conversation was Stephen's excitement over René Guyon's conclusions on the inalterability of the homosexual condition.

They sat waiting for lunch to be served, in the white dining room with its tall Jacobean chairs, octagonal table and concealed 'restaurant' lighting. And waited. No sign of food. Stephen announced that a Sleeping Beauty coma must have come over everybody in his kitchens. Then, when the food arrived, 'it was so typical of Stephen that it made one giggle. Punch was served – a horrible sticky mixture that looked like melted jewellery & matched the vermilion flowers on the table. The food was very highly-coloured – chaud froids of chicken highly creamed & decorated with circus decorations – many sweets & cut up fruits.'

After lunch, they perused Stephen's scrapbooks of old photographs, '& he translated the pictures to us – some very ordinary pictures of Garbo were brought to life by his rapt ecstasies. (In breathless voice) 'Look – look at the beauty of that. It's the Aurora Borealis. She is not a cinema star – She's something much greater,' exclaimed Stephen. 'Think of it – 3 continents to a man worship her – Look at that – it has the tragic quality of a child – and here she is rugged – almost rude with insolent health – and again, infinitely pathetic.'[19] When the time came for his guests to leave, Stephen amused them by telling them 'how much he had dreaded their coming and now quite regretted their going, though he could not answer which he hated the thought of most'. [20]

Cecil, as with all Stephen's friends, was acutely conscious of what Stephen's long-term future might be – how could he fulfil his early promise, so broken up in recent years by loss and ill-health? He was not particularly optimistic. 'Lord Grey said he should not draw,' Cecil noted privately, 'that he had a great talent for writing, that his language was excellent. That he could always find the telling word.' But Cecil thought Stephen's late stepfather 'only half-right – for Stephen's drawings are astonishing. He has genius – he can undertake great feats of endurance with pen & pencil unflinchingly – & yet I doubt if he will ever produce much. He could prove himself to be one of the most brilliant artists in England.'[21]

Stephen had begun to develop his own particular style. Using Indian ink, pens and brushes, he created 'decorative assemblies' of his favourite images and objects of desire. In one early 'collage' of this type, 'The Gay Life', the frame-effect of Stephen's accumulated objects – perfume bottles, cigarette packets, ribbon bows and roses – has already begun to dominate. It is as contemporary as any thirties fashion-plate, yet with an edge of a yet more modern aesthetic sensibility, a cult of the inanimate symbols of an age.

Stephen's style drew lightly on the neo-romanticism of Tchelitchew and Bérard. Yet his pictures, decorative as they were, seemed more like the product of his own sublimated sexual desires; as though Gauguin and Dufy had tried to teach Jean Genet to illustrate *Querelle of Brest* whilst the author-thief languished in a Toulon gaol. His sailor preoccupation was reflected in the work of contemporaries – Cocteau, Burra, Lorca. But there is a retentive gentility that holds back; Stephen's draughtsmanship, teetering between superb representation and tentative inconfidence, led to pictures that fell just short of what he wanted. He lacked the confidence to work it all up into true genius; perhaps the time-consuming illustration of journals dissipated the talent, as the writing of them leeched his literary ability. There, however, the images were sometimes incredibly accurate – a gloriously realistic pansy head in chromium yellow and the deepest purple, almost velvet to the touch; a New York tough, muscular and with an inner-city scowl upon his face; or a turquoise terrapin, precious and mysterious.

This was the visual language of his life; he drew to eternalize these longings (as his endless matelots indicate), drawing and painting for his own satisfaction, or that of a limited group of friends. He was the true English amateur, putting down these images, underlining an acquisition in his journals, or logging some natural beauty. Both Willa Cather and Julian Huxley praised Stephen's ability to draw from nature; Huxley, a distinguished biologist, told Stephen Spender that he thought Stephen one of the best naturalist artists he knew. Despite such accolades, Stephen could find no satisfaction. Rex Whistler asked him why he didn't paint more, telling him he could be as good as Beardsley: 'Is it because you think you won't be good enough?' Stephen had to agree.[22]

Chapter 18

A Story of the Maritime Boulevards

Nature I loved, and next to Nature, Art. Nature in the raw is seldom mild; red in tooth and claw; matelots in Toulon smelling of wine and garlic, with tough brown necks, cigarettes stuck to the lower lip, lapsing into unintelligible, contemptuous argot.

— Ambrose Silk, in Evelyn Waugh's *Put Out More Flags*

SUMMER 1937, and Stephen was off to Switzerland to sample the exhilarating air. This time he took his Rolls, driven by his new half-Spanish chauffeur/valet, Ivo Raphal-Ransome. The car was craned at Newhaven and from Dieppe they drove overland to Aix-les-Bains, and the Regina hotel, Bernascon. Shortly after his arrival, he received a telephonic summons from Gertrude Stein, to come and meet the celebrated American playwright, Thornton Wilder.

Stephen had met Stein before – probably through Edith Sitwell, during her brief flirtation with the American writer – before the battle for Tchelitchew had come between them. Soon Stephen was in their glorious garden at Bilignin on a hot summer's afternoon, enjoying the scent of Gertrude's roses, and Alice B. Toklas' famous cuisine. Stephen made a display for the benefit of his hosts – sea shells laid in a dish of cold, clear water; he thought they looked their best underwater, it brought out the colours and patterns so well. Gertrude talked of Pavlik, who had long fallen out of favour at her studio in the rue de Fleurus. She told Stephen how much Tchelitchew bored her now, and she no longer considered his paintings important. Stephen could not, even as the polite guest, agree with that.

From Aix, Stephen set off to explore the Swiss Alps, arriving at Andermatt, perched 2,000 feet above sea level. Here he chanced upon a shop called 'Gotthardmineralten, Prop. J. B. Meyer', and was delighted to discover some of the best examples of rock crystal he had yet seen. Stephen could not resist it: he bought several splendid specimens and an enormous five-foot pillar of opaline rock. It wasn't until 19 September that Stephen got round to sending Ivo off from Aix to collect the monster rock from Andermatt. Later that day he received a distressed telephone call from Herr Meyer's shop: Ivo was 'nearly snowed up',[1] unable to drive through a heavy fall in a car already handicapped by the weight of its crystalline burden. He finally struggled back to Bernascon the following day, triumphantly bearing the crystal, later to be erected on a pink and gold pillar at Wilsford, and dubbed 'a manly rock' by Michael Wishart.

It was Stephen's subsequent visit to Marseilles, from Aix, in the autumn of 1937, that consolidated and inspired the themes and ideas for his masterwork, *Lascar*. He arrived there in October, after spending three days in Toulon, 'sketching and watching'.[2] He found the latter a 'lovely place', especially the Ministère de la Marine buildings, but it was Marseilles' scale and cosmopolitan atmosphere that really impressed him.

He stayed at the Hôtel de Noailles, right in the heart of the city, on its most famous thoroughfare, the Canebière. The magic of that street and the Vieux Port was working into his head, filling it with ideas for a dark story set in those boulevards, of madames with shady pasts and occult powers; of burly seamen in sweaty singlets and tattered, patched jeans; of tattoo parlours and sleazy bars and mysterious alleyways – the world which he found just a walk away from the doors of his smart hotel.

Life in Marseilles had an enlivening quality for Stephen; the smallest incident was an adventure. He made friends with the Englishman, Mr Gray, who ran the Thomas Cook shop, and helped him discover the parts of the city tourists normally missed. Soon Stephen was adept at solo explorations. Even so, he was still very much an Englishman in a foreign town. One day he was in a tram going from one part of the city to another, and the ticket-collector somehow missed him. 'I said to an English lady next to me and a Frenchman next to her, "I can't get off the tram because I haven't paid for my ticket",' he recalled. 'And they said "Good heavens! Don't be such a fool! Go to the door and jump! Sautez! Sautez!" So I did jump, but I felt guilty that I had six centimes worth of ride for nothing!'[3]

One part of Marseilles that Stephen became particularly fond of was the old Parc Borely, the pleasure gardens at the eastern end of the town, where there was a small zoo. 'Many of the cages had leopards in them, and pumas – the doors were left open!' He admired two pumas especially, 'with emerald eyes . . . they were sitting with their paws spread out in front of them looking out over that inscrutable sea'. These became a symbol of the attraction Stephen felt for the place; exotic, only just tamed; the pumas 'staring eternally so far across the sea . . . It is an old, half derelict zoo . . . The red hibiscus burns to pink ash in the public gardens. The black pumas stare out to sea, alive within their miracle. Their durance which transcends all patience. Art is, after all, only superfluous contribution, the lyric fantasy. No man is a prisoner in his own heart.'[4]

Stephen fell ill whilst in Marseilles that October – 'a chill on my chest and in my right ear' – and Wilkie had to send out a male nurse to look after him. Stephen despatched Ivo back to England 'with a car filled up with sea-shells & rock crystals',[5] and took to his bed. Towards the end of the month, he sailed back to Southampton. Tired as he was, his head was full of the potency of the Vieux Port, and throughout that winter, at home in Wilsford, his plans for *Lascar* fermented.

The Manor was 'brimming' with workmen, busy redecorating a further four rooms when Stephen got back. He set about getting his new treasures in place. He wanted to combine his collection of rock crystals 'with dark red roses & white lilies', possible even in autumn, Stephen bragged to Cecil, because 'flowers seem to scorn the seasons at Wilsford!'[6]

He also returned to bound copies of *Leaves from a Missionary's Notebook*. In the nine years between its inception and publication, Stephen had lost track of his 'funny little book'.[7] When it appeared at last, the press notices made the obvious point: 'It is a long time since any work has been seen by Mr Stephen Tennant, the artist son of the late Lady Grey of Fallodon, who was one of the more bizarre figures of the nineteen-twenties,' wrote the *Evening Standard* on 4 November. 'To-day Mr Tennant "comes back" with a precious and limited book of entertaining drawings, entitled "Leaves from a Missionary's Notebook". It illustrates the adventures of an ingenuous missionary and the sad demoralization, in a tropical atmosphere, of his female helpmate, for whom "whereas before the passwords had been Faith, Hope and Charity, now they were Jack, Bob and Timothy." Mr Tennant lives at Wilsford Manor, in Wiltshire, which he inherited from his brother. He keeps a private zoo of lizards and snakes which have served as models for the drawings in his new book.'

It was clear to Stephen, and to his friends, just how little he had accomplished in the past ten years. Even his book seemed dated, and to belong to a former decade (and, more than likely, had been subsidized by its wealthy author). Whilst earlier efforts had been hailed as the work of a prodigy, *Leaves* was dismissed as the product of an aristocratic dilettante. Just as Stephen's one published adult work showed the influence of his youth, so it emphasized the apparent frivolity of his life. *Leaves* did not sell well; perhaps such a book could not hope to fare well in an increasingly political and threatened decade – the 'black Thirties', as Siegfried had called them.[*]

As if in answer to these implied criticisms, Stephen set to work on the very serious themes of his new book, developing his ideas in the months immediately following his return from France. 'One day in early spring I was reading a story by Herman Melville – Benito Cereno, from "Tales of the Piazza", translated into French & printed in the magazine "Revue des deux Mondes",' Stephen noted of the genesis of *Lascar* that year. 'After looking up a word in Larousse's Dictionary, I pottered about in those pleasant pages, among the "L's – *Lasso* – *Larme* – *Lapidaire* – *Lascif* – *Lascar*" – and reading the definition of the last, "*Mercenaire, matelot Indien, homme brave, hardi et malin*". It is like a poem, I thought, a voyage to strange lands – and the word Lascar is beautiful in itself, hard & sparkling, like a precious stone – *beau et force et nostalgique*. The name lay about in my mind for some days & became a prized possession. I was beginning a story about Marseille at the time – and the name *Lascar* fitted it admirably – it seemed as inevitable & splendid, glowing as a barbaric ring on a dark hand.'[†9]

Never one to keep anything of great importance to himself, Stephen announced his intended *roman à clef* to friends. Roger Senhouse, who had seen *Leaves* through to publication at Secker & Warburg,[‡] was one of the first to hear the news, and wrote Stephen a postcard on 21 February: 'How exciting about the new book!'

It was Stephen's intention to write a 'restless, glittering book, like the Canebière – a story of crude desires, lusts, fidelities, and treacheries. A story that shifts & changes like the lives of Lascar and his friends – a book about people, men, rather, that have no homes. A café on the Canebière, a

---

[*]There was one outstanding review, however, supplied by the critic Cyril Connolly (who had been at prep school with Beaton, and was already an acquaintance of the author's) for the *New Statesman*, 18 December, which saw positive virtues in Stephen's escapism, which he likened to Firbank's fantastic creations: 'The sprays and tendrils of the orchids, the feathery palms, the shells by the sea-shore are a kind of poetic vision of a better world . . .'[8]
[†]Another definite source of inspiration for Stephen's book was Joseph Conrad's *The Arrow of Gold*, also set in Marseilles and featuring the Canebière.
[‡]Roger Senhouse (1900–1970), a Bloomsbury figure, and former lover of Lytton Strachey, he was promised *Lascar* for his publishers by Stephen.

lodging-house in Buenos Aires, a tattooist shop in Puerto Rico; Formosa, Rangoon, Alexandria, Melbourne, the Cape of Good Hope, and the Roaring Forties – names of great sea ports – invested with the qualities of pleasure, loneliness, menace or despair according to the adventures recorded there. A book of the streets – with the blue maritime twilights mixing with the harsh glare of Café lustres – there are mornings and afternoons in the story but it is chiefly a nocturnal book – and the Vieux-port in Marseille – where the tale begins & ends is a sort of frame to the narrative.'[10] The preoccupation with this story was vital to Stephen's creative future; the world of *Lascar* was the only subject of Stephen's paintbrush, as well as his pen, for years to come. It became his alter-ego, his fantasy, his dream life.

Much of 1938 was devoted to the seemingly never-ending work on Wilsford Manor, and the flat in Mecklenburgh Square. In April, Cecil Beaton arranged a full-scale photo-session at Wilsford, photographing not just Stephen this time, but capturing every corner of his dream palace, Cecil regaling his host with 'witty tales of folk in Town' the while.

Syrie Maugham's influence on Wilsford is evident in Cecil's photographs; from the swagged and festooned velvet and silk curtains, to the mirror-topped tables. Stephen's contributions included golden ox-head and ribbon decorations above a mirrored library alcove, and a carved cherub group perched dramatically above a velvet swag, itself hung over a satin sofa. Beaton relished unique, near-surreal touches such as Bridport fish nets draped over the banisters, the wooden revolving postcard stand, complete with the old music hall postcards Stephen had bought in Italy in 1928, standing on a kidney-shaped dressing-table, glass-topped, under which Stephen had placed tram tickets from Marseilles.

Among the 'very crazy & exotic' poses recorded were Stephen and Cecil sitting on a huge white-quilted Syrie sofa in the drawing-room, holding up copies of *Photoplay* and *Moving Screen*, giving Stephen the face of Norma Shearer and Cecil, Katharine Hepburn. Stephen was a regular subscriber to these movie fan-magazines that proliferated in the thirties; they provided a rich source of illustration for his scrapbooks and collages (Beaton used this shot in his book on New York, published in October, captioning it 'Film-Fans').

Elsewhere Stephen made like a semaphorist with the day's newspapers, their remnants scattered about his feet in a presage of the clutter that was later to obscure the white carpets of Wilsford. Or he knelt with one ear to the ground in his lavish new study, flanked on one side by his fantastic Swan chair. One of the more 'sensible' shots has Stephen sitting at the grand piano on the expansive landing, looking rather serious, not very well, and just a little chubby around the jowls. The *pièce de résistance* was the dining-room, light, intimate, and now with white wood Venetian blinds. Its swags of plaster rope were carried through, along with mock-porthole mirrors, to one of the guest bedrooms, named the Sailor Room by Morgan Forster, who liked to stay there when he came down with his friend, Bob Buckingham.

On went the work at the Manor. A page from Stephen's journal for 1938 illustrates a veritable posse of Wiltshire workmen putting up new sunblinds outside the dining-room window. Stephen drew their bags being lowered past the window, and details of the rawl-plugs going in the walls; he loved the atmosphere of genial busyness, their whistling and workaday wear.

In late April, Stephen supervised another reptile delivery: wall lizards, edible and green frogs. The mauve clematis was out, so he spent an afternoon painting that, while elegant terrapins explored their new home.

Everything in the garden looked rosy, but still could be found in one corner of a page of his journals the quote from *Lascar*'s Madame Neffus: 'Only fools are happy.'

There was an outlet for Stephen's emotional longings in those days, evidently. All manner of uniforms are hinted at. Stephen boasted in old age of having had 'a wonderful love life', but he remained too well-mannered to elaborate. Certainly, visits to ports foreign and local – Marseilles and Toulon, Portsmouth and Southsea – all had their masculine attractions for Stephen, but there was never anyone to compete with Siegfried. No permanent relationship was established again, even if he had felt able to sustain such a friendship. That Stephen could not, and never felt able to, was part of the reason for his subsequent descents into severe depression.

But Stephen's attitude to sex was basically light-hearted, by turns naive or knowing. He might relish a streetwise saying from an American GI in the war – 'If only they would understand! Love's a commodity'[11] – or enthuse, in *Lascar*, over 'blue-cotton-covered bums', and stick advertisements for jockstraps cut from boxing magazines in his journals. 'I love an ass on that scale,' went one verse. 'Let us revel in glorious asses.' He was strongly against Victorian prudery, and in later years protested against Lord Longford's attempts to curb pornography. Whilst others deprecated the sex scenes in Joe Ackerley's autobiography when it was published, Stephen defended them as necessary to the artistic effect of the book. Yet he was careful never to overrate the physical side of love:

> I wonder why sex is so enthralling?
> Monotony is so very trite
> What is repeated can be galling
> But love has a mysterious right . . .[12]

Stephen spent a deal of time in London that summer and autumn. Staying at the Hotel Russell, he would visit the British Museum, where he might spend an entire morning sketching the tassel on an Assyrian bull, to reproduce it as a furnishing detail for Wilsford; other times he would simply loiter in Russell Square. One evening he wrote in his journal, 'Oh, if only I could ask time to stand still, it is so heavenly to be young . . .' (he was thirty-two). He had just finished a drawing for *Lascar*, and as he went to bed, Stephen heard the music drifting up from the hotel lounge: 'Very seductive at this distance. I am sniffing a delicious Wilsford rose – oh what a perfume! – a pale pink one. This evening I looked very beautiful.'[13]

*

Cecil Beaton had a chance to see Stephen's work that autumn, when he visited Wilsford after returning from France. 'It was very interesting to see his new drawings,' commented Beaton on the prolific sketches for *Lascar* Stephen had already done, 'which always remarkable are becoming more and more perverted. He now draws almost nothing but the coarsest types of labourer or sailor & it is his more poetic drawings of Nature that I like best.'[14] Yet Beaton thought *Lascar* could be successful, and he told Stephen it ought to be printed in the same ever-changing rainbow inks in which he was writing it.

Cecil's visit showed how far removed from reality – if political events are to be construed as 'reality' (for Stephen, they were not) – the world of Wilsford was, and how far advanced Stephen's *Lascar* obsession had already become. Late 1938 was an anxious time: Germany threatened Czechoslovakia, and Chamberlain's efforts to stabilize the European situation were frenetic. In this atmosphere, Beaton had been staying with Edith Olivier, who was busy distributing gas masks in Wilton. When they had motored over to see Stephen, 'in order to find some diversion from the depressing anxiety', they found 'someone quite unmoved by the events of the week. Stephen had not even read the papers – he said he liked Hitler's mysticism – the way he parted his hair – the mad starry look in his eyes – Stephen is only interested in himself & his health & now he was particularly occupied as he must enter a clinic tomorrow for a slight operation on his nose.'[15]

The following day, 2 October, Stephen went up to London, to the London Clinic in Devonshire Place. All he took with him was Siegfried's collection, *Vigils* (which contained the poems written during his time with Stephen). 'It was the only luggage I wanted,' wrote Stephen. 'These poems are wonderful.'[16]

The late nineteen-thirties saw a period of new meetings and new travels for Stephen, both of which served to prolong the creative progress of *Lascar*. Yet gregariousness, in measured quantities, was an inherent part of his personality, and the freedom his money and position gave him to acquire new acquaintances – especially literary ones, with whom he could discuss his own projects and feel a certain comradeship – was one which he exploited to the full. And in November Stephen made an important new friend through the painter Ethel Sands. An elegantly-dressed American, she had been a friend of Stephen's since the twenties, and was very much a figure of Chelsea society, as well as being a talented artist in her own right.

Stephen sought Sands' company, and lso that of her lifelong companion, Nan Hudson (he had an eye for these female *ménages*, noting that such women as Sands, Edith Sitwell and Willa Cather liked to have 'a dark companion, preferably with a moustache').[17] Ethel and Nan threw one of their renowned parties at their Chelsea home, 15 The Vale, on 11 November. Guests included Osbert Sitwell and David Horner, Violet Hammersley, and Max and Florence Beerbohm, newly arrived from Rapallo. Stephen arrived, 'preceded by a lovely bunch of orchids', and on entering the room, 'looked rather like an orchid himself'.[18] Ethel thought he might like to meet a friend of hers, an Anglo-Irish writer called Elizabeth Bowen.

Stephen and Elizabeth immediately fell into deep conversation, he charming her with his appreciation of her recent work, *The House in Paris* (1935), a tale of a little girl left to her own devices amongst grown-ups in a strange city. It appealed greatly to Stephen, not least because of the young heroine's love for her toy monkey, and the story's echoes of his own halcyon time in Paris in 1922. And the writer herself, with her distinctive features and intense intelligence, was very much to Stephen's taste. 'I want to see Elizabeth Bowen again,' noted Stephen in his journal.[19] It was to be a close and dedicated friendship, which became yet closer in the overshadowed years of the decade ahead.

Stephen spent late autumn between London and Wiltshire. 'War seemed round the corner,'[20] wrote Virginia Woolf. Life went on as normal. On 23 November there was David Tennant's second marriage, to Virginia Parsons, but Stephen, whose relationship with his brother was at its lowest point, did not attend. David accused his brother of being capricious, and certainly had a point. One day, deciding to go over to Wilsford, he was met by the butler at the front door, who went upstairs to see if Mister Stephen was receiving visitors. 'Is he fair or dark?' enquired Stephen. 'Dark, Sir.' 'Oh, I'm only seeing fair-haired people today,' he replied, and David was dismissed.[21]

By December, however, Stephen was busying himself making plans for 1939 which, given the political situation, were surprisingly, almost foolishly adventurous. Egypt was his destination, the furthest east he would travel. With such an exciting expedition ahead, Stephen couldn't wait for the New Year to begin.

Chapter 19

1939 and All That

I am well, and planning to go this weekend with Bob to Stephen
Tennant's mansion near Salisbury. It should be quite pleasant, if the
world holds.

— E. M. Forster to John Simpson, 3 July 1940

STEPHEN flew from Southampton by seaplane in January, *en route*
for the Mediterranean. 'It was dawn – I was flying. How could I ever
have thought that I had any other destination?' he wrote later. 'I
remember the seaplane as it rose above Southampton – slowly turning –
and then going on – straight – on & on into the first delicate radiance of
early sunrise. We stopped in Crete. I remember Canea – there was jasmine
in flower outside my window. Next day we went on to Alexandria – and I
had a bunch of jasmine in my lap.'[1]

Egypt, 1939. The reverberations from an unstable Europe had reached
even the Middle East. In Alexandria and Cairo, all nationalities were to be
found, and in the capital city of Egypt Stephen made the acquaintance of
the Countess Barbara Reventlow, née Hutton, the millionaire heiress
to the Woolworth fortune, and probably the richest woman in the world.
Stephen takes up the story:

'Every winter she used to go away with three or four very good friends –
generally a man and two beautiful women to make her look more
beautiful – I remember I had a valet with me, called Wade, a very nice
man.'[2] One of Hutton's friends with her that winter was Princess Sita of
Kapurthala. The Princess spotted Stephen sitting out on the hotel terrace,
and it was obvious they were talking about him. 'I was a little bit naughty,
really, because I was aware that they longed to know me . . . One day I
was sitting and reading on the beautiful veranda and on the other side of
the pathway out into the garden was sitting Barbara Hutton, reading, and
Sita Kapurthala came up to me and said, "Mr Tennant, will you excuse me

if I introduce myself to you? I am Sita Kapurthala, and Barbara, over there, longs to know you." So that's how we met! I went across to Barbara – she looked up and her face laughing told me, "Sita does all my dirty work for me!"'

Barbara Hutton was twenty-five, and all her life had been used to immense wealth. She was, when Stephen came to know her, already a figure of extravagance; Winfield House in Regent's Park was just one of her luxurious homes (later donated by Hutton to the American Ambassador) dotted around the world. With a legacy of twenty-five million dollars and a Fifth Avenue palace, she had created a glamorous life-style in the thirties that had not, for all its indulgences, brought happiness. The Danish Count Reventlow was the second of a total of seven husbands (who included Cary Grant), a symptom of her uneasy personal life which stemmed in part from a disastrous upbringing; her mother had committed suicide when she was young, and her father held her in little affection.

In her search for diversion, Barbara Hutton travelled endlessly, and would later turn to drink and drugs, dying a virtual recluse in a Californian hospital, after a number of suicide attempts, in 1979. But this degenerative process had hardly begun. At twenty-five, she was stunning to look at, with her bleached blonde hair, vivid blue eyes, and ineffable chic. The mutual attraction between Stephen and Barbara was obvious: she represented complete glamour to him, and he was a witty and good-looking companion for her, who posed neither a sexual nor a financial threat.

So these two golden creatures got together in Cairo. 'We had such fun together,' said Stephen; 'this'll make you laugh. Every week Barbara went into Cairo to have her hair dyed, and I went with her. We always went to the same scent shop after she'd had her hair done, and a wonderful lunch at the Shepherd's Hotel.' The scent shop was kept by a Mister Abi Abdullah, according to Stephen, 'and he gave us his card and I remember he said to me "You know, Mr Tennant, there is only one Abi Abdullah in Cairo", and I said, "Why is every other shop called that then? I can't believe you're the only one." Then he said to Barbara, "Miss Hutton, would you like to re-enter the portals of youth?" And she said, "Damn it all, I'm only twenty-six! – I think I've already had enough of the portals of youth to last me a long time . . . I've learnt very quickly what you men are worth – you're all rubbish, that's what you are, the whole pack of you!" Then he said, "You must have my unguent, my new unguent for exciting the passions" – it was made of the legs of a flamingo, the tusk of a rhinocerus, and lots of newts – "If you use this and put it on your shoulders in the evening everybody will fall in love with you." And so we bought a lot – we bought a lot of things . . .'

Barbara Hutton was one of the few people who could rival Stephen in her patronage of the cosmetics industry. 'It's rather naughty of you,' he admonished her one day, 'you've brought from Paris with you six crates of scent made by all the firms of Paris – it's rather naughty . . . to let all the other passengers around your room reek of scent! It may not appeal to other people.' He pointed out – albeit with some incredulity: 'There are some people who don't like scent at all.' And she said, 'I've never thought of that!'

Egypt entranced Stephen. The old towns of Cairo and Alexandria, full of European uniforms amongst the native costumes, and the Casbah thronged with hawkers, tarts, and servicemen, were very much the stuff of *Lascar*, he noted, especially 'the great gates leading onto the docks at Alexandria; guarded, & with warnings in Arabic'. Or 'the manor boy who disappeared into the doorway of the house in the Sharia Zaglal Pasha in a black and white check suit' who caught his eye, 'dressed rather like the country cousin in the Ziegfield Follies – ventriloquist doll. He was essentially the material of *Lascar*. I cannot say why.'[3] The book seemed ever closer. Stephen stayed in the grand Continental Savoy Hotel until May, when he booked his passage – back to Marseilles.

He sailed on the SS *Mariette Pasha* from Alexandria, and the voyage was in itself a new experience. The ship carried Syrian merchants, French militia, Egyptians, Turks, mothers with children – a Biblical scene. Most travelled steerage, but the French soldiers were under the supervision of a captain who went first class with Stephen, periodically going below decks to visit his men throughout the voyage. Stephen accompanied him, and found them playing cards at their leisure, in the bows of the ship.

They came into harbour 'under indigo grey clouds'. Here was Marseilles again, at last, and Stephen saw the docks, 'an impression of smoke-coloured chaos'. There were 'piles of crates & barrels and heaps of cement and coal & pig-iron' everywhere on the quay, and the 'greyness of the weather, the lowness of the clouds and the heterogeneous conglomeration of machinery each seemed a natural component of each other.' To Stephen, it was 'a scene of extraordinary power and sombre evocation'.

It was the territory of his fictional imaginings, and as he came into the Vieux Port on that murky summer's day, Stephen felt re-invested with the spirit of *Lascar*, its colourful characters, its thrilling plot; and above all, the city itself, brooding over his story like an ominous thundercloud moving slowly overhead. 'As the ship slid into her berth, the scene, from being a breathtaking backdrop, became one's own life again – not humdrum, Marseille could never be that, but by assimilating one into its texture, the sullen panorama lost something of its uniqueness.'

Once disembarked, however, the old magic returned. 'Rattling over the cobbles & railway junctures of the dock roads on the way to my hotel I noticed several ship names, Compiègne, Chenonceaux, and Ville d'Alger. How the names of ships carry one's heart away,' observed Stephen. 'With extasy [*sic*] knocking at my heart, I asked the taxi-driver to stop at one of the kiosks on the Vieux Port (quai des Belges) where sea-shells are sold. The deafening din of the quais was overwhelming – the clang of the girders, the shovelling of coal, the rumble of cranes of all types. Lascars & dockers in maillots & blue linen hurried or lounged.'

From his hotel on the Boulevard du Rhône, Stephen wrote to Cecil on 22 May, having arrived with 'wild roses & pinky-gold roses & *Lascar*'s mss. in two exquisite Egyptian trunks . . . made of fibre & chocolate tin-foil; and now I am here to work on *Lascar* – I have a friend in the French Police & we are going to visit factories & cargo boats – already my notebooks brim – I especially want to ask your advice about the colouring of the book & illustrations. I'm calling it *Lascar, A Story of the Maritime Boulevard*. The lists of cargoes & merchandise in the shipping reports here are so beautiful – beyond words – "*Belligeuse, venant de Shanghai, Samarang & Formosa; avec 1.367 tonnes de Vanille, Semoule, Opium, Amandes, Café, thé, et merchandises diverses, à la Joliette* (Joliette is a quai). So you see how busy I am – I hope to get home in early June . . .'

Stephen stayed in Marseilles for a week, roaming the Vieux Port with his policeman friend, Raoul, making copious notes for his book. Nothing of the city's intensity, its ineluctable romance escaped him; Raoul turned to him one night and said, '*Nous sommes parmi les étoiles.*'[4]

By the time he reached Paris on 27 May, Stephen was quite exhausted by the strains of his research. He told Cecil: 'Your letter brought such a pang of longing to see you – that I had to ring & ask for a cup of tea. I am so overwrought & worn out & repressed, just like you, that I only read dictionaries (there being no continuity no concentration is needed) and long to be home resting. I've been working so hard & travelling so much that my nerves are dreadful, my hand shakes – & I jump a yard into the air if anyone comes in suddenly.'[5]

The immensity of the literary task he had set himself was demanding much of Stephen's reserves. 'Oh dear – & there's still so much of *Lascar* to do,' he lamented. 'The whole scope of the book . . . must be enlarged . . .

since being in Marseille again – the town is far more complex & romantic
& tempting than I had remembered. Such thrilling exciting things keep
cropping up.' Stephen had been sung to by a barman on the Canebière,
and the air of abandonment there caught his romantic fancy. He added as
a postscript to his letter to Beaton: '*Lascar*. A story about dark eyes on the
boulevards – in the marvellous twilight of the South.' Ever after, that
phrase would recur in Stephen's notes: 'Dark eyes – I would go to the end
of the world for dark eyes.'[6]

Whilst in Paris Stephen got a telephone call from a reporter on the *Sunday
Express*. A Miss Isolene Thompson had heard about the amazing
refurbishment of Wilsford, and wanted a comment from the 'golden-
haired, rich . . . youngest brother of Lord Glenconner' who had, according to her informants, recently 'surprised his staff at Wilsford Manor . . .
by announcing his intention of engaging Arab or Moroccan servants'.

The story became a major feature in the paper's 4 June edition. 'This
young man, at thirty-three a brilliant artist and dress designer, has given
the countryfolk for miles around something to talk about. There are
twelve Nubian slaves and negroes installed in his house now – as statues.
Many are lifesize, painted by himself. Nine are the conventional black,
but one is white and two are golden!' Miss Thompson had evidently
spoken to Amy Gale, Stephen's housekeeper, 'plump and smiling, who
has adoringly indulged his "little ways" ever since he was a child', and was
now 'shaken out of her usual placidity. "He seems set on it", she said to
me. "I must say I don't fancy live coloured men about the house, but this is
Mr Tennant's house and I've got my orders. All I know is that he has
written to me asking me to inquire at the agencies for Arab or Moroccan
servants, and if I'm not successful he will see about it himself when he gets
home. He's been holidaying in Egypt and such-like places and I suppose
he has taken a fancy to black servants. But if you want to know any more
you must ask him yourself."'

The intrepid Isolene located the errant Stephen at the Hôtel Raphael via
a crackly cross-Channel telephone link. 'It's not that I think coloured
servants better than English ones, except individually,' he told Miss
Thompson. 'But my housekeeper told me of the difficulty of getting
servants down in the country just now and I told her to try to get Arab or
Moroccan ones.' This conversation was printed in bold type, as if the
notion were quite incredible to the readership of the *Sunday Express*.
Stephen spoke of *Lascar*, and ended the interview saying: 'I expect to be
home next week, but Paris is gay, very gay . . . Goodbye.'[7]

*

Still in Paris in early August, Stephen was introduced by Tchelitchew to France's most visible poet, Jean Cocteau. Cocteau had always been a magical figure to Stephen, and this meeting destroyed none of his illusions. Together with his friends Christian Bérard[*] and Boris Kochno, they lunched in a restaurant, and the poet was completely charming – and paid Stephen many compliments. He called him *'le Carnival de Venise'*, and regaled his elegant new English friend with his terse and witty epigrams, telling Stephen he was *'de pureté de pureté – de débauche en débauche'*. Cocteau was amused by Stephen; he remarked of a Lascar picture *'ca grouillent'* [*sic*] ('it's swarming') and, turning to Kochno, said: 'What he likes here, in France, is *ce qui est fort.*'[8]

Boris Kochno had been secretary and companion to Diaghilev, and probably first met Stephen in the twenties. Harold Acton described him as a 'small dark wiry Russian' with 'coal-black eyes . . . his *charme slave* was faintly macabre'.[9] He and Bérard lived together in an apartment near the Odeon. M. Kochno echoed his friend's sentiments when he described Stephen as 'this tall fair good-looking young man' who appeared to be 'a kind of broken lily – a sick flower who needed the constant care of a loving gardener. He was rather like the hero of a medieval story by Oscar Wilde; and might have served as a model to a Mannerist painter. It was surprising to hear vocal cadenzas worthy of the divine Sarah burst forth suddenly from the lips of an elegant English aristocrat, who, moreover, adored the murky underworld of Toulon and Marseilles.'[10]

Whilst in Paris Stephen went to a party given by Elsie Mendl at her Villa Trianon at Versailles. Here Lady Mendl – another of those seemingly interchangeable society interior decorators thrown up by the twenties' enthusiasm for the art – and her 'Bachelors' (her two female companions) reigned, in immaculate good taste, she with her gilded capes and clothes from the best Parisian designers, her hair dyed blue to match her poodles'. These were the last of the great parties, extravagant fêtes designed by Stephane Boudin. Stephen saw his hostess 'in chalk white greek chiffon – gold cracker jewellery on her head, & a crinkled watered ravishing Schiaparelli cloak'.[11] He also met Wallis Simpson, the Duchess of Windsor, '& thought her talk so puissant, & racy & fresh – I also liked her elegance,' he noted, '& great grace and brio – violet eyes & gardenia skin . . .'[12] All this while London dug trenches and filled

---

[*] One of the painters who, like Tchelitchew, had emerged as a 'neo-romantic' in the mid-1920s, 'Bébé' Bérard was a large man, with a sizeable opium habit to match, likeable and much admired by both Stephen and Cecil.

sandbags. Versailles was an apt setting, perhaps: partying by Marie Antoinette's toy farm at the Petit Trianon, while Europe geared itself for war.

The ever-growing tension in England did not make Wilsford – or London – happy places to be that summer, and even though Stephen could still escape back to the Continent, he found that the war's poisonous tentacles were grasping the whole of Europe in their dangerous embrace. He had left England and gone to France, hoping to get back to Marseilles. Staying at Bayonne in 'the first few weeks of the war', he recalled 'walking to the Caeserne at night. The Timailleurs – the hot dark night – the little French country town teeming with Militia, the Isere – the street – with men in cheehias in rows.'[13] On the day that Neville Chamberlain announced that Britain was at war with Germany, Stephen was in the Hôtel du Palais in Biarritz. He wrote to Sibyl Colefax that night: 'Yes, we must be very strong & brave now . . . Here the terrible carved deep grief on the poor people's faces is very terrible – unbearable . . .'[14]

Stephen's feelings about the crisis were not as devil-may-care as the bald facts of his 'holidaying' might belie. He cared about the fate of the civilized world – albeit in his own personalized way – deeply enough, in fact, for the psychological effects of the war to contribute to severe mental stress. It may have been for his own rarefied past existence that he was grieving, but that past embraced all things and peoples, not just his immediate surroundings and friends. 'I was on my way to Marseille,' he told Sibyl, 'but in Paris, that *Citta Morta*, friends said that M. being the big shipping port of the Midi it will be bombed so soon & so thoroughly. Lovely Europe – "look your last on all things lovely, every hour, let no night seal your sense" – but now we have not time & heart to trace quotations.' Stephen was travelling with a new friend whom he had met in Paris, an Indian ballet dancer, Edelgi Dinshaw, '& my plans are vague. Wilsford is already commandeered by the military & Christopher has asked if a room may be kept for Stephen,' he noted humbly. 'We must be cheerful, help each other – & never despair.'[15]

Stephen managed one last look at Marseilles before the Nazi bombs systematically destroyed the Vieux Port for ever. Within two weeks he was back, drawing a shell booth and its old sailor attendant, where he had found 'orange persimmon coloured sea-shells with big lips rolled back . . . from Madagascar'. He dawdled in the Parc Borely, in that Indian summer of 1939, and there, in 'heavenly hot sunshine, and such a feast of beauty as one rarely sees' – and which he would never see again –

he contemplated 'La Roserare with still lots of roses', and 'sat under a cedar & lazed blissfully . . . I took Monkey with me & we sat together in hot bliss.'[16]

London was a changed place when Stephen returned to it. As the street lights had gone out, so had much of the social life, as he had known it. Many of his friends had closed up their town houses for the duration; Barbara Hutton had packed up the treasures of Winfield House, and an armoured car had come to take her fabulous jewels to the vaults of Coutts Bank. Those that stayed in town moved into the large hotels – the Ritz, the Dorchester, and the Savoy.

The Savoy was Stephen's chosen London refuge during the war years. In this imposing riverside edifice, with its gracious and subtly-lit halls and lounges, he would entertain friends. On one occasion, when Morgan Forster and Bob Buckingham were invited to lunch there the following February, their host was three-quarters of an hour late. This 'enraged' Forster, and the two guests 'took revenge' by ordering the most expensive dishes on the menu: 'We were awfully vulgar,' admitted Morgan in a spirit of devilment.[17]

They were also guests at Wilsford in July 1940. Whilst Stephen still had his manor to himself, he often had his friends to stay in the early part of the war, though frequently people like Constant Lambert and Stephen Spender had to cry off when duty called; they hadn't Stephen's freedom of movement. That summer the world, which for a while had seemed unaffected by European events, suddenly became more dangerous. On 21 July Paris fell to the Germans, a bitter blow, much felt by Stephen who hated the idea of his favourite city so desecrated.

The Luftwaffe's raids that began on 7 September created sudden instability. A few days later, Mecklenburgh Square was bombed. Virginia Woolf returned on 10 September to find her house 'still smouldering . . . a great pile of bricks'.[18] Stephen's flat had merely had its windows blown out. However, the whole square had to be evacuated, and four days later, a UXB exploded. Roger Senhouse reported that Stephen's flat had even withstood that, but was 'somewhat shattered'.[19] Stephen arranged to have his furniture moved to Wilsford, and gave up any idea of re-inhabiting the flat.

Bed-ridden with 'a bronchial chill' (his weak constitution having made him unfit for active service, apart from other considerations), Stephen wrote to Sibyl Colefax on 21 September, apologizing for being unable to lunch with her and Virginia Woolf: ' . . . are you in London? I hope not –

do come & stay here while the bombing is so bad . . . I saw nice Leslie Hartley* the other day . . . London must be a nightmare now.' Even so, Stephen returned to the beleaguered capital for a visit, only to come into personal contact with one of the German bombs that rained on the town. He was leaving the Ritz when a bomb exploded in Stratton Street. Stephen said that the blast shot him and the page boy through the swing doors of the hotel 'like Peter Pan and Wendy'.[20] When the manager came down to ask 'Is everything all right?' he appeared to be concerned only that the chandeliers were intact.

Stephen entertained Cecil and friends at Wilsford on the first weekend in November. As ever, Beaton was concerned for his friend's health and future. 'By being so ill so often he has now realized the importance of preserving his strength & through this safeguard I have now come to look upon him as someone who will have beaten all of us & that he will be the last of us to go. That he has now contemplated old age & how best to cope with its disadvantages. He is now the tortoise & we his contemporaries are the hares.'

The war and its uncertainties made Cecil wax nostalgic. 'He will doubtless develop into something very remarkable in his maturity,' he observed. 'Nevertheless each time I visit him I feel it is as though I am privileged to know Firbank or Beardsley. For nearly twenty years now I have known him – & still we feel like the two rebellious bright young things we were. His house still thrills me in that same particular way . . .' In the past, Cecil had been 'sorry that so brilliant a person should have wasted so much time discussing nebulous artificiality . . . a piece of french blue ribbon, or pink carnation, a photograph . . . or a perfume.' Now he found a new maturity in Stephen; the war had made the bird of paradise return to earth. On this visit Stephen read aloud serious pieces from Emily Dickinson and Anna de Noailles, and 'the conversation was strictly literary'.

It was a full weekend party. Besides Beaton, there was Arthur Waley, the interior decorator Felix Harbord, the painter Derek Hill, Violet Trefusis[†], Tancred Borenius (the Finnish art historian who was Stephen's lecturer at the Slade), and Sheila MacDonald (daughter of the former Labour Prime Minister, Ramsay MacDonald, who knew Stephen through Princess Marthe Bibesco).

*L. P. Hartley (1895–1972), author of *The Go-Between*, whom Stephen had first met at one of Marie Belloc Lowndes' literary evenings at 9 Barton Street.
†Violet Trefusis (1894–1972), daughter of Edward VII's mistress, Mrs Keppel, was, after her divorce precipitated by her runaway affair with Vita Sackville-West, an expatriate member of the *beau monde*, coming back to England in 1940, homeless.

Sheila MacDonald was deeply impressed by the 'uncanny nebulous atmosphere' of the whole weekend. She recalls being invited down by Stephen to escape the air raids, 'but warned I mustn't mind being left to my own resources as he was very busy'. She also felt a little out of place among these people who moved in such different circles to hers, and knew few of the names whom they gossiped about: 'However, they most courteously tried to bring me into the conversation by always turning to ask me whether I knew them. It became a matter of routine for me to admit "No". Violet Trefusis was mentioned. Did I know her? "No." "Oh," said Stephen, "I've forgotten. I asked her to come to stay. I must send the car for her." In due course the sitting room door was flung open. "Miss Violet Trefusis and Professor Borenius." She immediately rushed up to me, flung her arms around my neck with "dear Sheila. How lovely to see you again." I forgot I had lunched with her at Mrs Keppel's.'[21]

'The whole place is gloriously, lavishly Stephen', wrote Sheila Mac-Donald in her diary. Her 'French' bedroom was done in tricolour shades, whilst elsewhere she found lobster pots vying with crystal candelabra as lampshades. In the yellow and white drawing room 'a great dais of steps spattered nonchalantly with shells leads up to a table with the most devious legs bearing a great basket of rushes and leaves with yellow bows bright amongst them. An imitation dog stands awkwardly around, and a slab of rock crystal rearing up from a carefully broken classical pillar placed in an imitation marble yellow alcove, at the top of which hangs a nondescript classical mask. All subtly floodlit.'

She was particularly impressed by the staircase. 'It was littered with scallop shells – which made it very difficult to walk up! And Stephen's bedroom was amazing. There were lush ferns everywhere, and dried flowers fixed with wires to the Gothic windows, so that it appeared they were falling down to the floor.' (Just as surprising that night was a 'sudden vision – sudden because the luxurious carpets eliminated sound – of Stephen floating into the room wearing yellow satin pyjamas, holding a lighted candle before him.')

Stephen read aloud from Conrad's stories, from Firbank's novels, and from books on 'sexual aberrations, the insect world, Sarah Bernhardt, Spiritualism', noted an impressed Cecil. This took up the whole weekend, as Sheila MacDonald wrote: 'We spent much of the time surrounded by cushions or lying on the thick pile carpets . . . I read Firbank's *Prancing Nigger* – who was it read *Cardinal Pirelli*? We talked very much, comparing the sensual qualities, the artificialities of different writings, the delight in oddities; the cynicism and lack of sympathy . . .'

It occurred to Beaton that Stephen was 'one of the strangest people. In his own home he is utterly delightful. At the Ritz or in a train* he is shaming and ridiculous – He is the greatest paradox of heart and heartlessness – sensibility and cruelty – taste and vulgarity.'

Cecil saw 'how alive & susceptible to impressions' Stephen was, despite being 'incarcerated in his ice cake fortress. Tancred said that the house should be made air-tight & preserved intact just as it is at the moment so that future generations may see these incredible delicate & vivid colours – the vases of artificial roses & lilac, the fish nets hanging over the banisters, the tinselled postcards in the revolving stand, the whole paraphernalia of Stephen's taste – just as it is now to the astonishment of his few intimate friends – & incomprehensible to most that see it today – so for future generations it will have an added mystery.' Beaton stayed only on Saturday night, 'though I hated to drag myself away, it was as well to quit before the house lost its freshness, & became, as it can, tawdry'.

One relative stranger who came to visit was the young writer Colin MacInnes. This in itself was a reminder of the pre-war world: MacInnes' mother was Angela Thirkell, a friend of both Stephen and his mother. The Thirkells had moved to Australia in the twenties, but after her marriage had broken down Angela brought her children back to England, where she made her career as a novelist. Colin, her second child, was described, at the age of sixteen, as 'extraordinarily beautiful, with an ethereal quality. He seemed to have stepped from one of his great-grandfather's works . . . "a pure throw-back to Burne-Jones"', although 'his temperament was not as angelic as his features'.[23] Later known for his art criticism, and novels dealing with the seedier side of life (*City of Spades, Absolute Beginners*), MacInnes was a bisexual who deliberately wrote on subjects that would shock his mother, whose own works were of a determinedly 'middle-brow' nature.

MacInnes recalls that the family were living in Melbourne in 1928, when his mother received a letter from Stephen describing, 'with a handwriting that spiralled over the leaves like the tendrils of a vine', the alterations to Wilsford. The young Colin hadn't thought much of such

*In *Love in a Cold Climate* Cedric persuades Norma's stern brother Jack to get his suitcase – full of resting-creams – down from the luggage rack. 'He says you gave him hypnotic stares through your glasses,' says Fanny. 'The thing is, he did have a rather pretty tweed on,' replied Cedric.[22] Edith Olivier noted in 1943 that Beaton was actively embarrassed to be seen in public with Stephen.

extravagance. 'It's a waste of money,' he had said. But in 1940, now with the British Army and stationed at Bulford, a mile or two due north of Wilsford, MacInnes' curiosity overcame his puritan censoriousness, and he took up an invitation to visit the manor. MacInnes later wrote up the experience in an essay for Stephen Spender's *Encounter* magazine, to accompany illustrations of *Lascar*. The circumstances 'for savouring its rare peculiarity could not have been bettered', he observed. 'By the end of 1940, the worship of "austerity" not as a positive virtue, but as the justification of the negation of all joy, was already settling like a sterile blight on England' – a blight which eventually sent Stephen into the life of an eremitic aesthete.

After a long trudge in army boots, MacInnes arrived at the Manor. 'The door was opened by a footman dressed like a barman in a white coat, and I was ushered into . . . but into which room was I ushered? The greatest strangeness of Stephen's alterations to Wilsford is that the individuality of each room is abolished, and the whole house has become one continuous, though constantly changing, apartment. It is as if the floors had been flooded by a sea of carpets, and the doors washed away, so that one sails through the walls, one room inviting you into the next.'

MacInnes drifted into this strange land, and awaited his host. Stephen made his appearance 'quite evidently as nervous as was I'. MacInnes saw evidence still of 'a fantastic physical beauty which seemed almost monstrous in its perfection' as Stephen crouched on cushions, 'looking like an exquisite, sad faun'. Conversation was, to begin with, very difficult. 'Searching desperately for safe gambits, we talked about "the war". "I was nearly killed", he told me, "last night in the Savoy Hotel."' The near-miss of an incendiary raid on the Embankment and the apparent disdain in which Stephen held the incident was quickly replaced by talk of his work. MacInnes mentioned *The Vein in the Marble*, hoping to flatter Stephen, saying he had been 'brought up on' the book, 'unintentionally implying that he was some artistic ancient, some Arthur Rackham of a venerable J. M. Barrie past. He writhed visibly, and rang for whisky.'

With spirits to help thaw the situation, the two relaxed, and MacInnes could relish Stephen's conversation, which he found 'poetical and imaginative, incisive and realistic – and enlightened, I am glad to say, by occasional asperities. But it is never – as is often the sad case with men of vivid personality and conversational virtuosity – an ultimately intolerable monologue. For Stephen is really absorbed by you and what you say – even when he may think you dull, and your notions idiotic. And with manners that are effortless, solicitous, and engaging, he invites his companion into a dialogue, in which the evocations of a person, or of a work of art, or of some natural object, make each of these seem to grow in stature and significance, and become more real.'[24]

The following April there were public glimpses of this private world, in the pages of the arts magazine *Horizon* (edited by Cyril Connolly and sponsored by Peter Watson). For the first and last time, this issue contained a full colour reproduction – one of the many projected covers for *Lascar* – in a fold-out section. Stephen Spender points out that, even though Stephen paid for the expensive colour separations himself, Cyril Connolly 'would never have accepted anything for *Horizon* for that reason alone – he genuinely thought Stephen to be talented – as he was'.[25] Underneath the illustration was the optimistic legend: 'DESIGN FOR BOOKJACKET from the forthcoming publication of *Lascar* by Stephen Tennant (Secker and Warburg).'[26] Forty years later, the publishers had still not received the author's manuscript.

Stephen's association with Connolly's *Horizon* resulted in a commission to review Cecil's new book, *Time Exposure*, a collaboration with Peter Quennell. It collected Beaton's photographs and Quennell's words, reflecting a lost world: 'All we can be sure of for the moment is that it has been lost for good.'[27] In that respect, it was an apt volume for Stephen's critical attention. 'This is a book in *paillettes*. A potent cocktail, the very newest bandbox or a flourish in electrics,' enthused Stephen. 'Mr Beaton's photographic skill and charm spill over and down a predestined course of fashionable popularity like a liqueur advertisement in coloured lights pouring and re-pouring down the side of the Eiffel Tower.'

Stephen's prose, effusive and florid, was not uncritical. 'Perhaps in an austere mood, the reader may sometimes feel that this gay confetti of camera clicks, of Mr Beaton's fantastic celluloid *fouettes* and Mr Quennell's clever asides is a little limited by its almost exclusively fashionable appeal, by its many reminders of the worlds of *Vogue* Magazine and *Harper's Bazaar* – i.e. that the "All is Vanity" motif inclines to tire one swiftly, to fade as quickly as new tissue paper,' he conceded. However, 'this book, this bouquet, a *corbeille de fleurs* real and false, evokes the *carnet de bal*, in pink cardboard, stamped in silver, new; newer than the freshest invitation; accompanied by the posy of moss-roses and blue forget-me-nots, corseted and framed in tulle and ribbon'. Only Stephen could have introduced such a list of his favourite things into a book review.

He also took issue with Quennell's piece on Cocteau. 'In that central estimate of the gifts of that unpredictable *enfant terrible*, Mr Jean Cocteau – his subject hardly seems snared. One has the impression that Mr Quennell's concise paragraph is a net from which his victim has escaped.' Even Cecil got a minor sideswipe. 'The edicts of fashion are notoriously capricious,' warned Stephen, 'and Mr Beaton's art is as volatile as the whim of his goddess.' He concluded triumphantly, however, that 'In Cecil Beaton's art it is always the birthday morning – the eve of the Ball, the rise of the curtain.'[28] Which could be Stephen's, too – never anything less than a child-like joy at the newness of things, even in the dark days of war.

Chapter 20

Lilacs in the Spring

You were very beautiful this evening, Stephen, your hair and skin were lovely, your eyelashes have grown, your eyes were very blue with just a *soupçon* of '*bleu argente*' on the lids . . . do you remember how Nannie used to say 'Steenie, when you're tired you have such a teeny face'? Tonight your face was teeny, for you are very tired and have given out a lot of nervous energy.

— Stephen Tennant's journal

WITH the threatened military use of Wilsford, and loss of his London flat, Stephen took a more southerly *pied-à-terre*. He had always found Bournemouth, the genteel seaside town, appealing, and so he leased 5 Sunbury Court, with its view of the palm-planted Pleasure Gardens.

Stephen's flat, at the top of the building, was minute in comparison to Wilsford's spaciousness, but cosy in a provincial manner. Inside, off a little hallway, opened the doors to two modest-sized bedrooms, a tiny kitchen, and a small living-room. With the art deco stained-glass designs above each door, and the rest of its suburban fittings, Stephen felt restrained and unostentatious there at a time when ostentation was very much frowned upon.

Stephen decorated it in muted Vogue Regency style – pink once more the predominant colour in its curtains and furnishings – and made it into a comfortable den, full of his favourite books and with his painting materials to hand. From this hidey-hole, he would walk out along lanes shaded by Scots pines, and mingle with housewives seeking some way round the rationing, or with the old men dozing in deckchairs in the park. There was good shopping, too. Brights, the large department store in the centre of town, was very much in the old tradition, with well-stocked luxury departments that thrilled Stephen (especially the perfume counter and its knowledgeable staff).

Work on *Lascar* proceeded apace. On sketching and note-taking expeditions to nearby Poole Harbour, Stephen found reminders of more exotic places.* In the old museum garden there, he was suddenly reminded of a similar park in Rhodes. 'I touched ancient gnarled rosemary bushes . . . Visited my beloved church – & wondered at the potency of Poole's harsh tough spell.' The town was still very much undeveloped at that time, and had a forlorn air. 'To feel tender towards so brutal & melancholy a place seems indefensible,' wrote Stephen. 'But the heart has strong allegiances – which dwarf the moralities . . . Chatted with a nice bloke – about his horse – a wise natural kind of man, full of the pith & kindness of human nature.'[2]

Stephen was not alone in Bournemouth during the early years of the war. Some, like Rosamond Lehmann and Cyril Connolly, made the trek down just to see him. If they were lucky, they were asked to stay, although Miss Lehmann, invited by Stephen one weekend, turned up at Sunbury Court to find no one in. She sat down on the steps and awaited Stephen's return. Soon she heard his distinct tip-tapping footsteps approaching. 'Rosamond, dear! What are you doing here?' 'You invited me for the weekend, Stephen, don't you remember?' 'But how could you be so cruelly literal, darling?'[3]

However, Philip Morrell, the Liberal MP husband of Lady Ottoline, was a visitor to the town on his own account, come to escape the bombs falling over Bloomsbury. He had declined noticeably since Ottoline's death in 1938. Stephen knew Philip and rather liked him. Morrell was staying, in March 1941, at the Norfolk Hotel, where Stephen often visited. Then suddenly came the awful news that Virginia Woolf had drowned herself in the river Ouse at Rodmell. Philip Morrell's reaction was one of great distress – for many years he had nursed an unrequited passion for the writer – and Stephen found that his friend required all his efforts of consolation. This was how Sir Fred Warner first came upon Stephen, 'having to administer wet towels around Philip's head'.[4]

Warner was later to rise high in the Foreign Office and become a NATO minister and an ambassador, but in 1941 he was a handsome young naval officer, awaiting his ship's departure at Weymouth. He had been given a letter of introduction to Stephen by a mutual friend, Alan Lennox-Boyd, who had told him Stephen was likely to be the only source of entertainment on the sleepy south coast. Stephen replied by inviting him

*In July 1943, a friend of Denton Welch's told him 'all about the gaiety of Poole Harbour where there are the dearest little pubs in which soldiers and sailors and civilians dance madly and feel awfully friendly. "Just like the South of France," he kept on saying.'[1]

to dinner at the Norfolk Hotel, where he habitually dined. Sir Fred remembers being very impressed by his host – his too-gold hair, beautiful blue suit, and exquisite silk shirt. Stephen talked impressively of his friends – Willa Cather, Jean Cocteau, Morgan Forster. They drank Bacardi cocktails ('Stephen liked them because they were pink!') and, later, he took his young friend back to Sunbury Court. Sir Fred was surprised at how small it was: 'I don't think he actually stayed there much – he seemed to live mostly at the hotel – but it was typically crammed with things. Candy-stripe curtains and walls in pink and white, books and drawings everywhere.'

Warner was stationed in the area for ten days, and spent eight of his evenings with Stephen: 'There was nothing much else to do – and anyway, he was very entertaining.' Stephen talked of Wilsford, and although Warner found it difficult to persuade him, he finally got Stephen to drive him up there. 'Personally, I found it all rather claustrophobic,' he confesses. 'There wasn't a sign of Syrie Maugham's spareness – all those fishing nets everywhere made it suffocating.' Warner was also a little surprised by Stephen's evident enthusiasm for what he saw as the 'second-rate'. 'He kept urging me to read the poetry of Anna de Noailles – which I found execrable! And his taste in music was very dubious, I thought – very "low-brow". It was strange that he should know so many first-rate people, yet have such bad taste himself.'

Which is not to say Sir Fred didn't find Stephen charming. After he left on his ship, he and Stephen corresponded fitfully, bemoaning the estranging effects of the war. Stephen would send him sweets and little presents. 'The next time we met was quite by chance in Glasgow, when I bumped into him in the street. He insisted we go for a drink, in one of those large hotels near the station. I remember feeling rather conscious of the attention he drew to us – but within half an hour, the hostility in the bar turned to interest, and he seemed to know everyone in the place, and they gathered in a circle around him.' Stephen was on his way to Glen. 'There was a story going round that he'd once ordered a taxi from Wilsford to Salisbury station – he was on his way to London – when they drove past two soldiers hitch-hiking on the road. Stephen got the driver to stop, and he asked the men where they were going. "Glasgow," they said. "What a good idea!" exclaimed Stephen, and ordered the taxi to drive there!' Stephen really was removed from the constrictions war had placed on ordinary people. Even his servants, Louis and Flora Ford, gave up their weekly chocolate ration so that Stephen would not miss his sweets – such was their devotion.

*

The winter of 1941 was harsh, and only as spring came did the visitors return to Wilsford. On the first weekend of March in 1942, Morgan Forster and Bob Buckingham came down to stay. The usually placid atmosphere was disturbed this time by Buckingham's 'tirade about crime and criminal horrors', of which, being a policeman, he could speak professionally. The gory detail and nasty realism aroused Stephen's ire, and suddenly he jumped to his feet, blew out the dinner candles, and ran furiously out of the room, leaving his guests in astonished darkness. Their host was soon mollified, apparently, for he finished the evening reading to them from *Lascar* – until 3 a.m., re-reading the parts he thought 'especially good', to their dismay.[5]

Generally, life hadn't changed too much for Stephen during the first half of the war; he pursued the same quiet pursuits as he had done for years – reading, writing, painting – and shopping. His appetite for glittering possessions was unabated. It was quite remarkable that Stephen could still be adding to the enormous collection of furniture and fittings at Wilsford in the middle of such austerity.[*] In November 1941 he had designed a huge zebra-skin pouffe, and the following January was visiting John Fowler's shop (later to team up with Sibyl as Colefax & Fowler) in the King's Road to oversee its manufacture.

But then, in July 1942, came Stephen's great sacrifice to the war. The Red Cross took over Wilsford for use as a convalescent hospital. Much of the furniture was removed for safe keeping to nearby Lake House, along with many paintings (among them a number of Tchelitchews which were subsequently lost). The large reception rooms of the house were converted into medical wards. Lady Janet Bailey, who lived at Lake and was the local organizer of the Red Cross, was asked by the staff to do something about the 'facilities'. 'They'd found that Stephen had had the lavatory bowls painted silver,' recalls Stephen Spender with amusement. '"One can't have servicemen using them," said the nurse!'[6]

Stephen's tenancy of his house became the few rooms of the thatched wing, where a flat was fitted out for him. A new bathroom was installed downstairs, and a separate staircase built next to it so that Stephen could come in and out without having to pass through the main part of the Manor. Thus relegated to a corner of his own home, Stephen found life cramped and the noisy intrusion of the constant coming and going of the medical staff next door disturbing. It was also difficult now to have friends down to stay, and he had to ask Lady Janet Bailey to put up excess

[*]One young man who came to work at the Manor in 1940 was amazed that Mr Tennant was ordering the moving of garden statuary while everyone else was sand-bagging.

bodies when his two spare rooms were full – or, failing that, send them to a local hotel. Stephen tended to spend much of his time in London or Bournemouth, although he did make his Wilsford flat more comfortable with some choice pieces from the greater part of the house. (And, one afternoon, he set about making his private entrance more stylish by the addition of a mural – a muscular Nubian acrobat and a crinoline lady – on the panelling; one of the few wall pieces he actually painted himself.*)

Sometimes Stephen, feeling that the poorly soldiers and sailors needed cheering up, would appear magically among them. Stephen Spender remembers him coming down one morning to announce to a wardful of tough men who had been wounded in action: 'Now, you're all going to have a treat today. If you watch carefully out of that window, you'll see a buddleia being transplanted from one end of the garden to the other.'[7] Strangely enough, this naivety, and his own quite opposite nature, appealed to some of the men. Although he might be jeered at by lorryloads of squaddies on the way to Bulford camp as he strolled along the Wilsford lanes with a straw basket on his arm, inside the Manor the same men became his friends. One, Tim, grew intimate enough to show off to Stephen his shell-splinter wounds, received in the Red Sea. Stephen thought he gave 'a very intense impression of being a real seaman. Navy through and through – he smokes a big pipe and has the walk of a real sailor.'[8] That part of Wiltshire had always been filled with training army men, and Stephen never felt abashed in their company; Edith Olivier later despaired of her friend's attraction to the American camps on North Hill. Richard Buckle recalls that Stephen's contribution to the war effort one year was to climb a nearby hill and plant lilies around a telegraph station. And in London, Stephen was found standing decoratively by the golden fountain in the Ritz foyer by Michael Duff, who had two American GIs with him. 'Darling boys, come all this way to save us', purred Stephen, adding 'Cru-el war.'[9]

Elizabeth Bowen's relationship with Stephen was strengthened by the war. He would often dine with her at her small flat in Clarence Terrace, close by Regent's Park. She would talk to her guests as she prepared dinner in her kitchenette, described in her novel of wartime London, *The Heat of the Day*, as a 'glazed, surgical-looking cabinet'[10] in which one person could just about stand and turn. Alan Pryce-Jones was another

---

*When renovation work began on the Manor after Stephen's death, uncovered above a recess on the landing was a painted swag, evidently done by Stephen in the early thirties. Christabel Aberconway also records Stephen as having decorated a bathroom at her house, Bodnant, but this has also disappeared.

regular guest, and wrote of one occasion, with Stephen and Natasha Spender, Stephen Tennant and himself just sitting down to eat when an air-raid began. 'Heavy crashes resounded, the curtains swung on their rods, the soup on the table broke into small waves. But the raid itself was never referred to. Talk turned on, say, Thomas Love Peacock, or the rhythmic subtleties of Meredith's "Love in a Valley". Thump, wheeee thump, from outside proclaimed war. But within Elizabeth was saying, "Emily Eden really ought to be reprinted . . ."'[11]

It was at another of Elizabeth Bowen's intimate, not to say cramped, dinner parties that Stephen made the acquaintance of T. S. Eliot. He was invited to Clarence Terrace for dinner on 28 May, and chatted to Elizabeth, who was wearing a 'crushed raspberry skirt, neatly pleated',[12] as she got the meal ready. Then he noticed the table was laid for three. 'Oh but Elizabeth, I don't want to be a gooseberry,' he exclaimed, having expected to meet Norman Douglas as well as Eliot. Then the poet himself arrived.

The evening started off coolly. There seemed to be no point of mutual interest between the poet and the aesthete, and Stephen was under the impression that Eliot did not approve of him. 'After being very silent at dinner, and, I thought, a little unresponsive to her, and to me,'[13] Stephen offered Eliot a lift back to his home in Isleworth. 'In the car he thawed very noticeably, smiled even, and when I spoke of an essay of his I much liked, he said, with real warmth, "I am so glad."' Stephen was then apparently invited in for a nightcap, and the two stayed up until two, discussing, among other subjects, American jukeboxes and Gertrude Stein (Eliot, who could be anti-Semitic, told Stephen that Stein had 'a real look of the Ghetto', and could not explain her use of split infinitives to him).[14]

Stephen often returned Elizabeth's hospitality. One house party at Wilsford with her, the Spenders, Roger Senhouse and Raymond Mortimer had Stephen 'all golden curls, ruffles and bracelets' reading out his poetry. 'That is so beautiful I am going to read it again,' he said – and did. 'Only kind Elizabeth remained totally patient and attentive during the second reading,' notes her biographer.[15] Elizabeth had a great deal of time for Stephen, and valued his opinion of her work as much as he did hers. It was not her first visit to Wilsford – Stephen was proud to have been instrumental in introducing her to Morgan Forster there – and he wrote inviting her to stay at his little Wilsford flat in the autumn. She arrived with Charles Ritchie, 'a nice "unadhesive" guest'.[16]

Ritchie, a Canadian attached to the diplomatic corps, and a close friend of Bowen's, was impressed. Stephen met their train at Salisbury dressed in a blue knitted helmet with his golden hair 'arranged in a becoming crest. Through the driving rain under a gun-metal sky with sodden leaves piled high in the ditches we drove to Wilsford and were wafted up into the pink rococo of his apartment. "Rich stains of former orgies", he said, giggling at the spots on the silver-satin cushion covers.'[17]

While Ritchie admired one of his host's journals, Stephen and Elizabeth discussed *Lascar* and writing in general. One of the most difficult tasks in fiction to get right, they concurred, was the dialogue: 'the sticky passages that haunt writers'. Elizabeth said that, in a sense, every novel was a detective novel, and they agreed that dialogue must always give clues. Stephen bemoaned the sheer hard graft writing seemed to require. For his part, Ritchie's judgement was that Stephen was 'too undisciplined to express his obsession in terms of writing' – that is, Stephen's world of 'matelots and tarts, procurers and pimps – faces which have obsessed him' could only find full expression in his art.

On New Year's Day, 1943, Stephen was woken in his Wilsford apartment, 'beside that humming swarming hospital', by a 'huge black haired sergeant' in the blue hospital suit: the tall dark stranger of the new year. 'So jolly,' thought Stephen. On that first day of 1943 he announced in a letter to Cecil that he had renounced the pleasures of London for the moment and was working full pelt on *Lascar*, and he was even learning to type.

Stephen decided that, with a great surge of effort, he could complete the book that year. Even greater events held happy portents. Allied successes were sending Rommel's desert army into retreat. Even to Stephen, this new spirit communicated itself. In early spring he discovered a new haven in which to work, this time in Southsea. It was the Queen's Hotel, an imposing nineteenth-century block situated on the sea front, overlooking an esplanade and the Solent beyond. The old Victorian charm of the seaside town appealed, as did the great naval establishments of Portsmouth nearby.

The hotel was Southsea's best, with its impressive marble pillared hall, and stained-glass domed ceiling. It had, like all of Stephen's favoured hotels, a quiet hushed air of untrumpeted luxury. He would take one of the first-floor rooms, with a balcony looking out over the promenade and green of Southsea, its castle and canons and strolling sailors. One of the porters at the Queen's, Charlie Taylor, remembered Stephen sitting in the lounge, gazing up at the dome: 'When I first saw him he was wearing a long fawn camel coat and a pixie hood!' Stephen quickly had the staff under his spell. 'He used to have his hair done at the ladies' hairdressers in town – brilliant blond – and he wore crocodile skin shoes. One day he was sitting in the hall, and called me over, and asked me to take them round to the shoe shop in Castle Road and get them dyed pink!'[18]

During February, fellow guests at the Queen's were Noël Coward and his troupe, who were performing at the King's Theatre in Southsea. Stephen did not know Coward well – although the latter often recounted a tale of seeing Stephen at the Savoy during a bombing raid, when, exactly at midnight, Stephen came down the staircase in a dressing-gown 'with every hair pinned on end'[19] – but any star of the theatre held limitless excitements for Stephen, and he and Coward chattered away. Stephen confessed later to finding the man and his work a little 'too much' for him (at the same time admitting to himself in a scribbled note on Coward: 'I may be jealous').

In March and April Stephen was back at Wilsford, in his 'beautiful elegant room, my boudoir' stacking armfuls of mauve lilac in a Sicilian marble jar in readiness for a visit from Leslie Hartley on 24 April, Easter Sunday. His house was no longer his, but one of the Red Cross ladies told him: 'We hope to put back the lovely rooms at Wilsford just as we found them.' 'This hope cheers me when I am pessimistic,' noted the owner, who wrote that evening in his journal: 'No one will ever know what the pleasure, the beauty of the pure cold white velvet curtains in this room mean to me. They hang so well, and now, in the twilight, an arctic prismatic shadow invades them.'[20]

That summer of 1943 was very sociable, with rounds of visits from, among others, Cyril Connolly, Sibyl Colefax, Roger Senhouse, Peter Quennell, the Huxleys and Stephen Spender.

Spender remembered Stephen very well from that time. They first met when he was editing *Horizon* with Cyril Connolly. 'I used to see quite a lot of him, because Rosamond Lehmann knew him very well, and I knew he had had a love affair with Siegfried Sassoon.'[21] Spender met Sassoon just before the war and didn't get on very well: 'I don't think he thought I admired him enough. Stephen was always very funny about Sassoon, I must say. He told me he drove – he liked to dress up in drag – he drove over to Sassoon's house in a pony cart or something to visit him, and on one occasion he nearly ran over Mrs Sassoon, which he thought was very funny.'

(It appears Stephen often liked to dress up in women's clothes. Felix Harbord was surprised when, on arranging to meet Stephen in the North British Hotel in Edinburgh during the war, his host came down for drinks in a tea-gown. Angus Wilson remembered Stephen coming into a restaurant with a bunch of violets in his lapel and with his overcoat half on, half off his shoulders, in a way that convinced the writer that Stephen had closely studied chic women-about-town. Spender recalls Stephen's restaurant behaviour, too. 'I remember him taking me to lunch one day at the Ecu de France – he liked it because it was full of generals and admirals, and he'd wear his bracelets and things. The waiter brought the menu and Stephen looked at it in a very puzzled way and said "You choose, waiter darling."')

One Wilsford weekend in 1943 Stephen had invited both Violet Trefusis and Sibyl Colefax, which Spender thought was very mischievous of him. 'He'd invited these two ladies because he knew that they hated each other – just for amusement. There was just the four of us at table, and Lady Colefax was talking away, and Violet Trefusis said to me "Drip drip drip, like an old tap. Why doesn't someone turn it off?" That delighted Stephen. The next day he took them to church and made them share a hymn book. Eventually Violet Trefusis left in a huff, and Stephen went to bed, and I was left alone for the rest of the weekend with Sibyl Colefax, who then announced "There's nothing more I like in life than being alone."'

Spender liked Stephen, for all his faults. 'He was a gifted artist – though not really a writer,' he observes, 'a very English character, the sort of person Shakespeare made fun of, like Sir Andrew Aguecheek – or in a Restoration comedy, where you find this sort of upper-class Englishman who seems made for dressing-up, and is regarded as a kind of joke – whom other people don't take seriously as a person.' But Spender thought Stephen 'very accomplished' in his own way, a 'gifted amateur . . . it's a very serious strain of the English character. The English are very gifted amateurs – it goes with all that eccentricity, I think.' Spender also respected Stephen's naive/knowing philosophy: 'He said that in the war, England was like a kind of large black dog, a retriever which occasionally goes splashing into the water and comes out and shakes the water off.' To Spender, Stephen was 'quite outside society except with the people he chose – you wouldn't find him at any old party – perhaps because he wouldn't get enough attention'.

Peter Quennell's wartime experience of the vagaries of Stephen's nature underlines the problems Stephen (and his friends) were beginning to experience. Quennell was working at the Ministry of Information, where he was sent letters by Stephen, resuming their old acquaintance. 'In the room where we all worked was a green baize board with tapes where the post was put up. Stephen used to write on rather wonderful paper with deckled edges, but my fellow censors complained that they were so heavily scented it distracted them from their work!'²² Stephen invited Quennell one weekend, 'but our friendship came to an end after I'd left Wilsford. He was sat up in bed with his make-up box, and I had to catch a train . . . He said, "Anytime you want to come again," et cetera. Anyhow, I got back to London which was not a pleasant place to be then, in every sort of way, and I wrote to Stephen saying, "Can I come and stay with you?" I thought it would be nice – he'd been so dear, "Oh you really must" and so on – and then – silence. Complete silence. I think he could be quite callous. He never answered my letters after that.'

It was not that Stephen obstinately ignored the war and its demands – just that he hated the enforced changes it had wrought upon his world. His socializing in 1943 was an attempt to forget, by losing himself in the company of friends. For people like Spender, Quennell and Forster, Stephen's invitations to Wilsford were a welcome escape from the war's discomforts. But for Stephen, there was nowhere to go, and he felt increasingly isolated. While Cecil was flying to war zones to document the fighting, and Rex had joined up and was training in the Guards, Stephen had recourse only to *Lascar*.

Stephen's life was approaching a critical point. Within the year he would suffer a major nervous breakdown, and spend the summer of 1944 attempting to recuperate. Why did this happen? He appeared to be so in control of his life, with his social engagements, his writing, and his painting. Yet what appeared to be self-sufficiency – and could seem cold, calculating and selfish behaviour – was in reality a severe and debilitating lack of self-confidence. A story is told of Sibyl Colefax awaiting a tardy Stephen in the Ivy restaurant in Covent Garden around this time. Derek Hill, entering the half-empty restaurant, went into the lavatory, and found Stephen seated on a chair. 'Sibyl is waiting for you!' admonished Hill. 'I know, but I can't enter an empty restaurant,' said Stephen.²³

Part of the problem lay in the lack of a stable emotional relationship. Stephen Spender is of the opinion that it would have been very difficult to have had a 'loving relationship with Stephen . . . Everything was an externalization of his own decorative desires, so you become part of the décor, really – and for that reason I think one can say that you could forget him without thinking you were betraying someone who "really loves me" . . . When he talked about Sassoon one never really had the feeling that he had the slightest real feeling for [him] – it was the idea that someone was in love with him rather than that he was in love with someone . . .'²⁴ It was this emotional frigidity – possibly underlain by a fear of sexual inadequacy – that resulted in Stephen's mental problems of the next few years. A steeled desire not to give love, just to receive it, stemmed initially from the fact that the people he had loved – Pamela, and more especially Nannie Trusler – had, as Freud would express it, betrayed his love by dying. Stephen attempted to disguise a great shyness by his outrageous behaviour and appearance; but within was a little boy who had not yet come to terms with the real world, and perhaps never would.

Chapter 21

Northern Gothic

I am one of those sad people who would like to be loved without
being known – to be a wonderful memory, a legend, a glory – the
essence that fame distils – that appeases my tired spirit.

— Stephen Tennant

SELF-DISCIPLINE was not entirely lacking in Stephen's life. He
made attempts at organization, as a memo to himself indicates:
'SCHEDULE WILSFORD. Now Stephen, I wish you to make your
working routine exact and punctual. Work from 7.30 to 9. Breakfast
9.30. Work until 1. Luncheon 1.30. Walk or rest for an hour. Work until
6. Vary this programme as you wish, adding or subtracting labour – but
keep to it in the main. A workout once started,' he added hopefully,
'maintains itself.'[1]

Such dedication did not impress Cyril Connolly, or, at least, the fruits
of this labour did not. He noted privately of Stephen (who often sought
Connolly's advice on the writing of *Lascar*: 'Ask Cyril if he thinks you
can write in these 2 mixed styles successfully,' he noted on one draft of the
novel), that 'he gets up to write before breakfast, lives without a
telephone, is completely dedicated and solitary'.

It was a bleak portrait to paint of Stephen. 'He lives absolutely alone,
without friends, without society, without sex,' wrote Connolly, 'moving
between his lonely flat in Bournemouth and his lovely corner of Wilsford,
giving all his time and thought to his art; his novel, his diary for his novel,
his investigations of technical affairs required for his novel, his covers for
his novel, his play, his study of the theatre for his play, his short stories, his
relations with editors and agents for placing his stories.' Cynical, too. 'His
friends, all writers, are a kind of dream audience invoked to listen to his
stories ("Elizabeth Bowen told me she had never contemplated anything
so ambitious as my novel *Lascar*!").' What Stephen had forgotten was

that one did not need to know great writers to create good writing; nor even to appreciate it, as often proximity to the creator destroys the myth: the initial appeal becomes tarnished. Perhaps that is why Connolly, supposedly a good friend, could conclude that Stephen Tennant was 'an interesting and pathetic phenomenon, a great writer who can't write'.[2]

Connolly noted that some literary friends of Stephen, whom he accused of using to get critical advice and possible leverage into publishing, had already been tested too far and had had to give their 'honest opinion', which had not pleased Stephen, who then 'threw them over'. Morgan Forster was said to be one of the hapless victims; Roger Senhouse another. Certainly Senhouse's reply to one of Stephen's queries about *Lascar* had provoked an exasperated letter from Senhouse at Secker & Warburg. In a journal entry for 18 August 1942, Stephen had consoled himself, noting, 'Rosamond Lehmann writes that she would like to read my novel – in such a sweet letter and all the sadness that Roger's caused me has been soothed – not erased. Alas bitterness is a very deep thing . . . One should hesitate to write a cruel letter – Artists especially never forget a slight.'[3]

Stephen may have suspected Connolly's real opinion of his work (it should be remembered that Cyril Connolly was himself famous for complaining at length that he could never write the novels he knew he could write). Years later he wrote to Hugo Vickers: 'Did you know that C. Connolly had a secret book full of reviews he'd invented on his own works? "Stupendous genius!!" "One is dazed with rapture", "This douche of wit". Cyril was very cross when a semi-friend found it and told us all.'[4] Stephen also gives Connolly's features to his reverend 'hero' in some *Leaves*-style sketches done for Vickers, as a 'priest' seducing a Dorothy Lamour lookalike.

In late January 1943, Edith Olivier lunched with Stephen at the Red Lion in Amesbury. She was afraid that the clientele, most of whom were military men, might take exception to her host's painted face and 'demand his dismissal from the Hotel! But they took him quite calmly and I think they thought him only a red-faced boy. I think I should,' she added, 'especially as he wore his flying hood, so that his dyed hair was hidden.'

Afterwards they went back to the nursery flat. Edith found heavy white curtains surmounted by gold pediments, and golden baroque columns in abundance. Mirrors set in the angles of the attic rooms extended their apparent size. 'Tables and shelves *cluttered* with knickknacks. No room to put a pin down . . . My room, hung with mirrors, curtains and draperies, has not got a speck of dust in it. *Who dusts it*?' she wondered, with only Louis Ford, 'still completely a stable hand . . . and a simple yokel', to wait on Stephen's needs. Indeed, her host even offered to cook dinner himself, but Lady Bailey had the hospital cook prepare it (Edith noted that Stephen had been surviving on meals 'cadged from the Red Cross kitchen').

Then Stephen talked till midnight, 'of the nine short stories which he says he *has* written, then he *has not*, then he *is* writing'. Edith thought that his ideas had originality, but feared they would never get down on paper. 'That requires more discipline than he possesses.'

The following morning they breakfasted off rare fried eggs, then Stephen packed for London. The clothes were jumbled about, 'and he threw them on the floor, saying he must hang up 3 golden balls as the room looked like a Pawnbrokers! . . . Then he packed *quite well* and we drank some exquisite hock from exquisite glasses and then drove to Salisbury station.' But back at Wilton that evening, Edith wrote in her journal: 'I feel he can't go on living in this magnificent squalor.'[5]

Stephen's own journal for January 1944 opens with his pessimistic quote from *Lascar*'s Madame Neffus, 'Only fools are happy.' His delight in the natural world around him was becoming Stephen's only discernible pleasure. 'I can never forget the beauty of a frosted morning some days ago. Tussocks of coarse grass in a field near Amesbury were jade green or silver white on casual sight, but on closer scrutiny, in sparkling sunshine, the frosted moisture was iridescent, like milky opals . . .' '*9th Sunday*, A pox on Sunday! Vile weather but good for my new shrubs & trees. I love to think of them drinking & breathing in the sweet fresh moisture. Indeed rain soothes me. I love it passionately.'[6]

Lascar was momentarily superseded by work on a novel conceived when Stephen was last in France, entitled *But in Brief Longing*, a social comedy set in Biarritz. 'When writing a novel like *But in Brief Longing* I believe one must be completely subjugated by one's characters. This book should be vivacious, farcical – packed with incident. The character study must be shrewd, acute, poetical & scintillating – from grim concentration the lightest frothiest dialogue must come.' Stephen intended this new work to be 'a wafer of subtle brittleness, a liqueur, a pastry – but although the flavour is in a sense ephemeral & frivolous the outbreak of war serves as a fine steadying background – a pervasive reality, surrounding the comedy and general absurdity and effervescence.'

Introspection was ever-present. Stephen set himself tasks of self-discipline which veer from the sublime to the ridiculous. '*Afternoon*, I'm pleased & excited by my new schedule for early '44. There is the new Eve Currie book to read, "Journey Among Warriors". My own novel to write: the Biarritz one. I am resting my eyelashes now – no mascara, no eyeshadow. Only a little orange skin food or Vaseline after the face is treated & powdered: I shall give my skin & hair a real rest for these next 3 months . . . I want to practise dialogue in my plays & novels, and endeavour to come to grips with human relationships more and more. Perhaps after all life is only habit.' Stephen attempted to realize the same sort of direct truths that he saw in Cather's or Forster's novels; but he knew he hadn't their diligence or application – or, possibly, their talent.

He could lose himself at Wilsford, planting new trees from Hillier's Arboretum, or in the woodpecker's 'odd call . . . lackadaisical, inane & wild . . . In this workaday world the best jobs are the most business-like,' he acknowledged, ' – the most studied and perfunctory – your approach is a little too ethereal and emotional, Stephen – you must learn to tackle the cold hard world with its own weapons.' The honesty which emerges in these reflective passages has an endearing quality which, if he had admitted it more to the outside world, might have helped him live within it. 'I wonder if the craving for love, affection in an ideal companion is really a wish to augment one's self love? To strengthen the . . . profound *amour propre* by a conviction that if another shares it – it is more deserved.' Stephen thus sought to explain his own position, almost to excuse his burgeoning misanthropy. '12th – I plan to engross myself in my writing . . . unless you take yourself seriously nobody else will.'

A clue to Stephen's psychological illness of 1944 can be found in his favourite book of the time. On the title page of his Everyman edition of *Wuthering Heights*, Stephen wrote: 'This is my own life – rare, unslaved.' He found the most intense poeticism and profundity in the book, 'pervaded by an unutterable sense of menace, like the breath of the arctic wind'. The combination of severed love and threatening, psychological horror struck a deep note of empathy with Stephen.

On his birthday that April, that bitter and lonely feeling of loss was still with Stephen. 'Peter [Watson] thinks the predominant urge beneath our daily life is the half-submerged wish for a perfect companion. This may be so.' Throughout his life Stephen had rejected the notion that one needed a partner to share one's life with. His upbringing, his temperament, his way of life had precluded the possibility of a long-term relationship.

Yet Stephen had not yet abandoned that notion. David Herbert told Edith Olivier that Stephen had designs on her lodger, Colonel Binns, allegations she light-heartedly dismissed. But she could not ignore the evidence that Stephen was also trying to resume his relationship with Sassoon. Edith Olivier found out about this from Hester, and disapproved. It seemed Stephen was trying to come between them, and Edith involved herself in a farce-like incident when Hester arrived one afternoon at the Daye House. She was 'desperately worried' that Stephen, who was just leaving, would see Hester's car and 'set off at once for Heytesbury'. When Edith realized he hadn't noticed it, 'she launched into an elaborate little farewell dance on the lawn to distract until he was safely out of the gates'.[7]

This unhappy emotional state of affairs took its toll. By early summer the deep unhappiness Stephen was suffering had resulted in a severe mental breakdown. He confided in Edith of his diagnosis, 'neuritis, neurosis and neuralgia . . . thinks he's dying and also afraid to live.'[8]

Whatever the real state of Stephen's health, it necessitated treatment far from Wilsford or London, where Stephen would only be reminded of the morass into which his life seemed suddenly to have sunk. So he went, under Lord Glenconner's direction, north to Scotland, to Broxburn, a small town west of Edinburgh. Here he spent weeks under the daily attendance of a Doctor Fairbairn, who attempted to treat his problems, which had externalized themselves in a general physical debility, as well as a mental exhaustion.

Stephen's lowness of spirits could not have been helped by the news that came to him on 20 July. During the Normandy landings, which at last heralded a foreseeable end to the war in Europe, Rex, leading his tank corps into action, had been killed instantly by a mortar bomb. To Stephen, the news was the sudden and harsh realization that this war was real. The shock could have only worsened his downward spiral, even taking into account his detached attitude to loss. Four years later, he was to write: 'His death was something I could never learn. There are some things the ear rejects.'[9]

Whilst in Scotland, Christopher invited Stephen over to Glen, hoping that being with his family might help. It was one of the few occasions when Stephen saw his siblings, and for one of Christopher's children the effect of seeing her flamboyant uncle was memorable. Emma Tennant fictionalized that experience in her novel *Wild Nights* (1979), in which Stephen is portrayed in both the characters of 'Uncle Wilhelmina' and 'Uncle Rainbow'.*

The book draws heavily on Glen as a setting, 'one of those atmospheres that a child receives'. Stephen's arrival at Glen that summer is still remembered by Emma Tennant with the vividness of a seven-year-old's memory. He came 'in a huge car full of bird cages . . . but left again quite quickly'.[10] The visit is expanded upon in her book. *Wild Nights* has a Gothic tone, filled with strange characters, of whom Stephen is just one. 'Aunt Zita' is Clare, his sister, and is seen descending for her annual three-week visit to the narrator's parents. The book blends fact and fiction in a stream-of-consciousness account of the family's stay together at their home in the wilds of the Scottish Borders. Zita appears tyrannical, smoking at table between courses and making demands on the household. The great bell in one of the turrets, rung only in emergencies, is sounded by Maurice, the narrator's young friend, and Zita is blamed for putting him up to it. '"Whatever it was," she said in her clipped, light voice, "the bell has heralded a new arrival. You didn't know Wilhelmina was coming to stay?"'[11]

He arrives in a large chauffeur-driven car. 'Uncle Wilhelmina took a long time to get into the house, and his cages of birds and boxes of lizards were carried up by the driver and by Minnie to his room. Immediately he released the birds, but it was some hours before they flew against the windows in a desperate attempt to get south . . . The lizards, which appeared on the backs of chairs in the hall and along the gilded frames of pictures long after he had gone, escaped early from the big room . . . and their bright blue eyes jumped like blue fire from their hiding-places.'

It was a dreamlike encounter, Emma Tennant remembers, for a young girl to meet an uncle who dressed in 'suede boots . . . purple and fringed with Robin Hood streamers' and a suit of 'cloth of gold'. He resembled 'a conjuror's trick', his suit with several pockets and a silk handkerchief fluttering from each one. His niece's account also says much about Stephen's relationship with the rest of his family, in particular the jealousy Clare felt for his position as Pamela's pet at Wilsford, as she remembers: 'when, running with her brothers, she had fallen on the concealed iron ring of the door in the grass and made a long-forgotten scar on her leg – in the jealousy of half-remembered rebuffs, and the

*Emma Tennant portrays Stephen in two other novels, *Alice Fell* (1980), in which he appears as the semi-parabolic 'Old Man', and *The House of Hospitalities* (1987), as 'Uncle Si' in djellaba, jewels and 'arsenic' white-green make-up.

cries behind the Racket Court when the youngest brother was scooped into his mother's arms . . .'

Wilhelmina is imagined as he 'lounged for ever in a smoky room above a quay, with pimps and harlots and criminals, with all the restless, heaving tripe of humanity that could ever be imagined . . . I supposed that my father's mother must be in there too, pale and out-of-place as an English watercolour in that bar. She would be searching too, but this time for both her sons, who had slipped into her maternal nightmares of homosexuality, hashish and release.'

Later, the book recalls an event from Stephen's past; couched in a semi-fictitious account, and the product of half-remembered tales of an eccentric uncle's misdeeds, it creates a scene that could have come straight from a film by Visconti. Maurice lives with his mother, and they visit an old woman who lives in The Street, a collection of farm workers' cottages near the big house. 'The old woman, who had seen so much, sometimes told Maurice's mother of the worst Hallowe'en night, when there had been a scandal from the big house.'

Whilst Wilhelmina's mother entertained dinner guests with cruel imper-sonations of a deformed boy from the village, the same age as Wilhelmina, he left the room, undetected. Going up to his bedroom, he made up his face 'as white as a porcelain doll. He drew black spokes around the hubs of his eyes. He purpled his lips from a pot stolen from his mother's table. He looked as if he had drowned in cold water.' Wilhelmina slips out of the house and into the night, his long hair tied in a black ribbon. 'He paused by a weeping ash, and picked a switch . . . In the dining-room, the party had at last assembled. Rich food was handed round. When the constables from the town came in . . . My father's mother's face went into an exquisite blur as the scandal was exposed.

'Uncle Wilhelmina had wandered along The Street, soliciting. He held the ash stick in his hand and asked to be beaten. One of the cowmen, a man of indignation . . . ran all the way to the town to report the scene. And Uncle Wilhelmina was smuggled down to the house and up to his room, for charges were not in the end brought. He lay exhausted on his bed, with his blue eyes rolling in the white paste surround. The old woman of ninety certainly remembered seeing him out there, but she couldn't know of the travesty of her idiot brother in the big house, which came before Uncle Wilhelmina's arrest, and the unforgiving century of his mother's shame.'

Not until mid-August did life come clear of its clouds and offer Stephen some optimism once more. On 14 August he noted, 'This is the first day since my illness that I have really noticed and loved the sky. Dr Fairbairn says this is only a psychological illness, and it will pass. A perfect summer day has come to emphasize the poignancy of newly arrived autumn, for autumn is here. But today we have a reprieve. Sweet soft breezes – intermittent – make me think of the sea – & shells & rock pools – of the agony of joy which shells give me. I am a child of ecstasy – no cousin but rapture.'[12]

That morning he visited Queensferry, the nearest sea-point to Brox-burn. He sat in the public gardens, overlooking the wide Firth estuary. 'My morning was tame – but is any vital experience tame?' he asked himself. 'I sat & watched the grasses swept up by warm winds, the coarse lowland grasses. And the hills of these lowlands were clearly seen, a soft dark viola blue . . . I basked in the hot sun & loved the sky. I nibbled a daisy and thought about Mr Day Lewis[*] & Rosamond & Stephen Spender. Absent friends can come very close sometimes, the irrelevant often conjures them.'

Stephen became excited by the war news: the Allied Army was nearing Paris. 'I devour headlines in the paper & slacken off while reading military details: War is dull unless you are a military strategist; but the thought of my beloved France being rescued – saved – is like an elixir in my blood – I become one burning transcendent idea, not a person.'

After his stay at Glen, Stephen went south, travelling by overnight train to London, and thence back at last to Wilsford – not yet well, however. 'I am very saddened and changed by my illness this summer,' he told Sibyl Colefax in despair, 'and I do not think that I shall ever come back – among you all again . . . I will not weary you with my boring illness . . . but I see no future – still, I can work a little at my novel – darling Rosamond has been such a comfort to me all this summer – She is a wonderful friend. So is Leslie, and Elizabeth. I've got three years of work here to pull into shape . . .'[13]

Stephen's recovery was slow, but in November he was well enough to go to one of Sibyl's London dinners, then settled into the quiet life of Wilsford again, spending the occasional evening at Larkhill, where he saw a play starring Eve Portman. He didn't care that it was a rather slow thriller, 'because the smell of the stage & the clothes – & the colours – had that eternal thrill about them, the thrill that pervades even the poorest play.'[14]

---

[*]Cecil Day Lewis (1904–72) the poet, a close friend of Lehmann's at the time.

Stephen's young niece, Pauline, daughter of David and Hermione,* now grown up and following in her mother's career footsteps, was working for ENSA, and also appeared in a production at one of the nearby army camps. She called to see Stephen. After an extended delay, her uncle appeared, apologizing for his lateness. ' "I had to look nice for you, darling," he said, and he did.'

Pauline (now Lady Rumbold) remembers being shown a 'wonderful room in the Thatched Wing – blue satin everywhere, inches of lace borders ... After tea Stephen took me into the hospital part of the house, where there were rows of beds. Stephen took me up to one man who was sitting up in bed darning his sock or something. He had the face of a real rascal – broken nose, cauliflower ears, the lot. Stephen pointed to him and said, "There, that's my favourite!" And this man just grinned and looked very pleased with the attention!' (The likely candidate for Stephen's favour was Tim, the Red Sea survivor.) Afterwards Stephen invited her to stay over, but Pauline pleaded that she had to be back at the camp. He looked rather disappointed. 'But he just didn't understand such things as duties – he was very much like my father in that respect. Stephen took it very personally, as though I didn't want to be with him, which was of course far from the case. There'd have been nothing I'd have liked better than to spend the night in comfort at Wilsford rather than in an army hut – but I had my duties to perform.'[16]

After Christmas, Stephen returned to the Queen's Hotel in Southsea for a spell of sea air. Sir Fred Warner met him in Portsmouth one day, and Stephen invited him to lunch at the hotel. Sir Fred noticed the change in Stephen. 'He seemed to be different somehow – less outgoing, or sociable than he had been ... I remember thinking "something's wrong here", but I couldn't place what it was.'[17] Portsmouth in January was exceptionally cold. Stephen saw 'men's breath freezing in the cold air' as he watched soldiers stacking their gear on the backs of lorries: 'coarse porridge white – stiff with frost. Snow, smooth & fine on trucks & sheds. Just spoke to a Navy man who is off to Belgium – Khaki battledress & navy cap. The tiniest snow is falling.' Stephen was contemplating yet another literary project, inspired, in part, by Portsmouth life – a short story entitled 'Next Gentleman Please'. 'I have to live in the climate of a story for some time while it is growing – deep in my consciousness – taking from irrelevant

---

*Stephen had written to Elizabeth Lowndes from Bavaria, in 1929, when Pauline was two years old: 'I'm so glad you love Pauline. She's a divine child – a combination of nursery greed & Roman Empress beauty.'[15]

daily life those little bits of vividness that go to make up the final ensemble.'*

Back in Bournemouth in April, Stephen basked in spring sunshine by the sea, 'a reparation of happiness after the winter hellish months', wearing sandals and his Hawaiian shorts. Again, it was the observation of common life that raised his spirits. In one of the sandy, pine-planted ravines that ran down to the beach from Bournemouth's cliffs, he watched two squads of Canadian soldiers at rifle practice. They were 'squatting in two groups on the hot short grass – among furze & old leaves. A seagull – wide winged – was blandly wheeling & turning in the pellucid air above them. A racketty crack of rifles . . . at long intervals. The Army boys – in khaki sweat clothes – were lounging as well as working – lying down – or standing, or chucking stones – & branches, some leaning on one elbow.'

It was exactly the kind of scene Stephen relished – carefree masculine gregariousness, comrades at ease – a world he could only observe, never be part of. 'The Canada boys had put out red flags – to warn of their rifle practice, which seemed however pretty desultory. Two of them waved at me – & sent a message in semaphore – which I did not understand.' Stephen's acute descriptions, perfervid and very slightly homoerotic, resemble the journal entries of Denton Welch,† another young man limited by illness to observation of English provincial life, with a similar eye for such detail. There is in both the idea of a tease, a near-contact, which never actually happens. The distance was all-important.

The soldier boys marched off up the hillside in their khaki drill suits and blue airforce caps, after 'a little stone-throwing match'. Stephen watched them go past 'ridiculous artistic little shelters – pagoda-roofed houses with seats & much writing on the walls'. That evening he read Auden, finding him 'puzzling, teasing and provocative – which I think a poet should be . . . It's potent charged stuff – a little perversely arid sometimes,

*Stephen's story was set in wartime London, in a Turkish bath bereft of all but a few of its male customers. The central figure is a hunchback named Johnnie, a 'sweet little chap' who dotes on young Ted, who has left to join the Navy. On Ted's return Johnnie is ecstatic, but becomes jealous when his friend is hijacked by the odd little barber whose cry gives the story its title. He was a 'living ventriloquist's doll' before the war, and is afraid his ex-boss, a threatening figure from whom he escaped, will come and find him, which he does, at the end of the tale. It is a strange story, one of Stephen's oddest. In it he describes the war as a 'hideous tunnel, black – and the world was a train hurtling through it, longing for the light'.
†A young writer patronised by Edith and Osbert Sitwell, Welch spent most of his brief life chronically ill after a bicycle accident in which he damaged his spine.

but I like his hectoring arrogant melancholy – queer verbal clowning & I respect his fundamental gravity. He is essentially a serious artist.'[18]

Stephen boasted of 'a hell of a spurt of work' that spring in Bournemouth. Remembering an evening at the Hôtel Splendide in Marseilles, which he noted was part of the inspiration for *Lascar*, he was also spurred on by a letter from Willa Cather, which he proudly pocketed as he left the Norfolk Hotel restaurant 'into an exquisite April twilight – to work on my book *Lascar* – Willa has sent me a sentence from a card of mine – sent to her from Marseilles in 1937 – This description of the old city has revived her faith in my book.'

Suddenly, on 25 May, came the news from Lady Janet Bailey at Lake that Stephen was to have Wilsford back. 'I want to whisper the wild joyful news to my amber necklaces – to my wisteria mauve lamps – to my lace curtains.' Lady Janet advised him to give the Red Cross official 'notice to quit' on 24 June – he would have his home back by September. This was more exciting even than the current Allied victories, the capitulation of the Germans, or the death of Hitler. Everything was in a rose light. Stephen spent that joyous day at Poole, where he had a shave in a tobacconist's and listened to the radio playing 'cheap raffish music – & I thought of my novel *Lascar* and Pierre & Manuel – & the slow ripening of that book. Ships sirens called, & I heard them differently – like old happy days, in Marseille – Can we dare to be happy again?'[19]

As the war ended, leaving his contemporaries to try and pick up the impetus of interrupted careers, Stephen saw the need to hasten his own efforts. Time he had in plenty, and always had had: time to write in his journal at length; time to write and re-write whole chapters of *Lascar* and stop to doodle a matelot's face or two, a bar scene, the lettering on a billboard. But this was time wasted, unless he were to steer a straight course for the actual completion of any of these tasks begun.

Stephen counted the days until he could have his home back; to be in full control of Wilsford once more would help him arrange his life in general. In June he stayed with Edith Olivier at the Daye House, where summer storms reminded him of Bavaria – and Siegfried. 'I long for France,' he wrote, recalling 'one May long ago, driving with S.S. in the forest of Saint Germain – & listening to nightingales pouring torrents of song among the flowering chestnuts. And the heat in Paris, & then that rainy night – of passionate storm – when we quarrelled . . .'[20]

Stephen was in sporadic communication with his old friend, exchanging letters and the occasional visits. One night he spoke to Siegfried on the

Willa Cather

Off to the New World, mid-1930s

Stephen in USA

Barbara Hutton

E. M. Forster

Lady Juliet Duff, Sir Michael Duff and David Herbert
at The Park School, 1938

Marseilles: *Stephen's postcards*

Lascar *cover, late 1930s*

Stephen with Tchelitchew portraits

The study

A study in Syrie Maugham

Wilsford interiors, 1939

A marbled alcove

The drawing room

The landing

The hall

Peter Quennell

Stephen Spender

Vita Sackville-West

Elizabeth Bowen

Stephen at his fountain, Wilsford, 1947

With Peter Watson, Wilsford, 1945

Tangier,
journal,
1948

Stephen's decorations
for the nursery flat

Stephen throws a children's party in
the Racquets Court, mid-1940s

David Tennant and daughter, Pauline, 1948

Flora and Louis Ford, Wilsford garden, 1950

telephone: 'he is very much his old self again', noted Stephen, 'now more vivid & contented, in his hard won solitude.'[21] That solitude seemed sad to other friends. Joe Ackerley spent a couple of weeks with Sassoon at Heytesbury around this time; Hester Sassoon was now living apart from her husband, a few miles away: 'He can't bear the sight of her any longer and treats her presence with no pretence of politeness,' noted Ackerley in his diary. 'S[iegfried] had already told me that Hester had alienated his friends from him – Blunden and Morgan who took her side, Rex Whistler who she fell for and would not leave alone . . . the battle, the fifteen years' battle, was still on.'

Ackerley compared Sassoon to Morgan Forster. While the latter's fame 'extends and expands, to cover the globe', Siegfried had seemingly taken a wrong turning, and 'with his short, selfish mind, sinks and sinks'. Could the blame for this man's broken life be laid in part at Stephen's feet? 'Dreadfully lonely', Sassoon would shamble about in clothes mended by himself, keeping strictly to his own territory during the day, taking Luminal to send him to sleep at night.

In their respective failures to approach life, neither Siegfried nor Stephen had come to an optimistic post-war future. They were both living off the past. Ackerley notes that Hester had made one of her frequent and unwelcome visits to Heytesbury just before he arrived. 'A couple of days later she came again, to upset S. with some story of a woman neighbour of hers who had come over and started talking in a pointed manner about S's affair with [Stephen], sixteen years ago! . . . He was very much upset over the [Stephen] business – out of all proportion, I think. I spoke to him sensibly and carefully – so bad for him to upset himself – and he soon recovered. Why was he so upset? Blackmail of his good and famous name? An odd, muffled man.'[22]

Stephen's behaviour here – his 'running over' of Hester, and flying visits – seems unnecessarily cruel. He even taunted Siegfried, as Patricia Lee Yongue discovered: 'Stephen started to tell Sassoon what he thought of him as a poet, called him a "stick-in-the-mud" poet and apparently accused him of excessive vanity'[23] – insults that could equally be turned around and aimed at Stephen himself.

Other friends besides Ackerley still felt the repercussions of Stephen's and Siegfried's tempestuous affair. On 21 January 1946 Edith Sitwell wrote to John Lehmann from Renishaw with her comments on Sassoon's newly published volume of memoirs, *Siegfried's Journey*, which she called 'one mass of treachery, fawning, and snobbishness. I didn't like old Lady Ottoline Morrell, and she hated me – but she adored Siegfried, and it is painful to see him "wishing she wouldn't look so extraordinary". (He has never wished that about Stephen Tennant, who might also be said to look rather outstanding) . . . Where is the man he was between 1914–18? Something very different has taken his place. Or do you suppose we only believed he was real?'[24]

Stephen and Siegfried appeared to correspond pleasantly enough over the next few years, wary of each other's emotions, neither wishing to be entangled again, but at the same time not wanting the friendship to sink into acrimonious memory. Stephen sent Sassoon regular reports from his travels in the coming years, and, in his own mind at least, retained wistful thoughts of their times together in Bavaria and Sicily. The thread between the two former lovers refused to snap. In January 1947, Stephen returned from a trip to Paris 'in tearing spirits', and boasted to Edith Olivier of having become 'passionately *lié* with Siegfried again' and was 'evidently being a very bad friend to Hester!'[25] And in 1951 Siegfried wrote to Stephen after a small celebration: ' . . . Kangaroos are a law unto themselves, and always enjoy a bit of fun. This one secretly drank to your health . . .'[26]

Reading John Donne's poems in that 'whispering gallery of the rain' which had started off his remembrance of the Siegfried past, Stephen observed that 'the exact limitations of one's taste should be an intense pleasure . . . Most people are never sure what they like. Pleasure should be a deep, as well as a light thing. You should name the book of your life "Serious Pleasures".' He added, 'and what is Love but everything's caprice? – the unwritten melody of an idle hour.' And so Stephen's idle hours drew on.[27]

Chapter 22

Wilsford Regained

'... My needs are very simple, admittedly, but such as they are they have been satisfied over and over again.'
'What are your needs?'
'I need a very great deal of beauty round me, beautiful objects wherever I look and beautiful people who see the point of One ...'
— Cedric in Nancy Mitford's *Love in a Cold Climate*

THE reacquisition of Wilsford was a major reversal of the depressing cycle of solitude Stephen had been experiencing over the latter years of the war. But to be home had mixed blessings. 'This is such happiness to me,' he told John Lehmann. 'I can't believe it – or sanction my heart to such a reprieve!' What he had witnessed over those years – 'the horror of watching my house slowly destroyed by dirt, vulgarity, ignorance, bombast, cheapness' – had 'nearly killed' him. 'I wish, sincerely, that I could feel towards these very kindly and hardworking strangers what Emily Dickinson calls a "transport of cordiality".'[1]

To adhere to such Christian ideals was hard when Stephen found his dream palace had been wrecked. He described the scene that faced him on his return in a letter to Laurence Whistler, starting with 'the perils undergone by the garden from the Red Cross deprecations ... The "patients" lit fires under the ilexes (on the roots!) & nearly killed these ancient noble trees – I only just caught them in time. Several trees were cut down – without permission ... Violent football almost wrecked the big yew hedges ... I stayed here during these vile years to guard the house – & certainly prevented many outrages taking place, but it took a great toll of my natural gaiety, reservance and threatened to badly warp any surplus human kindness I might possess! ... The horror of the noise was unbelievable! Screaming nurses & hospital staff. Radios unending – and both men & Red Cross staff threw their broken glass and china, medicine bottles into the flower borders beneath the windows so that it is dangerous to garden now.' Now that the house itself was given back, it required 'scouring & scrubbing. A terrible smell of unsavoury habitation pervades it – a queer sticky gummy smell & touch & stain & all their thoughts too – the thronging living thoughts – immobilized here – in cigarette ash, stains, food, hair grease; pin-up girls, facetious gags – footsteps – oh how strange, Laurie, an empty house can be – now the mild rain beats in at the windows – for I think any weather can exorcise this vile glutinous resonance !'[2]

Where on Bournemouth beach those army men had seemed romantic, jolly and vital, their counterparts, in his home, with their dirty habits and uncouth behaviour, had become contaminating. And the soldier's insults lingered long and unwanted in Stephen's all too retentive memory: 'White marble Louis Quinze mantelpieces are ruined (they built bivouac fires out in the room !)'[3] These excesses represented an unfeeling philistine humanity which seemed to be taking over the post-war world too.

To reinstate the rule of beauty at Wilsford, Stephen commissioned a new fountain to be built in the walled garden, and bought old stone urns, statues and columns to place among 'the blond flaking walls & ilexes'.

Stephen related, in jewel-coloured inks, the details to Laurence Whistler. The fountain was of particular interest: 'It's a little round Queen Anne wall fountain – with a wide leaden shell – with curly edge from which water falls into successive pools – with carved stone rims . . . A sequestered fountain – the colour of time. A leaden cherub pours the stream from an urn – I have put ferns & brilliant mosses all around & tall blue Agapanthus lilies, & pink Hydrangeas in masses.'[4] This pleasing feature, walled and hidden from immediate view behind the thatched wing, was just one of the myriad 'secret gardens' within the greater garden at Wilsford.

With the interior of the house so depressingly violated, and its renovation an intimidating task,[*] Stephen concentrated all his energies on the grounds. The green, almost overripe land came to be embellished by more and more artefacts, ranging from elegant classical busts to iron Japanese herons, as Stephen applied the same precepts of (over-)

[*]Stephen received a sum of compensation from the Government, with which to repair the wartime damage, but squandered it on other things; the house was never completely restored to the grandeur it had attained in the thirties.

decoration to his paradise-wilderness. He set no limits as to what might appear behind a tall clump of bamboo, or atop a new fountain, and the result was a child's idea of a fantasy garden; fantastic and quite surreal. And not to everyone's taste: Cecil later described it as resembling a Bournemouth municipal park, after Stephen had proudly shown him statuary newly painted pink. The coloured glass Victorian 'fairy lights' which illuminated the gardens created a similar effect to that of the pleasure gardens opposite Sunbury Court, where the same method was employed to light the 'woodland terraces'.

Whilst Wilsford was being disinfected of its former inhabitants, Stephen returned to Bournemouth. Here he could apply himself to his poetry. He asked Laurence Whistler, who had made his name as a poet, for advice. 'Words are savage, intransigent things, aren't they? – Years ago, I wrote to a friend [Cather] – "Not for the idle comment, things like these" – and sometimes I feel that in attempting poetry I am profaning something . . . age-old, sombre & fearful . . .'[5]

Stephen spent autumn 1945 at Sunbury Court, contemplating such profundities, and writing of them in letters so artfully decorated that they seemed works of art in themselves. On beautiful hand-made pink paper delicately embossed 'Wilsford Manor, nr. Amesbury' – pink on pink – he would intertwine the vivid tendrils of his script with ink illustrations which threatened to take over the whole of the page, leaving no room for literal communication. Moss-roses tumble dew-laden from a corner, meeting oak leaves and acorns across one page; another illustrates an intended fountain, impossibly ornate, with spouting tritons and Italian cypresses rising magnificently in the background, as if Wilsford had been transplanted to a Tuscan hill; and all in bright violets, viridians and pinks that appear to leap from the page.

These letters became Stephen's most immediate expression of his art, an ephemeral medium in which he could loose the reins of his febrile fantasies. They are impressive displays of a truly exotic imagination, and

a source of amusement and delight to those lucky enough to receive them, like Laurence Whistler, and Nancy Mitford. She exclaimed they were 'presents' in their own right, and framed them for the walls of her Parisian flat. (Stephen Spender did this too, but noted that when Stephen visited him and saw them, he became a little annoyed. 'He felt such things were private, and not for public display.')[6]

One new recipient of these pictorial missives was Vita Sackville-West, with whom Stephen had renewed his friendship – or, more properly, established a closer acquaintance. Stephen had first met her through Bloomsbury friends before the war, and found her an extremely glamorous figure. Vita's marriage to Harold Nicolson had not prevented either of them indulging their passions for members of their own sex; her torrid affair with Violet Trefusis in the twenties had ended in their respective husbands chasing the two eloping lovers across Europe. Since then, Vita had dallied with women – including Virginia Woolf – and men. James Lees-Milne, who knew her well, observed that she appeared to have developed a crush on Stephen: 'Vita was rather in love with him. I suppose he was a beautiful young woman to her.'[7]

Vita's very appearance was romantic. She seemed half-man, with her fine moustache and habitual riding-breeches, yet her dark eyes (her mother was half-Spanish) and handsome good looks proclaimed a sensual woman. She was best known for her exquisite gardens at Sissinghurst, but wrote novels and poetry too, and it was Vita's literary expertise, rather than her interest in horticulture, that was foremost in his mind when Stephen had sought her company in 1945. She returned the interest, finding him just as fascinating: Vita once addressed him as 'dear, strange, beautiful, gifted Stephen'. Replying to one of her letters, Stephen noted one frosty morning in March that 'some curious echoes and intimations haunt your suggestion that I am a creature of ice and fairy tale . . . why are there so many mirrors [in Wilsford]?' he mused. 'Is it because they suggest ice? . . . Last winter Cecil Day Lewis asked Rosamond Lehmann if I was 18 years old . . . Perhaps I have the agelessness of an enchanted creature. As a child, I read often with obsessed fascination *The Snow Queen* . . . She changed to foam, didn't she? There is a passage in my journal of six years ago, describing the quality of the foam of the eastern Mediterranean – which haunted me.'[8]

Stephen told Vita that he was at work on a new collection of stories, one of which, 'The Lynx', set in New Hampshire in winter, was obviously inspired by Cather: 'an analysis of a clever woman's state of mind – in panic-stricken rebellion against a pretentious & arty milieu – among New York intelligentsia'.[9]

In October Stephen wrote again, reminding Vita that 'some years ago we exchanged some letters about a cover design for your "Country Notes" ';[10] he was angling for a commission. This did not transpire, but they did exchange gardening tips, and soon Stephen found himself being invited to Sissinghurst for the weekend.

It was a memorable visit. 'She is the most beautiful & adorable person,' observed Stephen. 'I loved glimpsing, in these 2 days, her legend.'[11] Vita looked the part too. Hatless, her head ornamented by large gold gypsy earrings, and wearing riding breeches, she greeted Stephen holding a large Alsatian dog, which strained powerfully on its leash beside her.

They had 'heavenly talks' in Vita's tower, which Stephen described as the colour of 'squashed ripe pomegranates'.[12] Here she read 'The Phoenix and the Turtle' aloud, and quoted from Shakespeare's Sonnets. They discussed the post-war world. Vita announced: 'I loathe the Proletariat' (this despite her husband being a Labour MP). 'She has made the gardens so beautiful – with urns & statues from Bagatelle, in Paris', noted the visitor. Inside Sissinghurst there were treasures too; Stephen coveted 'a lapis table – with dull silver mouldings'.[13] During long walks Stephen bemoaned the 'intransigence' of *Lascar* – and the restlessness of his life. (Later he wrote to Vita asking if her son Ben knew of anyone who would go into partnership with him on a farm. This unlikely project was possibly a scheme to raise money; the running of Wilsford was proving to be expensive in the late forties, and Stephen found it hard to survive on his reduced income of £9,000 per annum.)

After Christmas 1945, Stephen encouraged Vita's desire to write a thriller. 'How I agree! a detective story is the supreme relaxation & stimulant combined.'[14] In February, he was in London, staying at the Connaught. He visited the Greek exhibition at the Royal Academy, which was 'very stirring' and 'fortifying . . . against the trivial clamour of London . . . the charm of a city's particular character always gets me,' he noted, 'but one's creative impulses dry up – a protective moronism descends. I become a non-entity.'[15]

Stephen had told Laurence Whistler of his intention to finish *Lascar* that winter. 'Wartime fixed leaden weights to my feet & hands, crushing out hope, chilling endeavours, & numbing all one's working resilience,' he explained.[16] 'I have never had one happy thought in my life that was not tinged with despair!! – And yet I am indestructible! . . . I feel more & more that this life is a passing husk – for our thoughts – a sheath – of no moment – except for the radiance it shields & shadows with such transience.'[17]

Throughout the first half of 1946 Stephen kept his mind off morbid thoughts by busying himself in town and country. In London he told Vita that he was 'glad to find all my prejudices & antipathies against it reinforced'.[18] He visited Sibyl Colefax in her shop. 'She is better [Lady Colefax had fallen and broken her hip] & was very sweet, I'm glad to say. She can be very spiteful.' He saw other friends, too: Elizabeth Bowen – 'what a heavenly person she is!'[19] – and Rosamond Lehmann, who had just published her collection of stories, *The Gypsy's Baby*.

Back at Wilsford at the end of April, there were new arrivals to celebrate Stephen's fortieth birthday: an Apollo statue, a 'little corn god', and 'a noble Charles II lead urn, so grandly floreated and carved'. However, Stephen declared to Vita: 'I have no possessions. No home. No name. But I exist far more intensely than most people. Like Virginia, I am formidable. A great power drives me.'[20]

Summer came, and with it more visitors. Vita brought her husband Harold to lunch at Wilsford on 7 August, but Stephen did not find the same charm in Nicolson as in his wife. His friendship with Vita lasted well into the fifties. She would often ask news of *Lascar*, of which she had high expectations: 'Your sense of the sea will make it like a shell held to the ear,' she told Stephen. 'I feel you have as many stories to tell as . . . Scheherazade.'

Although Stephen had declared to Vita in April that he was 'jibbing at the idea of even travelling again, anywhere!!'[21] by the end of the year he would be in Paris to see his beloved city once more. Meanwhile, he had a visit from Leslie Hartley, whose thank-you letter expressed much of the peculiar charm of Wilsford and its inhabitant: 'You put an enchantment on the minutes', he told Stephen, 'so that they no longer pressed. I never felt that more than I did last Sunday, when you seemed not only to have stopped the clock, but to have put it back, so that a great many pre-war sensations, anaesthetized for seven years, shyly made their appearance – and one became reunited to an almost forgotten personality . . . Some people's possessions are quite alien to them,' Hartley observed; 'others reflect their owner's personalities, but yours actively express you: they are beautiful always but the moment you appear they take on fresh meaning.' He added that he couldn't imagine how Stephen managed 'to read, & write, & be yourself with all those painters to direct, and . . . the decisions they must demand from you all day long.'[22]

Later that month William Plomer, writer, critic, and close friend of Morgan Forster, came to visit. He and Stephen went off for a long walk, and sat on a mac spread out under pollarded willows 'and spoke of many things', of the sadness of life, of the war, of friends. 'I keep thinking of William's words,' wrote Stephen: 'The War killed Virginia.' His own black thoughts were never far away.[23]

Stephen's trip to Paris in 1946 was a veritable reunion of old friends. He saw Jean Cocteau, Boris Kochno and Christian Bérard together again; Stephen recalled to Cocteau their first meeting, in Paris before the war: 'it was recognition' – to which the poet replied, 'If you are a friend, you are an old friend, there are no new friends.'[24] The company was genial, although Stephen had been less impressed with Cocteau's villainous-looking friend, M. Genet, who had stolen his sapphire cufflinks! Jean Genet, whom Cocteau had that year managed to free from gaol on the grounds that he was a great writer and moralist, could have been a character from *Lascar*, with his 'shifty eyes above a boxer's nose in a small tight skull with close-cropped hair', an appearance that had disconcerted Harold Acton when he met him around this time: 'One would not care to encounter him in the black-out.'[25] But Cocteau made up for Stephen's loss by giving him a copy of *The Beauty and the Beast* screenplay, in which he wrote '*À Stephen avec l'oeil et le coeur de Jean.*' (Stephen also apparently possessed a valuable copy of the original French edition of Cocteau's *Le Livre Blanc*, his 1928 semi-autobiographical, homoerotic fantasy illustrated with line drawings of matelots and their mates, an obvious influence on his own sketches for *Lascar*. Morgan Forster wrote to Stephen in the forties, telling him he'd seen a new English translation of the work, 'but all its truth and most of its heart had gone', and that he'd rather see Stephen's 'lovely blue leather' original.)[26]

Stephen also saw Nancy Mitford, who gave a drinks party at her flat in the rue Monsieur. She seemed to know all of Stephen's 'kind' in Paris. To her, people like Stephen and Brian Howard were 'blissikins', though she did complain one night of having twelve people 'in before dinner and afterwards I thought I was the only normal one . . . It is rather strange one must admit. Nature's form of birth control in an overcrowded world, I daresay.' Nancy noted that Paris in these liberated years had become 'quite giddy, people doing all sorts of things they will regret later'.[27] Nancy had a certain penchant for the sort of flamboyant homosexual who found expression easier in liberated Paris rather than in austerity London (homosexuality not being a criminal offence in France as it was in the United Kingdom). Stephen, the most elegant of such acquaintances, was to be the model for one of the most amusing characters in her success-ful book, *Love in a Cold Climate*, and it was his visit to Paris that autumn that gelled the characteristics of 'Cedric' in Nancy's mind.

Love in a Cold Climate, which was published in 1949, is full of barely disguised portraits of Nancy's family and friends. Lord and Lady Montdore are the two elderly parents of Polly, the central character. He is an ineffectual aristocrat who likes to pursue a quiet life; she is of a less refined nature, and the victim of her own snobbery. Together they await the arrival of their heir, long-lost cousin Cedric, a twenty-four-year-old Canadian whom they suppose to have been living the life of a lumberjack or some such outdoor pursuit. The butler announces:

'"Mr Cedric Hampton.":

'A glitter of blue and gold crossed the parquet, and a human dragon-fly was kneeling on the fur rug in front of the Montdores, one long white hand extended towards each. He was a tall, thin young man, supple as a girl, dressed in rather a bright blue suit; his hair was the gold of a brass bed-knob, and his insect appearance came from the fact that the upper part of his face was concealed by blue goggles set in gold rims quite an inch thick. He was flashing a smile of unearthly perfection; relaxed and happy he knelt there bestowing this smile upon each Montdore in turn.

"Don't speak," he said, "just for a moment. Just let me go on looking at you – wonderful, wonderful people!"'[28]

It could be no one else but Stephen, and Nancy Mitford's affectionate and funny portrait of her friend is one of the best glimpses one could have of Stephen Tennant as he appeared 'in society'. As Cedric floats 'jointlessly to his feet', Lady Montdore begs him to remove his goggles 'specially designed by Van Cleef', so as to see his eyes:

'Later, dear Lady Montdore, later. When my dreadful, paralysing shyness (a disease with me) has quite worn off.'

Cedric proceeds completely to charm both Lord and Lady Montdore, with special attention for the latter, whom he soon has dyeing her hair and using the most outrageous beauty treatments. Cedric's friendship with Lady Montdore develops through a veritable gamut of cosmetic treatments; together they dance 'a wild fandango of delight' – and he manages to win over everyone else in the process. Fanny notes that she gets on with him as well as a 'charming woman friend; better, because our friendship was marred by no tinge of jealousy'. This is very much Stephen as Nancy knew him, as it is the evasive Cedric, 'better than anybody I know at not answering questions if he did not want to'. He acquires a young friend, a lorry-driver named Archie, 'a nice handsome boy . . .

"For your ear alone, my darling, it was a stroke of thunder when I saw him. What one does so love about love is the time before they find out what One is like."'

'Sewer' – the ultimate condemnation of Uncle Matthew (Nancy's 'Farve') – becomes 'obsolete and inadequate' when he is faced with Cedric, and the slips of paper which he writes the names of offenders on and puts in a drawer now bear just one name, 'carefully printed in black ink, *Cedric Hampton*'. In a hilarious scene on Oxford station, Uncle Matthew sees Cedric go to buy a copy of *Vogue* at the bookstall, noticing at the same time 'that the seams of his coat were piped in a contrasting shade. This was too much for his self-control. He fell upon Cedric and began to shake him like a rat.' Luckily the train draws in, and Uncle Matthew 'who suffered terribly from train fever, dropped Cedric and rushed to catch it. "You'd never think," as Cedric said afterwards, "that buying *Vogue Magazine* could be so dangerous. It was well worth it though, lovely Spring modes."'[29]

Of the book, and the character of Cedric in particular, Sir Harold Acton wrote: 'The conquest of tough Lady Montdore by Cedric Hampton, "a terrible creature from Sodom, from Gomorrah, from Paris," was what reviewers used to call audacious, but many dowagers whose names I could mention found youthful companions like Cedric who subjected them to a course of rejuvenation.'[30] Acton observes that many of the Cedric incidents were based on real-life events witnessed by Nancy.[*] The author herself wrote to Billa Harrod (wife of Sir Roy Harrod, both friends of Stephen's too): 'America is taking exception to Cedric, the sweet pansy . . . It seems in America you can have pederasts in books so long as they are fearfully gloomy and end by committing suicide. A cheerful one who goes from strength to strength like Cedric horrifies them. They say "Cedric is too revolting for any enjoyment of the book." So I write back "how can you hate Cedric when he is such a love?"'[32]

There is no record of what Stephen thought of his literary portrayal. But the amusement he afforded so many people, and the fact that he knew he was 'entertaining' in that way, was to his credit. As the artist Eardley Knollys observed, after Stephen's visits to Raymond Mortimer at Long Crichel in the forties, 'his one great virtue was that he made one laugh.'[33]

*

[*]Sir Harold recalled that when he first met Stephen in the 1920s, his impression was of 'his extreme femininity, the coy mannerisms of a debutante eager to charm all and sundry. He seemed always to be dressing up for a fancy-dress party. Perhaps there was a serious vein under the surface frivolity but I was unable to discover it. Frankly, I found him rather embarrassing.'[31]

There was little to laugh about when Stephen left the pleasures of Paris, Nancy, Jean and Boris, to return to England (after a brief few days in Palma, and his 'passionate *lié*' with Siegfried). The winter of 1946–7 was one of the harshest within living memory. Britain froze under industrial action too, and petrol and food shortages exacerbated the already bleak situation when rationing still ruled, and regular power cuts added to the austerity. No one, not even Stephen, could escape the awfulness of the season.

Stephen, whose mood always seemed to swing with the vagaries of the weather like a human barometer, accordingly dropped into another depressive mood. Growing older, and in perpetual solitude, had made him more contemplative then ever. But the wisdom of his years was not like that of his contemporaries. Enclosed as he was, within the perimeters of a way of life he had deemed acceptable for himself – beauty, art, literature: serious pleasures – he developed a world view that was both archaic and modern at the same time.

Here then are the contradictions in his personality which determined Stephen's later years: liberal and reactionary, tolerant and disciplined, magnanimous and selfish – characteristics present in everyone to some degree, yet moderated by social behaviour and experience. For Stephen, who had never lived within society – not even from childhood, when he had been denied the peer group experience of school – there was no such tempering. And as quixotic, intemperate youth had given way to meditative, questioning middle age, there seemed to be even less hope for a stable future. By late spring of 1947 the strain was showing again, and manifested itself as another, and yet more acute, breakdown.

It was shocking for Cecil to meet his old friend in May 1947, for it was a very different Stephen that he saw now. Beaton was staying the weekend with David Herbert at Wilton when Stephen appeared, brought over by his brother Christopher. Cecil could hardly believe it was the same person. Stephen looked drawn and tired: 'rugged . . . with grey hair and no maquillage' – in fact, much older than his years. Stephen attempted an explanation: 'I got so tired of Gerry [?] saying "No" that I had a breakdown and had to be put away.'[34] Quite who "Gerry" was is a mystery, although one report had it that he was a naval man with whom Stephen had recently had an unhappy love affair in Portsmouth, and whose refusals had precipitated Stephen's mental illness.*

---

*Stephen had been friendly with 'a nice naval man', Roger Corbett Melaund, earlier that year.

Perhaps a contribution to his state was the news which Stephen had heard at the end of April. On 24 April, three days after Stephen's forty-first birthday, Willa Cather was found dead in her Park Avenue apartment by Edith Lewis. She had suffered a massive cerebral haemorrhage. The cruelty and the loss should have been greatly felt by Stephen: the woman whose talents he so admired, whom he counted as one of his greatest friends, the supporter of all his literary efforts – in effect, a surrogate mother/nanny figure – gone so suddenly out of his world. As Pamela's and Nannie's losses had brought on tuberculosis, as Rex's death had been at least part of the reason for his breakdown in 1944, so it seemed that this additional bereavement must have added to Stephen's sense of instability that spring.

Yet Stephen's attitude to death, even that of supposedly valued friends, remained equivocal. Back in 1933, when Lord Grey had died, Sassoon had noted Stephen's 'callousness' about it, showing no sign of real bereavement. In later years, friends noted this characteristic. A Wilsford retainer was shocked when Stephen exhibited no sadness on learning of the death of Lady Juliet Duff in 1965: 'He just seemed to wipe her from his memory.' The same happened when Beaton died in 1980. Perhaps, like the Snow Queen, Stephen had a glass splinter in his heart.

From very early on, it seemed, Stephen had hardened himself to the unpleasantness of past memories; he rejected the truth, and assimilated a myth of his own making. Yet the past could not be so easily dismissed, as such losses as Cather's showed. Her death, and Rex's, appeared to be catalysts for Stephen's illness, as reality intruded. In 1947, he had lost his continual struggle to keep it at bay, and the result was an intensification of an already present depression; and, apparently, a resumption of his old trouble. Penelope Middleboe, Edith Olivier's great-niece, notes that 'just when it looked as if the only thing bothering Stephen was the way the power cuts prevented him from making up, he had begun to cough up blood.'[35]

Three months' treatment was deemed necessary, at the Moorcroft private hospital for mental illnesses in Hillingdon, Middlesex. This included intramuscular injections of insulin, which had the effect of reducing tension, but also of inducing a stuporous state (and could cause coma); the sleeping draughts he was given also helped to make him sleep for long periods. But more dramatic than that, this was probably the first time that Stephen was given electro-convulsive therapy, still in its infancy as a method for treating clinical depression and other mental conditions.

It involved the administering of a general anaesthetic, during which time an electric current of 70–150 volts was passed through the patient's brain by means of electrodes placed on the temples. The sufferer woke later, thankfully ignorant of what had happened. ECT was, and is still, seen as one of the only effective therapies for severe mental conditions. By numbing the brain's neurones, the doctors sought to eradicate painful mental trauma. It was a radical method, hailed then as a miracle cure, and Stephen underwent treatment on a number of occasions.

Could it have had a deleterious effect on Stephen's subsequent life? ECT can damage brain tissue: a course of treatment can impair memory and concentration, and dull both imagination and perception; nowadays it is frowned upon by progressive psychiatry. But then its disadvantages were outweighed by the perceived benefits. Certainly patients seemed better, happier, afterwards, more able to cope with stress and ordinary living. Cecil, faced with a changed Stephen, was forced to conclude that 'so many of Stephen's eccentricities & poses were all part of his illness' and he hoped that 'when cured he may become quite a new person'.[36] That was the hope of all Stephen's friends, to whom this sad disintegration of such a vivacious, life-enhancing person must have been painful to observe.

Somehow, Stephen's will was strong enough to carry him through as he began to overcome this latest and most serious threat to his health. By 14 May, though still at Moorcroft, he was able to pick up his pen and write to Cecil. He was eager to know at which film set Beaton was working. In fact, it was quite near, for Beaton was busy on designs for Alexander Korda's *An Ideal Husband* and *Anna Karenina* at Shepperton Studios, 'lavish productions designed to compete with Hollywood'[37] (the latter starring Vivien Leigh, who also suffered mental illness – she too was a TB victim – and was, coincidentally, a later patient at Moorcroft as well).

'When are you coming to see me?' Stephen wrote sadly to Cecil. 'I shall be here until the 15th June . . .' Cecil replied by inviting Stephen on to the film set for the afternoon. Stephen, improved enough to enjoy all the costumes and sets, loved 'Vivien Leigh's toilette, the tart's ensemble, is exquisite and the hair-dressing accents her individuality perfectly, extreme though it is'.[38]

Stephen looked forward to returning to Wilsford, which he did on 14 June. 'I've been very ill,' he told Laurence Whistler, 'but I'm better now. I hope we shall meet before I go to Scotland, which will be in mid-July, I think. I think of Rex a lot – and lately I've been reading the *Masque* [a collection of essays on Rex's theatrical work]. It's admirable, though too short. Cecil Beaton's essay is good, don't you think? Very pungent & discerning criticism of Rex's stage world.'[39] So good, in fact, that Stephen asked Cecil where he could find another copy. 'I have promised the Queen that I will send it to her,'[40] he announced (one of many such gifts Stephen sent to the Palace, and which always elicited a polite note of thanks from one of Her Majesty's Ladies-in-Waiting).

Stephen's apparent return to normality – discussing books and clothes, flowers for Cecil's garden, Rex's art – belied the long-term effects of his illness. Its legacy was an eroded self-confidence which would eventually result in Stephen's sealing himself off from the world, to live 'in a bell under the sea',[41] as Beaton's secretary Eileen Hose put it. Mentally, he had been crippled. The carapace Stephen had built around himself since birth, via his mother's protectiveness, the protection of money, privilege and the castle-like defences of Wilsford itself, were all as nothing when faced by attack from within himself.

The summer dragged by, with protracted recuperation in Scotland, and short stays at Sunbury Court. An instinct for survival, and an ability to pull himself up, brought a victory of sorts, for by 7 September he was able to tell Laurence Whistler: 'I'm tackling loads of work: two novels and a long play in blank verse which is the best thing I've done. My need of solitude is very great – The granary of one's peace of mind & serenity, has, alas, no bolts or locks to keep out the inconsequent, importuning world, has it?' Within a week, he was back in Bournemouth – and bathing in the sea. 'The hot weather galvanized me, I felt six times more alive, more happy than usual.' A new mood of optimism had swept over Stephen. 'I feel as if all my life was newly mine to re-savour, to feast upon – and die of. The ripening year raises grim and grey ghosts . . . the heavy dews are like one's old tears, heaped up, and the starry nights make me forget to lament the summer.'

Throughout the winter of 1947/8 Stephen wrote, and built upon the growing mass of manuscripts, their foolscap pages of close-written coloured inks being written and re-written as his literary projects took on a cyclical quality, rainbow additions to Wilsford's already fantastic contents. Gradually recovering, feeling able to face the world once more, he began to plan new travels for 1948. Dreams of the Mediterranean, its exotic sun and historic places, grew vivid again. These would be Stephen's last great years of travel, a period that saw in a new decade, and a new world. In April 1948, quite suddenly and dramatically, the austerity of post-war Britain was left behind, as Stephen found himself flying over blue seas once more.

Chapter 23

Travels with Myself

Travelling does restore one's granary of spiritual energy and enterprise. I feel very soothed and serene, yet somehow kindled and expectant . . . Rarely have I woken to such a marvellous morning. The purity of the sunrise above the chalk white balcony edge, seen through the French windows, was startling. I lay as in an iridescent sheath of awareness . . . Yes, Tangiers is heavenly.

— Stephen Tennant's journal, 1948

SHORTLY before leaving England, Stephen consulted with Sir Ronald Storrs, an authority on the Near East, being the former governor of Jerusalem and of Cyprus. Stephen had written to Sir Ronald in October 1937, as a fan of his newly-published *Orientations*, and he had become friends with Storrs and his wife. Stephen stayed with them briefly in the country: 'Such subtle, delicate & luxurious hospitality . . . surely unique in England today?' he observed, as indeed it must have been, given the strictures of rationing. Sir Ronald had shown Stephen some snapshots of Anna de Noailles, and it moved him to see 'one who is so close to me, in thought & feeling'.[1]

Storrs had recommended Cyprus as a good destination for Stephen that spring, and so it was to that island he went first on his new adventure. He stayed in the capital, Famagusta, at the Savoy Hotel, and wrote to Sir Ronald to thank him for his advice. 'Famagusta exceeds my wildest expectations. The weather is paradisial – like July in England. The old town is exquisite, mysterious – and august. I shall stay here until June,' he announced, and proceeded to look for a house to rent. 'Please tell Lady Storrs that I was allowed to bring all my jewellery,' added Stephen, obviously having charmed customs in best Cedric manner – 'and with a kind smile, not a sour concessional air! (so important, this!).'[2]

289

Stephen revelled in the Mediterranean atmosphere, loving the red hibiscus, the camels, and geckoes: 'a lizard coloured like blond dust . . . The orange groves make the air fragrant – loaded with scent,' such a marked change from his recent times in England. Bathing in the blue sea, Famagusta was like 'a miraculous peacock – slowly spreading its tail – eyed with countless marvels & iridescences'.

Whilst in Cyprus Stephen heard of the loss of yet another old friend: Edith Olivier had died from a stroke at Wilton. This sad news contributed to his mood, 'dimmed – staccato & depleted', but Stephen hoped resumed work on *Lascar* would 'recreate' him, and help him forget recent traumas. 'Already I am ten times more alive than when I left England . . .'³

From Cyprus, Stephen did a Grand Tour of the Mediterranean lands, 'two months of voyaging', he reported to Laurence Whistler: 'France, Greece, Egypt, the Lebanon, Beirut, Italy, Cyprus – a wonderful succession of enduring and evanescent impressions . . . I loved Beirut, Laurie: a wonderful French-Syrian town and harbour, set among snow-peaked hills. Hibiscus & Plumbago flowering over the blond walls.' Everywhere Stephen travelled in those months, he found new observations to fortify the creative impulse. 'The shadows in hot countries are so beautiful . . . so flame-impregnated! The Middle East has a curious opaque sort of charm,' he noted. 'Egypt particularly is overwhelming – something carved in black basalt.'⁴

In June Stephen was back in the South of France, stopping at Hyères to visit his cousin Lucy Ellis at La Luquette (she was a Wyndham cousin, who had written *La Belle Pamela*, a biography of Stephen's romantic French ancestor, Pamela Genlis, and whose 'pungent, charming mind'⁵ he admired). Here he sent home cards to friends, extolling the beauties of this part of the Riviera, a rocky outcrop a few miles east of Toulon, which Nancy Mitford described in a letter to Stephen as 'very Edwardian' and living 'on memories of "*le gentry Anglais*" & how lovely & rich they were . . .'⁶ France had renewed Stephen's 'artistic enterprise, long dormant. I'm in love with Hyères . . . What a quietness of blue colour there is in my turquoise matrix box,' he noted. 'One can consult a heavenly colour as Goethe consulted the tendril of a vine. I feel very stilled and tranquillized this morning, as if a revelation of some great truth had come to me.'⁷ The thrill Stephen got from foreign places had not diminished with age; rather it had grown, and even ECT and sedative drugs could not dull these perceptions (indeed, the reverse may have been the case).

Stephen had become friendly with an American, Seymour Houghton, a 'large, very vigorous man in well-made pale grey clothes and a startling profligacy, plenitude of language' whom he found 'very American, very delightful'. Houghton invited Stephen and his cousin Lucy to dinner on 9 June, and impressed them when he arrived to pick them up in his smart Dodge car. Houghton was in Hyères to organize a children's home, and they spent the evening listening to his 'many stories, in both French & English. He joined the USA Army at Pearl Harbour,' Stephen noted with a certain admiration. Dinner was excellent, and served by an Italian prisoner of war. 'S.H. spoke of Marseille which he likes enormously.'

Stephen was obviously a little in love with this glamorous American, with his 'very masculine vocabulary – slangy, pithy, very expressive talk, with gestures and humorous moves. He is a big fleshy man, with full cut, very rounded lips and clear good eyes. Grey hair, large fine-grained pale hands – spectacles – a straight nose and a very intriguing and gay sparkle in his eyes . . . He drove us home – rather late – and when we had left Lucy at Laquette he drove me to Les Oliviers. There, in the car, at the moonlit entrance, we talked for quite a bit.'[8]

From Hyères, Stephen moved along the coast to make his first return trip to Marseilles since 1939. He found it sadly changed. German bombs had destroyed the heart of the Vieux Port, as occupation had marred the spirit of the city. So the war had done its worst; it had even managed to take Marseilles away from Stephen. He left after just a few days, never to return.

Travelling as he did, Stephen must have realized just how far everything was changing. Before the war, travel was easy, facilitated by valets, first-class passages, smooth interchanges and deferential treatment. In a war-torn Europe, that privileged world was dying out, replaced by modern ideas of travel and tourism. Soon the places to which only Stephen and his kind could have travelled would become accessible to the greater majority – and in the process, would lose their remote and exotic appeal, making them seem plebeian. Over these last few years of travel, Stephen would come to realize a different world lay in the future, one which seemed to have no place for him.

Stephen returned to England in July, albeit briefly. He saw Christabel Aberconway in London – they went to see a performance of Caribbean dancing – and she told him she had dined the previous evening with Osbert Sitwell. 'She had spoken to him of my letters – saying that my handwriting was so like Rex's – she added she thought I had copied Rex's handwriting and Osbert said he thought it more likely that Rex had copied mine – adding "Rex owed a lot to Stephen".'9 This prompted Stephen to embark on a memoir of Rex himself,* an essay which would be his testament to Rex's 'inexhaustible fancy rather than compelling intellect . . . Life was continually odd, quizzically fascinating . . . The alert restless child was constant in him.'10

It was, like all such pieces written by Stephen, a very subjective view, drawing a great deal on their time together at the Slade, and Rex's early influences. Its perceptions are astute, but within a limited scope; Stephen's very specialized arena. This technique of his, to sum up friends' genius in such a personal way (and one which often reflected well on Stephen's part in their careers, itself a comment on Stephen's own creative psyche), was very much the tone of the other monograph on which Stephen had begun to work, a preface to a volume of Willa Cather's critical essays, commissioned by Alfred Knopf, to be published the following year.

Meanwhile, there were other friends to attend to – Cecil in particular, who had Truman Capote staying with him at Reddish. Beaton had met Capote in the States, and had got on well with the new literary talent who was impressing New York with his angelic good looks, his high voice, his extraordinary behaviour – and his brilliant writing. That year he published his first novel, *Other Voices, Other Rooms*, which met with critical acclaim and a certain degree of notoriety. This was prompted by the author-photograph on the dust-jacket, which had Capote draped languidly over a Victorian couch, looking like a latter-day Aubrey Beardsley. His acquaintance with, and admiration for, Willa Cather also made Capote an obvious guest for Cecil to take over to amuse Stephen – and vice versa.

Capote was suitably impressed by Wilsford, and its owner, and together they had a long talk about Cather. However, Truman's slight suspicions about this strange place and his colourful host were confirmed when lunch was served. 'He gave me a meal with candy violets in the soup,' recalled Capote incredulously. 'After that I wasn't so keen . . . The house was quite extraordinary, and he was bubbly, out of a Charles Adams cartoon – we stayed quite awhile.'11 Stephen was impressed, and pleased, when, on leaving, Truman presented him with a copy of *Other Voices, Other Rooms*, which the author inscribed to him. After that,

*When Edith Olivier had been encouraged to write her own biography of Rex, Stephen had voiced the doubts of other friends: that she would romanticize the story. Now he was doing the same himself.

Stephen would often ask news of 'dear Truman' from Cecil (who saw a great deal of Capote thereafter), asking when he might come again. He wasn't to know that 'dear Truman' had been put off by the highly coloured menu at Wilsford.

Planning yet more travels for that summer, Stephen wondered what he should do about Wilsford, which was now being left empty for long periods, an expensive luxury. The solution was to let it for the summer, and he found suitable tenants in Oliver and Moira Lyttleton. Oliver Lyttleton was a distant cousin of Stephen's, later to become the first Lord Chandos. He was at that time a 'virile captain of industry', as David Herbert recalls (succeeded as Colonial Secretary of State in 1954 by an old friend of Stephen's, Alan Lennox-Boyd). Stephen was at Wilsford to show his tenants round, and took them through the various rooms, indicating their uses, who should have which bedroom and so on. 'At last he came to his room,' says Herbert, 'and said Oliver should have it, and pointing to his dressing-table full of cosmetic preparations, added: "And I shall leave this for you to use." '[12]

On 19 July Stephen travelled up to London on the Bournemouth Belle to lunch with Rosamond Lehmann. 'Perfect enjoyment – she is a darling and so sensitive & shrewd. Cecil Day Lewis & she have two rooms in Hampstead – temporarily – but she finds it very far from the hub of London.'[13] Rosamond had remained a staunch friend to Stephen through thick and thin, and he felt very grateful for her devotion. So grateful that he had bought her a bed, a huge pale-blue satin piece, 'a magnificent couch – far above my station', she remembered. 'I think I was much less grateful than I ought to have been.'[14] But at the time of his last illness, she had written: 'I think of you every time I stretch out on my ice-blue bed. When visitors admire it, & I say you gave it to me, they gasp with incredulous admiration of such generosity . . .'[15]

Stephen stayed in town only for the day, returning in the evening to Bournemouth and his little flat. 'I must finish *Lascar*,' he wrote that night. 'My poems I shall call "Flesh and Miracle".' (An apt title, for part of the reason for his London trip had been to buy new black corsets: 'So comfortable and elegant,' he noted, 'a godsend. One feels like a dancer in them – on tiptoe – winged – resilient.')[16]

The following week Stephen was staying at the Georgian Hotel in Haslemere, preparing to return to Europe, in company with Lucy. Stephen admitted that he was, like Edith Wharton, 'a passionate traveller',[17] and hoped to be able that summer to meet up with Percy

Lubbock, the critic, at Sevici – with a view, presumably, to having his opinion on *Lascar*, 'casual fragments' of which were, in Stephen's opinion, 'in the highest degree imaginative and original'.[18] Two days later, back from a sweltering hot day in London, Stephen noted that he had seen *Nightmare Alley*, starring Tyrone Power, whose '*maillot* & pants, his brio & muscular arrogance & guile' reminded him of *Lascar* characters. He added as an afterthought, 'It needs courage and enterprise to lead one's own life, fully. It is so easy to live . . . on the fringes of other people.'[19]

It was easy to live a peripatetic life, too. On the first day of August, he was back at the Queen's Hotel in Southsea, observing navy life. 'Portsmouth has all the charm & character I remember. I love the Navy canons on the grass in the public gardens . . . The square has a lot of Marseille charm. One sees Indian sailors & American Negro Joes, and New Zealand Navy. Ship names on caps I've noted are Daedalus, Theseus, Sirius.' It seemed Portsmouth had taken Marseilles' place, the latter being so changed. 'I leave for Spain tomorrow at 8. Can it really be true? – flying south! into the deepening warmth! I must pack now.'[20] By the following afternoon Stephen was checking into the Rock Hotel on Gibraltar. 'Bright colours, music in the air, flowers! Passion!'

Stephen was on the Rock for just a day before crossing the Straits to North Africa, and the unknown territory of Morocco. Its status as an 'international zone' made the country – and Tangier, in particular – an attractive place to escape to. Both David Herbert and Barbara Hutton made their homes there, as had Paul and Jane Bowles, and other 'bohemian' writers. Cecil, Truman Capote and Tennessee Williams were all visitors. Capote described Tangier on his visit the following year, 'looking like a white cape draped on the shores of Africa . . . magnificent beaches, really extraordinary stretches of sugar-soft sand and surf'. Then there was the Casbah, the old hub of the town, 'traditionally blue and white, like snow at twilight'.[21] To Beaton, one felt 'suspended in time there', where, 'apart from the exotic and strange Moorish life, there is the fantastic coterie of Europeans: black-market gangsters, Spanish crooks, French expatriates, the different Legations, and the eccentric English – the old ladies, dressed by Liberty's, who have lived here all their lives, and the decadent young ones who come here merely for *louche* reasons.'[22]

Tangier's notorious reputation as a homosexual playground had been established in the thirties, when it became a popular hunting-ground for those of Stephen's tastes. But Tangier meant Africa, too. 'I who so love &

long for summer in all its implications, find it much more fully realized here in Tangier,' he wrote. 'It's curious, but here – so near Spain – only thirty miles away – the sea is much warmer, and the sun much hotter. The sense of Africa, breathing, glowing up through the streets – exhaling from the earth and pavements, is strangely pleasurable to me.'[23]

All the romance of films like Sternberg's *Morocco* seemed to be here. Even *Lascar* could be transplanted to Tangier; Marlene Dietrich's lines murmured huskily to Gary Cooper in the Casbah, 'Do you think you can restore my faith in men?', could be Madame Neffus's. Stephen checked into the El Minzah hotel, where the head barman, Dean, was one of the characters of the town. The pleasures of Morocco were entirely sensual. Sketching in lamplit streets 'after a mood of rather grim depression', Stephen read about the mystic poet, Rilke, and was sold two tuberoses by an Arab boy. The flowers reminded him of Rilke, somehow, and had 'a passionate and complex significance for me – How strange this is! – I still feel troubled & exalted, as if some spirit had touched mine.'[24]

A dancer friend called Sergio Matta was Stephen's guide to the town, a Chilean who knew Elsie Mendl and Charles James 'and several other people I know slightly. He tells me that Elsie is at Versailles now – this moves me oddly . . . as if an old misted mirror of my life – being cleared – gleaming again.'[25] Matta was staying with Baron Favier at his apartment at 29 rue Grotus, and he took Stephen there for a tour.* Here the latter found an elegantly appointed apartment, 'modern, chic – no super-fluities . . . two absurd poodles, very eccentrically clipped', which dashed at them 'like tropical fish, Japanese fan-tails – most extraordinary'. Sergio also showed Stephen his own room: 'Dark gold . . . his avidity for life is everywhere,' Stephen concluded of his new friend, 'very clever & original and delightful. He is a very kind boy . . . so full of impulsive curiosity, aplomb & zest. He makes me feel more alive.'

Matta's curiosity took them to the Medina, the old town, where they explored the Casbah, whose high-walled gardens Stephen found fascinat-ing. Matta showed him the house of his friend David Herbert 'with its huge fig tree in the courtyard – Sergio suggested we take a photo of me in front of the house – to send to David. We saw Barbara Hutton's house also – that is most fascinating.'[27]

---

*Baron Favier was one of the shadier figures of the town. When Joe Orton stayed in Tangier in 1967, it was in a flat rented to him by Favier (the same flat in which Tennessee Williams wrote *Suddenly Last Summer*), and Orton noted in his diary that the Baron liked to 'dress young men up in military uniform', and was described by Kenneth Williams as a man who 'sometimes affects a lace blouse'.[26]

The absence of Miss Hutton herself from her crenellated white palace only stressed the loneliness which came upon Stephen. 'I miss my friends in lovely places – oh why isn't Rosamond here? Why isn't Vita? Elizabeth would love Tangiers so much.' The El Minzah made up for these lacks; the manager's solicitations brought appreciation from Stephen: 'Rarely have I liked any hotel so much . . . I dote on the place,' he noted before taking himself off for a bath, 'but I also want to write stories & poems – and write long exhaustive letters to my friends. Mais, que faire?'[28]

Amid many recollections of Cather's advice on *Lascar* ('the trouble is, you have not given yourself enough fun with the book! I think it would feed you, to do it . . . I have high hopes of that book'),[29] Stephen felt the recriminations of past and present friends when he addressed his own prevarication. 'You will have to put a spurt on now, Stephen, if you wish seriously to make a name for yourself,' he wrote whilst laid up at the Rock Hotel. 'Never expect the world to be indulgent or easy of conquest. Work & sweat – dedication are needed for even the beginning of a career.' Strange that he should know this so well, ten years after the beginning of *Lascar*, the manuscript still at his side. 'Success is the child of audacity and hard work,' he recognized. 'There are no short cuts. If you write regularly every day, the task becomes habitual. Willa's words "It is the practised hand that makes the natural gesture" are pertinent here.'[30] But how much notice did Stephen take of such advice? A deeply critical look at his attempts to write a 'great novel' might result in the opinion that here was someone who was trying too hard, and in the wrong way. The numerous re-writes of the book's ever-changing number of chapters betray a basic lack of self-criticism, or objectivity.

Was Stephen in fact deluding himself when he thought he could write at all? By surrounding himself with other writers, did he seek to circumvent a lack of real talent by some mysterious process of osmosis, to absorb the reflected talent of other, successful writers? It is true that the dialogue sequences of *Lascar* and other Tennant works – particularly the plays – do not ring true at all. The characters say what Stephen thinks they ought to say, not what someone in their position would say. They become mouthpieces for Stephen's obsessions, and the result is not a believable personality, but an extension of his own. Cather exhorted Stephen to be realistic, but he could not, in the end, grasp the realities by which this might be done. Even his risqué episodes in *Lascar* – using words like 'bum', and a scene in which one of the characters continues a conversation while 'making water' – are more dreamlike than real, and they fall short of a credible sexual or physical sensibility. Stephen was too polite for that, and only deceived himself when he declared that his book would be a rough and tough no-punches-pulled thriller.

Responding to one draft of *Lascar*, Morgan Forster told Stephen: 'It is lovely writing, and I think I see what you are up to, anyway what you are up against, to speak as an ex-don, pedantically. I think you are out for realistic action by stylized characters. This seems to me a most interesting line which might lead to very beautiful effects. Firbank tried it a little in Prancing Nigger [*Sorrow in Sunlight*] but usually stylized both characters & action. I have no criticism to make except to urge you to go on . . .'[31] Stephen's fiction is caught midway between Ronald Firbank's baroque artifice and the quayside sleaze of Jean Genet. As much as Firbank predated *Lascar*, so Genet postdated it; the latter took the same material to its logical conclusion. Perhaps Stephen sought, like Oscar Wilde, art in criminality, sin – but pulled back from the precipice. When Genet had demonstrated his thievery to Stephen, the latter had registered disbelief.[*]

Cyril Connolly observed that Stephen would 'intoxicate himself into a permanent creative ecstasy with his characters', even to the extent of apologizing for borrowing quotations from them: ' "As Madame Neffus says – you will like her, Cyril," [he] fills all his letters . . . with accounts of what his novel is going to be – "a great bleak cape jutting out in a stormy sea, the dark places of the soul" and so on. Yet when he reads it aloud, often reducing himself to tears, one cannot believe that anyone should so absolutely possess not only the soul but the vocabulary of a lovelorn and raffish housemaid.'

'Every cliché, every vulgarity, every banal and cheaply-scented expression is there, with thousands of words where one will do and long morbid exuberant second-hand expressions laboriously building up the theatrical characters. It is as if Proust, Virginia Woolf, Flaubert, Gide, living the same life as they did in reality, produced instead only erotic servants' hall fourpennies, snack-bar novelettes, heroes of Palais-de-Dance.' Connolly concluded that 'presumably no one will publish it, in which case he may be able to claim the incontestable greatness of being ahead of his time – but he is more likely to get it published somehow in which case it will either be a complete flop, or a *succès de scandale et de ridicule* like *The Well of Loneliness* or Amanda Ross.'

---

[*]Richard Ellman comments in his biography of Wilde: 'Like Genet after him, he proposed an analogy between the criminal and the artist, though for him the artist, not needing to act, occupies a superior place . . .'[32]

What Connolly said of Stephen is probably (albeit cruelly) true. 'If he ever admits his failure to himself he might commit suicide, become a permanent invalid – or, more likely, drop all his old friends and ways of life and let his narcissism branch out in a new part. Essentially he is an adolescent exhibitionist acting out the role of grand *écrivain méconnu*. Is writing really necessary to act out such a part?' pondered Connolly smugly. 'Or perhaps he really is a great writer and I shall live to eat these words? In which case something as remarkable will happen as for a fly which looks like a wasp, or a crab which covers itself with seaweed to become a wasp or a seaweed. Can mimicry become – through sympathetic magic – the object of imitation? *Lascar* will show.'[33]

Had Stephen known Cyril Connolly's opinions, he might have held up the praise of other friends – writers who, unlike Connolly, were successful creators of fiction. On 19 August Stephen was thinking of Elizabeth Bowen: 'I am longing to see her. She is the pivot, instigator, inspiration, guiding star of my writing – She believes tremendously that I can write.'

For Stephen to have taken his lead from Bowen's complex and meticulously structured books would have been difficult. Like Cather, she examined motive and emotion from within, but used urban settings instead of the great outdoors, in which her characters move in scenarios created by Bowen to expose their innermost thoughts. What Stephen was doing in his fiction was attempting to write about similar human motivations; but without Bowen's or Cather's skill to characterize, how could he attempt to do what they did so well? He noted that it was 'so hard – not to spotlight one character too much'[34] and that was part of the trouble, caused by his over-subjective approach. He later told Sheila Macdonald that he found it hard to write about the evil characters in his book, of which there were many. Likening them to the 'evil characters in the Brontës',[35] Stephen told his friend that he hated having them in the book, that he didn't like evil things. Yet they were necessary to the plot.

These struggles turned him to other media for satisfaction. Perhaps, he thought, he ought to pursue the muse of verse? 'I think that soon now, a strong wish to write poetry again will come to me. "I am in a poetry-writing area of my life", C.D.L. [Cecil Day Lewis] wrote me once – and I think it is important to write a little all the time . . .'[36]

Stephen's sense of futility continued to darken even the blazing sunshine: 'You must assert your poetic identity more conclusively, Stephen . . . Put aside a time each day . . . for serious writing. Don't spend all your energy on this journal and long letters [which is exactly what he did do]. Attack the more difficult problem – of work.'[37] Stephen attempted to discipline himself, to become his own nanny, but failed, a victim of his past. 'I think of Rex – and miss him – Last night, writing to Vita, I wept – with a longing for friends and home. I get very homesick sometimes . . . A crushing sense of loneliness came on me . . .'[38]

In happier mood, Stephen descended the El Minzah's white staircase one morning. 'I looked very beautiful,' observed the modest Mr Tennant. 'My gold hair, newly-washed (oh why doesn't one wash it every other day?) shone back a dare! to the sun. I fled like a creature down – down past mysterious grilled windows – past Villa Arellium – I wore white linen trousers, white Egyptian cotton shirt, dark blue silk tie – the blue & white Tahitian shirt from Hyères – under one arm a towel.'[39]

On the beach he watched 'men like teak and dark amber' playing ball or doing acrobatics. Stephen spent most of his time there, on 'white sands – sea like blue spring grass'.[40] A snapshot shows him tanned deep mahogany, still quite thin, leaning on one elbow, laughing into the camera, certainly happy; yet with discernible lines of sadness on his face.

As September came around, he was reminded of Sassoon's birthday. 'This is S.S.'s month . . .' Sassoon remained a source of concern for Stephen, and it is evident from journal entries at this time that there had been further unsatisfactory contact between the two back in England. 'I miss Siegfried this morning,' he noted after his traumatic ferry journey to Gibraltar, and on 19 August he wrote: '. . . thinking of S.S. a little sadly. But all will be well. He will understand,' and the next morning: 'Woke thinking of S.S.'[41]

As his time in Tangier drew to a close, Stephen watched 'moving & tragic, inexplicable figures of Arabs & negroes who lie in the white sand of the livid beach with their mouths buried – or on their backs – for the sun to devour like an eagle – the sun eats their hearts . . . They belong to these shifting silver-white & stark sands.' These 'nomadic sands' were 'a tragic symbol of man's evanescent thoughts, wishes, loves, hates' to Stephen, who concluded that such metaphysical musings were 'very healthy . . . to write of something unconnected with one's own life. That is why imaginative writing is so curative and strengthening . . . I am wearing my coral-flame pyjamas – they are very lovely – like a tropical flower. All men are angels. There is always some vigilant poetic sentinel standing apart, a little outside of one's life, who scrutinizes the curious day . . . He is the poetic voice, shining like a light, far into futurity. All men, and one.'[42]

Chapter 24

Stephen and Edith

One never knows if one is happy – one only knows if one is unhappy.
— Paul Bowles: *Without Stopping*

STEPHEN's friendship with Willa Cather's companion Edith Lewis began shortly after the death of their mutual friend. She was to become his link with Cather, a reminder of the respect and affection they had for each other, and as Stephen's friendship with Cather had begun by letter, so did his increasing closeness with Lewis. In September 1947 Edith had replied to an unexpected letter of Stephen's: 'How kind, how kind you were to write to me. Of course I remember the evening we had here with you. And Willa used to talk of you so much . . . We used to look at your beautiful drawings together. When she spoke of you, it was always with such affection and pleasure in her voice and look . . . I know that her friendship with you was one of her greatest treasures.'[1]

Edith Lewis told Stephen they should be grateful Willa had not suffered a long illness, and that she was now at rest, at Jaffrey, 'lying in a beautiful spot, just at the corner of the old burying ground where you look off over fields and woods to the mountains beyond' (and where Edith herself would eventually be buried too). Stephen was pleased to hear that Cather had kept all his letters: 'They are here, tied together in her secretary – just as she left them . . .'* Stephen's letters to Edith Lewis, initially about Willa and him, gradually established a bond between them. 'Yes, she had spoken to me of *Lascar*,' Edith confirmed. 'She said several times that she hoped so much you would finish it.'[2]

Soon Stephen and Edith were planning to meet, to tour Europe together. An initial plan to meet in Cyprus had to be put off, and it was

---

*Their whereabouts remains a mystery; Lewis promised to send them back to Stephen in 1948, but he never received them. It is likely that Lewis later burnt them in accordance with Cather's will.

not until 21 August 1948 that Edith sailed from New York for France, arriving a week later to find a telegram from Stephen welcoming her to her hotel in Paris.

Stephen arrived a week or so later. It was only his second meeting with her, and he found a silver-haired woman, a journalist by profession, with kindly features and an accommodating manner. Stephen knew at once this was the kind of person he could get on with. Despite a bad cold, he and Edith set off to explore Europe together. First was a visit to Switzerland; Edith recalled 'that first morning we dashed out of the train at Lausanne, and had a wonderful breakfast in the station. It was the best breakfast of my life.'3 They stayed at the Beau Rivage, a hugely luxurious hotel with balconies overlooking Lac Leman (used by Noel Coward as a setting for his *Private Lives*).

By early October they were in Venice, at Proust's Danieli hotel, 'doing' St Mark's Square, and loving it. Stephen and Edith found each other's company amiable and easy, and their common bond, their love of Willa Cather, seemed to be an invisible tie between them. Cather student Patricia Lee Yongue notes that Stephen was 'charmed by Edith Lewis's flattery and confidence. She knew immediately how to respond to him. He more than any of Cather's friends who continued a relationship with Lewis unwittingly allowed her to indulge herself . . . she seems, also unwittingly, gradually to appropriate Stephen away from Cather, under the guise of devotion to her.'4

It was already an equivocal relationship. Stephen met up with the actor Michael Redgrave and his wife, Rachel Kempson, at the Opera House in Milan, and Lady Redgrave recalls: 'We were at *Werther*, and Stephen came into the stalls. I'd met him briefly before – through John Fowler [Sibyl Colefax's partner] – and he said, "It's too wonderful to see you!" We were staying at the Danieli too, and Stephen said we must join him touring Venice. We weren't terribly well-off then – but he came into our room and threw thousands of lira in the air. We had a lovely time. He had that writer friend of his with him – I think he gave her rather a bad time, actually. He wanted to go out and about, and she, poor dear, was rather quiet, so I think he used to go off and leave her.'5

Edith judged the two weeks she and Stephen spent in Rome 'one of the great experiences of my life; it somehow means more to me than Paris, more than Venice – beautiful as they are.'6 Stephen brought her roses, tuberoses, carnations, and whisked her around the city showing her its famous sights. All too soon Edith had to return to the States, but plans were already drawn up for Stephen to make a return trip to New

York, to stay there with Edith, then explore Florida, and, perhaps, further south.

But one problem might prevent this happy schedule. Stephen intimated that his finances, already depleted by the post-war depression, and further run down by his recent travels, would not stand up to such an expensive trip (also stringent post-war currency rules meant British subjects could take only £25 out of the country with them). The solution was very simple, said Edith. She would pay. She had been the major beneficiary of Cather's will,* and nothing would please her more than to share her good fortune with such an old friend of Willa's.

Stephen arrived in snowy New York in the early spring of 1949. He stayed with Edith at 570 Park Avenue, last seen twelve years ago and here, with Edith's help, he put the finishing touches to his essay on Willa Cather for Knopf. Stephen loved being back in 'Babylonian New York', riding across the park in open horse-drawn carriages, or cruising his favourite shops. But Edith had even more exciting plans, and within a few days they were driving across the Florida countryside, past canals full of water-hyacinths, to Sarasota, where they settled down to enjoy spring.

From Palm Beach, it was overland to California, where Stephen stopped to draw the gigantic redwood trees and their massive roots; thence to Santa Barbara, and San Francisco, staying at the elegant Fairmont Hotel. Then came Stephen's most adventurous expedition yet – to Cuba, and Havana, where Stephen approved of 'the Catholic flavour . . . very pleasing – one meets very cultivated priests of great charm',[7] he noted, whilst admiring the coral-decorated cathedral in pre-revolutionary Havana.

On yet further, to America's Mexican playground, Acapulco. They stayed at the Hotel de las Americas. Stephen found it all 'so beautiful, a resort of fantastic Spanish-Mexican exoticism . . . vast sea-turtles basking on snowy coral beaches, lizards, mountain lions, crocodiles in a lake ! ! And a comical, musical comedy atmosphere.' Stephen saw everything in terms of theatre. There was 'barbaric colour everywhere – a purple-blue warm sea . . . Iguanas . . . Macaws, Parrots'. Stephen felt the ancient races of Central America, 'Maya, Aztec, Toltec, so close, more potent, to me, than any Spanish quality',[8] and bought a large plaster replica of a Pre-Columbian head to take back to Wilsford.

*Which had also left Stephen a modest bequest, money deposited abroad for use when Stephen travelled (a clever device to prevent him squandering it on Wilsford, rather than using it to broaden his horizons, and help him to write *Lascar*, as Willa wished).

But Stephen and Edith were not content with Central America. They wanted to go on, out into the Pacific – to Hawaii and Honolulu. It was the furthest from home Stephen had ever been, and he found it all very romantic, especially the native islanders, and Polynesian faces soon became part of his creative repertoire. Stephen's fertile imagination was particularly caught by the rocky coastline of Honolulu, where huge metal chains seemed to tie the land in. 'Can you think of anything more perfect than chains binding the sea?'[9] he said, and sketched the scene in his journal. It was June, and incredibly hot on the paradise island, the most exotic place he had yet visited; but perhaps that very remoteness induced homesickness in Stephen, for he felt sad and a little depressed. Reading the poems of Keats, in a volume illustrated by Michael Ayrton, at breakfast in his hotel, he found that he had signed his check on the page, and a carboned 'Stephen Tennant' had been left over the lines 'We rest in silence, like two gems upcurl'd /In the recesses of a pearly shell.' 'Fateful, perhaps?' added Stephen in the margin.

In early autumn Willa Cather's essays, *On Writing*, were published, with the proud announcement on the title page, 'Foreword by Stephen Tennant'. It was the first really serious piece of writing Stephen had had published. Stephen's critique, 'The Room Beyond', draws on the metaphor of the open door in Cather's work. 'There is for me a profound symbolism in this idea of seeing beyond the immediate room,' he observes, 'either to sky or sea or mountains, or to the Room Beyond ... Willa Cather's art is essentially one of gazing beyond the immediate scene to a timeless sky or a timeless room, in which the future and the past, the unspoken and the unknown, forever beckon the reader.' It is a wistful piece of allusion; like his own paintings with their distant views of a still sea and mountain peaks, Stephen sees the infinite in Cather's landscape. 'Art is not life, and it is not a substitute for it, or an aggrandizement of a dubious reality,' continues Stephen's concise analysis. 'It is a necessary commodity – compacted of many realities and fantasies, unrealities and dreams, which the artist commands and respects. It is a method, the only one, of preserving the beauty of transient things, the wonder of youthful happiness, the pleasures of controversy, wit and enterprise, and the finer aspects of intellectual discovery ...'
Stephen's thoughts on Willa have been assessed by Cather scholars to have caught her spirit better than anyone else. It is because Stephen's own longing for a lost past (his *nostalgie de la boue*, as his friend Lord Sudeley saw it) is so close to that spirit that he was able to sum it up so

well. 'When one thinks of the deep indelible impression made by some of her books – *A Lost Lady, My Mortal Enemy, My Àntonia* – I think it is the burden of unspent feeling one remembers; something gathered up, inviolably, delicately, almost denied one.' This is Stephen's own life: he maintains that 'a great writer is always an influence of expansion. He gives direction to the reader's thoughts. The world is more interesting when it is viewed by a subtle and invigorating mind that deals summarily with the inessentials, and lays bare in all their fascination and glory the great truths, the deathless power that is in man, and his irreducible and ever-changing eternity.'[10]

Contemporary critical response to Stephen's introduction was generally favourable. The writer Eudora Welty, whom Stephen met through Elizabeth Bowen,[*] was presented by the author with a copy of *On Writing*, and thought it very good. Welty later noted, on hearing that Stephen was planning to give a lecture on Cather in her home town of Red Cloud, Nebraska, that she 'almost wouldn't have batted an eyelid had he come dancing in his auburn camels hair coat with hair to match'.[11] Even Queen Elizabeth (who, Stephen remembered, liked Cather's work), was presented with a copy in November, and commanded her Lady-in-Waiting 'to thank you for the book of Essays, to which you have contributed a Preface . . . Her Majesty looks forward to reading this book with interest, and is very touched by your thought in sending it.'[12]

Not everyone was impressed with Stephen's scholarship, however. In October Stephen received a letter via Knopf which began: 'Dear Mr Tennant, I think he must be something of an egotist who would write a lengthy preface to a book of Cather's critiques. If Miss Cather's work is outstanding as you insist – and it is – it needs no embellishment, no explanation. I think, too,' wrote Miss Ruth Crone from the Senate Office in Washington, 'that one who would write a preface to any of Miss Cather's work must inevitably lend himself to comparison with her and must needs, thereby, suffer. To me, at least, one of your comments is preposterous.' Ruth Crone illustrated her complaint with one of Stephen's admittedly sweeping remarks about a writer having 'to produce an impression of veracity he must exaggerate'. 'Perhaps you, yourself, have exaggerated?' she concluded.[13]

Stephen replied, thanking her for her comments, and noting that he had had some 'wonderful' letters about his preface, 'and a superb press – a noble press. No,' he agreed, 'there is not a peak for truth, it is its own

[*]Possibly in late 1944. Welty gave Stephen a copy of her stories, *A Curtain of Green* (English publication, 1943), which Stephen thought exhibited 'the shock of excellence'.

peak: – I mean the clouds and vapours of fashion float past it – colouring it a little, sometimes, but never altering its essential probity – or verity. Thank you so much for drawing my attention to this point.'[14] It was a typically elegant riposte, and one which resulted in yet another trans-atlantic friendship. 'Our correspondence, though irregular . . . continued for almost 25 years', recalls Ruth Crone. 'Always Mr Tennant was a gentleman, always gracious. Always he found something to praise.' To Crone, who never actually met Stephen, he seemed 'filled with enthusi-asm, if not exuberance. Zeal . . . To Stephen, Cather was – to use a current American slang word – "the ultimate".'[15]

Stephen was back in Europe in October, at the Hotel Beau Rivage in Lausanne, working on *Lascar* and writing long letters to friends. Then he set off for Italy, stopping first in Geneva, where he had heard from Elizabeth Bowen that he might catch Charles Ritchie at the Hotel de la Paix. Ritchie was there on diplomatic business for his country. 'I was in the lobby of the hotel . . . with some rather stuffy Canadian officials, when suddenly this brightly-plumaged bird – that is the only way I could describe Stephen – rushed across the hall towards me,' he recalls. 'I saw the shocked look on my colleagues' faces – they were obviously completely taken aback that I should know this person . . . But it amused me very much that, after talking to them for half an hour, Stephen had subjugated them completely – catching them "off base" as he did . . . I thought it was very funny.'[16]

Stephen travelled on, back to Venice and the Hotel Gritti Palace. St Mark's Square inspired him, as he sat in the early morning, watching sailing boats in the 'grey early hours . . . the air is full of shouts – men calling from barge to barge . . . The air interwoven with mysterious greetings.'[17]

'I'm so tired of travelling now' he wrote; 'soon I will be home, thank God, & resting, & listening to the doves & pigeons at Wilsford', there to work on his poetry. He found Venice too 'noisy & glutinous & sticky & restless'[18] to be conducive to such concentration. A letter from Leslie Hartley (whose last novel, *Eustace and Hilda*, had used the city as its setting) replied to his complaints: 'I hope your mood of disappointment with Venice has passed. It always has been shabby, dirty, noisy & smelly, and full of vulgar people. From what you say, it may be more now than it was – but I think it always reflects one's moods very faithfully . . .'[19] Stephen visited Rome briefly, finding it noisy too, and then called on the Beerbohms at Rapallo. 'Yes, the Bristol is still there looking from the outside just as it did and I imagine as it was inside,' wrote Florence Beerbohm. 'I hope there will be only blue days of sea and sky when you come – no worries. Peace and quiet if possible, stories of what you have seen and felt and hearing and reading what you have written.'[20]

He resolved to return to the Beau Rivage. 'I could work there,' said Stephen confidently, despite the 'wonderful latitude' of Venice. 'This great book [*Lascar*] which is demanding experience will require calm and peace in the country. Wilsford is ideal for working. I need 8 or 9 months of quiet work – to feed and recharge my heart and soul with power – vigour – enterprise.'[21] Thus did Stephen draw closer to reclusion at Wilsford, convincing himself that only there could he finish his work. Travelling, even as comfortably as he did, had exhausted him – and the still emptiness in his heart when he did halt worried him deeply, too.

At the Beau Rivage in March 1950, Stephen completed an introduction for a collection of his poems he hoped Alfred Knopf would publish, provisionally entitled *Call Rapture by its Name*. The introduction, 'A Reassessment of Poetry', was a prime example of Stephen's prose: flowery, convoluted, personal – and sometimes profound. Poetry, he declared, is 'the realization of an absolute in intellectual expression'; and he cited the work of Keats, Emily Dickinson, Dylan Thomas, Laurence Whistler and Anna de Noailles as inspiration for his own verse. 'That kindler and inspirer of poets and writers, Blanche Knopf, asked me to say why I wrote these poems. I wrote them because the tangible, palpable world so perfectly mirrored the ideal and sublimated world of my imagination that I wished to make this fusion complete – with those airy, frail, yet indestructible words that, unified into a poem, make our spiritual boundaries secure.'[22]

Stephen's selection for Knopf never surfaced; it appeared that his ambition had overtaken his ability once again. In the light of the nineteen-fifties, Stephen's verse appeared old-fashioned and stilted, as the various editors to whom he submitted work tried gently to tell him. Later, Norah Smallwood of Chatto & Windus called them 'very accomplished writing', but also, 'for better or worse, out of fashion today'.[23] Neither John Lehmann nor Roger Senhouse disagreed. Much of Stephen's verse does not bear close examination. His serious poems contain the germ of inspiration, but he was unable to hone down his florid language into the tight cohesion needed to make them work. His more humorous pieces are much more successful: Stephen seems to find his voice in odes to Queen Victoria's gloominess or the attractiveness of life as an Army man. Yet reams of verse poured from his pen, and Stephen sought the advice of other poets very seriously. 'Let us put our heads together,' he told Laurence Whistler, 'since you are so kind as to wish to help me with the burgeoning of my volume of poems . . . Just now, I'm finding important notes on poetry which must go into my preface . . . I think you will say I'm a metaphysical poet, and perhaps a fantastic visionary . . .'[24] But Laurence could say nothing of the kind.

Stephen toured Switzerland, visiting St Moritz in early February, and Zurich after that. Edith Lewis was trying to persuade him to return to the States later in the year. 'Yes, yes, we can afford it,' she said. 'Come soon to America! . . . How you make all life into poetry! . . . How unswerving you are, Stephen, how absolute.'[25] She wrote again on 24 March, urging her friend to rest and get rid of the bronchitis he had contracted: 'Rest all you can, eat all you can at dear Beau Rivage . . . I think your money must be running low, I will send you some the first of the week.'

By April, Stephen had recovered sufficiently to return to Venice, and the Gritti. Leslie Hartley came out on a brief visit, and Stephen was grateful for his informed and erudite company. From there Stephen went to the Hotel Pont Royal in Paris for a week or so, but in May his bronchitis recurred, and he returned to Switzerland to recuperate. 'Everyone thinks I am flying to Switzerland to visit gay friends,' wrote Edith a week later, 'but what I am really going for is to settle down quietly at the dear Beau Rivage, where I can see trees and flowers and water and mountains, and finish my notes for Brown [Cather's biographer] and most of all get reports every day that you are better!'[26] When she arrived in Lausanne, Edith spent her time with Stephen discussing his recollections of Cather for the proposed biography and, of course, reading his 'Reassessment of Poetry' and his piece on Rex Whistler, both of which she judged excellent. Stephen proposed that Edith should be his guest now and, to that end, they returned to England together.

So Stephen, for the first time in years, had a guest at Wilsford that summer – an ever rarer occurrence over the following years. Edith wrote later: 'I think so often about Wilsford – about all your lovely kindness to me there, the way you gave me one beautiful thing after another, to keep forever, for I feel that I shall never lose any of it. No one was ever so generous.'[27]

The idea of Stephen's generosity was debatable to other friends. He certainly liked to give presents, but often regretted having parted with them. When staying in Jefferson in 1935 he had confessed to his diary that he felt sad, as he had given his landlady a cheap amethyst 'bubble' vase he had bought at the local post office, '& now I miss it! I'm not sure if she loves it as intensely as I do.'[28] Later, he gave his niece Pauline a copy of *On Writing*, only to tell her months after that he had only lent it to her, and could he please have it back? Cyril Connolly recorded a weekend visit to Wilsford in company with Elizabeth Bowen, when all they were given to drink was a bottle of cider between them, whilst a full bottle of gin stood unopened on the sideboard. And Caroline Blackwood, who met Stephen in the early fifties with her first husband, Lucian Freud, observes that on their visits Stephen was always promising champagne which never came.* His hospitality obviously had limits. Edith was one of the lucky ones: certainly Stephen owed her something.

Others, who might be turned away at the door, had to grin and bear it, if they were to remain friends. Stephen could be quite capricious, sometimes cruelly so. 'The meanest and bitchiest of men,' recalled one acquaintance sourly, perhaps with good reason. Around this time he met Margaret Rutherford, a superb character actress, but not known for her beauty. She and Stephen became friendly, and she fell for his charms. Sir John Gielgud observes that she was 'not only a wonderful actress but a naive and sweet woman . . . I was told he treated her very badly though I never ventured to ask her about the episode.'[29] The story went that Stephen actively cultivated the actress's company, and more or less proposed to her. 'He was treating her like a goddess,' recounts David Herbert. 'Then one day she came down for the weekend and he wouldn't let her in. She was terribly upset – she nearly had a nervous breakdown. The butler felt sorry for her and let her in, only to find her later, in the cellar, eating coal . . .'[30] There is no way to make excuses for such behaviour, only reasons – and those so complicated that many people who knew Stephen then would shake their heads and express no hope for him.

Stephen was ill again that summer, having contracted fibrosis, which necessitated daily visits to Salisbury Infirmary. By 16 August he had recuperated enough for a trip to London, where he lunched with Cyril and Barbara Connolly. Mrs Connolly noted a frustrating conversation with him. Asked by Stephen, 'I hear you know Cairo well?' she replied: 'Oh, do I?' 'But you were there?' 'Oh yes.' 'Were you there for long?'

*Yet there are many records of Stephen's generosity. In 1929 he presented Edith Olivier with a brand new Austin Seven, and the same year gave Rex Whistler £50 to repair his rather battered Vauxhall saloon; and in May 1933, whilst in hospital, he sent the Vicar of St Michael's Church at Wilsford £30 for church expenses, a gesture that gladdened Sassoon's heart at the time.

'Eighteen months.' 'Then you do know it well!' Long pause . . .[31] It was difficult to argue with that.

Edith flew back to Europe in September, and from Paris wrote to Stephen telling him she would finance another Italian tour. 'Let us not think about money! I went to my bank this morning and arranged to get more from New York if I should need it. What fun it would be to do just as we like – go where we like – for these few weeks – without having to do arithmetical sums . . . But it worries me, Stephen, when you say you are so tired. Do not hurry to come here. Why do you not rest for a week? . . . And please do not try and get along on £35. If you will let me share what I have with you, it will make me so wonderfully happy.'[32] Was Stephen using Edith? He certainly knew the power of his charm. It was a mutually beneficial arrangement: both wished to travel, neither had company. Stephen had always liked older women – caring, cosseting figures like Edith were nanny-figures – and she had the added charisma of her Cather connection.

Stephen joined her in Paris, and they took an overnight *wagon-lit* to Venice. Having sampled the delights of Italy, Edith persuaded Stephen to fly back with her to the States – his first long air journey, which he appears to have taken coolly. Thence to Palm Beach, to spend September at the Whitehall Hotel and the Palm Beach Country Club. The affluent atmosphere of the resort had only just begun to fade into the widow's paradise it later became; but to Stephen, it retained the mystique it had had for him when he first visited America with his mother all those years ago.

That winter Stephen spent in New York with Edith, preoccupied with his poems for Knopf. He was marshalling his thoughts on his creative future. 'Solitude is a kind of dignity,' he wrote. 'Poetry is the perenially new young love, of the great old world'[33] – and he hoped that therein lay his late vocation. Certain strands of his former life now came together to set a philosophy that would guide him. 'The world's conventional opinions are always wrong' he had written whilst still in Palm Beach in November 1950. 'But they do remain interesting.' Without that interest, what would he do? Become the hermit aesthete, studying Beauty? 'Gaze too long at anything,' he observed, ' – and you stare at ashes.'[34]

Stephen saw other friends in New York that autumn. Staying at the Colony Hotel, he heard that Elizabeth Bowen would be coming over in November, and was glad of a familiar English face. With her he saw Eudora Welty, who was impressed with Stephen's long coat and long hair, and Lionel Trilling, a literary critic particularly interested in

Forster's work, who heard all Stephen's reminiscences of the great writer. A great thrill was to meet W. H. Auden for tea; Auden recommended the work of e. e. cummings to Stephen. Stephen was pleased when, years later, Michael Wishart told him that Auden had read some of Stephen's poems – he had sent him a copy of his collected verse, *My Brother Aquarius* – and had pronounced them 'remarkable'. Stephen took the comment as a compliment.

But it was the place, more than anything, which excited him still. Stephen took 'prowls' along 'squalid, vast Broadway', but was punctually out of Central Park at dusk, lest something nasty happened in the dark. The people on the streets fascinated him, and all was eagerly logged in his visual memory bank; one youth was drawn from the back, his baseball jacket displaying the legend 'Carolina's Golden Gloves'.[35]

Escaping the winter, Stephen and Edith took off south, to Florida again. Stephen was determined to go further afield and, leaving Edith on the mainland, he flew to Jamaica. Stephen liked the island, and sketched its palms against the blue Caribbean. He wrote to Percy Lubbock, telling him he felt he could really work here. Lubbock replied, 'so much the better for Jamaica'. He added, 'Certainly no one can accuse you of monotony, and I hope your flights and excursion have all made for your pleasure and well-being.'[36]

In June, Stephen and Edith flew back across the Atlantic together. He had been invited to Portugal, to see Susan Lowndes, his childhood friend. Susan was now married, and lived with her husband, Luis Marques, the editor of *Anglo-Portuguese News*, in Estoril, just outside Lisbon. Stephen and Edith stayed in the Hotel Palacio in Estoril, and spent much of their time at the Marques' home, Palmerial. Susan remembered their visit with great affection, Stephen and Edith chatting with them in their drawing room, and visiting the galleries and sights of northern Portugal. 'Stephen got on very well with my husband – he even told him that, if he became a widower, Luis should go and live with him at Wilsford! Luis liked Stephen a lot, but I must admit he thought him very funny. After they left, Luis would imitate the way Stephen pranced into the house!'[37]

Susan Lowndes Marques observed that Stephen seemed to get a little impatient with Edith's unshakeable devotion. 'Stephen was very selfish, you know . . . I remember he left Portugal before her . . . I think he got bored having Edith around.'[38] Stephen returned to England, glad to be home. He told Susan that he hadn't liked New York this time: 'Nothing was right . . . It's so nice to be home. Beloved Wilsford. Why do I ever go away?'[39]

Chapter 25

Serious Pleasures

The only artists I have ever known who are personally delightful are bad artists. Good artists exist simply in what they make, and consequently are perfectly uninteresting in what they are. A great poet, a really great poet, is the most unpoetical of all creatures. But inferior poets are absolutely fascinating. The worse their rhymes are, the more picturesque they look. The mere fact of having published a book of second-rate sonnets makes a man quite irresistible. He lives the poetry he cannot write. The others write the poetry that they dare not realize.

— Oscar Wilde: *The Portrait of Dorian Gray*

THE Thomas Cook-controlled itinerary of Stephen's life continued, but he was becoming world-weary in a world all too evidently changing. It was easy to think that VE Day had not altered anything, that old lives could be picked up where they had left off. But new opinions and new ways had come with the late forties and early fifties: the Welfare State, the Cold War, Angry Young Men. The world had raced on, and Stephen had been left behind. Everywhere society was different. In London, the large Park Lane mansions had been demolished; huge chunks of the city were no longer recognizable after the bombing. What replaced it had little time for the antiquated ways and large retinues of servants. Many big country houses were now too expensive to run, and the National Trust came to the rescue of those that were not sold up. The very territory that he had inhabited was disappearing, and Stephen and his like became an endangered species. What Elizabeth Bowen had called 'the unwary civility of the old world, privilege, ease, grace', which had been a protective greenhouse for Stephen, had gone. Travel was but a temporary answer.

Stephen was back at Wilsford in the summer of 1951, house and garden so long neglected by their master. He spent those months resting, and reacquainting himself with peaceful Wiltshire life. But even that quiet county saw an invasion of glamour that autumn, for Cecil had at last persuaded Greta Garbo to come and stay at Reddish House: 'his greatest triumph'.[1] She had arrived at Southampton in mid-October, to be 'whisked away' to Broadchalke for a two-month stay. Stephen was let in on the secret, and it was thrilling for him to meet one of his all-time favourite film stars. When Cecil brought Garbo over to Wilsford, Stephen was quite overcome – and flattered when she admired his new blue Venetian blind hung on the landing wall. It was all too short a visit, however, so when he invited his own friends, Julian and Juliette Huxley, to stay for the second weekend in November, Stephen took the opportunity to arrange dinner at Reddish House so he could take in more of the actress himself.

The Huxleys arrived at midnight on the Friday, but Stephen 'had stayed up for us with a delicious champagne supper before the fire'. Huxley recalled the house as 'the embodiment of a fanciful dream . . . Was it perhaps part of the fantasy that he took us to dine with Cecil Beaton in his fine house, there to meet the fabulous Greta Garbo?' When Stephen and his guests arrived for dinner, they found Garbo 'looking as beautiful as in her haunting films, dressed merely in black slacks and sweater'. When Garbo learned of Huxley's profession, she sat at his feet and asked him 'in her deep, husky voice to tell her something interesting about animals'.[2] The biologist detailed the male-eating courtship of the praying-mantis, to Garbo's delight.

The fact that Stephen was not the centre of attention might well account for his own slightly acerbic reminiscence of his former idol. 'She was very lovable,' he recalled. 'We all simply loved her. But Tchelitchew thought she was a terrible bore. He said, "She's got a lovely face, lovely looks, but *elle est si bore, Mon Dieu, elle est si bore*!" She hadn't much to say. I took the Huxleys to dinner with her, and Julian Huxley was very struck by her intelligence. He thought her not imaginative, exactly, but . . . astute, and hard-headed – all different to what most people thought her.' Stephen added: 'It's very true when people laughed at her for wearing large goggles and enormous draperies over her head – because of course it meant everybody would look at her – nobody would've looked at her otherwise because she didn't use make-up. She was a home-town girl really,' Stephen concluded, although he did concede that Garbo had 'lovely hands – long, petal-like fingers'.[3]

*

Stephen began 1952 by renewing more old friendships. Lady Juliet Duff had a visit from him at Bulbridge House in Wilton, telling Cecil on 1 February that 'Stephen Tennant blew in the other afternoon, as fat as a pig & exuding gales of mad laughter. He was on his way to see Siegfried.'[4]

Elizabeth Bowen was one of the few friends who could still weather Stephen's caprice. She stayed at Wilsford in February, when Juliet Duff saw them again: 'I do like her so much,' she noted rather pointedly.[5] Stephen had Elizabeth sit for him, and the result, 'Elizabeth Bowen as seen by Modigliani',[6] was seized upon by Lady Juliet for her scrapbook.

Another attempt to pick up on an old friendship came with a series of letters and visits to and from Eddy Sackville-West. That month Stephen wrote to him, after a telephone call, 'You have a beautiful voice, Eddy – the voice of genius, I think. I want to make a sketch of you – your eyes are part of your voice – loaded with rich, timeless mysteries and poetic intimations.'[7] Sackville-West's biographer notes that this 'trowelling-on' of flattery was followed by another letter from the Queen's Hotel, where Stephen had gone for 'total peace and solitude' on 15 February: 'I wish you were here,' Stephen wrote, 'I long to draw a portrait of you.'[8]

Eddy Sackville-West, Vita's cousin, was a music critic, radio broadcaster and dilettante. He had bought Long Crichel House, near Wimborne, in 1945, where he lived with Raymond Mortimer and Eardley Knollys (described by Elizabeth Bowen as 'the Crichel Boys'), and Stephen had written to him in Venice in 1947, complaining that he never saw him. He finally managed to lure Eddy round to Wilsford in April 1952, for the first time since the legendary Wylie weekend of 1927. 'Do come soon again to see me please,' Stephen wrote after the visit. 'You enrich life for your friends. I have the deepest admiration for you, for your lovely gifts, and for the way you plan and carry out your life.'[9] Thus did Stephen attempt to snare new people into his web, and so eventually, by dint of his capriciousness, did he lose them.

There was another victim in Rosemary Olivier, who had known Stephen since their respective childhoods. Miss Olivier recalled staying one weekend at Wilsford in the late forties, with Peter Watson a fellow guest. 'Stephen went to bed early, and it was so cold in the house – there was only one fire – we had to sit huddled around it trying desperately to get warm.'[10] (Eardley Knollys remembers a similarly uncomfortable stay at Wilsford with Raymond Mortimer: 'very uncomfortable indeed and there was hardly anything to eat . . . it was very cold and we left early the next day.')[11]

These privations suffered by Stephen's guests might have been explained by post-war restrictions; not so Rosemary's subsequent experience. Stephen had promised to take her with him to Italy, a trip to which she was greatly looking forward. Together they went up to London and checked into the Hotel Russell, there to await the booking of tickets and passage. Rosemary had the room below Stephen's, and during the night heard him pacing the floor above. He was obviously in some sort of quandary, the nature of which did not transpire. Three times over the following day or so he put off their departure. Eventually he asked Rosemary to cancel the tickets. 'Stephen had decided to go and stay with Princess Bibesco in Paris,' recalls Miss Olivier, annoyance tempered now with subsequent experience of Stephen's whims. 'It was all called off.'[12]

And so in late March Stephen arrived in Paris – without Rosemary – to stay with Princess Bibesco on the Île St Louis. Marthe Bibesco was a near-legendary figure who had made much of a transient acquaintance with Proust, and had been a friend of the family since Stephen's childhood (her cousin, Prince Antoine Bibesco, had married Margot's daughter Elizabeth in 1919, and Stephen had been a page at the wedding at St Margaret's, Westminster, wearing a golden crown that made his head hurt). A Romanian with stunning red-gold hair, she was supposed to have been the object of the Crown Prince of Saxe-Weimar's affections before the Great War; for love of her green eyes, it was said, he had stopped the bombardment of Paris.

Stephen's correspondence with Princess Bibesco had become most fervent in the late thirties. He would call on her in Paris, and write from Marseilles, the subject of their letters being poetry – that of Bibesco's friend, Anna de Noailles, in particular. The Princess had sent Stephen a postcard of herself in March 1939, eyes heavy-lidded and sensual, features dark and very *fin de siècle*, and bearing the inscription, 'Marthe looking at Lascar and Stephen through *"une jalousie"*.'[13] They became closest in post-war years, however, when they met frequently in Paris and London, and on visits by the Princess to Wilsford. One of the reasons for Stephen's trip in 1952 was research for a book he planned to write on Anna de Noailles, and Marthe told him he should meet people who had known the poet in order to gather material from them.

Along with his afternoon visits to the Île St Louis, Stephen also saw Nancy Mitford in Paris. Nancy had seen Stephen on a fleeting visit to England the previous September. 'I am back here and pine for you,' Nancy had written to Stephen. 'Thank you for what you say about *The Blessing*. I am simply delighted you like it as I don't think you are an easy critic & I know you're not a great one for novels. It has been badly received by reviewers in England – comes out in America next month & is book of the month there so we shall see what they think. Not that I mind very much, except for the dollars!* Are you coming over at all? I don't think I shall go to England because I die so terribly of cold there . . . I suppose you weren't in Jamaica for the High Wind? [Stephen had escaped one of the Caribbean's most ferocious hurricanes of the century.] It must have been terrible & thrilling . . . Do write and tell me your plans.'14

When Stephen returned to England in September 1952, it was to new and exciting prospects for his artistic career. The Redfern Gallery in Cork Street had agreed to a one-man exhibition in January 1953. He could show all his new pictures, the designs for *Lascar*, and the work inspired by his travels of recent years. The gallery was quite small, but well situated, close to Bond Street in the heart of London's fine art district.

Stephen's second-ever exhibition – at the age of forty-six – opened on the first day of the New Year, 1953, with an introductory talk given by Stephen Spender. Some forty examples of his work were on display, with alluring titles like 'San Francisco', 'Tokyo Rose', and 'Sumptuous Nostalgia', which proclaimed their subject matter as well as any lengthy description could. But Spender's foreword to the exhibition catalogue encapsulated the appeal of Stephen's work: 'Among my most cherished possessions are letters from Stephen Tennant, on coloured writing paper, and with lettering inwreathed among drawings of plants and flowers, which combine the accuracy of an amateur botanist with the passion of someone who inhabits his own world of fantasy.'

He described the pictures on show as growing out of 'fragmentary writing: journals, letters, haunting lines of verse – this world is crowded with images suggested by poetic ideas; statues, ports, ships, sailors, dolphins, exotic brands of cigarettes, and Venice. It is a fervid, hot, sometimes overcrowded world, restored to its own kind of innocence, by flowers, trees, sea-shells, the sea. Just as Ronald Firbank, out of what seems extreme artifice, created his own peculiar vision of a paradise, so Stephen Tennant in these drawings creates the image of a unique personality.'15

The show ran until the end of January. It cannot have been widely attended after the afternoon private view on New Year's Day, but the satisfaction for Stephen was not the number of visitors, or the few

*In fact, *The Blessing* sold 'like the hottest of cakes' on both sides of the Atlantic.

paintings sold, but the knowledge that he was being taken seriously. That fact strengthened his resolve for the rest of the fifties, so much so that over the next five years he could boast a further four one-man shows of his work in London, New York, and Rome.

Stephen was in London for much of the autumn of 1952, visiting the British Museum and Library for *Lascar* researches,[*] drawing up new plans for Wilsford's embellishment, and going to the theatre. There he found Cecil's designs for *Quadrille* inspired, and told his friend so. However, relations between the two were soon to sour, a result of Stephen's increasingly changeable nature.

The paradoxes in Stephen's character seemed to heighten as he grew older. He loved to observe life; every little thing would be noted down, and described in journals and letters, and would come alive in his words, as essential experiences. Sitting alone in a public park on a summer's day, he would bask in hot sunshine and believe the world to be beneficent, on his side. It was an uninhibited joy in things – especially nature and natural phenomena – which one might find hard to reconcile with the underlying and burgeoning misanthropy in Stephen. This manifested itself in notes to himself such as '"There's nothing like a good hate" – Nan Hudson', or 'Chuck me without a qualm, Violet.' Perhaps he was less able to reconcile himself to the loss of youth and good looks (as Lady Juliet Duff had noted, Stephen had by now begun to expand in girth) than others. Stephen tried to harden himself to life by retreating from it and the demands of its society. In so doing he endangered almost every friendship he ever had.

Cecil had seen the vagaries of Stephen's volatile personality in operation on many occasions, and knew the victims – Sassoon, Rosamond Lehmann, Rosemary Olivier, Margaret Rutherford. He had seldom been on the receiving end himself, but that October, Stephen 'chucked' a lunch arrangement with Cecil. He should have known better. Cecil was not to be trifled with – he knew Stephen far too well – and in his letter of protest, Cecil decided it was time to tell Stephen a few home truths.

---

[*]Stephen's research for *Lascar* was nothing less than thorough, stretching even to a visit to a tattooist, a Professor Diamond, in the Old Caledonian Road back in 1940. Diamond had been so taken with Stephen's own fanciful designs for tattoos that he had traced some of them to use himself. Even now, there may be some wartime visitor in London unknowingly walking round with a Stephen Tennant design on his arm – or elsewhere. (In one chapter of *Lascar*, Manuel receives a rather painful tattoo on his bottom.) And on his last visit to Paris, Stephen had acquired *Les Tatouages du 'Milieu'* (1950), a comprehensive guide to the art which helped him with subsequent skin designs.

'My dear Stephen,' Beaton opened calmly enough, 'I don't want to appear unkind but I haven't been able to answer your messages during last week because I was hurt and angry at the appalling lack of consideration for others as exemplified by your sending, long after the appointed hour, a cursory message cancelling our arrangements. I remember many years ago your saying that you had absolutely no scruples about cutting or putting off at the last moment any social engagement, & I was slightly surprised at your offhandedness then, but circumstances have now changed so much that I doubt if you will find many people who would put up with such treatment today.

'We have been friends for many years – you have shown me many kindnesses – we have had some delightful times together – for which I am grateful. It is not a question of my "dropping you" now, but on several occasions in recent years you have shown me that your interests are only one-sided, & that everyone you see has to fit in with your wishes & plans. I am too overworked to risk downing tools whenever you are in the mood for a little diversion & to make arrangements which have to be cancelled because you are feeling tired. Most people have to go on with their plans once they have made them even if they are tired.

'I know nobody enjoys being told unpleasant things for their own good & I am not trying to be vindictive, but I think it is time one of your friends risked your displeasure by offering a little warning that without give & take one runs the risk of becoming lonely. It is for this reason that I have gone through the very unpleasant experience of writing you such a letter.

'I am rushing off to Paris on a business trip but will be down here again on the 25th – so if you feel like calling me then I'd be very pleased if you would come over & share the roast chicken which was neglected last week. Yours, Cecil.'[16]

Stephen's reply was apologetic; how could it be otherwise, if he were to keep one of his best and oldest friends? 'Dear Cecil . . . I was so sad to hurt you – and still feel very sad, & regretful – It was very rude of me – and I know I will never be invited again.'[17] But of course he was. Stephen's little-boy-lost charm and his plea for forgiveness could, like Cedric Hampton's, soften the most hardened of hearts.

Edith Lewis continued to be a close friend of Stephen's, but she too experienced his prevarications in the fifties. In late 1952 she was expecting him in New York, for a return visit to Acapulco, and she had sent Stephen the necessary forms and affidavits required for an extended stay in the United States; but, months later, there was still no sign of

Stephen stirring. It appears Edith's company was beginning to grate on Stephen, for he told Susan Lowndes Marques at the end of February, writing from the Queen's Hotel: 'Edith L. cables more happily now – she is a dear (but oh so tiresome! I can see you laughing!)'[18]

Perhaps he felt guilty at being off-hand with his friend, for Stephen wrote a gracious letter to Edith thanking her for all her financial help, and saying that she really couldn't afford to sponsor another trip to Florida they had planned for mid-March (which in fact did not transpire, as Edith could not leave New York). Edith replied on 29 May: 'How can you ever think of having "impoverished" me – when you have done nothing but enrich me in every possible way! . . . I hate to think of your being cut off from travel, when travel means so much to you – it feeds you as it does few other people . . . out of it you make beautiful works of art . . . Couldn't you, with $5,000, go out West to some of the places you want to see? I could spend that much without being "impoverished" at all. I would love to think of you exploring that Western country. Please think it over. Naturally I don't want anything that would be harmful for you – but would it be? I can't see how. I would like a few bright and beautiful things left in this dark world – not to see everything going into machine guns. Your last picture, in the Mexican shirt, I like best of all . . .'[19]

In August, Edith was still sure Stephen would arrive, but by the 19th it was obvious from the tone of his letters that he was 'reluctant to leave Wilsford', at which she didn't wonder. She was only grateful for Stephen's friendship. 'I feel that I have had the best life anyone with my limitations could possibly have. I have known you and Willa and that satisfies me . . .' She gave Stephen credit for having started her on a biography of Cather by 'urging it and urging it in your letters . . . You are like Prospero and Ariel combined.' Now she was the exhorter, saying Stephen must finish *Lascar* 'this summer. Please, Stephen, do it for her [Cather] . . . I feel that . . . it will bring her very close to you – and that another feeling will take the place of the sadness you feel now . . .'[20]

In spring 1954, the tantalus of travel beckoned Stephen again, but he pleaded a heavy bout of 'flu when Edith wrote enticingly on 16 March: 'Do you still want to go to Hawaii? . . . I suddenly remembered you had never taken up your passage home on the Holland–American line (1950!) . . . Rotterdam has now sent you the money. You also have credit with them for £25 . . .'[21] The passage would remain untaken. Stephen had made his last transatlantic trip. From the mid-fifties onwards, his tireless travel itinerary grew less ambitious, as age and accidie caught up with him. The prospect of roving the globe, although in theory always immensely attractive to Stephen, was no longer an essential part of his existence. He didn't like to be away from the comforting confines of Wilsford, or his Bloomsbury hotels. Like Des Esseintes, he preferred increasingly to stay at home and leave adventure to his imagination.

But there was always Paris, always full of friends awaiting his return. It was Stephen's home from home, glamorous, cultured, romantic – and not too far away to exhaust him. In July, he found a new travelling companion to accompany him. Richard Buckle was ten years Stephen's junior, the founder of *Ballet* magazine and then the dance critic for the *Observer*. He and Stephen had a fanatical admiration for the Ballets Russes in common, and in 1954 Buckle was busy trying to organize a major exhibition of the Diaghilev era. To this end, he was going to visit Boris Kochno, the master's friend and last collaborator.

Buckle, handsome and with a slight military bearing that belied his calling, remembers Stephen as still 'very striking in the fifties – very tall, although slightly portly', wearing 'pastel and pistachio-coloured suits'. He found his companion's presence very commanding, almost imperious, quite oblivious to the stares they attracted as they walked the streets together. 'He'd trained himself not to notice,' observes Buckle. 'His lips were always pursed – as though he were continually amused by some interior joke – self-mocking and assertive – and used to having his own way.'[22]

They arrived at the Hotel Raphael, Stephen's favoured Parisian hotel, described by Buckle as 'the sort of place where dukes stay when they come up from the country'. Stephen paid for Buckle's room, which turned out to be a rather small attic room, whilst he, Stephen, had a large first-floor suite. Buckle would have much preferred a better room in a more modest Left Bank establishment, but the Raphael it was: there was no arguing with Stephen. Together they visited Kochno at his flat on the rue Bleue. They chatted about old times, and Buckle and Kochno discussed plans for the exhibition. Stephen noted a fine portrait of Boris on the wall: 'Near it was a Beardsley "A Bachante"'.[23] Leaving his friend to do further ballet research, Stephen went off that evening to a party given by Coco Chanel, who had just launched her first post-war collection and was riding high on its success. Stephen had seen her back in the thirties, at Lady Mendl's, and to be invited to one of her parties now, as the fashion world once more looked to her for inspiration, was a great thrill. (Later, in the sixties, when Cecil was designing *Coco*, the musical production of the couturier's life, Beaton asked Stephen for his memories of Chanel. Within half an hour, Stephen had done a brilliant ink sketch which he delivered, still wet, to Cecil at Reddish.)

The next day, rejoining Dicky Buckle, Stephen announced that they would have a 'perfect luncheon' together at Fouquet's. It would be his treat, and he would draw on Cather's legacy to pay for it. Together they drove to the Chase Bank on the rue Cambon. 'We were ushered by bowing officials down porphyry steps, through gilded gates, into a Pharaoh's tomb. "Now," said the most tail-coated director, "I have my key here. If Monsieur will give himself the trouble to produce his key we shall open the two locks together." "Oh, how silly I am!" exclaimed Stephen, cooing with self-mockery, "I've left mine at Wilsford." We lunched at Fouquet's all the same. The taxi-driver who took us there went too fast for Stephen's liking. "*Pas si vite, s'il vous plaît!*" The man let out a stream of oaths. Not for nothing had Stephen ruled the waterfront. "*Je vous le répéte,*" he said in a voice of authority, "*NOUS NE SOMMES*

PAS PRESSÉS!" Silence. Nodding at me, Stephen remarked, "Never let them have the last word." '[24]

The coda to Stephen's friendship with Richard Buckle came when they had returned to London. Stephen asked if he could design the poster to advertise the Diaghilev exhibition, which was to open in Edinburgh in 1955. Buckle was living in Covent Garden at the time, and recalls that Stephen visited him frequently – rather too frequently, as the writer was trying to finalize arrangements for the exhibition, for which Stephen lent Buckle his own Tchelitchews – designs for *Ode*, and a study of Serge Lifar. Eventually Stephen delivered his design, which Buckle realized was too fanciful to use to publicize the show. He made his excuses and tactfully turned it down. In October Stephen wrote to him asking for his design back: 'I know you don't care much for my work; never mind . . . You've hurt me terribly about the Edin. poster.'[25]

Stephen sought the glamour of Cannes – 'that sexiest of towns . . . invented for pleasure' – as Ned Rorem saw it a year later.[26] He lodged at the Villa des Délices on the rue d'Antibes, and expected to stay there awhile, and perhaps go on to explore the Greek islands, but as Edith pointed out with maternal concern, 'You too are sometimes uncomfortable on boats.'[27] So Stephen went back to Wilsford, but briefly, before Paris summoned him once more. 'Oh good, I long for you,' wrote Nancy when she heard he was coming back. 'I don't know if Paris is gay because I never leave my 4 walls or hardly, but it's looking very pretty. Might Boris not put you in touch with all these *louche* gentlemen? (I feel they must be *louche*). Funnily enough I don't know any of them. I adored your 16 letters, which I found on getting home from a fitting, a lovely heap of pink envelopes & the insides will have to be framed . . . Now do ring me up as soon as you arrive & keep the number as I refuse to be in the book . . . P.S. Are you now the uncle of the Queen of England? Don't have your head cut off I beg.'[28] (Stephen's nephew Colin was being seen about town with Princess Margaret, which gave rise to certain tabloid rumours.)

Stephen stayed in Paris until just before Christmas, coming home for the festive season – and to terrible storms across the country. Stephen decided to invite himself to the Tennant family Christmas at Glen that year. Engaging the services of a chauffeur, he was driven up to Scotland in time to join Lord Glenconner and his family for Christmas Eve. His niece Pauline was there too, with her new husband, Euan Graham. As they were newly married Christopher gave the couple one of the best rooms, the Oak room. 'I think that's what caused the trouble,' recalls Pauline.

Stephen had to have one of the smaller rooms, one which he had had as a child, and which Christopher thought he might have preferred anyhow. Not a bit of it. Stephen thought he had been given an inferior room, and when the time came for him to distribute his Christmas presents, he called the family to his room for his 'levée' and present-giving, pointed to Pauline and said: 'You will know what I mean – this chill Scottish air is very bad for me.' He then ordered his bags to be packed, the chauffeur summoned – 'awful for him because he thought he was going to spend Christmas in Scotland' – and off they went. 'The last we heard was that they had to stop the night in an hotel in Leeds,' remembers Pauline.[29]

(A visit to Glen the following year had Stephen in a happier mood, being taken to tea at Bowhill, the home of the Duke of Buccleuch. Arriving in a rather *outré* suit, Stephen made himself at home with the Duchess, chatting happily away, telling her he would hold her handbag for her, it being a nuisance whilst she was seeing to things. Then the imposing figure of the Duke appeared. Stephen enquired sociably, 'What have you been doing today?' 'I've been selecting police constables', said the Duke, in his gruffest voice. 'Oh, what a lovely job!' said Stephen.)[30]

In the New Year the ever-patient Edith was still expecting Stephen in New York, if only to attend a new exhibition of his work that was being arranged at the Alexander Iolas gallery there. Stephen had written to Cecil in December, to enlist his help in setting up an American show of his work. Beaton had told him that having had a London show would help him to get one in New York. 'Pavlik wrote me that if Osbert asked Edwin Hewitt to give me a show there, he would certainly do so – and I know your name, your Celebrity is quite as great as Osbert's, if not greater – your influence would most certainly gain me a show . . . I think if I could have a little show after Christmas in N.Y. – it would cheer me up – & help to put me on the map.'[31]

Few people would so unashamedly use flattery as did Stephen. For few people would it work so well. Through both Beaton's and Tchelitchew's machinations, Iolas was persuaded to show Stephen's work. A Greek, he was a former ballet dancer who had sponsored the wartime refugee surrealists in the States, and had helped establish Max Ernst's post-war reputation in New York. He had had galleries in Paris, Geneva and Milan, but finances meant his sole remaining gallery was now the modest space he had at 46 East 57th Street, where, amongst others, he had shown Tchelitchew's work.

Stephen's first American show was a lavish affair, to judge from the brochure Iolas produced (subsidized by the artist). A full-coloured *Lascar* illustration was splashed across the 14 x 12 inch cover, with a large reproduction of a Beaton photo of Stephen inside, naked to the waist, with his hands posed aesthetically across his face. Underneath was the legend: 'Ballet – Stephen Tennant, as Echo, in his Ballet, "The Mirage and the Echo". Music by Debussy' – another of Stephen's flights of fancy. Inside were reproduced pages from Stephen's 1944 diary, his thoughts on *Wuthering Heights*, and two later photographs of Stephen, taken in the Wilsford garden in 1952, a rather more chubby chap, in Hawaiian shirt and short shorts, standing by yet another new fountain. The text alongside was a biographical sketch by way of an introduction,[*] supplied by the artist, and was, as the natives would say, something else. It treats the reader to Stephen's full provenance, from *La Belle Pamela*, to Aunt Margot, and the 'Three Graces' Sargent portrait (the latter being familiar to New Yorkers as it hung in the Metropolitan Museum). 'Stephen Tennant's brother is Lord Glenconner, who inherited the Tennant Collection [actually sold across the Atlantic before the first war] and is deeply interested in the arts. Lord Glenconner is also interested in business, and is a Director of Imperial Chemical Industries.'[32]

It was all calculated to appeal to a presumed American love of English history and aristocracy; Stephen was doing the hard sell. The piece concluded with a list of the famous people who owned pictures by him: Julian Huxley, Cecil Beaton, Stephen Spender, Elizabeth Bowen *et al.*; the implication being that any prospective purchaser would be exhibiting extreme good taste were he or she to buy likewise. A tantalizing synopsis of *Lascar* was also included for good measure, guaranteed to whet the reader's appetite 'with its bravura and tragic ecstasy' which 'gleams like a black pearl or fire opal, brimming with night'. The author had 'lived in Marseilles for considerable periods and has made researches on the old Marseilles during an eight months period of reading in the British Museum Reading Room before completing this very ambitious work',[34] it claimed. This intimation that *Lascar* was actually finished had an editor at Alfred Knopf writing eagerly to Edith Lewis, asking if they might see the manuscript. But Mr William Koshland never saw it, or even parts of it,

---

[*]There had been a plan for Tennessee Williams to write the introduction – Stephen had met him on his last visit to the States – but he politely refused. 'He says he knows nothing about art and paintings in particular,' reported Mr Rasponi, an associate of Iolas', 'that he would feel foolish and exceedingly self-conscious about it. I don't see any point in insisting,' he added. 'I feel Cecil would be an excellent choice and in many ways, his name for an art exhibit would mean infinitely more than Williams' who is known as a dramatist of dingy, back-alley problems . . .'[33]

for despite pleas from Edith, from Iolas, and others, Stephen refused – at the last minute – to come and publicize his show in person.* It opened on 25 April, and was moderately well attended. Edith bought one picture, a painting of a flight of doves, and others sold quite steadily. Only a dozen were left at the gallery by mid-May.

Edith pleaded with Stephen to pull himself 'out of this low state of health and feeling so tired all the time . . . do come over and go to Acapulco . . . the important thing is for you to get back a feeling of health and well-being and unused energy.'[36] Edith, even at that distance, knew Stephen had sunk back into the old trap of assuming the protective mantle of illness, wherein he allowed himself to think ill, and therefore be ill.

A newcomer to Wilsford-cum-Lake could have explained the trouble to Edith and Alexander Iolas. Dr Tony Davis moved to Wilsford in 1953, and came to know Stephen, and his problems, very well. He first called on him socially, when the doctor's first glimpse of Stephen was quite extraordinary. 'He was reclining on a sumptuous bed, reeking of perfume, and was dressed in a nightdress with ribbons in his hair . . . My wife couldn't believe it when I went back and told her about him. "What did you say?" "I said 'Hello' as normally as possible."'†[37]

Evidently Dr Davis' bedside manner impressed Stephen, for he asked the doctor to call on him regularly, in a professional capacity. Dr Davis consulted with Lord Glenconner, telling Stephen's brother that such frequent attention would not come cheaply. 'But he replied that anything that might keep Stephen out of an even more expensive psychiatric home was worth it.' Dr Davis took to seeing Stephen two or three times a week, as Stephen wished. His diagnosis was 'acute depression', but there was little he could prescribe to treat it (Stephen was already seeing a Harley Street psychiatrist in London). What Stephen wanted, Dr Davis soon saw, was someone to whom he could talk openly about his depression. 'I think he assumed I knew about his lack of any personal relationships,' observes

---

*Mr Rasponi had written to Stephen on 8 April in a last-minute attempt to persuade him to come over. '93 per cent of the success of your exhibit and the publicity hinges on your being here,' he told the artist, and tried to alert Stephen to the pressures of the modern art market. 'It's such a very personal business and your presence is a MUST . . . Mr Mann of the Iolas Gallery called this morning to say you might be going to Florence to visit Bernard Berenson. Nothing is more stimulating than a visit with B.B. but couldn't you put it off until June after your visit to the United States?'[35]

†A subsequent visitor found Stephen wearing just a gold shirt, lying in a cot in one of the nursery rooms at the top of the house. To Freud, such 'regression' of the libido to 'infantile wishes' was the 'almost inevitable' result of 'persistent rebellion against the real world'.[38]

the doctor, 'and that [lack] was probably the cause of it all . . . It was very sad, really.'

But Dr Davis' friendship with Stephen was not always so morose or introspective. Stephen had frequent periods of high spirits. One afternoon he invited the Davises over for tea; the doctor said he had friends staying, but Stephen insisted they come, too. 'Louis took us out round to the "Italian garden",' Dr Davis recalls – 'all surrounded by palms. We'd been there about twenty minutes or so, and there was no sign of our host appearing, when we heard a loud "coo-eee!" from above. We all looked up, and there was Stephen, in tight pink shorts, perched up high in a tree! He came down and was perfectly charming as we had tea, and remarked, "Isn't this lovely? So Wiltshire, don't you think?" Anything less like Wiltshire – the garden with its lizards and palm-trees – was hard to imagine!'[39]

Chapter 26

Genius Manqué

If you were born extremely rich but uninterested in power or making money, what is there to drive you on? If nevertheless you write or draw or compose, nothing much less than genius will get you taken seriously – the rich man's well-advertised difficulty in gaining the Kingdom of Heaven is child's play by the side of his trying to make the Republic of Letters.

— Philip Purser: *The Extraordinary Worlds of Edward James*

IN July 1955 Stephen sent a letter on pink notepaper from his hotel in Bloomsbury, round to the Palace Theatre, Shaftesbury Avenue. It was addressed to the star of the production of *King Lear* playing there, John Gielgud. With the letter was enclosed Stephen's play, *Madame is Resting*, which he hoped Gielgud would consider. 'I thought the play . . . was no good,' Sir John recalls, 'but he came across more than once to my dressing-room full of enthusiasm and flattery.' For once, Stephen's charm fell upon stony ground. 'I took a great dislike to him, I'm afraid. He had no trace of his much supposed good looks: his hair was dyed and he was very flabby,' observes the actor. 'His beauty and charm . . . had certainly left him by the time I met him.'[1] That Stephen knew his looks were not what they were is debatable; he certainly continued to act as though he were a man of thirty as he approached his fiftieth year. He did look younger than his age, but underneath the foundation and the peroxide, the cracks were beginning to show.

Despite long periods in bed, especially in cold weather, the New Year found Stephen busy on a new idea he had to publicize his work. He had a full-colour poster of one of his best *Lascar* pieces printed, to send off to friends. John Lehmann, Rosamond's brother, then editor of the *London Magazine*, was one surprised recipient. 'How very nice to hear from you again,' he told Stephen on 8 March, thanking him for the poster and the copy of Stephen's 'A Reassessment of Poetry'. 'I was deeply moved by this, and feel you understand what poetry is really about in a way that is rare nowadays . . . [but] alas I have such a long list of critical . . . articles waiting for publication that I do not think I can find space for it in the L. Mag before the book comes out: I look forward to that very much . . .'[2]

While Stephen failed that spring to get his literary work published, he did manage to secure another exhibition, this time in Rome (probably through Tchelitchew, who was spending a great deal of time in the city). A small gallery, the Sagittarius had a ten-day show of Stephen's 'Abstract Designs', the predominant theme of which was Mexico and Hawaii; Polynesian faces taking the place of lascars'. It ran from 1–10 April, and Stephen's work sold successfully. This prompted him to write an essay on abstract art, 'a revelation' to Edith. 'I wish everyone who hates the work of the new men would read it – it would disarm the bitterest foe . . . Are you having a gay time in Paris, dear Stephen?' she added. 'Are the horse chestnuts in bloom . . . ?'[3]

The spring spikes of the horse chestnuts did indeed bloom for Stephen, as did the rest of Paris. He stayed late into summer, seeing Nancy, and Pavel Tchelitchew, with whom he spent a pleasant evening that July. The painter was busy arranging his show at the Galerie Rive Gauche, on Gertrude Stein's old stamping-ground, the rue de Fleurus. His work had by now evolved into strange and delicate abstractions, of vein-like, luminous lines: 'I am doing a too serious work for many to be popular, and frankly, understood . . .' Pavlik told Stephen in a letter on 2 August.[4] It was the last time Stephen would see the charismatic Russian; in November Tchelitchew sent him an invitation to the *vernissage* of his exhibition (which opened on the 6th, and which Stephen was unable to attend), with the inscription, 'Dear Stephen, I miss you.' On 1 August the following year, Tchelitchew died in Rome.

Stephen was emboldened by his interpretation of 'abstract' art, which in reality was a playful attempt to juggle colour and shape ('An Abstract Drawing to amuse you!' he later announced to Hugo Vickers, only having to concede at the bottom of his sketch: 'It keeps being an Ordinary Picture'),[5] enough to launch himself into another heavy session of painting. The result – and the reason why he could not attend Pavlik's Parisian private view – was a new London exhibition.

The new Gallery One in D'Arblay Street, Soho, had been started by Victor Musgrave, whose wife, Ida Kar, was a talented photographer and had done one or two photo-sessions with Stephen. The show Musgrove gave of Stephen's work that autumn garnered the most attention yet – since the war, at least – for the artist and his work. Stephen Spender ran a long piece in *Encounter*, which combined Colin MacInnes' essay on meeting Stephen during the war with a selection of Tennant pictures printed full-page in the magazine. Added to this, he once again made the diary pages of the national press. The *News of the World*, no less, ran a piece:

'Question: How many celebrities can be crowded into a given area? Answer: No more (I should think) than artist *Stephen Tennant*, brother of Lord Glenconner, packed into a tiny Soho gallery for a private view of an exhibition of his drawings and designs.' The exhibition was opened on 2 November by Lady Juliet Duff, and Stephen Spender once more gave 'a few introductory words'. At this glittering occasion, the paper's columnist noted many famous faces. 'As I stood talking to *Loelia, Duchess of Westminster*, I was so hemmed in by notabilities that there was barely room to raise a champagne glass. *Lady Cynthia Asquith* and *Lady Aberconway* were busy buying a picture each. Poet *Stephen Spender* and *Lady Juliet Duff*, daughter of the fourth Earl of Lonsdale, were lavishing praise in short speeches . . . There was *Princess Bibesco*, a Roumanian who has become one of France's great literary figures, an astonishingly young-looking grandmother. And looking more like a successful businessman than an author and playwright, there was *Christopher Hassall*,* who composed the lyrics for some of Ivor Novello's most popular shows. At a guess, there were about 150 other folk. It was quite a party.'[6] So much so that the *Evening Standard* noted that the artist himself was crowded out: 'It was impossible to cram one more person inside. "I'm sorry I didn't hear the speeches",' Stephen told their reporter when he had finally pushed his way in.[7]

Art critic David Sylvester reviewed the show for the *Listener*. 'What is it that enables him to invest with such glamour that which in other hands would become boring and vulgar?' he asked of Stephen's work. 'Tennant gets away with the unsuitable because it never occurs to him to ask whether it is suitable, and that he has no such doubts because his tastes are his own and sure and precise.'[8] Doubts were raised, however, by *The Times*. In a piece headed 'Pleasures of Scent', it remarked: 'What is one to do about an artist like Mr Stephen Tennant? Go to his exhibition . . . with a few of the usual standards and be bored in consequence? He lays himself so blandly open to criticism on that score that it would be almost ungentlemanly to advance it as a legitimate cause of complaint.'

---

*Christopher Hassall, composer, poet, and lover of Ivor Novello, had met Stephen through their mutual friend, Laurence Whistler.

The reviewer went on to wonder, 'Is the alternative to sweep oneself from one complicated drawing to another in the general atmosphere of tinsel glamour and pretend not to notice that one would reject this jaded romancing out of hand if it were presented between the covers of a paper-backed novelette?' The line is clearly the Emperor's New Clothes. 'This, it is fair to say, would at least be to fall in with the artist's intentions. Mr Tennant, in his sophisticated way, has allowed himself to indulge in the unalloyed pleasures of a ripe, vulgar, shop-soiled sentimentality. He crowds into his drawings every fragmentary evocation he can lay his hands on of the twentieth century's dream of escape into romance, from moonrise over Hawaii to the glitter of the footlights. In so far as these are also the stock-in-trade of the travel brochure and the cinema poster he is able here and there to touch the springs of a genuine popular emotion. But it is altogether more questionable how far this has been translated into an art.'[9]

Whereas critics a decade later might have leapt on Stephen's work, in the Pop Art atmosphere of striking at – through that 'popular emotion' – basic aesthetic tenets, *The Times* could not see beyond the strict parameters of traditional taste. Even Stephen's exhibitor, Victor Musgrave, subsequently wrote of him: 'His unfashionable, obsessive, anachronistic world seems as if it could only have been created a few decades ago.'[10] (Art historian Timothy Prus observes that Musgrave felt a certain resentment towards an artist who arrived at a gallery in the depths of Bohemian Soho in a Rolls-Royce.)

Such were modern attitudes to Stephen. For friends such as Joe Ackerley, this denial of success because of an accident of birth – and the accidie that had overtaken Stephen – was very sad. Ackerley's friend, James Kirkup,[*] noted that he 'always spoke of Tennant with pride and affection, and wished he were better known. He would quote Robert Bridges' poem, "Low Barometer": "Tenants unknown/Assert their squalid lease of sin" . . . but that was just another example of Joe's macabre black humour.'[11]

Ackerley visited Stephen at Wilsford on a number of occasions, one of which saw his dog, the much-pampered Queenie, foul Stephen's white carpet. Stephen was not best pleased, but with Ackerley, it was a question of 'love me, love my dog', and he in turn took umbrage. As with all Stephen's friends, his attitude to the latters' own eccentricities was a

---

[*]James Kirkup (1923–), poet, translator, and novelist, was the cause of the first prosecution for blasphemous libel in fifty years when his poem 'The love that dares speak its name' was published in *Gay News* in 1977.

mixture of amusement, tolerance, and exasperation. In 1961, writing to Geoffrey Gorer about his book *We Think the World of You*, Ackerley noted that a publisher had complained of the pale pink typewriting on his manuscript, which made it hard to read, 'as if to imply I was a sort of pansy Stephen Tennant who preferred pale pink typewriting to any other, instead of being reduced to such extreme economies by poverty'.[12] Ackerley's biographer, Peter Parker, observes that 'I would guess that, ascetic and impoverished himself, Ackerley found Tennant's combination of aestheticism and unearned income rather galling.'[13]

The intricate arrangements made for Stephen's second American exhibition in December 1957 were carried out via a long correspondence between the artist and David Mann, the gallery director who had helped organize the Alexander Iolas show and had now started his own gallery, the Bodley, at 223 East 60th Street, New York. He had become a close friend of Stephen's, and had come over to England in June to stay at Wilsford, where they discussed the show. On 3 September Mann wrote: 'As you know, all was arranged with your brother for the show at Christmas and photographs were supposed to be coming this week. I hope that they are already on their way, as I must start on publicity at once . . .'[14] Mr Mann, should he have had psychic gifts of precognition, might never have embarked on his course. Arranging an art exhibition when artist and exhibitor are on opposite sides of the Atlantic was difficult enough; but when the artist was Stephen Tennant, things could, and did, become impossible.

Mann told Stephen in his letter that he had persuaded American *Vogue* to run some of Stephen's work, in colour, in their December issue. Yet Stephen's sluggish response was endangering this valuable exposition. 'It occurs to me that perhaps you do not wish to do the show,' Mann was driven to comment. 'I assure you it will not in any way alter the affectionate regard in which I hold you.'[15] The plan was for Stephen to go to New York, both to publicize the exhibition, and to see old friends like Edith Lewis. Lord Glenconner wrote to Stephen's pre-war friend, Edelgi Dinshaw, now in New York, telling him that Stephen had had 'a neurasthenic illness' over the past couple of months, but was now much better and eager for the show to take place. Christopher noted that Stephen's doctor thought him well enough to travel, but hoped that Dinshaw would take care of him whilst his brother was in New York, 'and perhaps . . . give him the help and encouragement which he may need . . .'[16]

Stephen proposed that Antony Armstrong-Jones should do the new press photographs; Christopher arranged this, but when David Mann received the prints, he thought that they didn't 'convey one ounce of flesh or charm you have . . . You look like a country squire and not the Artist and Poet you so undoubtedly are . . .' Mann's publicity director, Patrick O'Higgins, suggested that Stephen 'go to the London office of *Vogue* and *Harper's Bazaar*, both, and have yourself photographed by their man'.[17]

There were problems too with the actual work. Mr O'Higgins told Mann he couldn't take the *Lascar* pieces to the magazines for illustration, as they had been used before and were too distinctive to reprint for publicity. 'Patrick also suggested "Girls and the World" might be fun, but by all means rush on to me any Flowers or Theatre pieces you may have, also please try to send paintings that are in fresher condition, as the ones you sent were very fragmentary (two of them) and rather wrinkled . . .' David Mann added that he'd had 'a nice talk' with Edith Lewis, who had been ill and had undergone a series of operations. 'She sends her love and the poor dear thought that you were arriving in New York today . . .'[18] Not then, nor ever again, had they but known it.*

Large posters were printed, a full-colour 'Stephen Tennant' in the centre, with a large white border in which were set some of Stephen's favourite quotations. The poster proudly proclaimed that 'The Exhibition will be opened on 5th December 1957 at 4 o'clock by MRS MENUHIN – Diana Gould.' But David Mann wrote on 4 November that he had spoken to Mrs Menuhin, 'and she was very sweet about you. She said, however, that she hasn't heard from you, except for a cable on the boat . . . also she does not know whether she will be in New York during the first week in December, but she will see your show.' Mann was now in a state of despair. 'I still have no press release . . . I know this is a chore but it is part of the job we have to do, so please get along.' A mailing list was necessary. 'The various names you have included in your letters to me are very exciting, but sometimes as they are penned in as P.S.'s they are difficult to read.'[19]

So Stephen remained resolutely at home, while Mann beavered bravely away to get his show up on time, hanging the thirty-odd pictures himself. Diana Menuhin, wife of Yehudi, and a former Ballets Russes dancer, turned up. 'I went along to one of those hundreds of tiny galleries off Park Avenue, and I couldn't think what I would say about his strange paintings, which seemed so different to all the modern work that was

---

*Stephen was even sent an 'extended credit' privileges card for the Sheraton Hotels, giving his address as 570 Park Avenue. The card was still in his white suitcase, unsigned, thirty years later.

being shown at that time. But when I got to the gallery at the appointed time, there was only one other person there, so I asked the gallery owner to let me off.' The other person happened to be Madame Felia Doubrovska, a Russian-American with whom Diana had danced before the war: 'I was very surprised that she knew Stephen.'[20] Later, talking to Hugo Vickers about Cecil's 'deep love for fame', Stephen commented, 'Success was his fairy wand! When I told him that in New York, I'd met Felia Doubrovska, he said: "Failure, did you say? How awful!"'[21]

The anecdote points up the reason why Stephen wasn't there for his private view; he too was afraid of failure, of putting himself on show, exposing himself to public criticism. He liked the kudos of a one-man show, but held back from it too. Stephen remembered what Rex had said to him: why didn't he try harder, was it because he was afraid he wouldn't be good enough? 'Yes,' answered Stephen, 'I suppose it is.'[22] He was the true English amateur, who could not make Art all-important. On 14 December Stephen wrote to Susan Lowndes Marques: '. . . Here I love to give the children parties & fireworks & fun; & ordinary life seems nicer than Art, somehow.'[23]

However, such post-mortems did David Mann no good. 'Bodley Gallery. Jan 11th 1958 . . . It is so long since I last heard from you that I feared you might be ill again. But yesterday I had word from Zachary Scott who said he had seen you in London and that you were fine . . .' Mann's letter was full of implied reproach. 'Your lovely show is down . . . I have sent all the work back to Francis Leggatt.' His report was couched optimistically: 'Many people saw your work, and I have some lovely messages for you from an actor, Tony Selwart, who met you through Johanna Hirth . . . Farley Granger the movie star was in and oh so many nice people . . . I was a bit discouraged by the illness which kept you away [read: 'How come Zachary Scott saw you on the town?'] as again we missed the opportunity of having a great success in sales as well as esteem . . . I must see some of your flower works that Spender writes of. You did not send a single one across . . .'[24]

Stephen was in London intermittently before and after Christmas, when he picked up his old friend Angela Thirkell for lunch at the Carlton Grill. She was impressed by Stephen's new green Rolls-Royce, and found him 'always affectionate with the three generation background'.[25] Stephen was as fond of expensive accessories as ever he was; on 10 January he took delivery of a new evening suit from the

Savile Row tailors Anderson and Shepherd* (a departure from the usual Tennant family outfitters, Lesley & Roberts). They supplied a beautiful midnight blue wool suit, with moiré silk shawl lapels. The double-breasted jacket and capacious trousers indicate how large Stephen had grown: his waist now measured thirty-eight inches. Years of eating rich food and a great deal of sweets had transformed him from the slender twenty-year-old into a rather rotund man in his fifties.

The following months brought sadness: Lucy Ellis, Pavel Tche-litchew, Peter Watson all died that year. Stephen's old set was slipping away fast; even Cecil was off in Japan with his new chum, Truman Capote. Stephen longed to travel again, but something within curbed the urge.

Evidently the combination of loss and ennui led Stephen back into illness. Early in 1958 he was suffering from 'neurasthenia and nervous exhaustion', and was being treated with insulin again. Despite this, he still planned to go to New York, even telling Laurence Whistler that he had been given a flat there, and went as far as having stationery printed with his New York address. 'I may go there quite soon – it's very sunny there in May,' he told Whistler, writing his letter by the river in Salisbury's Cathedral Close. 'Misty sun & meadows & willows make the afternoon paradise. Beside me is a big bushel of poems I've written, gay & wistful and Romantic and Lyrical.'[26] His hope was still for publication. 'I'm revising 15 years of Nature poems – some are very beautiful,' he announced. '*Encounter* is giving my poetry in June, I think. Do please tell me your opinion. I think I shall be famous, Laurie, when these poems are out in the world . . . I love your poems – and I love mine also. Occupied as you are – now [Laurence was at work on a book about Rex's life and art] these lines will move you – "Ah, sweet, unfortunate Memory, pity me! Give me release – from too much crowdy joy!"'[27]

Two highly contrasting views of Stephen Tennant in the nineteen-fifties come from the writer Caroline Blackwood and the artist Michael Wishart, both of whom first encountered Stephen when he paid a visit to Combe Priory, Dorset, where Lady Caroline lived with her first husband, the artist Lucian Freud. Wishart describes his first glimpse of Stephen in his elegant autobiography, *High Diver*: 'He arrived at the priory on the arm of a chauffeur, enveloped in Thai silk and a cloud of wild musk. In

*They also supplied Stephen with his favourite sheepskin slippers, almost his only footwear in later years, when he wore them with the additional support of long ribbons, one pink and one blue, tied like a ballerina's.

each hand he held an orange and a lemon, made of soap. Stephen's unique beauty still hung around him like an old-timer at the stage door, hoping for employment . . . To call Stephen affected would be like calling an acrobat a show-off, or a golden pheasant vulgar.'[28]

'By being himself in an age of pervasive uniformity,' Wishart observed, 'Stephen is outstanding: yet no one is more reticent, often eremitic.' But for Caroline Blackwood, the romantic notion of Stephen as the hermit-aesthete cut no ice. 'Stephen Tennant was just an eccentric gay who didn't really do anything' is her opinion. 'He was highly narcissistic – really quite boring. It's only because of his background that anyone took any notice of him – if he weren't upper-class, no one would've cared . . .' She remembered that first visit, too. 'He looked at our house and said how wonderful it would be with stones around it, leaves in the corners, how divine it would look and so on. Of course that was all very amusing,' she conceded, 'but it becomes rather a bore after a while. He had a tremendous egocentricity. He wrote endless letters to Lucian, and they were all the same. In the end Lucian didn't bother to open them. Of course he only wrote if you didn't write back. If you did, he lost interest. Quite frankly, I thought him a semi-psychotic personality – all that writing around the edge of the page – it indicates a mind that can't contain itself . . .'[29]

Yet when Michael Wishart was invited to Wilsford, he was 'always impressed by the variety of his erudition . . . even while talking, Stephen draws. Page after page is traced in coloured inks with tattooed sailors, Greta Garbo, bordellos, petals, extinct cigarette card heroes.' To Wishart, Stephen resembled a rainbow, 'exquisite and seldom seen . . . the most loyal of friends to those who can penetrate the barriers of his irregular discernment'. When the Freuds called, Caroline recalled that 'we wouldn't even get a cup of tea . . . He was always pretending that champagne was about to arrive, and it never did. He was incapable of hospitality – his wretched housekeeper would open the door to you, and you'd know she wasn't being paid. I think he used his charm on them to make them think how wonderful it was to work for him – if they didn't know he was part of this great family, they'd never have stayed.' (Lucien Freud remembered Stephen more kindly, perhaps: 'I greatly admired him,'[30] he said, and as if to prove it, remained one of the few people able to quote from Stephen's verse by heart.)

Caroline Blackwood admitted: 'I disliked him, I think, looking back. I hated his stinginess, his determination not to spend a cent on anything or anyone . . . The gold-dust in his hair, and on the gravel-path too – which the rain rather spoilt. The bath full of leaves and stones and grass. To me, Stephen Tennant was just an exhibitionist. There was nothing behind it all – no art, or anything.' The comparison illustrates just how different the phenomenon of Stephen Tennant could appear. Susan Lowndes Marques comments that he was 'a chameleon, changing his skin to suit his surroundings'.[31] Diametrically opposed to Caroline Blackwood's opinion might be placed Edith Lewis's, who warned Stephen in April that year: 'Oh dear! In some ways you are so like Shelley, Stephen. With his angelic nature, he had no prejudices against any human being.'[32]

Chapter 27

'The Last Professional Beauty'

'I wish I could love,' cried Dorian Gray with a deep note of pathos in his voice. 'But I seem to have lost the passion and forgotten the desire. I am too much concentrated on myself. My own personality has become a burden to me. I want to escape, to go away, to forget.'

— Oscar Wilde: *The Portrait of Dorian Gray*

SO life continued at Wilsford Manor, as the seasons passed over Stephen, his house and garden, the whole becoming overgrown and submerged into the sleepiness of the Wiltshire valley. Fewer people came to stay, or even to visit its incumbent. Only occasionally would glamorous figures from the past slide into view again. In August Stephen visited Barbara Hutton at a clinic in East Grinstead, where she was having corrective plastic surgery. Her surgeon, Sir Hector Archibald McIndoe, was renowned for his work on movie stars and royalty alike. Stephen considered having 'a few stitches put in', but decided his natural beauty was still evident enough not to warrant it. He would cradle his face in his hands and announce, 'I'm still beautiful, aren't I?'[1]

He was still good-looking. Those years of rest and 'preparations' retained a youthful glow on a fuller face. Stephen's eyes still twinkled blue, although to the more observant there was sadness in their depths too. He had grown fatter, but his height and bearing helped him carry the extra weight regally; he never moved with anything less than grace and poise. His hair, only a little thinner, was yet longer, and going through an auburn stage – a more suitable colour for his age, Stephen thought, than the brassy blond he had been. Not for nothing had Osbert Sitwell declared him 'the last professional beauty'.[2] And Stephen's wardrobe, never conventional, now consisted of quite bright colours; a mustard yellow sports jacket specially made in Palm Beach was worn fashionably with baggy shorts and sandals. The long camel-hair coat he'd bought in

337

New York in 1935 still exuded American appeal, whilst his loudly patterned summer shirts might have put a Texan tourist to shame.

Nevertheless, beneath the outward signs of reclusive meditation – Stephen's newly-assumed 'visionary poet' role – turbulent waters still flowed. By 1959, things had begun to get on top of him again; as with many depressives, the condition's remissions never seemed to last long, and each attack grew in intensity. Once more that autumn, Stephen's doctors had recourse to the drastic treatment of electro-convulsive therapy. The awfulness was bravely borne, and Stephen was back at Wilsford for a long winter, under the care of Louis and Flora Ford.

The Fords had been at Wilsford for as long as they and their master could remember. Louis had been Pamela's coachman, and had married a local girl, Flora, who, as she grew older, took her place as Stephen's companion, accompanying him on his trips to London, Bournemouth or Southsea, once more the nanny figure. It was a pleasant life, going off on these jaunts with Stephen, who was charming company. Occasionally, Flora had to take the rough with the smooth, as when her employer's whims dictated sudden changes of plan. This might mean getting dressed up and into the car, setting off for a visit to Southsea, only for Stephen to decide a mile down the road that he didn't wish to go there after all. Or 'Mister Stephen's' changes of plans could be of a more radical variety. One Wilsford taximan recalls driving Stephen and Flora to Salisbury station, where at least six porters were required to entrain him and his extensive luggage. He was off to holiday with Princess Bibesco at her Cornish country retreat, Tullimaar. The next day there was a telephone call to Wilsford – from Bournemouth. Stephen had not liked Marthe's house, so he and Flora had taken a taxi to the Royal Bath Hotel, and would be spending the rest of their holiday there.

The Fords also had to cope with their master's ever-growing menagerie. Besides the lizards, terrapins, frogs and tortoises, there were the birds. In the loggia, now caged off with chicken wire, he kept two expensive cockatoos, and once introduced a wood ibis into the garden. An employee remembers the awful day it fell ill, and had to be captured, with great difficulty, and taken to the vet. 'Its blooming great wings were flapping up and down and the long bill snapping away! We got it to the vet, but whatever he gave it did no good, and the bird – which had cost an awful lot – died. But Stephen didn't seem to care much. Once things were dead, he just wiped them from his memory. He didn't like to discuss sad things . . .'

But Stephen loved his lizards: 'He liked their big eyes,' recalls the gardener. 'We would drive to Southsea to Taylor's pet shop and buy a boxful of green lizards, and on the way home he would open the box and say, "There, look at them." And they'd be gone! We'd have to close the windows of the car and wait till we got back to find them – then he would just let them free into the garden. Of course, as the cold weather came, most of them died – though sometimes they would find somewhere to spend winter, and hibernate, and then in spring you'd see this sudden flash of green scampering across the West Lawn.' Taylor's pet shop in Southsea was run by Charlie Taylor, the former porter who had known Stephen from the Queen's Hotel. Stephen became a regular patron of Taylor's business; when they had new stock in, Taylor would send Stephen long lists of merchandise, and Stephen would order the car and set off for another basketload of reptiles. Another supplier was Palmer's Pet Stores in Camden Town, who would send Mr Tennant's order down by train. Stephen would never tire of recommending these establishments to his friends – whether they wished to buy green lizards or not.

Two new friends of the fifties had come to Stephen via Willa Cather's departed spirit. Yehudi and Diana Menuhin had come to know Stephen through his brother, Christopher, but the real connection was their love of Willa. Cather had known the Menuhin family in America, and had doted upon the child prodigy Yehudi and his sisters. They had called her 'Aunt Willa', and to Stephen, friendship with the Menuhins was preordained: there could be no more strong a link of friendship than a love of Cather. He remembered Cather saying to him in her New York apartment in 1935: 'Yes, Yehudi is one of the most truthful people I know – he and I read Macbeth together last winter.'[3] In 1958, Menuhin was performing at the Bath Festival, and Diana recalls Stephen asking them both over to Wilsford for lunch. Yehudi had rehearsals to attend, but his wife was able to go. She found Stephen a sad person. 'He was trying to escape this world – I found him very touching, very generous . . . He was longing to find a place, some sort of position, but the war seemed to have killed all that for him.'

Lady Menuhin saw him as very much a product of the excesses of the between-the-war period, when 'all his generation were reacting against the horrors of the war, their parents' hypocritical mores . . . the reality of the second war changed all that'. Stephen was susceptible to 'scenes', she recalls. 'He could be very explosive. I remember I met him at Claridge's once, and he was becoming over-ebullient, saying "oh darling, darling" – I had to calm him down. I've had experience of coping with manic depressives, so I knew what was going on. After the shock treatment [in 1957] he seemed even more depressed. Stephen just didn't fit into society, and he was certainly the victim of unscrupulous people, like so many in his position are.' When she met up with Stephen in London, to go and see Enid Bagnold's *The Chalk Garden*, she saw how nervous he was in public. 'He sort of attached himself to us,' she observes, 'he was rather pathetic, really . . . I think truthfully that he was in the wrong sexual envelope – he wasn't effeminate so much as feminine.'[4] (Susan Lowndes Marques agrees with this opinion: 'Of course, there's been a lot of nonsense talked about Stephen . . . Quite simply, he was an hermaphrodite. Perhaps not in the physical sense, but certainly in every other.')[5]

The lack of self-confidence Lady Menuhin observed was apparent to others. Dr Davis and his wife remembered the beads of perspiration on Stephen's forehead when they invited him over for dinner. 'He was incredibly apprehensive of meeting people, of putting on a show. One could almost see the adrenalin going through him.'[6] The Marquess and Marchioness of Bath noted it too, on a rare visit Stephen made a few years later to their home, Job's Mill. 'He sat in the armchair sweating – he was obviously very nervous,' remembered Lady Bath, 'even though he knew us very well.'[7] Stephen's neurosis seemed to have sapped his social ability, which had hitherto been so practised. But more than being a product of illness, it was a symptom of Stephen's unwillingness to take part in the world. From now on, nearly all his appearances would be made on the Wilsford stage, the one he had created for himself.

Princess Bibesco remained one of the regular visitors. Addressing Stephen as *Incoronato*, she would write to thank him for 'heavenly gardens – the birds, the divine Chinese quail, the Persian lady torque . . .'[8] Their mutual friend, Sheila MacDonald (now Lochhead), observed that these two unworldly creatures shared a definite feyness, mixed with a certain spirituality. Writing from Tullimaar, the Princess longed for 'Salisbury's Cathedral cloister . . . and the white stones in the deep green grass'[9] they had enjoyed together, and promised later that spring to pray every evening for Stephen to *Notre Dame de Lourdes*, 'whose statue stands in a niche of the flower-house in our garden'.[10]

The cult of the Blessed Virgin Mary appealed to Stephen, and he often wrote to Catholic friends, such as the Countess of Iddesleigh and Susan Lowndes Marques, of how profound he thought the religion. Considering that both Siegfried Sassoon and Edith Sitwell were converts to Roman Catholicism in the nineteen-fifties (and Willa Cather had been a great sympathizer), the idea might have been attractive to Stephen, too. He told Susan in 1966: 'I love the Catholic faith – yes – Beauty is a part of religious belief. I share W. Cather's love of your Faith. She loved the colour & Beauty & zest. Perhaps I am a Catholic at heart . . .'[11] Like Oscar Wilde, and his hero, Dorian Gray, Stephen considered an intellectual flirtation with the Church of Rome as 'a superb rejection of the evidence of the senses'. Perhaps a stricter religious discipline might have given Stephen a way to 'flow out' of himself, as Victoria Glendinning observes it had done for Edith Sitwell, to channel his contained 'non-physical realities'[12] (that is, those emotions more often invested in marriage, children, home), into faith, as she had done. Instead of religion, however, Stephen sought poetry and art and literature as outlets; like his fellow poet, Wilde, he saw the secret of life as art – and placed his heart therein.

Thus Marthe Bibesco's paeans to her fellow poet lavished praise that was music to Stephen's ears. 'Incoronato! You hand your crown of light la couronne d'olivier sauvage to me by this Preface [Stephen's introductory essay to his poems, dedicated to the Princess], my dear Stephen, dearest Poet, my own friend since your boyhood and my youth. As a child, an English angel. As a man, this English archangel who stood before me in a sad dawn on a landing field near London and made it look like St Apollinaire in Classe at Ravenuese . . .'[13]

For Stephen to be so assailed by lyrical tributes was a panacea to the marches of time and a startling new decade. The nineteen-sixties promised yet more radical changes to the new world; the Princess kept the old alive. 'Your gentians have arrived,' she wrote from Cornwall, 'as blue as the Capri grotto when you and I sailed in, when all the world was young, in our happy past centuries under the reign of Tiberius . . .'[14] Yet advanced as the century had become, it still held excitement for him. In the coming years Stephen would publish his own verse, achieve further exhibitions of his work, and cultivate an entirely new set of 'swinging' friends, lured to his court by legendary stories of this fabled, eccentric, sleeping beauty.

Cecil Beaton, with his ever-widening circle of artistic, literary and other famous friends, was a primary source of entertainment for Stephen in the sixties. Beaton often brought house-guests to Wilsford, to amuse both them and his old friend. One such visit is brilliantly told in Cecil's diary for summer 1961. Cecil had Christopher Isherwood and his friend, Don Bachardy, to stay, during some of the 'best summer weather' of the year. Cecil knew a visit to Wilsford would impress, so he rang up Stephen to ask if they might come over. Stephen had just returned from a prolonged stay at the Branksome Towers Hotel in Bournemouth, and told them they would be his first visitors in six months.

'Stephen is in good health now and has been severely indulging his selfishness,' observed Cecil, '"resting" non-stop . . . I have seen Wilsford through many of its vicissitudes – but never – never have I seen it look so extraordinary as today,' he wrote. Since the late forties, Stephen's 'improvements' to Wilsford had consisted mainly of the application of numerous patterned and swagged wallpapers and borders, clashing with gay abandon across the walls of his home, with little thought for colour co-ordination. The décor had become overblown, without the sparseness of a Syrie Maugham to moderate his exuberance, and in consequence the result was a crazy mixture made yet more extraordinary by the further embellishments Stephen had devised. Cecil's party arrived 'to find an interior like that of a retired Ballerina of the Czar's day. All the old panelled rooms of Lady Grey's day . . . now of pink and tissue paper, & the oak stairs covered with fish net' was something Cecil had taken for granted. What astonished him was that the whole of the house was 'laid out . . . with still lives (on floors & chairs) consisting of lengths of material, pyjama tops, shells, bears, lots of soap (with carnation-pictured lids), with huge Italian straw hats . . . littering the staircase. One wonders how the house can be dusted. The effect is at first as if things were put out to a jumble sale – but in reality it is all *voulu*. The sketch books & diaries & pictures are displayed on the floor with a fan, a glove, a mask – a straw tray.'

Cecil was the first to be shown up to Stephen's bedroom, telling his two friends from America to have a good look round the house while he checked the lie of the land. Upstairs he found Stephen 'lying like a porpoise in one of the many bedrooms he inhabits . . . fat & appallingly painted with a bang of greasy dyed hair over his forehead, & greasy balding hair brushed forward from the crown & the head'. For Cecil, who made of his personal neatness a near-religion, the worst was yet to come: 'His fingernails were not very clean.'

'Oh what fun this is !' Stephen giggled. Cecil had secretly feared that he might become capricious, and decide he was too tired for visitors, but when Beaton announced that Christopher Isherwood was waiting downstairs, Stephen became positively animated, and 'in breathy bewilderment, marvelled that could it really be Christopher Isherwood, he who had written so many of his favourite books, that I had brought with me to Wilsford?' Christopher was summoned:

'Don & he came blinking into the room . . . "Can it really be

Christopher Isherwood? Come and sit by me on the bed. Is it really true? Can I touch you? I'm one of your greatest fans!" (Christopher later said that this sort of talk frightens the shit out of him!)' Having sat on the bed, the author was quickly discomposed by Stephen jumping to his feet:

'"Oh, I've got a very bad cramp, oh, oh" . . . and waddled ludicrously with his fat stomach & obtruding buttocks out of the door. Interval of five minutes.

'C & Don looked completely baffled at one another with broad grins on their faces. Stephen then reappeared carrying a garden basket of old potpourri, & got back into bed to talk about "life" & the dedication of an artist.'

Stephen proceeded to extol, in his deep bass voice, the philosophical virtues of Aldous Huxley and Morgan Forster, 'who said that the artist & the scientist were the only true practitioners of the spirit'. All the time, his 'childish plump hands flaying about his fat face', which was covered with foundation 'so that he soon started to sweat'. It was a very good performance, thought Cecil, 'dotted with aphorisms about Art & showing that he had read & remembered practically everything C.I. had written – including an article in *Horizon*'.

Talk was predictably turned to Cather, as Stephen recommended Isherwood read his 'Room Beyond' preface. '"Oh here it is. How I love California!"' he told his visitors, who lived there. 'When I come back from America I find everything here so dull. The sky in Europe is not interesting after Californian clouds, after Californian vitality – and the friendliness of the people – you feel enclosed here. I'd like to go and live in California,' he concluded. 'I feel so well there. Here it is always rain. But in California the sun is balm to one's soul – and the vegetation! Would you like to see a notebook I kept while in California?'

'Again Stephen waddles from the room. Interval of five minutes before the act continues. "Now sit here Mr Isherwood – on the sofa – let's get rid of these things!" The sofa, piled high with papers of all sorts, diary, pictures, books, was then denuded of its impedimenti by Stephen throwing everything sky-high over into a corner of the room. "You can't do that, Stephen!" I exclaimed in shock as a cloud of Tchelitchews and other valuable drawings went like confetti to the ceiling. "But it's such fun!" said Stephen with a mad glint in his eye.'

As Isherwood and Bachardy sat either side of their host, he turned the pages of his American journal, showing them his impressive sketches of Californian redwood tree roots, and the chainbound rocks of Honolulu. 'There was no time to read the extracts headed "At Sea",' noted Cecil, 'but Don remembered later that not one word was ever cut – or altered. There was no correction.' Stephen next produced sketches of 'wicked sailors': 'Isn't that a wicked face,' he enthused, ' – with sweat mixed with soot – making that deep purple look! Here is a cover for my novel. I'm getting on with it but Willa Cather said I'd already taken too long over it – "You've strangled it" she said (and twenty years ago!).' 'Still Stephen keeps it up', observed Cecil. 'He goes to Bournemouth to have his poems privately printed (the costs will be heavy!).'

At last tea was announced by 'Fred the old coachman' (Cecil habitually misnamed the staff at Wilsford, having a more cavalier attitude to domestics than Stephen). '"I must go and get it for you," said Stephen. Exit. Interval of five minutes. The tea was strong, & the food was crude. "This is the sort of tea Emily Dickinson would serve at Howth, New England" he chortled.'

To Cecil it was a 'funny performance which merited applause . . . In spite of the appalling, ludicrous, "sissy" behaviour, Stephen was impressive,' Cecil had to admit. "I realized that he really does read & absorb; that he remembers everything.' Whilst Beaton had imagined that Stephen's brain had 'rotted with introversion', the reverse was true: '. . . it is still a remarkable instrument – & he showed himself to be a real & true eccentric with deep passions for the things he loves, living in a hovel entirely of his own making with a frenzy & a zeal' that made Cecil feel his own existence was 'quite humdrum'.

Cecil had instinctively brought his camera along, and put it to good effect shooting twenty frames of Stephen, Christopher and Don in the garden, which looked idyllic as they walked down to the willow-planted banks of the Avon. When Stephen took them to see his new lily-pond, Cecil was suddenly reminded of the old Stephen, when 'his appalling taste or lack of the tenets of taste were not to be seen . . . he became as he used to be, a simple boy who loved his nannies, insects, nature . . . like Peter Pan among the trees'. But all too quickly they were back in 'the horrors of the garden he has created. A former orchard was now a mess of statues – some even painted pink & gold; iron heron, wire archways, potted palms, stone bordered beds that might have been part of Bournemouth's Municipal Gardens. Christopher, accustomed to the vulgarity of Hollywood, could yet not believe such things were possible.' The photo-session was, as always, an excuse for clowning and great exhibitionism, with Stephen posing 'like a pixie': 'Yes, show my legs please! . . . Come nestle close. Come Don – let's all be photographed together – so that I shall know you really have been to Wilsford!'[15]

The show over, Stephen's guests left, driving back to Reddish, laughing aloud over the extraordinary afternoon. And upstairs in his bedroom, Stephen chuckled too, quite well aware that they would be talking about him, and able to congratulate himself on another fine performance.

Stephen was, at the beginning of the decade, still relatively sociable. He turned to his friends to help him shake off the depression of last autumn which had occasioned hospital care. 'I had to have shock treatment for melancholy,' he told Cecil on 8 July, 'and I think I'm too much alone – will you please help me be my old self again? I think a little fun with you – a lunch party at Pelham Place [Beaton's London house] with gay friends – or a play with you would help me recover . . . I want to air my depression if I can now.' Stephen maintained that his doctor recommended 'only two things – Pleasure and Companionship . . . If you would ask me to a gay lunch, not dinner, as I have to go to bed early, to sleep a lot. I've had to take sedatives[*] now for 6 months which is not like me at all. I only tell you these things very privately; in confidence, because physically I am very well indeed. People do say there is a lot of depression about – is there? Is it England that depresses me? – and not my fault at all? I do love the tropics and the South so – but one needs a companion, to enjoy them with – will you give me your advice – London is so dull to me – has it grown duller?'[16]

That week Stephen had long London appointments with his dentist, having to have a number of rotten teeth in his upper jaw removed. He once again asked Cecil to cheer him up. 'I may still go to USA – having a flat in NY is so exciting,' he enthused, but even his love of America seemed to be waning, and now he admitted he sometimes found Americans wearying and boring: perhaps 'Tangiers would cheer me – or Nice or Cannes – I'd love to see your friend Mrs Vreeland if I go to USA . . .'[17] (In fact Stephen wrote to Diana Vreeland, Queen Elect of the New York fashion world, on a number of occasions. She was rather bemused by his attentions, but replied sending Stephen a postcard of New York at night: 'Here is Times Square waiting for you.')[18]

Isolated as he was, Stephen could sound paranoid at times. He asked Cecil, 'I wonder if you are really fond of me? I think you would vibrantly seek me out, if you loved me – You used to say to Hoyningen-Huené that I was such a lovely person! . . . You once touched me very deeply by saying that I appreciated & delighted in you, & helped you more than anyone

---

[*]Stephen was being prescribed Nembutal, a strong anti-depressant.

else did, in London long ago.' He continued in his accusatory tone, a belated rejoinder to Cecil's admonishing letter of 1952: 'So often I've brought you Bouquets of flowers to No. 8 [Pelham Place] – you've never given me any. Once – years ago in Paris, you did give me a bunch of flowers . . . Even if you don't love me any more, I think I have a significance for you of some kind – ' Stephen was calling in old debts '– old ties are very strong. I was cut to the heart this Christmas when I heard you were at home and never thought of sending me a loving word.'[19]

Later that summer, Cecil took his new friends Mark and Arabella Boxer to see Stephen. They arrived after dinner, in midsummer twilight, which made the house and gardens look all the more spooky. Stephen appeared at the front door in a shantung suit, 'smiling without any upper teeth in his mouth'. They sat in eerie half-light drinking champagne from quart-sized bottles, laughing at Stephen's jokes. 'Oh do you like it?' he said, referring to a new hairdo. 'It's a bit of a shock I daresay,' as he tightened his upper lip to make up for his lack of teeth, and parted his fringed hair, 'so red on top & white at the roots!'[20]

At times, it appeared that Beaton was showing Stephen off, treating him as a figure of fun rather than as a friend: at one point in the sixties he was planning a book about eccentrics, and proposed to make Stephen the star. This notion – Stephen as a weird figure, a source of diversion – could veer quite close to condescension, as an episode involving Sachie Sitwell (by then Sir Sacheverell) indicated. Stephen had written to him that summer, asking for advice on how to get his poems published. Sitwell replied that he no longer had any publishing contacts, and was only writing poetry for his own personal satisfaction, but that it was very nice 'seeing your characteristic writing again'.[21] It was not the only example of Stephen's hand that Sachie saw, for soon after Cecil sent him some of the letters he had himself received from Stephen.

'Please don't stop sending me the scented missives as I find them fascinating,' replied Sachie. 'I would love to have a graphologist's opinion of them. One or two of them could be written by a heavily drugged Cecile Sorel, or the "divine" Sarah.' To Sitwell, these (secondhand) letters looked 'incredibly old and crabbed, but this morning's moss rose is a kind of temporary rejuvenation, like an imagined aphrodisiac. And all the prattle about Pavlova, Gloria Swanson and Gina Valerine! He (or she) is heading for an old folk's home, and should be in the cast of that play of Coward's.'[22] (*Waiting in the Wings*, set in a home for retired actors and actresses, was produced that year in London with Sybil Thorndike in the leading role.) A later letter to Beaton from Weston Hall notes that Sitwell was being 'deluged with letters and books from Stephen, all written as though by someone like Deljora or Gina Valerine, long interned in some country lunatic asylum'.[23]

Stephen launched his poetry upon the world that winter, disregarding reluctant publishers by publishing himself. He began with a Christmas card: Two Poems for Christmas. 'Beatitude – Poem for a Christmas Child' exhibited his growing interest in Christianity, whilst 'Homage to Dylan Thomas' is self-explanatory:

> *Take your place, like Dylan Thomas;*
> *In the deepening sun of truth.*
> *Stand where the gods are idle, smiling,*
> *By the secret streams of youth.*

The following year, encouraged by favourable noises from friends, Stephen went to his friendly printer, George Nash of Bournemouth, with plans for a whole book of his collected verse. *My Brother Aquarius* was the result, a modest little hardback, with a dust-jacket in full colour, a painting by Stephen of his starry sibling of the heavens; his title came from a line of Keats that had been on his mind since his visit to Palm Beach in November 1950, when he had inscribed it in one of his books: 'Crystalline brother of the belt of Heaven: Aquarius'. (Stephen had long been interested in astrology, perhaps since discovering that those born under the sign of Taurus were supposed to be most blessed with beauty.)

The book is dedicated to an old friend. 'Many of these poems were inspired by my friend Barbara Hutton, whose great beauty and goodness have given so many people courage and enterprise, and serenity of heart.' This was followed by a lengthy preface, in the form of an open letter to Princess Bibesco, dealing with Stephen's favourite poets, a list that now included Ruth Pitter, Bruce Cutler (both acquaintances of his), and Dylan Thomas, along with his musings on the art. '"You have to live by the Heartbreak of things" as Pierre says in *Lascar* . . . Exactitude is purity . . . I, like Aphrodite, was born from the white foam of the Aegean, and it still laps my feet and bathes them in a timeless compassion and rapture.' Stephen hoped that his work would give the reader 'a delicate, haunting pleasure, like that which beautiful dancers – Anna Pavlova, Ted Shawn, Ruth Saint Denis – have given me; the delicious, troubling sense of an ecstasy only just withheld'.

My Brother Aquarius comprises some fifty-two poems, with titles like
'The Word Beloved Compared to the Sahara Desert' and 'Sea Harmonies:
Variations on a Theme', indicating the influence of the metaphysical
poets (to whom Stephen was first introduced by Laurence Whistler in the
late forties). Many are dedicated personally to friends: Barbara Hutton,
Laurence Whistler, Violet Bonham-Carter, Clara St John. Others recall
times and places, such as 'A Sandal from Delos': 'This poem brings back
memories of Rhodes and Crete.'

Which is what Stephen's verse always does – recalls events and travels
past; lost romance, a longing look back in the form of a homage to
Nature. Stephen seeks to recapture the beauty of a rose which reminded
him 'of an Italian purity', or 'Mother of Pearl', 'a shell from the Pacific'.
The influence of Sassoon's *Vigils* is evident in lonely, meditative pieces:

> *If you love the bark of a tree*
> *And the white moon of the Saints;*
> *Moss-roses on a summer night,*
> *The curlews silvered plaints . . .*

('The Happy Man')

Elsewhere there are direct references to Stephen's lost love:

> *I shall come dreaming to your heart . . .*
> *No memories, no past . . .*
> *Only the gardens of La Favorita, at Palermo – in*
> *Beloved Sicily – may hold the gentle glory of this*
>   *poem, safe . . .*
> *We speak in a garden – by a Sicilian Sea – alone, elate,*
> *To the God of Love, who never will depart –*
> *To worlds unknown, where joy is love and truth,*
> *Where the chalice of Spring bestows eternal youth.*
> *I shall come dreaming to your heart.*

April, 1961

Too late now, to come dreaming to Siegfried's heart – or anyone else's.
To those who knew Stephen and his unhappy past, such lines were
painfully poignant, if not brilliant verse. What was really going on, in
amongst all the sentiment, was Stephen's attempt, through poetry, to
express things in the written word he could never express in person. He
tried to externalize his longings, and his regrets, thus. Whether *My
Brother Aquarius* is good literature is almost beside the point. The
autobiographical content results in a sad, lyrical self-analysis, that nearly

reaches Stephen's real persona. But it is difficult to find a real heart here, and even the better poems go barely halfway to meeting his dispersed talents.

The mailing list for *My Brother Aquarius* read like a Who's Who of Literature and Society. The thank-you notes trickled in over the next few months. 'Christ Church, Oxford . . . Many thanks for your poems which I have been reading with enjoyment. I will bring Chester Kallman his copy when we meet in Brussels in Feb. at the première of our new opera . . . W. H. Auden.'[24] 'At first I thought it was a bunch of flowers – so light – so sunny . . . Christabel Aberconway.'[25] 'I find the production of the book admirable and the cover (and frontispiece) enchanting,' wrote Rosamond Lehmann to Lord Glenconner. 'But then I have always admired him as an imaginative artist more than as a writer.'[26]

Joe Ackerley was surprised to receive his copy of the book from out of the blue. 'How nice of you to remember me. Such a surprise. The book is charming, & since I never did see a starry man with so beautiful a face as your Aquarius, I would have liked to see more of your sapphire thoughts in their sapphire covers illustrated. How wonderful of you to have [attained] the sea-washed exultation that inspires your poems; I am no longer a bardsman to delight but have outlived my uses and interests. But bless your book & bless yourself for having remembered me.'[27]

So the notices kept coming: from Margaret Rutherford (now Mrs Stringer Davis), past slights forgiven; Edmund Blunden ('I'm so ashamed you had no "critical remarks" on your poems, but only because I am still rather tired after an illness of months');[28] and Clarence House, from the Queen Mother's Lady-in-Waiting. Despite the testament of such high-fliers, Stephen remained unable to persuade a 'proper' publisher to take his work. In November 1962 he had recourse to the vanity press again for *Some Poems for the Friends of Stephen Tennant*, this time a slimmer, less expensive tome, which was sprinkled with an assortment of quotations from Persian and Greek philosophers, and the odd epigram from the author: 'You should not need a precedent for any opinion you hold.' Rosamond Lehmann later donated her copy to the British Library, which copy bears a quotation written in violet ink: '"Il n'ya que la Poésie, C'est l'Antidote, et c'est la Vérité", Abbé Mugnier, in a letter.'*

There was a third Beaton visit to 'the Dreamland of Stephen Tennant', in the summer of 1964, this time with Cecil's new Californian boyfriend, Kin,

*Abbé Mugnier, secular and intellectual French priest, friend of Proust, and also of Princess Bibesco and Marie Belloc Lowndes.

a 6ft 4in American college boy, later described approvingly by Stephen as 'a great buffalo of a man'. Cecil noted that Stephen 'amazed the nice clean incredible Westerner in Kin'. They found Stephen 'looking quite mad' and in 'reverie – but shrewd reverie, not wandering', and the house covered with more 'rubbish ("Still Lives")' than before. His bath impossible of access – with its rim covered with powder & cream pots. Miss Havisham gone berserk.'[29] Also in Stephen's bathroom (which was not graced with its owner's body from October to March, as Stephen gleefully would announce with the onset of cold weather),* were yet more fantastic decorative additions for Beaton and his friend to see. Stephen had drawn up designs for a local artist, George Matthews,† to paint on mirrored panels in the small room which Stephen had renamed his 'Paris bathroom'.

It featured – in emblazoned household gloss – legends such as *l'Arlesienne by Bizet*, Paul Poiret, Dior, and *Les Biches*, under various fripperies and furbelows. There was a distinct similarity between the bows and ribbons, perfumes and hat-boxes of Stephen's designs and Cecil's own graphic works which showed how close their artistic influences – the worlds of theatre and fashion – were. Cecil took colour photographs of the new creation, which he called the '*Sans Souci Salle de Bain*': 'I see Cléo de Merode – Louise de Lavaillière – at your inspired elbow,' he told Stephen.[30] Thanking Beaton for the prints he sent afterwards, Stephen announced two new projects, along the same lines. 'Am writing on Cosmetics, and Scents & teagowns – this will be a little handbook on Charm – chic, mystical allure – thru' the ages – feminine wit and glamour,' he asserted, signing off 'all love & gratitude, Twinkletoes', with a sketch of Gaby Deslys'‡ mascara'd eye in one corner of his letter/ scenario. He included also an excerpt from his new play, in which the star, Lillian Russell,§ 'with the Beauty Chorus', performs the song:

> *We are tired of trying on stays!!!*
> *We are going to stick them on drays!!!*
> *We've sent dozens & dozens,*
> *To poor country cousins,*
> *A Kindness that nothing repays.*

---

*'No Bath now till May!' he told Hugo Vickers in the autumn of 1981. 'Too cold.'

†Matthews was also the painter of Stephen's later, abortive murals in the library at Wilsford, a mixture of Tahitian natives and Japanese-style scenery, ill-conceived and badly painted. Stephen had his haberdasher make up expensive curtains with which to cover them.

‡Gaby Deslys, theatrical star of the Edwardian era, greatly admired by both Stephen and Cecil.

§Lillian Russell, 'statuesque American singer-entertainer', who had died in 1922.

'. . . It is now called "Rhinestones: No Thank You!!!",' said Stephen,
'& opens in Lillian R's Corseteries shop near Tiffany's. They sing:

> *Black & Pink!! Black & Pink!!*
> *Paris Corsets make you think*
> *Lace and whalebone make you wink!!*
> *Black & Pink! Black & Pink!!*[31]

Cecil replied enthusiastically: 'Your book sounds very amusing. You
should write it just like the description in your letter. Masses of lists –
names – effects – just like your letters with Gaby Deslys' eye – Do do it in
a rush – no second thoughts. Just in frenzy. It must be unique.'[32] Cecil
sought to 'galvanize circumstances' as Stephen himself would put it, a
fruitless exhortation. It is a pity he did not succeed – Stephen's Manual of
Style could have been very amusing, and essential reading for every
aspiring chorus girl.

Chapter 28

Concerning the Eccentricities of Stephen Tennant

> When you have a cold & cough – revel in it; crow with joy at staying abed – when the Helena Rubinstein tube of eye-lash grower bursts – be jubilant – All the events of life can be made glorious – Enjoy especially the little things. Clothes – jewels; cosmetics – shells, silks, gay colours – Nature – revel in all weathers.
>
> — Stephen Tennant, marginalia

A S if to compensate for the self-imposed reduction in his social life, Stephen's correspondence grew to voluminous proportions in the nineteen-sixties. His vibrant-coloured letters pursued almost all his wide acquaintance. Some could not keep up the pace, some issued acknowledgements via their secretaries. But many were charmed or pleasantly surprised, or (in Sachie Sitwell's case) amused by Stephen's letters which reported in such vivid detail the progress of his latest painting, poem or play. Christabel Aberconway was particularly conscientious in her communication with Stephen in the sixties, always willing to proffer advice on water-lilies (from her gardeners at Bodnant), or to discuss the talents of the Indian dancer Ram Gopal, of whom both she and Stephen were great fans: 'The movements of his wrists and fingers and feet are breath-taking,' she reported to Stephen. 'He is as slim, as young, as gay, as beautiful as ever – there is a great deal to be said for the practice of Yoga, which Ram and Yehudi Menuhin follow.'[1]

Christabel was another of the privileged few to be allowed admittance to Wilsford in the years when the Fords' increasing elderliness and Stephen's truculence conspired to make overnight invitations a rare ticket. Not everyone would have relished Lady Aberconway's experience of the Wilsford table: '. . . But now, Stephen, I want to talk to you about the memories I have brought back from Wilsford,' Christabel wrote in late spring, 1965. 'Of course, of you and Mrs Ford ... I shall always remember our meal of lovely vegetables, raspberries, strawberries, cream – and Spam – washed down with bottle after bottle of champagne (perhaps I should add that they were half-bottles), and crème de menthe, like melted emeralds, to sip afterwards ... I confess that I regret the panelling on the walls of Wilsford Manor; but each generation must do as their "demon" urges. I shouldn't want to be a housemaid to dust all the objects on your tables – floors – & bannisters – but perhaps the Gods love you so much that no dust ever drifts your way.'[2]

Stephen had had Ernest Gimson's oak panelling ripped out, an alteration which even he came to regret. Such was the extent of Stephen's structural changes that friends wondered why he didn't just move to another house. To that end – and to economize on his upkeep – Lord Glenconner had a cottage built for Stephen in the grounds. But the tenant of Wilsford could never be persuaded to move into this tiny 'Teasel Cottage'. Stephen preferred to create his own world within his childhood home.

Affairs inside Wilsford reached an all-time low, as far as any 'respectable' notion of house-keeping was concerned. The contents of a hundred desk drawers and chests, filled with letters, postcards, photographs, magazines, jewellery, trinkets, shells and empty scent bottles, were tipped out on floors, beds, sofas, tables, chairs, stairs – any available surface. A sea of ephemera flowed across the sheepskin carpets and down limed staircases. Stephen had new icons: Elvis Presley postcards graced the famous postcard stand, alongside Tchelitchew's sailor's pom-pom card from Toulon. *Moviegoer* vied with a pop magazine featuring Cliff Richard as its cover star, grinning his wholesome grin under a half-pound of hair-grease. Stephen even began to cultivate a quiff of his own. Not that his musical tastes ran so youthful – *South Pacific* and *Carousel* were the records most frequently on the Wilsford gramophone, and soon Stephen knew all the words to *Oklahoma* too.

Yet however ludicrous this *mélange* of taste and clutter seemed, it remained an outpost of style that still reverberated, as did many of Stephen's more *outré* gestures, into an outside world. Even Caroline Blackwood commented that Stephen's taste for concealed lighting and fishnets predated the décor of certain New York night-clubs by years; and in the autumn of 1968, a major exhibition of Beaton's photographs at the National Portrait Gallery had as one of its set-pieces a revolving postcard stand displaying photographs of Marilyn Monroe – 'Even now his influence had effect,' observed Hugo Vickers.[3]

*

An important new member of the Wilsford household in the sixties was Miss Sylvia Grant, whom Stephen had taken on as his secretary. A good-looking woman in her thirties, she took Flora Ford's place as Stephen's travelling companion when Mrs Ford was grown old. She and her employer grew quite close; at one point Stephen asked her to marry him, and Christopher Glenconner was reported to have encouraged the match, which he thought would be good for Stephen. But it was the idea of marriage (to a quite glamorous young woman, who was also a good cook) that appealed, rather than the actuality. Miss Grant politely turned the offer down, and soon after left Wilsford to go and live in Andorra. Yet more changes were imminent at the Manor now. Lord Glenconner realized that the Fords were too frail to be looking after a huge house and its demanding inhabitant, and so in 1969 they were replaced by John and Mary Skull.

John Skull had known Stephen for some time – he had run taxi duties for him – and was already well acquainted with his idiosyncrasies and the often strange goings-on at Wilsford. An affable, commonsensical man, John Skull observed that when he and his wife first came to work at the house, Stephen was 'still getting out and about quite a bit . . . I would often have to drive to the station to pick him and Flora Ford up, after they had been staying at the Ritz . . . But slowly, over the years, he just didn't seem to get up any more. If the weather was bad, and he didn't feel like it, he would just stay in bed.'[4]

'And of course, he loved my wife's food – she was a good cook. He had four meals a day, a full cooked breakfast when he got up, followed by lunch, tea, and dinner.' Thus, without any physical exercise to speak of, Stephen began to gain a great deal of weight. Within two or three years, he weighed nearly twenty stone. His new doctor, Dr Batten, put him on a diet, remembered John Skull. 'He gave us a list of what Stephen could and couldn't eat', but when he was served his first meal under the new regime – 'a lot of fruit' – Stephen announced he might starve, and very soon was back to his old diet. Advice against the unhealthiness of corpulence cut no ice with him. 'But I'm beautiful,' he would reason, 'and the more of me there is the better I like it!'

Dr Davis left just before the Skulls took over at Wilsford, but he saw Stephen's growing reclusion even then. He remembered attending Stephen 'at the height of a boiling summer . . . in his bedroom with the curtains drawn, and with poor Louis lugging heavy logs upstairs to build up an already blazing fire. I suppose it made him feel cosy . . .' Louis Ford seemed often to have got the worst of it, often having to be the one to turn away unwanted guests. Dr Davis recalled Louis coming over to his house in a terrible state one day; Colin Tennant and Princess Margaret had called to see Stephen, and he had announced he wasn't receiving visitors. 'The Princess was turned away at the door!' remembered Davis, who was a secondary witness to the event. 'I think the friends gradually fell away – they seemed to give up on Stephen eventually.'[5]

One friend who had given up long ago was Siegfried. There is no record of what Stephen felt when he heard the news that Sassoon had died at Heytesbury on 1 September 1967. The poet appeared old and embittered to friends in his last years, and was, like Stephen, increasingly reclusive. His old age had not been a happy one: his relationship with his wife irretrievably broken down, he had only his new faith, and his son, George, to turn to. Stephen had not seen him for years (probably not since the mid-fifties), and each tried to forget about the other as they both came to terms with old age. If Stephen felt any remorse at Siegfried's death, he did not show it. He would rather remember the happiness of the distant past than the unhappiness of the events thereafter.

The decade had taken its toll on his friends. Edith Sitwell died in 1964, Lady Juliet Duff the year after. By the end of the sixties Stephen would lose Christabel Aberconway too, and his brother David, who died in Spain in 1968, 'having drunk himself to death on cheap Spanish brandy', as one friend bluntly put it. David was buried in the Wilsford churchyard, a dramatic occasion with his former wife Hermione (to whom he had been latterly reconciled) in 'black widow's weeds'. Dr Davis, in his house across the lane, was trying to keep his bantam cocks from crowing and disturbing the service. 'Stephen was invited, and expected to appear, but called off at the last moment', went one story. This was distressing for the mourners, as the funeral tea was supposed to have been served at the Manor. This report had the doors of the house firmly bolted and a mad-looking Stephen standing, laughing, at an upper window, a latter-day Mrs Rochester.

John and Mary Skull saw that, without any encouragement, 'Mister Stephen' would soon slip into worse health, and a more depressed state. They became determined not to allow this to happen to a man who, despite all his whims and eccentricities, still inspired absolute devotion. 'He had a silver tongue,' recalled John. 'That man could charm the butterfly off a flower.' Stephen had already been subject to certain liberty-taking by unscrupulous people, as Diana Menuhin had observed. 'A lot of people "took" him,' agreed John. 'He was so generous – to a fault – that people took advantage of him. When we moved into the Manor, we found a bill from his driver for a month in 1963. He had charged Stephen £680 for driving him around in his own Rolls-Royce!'⁶

Then there was the 'secretary' who looked after his financial affairs for Popkiss Ltd, Stephen's trustees. 'He would come down to Wilsford and ask me to help him load his car up with some furniture from the house he had been told to get rid of. I thought it was rather strange, so I asked Stephen if he knew anything about it. He didn't. Anyway, Mary and I were going on holiday, and she thought she could see things disappearing from the house, so she made a list of all the furniture stored in the Thatched Wing. Sure enough, when we came back, some of it had gone.' A quiet word with Christopher Glenconner sorted out the trouble. 'The chap was soon sacked,' recalled John with satisfaction. 'The funny thing is that he had persuaded Lord Glenconner that Stephen should sell his car – an Austin – to him – and buy a new one. This he did, and the secretary thought he'd got a real bargain, but a month later he broke down on the A40 – the cam-shaft had gone!'

The fact that Stephen had a big empty house full of valuable furniture was a great temptation. John remembered many an antique dealer 'coming up from Brighton "on spec" to try and persuade Stephen to sell some of it. Mary and I soon got wise, and we wouldn't let them in.' But Stephen himself did sell some possessions, among them a number of Tchelitchews, which Laura, Duchess of Marlborough, recalled were brought up to London stuffed in the back of Stephen's car, and sold to the dealer Micky Renshaw. All this was to provide Stephen with more spending money. Stephen sold a large Tchelitchew to Cecil for £800: 'He drove a hard bargain,' noted John, 'and he made Cecil come over and pay cash for it!'* Afterwards Stephen set off for a shopping expedition to Bright's of Bournemouth, his favourite store. 'He bought loads of cushions – mad on cushions, he was – and when he paid for them, he pulled this brown envelope out of his pocket and fivers went flying everywhere. Me and the assistant were scrambling around on the shop floor trying to pick them all up.' (Stephen once ordered from a shop in Salisbury a cushion large enough to fill an entire room. The order had to be cancelled out of practicality.)

Stephen's decorative fantasies were running amok. He would buy huge

---

*According to Bruce Chatwin, who had just left employment at Sotheby's, Beaton then proceeded to sell the Tchelitchew at the auction house for a sizeable profit. Chatwin believed that this caused a great rift between the two friends for a long period. The lack of correspondence between Stephen and Cecil in the late sixties could well be evidence of this.

lengths of materials that caught his eye at Bright's, and just drape them over furniture. 'It was a very modern effect, I suppose – very fashionable today,' observed John, 'but it drove Mary mad – after all, it was her who had to try and clean round the stuff.' And it was Mary who rescued Rex's beautifully illustrated letters to Stephen from the dining-room carpet, where Stephen's daily passage (to paint at the table) threatened to trample these works of art into mere litter. Only the efforts of his housekeepers kept the manor and master from complete anarchy.

With the encouragement of the Skulls, Stephen started to go out into the world more. He planned day trips with John, as his chauffeur, at the wheel. 'I was always driving him off for the day, and not knowing whether we'd have to spend the night in Southsea, or end up in Bournemouth. If he found lizards for sale at Wingates in Winchester, he had to have all of them. Once we were there and he saw a huge boa, and asked how much it was – £70 – and he said, "Oh John, do you think that is expensive?" and I said, "I don't know, sir, but if that's coming in the house I can tell you Mary won't be staying!" I didn't much like the look of it either!'[7]

The Queen's Hotel in Southsea lost its appeal for Stephen after its change of ownership in 1969. 'Oh, they've ruined my lovely hotel,' said Stephen; it had been refurbished 'and looked rather dark and gloomy', agreed John. The chosen successor was the Royal Bath Hotel in Bournemouth, a turreted and regal building sited high above the sea-front, old-fashioned and very much to Stephen's taste. 'One day let us stay at the Royal Bath Hotel,' Stephen told Violet Bonham-Carter, '& luxuriate. Heavenly food – nice *Vin de Pays* – I think you would like it – I've always loved it. And one can have a room on the garden – & go out in the dawn – so delicious. There are banks of peat turf – full of lizards – & camellias . . . I fill my pockets with pine needles & cones.'[8]

The porters at the Royal Bath remembered Stephen with affection, coloured, possibly, by the fact that he would habitually tip with five-pound notes – and this at a time when his personal finances were running quite low. His brother, in an attempt to limit Stephen's extravagances, put a ceiling on Stephen's spending; he had no personal cheques, and had to draw his 'allowance' via John. This meant that such luxuries as overnight stays at the Royal Bath had eventually to be curtailed, so Stephen would go there just for lunch. Staff recalled Stephen arriving in his long camel coat, and taking his favourite table. 'He would have one, and his manservant had another beside him' (thus maintaining the respectful master/servant distance) 'and they would chat to each other across the gap. He was always so charming,' remembered Pamela Benton. 'He wore a baggy brown suit, and he had a long strand of hair that hung down, which would blow away in the breeze.'[9]

Thus did time pass, driving around the south of England, shopping for new plants from nurseries, or new pets for the Reptillery. On one occasion, John drove past a house with a newly-gravelled drive. 'Stop!' shouted Stephen from the back of the Austin 1100. 'Go in and ask them where they got it from,' he told John. 'I was rather embarrassed,' confessed Mr Skull, 'but I went up to the door of the house and said, "My employer wants to know where you got your gravel, Madam." And the lady of the house told me I was the third person to ask them that day! It came from gravel pits at Romsey, and Stephen sent for 18 cubic feet of the stuff. When it arrived he told me to spread it by the West Lawn. I spent all morning doing this, and after he'd seen me take the fifth or sixth wheelbarrow loads across, Stephen said, "You must rest, John." He was always telling people to "rest". If he saw Mary working, he'd tell her to rest! Of course, he meant he was to rest, really . . .'[10]

One spring day in 1970, John Skull drove his master over to Reddish House to lunch with Cecil Beaton and his guest, Diana Cooper. Cecil noted Stephen's 'spectacular entrance . . . having "rested" all winter; he had not been out of his bed'. Each new sighting of his old friend seemed to bring new oddities. Cecil saw 'this extraordinary figure being helped across the hall. He had a long white beard, was incredibly fat, and under layers of coats and jerseys wore a red cotton, bobble-edged tablecloth as a skirt.' (John remembered having had to help Stephen into this costume.) 'As George [*sic*] his chauffeur assisted him upstairs, it fell around his ankles, much to Stephen's embarrassment. The cloth was being used to cover up the fact that he could not get into his trousers; an enormous gap displayed a pregnant stomach.'[11]

Once more Beaton was using Stephen's eccentricities to amuse; in fact, when the volume of his diaries with an abridged version of this episode was published, Stephen was said to be annoyed at the portrayal. But as Cecil was used to seeing Stephen 'as an elderly man' (Stephen was actually two years Cecil's junior), he found that 'the beard gave him nobility and distinction. He looked handsome like St Peter and it did not matter that he had no teeth.' Diana Cooper hardly knew Stephen,[*] but remained

[*] Although she had been in close contact with him on a number of occasions, the first of which had probably been her brother's marriage to Kathleen Tennant in 1917, when Stephen had been their page.

unfazed. She 'met him square on and would take no over-fine phrases – "Oh, Diana, you are as beautiful as ever!" "Oh, come off it, Stephen. Don't over-egg the pudding. You're hiding a big stomach. You can't do up your flies?"' That said, lunch was a great success. Stephen and Diana sparked each other off: he reminisced about Pamela, Margot Asquith, Harry Cust ('My father,' said Diana, her mother, like Stephen's, being a leading Soul), Anna Pavlova and Lady de Grey; all of which drew similar recollections from Diana. Cecil found the cross-table banter so fast it was difficult to follow. 'At one point Stephen asked Diana to sing some early songs as he knew she never forgot a lyric. This set Diana off on to Gilbert and Sullivan. Stephen lowered the tone by singing, "If you knew Suzie as I knew Suzie, oooooh what a girl!"'

Three years later, Stephen returned the hospitality and had Diana and Cecil over to Wilsford. 'Strangely enough we were welcomed,' noted Beaton, 'in fact Stephen was so over-excited at Diana's arrival that he never drew breath for an hour and a half.' Quoting from books on Emily Brontë and Pavlova, and relating the plot of one of Marie Corelli's novels, Stephen had time to remark on Diana's eyes: 'like those of a tiger', compared to those of Gary Cooper's, 'quartz – precious stone found embedded in rock – & fringed with ferns – dark & rather sticky'. Cecil thought Stephen's dictum, that 'most people's success came from their talent and by sticking to the job', ironic, to say the least: 'How would he know?'[12]

Stephen gave Diana a powder compact to admire, which she mistook for a cigarette box. 'She opened it and face-powder poured all over her!' he recounted with ill-suppressed amusement. 'I said I must warn people!'[13] She would have appreciated a warning about the other hazards of Wilsford as well. Walking outside, she broke her stiletto heel on the loose paving stones by the front door, a nasty fall only just averted by Cecil's proximity. Recalling this incident later, Stephen was reminded of Diana's accident-prone nature. She was a 'fascinating Being', he told Hugo Vickers. 'Years ago, during a Royal Night Pageant she was on the roof – with friends – admiring the fireworks. Then she stepped back onto a sky-light – which gave way!* For 2 years she was in a bath-chair – very made-up – & suave & calm. She is "formidable"!' he observed.[14]

Another guest at Wilsford in 1971 was the artist David Hockney, by now a good friend of Beaton's, and already world-famous for his work –

---

*Diana Cooper's accident happened in 1919, and was widely reported in the press at the time. It inspired D. H. Lawrence's characterization of her as 'Lady Artemis Hooper' in *Aaron's Rod* (1922).

and for his peroxide-blond hair and owlish round glasses. It was also the occasion of Beaton's last photo-session with Stephen. The prospect of meeting this odd-sounding old bird was not initially a source of great anticipation for the bluff Yorkshire painter. 'I didn't know until we got there how rare an occasion it was to see him – though I realized Cecil was excited, which meant it was something special. We'd been there about an hour when Stephen said, "Would you like something to drink?" and Cecil said, "Oh yes please." Stephen said, "Champagne for my guests," and the butler went off and brought back a cheap red plastic tray and on it was one half bottle and two quarter bottles of champagne and four glasses, none of which matched, and I thought, "This must be done on purpose!"'[15]

As Stephen regaled the painter with tales of the past, Cecil aimed his lens. Hockney sits on the edge of Stephen's bed, as Stephen, 'transform-ed . . . into a made-up Buddha',[16] lies out full-length. He is completely surrounded by chosen relics: his monkey, his jewellery box, letters, books and papers in profusion. In one frame, Stephen sweeps the still air of his Wilsford bedroom with a huge and ornate Japanese fan; in another, he toasts his friends with a glass of champagne. In this final attempt to capture an elusive butterfly on film, Beaton caught the dark, half-lit world of Wilsford, where this mysterious figure lay like a latter-day magician, or beached ballet dancer, swept up on an island by some tempest long ago, now languishing among the relics of a glamorous past. It was the last enduring image of Stephen Tennant, fittingly abed, corpulent and with a straggle of thinning hair – but as charismatic as ever he was.

Shortly after the Skulls took over at Wilsford Manor, there were other new arrivals on the estate. Teasel Cottage, the bungalow built in the grounds between the house and the Racquets Court for Stephen but never inhabited by him,* was let to the Indian writer V. S. Naipaul, who came to live there with his wife, Patricia. In the fifteen years he spent there, he never once met his landlord. He paid his rent and conducted any business with Lord Glenconner and the trust company. But he did see Stephen on occasion, and the strange tales he heard of his reclusive landlord sparked his imagination. The result is to be found in his novel, *The Enigma of*

*Teasel Cottage had formerly been occupied by Stephen's writer niece, Emma Tennant, and her family. After the Naipauls left, it was let to the publisher James Mitchell, whose friend, the astronomer Patrick Moore, became a frequent visitor. Stephen was seldom interested in these comings and goings; Emma Tennant was warned against 'bothering' her uncle-landlord and, like Naipaul, never visited the Manor during her time there.

Arrival, a semi-autobiographical work written about his time in Wiltshire. In it he uses Stephen as a metaphor for the decline of Britain in the twentieth century, for a forgotten empire, and for a lost past.

Stephen was told of his distinguished new neighbour (Naipaul had already won the Hawthornden Prize in 1964, and was acclaimed for his fiction), and after their arrival would send the Naipauls little messages and gifts via John and Mary Skull, who would trudge across to the bungalow to deliver a sheaf of poems dedicated to Krishna and Shiva which Stephen thought Mr Naipaul might enjoy. There were paintings too, of Indian gods, tentative attempts at a remote friendship that led to nothing as physical as an actual meeting, even though they lived only yards from each other. 'He was always going to have Mr Naipaul over for tea,' recalls John, 'but he never did.'[17] Yet Naipaul's received impressions, as expounded in *The Enigma of Arrival*, are lyrical and intense, and sum up the feeling of gentle decay around Stephen better than any other description of Wilsford in later days.

'Here in the valley there now lived only my landlord, elderly, a bachelor, with people to look after him. Certain physical disabilities had now been added to the malaise of which I had no precise knowledge, but interpreted as something like accidie, the monk's torpor or disease of the middle ages – which was how his great security, his excessive worldly blessings, had taken him. The accidie had turned him into a recluse, accessible only to his intimate friends.'* The author feels a 'great sympathy' for his landlord; he sees Stephen's 'malaise' as 'the other side of my own. I did not think of my landlord as a failure. Words like failure and success didn't apply. Only a grand man or a man with a grand idea of his human worth could ignore the high money value of his estate and be content to live in its semi-ruin.'[18] Naipaul was shown (by the Skulls) photographs of Stephen's early life. 'Blurred black and white photographs of parties in the grounds, the gardens not yet grown, undergrown; photographs of young people sitting in uncertain light (dusk or dawn?) on the rails of new timber bridges over the creeks in the water meadows',[19] all long since gone.

Then, unexpectedly, there is a glimpse of the man himself. Naipaul sees Stephen sitting in the back of his car, being driven along the beech-lined

---

*Naipaul portrays one visitor, 'Alan', seen as a failed homosexual writer who worked for the BBC, and eventually commits suicide. When *The Enigma of Arrival* was published in 1987, many people took exception to the character, whom they identified as Julian Jebb, a friend of Stephen's who was an arts producer for the BBC and had made documentaries on both the Mitfords and Virginia Woolf.

lane, giving a 'little low wave . . . I invested that wave with his shyness, the shyness of his illness, the shyness that went at the same time with a great vanity, the shyness that wasn't so much a wish not to be seen as a wish to be applauded on sight, to be recognized on sight as someone stupendous and of great interest . . . my imagination had played with a half-impression . . . now making him benign, now making him buttoned-up, with dark glasses and the long hair of a Howard Hughes recluse.'[20] The driver of the car later tells the narrator: 'He always wears dark glasses in the car. Otherwise his stomach gets upset, and then he gets a migraine.'[21]

Naipaul's second sighting – 'there was never another' – comes when he is walking along the river at the lower edge of the grounds.* Stephen was 'sitting (as I thought or felt afterwards) in a canvas high-backed easy chair in the sunlight, facing south, with his back to me. He was wearing a wide brimmed hat, that obscured the shape or baldness or otherwise of his head, just as the canvas back of his chair obscured the bulk or otherwise of his back or torso . . . From this second glimpse I again retained just one clear physical detail: it was of his crossed leg and his bare bent knee – shining in the sun. He was wearing shorts; they were tight around the plump thigh I saw.' In this Naipaul sees 'a wish . . . for nakedness and physical self-cherishing' – an echo of Stephen's past beauty that 'now went with an opposite reality: the fatness of self-indulgence and inactivity . . . I knew of course that he kept to his room in the cold weather, and went out of doors only in fine weather. He had been granted at birth a great house and a wide view in the dampest part of the country . . . But his instincts were Mediterranean, tropical; he loved the sun. Inertia, habit, friendships, a wish to be where his worth was known – perhaps these things kept him in his inherited house.'

The poems (carefully typed by Mary Skull) that arrived at Naipaul's cottage seemed to him to evoke all those lost ideas of Edwardian England, of 'a turning away from the coarseness of industrialism, upper-class or cultivated sensibilities almost drugged by money, the Yellow Book philosophy melting away into sensuousness, sensation – my landlord's Indian romance partook of all those impulses and was rooted in England's wealth, empire, the idea of glory, material satiety, a very great security . . . His fantasies (sensual rather than explicitly sexual, to judge by the poems) were unconfined but also unfocused: a warm blur,

*Naipaul's agent, Gillon Aitken, was with him at the time, and thought it quite surprising that his client should be so excited at seeing his landlord – until Naipaul explained how rare the sighting was.

something that was owed him but which might perhaps disappear with definition: something out there, outside himself, and eventually an aspect of his accidie, the curious death of the soul that had befallen him so early in his life.'[22]

What Naipaul saw in Stephen as a wish 'to be applauded on sight' was acutely observed. This was how Stephen appeared to the denizens of Wilsford and its environs: his ventures into quiet county towns like Wilton were akin to a royal progress or the arrival of some fabled movie-star – which is exactly how Stephen liked to be seen. Rosemary Olivier recalls the effect his appearance would have on Wilton when he went shopping there, in his tight pink shorts. In Salisbury, Stephen caused great concern in W. H. Smith's by asking the shop girls to pose for him; the manageress protested that they simply couldn't stop work for half an hour whilst Stephen sketched them. The town never got used to the sight of Stephen arriving to shop in Woolworth's gardening department in his long camel coat and red hair. If he saw someone he knew across the street, he would call out loud, thus occasioning acute embarrassment for everyone but himself.

A long stream of possibly apocryphal tales of Stephen's eccentricities date from this period. One story much-circulated around Wiltshire, told by impeccable sources, was of Stephen asking Lord Glenconner if, as he liked the town so much, Wilsford Manor could be moved to Bournemouth. Long-suffering Christopher managed to convince his brother that this was neither feasible nor wise. Consequently Stephen ordered two truckloads of fine sand, which he had spread over the Wilsford lawn. He then had a backdrop painted on a huge sheet of canvas, depicting the sandy cliffs of Bournemouth. This was then erected on the far side of the river Avon. Sitting out in his cane sun-lounger, Stephen could now announce to his friends, 'Bournemouth has come to me.'

Whilst Stephen's extraordinary appearances, in his long coat, trailing scarves and a cloud of perfume, could cause consternation among strangers, his friends and family exhibited bemused resignation. Lord Glenconner's reply to a request from Stephen, dated 1966, indicated a remarkable tolerance: 'Dearest Stephen, I think the first thing to find out about the seal pool is how much it would cost to maintain and look after the seals. I know one of the head people at the Zoo quite well and will write and ask him to give me this information. Love from Christopher.'[23]

That Stephen knew he appeared eccentric was obvious. In fact, there is evidence to suggest that he looked to great eccentrics of the past for inspiration. 'I am the Prince Youssoupoff of England,' he announced in one of his copy-books, comparing himself to Rasputin's killer who lived in exile in London, and used belladonna to enlarge the pupils of his eyes. Perhaps Mad Ludwig of Bavaria was a little *de trop* – but certainly William Beckford was a role model for Stephen, and had been since the early thirties, and he would quote from biographies of Beckford in his ever-more extensive marginalia. Beckford had lived nearby, at Fonthill, where he built his great Gothic folly. Beckford was Stephen's eighteenth-century equivalent; James Lees-Milne describes his prose as antedating modern writers like Firbank and Waugh, and, like Stephen, had spent much of his time travelling and recording his experience in detailed journals. He too was essentially child-like. 'Of all the favours gracious Heaven has bestowed on me,' he wrote, 'the one I esteem the most is still retaining the appearance, the agility and the fancy of a stripling.'*[24] Fonthill too seems to have predated Wilsford, with its owner, 'a mystery man, in a decor of echoing corridors, Gothic halls and galleries, opulent hangings, contrived lighting effects, dizzy heights, pictures, music, wonderful books'.[25]

Stephen was a peculiarly English eccentric; he never appeared anything but a gentleman, no matter how much powder might be on his face. He loved simple pleasures, and that was what life had to offer. In the winter of 1972–3, he was in Bournemouth, enjoying the annual pantomime at the Pavilion Theatre, and enthusing over the performances of Lonnie Donegan, Miss Terri Howard and Miss Barbara Hallwick. 'Magical dresses & scenery,' he told Cecil. 'The whole show is a whirl of iridescent gaiety, and talent.'[27] Again, it was his love of what might be called 'second-rate' that was most enlivening to Stephen.

But Cecil had new plans to stir Stephen out of his lethargy. Beaton was involved in the first Salisbury Festival of the Arts that year, and he thought it might be a good opportunity for Stephen to re-emerge into the artistic world. It was an invitation Beaton had cause to regret, involving as it did Stephen's temperamental approach to such happenings: only Stephen's endearing enthusiasms – often very funny, and knowingly so – stopped him from appearing a cantankerous old man. Already in February Stephen was having to apologize for a fit of 'pique'. He had planned portraits of Cecil, Laurence Whistler, Christopher and Elizabeth Glenconner, 'and several other distinguished people', but was frustrated in so doing and announced his withdrawal. Only Cecil's cajoling brought him

---

*Lees-Milne wrote: 'Hubris and euphoria were two besetting infirmities to which Beckford was not immune . . . As for homosexuality itself, André Parreaux sees in it a mixture of narcissism and nostalgia for the innocence of his lost childhood.'[26]

back. Stephen then decided: 'I want to sketch some Brigadiers and tall majors in their uniforms for my exhibition . . . But I don't know any – oh, dear, what can I do, to contact the Army in a big way ? ? ? Not too many ! – of course, yet some Sergeants, and Subalterns, and Army Cadets would look very romantic, arranged in tiers ? or lolling on a couch ? I can see you laughing !' he told Cecil. 'So many possible "models" seem to be now lurking in the new Wilton Barracks.'[28]

Stephen's daily painting and drawing habits at Wilsford in those years were fairly idiosyncratic. He worked at high speed to produce new work for his Arts Festival exhibition, sitting up to a dressing-table in the Rose Room, or to the hexagonal marble dining-table downstairs; or, like Christopher Robin, halfway between the two on the wide landing. Stephen worked fast, selecting his colours from a basketful of Windsor and Newton indian inks, with their acid-bright colours. He would sketch out a full-lipped actress or a python crawling up a Doric pillar, then, adding more and more objects until the composition was satisfactory, would begin to fill in with washes of iridescent colour, the excess ink from his brush being splattered by his side before he put it to the paper. This resulted in a graphic firework display of ink spots on the carpets below his working areas, like miniature abstract expressionist compositions.

Stephen painted because it gave him pleasure. He was immensely prolific in the designs he turned out: Michael Wishart put the Tennant Factory at three or four pictures a day at its peak – there was no danger of a market shortage. One way of getting to see Stephen, claimed Wishart, was to offer to buy a picture; there was ready admittance then.

Organization for the Festival was already at fever pitch. 'The Council-lor Mr Townsend has written a very contrite, gracious letter,' noted Stephen, after a minor disaster over arrangements to show his work, adding that the committee seemed 'in a maelstrom of doubts – all sixes & sevens! wondering – dazed with their own bungling !'[29] Stephen had a full-colour poster printed to advertise his show, which John Skull delivered to the Festival Office in early June – to the delight of a secretary there who told him that the organizer's own publicity was sadly lacking. 'You must have publicity if you wish for Success,' observed the artist.[30] He planned a series of poetry readings to coincide with his show, and was much encouraged in this by the publication of his ode to Willa Cather, 'The Old Prairies', on the front page of the current issue of the *Willa Cather Pioneer Memorial Newsletter*.[31]

Another exhibitor invited by Cecil to the Festival was the painter Patrick Procktor. He recalls that Stephen had brought over his pictures to

Reddish House, where Cecil had arranged for them to be framed. 'When the framer came, Stephen still couldn't decide what colour he wanted his mounts – so he was sent away again. I think Cecil was having quite a few problems with it all.'[32] Beaton's secretary and general wonder-worker was Eileen Hose. 'Quite often these plans of Stephen just didn't happen,' she said. 'You got used to it after a while.' She was percipient on the subject of Stephen. 'He was a broken cog in the wheel – I think he was always afraid of failure – he never brought anything to a conclusion. Cecil asked me to help with the exhibition, but he warned me what might happen. Stephen got terribly excited about everything, then tried to pull out at the last moment. I think he would have liked to be famous – but he just couldn't follow through. When he came to the Festival, he was dressed quite outrageously – and you could see how much he enjoyed the stares.'[33]

There was a pre-Festival lunch at Cecil's, with Patrick Procktor and Raymond Mortimer as fellow guests. Procktor remembered a good performance from Stephen: 'It was always one of Cecil's social coups, to be the only person who was able to winkle Stephen out of Wilsford.'[34] Beaton noted Stephen's appearance as 'a great comeback' (Stephen would appear to have made as many 'comebacks' as Frank Sinatra). 'His eyes & teeth have gone – he can hardly waddle along he is so fat – his hair white going down to beetroot is shoulder-blade length – yet his mind is as clear as ever it was & he is quite brilliant at times.' Over lunch, Stephen described seeing, as a boy, 'the staggering beauty' of Gladys Cooper, and afterwards, in Beaton's well-planned and tasteful garden, his 'great love of nature, birds & insects & flowers' made it all come alive.[35]

Stephen had been suffering for some time from cataracts, which had to be left until they 'ripened' so as to be operable. (Gallery owner Jamie MacLean observed that this was partly the reason for the garishness and lack of fine lines in Stephen's later work.) The operation – done in a Salisbury hospital – was so successful that the doctor told John Skull that, with his new bi-focals, Stephen 'had sight as good as an airline pilot's' – despite the fact that his glasses regularly got so dirty he could hardly see out of them anyway. His dental health was less successful. Stephen had had the rest of his teeth taken out in a clinic in Poole, and was given a pair of dentures, but refused to wear them, and reverted to the old bridge he wore. 'I think that's why he liked to eat alone,' commented John. 'Even Lord Glenconner couldn't eat with Stephen when he came. Stephen always ate upstairs, alone.'[36]

*

After the Reddish lunch party, Stephen wrote to thank Cecil for the 'fairy-tale food and wonderful flower-glut in the garden! . . . Do please coax Eileen to write an Essay "Garden Musings" . . . she is so clever! . . . P.S. Can I see you opening the Festival? On the 12th? Mr Townsend says you will conjure the marvels in the Double Cube Ballroom – at Wilton? at 11.30 (I think?) or is this news to you?? . . . Do please make a gracious speech thanking the committee for their outsize bungling of everything! for their Genius for inept, sedulous, apathetic, dilatory "Laissez-faire!" on the grand scale.'[37]

Whatever the shortcomings of the Festival committee (which included Geraint Jones and Elizabeth Jane Howard as artistic directors), at least, when Cecil declared it open, Stephen's paintings were on display. This was almost entirely due to the efforts of John Skull, who had had to borrow easels from the College of Art to set up in the Vestry of St Thomas's Church in the city. 'I had got them all up and ready for the opening, when the night before Stephen came along and wanted to go in. I thought, "Oh no, he'll want the whole lot rearranged if he does", but when he tried the door it was locked. "They can't lock bloody churches!" shouted Stephen for all to hear. I had to explain that it had been done to protect his pictures, but he was livid!'[38]

It was a strange location for Stephen's decidedly secular art. Cecil's retrospective 'Summer of '73' article for *Vogue* in December noted: 'Making a spectacular reappearance after years of retirement, Stephen Tennant showed his puce and magenta paintings of Marseilles low life in the People's Vestry of St Thomas's Church.' The exhibition also afforded bookseller John Byrne his one and only glimpse of 'the legendary beauty', whom he found 'in the dimmest corner' of the room. 'A long figure slouched in a crumpled silk suit, peering through pebble lenses, a few henna'ed ringlets falling to his shoulders from an otherwise bald pate . . . After a few minutes there was a writhing and a squirming and a high voice spoke: "Do say you like that one. Do say you like it," he gulped. "I feel I've captured that moment we who live in the South know so well", another gulp, "that time that is neither day nor night when the air somehow", gasp, "crepitates". I felt that I had been afforded a glimpse of how Ronald Firbank behaved in public.'[39]

The writer Angus Wilson was in Salisbury too, invited by Elizabeth Jane Howard to give a talk at the Festival, and was told by her that he ought not to miss Stephen Tennant's exhibition. 'She rushed me into the Vestry where the paintings were on show,' remembers Sir Angus. 'They were all explicit scenes of sailors in the South of France, crowding public lavatories, picking up men in the street and other naval activities. The Vicar appeared and was introduced. He turned to me and said, "So glad you are enjoying Mr Tennant's lovely paintings. He has such a lovely way with colour, don't you think?" '[40]

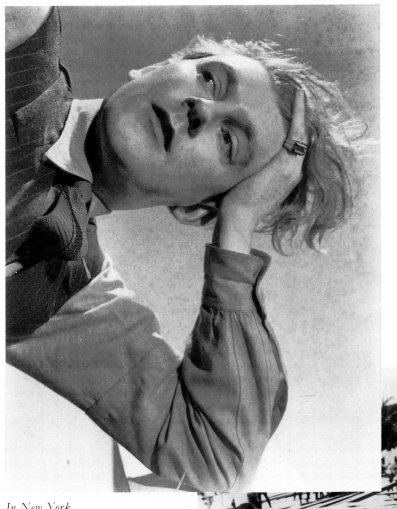

In New York

Edith Lewis, April 1951

On the beach, possibly Hawaii, 1949/50

Stephen
Tennant

at the

IOLAS GALLERY
46 East 57 Street
NEW YORK
22m

from April 25, 1955

Brochure for Iolas show, 1955

MEXICO   **HAWAII**

SAGITTARIUS
GALLERY
ROMA
April
1956
ITALIA
Stephen
Tennant

Introduction   Décors for Opera,   Burlesque.
by Stephen Spender.   and Ballet. Costumes. Sets.   Extravaganza.
                        Music Hall.
                        Circus.

Poster for Sagittarius show, 1956

Artwork, mid-1950s

Michael Wishart

Cecil Beaton

Marthe Bibesco

Siegfried, 1961

Christabel Aberconway

*Stephen by
Ida Kar,
mid-1960s*

Wilsford still life, 1967

*Fan photograph from the tenant
of Wilsford Manor*

Wilsford from the air, 1974

*John Skull laying
Stephen's tray, Wilsford
kitchen, 1981*

*Mary Skull with cuckoo,
Wilsford, 1960s*

Patricia Lee Yongue at Wilsford

Stephen entertains David Hockney, 1971

The garden

On the piano: Daphne du Maurier, Willa Cather, Pamela

*The sofa where
Stephen received
guests*

The landing

Last photograph of Wilsford before Stephen's death

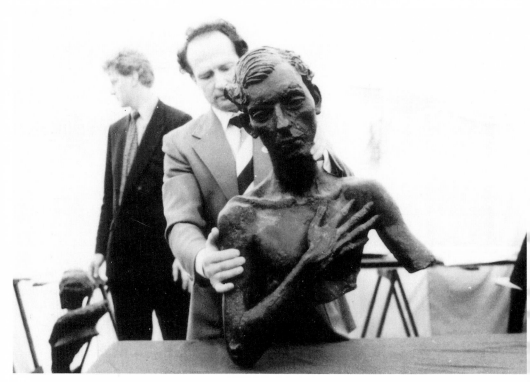

Wilsford auction, October 1987. The Epstein under the hammer.
(Maurice Lambert bust behind)

Chapter 29

Fallen Idle

...His sensibility he did not even try to control. But this was precisely where his gifts came from; they were not such as to generate genius – he needed concentration for that. Something of his lifelong dissatisfaction may have come from the feeling that he was a genius manqué.

— James Lees-Milne: *William Beckford*

O N 23 May 1973, Cecil had written in his diary that Stephen's recovery was almost absolute. 'After being almost blind for 2 years he has now had 2 cataract operations so that he can see perfectly. His spirits are high – he diets on melons – & is now a passable shape & has bought new clothes. His brain is incredibly flexible – he remembers everything he wishes, he quotes passages of prose & poetry – He is witty. He talked of the disadvantage of broken nails. "Oh I'm always breaking a nail – of course that means immediately breaking any social engagement."'[1]

Luckily there were no broken nails that month, for Stephen had arranged a reunion with two of the Mitford sisters. That winter he had sent Debo, now the Duchess of Devonshire, and a relation by marriage (her daughter Emma Cavendish having married Stephen's nephew Tobias in 1963), a copy of *My Brother Aquarius*. She wrote a letter of thanks couched in characteristic Mitfordese: 'I hardly can read, or I would really try the books you say are so good. My sisters say I have to point with one finger, I must say they are nearly right.'[2] A week or so later she returned from a sad visit to her sister Nancy in Paris, where she was dying from cancer. The Duchess had seen Stephen's drawings still framed on the walls of Nancy's flat: 'They adorn her dining room – marvellous.'[3] She told Stephen she was planning to go and stay with her sister, Pamela, in Gloucestershire at the end of May, and hoped to take him up on his offer and visit Wilsford then – which she did.

The visit was something of an eye-opener to both ladies. To Pamela, Wilsford was unrecognizable – her last visit having been in 1926 with Nancy and their mother – while Debo struggled to get a word in edgeways with Stephen's lectures on Sarah Bernhardt and Willa Cather. When she asked if they might go into the garden, Stephen said no, they were 'snowed in'. A 'strange bird', thought Debo,[4] but fascinating in the extreme. 'Pam and I so loved our visit,' she reported later to Stephen. 'I have so often wondered what Wilsford was like . . . It was so exciting to meet you after hearing about you for years, such a figure of glamour! . . . I told my sister [Diana, Lady Mosley] all about it and she was terribly jealous, you see she was invited by your mother all those years ago when my mother took Nancy and Pam to stay with you, but perhaps my mother thought three huge girls was far too many, anyway she was left behind and she minded dreadfully . . .'[5]

One of Stephen's later passions was for the Elizabethan era, 'that England of Gloriana', which, he informed Patrick Procktor, he had been studying for two years. 'Marlowe & Campion, Ben Jonson – Webster. And Raleigh & Drake & Essex – It's a thrilling epoch!'[6] For him, the romance of the sixteenth and seventeenth centuries held limitless appeal, greater than the Age of Reason and its rationality. Stephen felt himself a kinsman to the Metaphysical poets, whose 'thoughts were experiences which modified their sensibility'.[7] Stephen's poetical inspiration remained 'mystical, atavistic wisdom', and also, increasingly, theology.

Weaving in and out of his aesthetic and intellectual dalliances in the mid-seventies was a serious contemplation of things theological. He planned An Essay on Religion. 'E. M. Forster once said to me "I think 'Doubt' is the most important of all qualities for a writer or an artist; He must be free of all cramping doctrinism." Proust thinks this, & B. Russell & Aldous H.,' mused Stephen in a letter to his new friend, Patrick Procktor. 'Morgan Forster used to visit me, often. A radiant genius; we often talked of the Soul, the curious fact that Man demands Religious ethics & tenets, & then refuses to use them: strange anomaly!' Faith was 'a questionable Mecca! to be quite sure of anything – is to be duped by everything.' He considered that the modern world required 'a new religious feeling . . . but it must be a liberating of the spirit . . . On the whole, stupid people are the most religious – Clever men want to be free – to brood & experiment with a 1000 doctrines.'[8] Stephen's way of thinking was quite in line with a new and liberated generation, thought Patrick. 'He didn't need to smoke dope to get high – he was on a permanent high naturally!'[9]

Stephen's new-found liberalism even manifested itself in a tirade against the censorial attentions of Lord Longford's commission on the effects of pornography. 'No condemnation of physical joy can be admirable,' wrote Stephen in 1974. 'I do not think pornography should be unduly deformed. People need as many sensuous outlets as possible. A great psychologist said, "Whenever a patient of mine says how much he dislikes this subject, I know he has a secret obscene library."' Stephen observed that some of Aubrey Beardsley's 'great drawings are scata-logical . . . Some improper pictures have a great vitality, charm, punch and even power; Beauty! . . . Christian teaching attacks the natural functions of the body – this, of course only increases the licentious interest . . . I think personally that pornography in prose or sketches is simply a healthy overflow of the rich, natural products of body, mind & soul.'[10] To Stephen, his homosexuality had never been a 'problem', and on this subject, his thoughts appeared very liberal to new friends. He liked to quote Sassoon, who had reminded him that many 'great people of the past' were that way: 'one can hardly be ashamed of being among the very great. Plutarch, Gloriana, Shakespeare, Proust, Wilde, Sappho,' went his selective list. Stephen opined that 'most people are asses & bores whose opinions are negligible. I loathe conventional people . . . To be a Rebel! . . . Conventional asses bray uneasily, of moral redemption – they say what is proper, the right thing, at the right moment – they dread any subversive gleam of sincere passion.'[11]

Stephen's remained an unsensational attitude to sex. Sent 'muscle men' magazines by friends, he would relish the earthy pleasures in a supremely innocent manner: 'Oh, what a sexy book! quite uplifting! ah yes, to aspire! that is our aim! Erections! to rise! glorious! oh what a happy toffee-slide of fun!'[12] After reading Ackerley's frank autobiography *My Father and Myself*,* Stephen observed that it was a 'little improper – but so witty & wise. It shows that the treatment is more important than the subject-matter . . . Society dreads this frankness – prefers any circum-navigation, any lies, fibs are preferable to the searing truth . . . Adorable sex! How I love it. Let yourself go! Be a minion of the sun; & of joy! Be a glorious amorist', he advised. 'Love is the best tonic . . . Enjoy all the languors & ardours of Love – the beach in Tunis. Sunshine peaches!

---

*Joe Ackerley had passed on one piece of pick-up advice to Stephen: to go into pubs wearing a scruffy overcoat.

Glorious men! Enjoy the ultimate fruition of LOVE. Yes, sir! Worship –
Hug! squeeze! Study a manual on love.'[13] (Stephen occasionally liked to let
himself go, and would report in mock shocked tones the comments of
friends such as Julian Huxley, who was 'fond of rather improper stories . . .
he loved a flower catalogue which said "good in a bed, but better still up
against a wall" !')[14]

The spirit of the swinging sixties and seventies seemed to have caught
Stephen, and with friends like Michael Wishart, he came into direct contact
with a new social world. Wishart had been a friend since the late fifties, and
had also been responsible for bringing the modern world to Wilsford's
door. In August 1965 he told Stephen that his friend, Sir Mark Palmer, was
anxious to meet him: 'He is the most exquisitely beautiful boy with the
most lyrical and extravagant clothes as befits a leader of the Peacock
Revolution.'[15] Sir Mark was also the Queen's godson, the only person
known to have called the Queen directly from a public call-box to cancel a
dinner engagement at Windsor Castle. A trained jockey, and very handsome, Palmer had taken to life in a gypsy caravan for a while (a Bohemian-
ism that was nothing new to Stephen, who had been caravanning before
the Flower Children were even thought of). Sir Mark was very impressed
with Stephen when Michael brought him to Wilsford; he found his host
lying upstairs in the nursery, loosely attired. Palmer came on other visits,
and in 1976 he became a relation of Stephen's when he married his niece,
Catherine.

Michael Wishart brought another fashionable friend to Wilsford – the
cult film-maker, Kenneth Anger. Anger had started his career at the age of
four, playing the Changeling in Max Reinhardt's *A Midsummer Night's
Dream*, but since then had been behind the camera, making such underground classics as *Scorpio Rising*, a paean to leather-jacketed bikers done
to the soundtrack of the fifties song 'Blue Velvet'. It was a strange
combination, but Anger was very taken with Stephen and his house when
he met him in 1969, especially Stephen's 'colour sense – as reflected in the
"arrangement" of your rooms . . . I should be delighted to attempt to
capture its unique beauty in a colour-film poem.'[16] Stephen was enthusiastic, ever one for the glamour of the silver screen. He and the film-maker, and
Michael Wishart, exchanged fervid ideas. The scenario was to be, loosely,
'Sleeping Beauty', and Anger hoped to 'take a few scenes in your "Garden
of Pan" if the weather's fine – I would so much like to catch a glimpse of
your jewelled lizards on film!'[17]

Circumstances (mostly Stephen's prevarication) prevented filming that
year, but in 1973 Wishart was writing to Stephen again, proposing that

Anger bring down 'some of his films and his private silver screen . . . He would like to show you his film *Scorpio Rising*.'[18] Stephen looked forward to it, but decided things must be kept very quiet. 'Of course the embryonic *chef d'oeuvre* of the genius Anger must remain a secret, absolutely,' agreed Michael.[19] Throughout January and February of that year they exchanged ideas on the proposed film. Stephen aimed high: 'I absolutely agree with many of your suggestions for "extras",' wrote Michael. 'The trouble with people like Dame Margot and Rudolf and Peter Finch is that they have, usually, previous commitments, and to relative trivia always, which is so dull of them.'

Michael Wishart thought his friend Paul Getty 'might appear in the film if offered something in the region of Elizabeth Taylor's fees. He is not a spendthrift I fear, though highly intelligent but a total recluse.'[20] So it continued. Wishart observes that Stephen's 'Sleeping Beauty' scenario was 'a masterpiece . . . exactly like the film Anger would have made, even though Stephen had never seen any of his work.'[21] Sadly, all these plans to film Stephen and Wilsford, which under Anger's direction might have captured something of the strangeness of the place and the charm of the person, came to nothing. As with so many such projects, Stephen backed out at the last minute, and Anger's cameras never came to Wilsford Manor.

In the nineteen-seventies, Stephen discovered that he was already part of social history; in fact, he was positively sought after by writers seeking his valuable reminiscences of the famous people he had known. The biographer Michael Holroyd had alerted a new literary audience to Stephen in his two-volume *Lytton Strachey*, published in 1968, a book which Stephen greatly admired. 'I long to know Michael Holroyd,' noted Stephen. 'I do admire him so (bum chance!).'[22]

But in December 1972 Holroyd himself wrote to Stephen, asking if he had ever known Augustus John (who had lived nearby in Fordingbridge), and whose life he was now embarked upon. Stephen had not, but replied enthusiastically, recommending Cecil and Iris Tree as good sources (although the latter had died four years previously). Thus began a short friendship-by-post, wherein Stephen, anxious to lure the writer down to Wilsford, would prevail upon him to come and stay, whilst Holroyd, in the thick of his research, pleaded to be excused: he was immured, with the curtains drawn, busy on his book. *My Brother Aquarius* arrived at Holroyd's house, along with many letters, now written in blue and purple felt-tip pens, on blue stationery. Willa Cather, the Royal Bath Hotel, and Palmer's Pet Stores all came highly recommended, along with outlines for

Lascar and exhortations to rest. 'Please don't overwork,' Stephen told him. 'You are an Important, very gifted man – a genius indeed . . . What fun we shall have, when we meet.'[23]

Michael Holroyd regrets that that promised meeting never happened, 'though we exchanged messages through people like Stanley Olson' (who did see Stephen around that time, in the process of writing a biography of Elinor Wylie). 'I think he took the Strachey quotes all in good humour,' recalls Holroyd, 'which was rather generous of him, as it suggested that he might be of a less intellectual streak – "few feathers where brains should be" and so on – I think it was rather nice for Stephen to be in vogue once more. He'd been through something of a trough, then had come out of it as the world took interest in him once more.'[24]

Stephen's new role as oracle gained apace. He supplied valuable information and observations on Sir William Walton to Dr Stewart Craggs and Neil Tierney, both Walton scholars, and on 'dear Morgan Forster' to his biographer, P. N. Furbank, who also received a torrent of Stephen's letters. 'Actually I thought them extremely good,' notes Furbank. 'I got quite a bit from them.'[25] Furbank particularly valued Stephen's ideas on the novelist's more exotic tastes. There were detailed mauve-on-blue reports on Elinor Wylie to Stanley Olson, and when Sandra Jobson Darroch got in touch about Lady Ottoline Morrell, Stephen supplied a deluge of recollections and philosophical observations. He seemed eager to build up a relationship with each enquirer – perhaps out of loneliness, but also as an indication of a continuing vivacity and interest in life, and his own past in particular. An inveterate letter-writer and certainly an egotist, there was nothing Stephen liked better than to dash off two or three letters before lunch, detailing his thoughts on old friends and acquaintances who were now – as he was becoming – the subject of myth and legend.

The one subject which remained difficult for him to talk about was Sassoon. In 1971 Stephen kept up a short correspondence with a French Sassoon scholar, Gilles David, commenting on his erstwhile lover's lack of social sense, his possessiveness, and eccentricity. 'S.S. like all Oriental men was very secretive – reticent . . . on the whole I think, he was very remote . . . a very moody man, silent sometimes – but in a good mood he told funny stories, & then he roared with laughter & charmed everyone . . .'[26] But further comments in other letters, when Stephen could be drawn on the subject, show little objectivity, even at this remove, and could still exude resentment, with comments about his lost lover's selfishness. 'I haven't kept any of his letters,'[27] Stephen told his

French correspondent, and it appears that the majority of what must have been a voluminous correspondence between the two had been destroyed (only a handful of postcards and one or two letters survived Stephen's death to be sold at auction in 1987). It is possible that they had been burnt, as long ago as 1939, when Stephen wrote in a poem:

> *Old love letters will burn as bright*
> *as when they scalded me*
> *And time will set you free.*

But he also wrote, at the same time:

> *But time is not a peal of bells*
> *And life is bloody true*
> *And winter wild is all my lot*
> *since ever I lost you.*

Following Stephen's Festival show, further advancement of his artistic fame presented itself. Peter Maas ran an art shop in Crane Street in Salisbury, which supplied Stephen's Indian inks, and the owner had been thinking of starting a small gallery above it. He wrote to Stephen after seeing his exhibition, saying it was his pictures that inspired him to do it. Stephen leapt at the chance, and proposed a show that autumn, but Maas put him off till the following July, when once again the Festival was in full swing. The 'Compleat Artist' showed a selection of Stephen's work from 6–20 July, and was reviewed in the local paper, which likened his pictures to Toulouse-Lautrec's 'painted drawings' and discerned a baroque influence: 'His pen and brush do not define decisively the forms they bring to life but grow outwards over the surface of his pictures like the tangle of wild plants in a lush Wiltshire hedgerow . . . Sex is everywhere. But it is the sex of the Kingfisher's courting ritual – where human thought seeks nothing beyond the flamboyant spectacle.' The critic, like so many before him, posed the same questions: 'Is Stephen Tennant a good draughtsman? Are his characters convincing? Even if the answer is no, it is of no importance. What matters is that in his youth he lived in and for the theatre, the ballet, and the people who belonged to the world of make-believe . . .' He concluded that 'the story is unbelievable, fascinating, full of the joy of living . . . and almost painfully nostalgic'.[28]

Stephen's show was only moderately successful, but it did lead indirectly to his first television appearance. Dicky Buckle recalls being with Beaton and Patrick Procktor when they bumped into Stephen on Crane Street. 'Cecil saw him coming out of the art shop, with his long trail of purple hair . . . We were going to an hotel where the local television station were doing a piece on the Festival, so Cecil brought him along. Stephen sat in the only available chair in the room, dead centre, completely hogging the limelight. To his credit, Cecil wasn't embarrassed at all. I felt that he was very loyal to Stephen.'[29] Patrick Procktor also met Stephen by chance in Maas' shop, and urged him to come to his own opening. Stephen was indecisive, and Patrick playfully – and physically – insisted. 'I'm being kidnapped!' exclaimed Stephen. 'He came along anyway,' remembers Procktor, 'and he was very pleased because someone made a favourable comment on the "autumn colour" of his suit. "A compliment! At my age!" he said, adding, "Thank you for kidnapping me!"'[30]

Bournemouth and its shops continued to delight Stephen. 'When you need some really glamorous Silks & Metallic Brocades,' he told Cecil, 'either for your lovely house or for a shawl – do remember Bright's in Bournemouth Avenue.' Stephen sounded like an advertising trailer at a provincial cinema as he recommended the department store, more usually the habitat of blue-rinsed ladies (as opposed to hennaed gentlemen). In his description, Bright's takes on the more exotic aspects of the Tangier Casbah: 'Splendid for rich gold lamés & tissues de gloires: of all nuances & calibres. Exquisite chiffons from Lyons – very large, voluptuous! Also their silk scarves; Japanese . . . The Cosmetics Dept. is so Heavenly. Such pretty happy girls – spraying each other with "Fenime" or "Arpège".' (The image of ecstatic shop-girls wantonly dousing each other with perfume could only be Stephen's – and what would the floor-walker say?) 'The new rouges appease even me! the Blush Flairs of Estée Lauder on all sides – Egyptian eyeshadows – It is fun to shop there. Take a Huge Basket with you Cecil – and lovely gay Eileen to enjoy it all with you!'

Stephen returned from this particular trip with his straw basket packed full of stuffs 'for my new Lotus Dress. Rouge – Yes! Well, Yes!! . . . to give me moral support – & Élan! Verve! I love rouge so!' Stephen was reputed to have sixty-six shades of eyeshadow in his make-up box. The planned costume was to be made the following spring. 'Can I get some rubber foams to make Brassières at Gamages in Holborn?' he asked Cecil. 'I think I can,' he added, without waiting for an answer. 'My fertility Goddess of the Lotus Dress – this Dress will be becoming (I hope?) . . . I need a Brassière.' Stephen included a drawing with his letter, portraying himself: 'ST in his Fertility Goddess Dress as Ishtar-Cum-Venus – Miss Gethsemane Wallace in my play (*The Careless Rendezvous*) wears a dress like this for her Dance called "Samoa! Are you ready??" Her Swedish dance is called "Norsemen Unleashed!" (She is a Riot!)'

His new theatrical production necessitated 'writing comic songs and jingles. Really outrageous lyrics – full of Sporty, Happy-go-lucky innuendo . . . Wasting my Time on You! oh so naughty! so sporty, so showbiz! I feel quite shy . . . so erotic!' Then there was Stephen's *magnum opus* on foundation garments: 'Military men (so E. M. Forster says) used to wear "Stays",' he observed whilst selecting material for his 'Book of Corsets'. 'Also, of course, Gaiety Girls, Duchesses & Lost Ladies of all kinds . . . I adore the Corset advertisements in the Play Pictorial – do you? so gay!! "Our new Shimmerlastic Corset de Luxe – a miracle – it shimmers! Yet also grips you like a vice – you are as Svelte as a Python, & as cunning & wily! You undulate – yet you are as Serene as a bland Rose."'[31] Stephen boasted that the Maas gallery had already sold one of his corset designs – and he was about to take four more down.

Stephen's correspondence flowed on, trimmed like his corsets to the interests of each individual friend, although the same underlying themes were there: his (imagined) literary output; philosophical musings; poetry; and artistic endeavour, frequently accompanied by a sketch of a full-lipped Mae Murray or a pipe-smoking man of the sea. Whilst with Cecil he was whimsical, outrageous and silly, with others, such as Mildred Bennett of the Willa Cather Pioneer Memorial (of Red Cloud, Nebraska), he would wax lyrical and serious. Two new friends receiving Tennant letters now were actually old connections: Pauline, Stephen's niece, now married to her third husband, Sir Anthony Rumbold, was one; and Virginia, the Marchioness of Bath, formerly David Tennant's second wife, and now married to the Marquess of Bath, was another re-established relationship. Stephen's friendship with Virginia Bath began properly in the spring of 1974, although she had met and seen Stephen many times before (notably on one post-war occasion, when she and her husband ran into him choosing some purchases, quite unselfconsciously, from the cosmetics counter at Galerie Lafayette). But it was not until now that Stephen decided she might be worth cultivating. Lady Bath visited Wilsford, and Stephen was very taken by her fine looks, and those of her daughter, Silvy, too. 'I like young people to enjoy themselves,' he told her, and recommended Chipperfield's 'sublime Circus – Christchurch this week – Southampton next – Pure atavistic, Pantheistic Rapture & Ecstasy. Will you come for Afternoon tea?'[32]

That July was hot. 'How lazy one feels in this Heavenly summer . . . "Ah'm takin' ma ease," as negroes say. Really every social chore is pure

Hell! Oh dear! Ought we to say this?' he asked jokingly of Virginia, adding that he had had a new jewel case made by Hermès in Paris, '& the Customs Gentlemen are so in love with it that the odds are I may never get it! – they keep bleating, "Is it for your personal use?"'[33] A week or so later, the Baths called for tea, after an invitation which conspiratorially extolled the virtues of seeing very few people. 'How naughty we are!! We will grumble delectably & run down all our friends for their odious pertinacity in wanting to see one. I growl if the feeblest message is brought me by the quailing trembling housekeeper. "Say I'm in the Philippines – my Hacienda near Manila." Oh, Virginia ... Please say "NO" to all social overtures except mine!!!' The visit gave Stephen 'rare, exquisite pleasure ... Henry so amused me by saying "You don't sleep in that bed?" ... You are pure fairy-tale: Legendary loveliness. You remind me of Elsa von Brabant in Lohengrin.'[34]

Pauline, now Lady Rumbold, resumed her visits to Uncle Stephen in August 1971. She remembers stopping at Wilsford with Michael Wishart *en route* for a reading, hoping Stephen might consent to see them. 'He saw very few female members of his family,' she notes, 'so I was honoured when he said we could come in.'[*] Three hours later, the guests realized Stephen's monologue had erased all notion of time, and they were late for their engagement. Cecil was waiting for them there, and required no explanation for their tardiness when he realized where Pauline and Michael had been – in fact, 'he looked frankly envious!'[35]

Thereafter Pauline was granted a number of audiences with her uncle, and they enjoyed discussing poetry, and ideas for 'lassoing a publisher', as Stephen put it. Other plans were more exotic. In April 1974 Stephen asked if she knew of '2 or 3 strong amiable men' to help him with his new project; he was going to build a 'jungle cage' at Wilsford. 'I've got 20 pine tree posts 18 foot high – It will hold some monkeys, Apes, a goat or two, a small Bear ...' 'I love unexpected friendships in various animals,' observed Stephen (although a Wilsford retainer recalls that a pet monkey he had drove Stephen mad by running uncontrollably around the house, and had to be got rid of). He maintained his Wiltshire chain-gang would be well-treated, and would enjoy their labour under his direction, 'as the water-lilies are awaking' and his 'kind helpers' would 'really enjoy the green Italian lizards (45 on the lawn free!) and the Carp & Golden Orfe in my 6 pools.' They would receive 'delicious meals' and a 'Pavillon d'Armide' atmosphere would prevail – complete with pink champagne to refresh the 'stalwart helpers'.[36]

[*] Clare's grandson, Simon Blow, was another regular visitor in the later years.

Such fantasies grew abundantly in summer months, when Stephen, like his lizards, came to life. Warm weather awoke many instincts in him, and he acknowledged that autumn the effect of the seasons on his writing. 'I wrote *The Careless Rendezvous* – an outrageous farce – & felt high-spirited,' he told Pauline in November. 'When the cooler weather came I completely lost all interest in the play.'[37] Likewise *Lascar*, which he had described as 'thrilling! a sombre very sinister tale . . . like a fugue of Proust's despair',[38] but was now a source of his own despair. 'I've decided not to publish my Marseilles Super-Thriller,' he wrote. 'The very luscious over-spiced passages hold up the action – the whole novel is too perfervid.'[39]

And so Stephen would spend the winter months tucked up in bed, resting. Many people would like to have taken his oft-proffered advice to do as he did, and rest for long periods. But even then, Stephen was not completely idle. When he was not writing or painting, he might be sifting through the mementoes he had acquired over his long life: looking for a photograph of Willa Cather 'in a fancy hat' he had promised to send to Mildred Bennett in Red Cloud; or for one of Rex's early drawings, long since forgotten, which Laurence Whistler must see. It was a constant referral to the past; Stephen's preternatural ability to telescope time created a ceaseless flow of nostalgia. Like many old people, memories of his youth, even his childhood, became more vivid than those of middle age. His beginning and his end were joining up seamlessly, with the nasty things forgotten. 'Let's only talk of nice things, shall we?' he said to Virginia Bath when she asked him about David and the Gargoyle Club. Stephen was forever telling friends to 're-read' books (ones which they might never even have heard of), as he did, always going back to what he liked, and knew, and trusted. The past was no longer another country to him; it existed in the same way as the day before had done. 'Somewhere in Time' was often the only heading Stephen put on his letters written from Wilsford.

In November a sharp illness, probably the first signs of the stomach problems caused by years of bad eating habits, brought some days of pain for Stephen. It made him 'tigerish', and through 'rage and tears and agony' he hurled abuse at John Skull. 'I'm glad to say he became furious; and I was so horrified by my own ingratitude that I said humbly, "People do say horrid things when in fearful pain" (He is still only partly mollified),' Stephen told Virginia. 'Mary, his wife, is such an angel. She really does sympathize – but when I said (in tears!) to John, "I know I can't recover," he said crossly, "Pull yourself together, sir, we all have our ups and downs." This sobered me – that I subsided into pitiful sobs, and fell asleep.'⁴⁰ Yet Stephen's suffering seemed minor when set against what Cecil Beaton had undergone that summer: he had had a severe stroke, which had cruelly curtailed his working life. He could no longer write or draw (although he later learned to use his left hand), recall names easily, or look after himself physically. Stephen heard about it from the Skulls, and later in a letter from Cyril Connolly: 'I went to lunch there the day he had it, about 2 weeks ago, & was told he had fainted in his bath – so we all went out instead ... Nature is determined to yank us all out of circulation, I fear.'*⁴¹

Stephen wrote Cecil letters of support and sympathy – 'All your friends miss you so much'⁴² – but when Cecil began to recover a little, and came to visit Stephen at Wilsford, the side of Stephen's character that many saw as sheer callousness emerged. John Skull recalled: 'Sir Cecil [Beaton was knighted in 1972] arrived unannounced. I went up to Stephen and said, "Sir Cecil's here to see you," and he said, "Oh, I don't think I want to see him." I thought this was very bad. Anyway, Sir Cecil had presents – books – for him, and insisted on coming up the stairs. It was very difficult for him, but he got up to Stephen's bedroom, and spent two hours with him. When he left it took us nearly quarter of an hour to get him back down.

'I was very annoyed with Stephen, but when I took him his tea I said nothing. The next day he asked me what was wrong with me, and I said, "Well, sir, I don't think it was right to make Sir Cecil come all the way up to see you when you could have easily gone downstairs and had tea with him in the dining-room." "But I didn't feel like it," said Stephen, "and he came up here anyway." He had this wronged expression on his face, like a little boy. You had to forgive him – although I didn't want to.'⁴³

Beaton himself appeared unhurt by this display; perhaps, even in his illness, he knew what to expect. In a shaky left hand, he replied to a later letter from Stephen: 'I am so glad you like my scouting around. The book was a present & so were the magazines. I have been to London – & enjoyed 3 plays & 3 visits to doctors – but now I don't know quite what to do! There is television but one can't keep running to London. What do you do to keep in trim?'⁴⁴ Such agonized communications disturbed Stephen, who did nothing to 'keep in trim', and never watched television. He disliked any form of defect, and hated seeing his old friend crippled,

---

*Stephen had written to Connolly for advice on how to sell some of his letters from famous friends. Connolly advised him to separate them into manila envelopes, and send them to Christie's for auction, noting that Bloomsbury ones were particularly sought-after now.

walking with a stick. 'He couldn't stomach Cecil's disability,' observed Eileen Hose. 'Cecil would have reacted in the same way – neither of them liked any imperfection – everything was so visual to them. Stephen couldn't bring himself to see Cecil after that visit.'[45]

Chapter 30

The Blue of Redemption

I have put my talent into my works. I have put all my genius into my life.

— Oscar Wilde to André Gide

FOR a man regarded as a recluse, Stephen continued to make a surprising number of new friendships in the 1970s. It seemed as though he had got a second wind even as he approached old age. One such relationship, which blossomed from a mutual appreciation of the works of Willa Cather, was with a young American scholar, less than half Stephen's age. Patricia Lee Yongue first wrote to him in 1973, enthusing over his preface in *On Writing*. 'Ours was very much like the other [correspondences], rhetorically quite outrageous. Throughout that year, Stephen kept inviting me to come to Wilsford and described the delights of the place, not to mention the Cather memorabilia. So, having never been outside the country before and rather excited by Stephen's attentions, I borrowed $1,000 and took him up on his offer.'[1]

Preparations for Miss Yongue's departure from California were well under way when her mother wrote to Stephen, expressing her reservations about her daughter 'making this trip alone . . . My mother would never hear of my taking a trip such as Pat is doing . . . Your reassurance that you will look out for her was and is greatly appreciated.' Mrs Yongue added: 'You know, Mr Tennant, before I close, might I make one request, just don't tell Pat, please try to fatten her up some. She has grown so thin which worries me more than anything.'[2]

Pat had imagined that 'a cross between Henry James and Henry Higgins' would greet her at Salisbury station when she and her travelling companion, the photographer Lucia Woods, arrived. 'Imagine my surprise! John and Mary Skull roared for years after over the look on my face when I first alit at Wilsford and espied Stephen James Napier

Tennant.'³ John Skull takes up the story: 'Professor Yongue was invited
to stay for a month, we were told, but when we got a call to say they
would be arriving at Salisbury station, Stephen said, "Oh, but I'm going
out to buy flowers," and had me call him a taxi!' The two young American
girls eventually turned up, a little lost and bemused, having been given a
lift to Wilsford by a kindly stranger. Within minutes of John and Mary
coming out to meet them, Stephen appeared, clad in a pair of white
trousers that had seen better days – belted with a tie – an open-neck shirt
and his hair flying out behind. He was waving some Cather letters in his
hand. 'Miss Yongue! Miss Woods! Welcome to Wilsford!' 'You should
have seen Pat's eyes!' said John. 'Like saucers, they were!'⁴

Their stay was not to be a long one. Lucia had received a warning note
from Stephen via Wilsford's internal mail service: 'I'm so sorry you and
Patricia must leave me!! . . . But I am very busy – writing my novel *Lascar*
– and some essays AND revising 368 new poems – so it is best, really,
that I should be alone . . . Solitude is the school of genius: one must be
alone to create! . . . I value your friendship – and Patricia's . . . I've a little
neuralgia – so am resting – for a bit. Do please write to me – sometimes.'⁵

Lucia Woods packed her bags – she had planned to stay just a few days
– and when she left, Stephen told John, 'Tell Miss Yongue she may go
too.' Pat, who had happily taken up residence in the Rose Room, was
dumbfounded. 'Although Stephen had invited me for the summer, I
quickly learned that he really meant two or three days.'⁶ Having nowhere
else to go, and no money for an hotel, Pat didn't know what to do.
Luckily, the Skulls came to her rescue. John persuaded Stephen to let Pat
move into their part of the house, out of the way, where they would look
after her. And there she stayed for three weeks. 'We enjoyed her
company,' recalls John. 'She would go up for audiences with Stephen
every so often, and we joked about him always saying, "I think this will
amuse you." Pat would come down saying, "I think I've been amused
again!"'⁷

Miss Yongue was, on the whole, 'entranced' by her stay. 'My only
duties were to oblige Stephen's requests for visits and not bother him for
the rest of the time. I was invited usually in the morning and then in the
afternoon, for sherry. Normally, we/he talked about an hour. Sometimes,
he went on for several . . . At first John and Mary had a time with the
American girl who did not like to be summarily summoned and
dismissed. But I really did start to enjoy it all. Stephen was absolutely
generous and let me run loose in his library and gardens. In time, I grew to
love all that wilderness outdoors and shabbiness indoors. I must admit,

however, that I did try to get out of a few sherry hours,* but John and Mary were adamant about granting Stephen his wish for my company. And they were right. Stephen was my host, and he asked precious little in return for all that he gave me.'[9]

Pat was obviously the right kind of house-guest for Wilsford, for Stephen invited her back, and over the next ten years she spent alternate summers with him. One service she performed was to try and sort out some of Stephen's treasure-trove of literary correspondence, especially the few surviving letters from Cather, and from Edith Lewis, which had 'reached the death throes stage . . . Stephen played with the letters and often broke them up, pasting a page here or there, as it suited him.'[10] This was heartbreaking behaviour to a Cather aficionado who knew that the great majority of the writer's correspondence had long since been destroyed on her own insistence.

Over such a prolonged period of attendance on Stephen, Pat was able to make some acute observations. 'You know, the more I think about it, the more convinced I am that Stephen was very crafty, devilishly crafty. All those extravagant letters and the flamboyant conversation – a good deal had to be prepared, tailor made to fit the occasion, and the guest! He had carefully planned his medley to meet the interests of his visitor. With me, for example, it was all Edith Lewis and Willa Cather, of course – and, curiously enough, other women, such as Virginia Woolf, Elizabeth Bowen, and Elinor Wylie. He was not at all concerned with male writers, unless I brought them up. Oh, he would go off at times; he sang songs from American musicals to me and a friend for three hours (he thought my friend looked like a star he once knew or liked who had done *Oklahoma* and assumed, therefore, that my friend would like to hear *Oklahoma et al*), and John had to rescue us. He made three unsuccessful attempts, I think.

'But Stephen wanted to amuse as much as he wanted to be amused, and so his performance started out at least to play to his hearers. I don't think he had the slightest real feeling for any of us, none that he acknowledged or even recognized. I've never had that experience before. I do not feel trifled with; I just felt odd that I spent so much time in Stephen's house and in his presence and had not the slightest sense that he cared in any

---

*V. S. Naipaul was told by Mary Skull ('Margaret' in *The Enigma of Arrival*) of Stephen ringing for sherry, and being brought the bottle and a glass by a new member of staff 'looking as though she herself had had a drop too much . . . He didn't like it. "A little formality, Margaret," he said to me. "A little formality. It's all I ask. A drink isn't just a drink. It's an occasion." And I think he's entitled to a little formality. I told her, you know. Take nothing in without a tray. I told her.'[8]

remotely human way for me. I established the normal, expected relationships with others I met through Stephen, including a wonderful one with John and Mary. But Stephen's whole approach to me was performance.'[11]

It was the 'other side' of Stephen, that kept him apart from the rest of the world, a wall he had erected which remained steadfastly between him and humanity. The cool, cold side that had spurned Siegfried and rejected Cecil ensured a life lived completely alone. It was not to be altered now.

The shabbiness Pat encountered at Wilsford was the result of years of neglect. The Norfolk straw of the Thatched Wing was hanging loose, there was trouble in the boiler room, and the Edwardian plumbing system was cracked underground. In 1973, water had burst through the roof where a pigeon's nest had blocked a drainpipe, showering the rooms below. Carpets were ruined, and the wallpaper had to be replaced (although not matched, as the hand-printed papers – dusky pink with gold stars or white with Napoleonic wreaths – were too expensive). It was discovered that none of the contents of the manor were insured: a valuation was made and they were insured for £66,000. But the general financial problems of Wilsford were becoming critical. The central heating was oil-fired (according to one estimate it was costing £5,000 every year), and after the oil crisis of the mid-seventies, it became impossibly expensive to heat the whole house for just one person. As a result, only the rooms used regularly by Stephen were heated, which in turn left the greater part of the house damp and neglected.

Outside, there was only John to keep the huge garden in order. The bamboo grew high, the grass grew long, and ivy overwhelmed the statuary. The Skulls did what they could, but they were fighting a losing battle. Inside, mice were seen in Stephen's bedroom, and traps were set, but then forgotten. Weeks later, someone noticed an awful smell. The only time Stephen's rooms could be cleaned was when he was away, and overnight absences were becoming rarer. Latterly, he would be driven to Bournemouth once a week, for a shave and haircut in his favourite hairdressers, Mr Orton's, in Old Christchurch Road, and he would lunch in the 'Buttery' at the Royal Bath. This was his only travel now, yet to friends like Pat, Stephen always wrote 'as if he had just returned from or was on his way to New York, Paris, Corfu etc. . . . . He often asked me to look up dear friends in San Francisco, as if he had recently seen them. I came to learn that he was writing at least forty years in the past, that the years since World War II were not a reality to him.'

But Miss Yongue also wondered if Stephen didn't 'interiorly consider the present, though, as we have to do, and whether his condition was a manifestation of depression rather than an expression of his deletion of the last forty years. Although he talked always of a past world and a life of beauty and excitement, he turned his present life, except for his memories and the aristocratic privileges, into near squalor. His clothes and hair and room were exactly the opposite of what they were when he was a young man. Yet he always talked of his physical beauty and fastidiousness; how he would not think of going anywhere without a valet.'[12]

Not that he could even think of such luxuries now. Stephen's personal finances were strictly regulated by his trustees. Lord Glenconner had imposed the limitations out of necessity; he had once, long ago, asked Stephen what he spent all his money on. Stephen told him he bought useful things. 'Such as?' said Christopher. 'Well, that polar bear skin over there, for example.'[13] Stephen's fondness for animal skins would not endear him to modern conservationists. When Southsea pet-shop owner Charlie Taylor visited Wilsford, he was amazed to find on the stairs 'eight Columbus monkey skins – the world's rarest monkey – sewn together for a rug!'[14] (Stephen also boasted to Rosemary Olivier in 1961 of opening 'a crate of leopardskins from Nairobi – zebras also – so lovely'.)[15] It was only late in life that Stephen could be trusted with a cheque book, when he was no longer going out so much, and wouldn't be tempted to make exotic purchases. Even then he had just £45 a week to spend. 'He was always giving things away,' recalled John Skull; 'eventually Mary and I stopped saying we liked anything in the house, because if we did, he'd give it to us, and would get very depressed if we didn't take it. He would often try to give me money – sometimes more than my week's wages – and got very upset when I refused to take it. Of course I knew exactly how much he had – I drew his pocket-money from the bank for him.'

During the heat wave of 1976, when the heat made tempers fray, John Skull, despite the affection he felt for Stephen, very nearly resigned from his master's employ. Stephen had already become irritable with the protracted drought, and the Skulls put the moods down to the weather. 'I think he nearly got sun-stroke that summer,' recalls John. 'He would sit outside all day, and it did make him bad-tempered.'[16]

Stephen liked to spend his summer days in the garden, painting and writing. He sat on the West Lawn, which he liked to grow wild, only occasionally asking John to cut the grass when the nettles stung his legs.

Each day John would spend half an hour taking Stephen's things outside and setting them up: his sun-lounger, his painting materials in his little basket, his hats and books and papers and Ambre Solaire. Having done this one very hot afternoon, John left Stephen to his own devices, hoping for an hour's peace. He wanted to go into Amesbury to run some errands. 'When I came back into the house, I must have inadvertently locked the West door. Anyway, I went off to Amesbury, and when I came back, Mary was at the door. She said, "You're in trouble!"'

'She had heard knocking at the front door, and because of antique dealers coming up from Brighton and places like that, we used to look round the side window first to see who was at the door. And she saw Stephen leaning against the door, banging away. He was furious. "WHO LOCKED THAT BLOODY DOOR!" he shouted. Mary tried to explain when she let him in, but he had just stormed up to his room.'

John summoned up the courage to go up and apologize. 'But all he said was, "You locked me out of my own house!" I tried to apologize, but he wasn't having any of it. I took him his tea, and his supper – not a word. Then he shouted something at me again, and I said, "If you can't accept an apology like a man, then you'll have to accept my notice." I came down steaming! Later he rang the bell again, so I went up. "I don't want you, I want Mary," he snapped. So Mary went up and he started shouting at her too, telling her to "come here". She said, "You're not speaking to me like I was a little girl," and stormed off too!'

The next morning John took Stephen his breakfast. 'He was full of the joys of spring, making arrangements for an exhibition he was going to have. And I said, "But I won't be here, Sir." He couldn't understand what I was talking about, and I explained that I'd given him my notice.'[17] But Stephen's old charm had not left him, and by the end of the morning peace was restored to Wilsford, and John and Mary Skull agreed to stay.

Stephen's artistic endeavours continued to interest the outside world in the late seventies as a new audience, nostalgic for the twenties and thirties, came to hear of this extraordinary survivor of those wild days. In 1976, there was another show of paintings, at the fashionable new Bond Street gallery of Antony d'Offay. It was the high point of Stephen's revival, and was celebrated by a piece in the *Guardian* headed 'The Romantic Englishman', complete with a photograph of Stephen hiding coyly behind his Japanese fan.[18] Unfortunately, despite cajolements from friends and relatives, Stephen couldn't be persuaded to come up for the private view on 24 June, which was announced on a splendid invitation card illustrated with a reproduction of the famous 'Wilsford Bridge' photo-graph of Stephen and his bright young friends. More than anything else, these images helped to establish Stephen as a legendary and flamboyant figure of the 'roaring twenties'.

With advancing old age, Stephen's appearance began to change. His face became a little sharper; the fine-chiselled nose, inherited from Pamela, gained prominence, as did a well-defined chin. His weight continued to fluctuate. But despite his puffy cheeks and threadbare hair, he was still vain of appearance. He would spend hours in front of his dressing-table mirror, choosing his day's maquillage from a huge array of cosmetics. 'He was very vain,' recalls John Skull, 'and he had good reason to be, when he was young. I think he still thought he was a god – he used to spend ages in front of his mirror before going out, and even then, he'd stop at the first shop window and admire himself . . . His hair was going very thin, so he grew it long and would pile it up on top.' This coiffure, coloured with 'Sea-Witch' hair dye, was 'seen to' by Mr Orton on Wednesday afternoons; until one day Stephen fell over the step coming out of the shop, and John had to ask a passer-by to help get his master on his feet, so heavy had he become: 'It was very frightening, actually, for both of us . . . Stephen stopped going after that.'[19]

Age and infirmity were creeping up, and Stephen did not like it. He found it hard to accept his own mortality, as he had done with Beaton when he fell ill. Their friendship had an unhappy end. Stephen wrote Cecil a last letter, in effect a notice of the termination of their relationship which had lasted, through thick and thin, since that first meeting of Christmas, 1926: 'I don't want to see any friends or neighbours ever again', Stephen announced in 1978. 'I am a total sad recluse alas. I'm a complete failure in every way. How sweet you are. Infinitudes of Blessings to you . . . What a vile HELL of boredom the country is! no more fun now – ever . . . I'm so frail now.'[20]

Stephen's self-pity was all the more sad because so true. Cecil, who despite his disability had secretly resumed his diary, struggled to express his own pessimism in it after receiving Stephen's valediction: 'I have a frantic letter from Stephen . . . I cannot bear to think of his idleness & wonder what it consists of! I think most of his ideas are gone. It is difficult to know how to answer him! I have sent off a letter of bromides but I feel they are not worth sending, let alone his answering – It is an end of an epoch! A very frail one – but still it held forth a lot for me during the time I spent with him when he filled with birthday bright-day in London surrounded by people of his eye and temperament. Oh dear!'[21] 'Thereafter, if Cecil called, the message was that Mr Tennant was unwell,' wrote Hugo Vickers. 'The doors of Wilsford, so often closed in the face of a friend, foe or stranger, now rejected Cecil for ever.'[22]

There were few human reminders left of Stephen's old life now; as Beaton and others had predicted, by sheer willpower and 'preservation of his strength', he had survived them all. In 1972 Edith Lewis had died, leaving an ambiguous will in favour of her nurse, which was contested by Stephen and the other beneficiaries of the first will. All Stephen really wanted was the collection of sea shells and coral Edith had inherited from Willa Cather, although some extra financial support would have been helpful too. To deal with such matters there was only Christopher Glenconner, and he instructed Stephen's trustee, Mr Popkiss, to liaise with the solicitor in New York. Stephen neither understood nor liked legal matters, and it was probably this that put him off making a will of his own.

Lord Glenconner was practically the only close contemporary Stephen had left. He had always corresponded with his brother, and thought highly of Stephen's letters, keeping them carefully, and advised people like his niece Pauline to do likewise (Stephen made similar exhortations: 'Keep my letters, Eileen,' he told Miss Hose, 'they may be important.')[23] He was always pleased to hear of Stephen's advances in the artistic world. 'I am so glad – & impressed – that you have sold more pictures,' he wrote after Stephen's 1974 show, 'and now Essays on Theology & 2 plays! This is proving your most productive period!'[24] There was even a plan for Stephen to visit his brother at the villa in Corfu to which he had retired. Detailed flight and transport arrangements were made but, as ever, called off before Stephen got as far as packing his bags. Then, in 1977, Stephen sent a concerned letter to Corfu. Christopher replied: 'I'm so sorry you have been worried about Elizabeth & me. We are both very well . . . I haven't written because all our correspondence for years past has been that you write and I reply . . . I do indeed have a special & deep love for you – ever since you were very small & I used to cut up your bacon & eggs & mix them with breadcrumbs, which you liked very much, & which you would eat when you would have nothing else.'[25]

Who really cared for Stephen? Whom did he really care for? The Skulls were devoted, but were, after all, hired hands. A coterie of close friends like Pauline, Virginia, and Michael would give up what time they could, and made him feel that he remained a precious person. But they had their own lives to run. And with Stephen, there was always a distance – created by himself, by his past and present behaviour – that self-imposed gulf between him and the rest of the world, perhaps in the whole of his life only ever crossed by one person – his Nannie.

Two of Stephen's most glamorous visitors in the late seventies were David Bailey, the fashion photographer, and his wife, the beautiful model Marie Helvin. They were taken to Wilsford in early summer, 1979, by Nicholas Haslam, who had got to know Stephen through Simon Fleet (Lady Juliet Duff's 'walker'), and was now an interior decorator. Having had lunch at Broadchalke with Cecil, who told them they wouldn't get any sense out of Stephen (Haslam intended to write up the visit for David Litchfield's magazine *Ritz*, with Bailey's photographs to illustrate the piece), they left for Wilsford.

The three visitors found Stephen lying fully dressed on an unmade bed. He was very taken with Marie Helvin's Hawaiian looks. She remembered thinking that Stephen must have seen few women: 'I got that impression, from the way he talked to me . . . quite excitedly. He got out wonderful little diaries, with tiny sketches and beautiful handwriting – one had a lovely picture of Josephine Baker. Apparently he'd got backstage at one of her shows, and had sketched her . . . There were lots of drawings of Marseilles, and this sailor friend of his – he wound all these pieces of material around himself – "This was what I was wearing when I met him," he told us . . . He was wearing bright blue eyeshadow, rouge and powder,' she recalls, 'and his long hair was trailing over his shoulder. But under the powder you could see that the skin was actually quite good.' Within minutes Stephen and Marie were in deep conversation about cosmetics. 'He showed me his legs, which he'd painted brown with pancake make-up, which had come off on the sheets. I told him there was special body make-up you should use for that.' Bailey managed to drag Stephen away to pose him for a photograph on the landing, sitting on a chair by the stairs, his tweed jacket shrugged stylishly on to his shoulders, and baggy khaki shorts to show off the famous legs. White socks, loafers, a clutch-bag and a handful of silk scarves completed the ensemble, which was later revealed in a full-page photograph to the readers of *Ritz*.

'Stephen posed with his toes pointed,' said Marie. 'He seemed very proud of his legs. He walked with a little difficulty, but we had a good tour of the house and garden.'[26] The talk continued all the while, as Stephen described the exotic contents of his domain. Helvin went into the bathroom, where she found the sink and bath full of shells, the water tinted pink and blue. Stephen liked to keep some of his shells under water;

as he had demonstrated to Gertrude Stein back in 1937, their colours came out so much better. Sometimes he left the tap running water over them, thus threatening to flood his bathroom. No matter; it wasn't as if he actually used it for the purpose for which it was intended.

Just a few days into the new decade, Cecil Beaton died at Reddish House. He was buried on 23 January at Broadchalke, and a message of condolence came from John and Mary Skull at Wilsford. Eileen Hose read their note of sympathy, which bore an odd postcript: 'Mr Tennant wishes to be associated with this message . . .'[27] Even now Stephen could not bear to acknowledge death. Cecil would not have been surprised at this apparent coldness. He had known, as did everyone else who knew Stephen well, that his friend's attitude to death was not one which encompassed normal ideas of bereavement. Stephen thought grief 'a very private thing'. But the apparent decline announced in his last letter to Cecil had already receded. The cloud passed, and the sun shone on Palazzo Wilsford once more.

Before he died, Beaton had decided that Hugo Vickers should write his biography. Vickers had started work just two days before his subject's demise. 'His sudden death was more than disappointing and it changed the nature of the book I was to write,' observed the writer.[28] Now he would be heavily reliant on the letters and diaries left by Beaton – and on the memories of people who had known him. As Vickers began to delve into Beaton's huge mass of correspondence, he realized how important Stephen had been to Cecil in his formative years. Working at Reddish that February, he noted in his diary, 'Already in my research Stephen Tennant comes to life . . . I must ask Eileen about him.'[29]

What he was told by Cecil's secretary fascinated him. Eileen said Stephen was 'quite mad' and a recluse.[30] After Beaton's death, Stephen had started up a correspondence with her, sending his poems, and discussing *Lascar*, which, he admitted, had become 'more of an occupation than a novel'.[31] When Hugo left that evening, he took a detour past Wilsford. 'There was a light on in the park – I wondered if that was where the house was with that strange recluse living inside. And what would he be doing? Playing with his beads or jewels – reading his cine-magazines or reciting poetry . . . The whole thing becomes more and more mysterious.'[32]

Vickers was soon to find out more, in a close encounter of his own. Talking to Beaton's old friends, he kept hearing new stories of Stephen. Diana Cooper alleged that Stephen had been 'one of Aaron's babies',[33] whilst Peter Quennell told Hugo a little of the affair with Sassoon, how extraordinary it was that Stephen could make the great poet return to their hotel room to fetch his necklace. Caroline Blackwood described the extraordinary interior of the house. In turn, Vickers told a society lady about Stephen. She bought some of Stephen's journals (which had been given to Beaton, and were sold off by mistake after his death), and began to write to him. In due course Stephen heard of Hugo, and his work on Cecil – and was intrigued by Vickers' first biography, *Gladys*, the product of his obsession with the equally reclusive and strange Duchess of Marlborough (whom Stephen had visited with Pamela as a young boy), a copy of which the author now sent to Wilsford. The bait was taken.

On Thursday 18 September, the telephone rang in Vickers' flat. John Skull announced: 'The Honourable Stephen Tennant would like to speak to you. Can you hang on?' Hugo waited, then Stephen came to the telephone. 'He sounded like an actor with a rich, fruity voice, deep and intellectual.' The opening gambit was Gladys, and how much social life Hugo needed. 'He spoke of Willa Cather . . . He felt the same way about her as I did about Gladys.' *Lascar* soon entered the conversation, and Stephen talked about his love of sea-ports: 'They are partly sinister, partly displeasing . . . Marseilles had a rich, drowsy languor.' Then suddenly across the world to Mexico, and 'avenues of tuberoses . . . All our roses grow in Mexico . . . I adore a black velvet rose.' Talk of hot climes seemed to chill Stephen, for he declared, 'I don't like the telephone. It's in a cold part of the house. I just want to go and get a wrap to put around me.'

After one of Stephen's dramatic interludes, he returned to pick up the conversation. Beaton, and the biography, was the subject. 'He's too complex,' Stephen maintained. 'There are so many contradictions, though each may be right.' Stephen then suggested Hugo come to Wilsford to talk at greater length, suggesting he leave London in his 'motor' at 'about 9.30, passing through Virginia Water and Bagshot, and lunching at the Cricketers Inn. I would be with him at four. The plan was for Saturday . . . He ended by talking of the world in general, the strange bombs and said "We're all in this together."'[34]

'In due course I set off to make my pilgrimage,' wrote Hugo. John Skull met him in the courtyard at Wilsford. '"Mr Vickers? Would you go round to the front door please." A bolt was drawn back, a chain clanked, but no, the door did not actually creak on its hinge. Apart from the faded, musty air I could not take in the hall – no time – but through I went, following John to the staircase and up. "Mr Tennant is on the landing" he said . . . Turning the corner there he was, the lone occupant of Wilsford Manor.'

Stephen did not appear as eccentric as Hugo had hoped. 'He looked younger than his 74 years due to a powdered face. His fingers were small and feminine and tapered. A huge turquoise ring was on the "wrong" finger of the left hand.' Stephen's hair was still shoulder-length, however, and hennaed, and he wore his sheepskin slippers tied like a ballerina's. 'And of course awful scent. But the overall impression though odd was not from another world. He could have been an old actress, or an old school-master gone to seed . . . If you saw him in the street, you'd say "Good God" but the image would pass. Cecil B. said "a mad tramp". Perhaps. I have a feeling that he wanted to look as normal as possible on this, my first visit.' Stephen greeted his guest with the usual 'little noises of delight'. Cushions were sent for his guest to 'loll onto', and tea and cucumber sandwiches were served. 'He urged me to eat them to please Mary, John's wife. He praised them both so highly: "We've had some adventures in the last ten years but she's never lost her temper."'

Conversation revolved around the familiar *dramatis personae* of Stephen's life – Cather, Sassoon, Beaton. Stephen told Vickers that his eyes were tired and 'that I should not read at night for two months . . . Now and again he recited a poem – now and again he sent me on a mission – to see the room with the zebra rug – to see his mother's room, and then the drawing-room.' They all looked untouched to Hugo. 'The beds were unmade – I feel sure his mother's clothes were still in the house . . . Then there was the expedition to his bathroom. There was a small bath, many mirrors, painted panels and again shells placed one here, three there on the floor. His bedroom into which I peeped was the most squalid room I've ever seen. A bed had been crawled out of. On it were letters, drawings, scribblings, jars of cream, beads, shells, screwed-up bits of tissue, old press photographs. It was extraordinary.'

Vickers vacillated between fascination and disapproval. 'He was at his worst when he said things like "I'm a bit over-weight, but I'm still rather beautiful, aren't I?" And "Some people say I'm a genius..."'[35] Eventually, after three and half hours of Stephen's monologue, Hugo made his excuses, was lent two Willa Cathers, and left, promising to return. He kept his word, and thereafter came back to Wilsford on many occasions, each time discovering new aspects of its strange incumbent – and liking him more on each visit. A fervent correspondence started up, initially based on Stephen's recollections of Cecil and advice for Hugo's book, but later on all manner of things. Vickers found Stephen's sense of humour close to his, and they enjoyed swapping caricatures of mutual acquaintances that would have scandalized their victims. Of course, *Lascar* and Stephen's literary output *manqué* were always major topics – all expressed in Stephen's stressed and underlined felt-tip script:

'My procrastination and relish weary everyone,' Stephen told his new friend in one of his first letters. 'Cecil B. said choose "Sardonyx"' (a proposed title for a collection of poems) 'and stick to it! (I was huffy for weeks at this martial tone!)' He described the plot of *Lascar* at length – still the conception of his great work, all seven versions of it – which could excite Stephen into paroxysm of descriptive prose, as could his poetry. 'I am sure my poems would sell, Hugo – they are really waiting for the shrewd opinion of some very intellectual friends,'[36] the hint being obvious: that Hugo should be the latest in a long line of 'intellectual friends' to embark upon the search for that ever-elusive publisher.

Stephen wondered too if Vickers knew of a 'nature-loving friend' who might want to share Wilsford. 'Oddly enough, I like jolly, genial men,' said Stephen. 'If we could find him – I'm sure he's there!!'[37] He had conceived a notion – after years of solitude – that it might be nice to have a companion again. He even joked to Virginia Bath that he should wed. 'I'm thinking of marrying – will you and Silvy help me? Wistful clauses: A modicum of charm – Much business calling her away, Urgently, Monthly. The one Vital stipulation is Vast Wealth; Reserves of financial Power, to wallow in, & gloat over. A wife-hunting Safari would be fun, a lark,' he decided, but 'it would be a "Marriage Blanc" ... A plain, homely face keen with religious zeal, self-effacement essential. Also, endless apologies for her lack of erudition. As silent as a Trappist priest. Ailing relatives in Finland, or Key West, calling her constantly to their protracted demises. She must have a passion for funerals & fasting, and Awe of Me.'[38] (Stephen also wrote to Eileen Hose around this time that he thought 'A man is happier married – He's all the man, nearly ...')[39]

A subsequent letter to Lady Bath has this unfortunate would-be mate devil-worshipping in Assam, where 'she was Goddess of fecundity, Devil cults in Burma were a strain! Yet? Satanic Blisses – of a sort? oh dear! Python worship temple! – she had to sit on the Altar! with an Ape while 3 priests kneeling, a Boa Constrictor and a Llama, & a Yak!'[40] It recalls Stephen's *Leaves from a Missionary's Notebook*, to which he drew Hugo's attention in 1980. 'My comic *Missionary* book would amuse you,' he told Vickers.[41] As it did – so much so that the biographer eventually secured its republication.

In between time, Stephen's Muse was hard at work. 'My dear Hugo,' he wrote in 1981, 'do come & see me please. A quick torrent of Poetry is now Battering at my portcullis . . .' New fan letters were arriving at Wilsford, he said, 'saying the public must now know my work.'[42] How could anyone disagree when Stephen delivered such lines as 'What fun it is being Geniuses like you & I.' One of the most amusing comments came on the back of an envelope Vickers found one morning on the doormat, writ large enough for the least inquisitive of postmen to see, in vibrant cyan ink: 'Guard your Talents carefully, Hugo – I sense Genius in you.' 'That cheered breakfast up,' observed Hugo.

On his fourth visit to the 'ageless and unreal' Stephen, they talked of his family. His nephew Colin, observed Stephen, was always to be found at the Ritz in tennis clothes, while he confessed he didn't understand the books of his niece Emma Tennant. Stephen was not completely starved of news of the modern world: although Lady Emma Tennant could not persuade him to sample the diversions of television, he did receive *The Illustrated London News* weekly; and he exhibited his knowledge of current affairs by commenting on Prince Charles' engagement to Lady Diana. (The royal family continued to be of interest to him, though his observations were not always polite. He wrote once of Princess Anne 'and her Great Barrier Reef' of teeth, and noted that the Queen Mother was now 'too Royal to carve the joint'.) Then Stephen described the opening passage of *Lascar*: 'A lorry sets off – someone has forgotten to do up the back – a pile of boxes tumble out containing oranges and pineapples which spill out over the quayside. This is heard by Mme Seraphim Neffus and her Dame de Compagnie, Mme Hortense.' Hugo was fascinated: 'I wish he would write it or hand over the drafts.'[43] (Vickers later bought the collected MSS. of *Lascar* at the Wilsford sale.)

In the spring of 1981, blossom and sunlight flooding into the valley, Hugo found Stephen still in the dark, dressed in his pyjamas, the curtains drawn. It was the first time he had been greeted by his host actually in bed. Stephen gave him his essay on poetry to read, and talked of famous friends – 'I wish you could have known Virginia.' On this occasion, Hugo had a chance to chat with John about his master. He was pessimistic, telling him Stephen was 'living on borrowed time. He was in a bad way, to hear John talk. He'd gone to Bournemouth, and eaten rich food, as a result of which he became terribly constipated and had to go to hospital. "He never told me", said John, referring to a previous occasion when there had been a terrible mess to clear up in his room.' John told him that they kept Stephen informed of the outer world, 'especially to do with the Royal Family – he doesn't tell him the gory details of Ireland, for

Serious Pleasures

example'. Vickers left Wilsford and its sleeping, ailing inhabitant, 'reeking of that awful scent that pervades the atmosphere'.[44]

That same scent was the cause of an unhappy episode for Hugo on his next trip, this time with Eileen Hose. 'He made Eileen close her eyes and then handed her various bits of jewellery first to hold, then to see. And he squirted Max Factor on our hands. That's what did it, I think. I had to go out and be sick. Not once but twice.'[45] Hugo asked John if he could lie down for a few minutes. Mr Skull remembers the writer's face, 'as white as the marble fireplace!'[46] Nausea grew to feverish shivering, and Hugo found that he couldn't get up, and had to spend the night there, alone. In the middle of the night he nearly got up to go to the bathroom, but heard strange footsteps, and having seen too many horror films, decided to stay where he was.* It was a relieved young biographer who got into his car the next morning and drove back to London, where he collapsed with 'flu for several days.

---

* 'Strange things used to happen in the Manor,' said the lady in the local post-office after Stephen's death. 'Plants used to water themselves,' she added, hinting darkly at other weird happenings in those lofty beamed upper rooms.

Chapter 31

Final Act

I'm going to be a Bird of Paradise this Spring.
— Stephen Tennant

IN March 1982 Stephen was in hospital once more, in the Tatum Ward of the Salisbury Infirmary, having had trouble with his digestion. Prolonged periods in bed, and taking his meals there, without proper exercise, had resulted in many problems. However, he seemed well enough to be discharged a few days later – only to return soon after, his condition having become serious. Stephen hated his illness, and the necessity of medical treatment. Hugo offered to visit him, but he was politely turned down; Stephen didn't want to be seen in that state, in the same way as he didn't want to see anyone else like it. Mary Skull reported that the hospital staff were having difficulties with him: 'They think "what a nice old man". But then he roars at them like a lion and they realize.'[1]

Back at Wilsford, Stephen found it difficult to walk unassisted, and Toby Tennant recommended he have hand rails fitted, saying that their friend, Sir John Betjeman, managed very well on them. But Stephen was not convinced, and on his return, crawled upstairs on all fours. 1983 saw further loss – the death of Christopher Glenconner, and also of Mary, John's wife. Stephen's affairs had been delegated to the care of his nephew, Toby, before Lord Glenconner's death. Stephen wrote to him that Christopher, Toby's father, had been 'a creed of life to emulate'.[2]

Mary Skull had been ill for some time, and officially retired in November. Her sudden death from cancer was a blow to both John and Stephen. Besides being a stalwart and resourceful housekeeper-cum-nurse to him, she had been part-time secretary too, ever willing to read Stephen's often impenetrable poems and type them out for him. With her death, Stephen lost a friend as well as a housekeeper. John felt unable to stay on at Wilsford on his own. He remained there for nine months after

Mary's death, doing everything for Stephen, until Sylvia Blandford, who had been nursing Stephen latterly, could take over as housekeeper proper. (John remarried, and went to live in London. He returned on a social visit to Wilsford a year or two later, and recalls Stephen asking his new wife to come and sit with him 'while he ordered me off on an errand, as if I still worked for him!')[3]

It was Sylvia Blandford who looked after Stephen for the final few years of his life, and she was as devoted to him as had been her predecessors. Her duties ranged from the Herculean task of keeping the house and its contents clean, to mending Stephen's favourite teddy bear: 'If I sewed his leg on once, I sewed it on a thousand times,' she said.[4] Toby Tennant took the business affairs of Wilsford in hand, and managed to save Stephen some money by changing the firm who handled his finances. Even so, there was still only just enough to meet costs, and to pay for nursing home and medical expenses part of the estate had to be sold off. Stephen now had to stay for long periods in homes; after his second return from the Salisbury Infirmary, he had contracted pneumonia, and this required further rest and recuperation at a nursing home in Nether Wallop, where he could be looked after properly.

Despite such serious complications (pneumonia could be fatal at his age), Stephen's strength of spirit carried him on. His last years were characterized by the same flow of correspondence, but with a perceptible slowing-down after 1984. He wrote to Virginia Bath on 30 September 1985: 'I've had a long illness (I'm 79) a curious kind of breakdown, Virginia, only a nervous breakdown, my body & mind are quite all right.* But Wilsford is too lonely. Could I marry do you think? I know so many lovely people who would marry me . . .' He insisted that he would still be a good 'catch': 'there is nothing wrong with me', though he admitted 'I walk with a "frame" (I had some "falls" & this frightened me).'

Yet he still had visits from 'lovely friends'. Hermione Baddeley, Pauline's mother, came whenever she was in England; John Skull recalls her looking 'very chic in a white trouser suit, still beautiful at seventy-odd',[†5] and her daughter Pauline came on a number of occasions. She

---

*Stephen had told Hugo Vickers in April 1982: '. . . I've got a strange horrid Neurosis. It will fade away I hope – the price we pay for being a Genius!'

†After her separation from David Tennant, Hermione Baddeley had continued her successful career on the stage and in films, starring in, amongst others, *Passport to Pimlico*, *Brighton Rock*, and, latterly, *Mary Poppins* (in which she played the housemaid). Baddeley never lost touch with Stephen's brother, despite their respective marriages, and in his later years she had become quite close to him again, and there were even suggestions of remarriage. She died in 1986, and was buried in the same grave as David in Wilsford churchyard.

recalls one visit, when she took her aunt, Muriel,* along with her husband
Sir Anthony Rumbold, and her young adopted son, Andrew:

'Stephen had invited me for tea, and I knew that he was strange and shy
about other visitors, so I told Tony and my aunt to wait in the car whilst I
went in to ask Stephen about it.' She was shown in to Stephen, where he sat
with the tea-tray laid. 'I told him I wanted to introduce him to my husband
and my aunt, whereupon he turned to me and said, "I think tea for two is so
nice, don't you?" So I said, "Well, they're waiting in the car, I'll have to tell
them something." So Stephen sent Andrew, who was quite small at the
time, to go and tell them.' Unfortunately young Andrew got waylaid by the
sand on the West Lawn, and started to play in it. 'Stephen talked
mesmerizingly until I left. When I got back to the car, I realized what had
happened. My aunt was furious, but Tony had understood. "I guessed
what had happened," he said, "and went for a walk."'[6]

There was still time for a last exhibition of Stephen's work, in 1983 at the
Maclean Gallery. Jamie Maclean had already sold one of Stephen's
Lascar pieces for £300, and it was obvious that, after the d'Offay Gallery
show and recent publicity, his work was fetching higher and higher
prices. Maclean visited Wilsford to help Stephen choose the pictures for
the show, which was his most successful yet. Some fifty paintings were
shown at the St George Street Gallery, from 6 September to the end of the
month. Total sales came to £5,825,[†] with only seven pictures left unsold.
It was a great triumph for Stephen's art and, in its own small way, a
vindication of his struggle to be known as an artist.

There was yet more excitement a year later, for in 1984 the BBC
descended upon Wilsford to collect Stephen's impressions of Cecil for a
documentary on him. Nicholas Shakespeare was the interviewer; the
interviewee, in his thick-rimmed glasses and silk cravat, spoke know-
ledgeably about his old friend (pointing to one of the Lancret Affair
photographs and exclaiming, 'I hope I really did look like that!'),[7] whilst
completely transfixing viewers. Stephen, it seemed, was as much a
'natural' in front of the moving camera as he was before the still. There
were to be another two occasions over these last years when the spotlight
was literally turned upon the legendary inhabitant of Wilsford.

*Hermione's eldest sister. Her younger sister, Angela, had married Glen Byam Shaw (Sassoon's
former lover) in 1929, and was also a well-known actress, a familiar face to millions as 'Mrs
Bridges' in the TV series *Upstairs, Downstairs*.
†Although after 40 per cent commission and a £553 framing bill, Stephen actually received only
£3,007.32.

A year later the Earl of Pembroke succeeded, where Kenneth Anger had failed, in making a full length film of Stephen. The Pembrokes as a family had retained a close connection with Wilsford since Pamela's days, and the present Earl, Henry, and his young family were very attached to Stephen, and often visited him. The children loved him, regarding him as an interesting variation on the usually dull sort of uncle, and when they came to Wilsford there would be much fun and games in the garden. John Skull recalled them being out there for hours one sunny afternoon, 'all shrieking with laughter'.[8] Stephen would entertain the company with songs from *Oklahoma*, and they thought it was very funny that, when the record came to the song 'Poor Jud', Stephen would stuff bits of tissue in his ears because he hated it.

Henry Pembroke liked Stephen's company, and thought him good for the children, and vice versa. That was not the case when he first remembered meeting Stephen in his early teens. 'I was out walking with my father in the grounds, and as we crossed the Palladio bridge, there was Stephen, lying in the grass with a flower behind his ear, admiring the house from the far bank. My father hurried me along after we'd said hello – I think he rather disapproved, and thought Stephen might be a bad influence on me!' Lord Pembroke took many friends on later visits to Wilsford, including the filmmaker James Ivory, who was impressed and thought it all a good subject for a film. Another visitor was Princess Elizabeth of Yugoslavia, to whom Stephen insisted on showing off his beautiful legs. To do so, he proceeded to undo his trousers, and take them off, with great difficulty. He asked for assistance. 'There was this extraordinary scene of a princess yanking off this old man's trousers,' laughed Lord Pembroke. 'Stephen used to be very proud of the tan he got on his legs – it was only [when he] turned that you saw they were painted – and he'd only done the front. The backs were completely white.'[9]

Henry Pembroke was also a film producer of note (he had directed Koo Stark in her film début, *Emily*), and since 1978 had been trying to persuade Stephen to allow him 'to make a little film . . . Just you talking about yourself and your house and your life and your likes and dislikes. Would you agree to it? It is so important that you be remembered for ever . . .'[10] This was an attractive notion to Stephen, who liked the idea of immortality, and so the date was set. Henry Pembroke enlisted the interviewing services of Nicholas Haslam and, once at Wilsford and in Stephen's den, they set up the movie camera. As he got used to the attention and the whirring camera, Stephen became loquacious. The result was one of his best monologues, as Stephen reminisced over famous friends: Willa Cather, Barbara Hutton, Tallulah Bankhead, Mistinguett, Greta Garbo and Virginia Woolf all starred in this one-man show. His talk was steady, humorous, almost bitchy at times – and quickly became rapturous and elegiac at others.

Stephen directed his friends to look round the house; the camera panned over a dusky interior, with faint glimmers of Venetian glass and swagged silk. Back inside, the talk continued. His plants needed watering – 'Would you give them a drink, Nicky?' – and then out came the jewellery box, from which he extracted all manner of gems, doused in 'sacred saliva' to make them sparkle for the camera. He spoke of finishing *Lascar*: 'I've delayed all this time . . . but there still is time – that is a joy . . .'[11] It was a virtuoso performance, one of his best.

And still his filmic career had seemingly not yet ended. Stephen, normally so shy, had begun to be quite used to this glamorous attention, so when BBC2 came down to film him for the last time, he had everything ready. They were at Wilsford two days, and filmed him at length, but left abruptly as Stephen was setting out his lipsticks for the last session. He was very disappointed.*

Patricia Lee Yongue was another of the rare visitors to Wilsford in Stephen's declining years. She found Stephen's inability to walk 'a mystery. Clearly there was atrophy, though probably not from disease . . . His legs died. I think he may have developed – cultivated – a terror about being alone, and illness and immobility guaranteed him the presence of human beings.' Like other friends, she saw that Stephen wanted to stay at Wilsford, and not end his days in a nursing home, 'so he had to find a way to be both helpless and independent . . . Listen to me, I sound like a psychiatrist,' said Pat. 'It's just that I've thought this over and over and over. I've agonized over Stephen's many refusals. When I first knew him, he at least roamed the manor inside and out. He liked to sun and to watch his terrapins. He picked flowers. Then he started not going out at all, just stayed inside and trotted about. At last, he kept to his room and then to his bed. It was all so bizarre.'[12]

She last saw him in the summer of 1984. 'Mary had died the previous year, and so it was only John and I for company. Stephen was mostly in a temper, and neither of us was called in for chats too frequently. It was pathetic to see Stephen deteriorating so, to see him just lying on that bed in that darkened little bedroom of his piled high with playthings.'[13]

---

*Kit Hesketh-Harvey, the producer, recalled that, sadly, Stephen's mental and physical state was not up to the demands of filming.

There was to be just one more outing for Stephen. In the summer of 1985, Stephen decided he would go to town. It was his last trip to London. He was driven up to see an exhibition, 'Cecil Beaton and Friends', at the Michael Parkin Gallery in Knightsbridge. The sudden appearance of this extraordinary figure in front of his own pictures (two of which he apparently bought back himself) astounded the gallery staff. Then, on to lunch. 'The Ritz', Stephen had decided, and so there it was that he and Sylvia Blandford lunched in regal splendour, attracting sideways glances from other customers wondering who on earth this old man could be – obviously someone famous, and probably immensely rich. The staff reacted with suitably awed service. Then it was back into the car, and home to Wilsford, for the final run.

But even at the last act, there was time for a concluding twist in the tale of Stephen Tennant. Throughout 1984 and 1985, Hugo Vickers had been lobbying publishers to reprint *Leaves from a Missionary's Notebook*. Negotiations were begun with Hamish Hamilton, and proceeded slowly. Stephen asked occasionally, 'Where is it?' but had given up hope of seeing his 'funny little book' relaunched. But on 27 February 1986, Hugo wrote him an excited letter. 'How would an American begin this . . . "You're going to love this" – or "This'll make your day". The point is that I have some really good news to tell you.' Christopher Sinclair-Stevenson at Hamish Hamilton had agreed to the republication of *Leaves*.

The proposal was to offset the edition from Hugo's copy (which was the original given by Stephen to Cecil in 1937); 2,500 copies would be printed, selling at £10, with a royalty of 5 per cent – low because of production costs. And if Stephen approved, Hugo would write a preface. By September, Hugo could report that he had seen the first copy. 'I am thrilled with it and so hope you are too. I am asking Hamish Hamilton to send you one as soon as possible – and they will also send you nice pieces from *Vogue*, *Harpers & Queen*, & *Blitz* magazine. There is to be a big spread in the *Observer* on 14 September, I gather . . . After years of battling we did it! It's out!'[14]

Stephen was flattered by all this attention, though characteristically he never saw or wrote to Vickers again. He particularly relished the article in *Blitz*, which used the famous Beaton 'mackintosh' photograph of himself. 'Take it to the window,' he told Sylvia Blandford from his bed, as he lay covered with rugs in the darkened room. 'Isn't it wonderful?'[15]

After another visit to the nursing home in Nether Wallop, Stephen made a superhuman effort to get back to Wilsford. He was determined to end his life where he had begun it. Pauline came to visit, in time to see him being carried out on a stretcher to the ambulance that would take him home. He saw her and muttered, 'No teeth, no eyes' – he was without his glasses or dentures. But to Pauline, he looked dignified. 'It reminded me of Shakespeare's Seven Ages of Man – "Sans teeth, sans eyes, sans everything."'[16]

So Stephen returned to Wilsford Manor, to die. In the last few months of his life, all the excess flesh had fallen away from his face, the high cheekbones showed through, and the elegant hands, with the large turquoise ring, were supremely beautiful again. As the winter of early 1987 faded into spring, his favourite season, Stephen Tennant sat propped up in bed, monkey and teddy either side of him, the last surviving maharajah of a lost empire, an empire of his senses. He grew weaker, until, as the first definite signs of warmer weather came once more to Wilsford, he died, on the very last day of February, in his eighty-first year.

Chapter 32

Coda

Who counts them all? Those poor lives,
All gone, disappeared, departed,
Just a sod and a stone.

And not only people, but things, houses – gardens – trees – loved haunts – where are they? Do they live only among the mists of memory that must fade and grow less remembered with every passing year? Strange are the workings of Him who knows. Is this all? No. Somewhere out of time, out of space, they live unshackled by earthly ties. Somewhere, encircled by reality, they wait and are, and always will be.

— Stephen James Napier Tennant: *The White Wallet*

STEPHEN's death certificate gave two causes of death: haematemesis (vomiting of blood, a result of his bowel cancer), and senile myocardial degeneration – his heart had given up. His body was cremated a day or so later, and the funeral arranged for 4 March. To the service in the little church of St Michael's at Wilsford, where his mother and brother were buried, came the family, and surviving friends: Michael Wishart, Eileen Hose, Laurence Whistler and Rosemary Olivier. It was a quiet, low-key ceremony, given a certain pathos by the singing of 'All Things Bright and Beautiful', and readings from two of Stephen's favourite poems, by Emily Dickinson and Robert Frost. Then the tiny casket containing his ashes was taken out to be interred by the chancel wall.

His wake was a strangely happy affair, for the memories of Stephen seemed to be only amusing ones. His house had woken up to throw its last party: there were bunches of snowdrops everywhere, gathered up and placed in shells, lights behind plaster shells came on, and the curtains were pulled back for the first time in years. Mrs Blandford's husband had great difficulty in opening the front door, and clearing the path of moss, but as the mourners came into the Manor – for most of them, their first visit in a long while – they entered a brightly-lit fairy land ready to bid goodbye to its creator. Only the commode and the walking-frame, still in the room in which Stephen had died, bespoke the cruel physicalities of decay. The house itself seemed to be fading. Wilsford had been conceived as Stephen was conceived; it had been the only constant thing throughout his life, changing with him, witnessing his vicissitudes, his ups and downs. Its stones had lived the same life as he had, and lived as long. Now that its owner was gone, the spirit of the house died too.

Stephen's death was announced by obituaries of unprecedented length in the national press. The *Daily Telegraph* ran a three-column notice, complete with Beaton photograph of Stephen in his 'Romeo' costume, pearls and all, which astounded readers by taking up the entire length of that august journal's page.[1] The *Independent* had a less fervid tribute to Stephen from Hugo Vickers, again accompanied by a Beaton shot, this time from the 1971 'Hockney' session.[2] *The Times* was, as ever, the most staid of obituarists, yet still managed to give a posthumous accolade to the life and work of a poet and painter of whom few people had ever even heard.[3]

The fact was that Stephen Tennant was, in death, even more of a legendary figure than he had been in life. The British love of eccentricity had embraced this most photogenic of eccentrics, and the fascination with his extraordinary life kept a grip on the media for the rest of the year. The long obituaries brought predictable derision, from *Private Eye*, who satirized what they saw as such silliness by over-excitable devotees of old aesthetes of dubious distinction, to the *Sunday Times*, whose columnist Edward Pearce (in a piece entitled 'Let's lop off noble toadies', published 8 November) vented his bile on the fact that sensible newspapers should print such frivolous and ultimately meaningless tributes. What these writers underestimated was the British appreciation of someone who had not tried too hard, who was not a success, but rather an amateur, more especially appealing because of his presumed eccentricity. The late eighties' predilection for such flamboyant figures, for deviation from the norm, combined with a visual eye for outrageousness – itself a product of popular culture and its promulgation of identifiable personalities – made Stephen eminently newsworthy. He was an incredible figure from the recent past; and the fact that he lived, Miss Havisham-like, in a decaying fairy castle made the whole story all the more attractive to editors and readers alike.

What would be done with that palace? Tancred Borenius' proposal – forty years previously – that it should be hermetically sealed for generations to come was, despite its attractiveness, an impractical notion. And so, Stephen having died intestate, it fell to his appointed family executors to dispose of Wilsford and its contents in as fair a manner as possible, to give the many nephews and nieces of 'Uncle Stephen' their share of the inheritance. Thus Sotheby's was called in to supervise a grand sale of the house's amazing contents.

The result was a two-day country house sale, the like of which had never been seen before. Only the sale of Beaton's Reddish House, and Edward James' surrealist fantasy at West Dean, came close to the unprecedented fuss caused by the auction. In the weeks preceding the sale in the autumn of 1987, the national press ran innumerable articles, detailing the polar bear skins, the Syrie Maugham sofas, the Venetian grotto furniture that were to come under the hammer – all made fascinating by the fact that the house's interior seemed to have been untouched since its owner went into 'decline' after the Second World War.

The *Daily Telegraph*'s Godfrey Barker reported on 'the rococo madhouse of the Hon. Stephen Tennant', and alleged that 'Wilsford only matters because it is a statement about its beautiful hero . . . it exemplifies nothing serious – surrealism, for example – other than one individual Englishman's sublime indifference to the main currents of European art in the mid-20th century.'[4] In their attempts to grasp the unreality, the reporters fell to savaging Stephen. *Homes & Gardens* magazine* noted that 'the auctioneers' hype managed to obscure the stark reality that Wilsford Manor was a raddled grotesque of a house. As its owner turned from bright young thing into pudgy, over-blown old queen, so he turned his house into the same. Its interior decoration had about as much originality as the myth that Stephen Tennant was a recluse had to the truth. (In fact, he was still making trips to America in the 1970s and he was in London visiting friends just before he died.)'[5]

The obvious fallacy of such reports did nothing to deter the true connoisseur of British aestheticism. Beyond the hype and furore was the actuality – one to which the hundreds of visitors on the four viewing-days prior to the mid-October sale at Wilsford Manor attested. It really was unbelievable, this mysterious Wiltshire manor set deep in bosky grounds, in a misty river valley, like something from a Gothic tale. The

---

*There were also major features on Stephen and Wilsford in *Country Life*, *The World of Interiors* and *Harpers & Queen*.

prospective buyers came and crowded that quiet lane with their cars, and entered the grounds along a coir mat pathway, the bamboo clumps on either side lit by strategically-placed lamps. They were literally agasp at the interior.

Despite the tidying-up and ticketing done by Sotheby's, the house still retained some magic. Each room held more furniture than might be thought possible, and in such multi-coloured profusion that much of it had had to be removed to an adjoining marquee to allow access. Now strangers trod Avon mud into the sheepskins, fingered the satin seats, or sat on dining-room chairs which had once been graced by Bloomsbury bottoms, the room ringing to Stephen's caustic witticisms. Saddest of all was the bedroom in which he had died, where the blankets were rolled back and even the bed was for sale. His toy bear and monkey stood forlornly on the window-shelf awaiting new homes. In the Thatched Wing were laid out a selection of the huge cache of Stephen's paintings that had been found scattered around the house. A cardboard grocery box contained his life's correspondence, with a few more saleable letters – from Willa, from Cecil, from Morgan and from Siegfried, taken aside to be auctioned off to the highest bidder, most eventually finding their resting place across the Atlantic. Stephen's library, a collection of signed first editions from beloved friends, was stacked up in serried rows for disposal.

On 13 and 14 October, these contents were marched out of the house and into Sotheby's auction tent. Here was the Epstein bust, held up by the porters' shaky hands, shouted down for £24,200. Here a miniature of Stephen as Shelley, by Rex Whistler – £8,580. Here the Beaton 'mackintosh' portraits – one sold for a staggering £3,740, another for £1,760 to a Japanese department store. The prices went up and up. The most expensive was a pair of oils, views of Rome by Vanvitelli (remnants of the Tennant Collection) which made £220,000 (estimate: £25,000). The cheapest, a Creda Compact tumble dryer, for £5. But people wanted anything, as long as they could get it home and tell friends, 'Oh, that? That was Stephen Tennant's.'*

Uri Geller bought the Alpine rock crystal (for psychic experiments) for £5,720, and caused consternation by bending the Earl of Pembroke's car keys for him. The presence of Lord Snowdon and his son, Viscount Linley, drew the attention of television cameras and gossip columnists, as did the full force of the Tennant family. Pauline, Lady Rumbold, was

---

*Just a week later, buyers might have been more reticent, as the Monday following the Wilsford sale saw the biggest stock market crash since 1929 – so-called 'Black Monday'.

photographed for the *Daily Telegraph*, and told reporters she thought her uncle would have been very amused by all the fuss. Colin's son, Henry Tennant, came closest to Stephen's own breed of chic; tall, blond and elegant and looking very late eighties in designer leopard-skin.

Stephen would have been gratified to hear a *Lascar* picture go down at £1,100, more than double its estimate, and would doubtless have been astounded to learn, in his celestial parlour, that the sale had raised a total of £1.59 million for his heirs (although he might have wondered why, in the latter years of his life, he had had to sell Tchelitchews to pay for his own little luxuries). The house itself, which Stephen's trustees had bought from his brother back in 1928 (for £30,000), was sold for £1.5 million pounds. One prospective buyer who had looked it over was Mick Jagger; but it went to a young couple who intended to renovate the whole building, and establish it as a family home once more. The history of Wilsford Manor had come full circle.

News items were run on Channel Four, ITV and BBC, and the country looked in on those incredible interiors and wondered that anyone could live like that. The tabloid press got excited about the more outrageous aspects of Stephen's life – and appearance – and old friends were sought out for their comments. Loyal to a man and woman, they had nothing but praise and love to evoke of the lost boy. There were even intimations that Stephen might still be hanging round, 'like an old-timer at the stage door',[6] as Michael Wishart had put it; Sotheby's staff detected a powerful smell of incense in the upper rooms of the house on the first day of the sale. And months later, when the last traces of Stephen's gold-starred wallpaper had been ripped down, and the yew tree around which his mother had had the corner of the house angled had been felled, the new owners of Wilsford Manor had recourse to an exorcism, after workmen downed tools and refused to carry on working. They had seen, they said, the apparition of a male figure in the upstairs rooms.

Then, suddenly, it was all over. Purchases were collected; cars and vans stacked full of books, or groaning under the weight of garden statuary, rumbled off up the gravel drive. That great stone house was empty again, denuded of its finery, its gardens stripped of their fountains, and the autumn mists crept up from the river to cover the scars. The next day, the greatest storm England had seen for decades blew across the countryside, and a tree demolished Stephen's pink-painted conservatory. It marked the irrevocable end of his eighty-year reign.

Appendix I

Stephen Tennant: Works
Bibliography

The Bird's Fancy Dress Ball – Illustrations (privately printed, 1921).

The Vein in the Marble – Illustrations (Philip Allen, 1925).

The Mildred Book – Edith Olivier, portrait drawing, High House Press, Shaftesbury (privately printed, 1926).

The Treasure Ship – Illustrations to 'Round the Bird Shops' (S. W. Partridge & Co., 1926).

The Charm of Birds – Lord Grey of Falloden, dust jacket (1928).

The White Wallet – Quotation and illustrations (J. M. Dent & Sons, 1928).

To My Mother – Siegfried Sassoon, cover and frontispiece (Faber 'Ariel' series, 1928).

In Sicily – Siegfried Sassoon, cover and frontispiece (Faber 'Ariel' series, No. 2, 1930).

To the Red Rose – Siegfried Sassoon, cover and frontispiece (Faber 'Ariel' series, No. 34, 1931).

Leaves from a Missionary's Notebook – (Secker & Warburg, 1937; republished Hamish Hamilton, 1986).

Horizon – *Lascar* colour illustration, April, 1941.

Horizon – Review of *Time Exposure*, September, 1941.

On Writing – Willa Cather, preface (Alfred Knopf, 1947).

Two Poems for Christmas – (Nash Publications, 1960).

My Brother Aquarius – Poems and frontispiece (Nash Publications, 1961).

Some Poems for the friends of Stephen Tennant – (Nash Publications, 1962).

Exhibitions

Dorien Leigh Galleries, Cromwell Place, London, 5 April–June 1921.

Dorien Leigh Galleries – 'Amateur Art', November 1921.

Redfern Gallery, Cork St, London, 1–24 January 1953.

Alexander Iolas Gallery, 46 East 57 Street, New York, from 25 April 1955.

Sagittarius Gallery, Rome – 'Abstract Designs', 1–10 April 1956.

Gallery One, D'Arblay St, London, from 29 November 1955.

Bodley Gallery, 223 East 60 Street, from 5 December 1957.

The Vestry, St Thomas' Church, Salisbury, 16–21 July 1973.

The Compleat Artist, Crane St, Salisbury, July 1974.

Palm Beach Gallery, Florida, 1975.

Anthony d'Offay Gallery, Dering St, London – 'Stephen Tennant, Drawings and Watercolour', 24 June–23 July 1976.

Maclean Gallery, St George St, London – 'Stephen Tennant: A Story of the Maritime Boulevard', 7–30 September 1983.

Michael Parkin Gallery, Motcomb St, London – 'Cecil Beaton and Friends', 29 May–19 July 1985.

Michael Parkin Gallery – 'Rex Whistler, Stephen Tennant and their two semi-circles', 7 October–6 November 1987.

Appendix II

Lascar: A Story of the Maritime Boulevards

STEPHEN TENNANT ADMITTED to having written at least seven different versions of *Lascar*, yet not one of these could be said to be complete. There exists instead a great pile of rainbow-coloured manuscript chapters, written in his inimitable hand; Stephen wrote more than 500,000 words of text, with intricate scene-directions, plot summaries and character analyses. But the paperclips were left to rust on the finest foolscap and yellowing pages of Savoy Hotel writing paper. Why did he remain unable to conclude his masterpiece?

It is a novel *manqué*, full of cinematic dissolves and theatrical fantasy effects, of author asides and intrusion: Stephen Tennant playing the God of Fate with his characters. There is a prevailing mood of doom; Madame Neffus is described as 'a head on a coin, that has been struck in the mould of grief', to whom 'memory . . . is the most wonderful thing in the world . . . the one real respite'. Yet there are lighter moments — many very funny, some frankly homoerotic. Stephen runs away with his descriptive passages, such as that of Mme Neffus' nephew's room, which she keeps as a shrine to 'sporting men', full of punchballs and dumbbells, and 'prize boxing belts, photos of wrestlers . . . jock straps . . . a kind of pervasive bombast and rugged obscenity'.

Stephen wrestled with such themes for days on end, adding to and subtracting from his text. His ideas as to how the book should read changed from day to day as much as from decade to decade. '*Lascar*: I want the book to be a tough straightforward yarn with the minimum fantasy and spirituality,' he wrote early in its inception; 'lots of shipping facts & Marseille atmosphere and sea lore & yarns of men . . .' At other times he wanted to make it deeper, and yet felt more foreboding. 'I feel such a sense of responsibility towards it,' he admitted, 'there are some passages I am not ready to write.' Twenty years later, it seems that this was still the case. Stephen's comment on *Lascar*, in May 1975, was one of the bleakest regarding his great work '. . . My book is, I think, so Bad; pretentious clap-trap,' he told his old friend Elizabeth, now Countess of Iddesleigh, announcing he was about to send a copy to Norah Smallwood at Chatto &

Windus; 'but I have a queasy feeling the Public might like it. It's really Rubbish – I think – so over-coloured,' he deprecated, professing that his was 'an eccentric, very aberrational talent, really'. But in September 1980, only six years before his death, he told Hugo Vickers that he was 'working on a novel so exciting, a Thriller set in Marseilles in the 20s – Dazzling cafés, Cheap music hall actresses & Tunis prayer rug vendors and the plot is very subtle: Stevedores, factory "Bosses" – A sinister, haunting book, narrative – very vivid in Colour – Sea-Captains – Shady loafers & Tattoo Parlours – it is called *Lascar*: A story of the Maritime Boulevards.'

Stephen even went to the length of having at least the first chapter of his novel typeset in Bournemouth, and told Stephen Spender how exciting it was to come back in the London train reading 'his proofs'. The endlessly drawn-out procedure was too much for Willa Cather, who wrote to him in the forties: 'Why didn't you go on with *Lascar*? – were you afraid of its not being a Great Novel, from vanity, Malvolio? . . . No one ever wrote a great novel by intending to do so. Ten years ago you began to write it – you've strangled it now I think? The world won't come to an end, and you won't come to an end, if you give it up.' Still he went on, but spending more time on its illustration than on the text: '*Lascar* endpapers', he noted in the forties, 'tattooing designs – advertisements – torn through the middle'.

Stephen acknowledged to Sheila Macdonald that much of *Lascar* was autobiographical in content, which is borne out by the uncanny assimilation of their creator's characteristics by many of the book's personae. But despite the fact that supposed rough, tough sailors have conversations about flowers, and exhibit an unnatural predilection for wallpaper designs and furniture rearrangement, there is enough of the real atmosphere of Marseilles and its Vieux Port in the twenties and thirties to make the reader of *Lascar* believe that its author knew his stuff. What comes out of the few surviving fragments of Stephen's novel is a sense of his own experience of that particular time and place, highly-coloured and unrealistic – but only in that it was a highly-coloured place, and his was an unrealistic existence. Given those qualifications, and these fragments, one can just start to imagine what Stephen's finished edition of the book could have been like. Perhaps he knew too much of what was expected of a work of genius, and was too critical of his own efforts, too aware of the standards set by his great literary friends. The fact that the book was not finished is a crucial key to the whole of Stephen's life – the holding-back that defines his life and work. If *Lascar* had been completed, the phenomenon of Stephen Tennant as a 'decorative recluse' would, perhaps, never have existed.

Lascar: Dramatis Personae

Madame Neffus is (or, rather, was) Helene Laperouse, a popular stage actress, now faded and of indeterminate age. She is an adept dealer of Tarot cards, and still retains a certain attraction for men. Her husband was George Neffus, 'an advocate of debatable distinction', long gone. Her brother Paul (the first) was a banker, 'of a certain rather phlegmatic temperament, very different to fiery, passionate boy, Paul the second.' Paul is now fifty-five. He was forty-six when, nine years before, the ill-fated escape from the prison colony took place.

Hortense Buist is Mme Neffus' *dame de compagnie*, the sister of an artist who painted Mme Neffus' portrait. Hortense became Mme Neffus' secretary when her brother died. She is described as 'a country cousin', resembling a 'female impersonator'.

Philippe Carmisnil is a shipping boss, an old friend of Paul the second, 'a wealthy Marseillais of dubious origin', who 'controlled much of the commerce of the docks'. He poses as a philanthropist, but is a gambler, and all-round mysterious character.

Manuel de Cubas is the half-Spanish port stevedore who, like Paul, carries 'the stamp of prison life'. He is 'Lascar'.

Ange is his lost love, a former singer at the Folies Bergère, who died as a result of Paul's perfidy, nineteen years ago in the prison colony. He was aged twenty-four.

Other minor characters include: *Lucie*, the maid, and *Ari*, the gardener, at Villa Persane. Then there is *Bertrand*, a 6ft 2in black sailor, very religious and amorous, a champion boxer and 'very lovable'. *Marie Petrain* is the erratic landlady of the lodgings shared by Pierre and Manuel, who is always after Manuel's body. Her sister, *Jeanette Petrain*, is described as a 'religeuse'.

Kurt Svensson (a.k.a. Captain Cederstrom) is a Swedish ship owner, and *Jean*, 'a dark young man, very spruce and sleek, with a touch too much pomatum and ondulation about his head', is a hairdresser. *Lucille* is his girlfriend. *Moustaffa* is an Algerian tattooist, and *Charles Rubin* is 'a fat sailor, an Artilleur, down from Boulogne . . . posted at Toulon', who 'came into Marseilles whenever he could'.

And last but not least is *Pierre*, the 'narrator' and central character, who observes these events and peoples of the maritime boulevard. He is 'witty, a capricious, rather sulky boy, very touchy and fastidious', and Manuel's best friend.

Stephen wrote a useful synopsis of his novel, which was divided into three parts and seventeen chapters, and although only the first two-thirds survived, it is clear from the following extracts what the author was aiming for:

PART ONE

1. Escalier Monumental
2. Villa Persane
3. 'I will escape'
4. Madame Hortense's shopping morning
5. Manuel and Captain Cederstrom
6. Madame Neffus' farewell party
7. Madadrague Sud

PART TWO

PART THREE

PART ONE

1. Escalier Monumental:
   'Manuel & Pierre talk far into the night – the glittering cafés of the Canebière, the suffocatingly hot July night – the full moon – the seething crowds – & in Pierre's disjointed picture of Mme Neffus . . . a few glimmers of her strangeness & power come through.'
2. Villa Persane:
   'Pierre & Mme Neffus. The Villa – Mme Hortense. This scene actually takes place before the opening chapter, but I want it to come second – because it is Pierre's narrative actually happening.'
3. 'I will escape':
   'Mme Neffus has the 2 sailors to dinner & explains her plan – & then her memories of Paul overflow – & we see her view of Paul – the last words of her narrative introduces M. Philippe – the white slaver & drug smuggler – & secret power in various Mediterranean ports.'
4. Madame H's shopping morning:
   'Pierre, Bertrand, Charles & Mme Hortense have a snack in a café on the Canebière. Pierre says he is almost sure Manuel will agree to Mme Neffus' scheme – Captain Cederstrom & M. Philippe appear in this chapter.'
5. Manuel & Captain Cederstrom:
   'In the Captain's office near the Docks – Manuel & Cederstrom & Jules talk later at the Villa. M. Philippe calls – & Mme Neffus realizes that she is bringing Paul back to a place where he will be in peril. Thrilling talk between them, the old enemies who each thought the other's string had gone.'

6. Mme Neffus' farewell party:

'Mme N. & Pierre have lovely scenes of wit & charm together. She grows to love Pierre deeply – & he her. She would like to keep him in Marseille, but realizes how Manuel depends on him, so lets him go – Pierre is keeper of his fears.'

PART TWO

1. Two days from Casablanca:

'This describes the arrival at Dakar – the meeting with Paul – & Fleur de thé. Pierre is kidnapped – & Manuel thinking Fleur may know something goes to her – then to Paul. The terrific scene of revelation follows, & M. kills Paul: – then with Mme N.'s money goes to hunt for Pierre – determined that since he can't take Paul back to her, he will take Pierre instead – who she so loves. Pierre meanwhile gets back to Marseille – & Manuel arrives last. This action covers Nos. 1, 2, 3, 4.'

5. Manuel's Dream:

'Manuel dreams that he is climbing over the roofs of Marseille because Mme N. is calling him, telling him that Pierre has come home. The dream occupies all Chapter 5. Moonlight over the harbours, lighted ships.'

6. Manuel returns to Marseille:

'Pierre, Manuel & Mme N. are reunited in the Villa – we find them playing cards with Mme Hortense – only M. Philippe thinks that Paul is home, & lies in wait for him under the arches on the docks below the Cathedral – but it is Manuel who comes – & in the starlight Philippe stabs him. Pierre & Jules & B[ertrand] & C[harles] trap M. Philippe & in his own warehouse hang him as revenge. Bertrand & Charles go to Marie Petrain & give her Manuel's sea chest – & Pierre signs on the Andalusian that is going to the Far East. Before he goes he says goodbye to Mme Neffus – who he so loves – "You will always be a part of the wonder of my life," he says to her, sitting at her feet – "let's pretend that this isn't goodbye – that it's just one of our lovely afternoons together – with Mme Hortense bringing in the tea tray, & Tibere asleep at the fire – & Manuel coming soon to join us – with his remote farouche beauty." And she, who has played so many games, plays this one like the great artist she is.'

Unfortunately, the latter part of Stephen's synopsis is missing, but further notes for the novel extant make clear its dramatic finale:

'Mme Neffus doesn't know all about Paul's shady life, but she knows a certain amount. Piere, who loves her, conceals much from her, and struggles to prevent M. Philippe from telling her. In the end she doesn't know the whole truth. In a way, they are all sacrificed to Paul. Manuel nearly loses Pierre's friendship. Kurt Cederstrom kidnaps Pierre to get him away from Paul. The money that should be left to Mme Hortense goes to Paul. Important: the reader must believe in Mme Neffus' love for Paul. If I can't make him do that the story fails. Manuel has a memory that haunts him, and times of recurrent ferocity, and Pierre learns to cope with these – to humour and help him dominate them – Manuel is dependent on Pierre more than he realizes (Pierre's disappearance at Dakar shows him the extent of his affection). Mme Neffus thinks that Manuel has known Paul years ago and that the incident in his life that haunts him would, if revealed to her, help in her knowledge of Paul. Manuel does not much like her. He distrusts her "elaborateness" and female liking for a situation of giving sympathy and reciprocation of fussy relationships. Pierre is like her in this respect, and in a sense, neither really succeeds in capturing Manuel. He is very masculine and independent, with an easy contempt for the social graces and amenities, doesn't care for women's company, farouche and awkward, he fascinates them but neither can stake out a claim on his affections – though he likes Pierre in a crude enigmatic way, – and when he loses him, feels unexpectedly desolate.'

Stephen had already decided the ending of *Lascar* when he was in Egypt in 1939. He scribbled it in pencil on a piece of writing paper from the Continental-Savoy Hotel in Cairo: 'In last chapter the reader mustn't know till the very end that Lascar isn't sailing on the Andalusian. He & Pierre are sitting on a bench near the vieux port. Paul & Philippe have a terrible fight, & Paul, before he dies, makes a will leaving Villa Persane to Pierre & Manuel. They ask Mme Hortense to come & keep house for them. The fight takes place in the docks below the Cathedral, where the arches are – & crates etc . . .'

Stephen wrote soon after, of Manuel, that he wanted 'the young people of my day, when they read of him, to cry & cry with the intensity of their love for him. He is a symbol of man's deathless courage, an eternal verity – flesh & blood, because we can only love flesh & blood . . . A principle has too much of doctrine about it. I want above all – from readers – I would like the tribute of their tears. Il se fut que [la] vérité est triste . . .

'There is no going back. Life is a remorseless pilgrimage of sorrow: Man's eternal dilemma – In the chapter called Manuel – the love, the timbre, the heart beat of this wonderful book is set. There is no going back – only the implacable hours, the days & the nights, the pitiless years can heap themselves upon the reader – perhaps there is a kind of sweet hesitating melancholy in these pages – gleams of pleasure – & strange extasy [sic] – but the momentum is principally governed by an implacable fate: – Paul's figure – dominates, & Manuel's – set in shadow, against the sea – demand a kind of shrinking magnetized attention from the reader – & Mme Neffus' wonderful words "It is on the boulevards of the world that we learn the map of our own hearts" – spans the book – her wild strange reveries – extasies float like autumn cobwebs in the dreamy southern air of the great seaport. Her augmenting solitude – her distinctive charm, her passion & desolation – wash through the book – like the sound of the sea. But it is to Manuel we return. A man against the sea. The seaman of 100 legends, stalking through this nocturne of the trading ports – skulking in the shadows of mean streets, lingering to light his cigarette on the edges of the pavement – his eyes – seething restless, the eyes of the fugitive – dark eyes seen through tobacco smoke.'

Acknowledgements

My first debt is to Hugo Vickers, godfather of this book. Without his unerring assistance, advice and encouragement it certainly would not have been started, let alone completed. Through his generosity I have had access not only to Cecil Beaton's unpublished diaries, letters and papers, but also to the great mass of Stephen Tennant's correspondence, manuscripts, artwork and papers which are now in his care.

Stephen's niece, Pauline, Lady Rumbold, was exceptionally helpful throughout the gestation period of this book, and Susan Lowndes Marques, her sister, the late Dowager Countess of Iddesleigh, and the Earl of Iddesleigh put at my disposal a treasure-trove of letters which made the documentation of Stephen's early life possible. Laurence Whistler was ever ready to make valuable observations on Stephen's relationship with Rex. I am glad to be able to thank them once more.

Stephen's love of the works of Willa Cather led me to her redoubtable circle of supporters and scholars in America. Patricia Lee Yongue, friend and observer of Mr Tennant in his later years, was forthcoming with detailed missives analysing the phenomenon. The late Mildred Bennett, Dr Ruth Crone and Lucia Woods Lindley all produced vital material. Patrick Quinn was perceptive on the Tennant–Sassoon relationship. The late Eileen Hose, Beaton's stalwart secretary, proved a great ally until her untimely death in 1988. Fred and Eileen Newton of Wilsford-cum-Lake provided great assistance, and John Skull spoke wittily, and sympathetically, of his former master. John Culme's excellent work on Stephen's diaries was indispensable.

For dedication above and beyond the call of duty: my sisters, Christina and Katherine; for their advice, Peter Goddard and Robert Holden; and for all of this, and much more, my parents, Leonard and Theresa.

Many of the following offered me generous hospitality in the course of my research; all were unstinting in giving time and consideration to endless enquiries, copied or lent letters, and gave extended interviews or wrote of Stephen Tennant to myself:

Her Majesty Queen Elizabeth The Queen Mother.

Lord Aberconway; Sir Harold Acton.

Dr Wendy Baron; Ann Barr; the Marchioness of Bath; Sir Brian Batsford; Nicola Beauman; Sir Alfred Beit; Quentin Bell; Lady Caroline Blackwood; Sylvia Blandford; Lord Bonham-Carter; Paul Bowles; Brigid Brophy; the Dowager Duchess of Buccleuch; Richard Buckle; Nigel Burwood.

Lady Camrose; William Chappell; Paul Chipchase; the late Michael Colefax; Louise Corrigan; Dr Stewart Craggs; Lydia Cullen and the Sotheby Beaton archive.

Gilles David; Dr Anthony Davis; Michael de-la-Noy; the Duchess of Devonshire; the late Dame Daphne du Maurier.

Lord Egremont; Natasha Edwards; Meredith Etherington-Smith.

The Hon. Mrs Fielding; Alastair Forbes; Charles Henri Ford; Ruth Ford; P. N. Furbank.

Sir John Gielgud; Robert Gittings; Victoria Glendinning; the late Francis Goodman.

Allanah Harper; Sir Rupert Hart-Davis; Lady Selina Hastings; Marie Helvin; William Henderson; the Hon. David Herbert; Derek Hill; Bevis Hillier; David Hockney; David J. Holmes; Michael Holroyd; David Howard and Old West Downians Society.

Helen Ingmire and Westminster School.

Barbara Ker-Seymer; Francis King; James Kirkup; Lincoln Kirstein; Eardley Knollys; Boris Kochno.

Diana Lawson and the Cassel Hospital; Hermione Lee; James Lees-Milne; the late Rosamond Lehmann; the Hon. Lady Lindsay; Sheila Lochhead; Michael Luke.

Kirsty Macleod; the late Laura, Duchess of Marlborough; Brian Masters; Lady Menuhin; Michael Meredith and Eton College; the Hon. Lady Mosley; Andrew Motion; Dr Patrick Mounsey; Lawrence Mynott.

The late Duke of Northumberland; Viscount Norwich.

Rosemary Olivier.

Peter Parker; Michael Parkin; the Earl of Pembroke; Anne Powell; Anthony Powell; Patrick Procktor; Timothy Prus.

Peter Quennell.

Jean Ralph and the Moorcroft Hospital; Lord Ravensdale; Lady

Acknowledgements

Redgrave; Ned Rorem; the late Dowager Duchess of Rutland; George Rylands.

Tim Satchell; the late Sir Peter Scott; Reginald Severn and West Downs School; Reresby Sitwell; Sir Stephen Spender; the Lord Sudeley.

Alan Tagg; Charles Taylor; Julian Tennant; the Hon. Tobias Tennant; Marianne Thorne and the Swaylands Study Centre; Neil Tierney.

Gore Vidal; the late Mrs Igor Vinogradoff.

Lady Walton; Sir Fred Warner; Auberon Waugh; Linda Collin Wileman; Sir Angus Wilson; Michael Wishart; Ursula Wyndham.

My thanks to the following institutions for permission to quote letters and papers in their collections:

The British Library for Edith Sitwell's letter to John Lehmann; Eton College library; Humanities Research Center, University of Texas, for Sassoon's letters to Henry and Ruth Head; Pembroke College library, Cambridge, for Sir Ronald Storrs' papers; the Provost and Scholars of King's College, Cambridge, for E. M. Forster's diaries and letters; Public Records Office; the Slade School of Art; the University of Sussex library for J. R. Ackerley's letter to Geoffrey Gorer; the Hogarth Press for Virginia Woolf's papers; Curtis Brown, London, literary executors of the late Elizabeth Bowen; Her Grace the Duchess of Devonshire, for Nancy Mitford's letters; the Virago Press for permission to quote from Willa Cather's published works, except *My Àntonia*, for which I have to thank Houghton Mifflin; George Sassoon for permission to quote from his father's poetry; Faber for use of Sassoon's published letters and diaries; Aitken & Stone for *The Enigma of Arrival*; A. D. Peters for quotations from the works of Evelyn Waugh and Nancy Mitford; the Society of Authors, agents for the Lytton Strachey Trust; Edward Arnold for *Howard's End*; Rogers, Coleridge & White and Mrs Deirdre Levi for Cyril Connolly's unpublished work; and Sir Reresby and Francis Sitwell, Sir Sacheverell's executors, for permission to use his letters to Stephen.

I would also like to thank the executors of Stephen Tennant's estate for their kind permission to quote from Stephen's unpublished letters and journals.

And last but not least, I must thank my agent, Gillon Aitken, my former publisher, Christopher Sinclair-Stevenson, my current publisher, Andrew Franklin, and my editors, Sophie Ovenden and Annie Lee, Karen Geary, and everyone else at Hamish Hamilton, for their patient efforts in assisting this book to eventual publication.

Philip Hoare
London 1990

Illustration Acknowledgements

Grateful acknowledgement is made for permission to use photographs taken or supplied by the following:

Associated Newspapers: cuttings on plates 5 and 12

Associated Press/Topham Picture Source: plate 22, top right and bottom; plate 27 top right

Cecil Beaton, courtesy of Sotheby's: plate 8, top and bottom left; plate 9, top and bottom; plate 10, top; plate 11; plate 12, top; plate 16, top left; plate 20; plate 28, centre; plate 30

Mark Gerson: plate 22, top left

David Herbert: plate 18, bottom

Dowager Countess of Iddesleigh: plate 3, right; plate 5, right; plate 6, top

Hon. Lady Lindsay: plate 6, bottom

Millar & Harris: plate 21, top left, centre, bottom left

National Portrait Gallery: plate 18, top right

Eileen Newton: plate 24, centre and bottom right

Rosemary Olivier: plate 13, right; plate 14, right; plate 17, left

Michael Parkin: plate 26, bottom

Popperfoto: plate 10, bottom left; plate 18, top left; plate 27, bottom left

Timothy Prus: plate 1; plate 3, top left; plate 4, top; plate 5, bottom left; plate 14, top left; plate 15, right and bottom; plate 16, centre right; plate 17, top right; plate 23, bottom; plate 25, top and right; plate 28, top left

Lady Rumbold: plate 24, bottom left

John Skull: plate 29

Hugo Vickers: plate 2, top right; plate 4, bottom; plate 6, centre; plate 13, top and left; plate 14, bottom; plate 17, bottom; plate 23, top; plate 25, left; plate 26, top left and right; plate 27, top left and bottom right

Victoria and Albert Museum and Weidenfeld & Nicolson Archives: plate 7, top

Weidenfeld & Nicolson Archives: plate 7, bottom

The photographs on plate 16, top right; plate 24, top left and centre left; plates 31 and 32, were take by the author.

Notes

All dates are as accurate as possible. Stephen Tennant's letters vary in their dated accuracy – earlier missives were more likely to be properly dated than the later, when Stephen's sense of time was somewhat abstract. Christabel Aberconway noted when replying to one letter of Stephen's received in March 1965: 'Your letter was just dated 1964, so bewildering for future historians . . .' (Christabel, Lady Aberconway, to Stephen Tennant, 21 March 1965).

Chapter 1: The Web of Childhood

1. Lady Menuhin, conversation with author 17 February 1988.
2. Raymond Asquith, 9 September 1902, quoted in John Jolliffe, *Raymond Asquith, Life and Letters* (Collins, London, 1980) p. 99.
3. Daphne Bennett, *Margot* (Gollancz, London, 1984) p. 162.
4. Stephen Tennant, journal fragment, ?1940s.
5. Nikolaus Pevsner (revised Bridget Cherry), *The Buildings of Wiltshire* (Penguin, Harmondsworth, 1973) p. 576.
6. Lady Diana Cooper to Hugo Vickers, 21 March 1980.
7. Susan Lowndes Marques, conversation with author, 7 July 1988.
8. ibid., 18 July 1988.
9. Osbert Sitwell, *Laughter in the Next Room* (Macmillan, London, 1949), pp. 96–7.
10. Peter Quennell, conversation with author, 18 March 1987.
11. Stephen Tennant, marginalia.
12. Pamela Glenconner, *The Sayings of the Children* (Blackwell, Oxford, 1918), pp. 115–16.
13. Susan Lowndes Marques, conversation with author, 7 July 1988.
14. Osbert Sitwell, *Laughter in the Next Room*, p. 98.
15. Edith Olivier to Cecil Beaton, January 1929.
16. Rosemary Olivier, conversation with author, 18 April 1987.
17. The Dowager Duchess of Rutland, conversation with author, 23 October 1988.
18. Stephen Tennant, journal, September 1935.
19. This and the following from Pamela Glenconner, *The Sayings of the Children*, pp. 119ff.

Chapter 2: The Never-Land

1. Osbert Sitwell, *Great Morning* (Macmillan, London, 1948) p. 230.

2. ibid.
3. Stephen Tennant to Cecil Beaton, 12 October 1929.
4. Sir Stephen Spender, conversation with author, 30 August 1987.
5. The Dowager Duchess of Rutland, conversation with author, 23 October 1988.
6. Typescript in possession of Hugo Vickers.
7. Sir Steven Runciman, conversation with author, 1 June 1987.
8. William Chappell, conversation with author, 11 March 1987.
9. Simon Blow, *Tatler*, July 1983.
10. Papers in possession of Timothy Prus.
11. Pamela Glenconner, *Edward Wyndham Tennant* (John Lane, London, 1919).
12. Susan Lowndes Marques, conversation with author, 7 July 1988.
13. Pamela Glenconner, *Edward Wyndham Tennant*.
14. Rev. A. E. Ford, conversation with author, summer 1987.
15. Susan Lowndes Marques, conversation with author, 7 July 1988.
16. Stephen Tennant to Cecil Beaton (Cecil Beaton, diary, summer 1973).
17. Stephen Tennant in a filmed interview with Nicholas Haslam and the Earl of Pembroke, summer 1985.
18. Dame Daphne du Maurier to Stephen Tennant, 26 September 1972.
19. Sir Oliver Lodge's obituary of Lady Grey, *Salisbury & Wiltshire Journal*, 23 November 1928.
20. Papers in the possession of Hugo Vickers.
21. Alan Jenkins, *The Twenties* (Heinemann, London, 1974), p. 214.
22. Stephen Tennant to Cecil Beaton, 15 February 1929.
23. Stephen Tennant, manuscript fragment, 1951.
24. Stephen Tennant to Mildred Bennett, July/August 1974.
25. Haslam/Pembroke interview.
26. Stephen Tennant to Cecil Beaton, 15 February 1929.
27. Haslam/Pembroke interview.
28. Simon Blow, *Broken Blood* (Faber, London, 1987) p. 151.
29. Last Will and Testament of Edward Priaulx Tennant, First Baron Glenconner (Somerset House).
30. Brian Masters, *Now Barabbas Was a Rotter* (Hamish Hamilton, London, 1977) p. 278.
31. E. F. Benson, *Final Edition* (Hogarth Press, London, 1988) p. 71.
32. This and the following from the Haslam/Pembroke interview.
33. ibid.
34. Manuscript fragment.
35. This and the following from the *Daily Mail*, 5 April 1921.
36. This and the following from the *Daily Mirror*, 8 April 1921.
37. The Hon. Lady Mosley, letter to author, 5 March 1987.
38. Stephen Tennant, marginalia.
39. This and the following from Sir Steven Runciman, conversation with author, 1 June 1987.
40. Hermione Baddeley, *The Unsinkable Hermione Baddeley* (Collins, London, 1984) p. 47.
41. This and the following from manuscript fragment, 'Parc Morceau'.
42. Rosamond Lehmann, letter to author, 26 March 1987.
43. This and the following from the Haslam/Pembroke interview.

Chapter 3: *The Kingdom by the Sea*

1. Stephen Tennant to Elizabeth Lowndes, 14 April 1923.

2. Oliver Messel, quoted in Charles Castle, *Oliver Messel* (Thames & Hudson, London, 1986) p. 39.
3. Rex Whistler to Stephen Tennant, 13 October 1924.
4. Laurence Whistler, *The Laughter and the Urn – The Life of Rex Whistler* (Weidenfeld & Nicolson, London, 1985) p. 52.
5. Charles Castle, *Oliver Messel*.
6. Laurence Whistler, *The Laughter and the Urn*, p. 56.
7. Stephen Tennant to Laurence Whistler, undated (?mid-50s).
8. Stephen Tennant, essay on Rex Whistler, written summer 1948.
9. Laurence Whistler, *The Laughter and the Urn*, p. 62.
10. Stephen Tennant, essay on Rex Whistler.
11. Rex Whistler to Stephen Tennant, 5 August 1924.
12. Laurence Whistler, *The Laughter and the Urn*, p. 62.
13. Mary Adshead, conversation with author, 18 September 1987.
14. Stephen Tennant, essay on Rex Whistler.
15. Laurence Whistler, *The Laughter and the Urn*, p. 81.
16. Stephen Tennant, inscription on a watercolour, (?mid-50s).
17. Rex Whistler to Ronald Fuller, July 1923, quoted in Laurence Whistler, *The Laughter and the Urn*, p. 64.
18. Laurence Whistler, *The Laughter and the Urn*, p. 81.
19. ibid, p. 65.
20. Rex Whistler to Stephen Tennant, 1931, undated.
21. Cecil Beaton, *The Wandering Years* (Weidenfeld & Nicolson, London, 1961), p. 164.
22. Stephen Tennant to Hugo Vickers, autumn 1980, quoted in Hugo Vickers, *Cecil Beaton* (Weidenfeld & Nicolson, London, 1985) p. 96.
23. Laurence Whistler, *The Laughter and the Urn*, p. 65.
24. *Daily Graphic*, 5 February 1923.
25. Rosemary Olivier, conversation with author, 18 April 1987.
26. *Daily Graphic*, 5 February 1923.
27. *Sketch*, 31 January 1923, pp. 202–3.
28. Edith Olivier, *Without Knowing Mr Walkley* (Faber, London, 1938), p. 253.
29. Susan Lowndes Marques, conversation with author, 7 July 1988.
30. Stephen Tennant, journal fragment, December 1925.
31. Stephen Tennant to Elizabeth Lowndes, 22 July 1924.
32. Rex Whistler to Stephen Tennant, 27 August 1924.
33. Rex Whistler to Stephen Tennant, 10 October 1924.
34. Rex Whistler to Stephen Tennant, 5 August 1924.
35. Laurence Whistler, *The Laughter and the Urn*, p. 73.
36. *Daily Mirror*, 20 October 1924.
37. Stephen Tennant, journal, October 1924, quoted in Laurence Whistler, *The Laughter and the Urn*, p. 73.
38. Stephen Tennant, essay on Rex Whistler.
39. Rex Whistler to Ronald Fuller, July 1923, quoted in Laurence Whistler, *The Laughter and the Urn*, p. 64.
40. Stephen Tennant, journal, 24 October 1924, quoted in Laurence Whistler, *The Laughter and the Urn*, p. 74.
41. This and the following, ibid., p. 75.
42. This and the following from Stephen Tennant, journal, October 1924, quoted in John Culme's introduction to the catalogue *The Contents of Wilsford Manor* (Sotheby's, London, October 1987), p. 9.
43. Stephen Tennant to Elizabeth Lowndes, spring 1927.

44. Laurence Whistler, *The Laughter and the Urn*, p. 75.
45. Stephen Tennant to Elizabeth Lowndes, 16 January 1925.
46. Stephen Tennant to Elizabeth Lowndes, 21 January 1925.
47. ibid.
48. Rex Whistler to Lady Grey, 4 February 1925.
49. Rebecca Trusler to Elizabeth Lowndes, undated, spring 1925.
50. Edith Olivier, unpublished diaries, March–April 1925.
51. Laurence Whistler, *The Laughter and the Urn*, p. 78.
52. Rebecca Trusler to Elizabeth Lowndes, 19 April 1925.
53. Rebecca Trusler to Elizabeth Lowndes, 29 April 1925.

Chapter 4: *Napier and Eloise*

1. Rebecca Trusler to Elizabeth Lowndes, May 1925.
2. Stephen Tennant to Elizabeth Lowndes, May 1925.
3. This and the following from manuscript of *The Second Chance*.
4. Elsa Schiaparelli, *Shocking Life* (Dent, London, 1954).
5. Stephen Tennant to Elizabeth Lowndes, 8 July 1925.
6. Stephen Tennant to Elizabeth Lowndes, undated, (? summer 1925).
7. This and the following from Susan Lowndes Marques, letter to author, 17 November 1988.
8. Pamela Grey to Marie Belloc Lowndes, 13 May 1925.
9. Stephen Tennant to Marie Belloc Lowndes, 8 July 1925.
10. This and the following, ibid.
11. This and the following from Susan Lowndes Marques, conversation with author, 7 July 1988.
12. The Dowager Countess of Iddesleigh, conversation with Susan Lowndes Marques, told to author, 18 July 1988.
13. Stephen Tennant to Elizabeth Lowndes, 17 July 1925.
14. Stephen Tennant to Elizabeth Lowndes, 22 July 1925.
15. Sir Steven Runciman, letter to author, 30 September 1988.
16. Stephen Tennant to Elizabeth Lowndes, 5 August 1925.
17. Stephen Spender, *World Within World* (Faber, London, 1977), p. 143.
18. This and the following from the *Alnwick & County Gazette & Guardian*, 29 August 1925.
19. Rosamond Lehmann, *Rosamond Lehmann's Album* (Chatto & Windus, London, 1985), p. 46.
20. Stephen Tennant to Elizabeth Lowndes, 19 September 1925.
21. *Vogue*, autumn 1925.
22. *Sketch*, 7 October 1925.
23. Stephen Tennant to Elizabeth Lowndes, 26 September 1925.
24. Daphne Fielding, *The Duchess of Jermyn Street* (Eyre & Spottiswode, London, 1964), p. 124.
25. Edward Burra to Barbara Ker-Seymer, in William Chappell (ed.), *Well Dearie: The Letters of Edward Burra* (Gordon Fraser, London, 1985), p. 52.
26. Stephen Tennant to Elizabeth Lowndes 26 October 1925.
27. Stephen Tennant to Elizabeth Lowndes, 2 December 1925.
28. Stephen Tennant to Elizabeth Lowndes, early December 1925.
29. Susan Lowndes Marques, conversation with author, 18 July 1988.
30. Stephen Tennant to Elizabeth Lowndes, December 1925.
31. Stephen Tennant to Elizabeth Lowndes, 15 February 1926.
32. This and the following from Stephen Tennant, journal, 18 December 1925.

33. This and the following from Stephen Tennant, journal, December 1925.
34. Stephen Tennant to Elizabeth Lowndes, undated (early 1926).
35. ibid.
36. Stephen Tennant to Elizabeth Lowndes, 3 February 1926.
37. Stephen Tennant to Elizabeth Lowndes, late February 1926.
38. Stephen Tennant to Elizabeth Lowndes, 10 April 1926.

Chapter 5: Overture . . .

1. Sir Steven Runciman, conversation with author, 1 June 1987.
2. Willa Cather, *My Àntonia* (Virago, London, 1980) p. 7.
3. Phyllis C. Robinson, *Willa: The Life of Willa Cather* (Doubleday, New York, 1983), p. 128.
4. Willa Cather, *My Àntonia*, p. 263.
5. Willa Cather, *A Lost Lady* (Virago, London, 1983), p. 124.
6. ibid., p. 133.
7. This and the following from the Haslam/Pembroke interview.
8. This and the following from Prof. Patricia Lee Yongue, essay in *Southern Humanities Review*, Vol. XIV, No. 1 (University of California, winter 1980).
9. Stephen Tennant, journal, 24 September 1927, quoted in Sotheby's Wilsford catalogue, p. 172.
10. This and the following from Stephen Tennant to Elizabeth Lowndes, 15 April 1926.
11. Stephen Tennant to Elizabeth Lowndes, 19 April 1926.
12. This and the following from Stephen Tennant to Elizabeth Lowndes, 10 May 1926.
13. Stephen Tennant to Dr Stewart Craggs, 'Uncouth June' 1975.
14. This and the following from the Haslam/Pembroke interview.
15. Stephen Tennant to Elizabeth Lowndes, July 1926.
16. Stanley Olson, *Elinor Wylie* (The Dial Press/James Wade, New York, 1979), p. 269.
17. ibid.
18. Rebecca Trusler to Elizabeth Lowndes, 21 July 1926.
19. Stephen Tennant to Elizabeth Lowndes, summer 1926.
20. Stephen Tennant to Elizabeth Lowndes, 2 November 1926.
21. This and the following from Stephen Tennant to Elizabeth Lowndes, 12 September 1926.
22. Stephen Tennant to Elizabeth Lowndes, 13 September 1926.
23. Stephen Tennant to Elizabeth Lowndes, 17 September 1926.
24. Stephen Tennant to Elizabeth Lowndes, 27 September 1926.
25. Rebecca Trusler to Elizabeth Lowndes, undated (early 1926).
26. Stephen Tennant to Elizabeth Lowndes, 2 November 1926.
27. Rebecca Trusler to Elizabeth Lowndes, undated (late 1926).
28. Edith Olivier, *From Her Journals*, ed. Penelope Middleboe (Weidenfeld & Nicolson, London, 1988), p. 44.
29. Hugo Vickers, *Cecil Beaton*, p. 84.
30. Mrs Edward Phillips, conversation with author, 29 May 1987.
31. Stephen Tennant to Elizabeth Lowndes, 20 December 1926.
32. Hugo Vickers, *Cecil Beaton*, p. 54.
33. Cecil Beaton, diary, 21 December 1926.
34. Hugo Vickers, *Cecil Beaton*, p. 85.
35. Cecil Beaton, diary, 22 December 1926.

36. Stephen Tennant to Eileen Hose, spring 1981.
37. P. N. Furbank, *E. M. Forster: A Life*, Vol. II (Secker & Warburg, London, 1977), p. 136.
38. Cecil Beaton, *The Wandering Years*, p. 152.
39. Stephen Tennant to Hugo Vickers, 'Magic Spring', 1981.
40. Cecil Beaton, diary, 22 December 1926.
41. Stephen Tennant to Cecil Beaton, undated (early 1927).
42. Cecil Beaton, diary, 2 January 1927.
43. Stephen Tennant, marginalia.
44. Cecil Beaton, diary, 6 January 1927.
45. ibid., 15 January 1927.
46. Stephen Tennant to Elizabeth Lowndes, 2 March 1926.
47. Cecil Beaton, diary, 15 January 1927.
48. Quoted in Hugo Vickers (ed.), *Cocktails & Laughter: The Albums of Loelia Lindsay* (Hamish Hamilton, London, 1983) p. 12.
49. Cecil Beaton, diary, 15 January 1927.
50. Cecil Beaton, *The Wandering Years*, p. 152.
51. Edith Olivier, *Without Knowing Mr Walkley* (Faber, London, 1939), pp. 255–6.
52. Cecil Beaton, diary, 15 January 1927.
53. ibid., 16 January 1927.
54. ibid., 17 January 1927.

Chapter 6: ... And Beginners

1. *Sunday Express*, 6 February 1927.
2. This and the following from Stephen Tennant to Elizabeth Lowndes, 9 February 1927.
3. Stephen Tennant to Elizabeth Lowndes, 11 February 1927.
4. Edith Olivier, diary, quoted in Laurence Whistler, *The Laughter and the Urn*, p. 99.
5. Edith Olivier, *From Her Journals*, p. 48.
6. Stephen Tennant to Cecil Beaton, undated (early 1927).
7. Hugo Vickers, *Cecil Beaton*, p. 95.
8. Cecil Beaton, *The Wandering Years*, p. 164.
9. Hugo Vickers (ed.), *Cocktails & Laughter*, p. 35.
10. This and the following from Laurence Whistler, *The Laughter and the Urn*, p. 100.
11. Stephen Tennant to Cecil Beaton, undated (March 1927).
12. ibid.
13. *The Lady*, 5 May 1927.
14. *Westminster Gazette*, undated clipping (Beaton scrapbooks, Victoria and Albert Museum), May 1927.
15. ibid.
16. Edith Olivier, *From Her Journals*, p. 51.
17. ibid.
18. Stephen Tennant to Elizabeth Lowndes, 21 July 1927.
19. Jacob Epstein to Stephen Tennant, 14 September 1927.
20. Stephen Tennant, journal, 27 September 1927, quoted in Sotheby's Wilsford catalogue, p. 161.
21. Michael Wishart to Stephen Tennant, 27 October 1967.
22. This and the following from Rosamond Lehmann, letter to author, 4 April 1987.
23. Cecil Beaton, *Ashcombe* (Batsford, London, 1949), p. 44.

24. Rosamond Lehmann, letter to author, 4 April 1987.
25. This and the following from Stanley Olson, *Elinor Wylie*, p. 271.
26. Elinor Wylie to Stephen Tennant, August 1927.

Chapter 7: Stage Centre

1. Edith Olivier, *From Her Journals*, p. 40.
2. Susan Lowndes Marques, conversation with author, 7 July 1988.
3. William Henderson, conversation with author, 5 August 1987.
4. Hugo Vickers, *Cecil Beaton*, p. 97.
5. Laurence Whistler, *The Laughter and the Urn*, p. 101.
6. ibid., p. 102.
7. Michael Davie, (ed.), *The Diaries of Evelyn Waugh* (Weidenfeld & Nicolson, London, 1976), pp. 285–6.
8. Stephen Tennant, marginalia.
9. Stephen Tennant to Cecil Beaton, 30 August 1927.
10. The Hon. Lady Lindsay to Hugo Vickers, 10 July 1981.
11. Cecil Beaton, *The Wandering Years*, p. 171.
12. Evelyn Waugh, *Brideshead Revisited* (Penguin, Harmondsworth, 1959), p. 49.
13. Lord Head to Hugo Vickers, 1 April 1982.
14. The Hon. Lady Lindsay to Hugo Vickers, 10 July 1981.
15. Edith Olivier, *From Her Journals*, p. 62.
16. ibid., p. 53.
17. Stephen Tennant to Hugo Vickers, 'Heavenly Sacred Winged January', 1984.
18. Stephen Tennant, marginalia.
19. Stephen Tennant to Elizabeth Lowndes, 12 September 1927.
20. Stephen Tennant to Cecil Beaton, undated (summer 1927).
21. Michael Holroyd, *Lytton Strachey*, Vol. II (Heinemann, London, 1968), p. 646.
22. Stephen Tennant to Elizabeth Lowndes, undated (October 1927).
23. Stephen Tennant to Cecil Beaton, undated (1927).
24. ibid.
25. Dame Felicitas Corrigan, *Siegfried Sassoon: A Poet's Pilgrimage*, (Gollancz, London, 1973), p. 47.
26. ibid., pp. 105–6.
27. Rupert Hart-Davis (ed.), *Siegfried Sassoon's Diaries 1920–1922* (Faber, London, 1981), p. 103.
28. ibid., p. 71.
29. Stephen Tennant to Gilles David, 4 December 1971.
30. Rupert Hart-Davis (ed.), *Siegfried Sassoon's Diaries 1923–1925* (Faber, London, 1985), p. 300.
31. Siegfried Sassoon, 'A Breach of Decorum', *Collected Poems 1908–1956* (Faber, London, 1956).
32. Rupert Hart-Davis (ed.), *Siegfried Sassoon Diaries 1915–1918* (Faber, London, 1983) p. 103.
33. Siegfried Sassoon, *Siegfried's Journey* (Faber, London, 1945), p. 11.
34. Stephen Tennant to Gilles David 4 December 1971.
35. Patrick Quinn, conversation with author, 25 February 1989.
36. Siegfried Sassoon, diary, quoted in Laurence Whistler, *The Laughter and the Urn*, p. 113.
37. Stephen Tennant, journal, quoted in Sotheby's Wilsford catalogue, p. 184.
38. Stephen Tennant, journal, October 1927, quoted in Sotheby's Wilsford catalogue, p. 12.

39. Sotheby's Wilsford catalogue, p. 12.
40. Sacheverell Sitwell to Stephen Tennant, 18 October 1927.
41. Siegfried Sassoon to Henry Head, 13 September 1928.
42. *Salisbury & Wiltshire Journal*, 29 April 1932.
43. Michael Holroyd, *Lytton Strachey*, p. 559.
44. ibid.
45. Haslam/Pembroke interview.
46. Michael Holroyd, *Lytton Strachey*, p. 765.
47. Stephen Tennant, journal, 14 October 1928, quoted in Sotheby's Wilsford catalogue, p. 22.
48. *Daily Sketch*, 7 November 1927.
49. *Lady*, 1 December 1927.
50. John Pearson, *Façades* (Macmillan, London, 1978).
51. *Daily Herald*, 23 November 1927.
52. Stephen Tennant to Elizabeth Lowndes, 3 December 1927.
53. Laurence Whistler, *The Laughter and the Urn*, p. 123.
54. Stephen Tennant, marginalia.
55. Laurence Whistler, *The Laughter and the Urn*, p. 123.
56. Stephen Tennant, marginalia.
57. Laurence Whistler, *The Laughter and the Urn*, p. 123.
58. Stephen Tennant to P. N. Furbank, undated (1975).
59. *Diary of Virginia Woolf: Vol. III* (Hogarth Press, London, 1980), p. 96–101.
60. Robert Gittings, letter to author, 3 March 1988.
61. Robert Gittings and Jo Manton, *The Second Mrs Hardy* (Heinemann, London, 1979), p. 132.
62. Stephen Tennant to Elizabeth Lowndes, 10 December 1927.
63. *Daily Mirror*, undated clipping (December 1927), Beaton scrapbooks (Victoria and Albert Museum).
64. *Vogue*, late winter 1927.
65. Edith Olivier, *A Guide to the Pursuit of Rare Meats*, Rex Whistler Tate Gallery Restaurant mural (galley proof).

Chapter 8: Intermezzo

1. This and the following from Stephen Tennant to Elizabeth Lowndes, 24 January 1928.
2. Stephen Tennant to Elizabeth Lowndes, 28 January 1928.
3. Stephen Tennant to Cecil Beaton, undated (1928).
4. ibid.
5. Mrs Igor Vinogradoff, conversation with author, summer 1988.
6. Stephen Tennant to Cecil Beaton, undated (1928).
7. ibid.
8. *Vogue*, 4 April 1928.
9. Stephen Tennant to Eileen Hose, undated (July 1981).
10. Stephen Tennant to Elizabeth Lowndes, undated (1928).
11. Stephen Tennant to Elizabeth Lowndes, 14 February 1928.
12. Stephen Tennant to Elizabeth Lowndes, 4 March 1928.
13. Hermione Baddeley, *The Unsinkable Hermione Baddeley*, p. 13.
14. *Daily Express*, 23 April 1928.
15. Peter Quennell, conversation with author, 18 March 1987.
16. *Daily Express*, 23 April 1928.
17. Stephen Tennant to Elizabeth Lowndes, 24 April 1928.

18. Stephen Tennant to Elizabeth Lowndes, undated.
19. Rupert Hart-Davis (ed.), *Siegfried Sassoon's Diaries 1923–1925*, p. 251.
20. Sotheby's Wilsford catalogue, p. 12.
21. *Daily Chronicle*, 2 May 1928.
22. *Evening Standard*, 4 May 1928.
23. Nicholas Mosley, *Rules of the Game* (Secker & Warburg, London, 1982), p. 114.
24. Rex Whistler to Stephen Tennant, undated.
25. *Everyman's Dictionary of Literary Biography* (Dent, London, 1958), p. 614.
26. Selina Hastings, *Nancy Mitford* (Hamish Hamilton, London, 1985), p. 63.
27. Stephen Tennant, journal, 25 September 1928, quoted in Sotheby's Wilsford catalogue, p. 159.
28. Cecil Beaton's scrapbooks (Victoria and Albert Museum).
29. *Sphere*, 16 June 1928.
30. *Evening News*, 10 May 1928.
31. Rebecca West, *Ending in Earnest*.
32. Hugo Vickers, *Cecil Beaton*, p. 103.
33. ibid.
34. ibid., p. 104.
35. *Daily Express*, 11 July 1928.
36. Patricia Lee Yongue, essay on Stephen Tennant and Cather.
37. *Star*, 11 July 1928.
38. *Morning Post*, 12 July 1928.
39. Hugo Vickers, *Cecil Beaton*, p. 106.
40. *Daily Mail*, 13 July 1928.
41. *Evening Standard*, 13 July 1928.
42. Susan Lowndes Marques, conversation with author, July 1988.
43. Edith Olivier, *From Her Journals*, p. 77.
44. Quoted in Hugo Vickers, *Cecil Beaton*.
45. Hugo Vickers, *Cecil Beaton*, p. 105.
46. Hermione Baddeley, *The Unsinkable Hermione Baddeley*, p. 86.
47. *Daily Express*, 14 July 1928.
48. Quoted in Marie-Jacqueline Lancaster (ed.), *Brian Howard: Portrait of a Failure* (Anthony Blond, London, 1968), p. 266.
49. This and the following from the *Daily Express*, 14 July 1928.
50. Marie-Jacqueline Lancaster (ed.), *Brian Howard: Portrait of a Failure*, p. 266.
51. ibid.

Chapter 9: *Southern Baroque*

1. Stephen Tennant to Cecil Beaton, undated (1928).
2. Siegfried Sassoon, *Siegfried's Journey*, p. 135.
3. Ronald Firbank (introduction by Osbert Sitwell), *Five Novels* (Duckworth, London, 1949), p. xxiii.
4. Sir Harold Acton, letter to author, 9 June 1987.
5. Siegfried Sassoon, *Siegfried's Journey*, p. 137.
6. Stephen Tennant to Cecil Beaton, undated.
7. Susan Lowndes Marques, conversation with author, 17 July 1988.
8. Sotheby's Wilsford catalogue, p. 13.
9. Stephen Tennant to Cecil Beaton, undated.
10. Stephen Tennant, journal, 11 September 1928, quoted in Sotheby's Wilsford catalogue, p. 13.

11. Siegfried Sassoon to Henry Head, 13 September 1928.
12. Stephen Tennant, journal, 15 September 1928, quoted in Sotheby's Wilsford catalogue, p. 13.
13. Christabel Aberconway, *A Wiser Woman?* (Hutchinson, London, 1966), p. 90.
14. Stephen Tennant, conversation with Hugo Vickers, 20 September 1980.
15. Stephen Tennant to Elizabeth Lowndes, 21 September 1928.
16. *A Reflection of the Other Person: The Letters of Virginia Woolf 1929–1931* (Hogarth Press, London, 1978), p. 27.
17. Victoria Glendinning, *Edith Sitwell* (Weidenfeld & Nicolson, London, 1981), p. 296.
18. Stephen Tennant to Elizabeth Lowndes, 21 September 1928.
19. Stephen Tennant, journal, 23 and 24 September 1928, quoted in Sotheby's Wilsford catalogue, p. 191.
20. Stephen Tennant to Cecil Beaton, undated (September 1928).
21. Edith Olivier, *From Her Journals*, p. 85.
22. Stephen Tennant to Cecil Beaton, 10 October 1928.
23. ibid.
24. Evelyn Waugh, *Decline and Fall* (Penguin, Harmondsworth, 1937), p. 128.
25. Auberon Waugh, letter to author, 28 May 1987.
26. Stephen Tennant to Cecil Beaton, undated (1928).
27. ibid.
28. Stephen Tennant, journal, 10 November 1928, quoted in Sotheby's Wilsford catalogue, p. 14.
29. Anne Douglas Sedgwick to Stephen Tennant, 15 November 1928.
30. Stephen Tennant, journals, 9 and 15 November 1928, quoted in Sotheby's Wilsford catalogue, p. 192.
31. Edith Olivier to Cecil Beaton, 23 November 1928.
32. Stephen Tennant, journal, 20 November 1928, quoted in Sotheby's Wilsford catalogue p. 154.
33. Cecil Beaton, diary, 20 November 1928.
34. ibid., 23 November 1928.
35. ibid.
36. Eleanor Brougham to Cecil Beaton, 23 November 1928.
37. Georgia Sitwell to Cecil Beaton, 4 December 1928.
38. Edith Olivier to Cecil Beaton, 10 December 1928.
39. Stephen Tennant to Mildred Bennett, 6 April 1973.
40. Edith Olivier to Cecil Beaton, 10 December 1928.
41. ibid.
42. Lady Rumbold, conversation with author, 26 August 1987.
43. Edith Olivier to Cecil Beaton, 10 December 1928.
44. ibid.
45. Stephen Tennant to Cecil Beaton, 27 December 1928.
46. Hermione Baddeley, *The Unsinkable Hermione Baddeley*, p. 68.
47. ibid., pp. 68–9.
48. Edith Olivier, *From Her Journals*, p. 88.
49. Stephen Tennant to Elizabeth Lowndes, 29 December 1928.

Chapter 10: The Siegfried Idyll

1. Stephen Tennant to Cecil Beaton, 27 December 1928.
2. Edith Olivier, *From Her Journals*, p. 87.
3. Laurence Whistler, *The Laughter and the Urn*, p. 130.

4. Siegfried Sassoon, diary, quoted in ibid.
5. Rupert Hart-Davis (ed.), *Siegfried Sassoon: Letters to Max Beerbohm* (Faber, London, 1986), pp. 4–5.
6. *Diary of Virginia Woolf*, Vol. III (Hogarth Press, London, 1980), p. 193.
7. *Siegfried Sassoon's Diaries 1923–1925*, p. 34.
8. Ruth Head to Stephen Tennant, 23 December 1928.
9. Ruth Head to Stephen Tennant, 26 December 1928.
10. Peter Quennell, conversation with author, 18 March 1987.
11. Mrs Igor Vinogradoff, conversation with author, spring 1988.
12. Anthony Powell, *To Keep the Ball Rolling*, Vol. 11 (Heinemann, London, 1978), p. 37.
13. Stephen Tennant to Cecil Beaton, undated (1929).
14. Stephen Tennant to Elizabeth Lowndes, 8 February 1929.
15. Ruth Head to Stephen Tennant, 12 February 1929.
16. Stephen Tennant to Cecil Beaton, 15 February 1929.
17. Edith Olivier, *From Her Journals*, p. 17.
18. Ronald Firbank, *Three More Novels* (New Directions, London, 1986), p. 341.
19. Stephen Tennant to Cecil Beaton, 19 February 1929.
20. Paul O'Prey (ed.), *In Broken Images: Selected Letters of Robert Graves* (Hutchinson, London 1982), p. 204.
21. Stephen Tennant to Cecil Beaton, 19 February 1929.
22. Stephen Tennant to Cecil Beaton, early April 1929.
23. Stephen Tennant to Elizabeth Lowndes, 24 February 1929.
24. William Walton to Siegfried Sassoon, undated (1929).
25. Laurence Whistler, *The Laughter and the Urn*, p. 136.
26. Edith Olivier, *From Her Journals*, p. 92.
27. Laurence Whistler, *The Laughter and the Urn*, p. 137.
28. ibid.
29. ibid.
30. Stephen Tennant to Cecil Beaton, 3 April 1929.
31. ibid.
32. Stephen Tennant to Cecil Beaton, 16 April 1929.
33. Laurence Whistler, *The Laughter and the Urn*, p. 138.
34. Stephen Tennant to Cecil Beaton, undated.
35. Stephen Tennant to Elizabeth Lowndes, 26 May 1929.
36. ibid.
37. Stephen Tennant to Cecil Beaton, undated.
38. Ruth Head to Stephen Tennant, 13 July 1929.
39. Paul O'Prey (ed.), *In Broken Images*, p. 204.
40. Ruth Head to Stephen Tennant, 13 July 1929.
41. Eddie Marsh to Stephen Tennant, 12 July 1929.
42. Rex Whistler to Stephen Tennant, 16 July 1929.
43. Laurence Whistler, *The Laughter and the Urn*, p. 135.
44. Stephen Tennant to Gilles David, 4 December 1971.
45. Stephen Tennant to Elizabeth Lowndes, 28 July 1929.
46. Stephen Tennant, marginalia.
47. Siegfried Sassoon to Ruth Head, 19 August 1929.
48. Laurence Whistler, *The Laughter and the Urn*, p. 149.
49. Stephen Tennant to Elizabeth Lowndes, 15 August 1929.
50. Michael Holroyd, *Lytton Strachey*, p. 645.
51. Laurence Whistler, *The Laughter and the Urn*, p. 149.
52. Siegfried Sassoon to Henry and Ruth Head, 7 October 1929.

53. Geoffrey Elborn, *Edith Sitwell* (Sheldon Press, London, 1981), pp. 82–3.
54. Edith Olivier, *From Her Journals*, p. 104.
55. Stephen Tennant to Cecil Beaton, 5 October 1929.
56. Stephen Tennant to Cecil Beaton, 12 October 1929.
57. Stephen Tennant to Cecil Beaton, 19 October 1929.
58. Edith Olivier, *From Her Journals*, p. 104.
59. Stephen Tennant to Cecil Beaton, 12 October 1929.
60. Stephen Tennant to Cecil Beaton, early November 1929.
61. Siegfried Sassoon's inscription, quoted in Sotheby's Wilsford catalogue, p. 15.
62. Laurence Whistler, *The Laughter and the Urn*, p. 149.
63. Stephen Tennant to Elizabeth Lowndes, 2 November 1929.
64. Michael Holroyd, *Lytton Strachey*, p. 646.
65. Stephen Tennant to Cecil Beaton, 28 October 1929.

Chapter 11: In Sicily

1. Stephen Tennant to Cecil Beaton, 19 November 1929.
2. Stephen Tennant to Cecil Beaton, 22 December 1929.
3. Stephen Tennant to Elizabeth Lowndes, 15 November 1929.
4. Rupert Hart-Davis (ed.), *Siegfried Sassoon: Letters to Max Beerbohm*, p. 5.
5. ibid., p. 11.
6. ibid., p. 5.
7. ibid., pp. 37ff.
8. ibid., p. 5.
9. ibid., p. 6.
10. ibid., p. 7.
11. Stephen Tennant, marginalia.
12. Stephen Tennant to Elizabeth Lowndes, 7 December 1929.
13. ibid.
14. Stephen Tennant to Cecil Beaton, 22 December 1929.
15. Stephen Tennant, marginalia.
16. Siegfried Sassoon, *Vigils* (Faber, London, 1935).
17. Stephen Tennant to Cecil Beaton, 29 January 1929.
18. Stephen Tennant, marginalia.
19. ibid.
20. Stephen Tennant, journal, (?)29 July 1938, quoted in Sotheby's Wilsford catalogue, p. 15.
21. Stephen Tennant to Cecil Beaton, 22 December 1929.
22. William Walton to Siegfried Sassoon, 22 March 1930.
23. Stephen Tennant to Cecil Beaton, 10 March 1930.
24. Hugo Vickers (ed.), *Cocktails & Laughter*, jacket notes.
25. Stephen Tennant, marginalia.
26. Rupert Hart-Davis (ed.), *Siegfried Sassoon: Letters to Max Beerbohm*, p. 9.
27. Stephen Tennant to Cecil Beaton, 10 April 1930.
28. Geoffrey Elborn, *Edith Sitwell*, p. 83.
29. *Diary of Virginia Woolf*, Vol. 111, p. 299.
30. Stephen Tennant to Cecil Beaton, 15 April 1930.
31. Stephen Tennant, marginalia.
32. Siegfried Sassoon to Ruth Head, undated.
33. Stephen Tennant to Sibyl Colefax, 12 April 1930.
34. Stephen Tennant, marginalia.

35. Parker Tyler, *The Divine Comedy of Pavel Tchelitchew* (Weidenfeld & Nicolson, London, 1969), p. 346.
36. Stephen Tennant to Cecil Beaton, undated.
37. James Thrall Soby, *Tchelitchew* (Museum of Modern Art, New York, 1942), p. 23.
38. Stephen Tennant to Elizabeth Lowndes, 12 May 1930.

Chapter 12: *There's Something Wrong in Paradise*

1. Stephen Tennant to Cecil Beaton, 8 July 1930.
2. Stephen Tennant to Cecil Beaton, undated.
3. ibid.
4. Stephen Tennant to Cecil Beaton, 16 July 1930.
5. This and the following from Stephen Tennant to Cecil Beaton, undated.
6. Stephen Tennant to Cecil Beaton, 16 July 1930.
7. Stephen Tennant to Eileen Hose, summer 1981.
8. Stephen Tennant to Cecil Beaton, August 1930.
9. Stephen Tennant to Cecil Beaton, undated.
10. Stephen Tennant to Hugo Vickers, January 1982.
11. Stephen Tennant to Cecil Beaton, undated.
12. Sassoon, diary, quoted in Laurence Whistler, *The Laughter and the Urn*, p. 154.
13. Stephen Tennant to Lord Egremont, told to author, 11 June 1987.
14. Siegfried Sassoon to Cecil Beaton, 8 August 1930.
15. This and the following from Susan Sontag, *Illness as Metaphor* (Allen Lane, London, 1979).
16. Siegfried Sassoon to Cecil Beaton, 8 August 1930.
17. Rupert Hart-Davis (ed.), *Siegfried Sassoon: Letters to Max Beerbohm*, p. 14.
18. Sassoon, diary, quoted in Laurence Whistler, *The Laughter and the Urn*, p. 155.
19. ibid.
20. ibid.
21. Siegfried Sassoon to Henry and Ruth Head, undated.
22. ibid.
23. Siegfried Sassoon to Henry and Ruth Head, 16 June 1930.
24. Siegfried Sassoon to Henry and Ruth Head, undated.
25. ibid.
26. ibid.
27. Siegfried Sassoon to Henry and Ruth Head, 21 June 1931.
28. ibid.
29. Siegfried Sassoon, *Vigils*.
30. Siegfried Sassoon to Henry and Ruth Head, undated.
31. Laurence Whistler, *The Laughter and the Urn*, p. 155.
32. Stephen Tennant, marginalia.
33. Felicitas Corrigan, *A Poet's Pilgrimage*, p. 207.
34. Siegfried Sassoon to Henry and Ruth Head, 23 May 1933.
35. Laurence Whistler, *The Laughter and the Urn*, p. 156.
36. Edith Olivier, *From Her Journals*, p. 111.
37. ibid., p. 112.
38. William Walton to Siegfried Sassoon, 8 March 1931.
39. Edith Olivier, *From Her Journals*, p. 120.
40. Rupert Hart-Davis (ed.), *Siegfried Sassoon: Letters to Max Beerbohm*, p. 17.
41. ibid., pp. 19–20.
42. ibid.

43. William Walton to Siegfried Sassoon, 2 June 1932.

Chapter 13: *The Fatal Gift of Beauty*

1. This and the following from Laurence Whistler, *The Laughter and the Urn*, p. 163.
2. Siegfried Sassoon to Henry and Ruth Head, 29 June 1932.
3. William Walton to Siegfried Sassoon, 10 August 1932.
4. T. A. Ross, *An Enquiry into Prognosis in the Neurosis* (Cambridge University Press, 1936), p. 6.
5. Information supplied to the author by Marianne Thorn/Swaylands Study Centre, November 1988.
6. T. A. Ross, *The Common Neuroses* (Cambridge University Press, 1923).
7. Siegfried Sassoon to Henry and Ruth Head, 20 November 1932.
8. Siegfried Sassoon to Stephen Tennant, 14 and 19 December 1932, quoted in Sotheby's Wilsford catalogue, p. 184.
9. Siegfried Sassoon to Henry and Ruth Head, 16 January 1933.
10. Siegfried Sassoon to Henry and Ruth Head, 26 January 1933.
11. T. A. Ross, *The Common Neuroses*.
12. T. A. Ross, *An Enquiry into Prognosis in the Neurosis*, p. 7.
13. Siegfried Sassoon to Henry and Ruth Head, 26 January 1933.
14. ibid.
15. Siegfried Sassoon to Henry and Ruth Head, 25 February 1933.
16. Siegfried Sassoon to Henry and Ruth Head, undated April 1933.
17. Siegfried Sassoon to Henry and Ruth Head, 23 May 1933.
18. Siegfried Sassoon to Henry and Ruth Head, undated (May 1933).
19. Siegfried Sassoon to Henry and Ruth Head, 20 May 1933.
20. ibid.
21. Transcribed by Sassoon, letter to Henry and Ruth Head, 22 May 1933.
22. Siegfried Sassoon to Henry and Ruth Head, 29 May 1933.
23. Edith Olivier, *From Her Journals*, p. 145.
24. Siegfried Sassoon to Henry and Ruth Head, 31 May 1933.
25. Laurence Whistler, *The Laughter and the Urn*, p. 164.
26. Stephen Tennant, marginalia.
27. Stephen Tennant, journal, 17 September 1939, quoted in Sotheby's Wilsford catalogue, p. 184.
28. Stephen Tennant, marginalia.
29. Felicitas Corrigan, *A Poet's Pilgrimage*, p. 25.
30. Stephen Tennant to Laurence Whistler, 3 May 1946.
31. Stephen Tennant, journal, October 1939, quoted in Sotheby's Wilsford catalogue, p. 15.
32. Stephen Tennant, marginalia.
33. ibid.
34. ibid.
35. Rex Whistler to Stephen Tennant, undated (summer 1933).
36. Edith Olivier, *From Her Journals*, p. 14.
37. Siegfried Sassoon to Henry and Ruth Head, 12 September 1933.
38. Cecil Beaton, diary, October 1933.
39. Stephen Tennant to Cecil Beaton, 29 November 1933.
40. Geoffrey Elborn, *Edith Sitwell*, p. 83.

Chapter 14: New Horizons

1. Charles Ritchie, conversation with author, summer 1988.
2. Edith Olivier, *From Her Journals*, p. 153.
3. Stephen Tennant, journal, 14 June 1934, quoted in Sotheby's Wilsford catalogue, p. 15.
4. Edith Olivier, *From Her Journals*, p. 156–7.
5. Stephen Tennant, marginalia.
6. ibid.
7. ibid.
8. Constant Lambert to Anthony Powell, summer 1930, quoted in Andrew Motion, *The Lamberts* (Chatto & Windus, London, 1988), p. 178.
9. Stephen Tennant, marginalia.
10. Stephen Tennant, journal, 20 September 1934, quoted in Sotheby's Wilsford catalogue, p. 126.
11. Haslam/Pembroke interview.
12. Stephen Tennant, marginalia.
13. Stephen Tennant to Cecil Beaton, 27 October 1934.
14. Siegfried Sassoon, *Siegfried's Journey*, p. 219.
15. Laurence Whistler, *The Laughter and the Urn*, p. 198.
16. This and the following from David Herbert, *Second Son* (Peter Owen, London, 1972), pp. 47–8.
17. ibid. p. 48.
18. Stephen Tennant, conversation with Hugo Vickers, 20 September 1980.
19. Edith Olivier, *From Her Journals*, p. 162.
20. This and the following from Cecil Beaton, diary, May 1935.

Chapter 15: Bloomsbury-by-the-Sea

1. V. S. Naipaul, *The Enigma of Arrival* (Viking, London, 1987) p. 195.
2. *Diary of Virginia Woolf*, Vol. IV (Hogarth Press, London, 1982), p. 319.
3. Sir Stephen Spender, conversation with author, 30 August 1987.
4. John Lehmann, *Virginia Woolf and Her World* (Thames & Hudson, London, 1975), p. 61.
5. *Diary of Virginia Woolf*, Vol. IV, p. 328.
6. Stephen Tennant, marginalia.
7. Professor Quentin Bell to author, 26 July 1989.
8. *Diary of Virginia Woolf*, Vol. IV, p. 340.
9. Haslam/Pembroke interview.
10. Stephen Tennant, MS fragment.
11. *The Sickle Side of the Moon: Letters of Virginia Woolf 1932–1935* (Hogarth Press, London, 1979), p. 419.
12. Stephen Tennant to Sibyl Colefax, 21 August 1935.
13. Francis King, *E. M. Forster and His World* (Thames and Hudson, London, 1978), p. 5.
14. ibid.
15. Stephen Tennant, marginalia.
16. P. N. Furbank, *E. M. Forster*.
17. Stephen Tennant, journal, 17 September 1935.
18. ibid.
19. ibid., 18 September 1935.
20. ibid., 22 September 1935.

21. ibid., 21 September 1935.
22. Stephen Tennant to Cecil Beaton, 4 October 1935.
23. Stephen Tennant, marginalia.
24. Stephen Tennant, journal, 5–7 October 1935.
25. Stephen Tennant, journal, 5–7 October 1935.
26. Stephen Tennant, journal, 5 March 1937, quoted in Sotheby's Wilsford catalogue, p. 22.

Chapter 16: O Pioneer

1. Stephen Tennant, journal, 24 November 1935.
2. Cecil Beaton, diary, November 1935.
3. Laurence Whistler, *The Laughter and the Urn*, p. 198.
4. ibid.
5. Stephen Tennant, journal, 28 November 1935.
6. ibid., 29 November 1935.
7. Haslam/Pembroke interview.
8. Phyllis C. Robinson, *Willa Cather*, p. 264.
9. Stephen Tennant, journal, 3 December 1935.
10. ibid., 5 December 1935.
11. Stephen Tennant, manuscript fragment.
12. Stephen Tennant, journal, 5 December 1935.
13. Phyllis C. Robinson, *Willa Cather*, p. 55.
14. Hermione Lee, conversation with author, 16 December 1987.
15. Stephen Tennant, journal, 7 December 1935.
16. Stephen Tennant, marginalia.
17. Stephen Tennant, journal, 7 December 1935.
18. ibid.
19. ibid., 9 December 1935.
20. ibid., 14 December 1935.
21. ibid., 5 January 1936.
22. ibid., 23 February 1936.
23. ibid.
24. Stephen Tennant to Mildred Bennett, 14 May 1973.
25. Stephen Tennant to Mildred Bennett, 2 May 1975.
26. Stephen Tennant to Mildred Bennett, 29 October 1969.
27. Stephen Tennant to Mildred Bennett, undated.
28. Stephen Tennant to Mildred Bennett, 18 November 1971.
29. Willa Cather to Stephen Tennant, quoted in Sotheby's Wilsford catalogue, p. 172.
30. Willa Cather, *My Ántonia*, p. 260.
31. Willa Cather to Stephen Tennant, quoted in Sotheby's Wilsford catalogue, p. 172.
32. Stephen Tennant to Mildred Bennett, 5 May 1975.
33. Sotheby's Wilsford catalogue, p. 172.
34. Willa Cather to Stephen Tennant, 6 March 1974.

Chapter 17: Palazzo Wilsford

1. Stephen Tennant, marginalia.
2. Stephen Tennant, journal, 13 June 1941, quoted in Sotheby's Wilsford catalogue, p. 168.
3. Ottoline Morrell to Stephen Tennant, undated.

4. *Diary of Virginia Woolf,* Vol. V (Hogarth Press, London, 1984), p. 38.
5. Stephen Tennant, journal, 24 May 1942, quoted in Sotheby's Wilsford catalogue, p. 168.
6. *Leave the Letters till We're Dead: Letters of Virginia Woolf 1936–1941* (Hogarth Press, London, 1980), p. 57.
7. Sir Alfred Beit, letter to author, 1 February 1988.
8. Lady Templer, letter to author, 13 January 1989.
9. Her Majesty Queen Elizabeth The Queen Mother, in conversation with Hugo Vickers, 26 March 1981; also letter to author, 10 May 1988.
10. This and the following from Stephen Tennant to Cecil Beaton, 11 December 1936.
11. Sotheby's Wilsford catalogue, p. 17.
12. Stephen Tennant, journal, February 1937, quoted in Sotheby's Wilsford catalogue, p. 17.
13. Richard B. Fisher, *Syrie Maugham* (Duckworth, London, 1978), p. 56.
14. Stephen Tennant to Sibyl Colefax, 25 April 1937.
15. Stephen Tennant to Cecil Beaton, 10 May 1937.
16. Stephen Tennant, journal, 14 May 1937, quoted in Sotheby's Wilsford catalogue, p. 23.
17. Stephen Tennant to Cecil Beaton, 11 July 1937.
18. Francis Goodman in conversation with the author, 8 December 1987.
19. This and the following from Cecil Beaton, diary, July 1937.
20. Edith Olivier, *From Her Journals,* pp. 189–91.
21. Cecil Beaton, diary, July 1937.
22. Stephen Tennant, marginalia.

Chapter 18: *A Story of the Maritime Boulevards*

1. Stephen Tennant, journal, 19 September 1937, quoted in Sotheby's Wilsford catalogue, p. 82.
2. ibid., 17 October 1937, quoted in Sotheby's Wilsford catalogue, p. 82.
3. Haslam/Pembroke interview.
4. Stephen Tennant, manuscript fragment.
5. Stephen Tennant to Cecil Beaton, 17 October 1937.
6. ibid.
7. Stephen Tennant in a letter to the author, November 1986.
8. Cyril Connolly, *New Statesman,* 18 December 1937.
9. Stephen Tennant, manuscript fragment.
10. ibid.
11. Stephen Tennant, marginalia.
12. ibid.
13. Simon Blow, *Broken Blood,* p. 180.
14. Cecil Beaton, diary, autumn 1938.
15. ibid.
16. Stephen Tennant, journal, 2 October 1938, quoted in Sotheby's Wilsford catalogue, p. 183.
17. Haslam/Pembroke interview.
18. Dr Wendy Baron, letter to author, 12 May 1988.
19. Stephen Tennant, journal, 11 November 1938, quoted in Sotheby's Wilsford catalogue, p. 169.
20. *Diary of Virginia Woolf,* Vol. IV.
21. Lady Rumbold, conversation with author, 26 August 1987.

Chapter 19: 1939 and All That

1. Stephen Tennant, journal, 2 August 1948.
2. This and the following from Haslam/Pembroke interview.
3. This and the following from Stephen Tennant, manuscript fragment.
4. Stephen Tennant, marginalia.
5. This and the following from Stephen Tennant to Cecil Beaton, 28 May 1939.
6. Stephen Tennant, marginalia.
7. *Sunday Express*, 4 June 1939.
8. Stephen Tennant, marginalia.
9. Harold Acton, *More Memoirs of an Aesthete* (Hamish Hamilton, London, 1986), p. 159.
10. Boris Kochno to Richard Buckle, 27 September 1987.
11. Stephen Tennant, journal, 13 November 1939, quoted in Sotheby's Wilsford catalogue, p. 16.
12. Stephen Tennant, marginalia.
13. Stephen Tennant, manuscript fragment.
14. Stephen Tennant to Sibyl Colefax, 3 September 1939.
15. ibid.
16. Stephen Tennant, journal, (?)28 September 1939, quoted in Sotheby's Wilsford catalogue, p. 83.
17. E. M. Forster, unpublished diary, 13 February 1940, quoted in P. N. Furbank, letter to author, 23 August 1987.
18. *Diary of Virginia Woolf*, Vol. V, p. 316.
19. Stephen Tennant to Sibyl Colefax, 21 September 1940.
20. This and the following from Cecil Beaton, diary, November 1940.
21. Sheila Lochhead, diary, November 1940.
22. Nancy Mitford, *Love in a Cold Climate* (Hamish Hamilton, London, 1949), p. 239.
23. Margot Strickland, *Angela Thirkell*, (Duckworth, London, 1977), p. 72.
24. Colin MacInnes, *Encounter*, January 1957.
25. Sir Stephen Spender, conversation with author, 30 August 1987.
26. *Horizon*, April 1941.
27. Hugo Vickers, *Cecil Beaton*, p. 250.
28. *Horizon*, September 1941.

Chapter 20: Lilacs in the Spring

1. Michael De-la-Noy (ed.), *The Journals of Denton Welch* (Penguin, Harmondsworth, 1987), p. 92.
2. Stephen Tennant, journal, 1942.
3. This story was told to the author by a number of different sources.
4. This and the following from a conversation between Sir Fred Warner and the author, 15 June 1988.
5. P. N. Furbank, *E. M. Forster*, Vol II, p. 184.
6. Sir Stephen Spender, conversation with author, 30 August 1987.
7. ibid.
8. Stephen Tennant, journal, quoted in *Andy Warhol's Interview* February 1987.
9. Simon Blow, *Broken Blood*, p. 195.
10. Elizabeth Bowen, *The Heat of the Day*, (Jonathan Cape, London, 1954), p. 44.
11. Alan Pryce-Jones, *The Bonus of Laughter* (Hamish Hamilton, London, 1987), p. 135.

12. Stephen Tennant to Lady Rumbold, told to author, 26 August 1987.
13. Stephen Tennant, marginalia.
14. Sotheby's Wilsford catalogue, p. 16.
15. Victoria Glendinning, *Elizabeth Bowen* (Weidenfeld & Nicolson, London, 1977), p. 141.
16. Elizabeth Bowen to Stephen Tennant, undated.
17. This and the following from Charles Ritchie, *The Siren Years* (Macmillan, London, 1974), pp. 153–4.
18. Charles Taylor, conversation with the author, autumn 1987.
19. Derek Hill, letter to author, 4 November 1988.
20. Stephen Tennant, journal, April 1943.
21. This and the following from a conversation between Sir Stephen Spender and the author, 30 August 1987.
22. This and the following from a conversation between Peter Quennell and the author, 18 March 1987.
23. Richard Buckle, letter to author, 9 October 1987.
24. Sir Stephen Spender, conversation with author, 30 August 1987.

Chapter 21: *Northern Gothic*

1. Stephen Tennant, marginalia.
2. Cyril Connolly, manuscript.
3. Stephen Tennant, journal, 18 August 1942, quoted in Sotheby's Wilsford catalogue, p. 192.
4. Stephen Tennant to Hugo Vickers, 'Magic Spring 1981'.
5. Edith Olivier, *From Her Journals*, pp. 268–9.
6. This and the following from Stephen Tennant's journal, reproduced in the Alexander Iolas exhibition catalogue, New York, 1955.
7. Edith Olivier, *From Her Journals*, p. 286.
8. ibid., p. 285.
9. Stephen Tennant, marginalia.
10. Emma Tennant, conversation with author, 23 June 1987.
11. This and the following from Emma Tennant, *Wild Nights* (Jonathan Cape, London, 1979) pp. 58ff.
12. This and the following from Stephen Tennant, journal fragment.
13. Stephen Tennant to Sibyl Colefax, 7 September 1944.
14. Stephen Tennant to Sibyl Colefax, 14 November 1944.
15. Stephen Tennant to Elizabeth Lowndes, 8 February 1929.
16. Lady Rumbold to the author, 26 August 1987.
17. Sir Fred Warner, conversation with author, 15 June 1988.
18. Stephen Tennant, journal fragment.
19. ibid.
20. ibid.
21. Stephen Tennant to Laurence Whistler, 28 January 1947.
22. J. R. Ackerley, *My Sister and Myself: The Diaries of J. R. Ackerley* (Hutchinson, London, 1982), pp. 175–7.
23. Patricia Lee Yongue, letter to author, 18 February 1988.
24. Edith Sitwell to John Lehmann, 21 January 1946.
25. Edith Olivier, *From Her Journals*, p. 306.
26. Siegfried Sassoon to Stephen Tennant, undated (1951), quoted in Sotheby's Wilsford catalogue, p.184.
27. Stephen Tennant, journal fragment.

Chapter 22: *Wilsford Regained*

1. Stephen Tennant to John Lehmann (unposted), July 1945, quoted in Sotheby's Wilsford catalogue, p. 19.
2. Stephen Tennant to Laurence Whistler, 4 October 1945.
3. ibid.
4. ibid.
5. Stephen Tennant to Laurence Whistler, 18 October 1945.
6. Sir Stephen Spender, conversation with author, 30 August 1987.
7. James Lees-Milne, letter to author, 13 February 1988.
8. Stephen Tennant to Vita Sackville-West, 10 March 1945.
9. ibid.
10. ibid.
11. Stephen Tennant, journal, 15 December 1945, quoted in Sotheby's Wilsford catalogue, p. 180.
12. Stephen Tennant to Cecil Beaton, 17 December 1945.
13. ibid.
14. Stephen Tennant to Vita Sackville-West, 15 February 1946.
15. Stephen Tennant to Vita Sackville-West, 19 February 1946.
16. Stephen Tennant to Laurence Whistler, (?)24 October 1945.
17. Stephen Tennant to Laurence Whistler, 31 October 1945.
18. Stephen Tennant to Vita Sackville-West, 14 March 1946.
19. Stephen Tennant to Vita Sackville-West, 24 April 1946.
20. ibid.
21. Vita Sackville-West to Stephen Tennant, 18 July 1950, quoted in Sotheby's Wilsford catalogue, p. 180.
22. L. P. Hartley to Stephen Tennant, 30 August 1946.
23. Stephen Tennant, journal, 26 and 28 August 1946, quoted in Sotheby's Wilsford catalogue, p. 180.
24. Stephen Tennant, manuscript fragment.
25. Harold Acton, *More Memoirs of an Aesthete*, p. 160.
26. E. M. Forster to Stephen Tennant, undated.
27. Harold Acton, *Nancy Mitford* (Hamish Hamilton, London, 1975), p. 75.
28. Nancy Mitford *Love in a Cold Climate* (Hamish Hamilton, London, 1949), pp. 210ff.
29. Nancy Mitford, *Love in a Cold Climate*, pp. 230–31.
30. Harold Acton, *Nancy Mitford*, p. 75.
31. Sir Harold Acton, letter to author, 9 June 1987.
32. Harold Acton, *Nancy Mitford*, p. 77.
33. Eardley Knollys, letter to author, 8 June 1988.
34. Cecil Beaton, diary, May 1947.
35. Edith Olivier, *From Her Journal*, p. 307.
36. Cecil Beaton, diary, May 1947.
37. Hugo Vickers, *Cecil Beaton*, p. 307.
38. Stephen Tennant to Cecil Beaton, 14 May 1947.
39. Stephen Tennant to Laurence Whistler, 4 June 1947.
40. Stephen Tennant to Cecil Beaton, 6 June 1947.
41. Eileen Hose, conversation with author, 16 February 1987.

Chapter 23: *Travels with Myself*

1. Stephen Tennant to Sir Ronald Storrs, April 1947.

2. ibid.
3. ibid.
4. Stephen Tennant to Laurence Whistler, 3 July 1947.
5. Stephen Tennant, journal, August 1948.
6. Nancy Mitford to Stephen Tennant, 18 September 1951.
7. Stephen Tennant, journal fragment, July 1948.
8. ibid.
9. ibid., 19 July 1948.
10. Stephen Tennant, essay on Rex Whistler.
11. Truman Capote, interview with Hugo Vickers, 28 June 1983.
12. The Hon. David Herbert, conversation with author, 7 June 1988.
13. Stephen Tennant, journal, 19 July 1948.
14. Rosamond Lehmann, letter to author, 14 December 1987.
15. Rosamond Lehmann to Stephen Tennant, undated.
16. Stephen Tennant, journal, 19 July 1948.
17. ibid., 24 July 1948.
18. ibid., 25 July 1948.
19. ibid., 27 July 1948.
20. ibid., 1 August 1948.
21. Truman Capote, 'Tangier', *The Dogs Bark* (Weidenfeld & Nicolson, London, 1974), p. 87.
22. Cecil Beaton, *The Strenuous Years* (Weidenfeld & Nicolson, London, 1973), p. 34.
23. Stephen Tennant, journal, 4 August 1948.
24. ibid.,
25. ibid., 12 August 1948.
26. John Lahr (ed.), *The Orton Diaries* (Methuen, London, 1986), pp. 161 and 183.
27. Stephen Tennant, journal, 12 August 1948.
28. ibid., 15 August 1948.
29. ibid., 17 August 1948.
30. ibid.
31. E. M. Forster, quoted in Sotheby's Wilsford catalogue, p. 16.
32. Richard Ellman, *Oscar Wilde* (Hamish Hamilton, London, 1988), p. 311.
33. Cyril Connolly manuscript.
34. Stephen Tennant to Sheila Lochhead (née Macdonald), undated.
35. Sheila Lochhead (née Macdonald), conversation with author, 23 November 1988.
36. Stephen Tennant, journal, 20 August 1948.
37. ibid., 29 August 1948.
38. ibid., 24 August 1948.
39. ibid., 2 September 1948.
40. ibid., 4 September 1948.
41. ibid., 16, 19 and 20 August 1948.
42. ibid., 4 September 1948.

Chapter 24: *Stephen and Edith*

1. Edith Lewis to Stephen Tennant, 5 September 1947.
2. Edith Lewis to Stephen Tennant, 3 February 1948.
3. Edith Lewis to Stephen Tennant, 12 May 1950.
4. Patricia Lee Yongue, 'Edith Lewis Living', essay.
5. Lady Redgrave, conversation with author, 12 November 1988.

6. Edith Lewis to Stephen Tennant, 17 March 1959.
7. Stephen Tennant to Susan Lowndes Marques, 28 February 1953.
8. Stephen Tennant to Susan Lowndes Marques, undated.
9. Cecil Beaton, diary, summer 1961.
10. 'The Room Beyond', in *Willa Cather: On Writing* (Alfred Knopf, New York, 1949).
11. Quoted in a letter from Ruth Crone to Stephen Tennant, undated.
12. Letter from Buckingham Palace, 24 November 1949.
13. Ruth Crone to Stephen Tennant, 13 October 1949.
14. Stephen Tennant to Ruth Crone, 17 October 1949.
15. Ruth Crone, letter to author, 27 July 1987.
16. Charles Ritchie, conversation with author, summer 1988.
17. Stephen Tennant, journal fragment, 1949.
18. ibid.
19. L. P. Hartley to Stephen Tennant, 27 April 1950.
20. Florence Beerbohm to Stephen Tennant, (?)29 December 1949.
21. Stephen Tennant, journal fragment, 1949.
22. 'A Reassessment of Poetry', Stephen Tennant manuscript.
23. Norah Smallwood to Stephen Tennant, (?) January 1973.
24. Stephen Tennant to Laurence Whistler, (?)8 January 1954.
25. Edith Lewis to Stephen Tennant, 16 February 1950.
26. Edith Lewis to Stephen Tennant, 2 May 1950.
27. Edith Lewis to Stephen Tennant, 8 August 1950.
28. Stephen Tennant, journal, December 1935.
29. Sir John Gielgud, letter to author, 28 November 1987.
30. The Hon. David Herbert, conversation with the author, 7 June 1988.
31. Barbara Skelton, *Tears Before Bedtime* (Hamish Hamilton, London, 1987), pp. 87–8.
32. Edith Lewis to Stephen Tennant, (?)20 September 1950.
33. Stephen Tennant, marginalia.
34. ibid.
35. Stephen Tennant to Hugo Vickers, 14 May 1981.
36. Percy Lubbock to Stephen Tennant, 15 May 1951.
37. Susan Lowndes Marques, conversation with the author, 7 July 1988.
38. ibid.
39. Stephen Tennant to Susan Lowndes Marques, undated.

Chapter 25: *Serious Pleasures*

1. Hugo Vickers, *Cecil Beaton*, p. 321.
2. Julian Huxley, *Memories II* (Allen & Unwin, London, 1973), p. 102.
3. Haslam/Pembroke interview.
4. Lady Juliet Duff to Cecil Beaton, 1 February 1952.
5. Lady Juliet Duff to Cecil Beaton, February 1952.
6. Lady Juliet Duff's scrapbooks.
7. Stephen Tennant to Eddy Sackville-West, February 1952.
8. Stephen Tennant to Eddy Sackville-West, 15 February 1952.
9. Stephen Tennant to Eddy Sackville-West, April 1952.
10. Rosemary Olivier, conversation with author, 18 April 1987.
11. Eardley Knollys, letter to author, 8 June 1988.
12. Rosemary Olivier, conversation with author, 18 April 1987.
13. Marthe Bibesco to Stephen Tennant, 14 March 1939.

14. Nancy Mitford to Stephen Tennant, 18 September 1951.
15. Stephen Spender, foreword to Redfern Gallery catalogue, January 1953.
16. Draft of Cecil Beaton's letter to Stephen Tennant (Cecil Beaton papers).
17. Stephen Tennant to Cecil Beaton, October 1952.
18. Stephen Tennant to Susan Lowndes Marques, 29 February 1953.
19. Edith Lewis to Stephen Tennant, 29 May 1953.
20. Edith Lewis to Stephen Tennant, 19 August 1953.
21. Edith Lewis to Stephen Tennant, 16 March 1954.
22. This and the following from a conversation between Richard Buckle and the author, 5 August 1987.
23. Stephen Tennant to Richard Buckle, undated.
24. *The World of Interiors*, October 1987, pp. 146–59.
25. Stephen Tennant to Richard Buckle, 6 October 1954.
26. Ned Rorem, *Paris Diary* (Barrie & Rockliff, London, 1957), p. 208.
27. Edith Lewis to Stephen Tennant, 6 October 1954.
28. Nancy Mitford to Stephen Tennant, 5 October 1954.
29. Lady Rumbold, conversation with author, 10 September 1988.
30. ibid.
31. Stephen Tennant to Cecil Beaton, December 1954.
32. Alexander Iolas catalogue, 1955.
33. Mr Rasponi to Stephen Tennant, (?)8 April 1955.
34. Alexander Iolas catalogue, 1955.
35. Mr Rasponi to Stephen Tennant, 8(?) April 1955.
36. Edith Lewis to Stephen Tennant, 19 May 1955.
37. Dr Anthony Davis, conversation with author, 24 September 1987.
38. Sigmund Freud, *Introductory Lectures on Psychoanalysis* (Penguin, Harmondsworth, 1982), p. 81.
39. Dr Anthony Davis, conversation with author, 24 September 1987.

Chapter 26: *Genius Manqué*

1. Sir John Gielgud, letter to author, 28 November 1987.
2. John Lehmann to Stephen Tennant, 8 March 1956.
3. Edith Lewis to Stephen Tennant, 13 May 1956.
4. Pavel Tchelitchew to Stephen Tennant, 2 August 1956.
5. Stephen Tennant to Hugo Vickers, January 1984.
6. *News of the World*, 2 December 1956.
7. *Evening Standard*, 3 December 1956.
8. David Sylvester, *Listener*, 13 December 1956, quoted in Sotheby's Wilsford catalogue, p. 20.
9. *The Times*, undated clipping, 1956.
10. Publicity handout for Gallery One.
11. James Kirkup, letter to author, 13 June 1988.
12. J. R. Ackerley to Geoffrey Gorer, undated, 1961.
13. Peter Parker, letter to author, 9 June 1988.
14. David Mann to Stephen Tennant, 3 September 1957.
15. ibid.
16. Lord Glenconner to Edelgi Dinshaw, quoted in a letter to Stephen Tennant, 1 October 1957.
17. David Mann to Stephen Tennant, 24 October 1957.
18. ibid.
19. David Mann to Stephen Tennant, 4 November 1957.

20. Lady Menuhin, conversation with author, 17 February 1988.
21. Hugo Vickers, *Cecil Beaton*, p. xxiv.
22. Stephen Tennant, marginalia.
23. Stephen Tennant to Susan Lowndes Marques, 15 December 1957.
24. David Mann to Stephen Tennant, 11 January 1958.
25. Margot Strickland, *Angela Thirkell*, (Duckworth, London, 1977) p. 169.
26. Stephen Tennant to Laurence Whistler, 22 April 1958.
27. Stephen Tennant to Laurence Whistler, April 1958.
28. This and the following from Michael Wishart, *High Diver* (Blond & Briggs, London, 1977) pp. 163–5.
29. Caroline Blackwood, conversation with author, 17 May 1987.
30. Lucian Freud, conversation with author, 23 May 1989.
31. Susan Lowndes Marques, conversation with author, 7 July 1988.
32. Edith Lewis to Stephen Tennant, 14 April 1958.

Chapter 27: 'The Last Professional Beauty'

1. Haslam/Pembroke interview.
2. Simon Blow, *Tatler*, July 1983.
3. Stephen Tennant, journal, 19 December 1935.
4. Lady Menuhin, conversation with author, 17 February 1988.
5. Susan Lowndes Marques, conversation with author, 7 July 1988.
6. Dr Anthony Davis, conversation with author, 24 September 1987.
7. Marchioness of Bath, conversation with author, 31 March 1987.
8. Princess Bibesco to Stephen Tennant, 16 August 1956.
9. Princess Bibesco to Stephen Tennant, 20 January 1960.
10. Princess Bibesco to Stephen Tennant, ibid., 20 April 1960.
11. Stephen Tennant to Susan Lowndes Marques, 26 July 1966.
12. Victoria Glendinning, *Edith Sitwell*, p. 317.
13. Princess Bibesco to Stephen Tennant, 29 July 1961.
14. Princess Bibesco to Stephen Tennant, 17 September 1961.
15. Cecil Beaton, diary, summer 1961.
16. Stephen Tennant to Cecil Beaton, 8 July 1961.
17. Stephen Tennant to Cecil Beaton, undated.
18. Diana Vreeland to Stephen Tennant, 3 April 1966.
19. Stephen Tennant to Cecil Beaton, undated.
20. Cecil Beaton, diary, summer 1961.
21. Sir Sacheverell Sitwell to Stephen Tennant, June 1960.
22. Sir Sacheverell Sitwell to Cecil Beaton, June 1961.
23. Sir Sacheverell Sitwell to Cecil Beaton, 13 July 1965.
24. W. H. Auden to Stephen Tennant, 20 November ?1961.
25. Christabel Aberconway to Stephen Tennant, 7 February 1962.
26. Rosamond Lehmann to Lord Glenconner, 25 March 1962.
27. J. R. Ackerley to Stephen Tennant, undated, 1966.
28. Edmund Blunden to Stephen Tennant, 23 May 1965.
29. Cecil Beaton, diary, summer 1964.
30. Stephen Tennant to Cecil Beaton, undated.
31. ibid.
32. Cecil Beaton to Stephen Tennant, undated.

Chapter 28: Concerning the Eccentricities of Stephen Tennant

1. Christabel Aberconway to Stephen Tennant, 21 March 1965.
2. Christabel Aberconway to Stephen Tennant, undated.
3. Hugo Vickers, *Cecil Beaton*, p. 527.
4. John Skull, conversation with author, 17 November 1987.
5. Dr Anthony Davis, conversation with author, 24 September 1987.
6. John Skull, conversation with author, 17 November 1987.
7. ibid.
8. Stephen Tennant to Violet Bonham-Carter, undated.
9. Pamela Benton, conversation with author, summer 1987.
10. John Skull, conversation with author, 17 November 1987.
11. This and the following from Cecil Beaton, diary, spring 1970.
12. Cecil Beaton, diary, 1973.
13. Haslam/Pembroke interview.
14. Stephen Tennant to Hugo Vickers, January 1982.
15. David Hockney, conversation with author, 18 July 1987.
16. Hugo Vickers, *Independent*, 4 March 1987.
17. John Skull, conversation with author, 17 November 1987.
18. V. S. Naipaul, *The Enigma of Arrival*, p. 53.
19. ibid., p. 173.
20. ibid., p. 191.
21. ibid., p. 172.
22. ibid.
23. Lord Glenconner to Stephen Tennant, 23 June 1966.
24. James Lees-Milne, *William Beckford*, (Allanheld and Schram, New Jersey, 1979), p. 27.
25. ibid.
26. ibid., p. 18.
27. Stephen Tennant to Cecil Beaton, January 1973.
28. Stephen Tennant to Cecil Beaton, 18 May 1973.
29. Stephen Tennant to Cecil Beaton, 6 May 1973.
30. Stephen Tennant to Cecil Beaton, 6 June 1973.
31. *Willa Cather Pioneer Memorial Newsletter*, spring 1973.
32. Patrick Procktor, conversation with author, 27 March 1987.
33. Eileen Hose, conversation with author, 18 February 1987.
34. Patrick Procktor, conversation with author, 27 March 1987.
35. Cecil Beaton, diary, 1973.
36. John Skull, conversation with author, 17 November 1987.
37. Stephen Tennant to Cecil Beaton, undated.
38. John Skull, conversation with author, 17 November 1987.
39. John Byrne's Introduction, 'The Two Semi-Circles', in *Rex Whistler, Stephen Tennant and Their Two Semi-Circles* (Michael Parkin Gallery, 1987).
40. Sir Angus Wilson, letter to author, 30 May 1988.

Chapter 29: Fallen Idle

1. Cecil Beaton, diary, 23 May 1973.
2. Duchess of Devonshire to Stephen Tennant, 17 January 1973.
3. Duchess of Devonshire to Stephen Tennant, 18 February 1973.
4. Duchess of Devonshire to Mrs Pamela Jackson, undated.
5. Duchess of Devonshire to Stephen Tennant, 17 June 1973.

6. Stephen Tennant to Patrick Procktor, 28 April 1973.
7. Christopher Hill, *Century of Revolution*, (Cardinal, 1974), p. 15.
8. Stephen Tennant to Patrick Procktor, undated.
9. Patrick Procktor, conversation with author, 27 March 1987.
10. Stephen Tennant, manuscript.
11. Stephen Tennant, marginalia.
12. Stephen Tennant to Patrick Procktor, 12 May 1973.
13. Stephen Tennant, marginalia.
14. Haslam/Pembroke interview.
15. Michael Wishart to Stephen Tennant, 4 August 1965.
16. Kenneth Anger to Stephen Tennant, 8 September 1969.
17. Kenneth Anger to Stephen Tennant, 10 September 1969.
18. Michael Wishart to Stephen Tennant, 13 January 1973.
19. Michael Wishart to Stephen Tennant, 27 January 1973.
20. Michael Wishart to Stephen Tennant, 6 February 1973.
21. Michael Wishart, conversation with author, 22 May 1987.
22. Stephen Tennant, marginalia.
23. Stephen Tennant to Michael Holroyd, undated.
24. Michael Holroyd, conversation with author, summer 1987.
25. P. N. Furbank, conversation with author, 23 May 1988.
26. Stephen Tennant to Gilles David, 12 November 1971.
27. Stephen Tennant to Gilles David, 20 October 1971.
28. Cutting in Stephen Tennant's papers, *Salisbury Journal*, undated.
29. Richard Buckle, conversation with author, 5 August 1987.
30. Patrick Procktor, conversation with author, 27 March 1987.
31. Stephen Tennant to Cecil Beaton, autumn 1974.
32. Stephen Tennant to the Marchioness of Bath, 1 March 1974.
33. Stephen Tennant to the Marchioness of Bath, 26 July 1974.
34. Stephen Tennant to the Marchioness of Bath, summer 1974.
35. Lady Rumbold, conversation with author, 26 August 1987.
36. Stephen Tennant to Lady Rumbold, 22 April 1974.
37. Stephen Tennant to Lady Rumbold, 3 November 1974.
38. Stephen Tennant to Lady Rumbold, undated.
39. Stephen Tennant to Lady Rumbold, 8 February 1976.
40. Stephen Tennant to the Marchioness of Bath, November 1974.
41. Cyril Connolly to Stephen Tennant, undated.
42. Hugo Vickers, *Cecil Beaton*, p. 579.
43. John Skull, conversation with author, 17 November 1987.
44. Cecil Beaton to Stephen Tennant, undated.
45. Eileen Hose, conversation with author, 18 February 1988.

Chapter 30: *The Blue of Redemption*

1. Patricia Lee Yongue, letter to author, 22 August 1987.
2. Mrs E. W. Yongue to Stephen Tennant, 25 May 1974.
3. Patricia Lee Yongue, letter to author, 22 August 1987.
4. John Skull, conversation with author, 17 November 1987.
5. Stephen Tennant to Lucia Woods Lindley, undated.
6. Patricia Lee Yongue, letter to author, 22 August 1987.
7. John Skull, conversation with author, 17 November 1987.
8. V. S. Naipaul, *The Enigma of Arrival*, p. 293.
9. Patricia Lee Yongue, letter to author, 22 August 1987.

10. ibid.
11. Patricia Lee Yongue, letter to author, 29 March 1987.
12. Patricia Lee Yongue, letter to author, 19 October 1987.
13. Sir Stephen Spender, conversation with author, 30 August 1987.
14. Charles Taylor, conversation with author, summer 1987.
15. Stephen Tennant to Rosemary Olivier, undated (1961).
16. John Skull, conversation with author, 17 November 1987.
17. ibid.
18. *Guardian*, 29 June 1976.
19. John Skull, conversation with author, 17 November 1987.
20. Stephen Tennant to Cecil Beaton, undated.
21. Cecil Beaton, diary, 1978.
22. Hugo Vickers, *Cecil Beaton*, p. 579.
23. Stephen Tennant to Eileen Hose, July 1981.
24. Lord Glenconner to Stephen Tennant, 18 April 1974.
25. Lord Glenconner to Stephen Tennant, 22 November 1977.
26. Marie Helvin, conversation with author, 17 June 1987.
27. Hugo Vickers, diary, 4 March 1980.
28. Hugo Vickers, *Cecil Beaton*, p. xxi.
29. Hugo Vickers, diary, 21 February 1980.
30. ibid., 22 February 1980.
31. Stephen Tennant to Eileen Hose, undated (1981).
32. Hugo Vickers, diary, 4 March 1980.
33. Lady Diana Cooper to Hugo Vickers, 21 March 1980.
34. Hugo Vickers, diary, 18 September 1980.
35. ibid., 20 September 1980.
36. Stephen Tennant to Hugo Vickers, 17 September 1980.
37. ibid.
38. Stephen Tennant to the Marchioness of Bath, November 1979.
39. Stephen Tennant to Eileen Hose, undated (1981).
40. Stephen Tennant to the Marchioness of Bath, November 1979.
41. Stephen Tennant to Hugo Vickers, September 1980.
42. Stephen Tennant to Hugo Vickers, undated.
43. Hugo Vickers, diary, 1 March 1981.
44. ibid., 9 May 1981.
45. ibid., 21 July 1981.
46. John Skull, conversation with author, 17 November 1987.

Chapter 31: *Final Act*

1. Hugo Vickers, diary, 2 April 1982.
2. Hon. Tobias Tennant to Stephen Tennant, 12 October 1983.
3. John Skull, conversation with author, 17 November 1987.
4. Sylvia Blandford, conversation with author, 17 October 1987.
5. John Skull, conversation with author, 17 November 1987.
6. Lady Rumbold, conversation with author, 26 August 1987.
7. *Cecil Beaton*, BBC film, 1984.
8. John Skull, conversation with author, 17 November 1987.
9. Earl of Pembroke, conversation with author, 7 April 1987.
10. Earl of Pembroke to Stephen Tennant, 9 February 1978.
11. Haslam/Pembroke interview.
12. Patricia Lee Yongue, letter to author, 19 October 1987.

13. Patricia Lee Yongue, letter to author, 22 August 1987.
14. Hugo Vickers to Stephen Tennant, 4 September 1986.
15. Stephen Tennant, conversation with author, 25 October 1986.
16. Lady Rumbold, conversation with author, 26 August 1987.

Chapter 32: *Coda*

1. *Daily Telegraph*, 3 March 1987.
2. *Independent*, 4 March 1987.
3. *The Times*, 21 March 1987.
4. *Daily Telegraph*, 13 August 1987.
5. *Homes & Gardens*, February 1988.
6. Michael Wishart, *High Diver*, p. 164.

Index

Lehmann, John Frederick, 50, 273, 275, 327–8
Lehmann, Rosamond Nina (1903–90), 166, 170, 217, 252, 258, 263, 269, 293, 317; with ST in Northumberland, 49–51; at Wilsford, 78–9
Leigh, Vivien, 286
Lenare, 132
Lennox-Boyd, Alan, 252, 293
Leonard, Mrs, 15
Lesley & Roberts, 52, 333
Lewis, Edith (?1883–1972), 211, 212, 285, 384; ST's friendship with, 300–303, 307, 309–11; expects ST in New York, 318–19, 323, 331, 332; compares ST to Shelley, 336; death, 389
Linley, Viscount, 407
Lindsay, Hon. Lady Loelia, 74, 84–5, 151
Lodge, Lady, 135
Lodge, Sir Oliver, 14–15, 160
Longford, Lord, 234, 371
Lopokova, Lydia (Lady Keynes), 199n
Losch, Tilly (Countess of Carnarvon), 107
Lowndes, Elizabeth (Dowager Countess of Iddesleigh) (1900–   ), 6, 13, 19, 43, 56, 57, 62, 64, 72, 74, 76, 77, 87, 96, 101, 103, 106, 117, 121, 128, 135, 141, 166; 'I LOVE "Elizabeth"', 26; at San Remo, 38–9; ST petitions, 46–8; at Fallodon, 49–51; fetches rat, 52; at Wilsford, 59–60; at Cap Ferrat, 73; Ellesmere Affair, 111–13; marries, 153
Lowndes, Susan Marques, 6, 7, 13, 14, 19, 64, 106, 113, 333, 340; ST visits in Portugal, 310–11
Lubbock, Percy, 293–4, 310
Ludwig II, King, 103, 118, 137, 364
Lutyens, Sir Edwin, 63, 130
Lynn, Olga, 98, 127
Lyttleton, Oliver (1st Lord Chandos), 293

Maas, Peter, 375, 376
Macdonald, Ramsay, 83n, 245n
Macdonald, Sheila (later Lochhead), 245–6, 298, 340
McEachran, Captain Neil, 82–3
Macfie, Dr Ronald, 36–8, 41, 42, 46
McIndoe, Sir Archibald, 337

MacInnes, Colin, 247–9, 329
McLaren, Denham, 143, 144
Maclean, James, 366, 399
McClung, Isabelle, 202
Mann, David, 331–3
Mann, Klaus, 203
Mansfield, Katherine, 33, 87, 159
Margaret, Countess of Snowdon, HRH the Princess, 322, 355
Marlborough, Gladys, Duchess of, 392
Marlborough, Laura, Duchess of, 356
Marques, Luis, 310–11
Marsh, Edward, 138, 140
Massine, Leonide, 81
Matta, Sergio, 295
Matthew, the pigeon, 205
Matthews, George, 350
Maugham, William Somerset, 98, 186
Maugham, Syrie, 98, 143, 156, 206, 221–4, 253, 242
May, Nurse, 164–5, 169
Melaund, Roger Corbett, 285n
Melville, Herman, 231
Mendl, Lady Elsie, 223, 242, 295
Menuhin, Lady Diana Gould, 1, 332–3, 339–40, 355
Menuhin, Sir Yehudi, 332, 339, 352
Messel, Oliver, 27, 65, 95, 98, 105, 109
Mistinguett (Jeanne Marie Bourgeois), 123–4, 188
Mitchell, James, 360n
Mitford, Hon. Nancy (1904–73), 43, 72, 80, 109, 275, 290, 322, 370; visits Wilsford, 59–60; *Love in a Cold Climate*, 281–3; ST visits in Paris, 315–16; death, 369
Moat, Alice Leone, 133, 137
Monkey, Plush, xvii, 199, 244, 360, 403, 407
Moorcroft Hospital, 285–6
Moore, Patrick, 360n
Morrell, Lady Ottoline, 90, 102, 130, 219–20, 224, 252, 273, 374
Morrell, Sir Philip, 252
Morris, Cedric, 105
Mortimer, Raymond, 152, 256, 366
Mosley, Lady Cynthia, 107–8
Mosley, Hon. Lady, 107n, 370
Mosley, Sir Oswald, 107–8
Mounsey, Patrick, 118
Mountbatten of Burma, Countess, 171n

FOR THE BEST IN PAPERBACKS, LOOK FOR THE

In every corner of the world, on every subject under the sun, Penguin represents quality and variety—the very best in publishing today.

For complete information about books available from Penguin—including Pelicans, Puffins, Peregrines, and Penguin Classics—and how to order them, write to us at the appropriate address below. Please note that for copyright reasons the selection of books varies from country to country.

In the United Kingdom: For a complete list of books available from Penguin in the U.K., please write to *Dept E.P., Penguin Books Ltd, Harmondsworth, Middlesex, UB7 0DA.*

In the United States: For a complete list of books available from Penguin in the U.S., please write to *Dept BA, Penguin*, Box 120, Bergenfield, New Jersey 07621-0120.

In Canada: For a complete list of books available from Penguin in Canada, please write to *Penguin Books Canada Ltd, 10 Alcorn Avenue, Suite 300, Toronto, Ontario, Canada M4V 3B2.*

In Australia: For a complete list of books available from Penguin in Australia, please write to the *Marketing Department, Penguin Books Ltd, P.O. Box 257, Ringwood, Victoria 3134.*

In New Zealand: For a complete list of books available from Penguin in New Zealand, please write to the *Marketing Department, Penguin Books (NZ) Ltd, Private Bag, Takapuna, Auckland 9.*

In India: For a complete list of books available from Penguin, please write to *Penguin Overseas Ltd, 706 Eros Apartments, 56 Nehru Place, New Delhi. 110019.*

In Holland: For a complete list of books available from Penguin in Holland, please write to *Penguin Books Nederland B.V., Postbus 195, NL-1380AD Weesp, Netherlands.*

In Germany: For a complete list of books available from Penguin, please write to *Penguin Books Ltd, Friedrichstrasse 10-12, D-6000 Frankfurt Main 1, Federal Republic of Germany.*

In Spain: For a complete list of books available from Penguin in Spain, please write to *Longman, Penguin España, Calle San Nicolas 15, E-28013 Madrid, Spain.*

In Japan: For a complete list of books available from Penguin in Japan, please write to *Longman Penguin Japan Co Ltd, Yamaguchi Building, 2-12-9 Kanda Jimbocho, Chiyoda-Ku, Tokyo 101, Japan.*